Research Anthology on Implementing Sentiment Analysis Across Multiple Disciplines

Information Resources Management Association
USA

Volume III

Published in the United States of America by
    IGI Global
    Engineering Science Reference (an imprint of IGI Global)
    701 E. Chocolate Avenue
    Hershey PA, USA 17033
    Tel: 717-533-8845
    Fax: 717-533-8661
    E-mail: cust@igi-global.com
    Web site: http://www.igi-global.com

Library of Congress Cataloging-in-Publication Data

Names: Information Resources Management Association, editor.
Title: Research anthology on implementing sentiment analysis across
  multiple disciplines / Information Resources Management Association,
  editor.
Description: Hershey PA : Engineering Science Reference, [2022] | Includes
  bibliographical references and index. | Summary: "This reference book of
  contributed chapters discusses the tools, methodologies, applications,
  and implementation of sentiment analysis across various disciplines and
  industries such as the pharmaceutical industry, government, and the
  tourism industry and presents emerging technologies and developments
  within the field of sentiment analysis and opinion mining"-- Provided by
  publisher.
Identifiers: LCCN 2022016823 (print) | LCCN 2022016824 (ebook) | ISBN
  9781668463031 (h/c) | ISBN 9781668463048 (ebook)
Subjects: LCSH: Sentiment analysis.
Classification: LCC QA76.9.S57 R47 2022 (print) | LCC QA76.9.S57 (ebook)
  | DDC 005.1/4--dc23/eng/20220622
LC record available at https://lccn.loc.gov/2022016823
LC ebook record available at https://lccn.loc.gov/2022016824

British Cataloguing in Publication Data
A Cataloguing in Publication record for this book is available from the British Library.

The views expressed in this book are those of the authors, but not necessarily of the publisher.

For electronic access to this publication, please contact: eresources@igi-global.com.

List of Contributors

Table of Contents

Section 2
Development and Design Methodologies

Volume II

Section 3
Tools and Technologies

Section 4
Utilization and Applications

Section 5
Organizational and Social Implications

Section 6
Critical Issues and Challenges

Preface

Sentiment analysis is a field that is gaining traction as more organizations and fields discover the myriad benefits and opportunities it offers. Regardless of industry, it is always useful to know what consumers think, whether that be about a product, a service, or a company in general. With sentiment analysis technology, it has never been easier to understand what audiences want and need. Organizations must embrace this technology and integrate it into their business strategies and tactics in order to successfully reach and communicate with their audience.

Staying informed of the most up-to-date research trends and findings is of the utmost importance. That is why IGI Global is pleased to offer this four-volume reference collection of reprinted IGI Global book chapters and journal articles that have been handpicked by senior editorial staff. This collection will shed light on critical issues related to the trends, techniques, and uses of various applications by providing both broad and detailed perspectives on cutting-edge theories and developments. This collection is designed to act as a single reference source on conceptual, methodological, technical, and managerial issues, as well as to provide insight into emerging trends and future opportunities within the field.

The *Research Anthology on Implementing Sentiment Analysis Across Multiple Disciplines* is organized into six distinct sections that provide comprehensive coverage of important topics. The sections are:

1. Fundamental Concepts and Theories;
2. Development and Design Methodologies;
3. Tools and Technologies;
4. Utilization and Applications;
5. Organizational and Social Implications; and
6. Critical Issues and Challenges.

The following paragraphs provide a summary of what to expect from this invaluable reference tool.

Section 1, "Fundamental Concepts and Theories," serves as a foundation for this extensive reference tool by addressing crucial theories essential to understanding the concepts and uses of sentiment analysis in multidisciplinary settings. Opening this reference book is the chapter "Fundamentals of Opinion Mining" by Profs. Ashish Seth and Kirti Seth from INHA University, India, which focuses on explaining the fundamentals of opinion mining along with sentiment analysis and covers the brief evolution in mining techniques in the last decade. This first section ends with the chapter "Sentiment Analysis in Crisis Situations for Better Connected Government: Case of Mexico Earthquake in 2017" by Profs. Rodrigo Sandoval-Almazán, Asdrúbal López Chau, and David Valle-Cruz from the Universidad Autónoma del Estado de México, Mexico, which adapts the methodology of sentiment analysis of social media posts to an expanded version for crisis situations.

Section 2, "Development and Design Methodologies," presents in-depth coverage of the design and development of sentiment analysis for its use in different applications. This section starts with "Integrating Semantic Acquaintance for Sentiment Analysis" by Profs. Rashmi Agrawal and Neha Gupta from Manav Rachna International Institute of Research and Studies, India, which focuses on semantic guidance-based sentiment analysis approaches and provides a semantically enhanced technique for annotation of sentiment polarity. This section closes with "An Extensive Text Mining Study for the Turkish Language: Author Recognition, Sentiment Analysis, and Text Classification" by Profs. Durmuş Özkan Şahin and Erdal Kılıç from Ondokuz Mayıs University, Turkey, which provides theoretical and experimental information about text mining and discusses three different text mining problems such as news classification, sentiment analysis, and author recognition.

Section 3, "Tools and Technologies," explores the various tools and technologies used for the implementation of sentiment analysis for various uses. This section begins with "Tools of Opinion Mining" by Profs. Neha Gupta and Siddharth Verma from Manav Rachna International Institute of Research and Studies, India, which examines how opinion mining is moving to the sentimental reviews of Twitter data, comments used on Facebook, videos, or Facebook statuses. This section closes with the chapter "Opinion Mining for Instructor Evaluations at the Autonomous University of Ciudad Juarez" by Profs. Abraham López, Alejandra Mendoza Carreón, Rafael Jiménez, Vicente García, and Alan Ponce from the Universidad Autónoma de Ciudad Juárez, Mexico, which considers how opinion mining can be useful for labeling student comments as positive and negative and, for this purpose, creates a database using real opinions obtained from five professors over the last four years, covering a total of 20 subjects.

Section 4, "Utilization and Applications," describes how sentiment analysis is used and applied in diverse industries for various applications. The opening chapter in this section, "A Survey on Implementation Methods and Applications of Sentiment Analysis," by Profs. Sudheer Karnam, Valarmathi B., and Tulasi Prasad Sariki from VIT University, India, compares different methods of solving sentiment analysis problems, algorithms, merits and demerits, and applications and also investigates different research problems in sentiment analysis. The closing chapter in this section, "Communicating Natural Calamity: The Sentiment Analysis of Post Rigopiano's Accident," by Profs. Nicola Capolupo and Gabriella Piscopo from the University of Salerno, Italy, aims at understanding the dynamics that led to the exchange and value co-creation/co-production in the interaction between P.A. and citizens during natural calamities and proposes a horizontal communication model in which both actors cooperate to respond to a crisis.

Section 5, "Organizational and Social Implications," includes chapters discussing the impact of sentiment analysis on society and shows the ways in which it can be used in different industries and how this impacts business. The chapter "Open Issues in Opinion Mining" by Profs. V. Uma and Vishal Vyas from Pondicherry University, India, explains the various research issues and challenges present in each stage of opinion mining. The closing chapter, "eWOW of Guests Regarding Their Hotel Experience: Sentiment Analysis of TripAdvisor Reviews," by Profs. Zelia Breda and Rui Costa from GOVCOPP, University of Aveiro, Portugal; Prof. Gorete Dinis from GOVCOPP, Polytechnic Institute of Portalegre, Portugal; and Prof. Amandine Angie Martins of the University of Aveiro, Portugal, focuses on sentiment analysis of comments made on TripAdvisor regarding one resort located in the Algarve region in Portugal.

Section 6, "Critical Issues and Challenges," presents coverage of academic and research perspectives on the challenges of using sentiment analysis in varied industries. Opening this final section is the chapter "Multimodal Sentiment Analysis: A Survey and Comparison" by Profs. Ramandeep Kaur and Sandeep Kautish from Guru Kashi University, India, which provides a full image of the multimodal sentiment analysis opportunities and difficulties and considers the recent trends of research in the field. The closing chapter, "A Sentiment Analysis of the 2014-15 Ebola Outbreak in the Media and Social Media," by Prof. Nilmini Wickramasinghe from Swinburne University of Technology, Australia & Epworth Health-Care, Australia; Prof. Blooma John of the University of Canberra, Australia; and Dr. Bob Baulch from the International Food Policy Research Institute, Malawi, analyzes news articles on the Ebola outbreak from two leading news outlets, together with comments on the articles from a well-known social media platform, from March 2014 to July 2015.

Although the primary organization of the contents in this multi-volume work is based on its six sections, offering a progression of coverage of the important concepts, methodologies, technologies, applications, social issues, and emerging trends, the reader can also identify specific contents by utilizing the extensive indexing system listed at the end of each volume. As a comprehensive collection of research on the latest findings related to sentiment analysis, the *Research Anthology on Implementing Sentiment Analysis Across Multiple Disciplines* provides social media analysts, computer scientists, IT professionals, AI scientists, business leaders and managers, marketers, advertising agencies, public administrators, government officials, university administrators, libraries, instructors, researchers, academicians, and students with a complete understanding of the applications and impacts of sentiment analysis across fields and disciplines. Given the vast number of issues concerning usage, failure, success, strategies, and applications of sentiment analysis, the *Research Anthology on Implementing Sentiment Analysis Across Multiple Disciplines* encompasses the most pertinent research on the applications, impacts, uses, and development of sentiment analysis.

Chapter 32
Building Sentiment Analysis Model and Compute Reputation Scores in E-Commerce Environment Using Machine Learning Techniques

Ishrag Ibrahim Elhafni

Abdelouahed Gherbi
https://orcid.org/0000-0001-9419-4526

ABSTRACT

Online reputation systems are a novel and active part of e-commerce environments, such as eBay, Amazon, etc. These reputation-based applications allow for trust calculation by measuring the overall feedback ratings given by buyers, which enables buyers to compare the reputation score of their products...

DOI: 10.4018/978-1-6684-7207-1.ch032

Chapter 52

Building Sentiment Analysis Model and Compute Reputation Scores in E–Commerce Environment Using Machine Learning Techniques

Elshrif Ibrahim Elmurngi

École de Technologie Supérieure, Montreal, Canada

Abdelouahed Gherbi

ⓘ https://orcid.org/0000-0001-9117-5743

École de Technologie Supérieure, Montreal, Canada

ABSTRACT

Online reputation systems are a novel and active part of e-commerce environments such as eBay, Amazon, etc. These corporations use reputation reporting systems for trust evaluation by measuring the overall feedback ratings given by buyers, which enables them to compute the reputation score of their products. Such evaluation and computation processes are closely related to sentiment analysis and opinion mining. These techniques incorporate new features into traditional tasks, like polarity detection for positive or negative reviews. The "all excellent reputation" problem is common in the e-commerce domain. Another problem is that sellers can write unfair reviews to endorse or reject any targeted product since a higher reputation leads to higher profits. Therefore, the purpose of the present work is to use a statistical technique for excluding unfair ratings and to illustrate its effectiveness through simulations. Also, the authors have calculated reputation scores from users' feedback based on a sentiment analysis model (SAM). Experimental results demonstrate the effectiveness of the approach.

DOI: 10.4018/978-1-6684-6303-1.ch052

1. INTRODUCTION

E-commerce has become one of the major way of shopping for products ranging from simple electronics to valuable items. Almeroth, and Zhao (2010) where collective unfair ratings are referred to as collusion Sun and Liu (2012); Swamynathan et al. (2010) and are more complicated and much difficult to detect than the single unfair ratings Sun and Liu (2012). For that reason, in the present work, we are focusing on understanding and identifying unfair rating scores, all good reputation problems, and collusion and manipulation detection. In online shopping, the customers often depend on other customers' feedback posted through a rating system, before deciding on buying a product (Mukherjee, Liu, & Glance, 2012). Online feedback-based rating systems, also known as online reputation systems, are systems in which users provide ratings to items they bought. Based on the feedback of the product, the consumer decides whether to buy the product or not. This motivates the seller to promote or demote a product of their interest depending on their competitors' product, by posting rating scores which are unfair (Brown and Morgan, 2006; Harmon, 2004). For example, fraudulent sellers may try to increase their income by submitting positive feedback which increases their product rating (Harmon, 2004). In addition, occasional sellers on eBay boost their reputations unfairly by selling or buying feedbacks (Brown and Morgan, 2006). Unfair rating scores are given singularly or collectively Swamynathan,

In the present work, we are focusing on understanding and identifying unfair rating scores, all good reputation problems, and collusion and manipulation detection.

Figure 1. Generic process of "all good reputation" problem

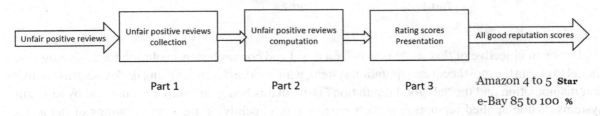

An online rating system needs truthful feedback in order to work properly. An important part of a rating system is creating honest and representative feedback. It should not only have qualitative, quantitative facts opinion-based process, but also should detect situations where some users may try to mislead the system by providing unfair positive and negative reviews, which is likely to lead to collusion and manipulation. Figure 1 Generic process of a reputation system and consists of three main components: feedback collection, computation and rating scores presentation (Noorian and Ulieru, 2010; Sun and Liu, 2012). Feedback Collection is responsible for collecting feedback from community and feeding it to the rating system. A feedback is the opinion of an evaluator on the quality of an item or a person. Generally, a feedback can be expressed either as a number, such as a textual review, or a rating score (Adler, de Alfaro, Kulshreshtha, and Pye, 2011). A numeric feedback can be a negative or positive number chosen from either a discrete list of options, for example, an integer choice between 1 and 5 representing quality of an item. Feedback computation is responsible for computation of all feedbacks received from evaluators to calculate correct rating scores for people and items. Investigating the feedback computation part after using sentiment classification algorithm is the focus of this study.

According to Reyes-Menendez, Saura, and Martinez-Navalon (2019), it is improbable for all consumers to be satisfied with a product, very positive ratings might be interpreted by users as incredible information. Consequently, it is recommended that companies ensure that the feedback made to them on platforms such as TripAdvisor, contains only actual comments, as well as several less positive comments; this can generate greater customer credibility and reliability of an offered product.

Figure 2 shows how unfair positive and negative reviews affects negatively on reputation scores computation. If the collection part collects unfair positive and negative reviews, the computation part will compute unfair positive and negative reviews and then the rating scores presentation part will present unfair rating scores as output.

Both the research community and the e-commerce industries has accepted unfair reviews to be a crucial challenge to the e-commerce industry Feng, Xing, Gogar, and Choi (2012) and Breure (2013); Sussin and Thompson (2012). Any (positive or negative) review that is an unfair review and not an actual consumer's honest opinion will affect reputation scores negatively.

Figure 2. Impact unfair positive and negative reviews on the reputation system

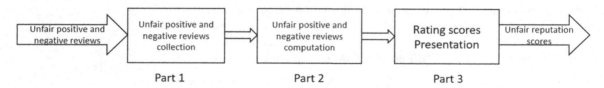

The main objective of this study is to offer a novel and comprehensive solution for designing a new model to obtain the most accurate reputation system, which addresses the existing issues, such as collusion and manipulation and the "all good reputation" issue that is being currently encountered by reputation systems. While applied reputation models currently rely mainly on the overall ratings of items, they do not involve customer reviews in their assessment. Conversely, few of the reputation models focus only on the overall reviews of products without considering the ratings provided by the customers. This research aims to compute feedback rating based on feedback reviews. Subsequently, in order to get accurate reputation scores, we propose a simple calculation method that calculates feedback ratings and feedback reviews to obtain real feedback ratings and real feedback reviews, after detecting unfair feedback ratings and unfair feedback reviews, as opposed to, Amazon or eBay websites that calculate reputation scores from unfair feedback ratings and unfair feedback reviews. As mentioned above and based on the limitations of the existing methods employed, our main contributions to enhance Reputation systems are summarized as follows:

1.   This study uses the Scikit-learn machine in Python tool, an open source software for implementing machine learning algorithms Brunner and Kim (2016), to apply sentiment classification with the Logistic regression algorithm which classifies the Amazon reviews datasets into unfair and fair reviews and unfair and fair ratings.

2. The sentiment classification algorithm is applied with CountVectorizer Selection and TfidfVectorizer Selection, using two different Amazon reviews datasets. We observed that it is more effective to use the CountVectorizer Selection method than using TfidfVectorizer Selection and that it is more efficient to detect unfair reviews, "all good reputation" issues, collusion, and manipulation.

3. We propose a statistical method to detect unfair reputation scores. Subsequently, we have designed and implemented a logistic regression algorithm to calculate new ratings from real feedback ratings and real feedback reviews in order to obtain fair reputation scores.

4. To evaluate the effectiveness of the proposed mechanism:
   ○ Reducing the collusion and manipulation done by, both sides, customer and seller.
   ○ Establishing the confidence between customer and seller.
   ○ Provide the developer with the ability to improve current reputation systems and take into consideration all of the issues focused on in this study.

The remainder of this paper is organized as per the following: Section 2 shows Background and Related Work. Section 3 presents the applied methodology. Section 4 displays the results of the experiment and lastly, Section 5 presents our conclusion and future studies.

2. BACKGROUND AND RELATED WORK

In this study, we demonstrate some background regarding Reputation System issues in E-commerce environment and discuss some related work to set the present study in the context of other studies.

2.1. Background

2.1.1. Definition of Reputation System

The Reputation, in general, is information used to make a value judgment about one thing within the context for a limited period Farmer and Glass (2010). As a first definition, a Reputation system can be considered as one of the established mechanisms to help customers in making decision in online shopping Gutowska and Sloane (2009). The second definition of a Reputation system is a process that collects, distributes and aggregates feedback about the participant's behavior.

2.1.2. Benefits and Limitations of Reputation System

We have identified the benefits and limitations of reputation systems in general as the following:

Benefits
   ○ Several websites currently provide a rating system for products, which allows customers to rate their online shopping experiences. The online ratings are aggregated and collected by Reputation systems to calculate all reputation for products, users, or services (Resnick, Kuwabara, Zeckhauser, and Friedman, 2000).
   ○ The insight gained from customer ratings about a product or service being good or bad can help improve customer satisfaction.

- ○ Creating opportunities to listen and involve customers to promote a particular brand.
- ○ Valuable insight can be gained about competitors by obtaining their customer's perception about their products and services.
- ○ The buyer can be aided by reputation systems to select the best seller for their transaction and avoiding getting cheated by the seller.
- ○ Marketing expenses can be reduced by knowing how the customers can be reached.
- ○ The services which require less time and money can be employed, thus reducing internal costs.

Limitations

- ○ Manipulation of a reputation system cannot be detected if there are no robust technical mechanisms (Jøsang, 2012)
- ○ It is difficult to stop collusion and potential attack due to the behavior of malicious identities (Saini, Sihag, and Yadav, 2014)
- ○ On online social networks, the mitigating and detecting the manipulated Reputation effect is an important drawback of Reputation systems (RSs) (Aggarwal, 2016).
- ○ The "all good reputation" problem is common in the e-commerce field, making it hard for buyers to choose credible sellers (Jha, Ramu, Shenoy, and Venugopa, 2017).

E. Elmurngi and Gherbi (2017a), E. Elmurngi and Gherbi (2017b), E. I. Elmurngi and Gherbi (2018) and Barbado, Araque, and Iglesias (2019) presented sentiment classification techniques, and they have detected unfair reviews. However, they have not computed reputation scores, after detecting unfair negative reviews and unfair positive reviews. In our study, we have detected unfair positive reviews and unfair negative reviews and computed reputation scores and, after having computed reputation scores, this article have detected other issues such as "all good reputation" problems, collusion and manipulation issues.

2.1.3. Generic Architecture of a Reputation System

According to Resnick, Zeckhauser, Friedman, and Kuwabara (2000) a rating expresses an opinion as a result of a transaction through the feedback of the customer. Reputation systems, through monitoring, collect, combine and distribute this feedback. Figure 3 shows the main components of a reputation system and its actors: The collector gathers ratings from agents called raters. The goal of a rating is called ratee. This information is aggregated and processed by the processor. The algorithm used by the processor to calculate an aggregated representation of an agent's reputation is the metric of the reputation system. The distributor makes the outcome available to other requesting agents.

2.1.4. Sentiment Analysis

Sentiment analysis (SA), also called opinion mining, is an approach to natural language Processing (NLP) that extracts subjective information behind a body of text Gamal, Alfonse, M El-Horbaty, and M Salem (2019). Text mining techniques consist of huge repository of unorganized data. To extract latent public opinion and sentiment through analysing this data is a challenging task. The aim of Sentiment Analysis is to study the reviews and evaluate the scores of sentiments. This analysis can be divided into several levels: document level Moraes, Valiati, and Neto (2013), sentence level Shoukry and Rafea (2012), sentence level Shoukry and Rafea (2012), word/term level Engonopoulos, Lazaridou, Paliouras, and

Chandrinos (2011) or aspect level Zhou and Song (2015). The main aim of the analysis is to predict the sentiment inclination (i.e. positive, negative or neutral) by studying opinion words or sentiments and expressions in sentences and documents.

Figure 3. Architecture of a reputation system

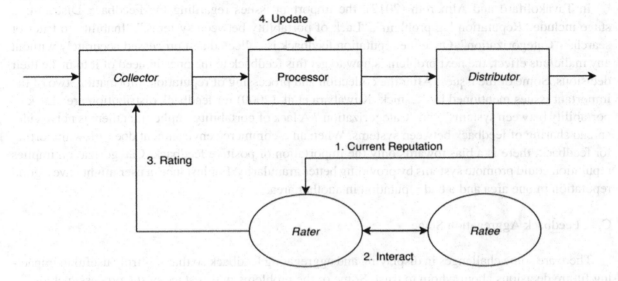

2.2. Related Work

The aim of this section is to set the present study in the context of other studies of reputation system vulnerabilities evaluation. This section employs a statistical method to vulnerability assessment; the related work emphasizes those studies that have applied statistical methods to this issue. Finally, this section compares these approaches outlining their weaknesses.

2.2.1. The Fundamental Problems and Available Solutions on Reputation Systems

There are three stages of operation on reputation systems, namely: first stage is feedback generation, second stage is feedback distribution, and third stage is feedback aggregation. Each stage of these components needs protecting against a variety of adversarial threats.

A.   Feedback Generation Stage

Representative feedback is one of the most significant tasks in a reputation system. Actually, users will occasionally try to trick the system and we have identified some issues as follows:

Unfair feedback reviews: This issue results from incorrectly presenting some users feedback reviews, which leads to create some errors in the system.

Unfair Review Detection: Presently, Amazon website uses some machine learning algorithms to select relevant features and decide the final rating of a product. However, it does not apply any algorithm to detect whether a review is unfair or not. Few websites, like Yelp.com and Fakespot.com, can be used to detect unfair reviews online, but there is no particular algorithm to filter reviews Mane, Assar, Sawant, and Shinde (2017).

B.   Feedback Distribution Stage

In Tavakolifard and Almeroth (2012), the important issues regarding the Feedback Distribution stage include "Reputation lag problem", "Lack of portability between systems," "Inability to filter or search," "Categorization". Once the reputation feedback is collected and processed accurately without any malicious effect, the next problem is how to get this feedback to the ones in need of it to make their decisions. Some of the issues: After the collection and processing of reputation information, two of the important issues mentioned by Resnick, Kuwabara et al. (2000) for feedback distribution are "Lack of portability between systems" and "Categorization." A lack of portability implies that there is not a widespread sharing of feedback between systems. When an e-commerce environment does allow importing for feedback, there is a bias towards only the importation of positive feedback. Categorization implies reputation could promote systems by providing better granularity. For instance, a user might have a good reputation in one area and a bad reputation in another area.

C.   Feedback Aggregation Stage

There are some challenges in displaying and aggregating feedback so that it is truly useful in impacting future decisions about whom to trust. Some of the problems in this stage of the process include:

Inaccurate equations: Some of E-commerce websites, such as eBay, use a simple reputation schema that could be misleading for users. For instance, an equal reputation score would be assigned to two users on eBay, one of them with ten negative ratings and 100 positive ratings; while the other with no negative ratings and 90 positive ratings. This is likely to lead to raise the vulnerability issue caused by "increased trust by increased volume" (Tavakolifard and Almeroth, 2012).

The publishing of false rumors: This issue occurs when the reputation of the feedback providers is not considered. According to Hoffman, Zage, and Nita-Rotaru (2009), one approach to this issue is to employ statistical methods to build Bayesian framework and robust formulations as an example that can be reasoned about in a precise method.

2.2.2. Reputation System for E-Commerce Applications

In online marketplaces like eBay, reputations of E-Commerce Marketplaces now act as an essential role in the decision to start a transaction and in the pricing of goods or services. A user's reputation as the sum of the lifetime ratings are computed by eBay's Feedback. These lifetime ratings then create reputation profiles which are tailored to forecast future performance and to aid users. Resnick and Zeckhauser (2002) The sellers that have excellent reputations can request for higher prices of their products, whereas poor reputation holders can only interest a fewer buyers. Ert, Fleischer, and Magen (2016) shows that a seller's reputation, given by review scores in online marketplace, does not influence the listing price or possibility of consumer purchases. They proved that changing a review score or reputation score has an effect on the buyer's decision, but the task of the visual cues is still substantial for tourism industry.

2.2.3. Textual Reviews to Provide Detailed Opinion about the Product

Current reputation models mostly rely on numerical data from different fields, such as ratings in e-commerce. These reputation models only consider the overall ratings of the products without taking into account reviews given by customers Xu et al. (2016). On the other hand, many online websites admit consumers to give textual reviews of their opinion About the product Tian, Xu, Li, Abdel-Hafez, and Josang (2014), Tian, Xu, Li, Abdel-Hafez, and Jøsang (2014).Thus, some of the reputation models only use the textual reviews of products, not taking into account ratings which were provided by customers. Consumers can read these reviews, and now an increasing number of users rely on these reviews more than the ratings. Reputation models could use sentiment analysis methods to obtain users opinion which can be used by reputation systems having included consumers opinion on different features (Abdel-Hafez and Xu, 2013; Abdel-Hafez, Xu, and Tjondronegoro, 2012).

2.2.4. Sentiment Analysis Based on User Behavior

Many researchers are working on opinion mining and sentiment analysis on textual information gathered from social network platforms. These opinions and sentiments are being used to improve business productivity (Iqbal, Zulqurnain, Wani, and Hussain, 2015).

To understand the behaviors of people are difficult and complex. In order to understand people's behaviors, it takes many resources to collect and analyze a large amount of information such as posts, comments, clicking likes, and sharing of thoughts. However, the difficulty is to get real business and customer data, since it is challenging to get confidential data (Chang, 2018). A Social Network Analysis Platform is designed to understand the strength of the relationship between social networks and sentiment analysis. Karyotis, Doctor, Iqbal, James, and Chang (2018) aim to show the usefulness of implementing the proposed fuzzy emotion representation model and to demonstrate its effectiveness and applicability in big data settings. However, the authors approach does not use sentiment analysis and opinion mining for detecting unfair feedback ratings and unfair feedback reviews from a Social Network. This study proposes a new method to build a Sentiment Analysis Model and compute Reputation scores in an e-commerce environment using machine learning techniques.

2.2.5. Importance of Logistic Regression (LR) on Sentiment Classification Techniques

The researchers E. I. Elmurngi and Gherbi (2018) used Sentiment classification techniques against a dataset of consumer reviews. The experiments were carried out using classification algorithms: Naïve Bayes (NB), Decision Tree (DT-J48), Logistic Regression (LR) and Support Vector Machine (SVM) for sentiment classification using three datasets of reviews. The experiments' results show that the Logistic Regression (LR) algorithm achieves better performance and is the best classifier with the highest accuracy as compared to the other three classifiers, not merely in text classification, but in unfair reviews detection as well. The researchers Gamal et al. (2019) and Lin, Lei, Wu, and Li (2015) presented an empirical study on Sentiment Classification and Logistic Regression which is constructed to combine different machine learning methods and get an outstanding performance in precision and recall.

2.2.6. The Impact of Feature Selection on Classification Accuracy

Techniques for feature selection are very beneficial for text classification in general and specifically in sentiment analysis. Fattah (2017), Guyon and Elisseeff (2003). These techniques rank features by given less weightage to non-informative features so that these features can be removed while valuable features are given more weightage to be kept for better classification accuracy and efficiency based on a specific measure. In this work, we study two feature selection techniques with the Logistic Regression, including CountVectorizer selection and TfidfVectorizer selection.

3. METHODOLOGY AND PROPOSED APPROACH

Our methodology was organized in the next six steps, as shown in Figure 4, steps that involve the supervised sentiment classification approaches using the scikit-learn in python tool for text classification, as described below.

3.1. Amazon Reviews Collection

Datasets of Amazon are used by many researchers such as Catherine and Cohen (2017), E.I. Elmurngi and Gherbi (2018), Ling, Lyu, and King (2014), Tan, Zhang, Liu, and Ma (2016). The datasets are available and have been collected and released by McAuley and Leskovec (2013). We have based our experiment on analyzing the standard datasets of Amazon reviews to sentiment value using Logistic regression algorithm and classification methods. Datasets of Amazon have many different kinds of products, however here we focus on two datasets: The Baby reviews dataset, and The Sports and Outdoors dataset, with raw data size of 30.5 MB and 65.1 MB, respectively. According to Chen, Chai, Liu, and Xu (2015) the category list provides all reviews of top customers. The kinds containing most reviews are "Sports and Outdoors" (296,337 reviews), "Baby" (160,792 reviews), while consumers' reviews in "Digital Music" (64,706 reviews), "Musical Instruments" (10,261 reviews), and "Amazon Instant Video" (37,126 reviews) have the least reviews. Each product review of dataset is provided with the following labels: ReviewerID, asin, reviewerName, helpful, reviewText, overall, summary, unixReviewTime, reviewTime.

3.2. Data Cleaning and Preprocessing

The Python programming language with Scikit-learn is a free software machine learning library that was used for the cleaning and preprocessing process. This language was chosen because of the ability to deal with several languages, and the available libraries and packages for English text. Data cleaning and preprocessing was done in some steps in order to get the dataset cleaned and ready for learning by the classification algorithm.

Figure 3 shows all the steps and their order for the cleaning process. The datasets used in our experiment are obtained from Amazon product and was divided into five scales rating: 1 star, 2 stars, 3 stars, 4 stars and 5 stars. The original datasets are not cleaned and not easy to model for classification. We have separated the datasets before cleaning and applied the sentiment classification classifiers after cleaning and after using Logistic regression algorithm.

Figure 4. Research methodology

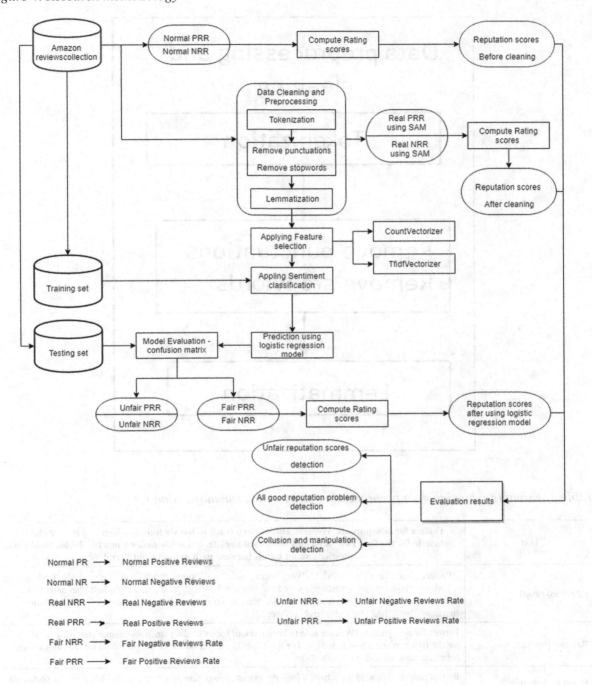

Pre-processing of data is an important step in the text mining process and plays a significant part in a number of supervised learning techniques, Figure 5 and Table 1 show all the steps for the Pre-processing of data process using SAM. Pre-processing of datasets are majorly done in three steps, as per the following:

Figure 5. Data preprocessing steps

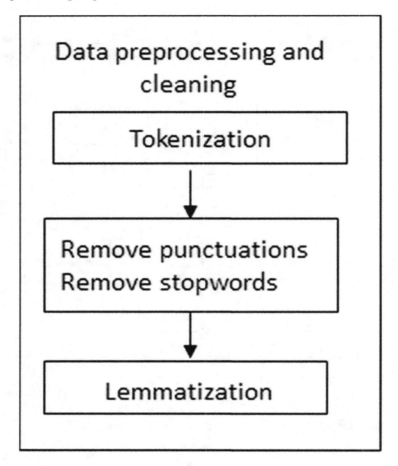

Table 1. Examples showing data preprocessing steps of text summarization

text	Perfect for new parents. We were able to keep track of baby's feeding, sleep and diaper change schedule for the first two and a half months of her life. Made life easier when the doctor would ask questions about habits because we had it all right there!
tokenized_word	['Perfect', 'for', 'new', 'parents', '.', 'We', 'were', 'able', 'to', 'keep', 'track', 'of', 'baby', "'s", 'feeding', ',', 'sleep', 'and', 'diaper', 'change', 'schedule', 'for', 'the', 'first', 'two', 'and', 'a', 'half', 'months', 'of', 'her', 'life', '.', 'Made', 'life', 'easier', 'when', 'the', 'doctor', 'would', 'ask', 'questions', 'about', 'habits', 'because', 'we', 'had', 'it', 'all', 'right', 'there', '!']
Remove punctuations	Perfect for new parents We were able to keep track of babys feeding sleep and diaper change schedule for the first two and a half months of her life Made life easier when the doctor would ask questions about habits because we had it all right there
Remove stopwords	Perfect parents. We able track baby's feeding, diaper change schedule half months. Made easier doctor ask questions habits right!
Lemmatized	perfect for new parent. we be able to keep track of baby 's feeding, sleep and diaper change schedule for the first two and a half month of her life. make life easy when the doctor would ask question about habit because we have it all right there!

Step One: Tokenization

In this process, after the data is retrieved from the datasets, we tokenize the sentences into words, so that it is easily to understand and count.

Step Two: Punctuation and Stopwords Removal

- Punctuation Removal

Punctuation is a string containing numbers, whitespace, and letters, including periods, semicolons, and commas. Basically, we believe that removing punctuation from a string is the best way in Python or any other tool in machine learning techniques.

- Stopwords Removal

Stopwords are the English words, which does not add much meaning to a sentence, and must be filtered out. For example, the words such as "the," "he," "a," "of," "you," "and," "have," etc.

Step Three: Lemmatization:

Lemmatization is called word normalization techniques in the field of Natural Language Processing (NLP) that are used to prepare text, words, and documents for further processing. The main function of lemmatization is the process of converting the words into their root words. In our study, we have used lemmatization, not steaming, because throughout our implementation we have compared between both, applying some words, such as feeding and flying: the conversion of feeding using steaming is feed, and the conversion of feeding using lemmatization is also feed. However, the conversion of flying using steaming is fli, and the conversion of flying using lemmatization is fly. Some special words using steaming are not given meaning and it will have an effect on sentiment classification and that is the reason why we are using lemmatization and not steaming.

3.3. Feature Selection

In data pre-processing, in order to gain efficient data reduction, feature selection (FS) methods in sentiment analysis can be employed. This helps to find precise data models and in finding the important attributes Koncz and Paralic (2011). In the recent paper, the list of features applied to classify sentiments include N-gram features, this feature has been the baseline in most related research Agarwal and Mittal (2016); Dashtipour et al. (2016). In this study, bigrams are applied as feature sets, and these features are consisting of every two consecutive words and capable of incorporating some contextual information.

Our research has implemented two-feature selection methods as show bellow:

- **CountVectorizer:** The CountVectorizer gives an easy method for tokenizing a compilation of text and for building terminology of known words.
- **TfidVectorizer:** The TfidfVectorizer will tokenize documents, learn the vocabulary and inverse document frequency weightings, and allow you to encode new documents.

In our study, the Logistic Regression algorithm with CountVectorizer feature selection achieved better performance than TfidfVectorizer.

3.4. Sentiment Classification Method

To apply sentiment classification, several supervised methods have been applied to these systems using supervised methods based on manually labelled samples Pang, Lee, et al. (2008). The sentiment in sentiment classification method is determined by training on a known dataset, and classifying feedback reviews as positive or negative. Actually, logistic regression is a robust algorithm fortwo-class classification. In our study, we used Logistic Regression algorithm with two-feature selection methods. A really fast and well-known classification algorithm is Logistic Regression (LR), also known as the logistic function, and is used to assign observations to a discrete set of classes. In our work, we employ this algorithm with CountVectorizer as feature selection and found that it is the most suitable and precise method.

3.5. Detection Processes

The original datasets, which we used in our study, are not labelled as positive and negative reviews. However, we prepared the datasets and we labeled them as positive and negative reviews based on ratings scores provided by users, as shown in Tables 5a and Table 5b. In our study, we built a sentiment classifier to identify whether the review has a positive or negative sentiment. The Logistic Classifier model used the CountVectorizer Selection and TfidfVectorizer Selection from the training data to develop a model predicting True positive reviews, False positive reviews, True negative reviews, and True negative reviews. We noted the numbers of positive and negative reviews from the original datasets, as shown in Tables. 5a and Table 5b, which are not the same numbers of positive and negative reviews found when we used the sentiment classification, as shown in Tables 7a and Table 7b.

In order to evaluate the performance of our classification model and test our results, there is a very common method called confusion matrix, which is shown in Table 4. The confusion matrix displays the methods in which the classification model is confused when making predictions Hinton, Vinyals, and Dean (2015). Reviews are classified based on the generated confusion matrix to positive and negative. In our classification of reviews, unfair is made up of the set of reviews considered to be False, which in this case involves both False positive reviews and False Negative reviews. On the other hand, Real is defined to combine the set of reviews to be considered as True, which in this case involves both True positive reviews and True Negative reviews. The fair reviews and unfair reviews are determined according to equations 1 to 4 as shown in Table 3.

- True Positive Reviews (TPR): when the actual class of the positives reviews point was 1 (True) and the predicted is also 1 (True)
- True Negative Reviews (TNR): when the actual class of the negatives reviews point was 0 (False) and the predicted is also 0 (False)
- False Positive Reviews (FPR): when the actual class of the positives reviews point was 0 (False) and the predicted is 1 (True).
- False Negative Reviews (FNR): when the actual class of the negatives reviews point was 1 (True) and the predicted is 0 (False).

Evaluation measures from the confusion matrix, (1)-(7) as shown in Table 3 display numerical parameters that apply below the mentioned measures to assess the Detection Process performance. In Table 2 the confusion matrix shows the Predicted actual reviews and Predicted unactual reviews forecasting found through known data, and for each algorithm used in this study are different confusion matrix and performance evaluation.

Table 2. The confusion matrix

	Predicted actual reviews Fair	Predicted actual reviews Unfair
Actual reviews Fair	True Negative Reviews (TNR)	False Positive Reviews (FPR)
Actual reviews Unfair	False Negative Reviews (FNR)	True Positive Reviews (TPR)

For each feature selection with Logistic Regression algorithm used in our study different Performance evaluation and confusion matrix.

Table 3. Evaluation measures from the confusion matrix

Measure	Formula	
Unfair PRR	FP / (TN + FP)	(1)
Unfair NRR	FN / (TP + FN)	(2)
Fair PRR	TP / (TP + FN)	(3)
Fair NRR	TN / (TN + FP)	(4)
ACC	(TP + TN)/ (TP + TN + FN + FP)	(5)
PREC	TP / (TP + FP)	(6)
REC	TP/(TP+FN)	(7)
Unfair PRR: Unfair Positive Reviews Rate; Unfair NRR: UnfairNegative Reviews Rate; Real PRR: Real Positive Reviews Rate; Fair NRR: FairNegative Reviews Rate; ACC: Accuracy; PREC: Precision; REC: Recall;TPR: True Positive Reviews; TNR: True Negative Reviews; FPR: False PositivesReview; FNR: False Negatives Review		

3.6. Calculation Processes

Feedback scores, stars and percentages on eBay or amazon are the original and best-known marketplace reputation system. The system has become more developed in recent years. In Figure 6a and Figure 6b show an example of eBay overall rating and an example of Amazon overall rating, respectively. Feedback is generally reciprocal; users almost always give positive feedback. The techniques for calculating rater's credibility in most of the existing models are not sufficient either. The authors in Malik and Bouguettaya (2009) propose an extremely complicated method to calculate rater's credibility. In our study, we have used a simple calculation method in order to compute reputation scores from real feedback reviews, after detecting unfair reviews.

Figure 6. Examples of overall ratings (Figure a. Example of overall rating from Amazon.com; Figure b. Example of overall rating from ebay.com)

3.7. Reputation Scores Calculation

On eBay

On eBay, the reputation score is represented by the Positive Feedback Percentage (PFP), which is computed through the transaction which ended within the last year based on the total number of positive and negative Feedback ratings using this formula:

$$PFP = positive / Positive + Negative \tag{8}$$

We have transferred positive Feedback percentage to positive Feedback star in order to calculate the reputation scores calculation on amazon using this formula:

$$Reputation\ scores = (PFP * 5) / 100 \tag{9}$$

Example

Positive: 850 Negative: 10

PFP = 850 / (850 + 10) = 98.8

Reputation scores = (98.8 * 5scores) / 100 = 4.9scores

On Amazon

Amazon calculates a product's star ratings using a machine learned model instead of a raw data average. However, we did not find the formula that Amazon uses to calculate the Reputation scores. In our study, we have used the same formula which eBay used to calculate the positive Feedback percentage and then we have transferred the positive Feedback percentage to the positive Feedback star in order to create the reputation scores calculation on Amazon, as shown in equation 9.

Example 1

Figure 7. A review example of Android 7.1 TV Box, ABOX A1 Max from Amazon.com

Figure 7 displays a webpage screenshot of customer reviews, showing 1-10 of 206 reviews (5 star), Showing 1-10 of 79 reviews (4 star), Showing 1-10 of 27 reviews (3 star), Showing 1-10 of 18 reviews (2 star), and Showing 1-10 of 52 reviews (1 star).

$\sum$reviews (1star) + $\sum$reviews (2star) = Negative reviews

$\sum$(4star) + $\sum$(5star) = Positive reviews

Negative reviews = 70

Positive reviews = 285

PFP = Positives / (Positives + negatives)

PFP = 285 / (285 + 70) = 80.28

Reputation scores = (PFP * 5) / 100

Reputation scores = (80.28 * 5) / 100 = 4.0scores

Example 2

Figure 8. A review example of Slim Rechargeable Bluetooth Wireless Mouse from Amazon.com

Figure 8 displays a webpage screenshot of customer reviews, showing 1-10 of 216 reviews (5 star), showing 1-10 of 72 reviews (4 star), showing 1-10 of 18 reviews (3 star), showing 1-10 of 17 reviews (2 star), and showing 1-10 of 41 reviews (1 star).

$\sum$reviews(1star) + $\sum$reviews(2star) = Negative reviews

$\sum$reviews(4star) + $\sum$reviews(5star) = Positive reviews

Negative reviews = 58

Positive reviews = 288

PFP = Positives / (Positives + Negatives)

PFP = 288 / (288 + 58) = 83.23

Reputation scores = (PFP * 5) / 100

Reputation scores = (83.23 * 5) / 100 = 4.1scores

In our results, we have calculated Reputation scores before cleaning and after using Logistic regression algorithm with two different feature selections.

3.8. Evaluation Results

In this step, we have compared the different Reputation scores before cleaning, after cleaning, and after using Logistic Regression algorithm with diverse datasets from amazon.com, which are Baby reviews dataset, and Sports and Outdoors dataset. Accuracy and time required for execution by the Logistic Regression technique is observed with two different feature selections. The expected result is to obtain the detection of unfair reputation scores detection, all good reputation issue, and collusion and manipulation.

4. EXPERIMENTS AND RESULT ANALYSIS

In this section, we present experimental results based on a logistic regression technique borrowed by machine learning with two different feature selections to classifying sentiment on two different real datasets, which are Baby reviews dataset, and Sports and Outdoors dataset. In addition, we have used the same method at the same time to detect unfair reviews, and "all excellent reputation" problem and collusion and manipulation using the scikit-learn, which is the free software machine-learning library of the Python programming language.

The datasets that were used in our experiments come in json file and we have converted them to csv files before preparing the datasets for learning.

4.1. Basic Statistics of All Reviews Datasets and Overall Distribution of Ratings

Amazon's product reviews and ratings are a very important business. Customers on Amazon often make purchasing decisions based on those reviews, and a single bad review can cause a potential purchaser to reconsider. The primary difference between the two distributions is that there is a significantly higher proportion of Amazon customers giving only 5-star reviews. On dataset of Baby reviews, we first analyzed all reviews dataset and overall distribution of ratings. Table 4a and Figure 9a show that 58% of the reviews have an overall rating of 5 Star, 20% of the reviews have an overall rating of 4 Star, 11% of the reviews have an overall rating of 3 Star, 6% of the reviews have an overall rating of 2 Star, and 5% of the reviews have an overall rating of 1 Star. On the dataset of Sports and Outdoors reviews, we first analyzed all reviews dataset and overall distribution of ratings. Table 4b and Figure 9b show that 64% of the reviews have an overall rating of 5 Star, 22% of the reviews have an overall rating of 4 Star, 8% of the reviews have an overall rating of 3 Star, 3% of the reviews have an overall rating of 2 Star, and 3% of the reviews have an overall rating of 1 Star.

The distribution of ratings among the reviews show that most of the reviewers have given 5-star and 4-star ratings with relatively very few giving 1-star and 2-star ratings.

We prepared datasets on Baby reviews and Sports and Outdoors reviews and we Labeled them as Positive and Negative. As shown in Table.5a, Label of ratings and Reviews as Positive and Negative on dataset of Baby reviews and Table 5b, Label of ratings and Reviews as Positive and Negative on dataset of Sports and Outdoors reviews.

Figure 9. Distribution of ratings on datasets (Figure a. On Baby reviews dataset; Figure b. On Sports and Outdoors reviews dataset)

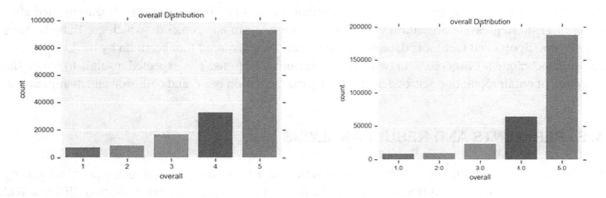

Table 4. Number of reviews and ratings

a: On Baby reviews dataset		b: On Sports and Outdoors reviews dataset	
Actual (Star)	**No. of Reviews**	**Actual (Star)**	**No. of Reviews**
1 Star	93526	1 Star	188208
2 Star	32999	2 Star	64809
3 Star	17255	3 Star	24071
4 Star	9193	4 Star	10204
5 Star	7819	5 Star	9045

Table 5. Label of ratings and reviews

a: On Baby reviews dataset			b: On Sports and Outdoors reviews dataset		
Actual (Star)	**No. of Reviews**	**Label of ratings**	**Actual (Star)**	**No. of Reviews**	**Label of ratings**
5.0 Star	126525	Positive	5.0 Star	253017	Positive
4.0 Star			4.0 Star		
3.0 Star	———	———	3.0 Star	———	———
2.0 Star	17012	Negative	2.0 Star	19249	Negative
1.0 Star			1.0 Star		

4.2 Reputation Scores before Cleaning

With the polarity results, Table 6a and Table 6b provide the basic of Sentiment and Number of reviews, which gives a high-level insight into what percentage and visualization of Sentiment and number of reviews are positive or negative, shown in Figure 10a and Figure 10b.

We have calculated Reputation scores before cleaning as the following:

1- On dataset of Baby reviews

Reputation scores = (PFP * 5scores) / 100

PFP = Positives / (Positives + Negatives)

PFP = 126525 / (126525 + 17012) = 88.14

Reputation = (88.14 * 5) / 100 = 4.4scores

2- On dataset of Sports and Outdoors reviews

Reputation scores = (PFP * 5scores) / 100

PPF = Positives / (Positives + Negatives)

PFP = 253017 / (253017 + 19249) = 92.93

Reputation scores = (92.93 * 5) / 100 = 4.6scores

Table 6. Sentiment and number of reviews

a: On Baby reviews dataset		b: On Baby Sports and Outdoors reviews dataset	
Sentiment	**No. of Reviews**	**Sentiment**	**No. of Reviews**
NEGATIVE	17012	NEGATIVE	19249
POSITIVE	126525	POSITIVE	253017

Figure 10. Percentage of sentiment and number of reviews on datasets (Figure a. On Baby reviews dataset; Figure b. On Sports and Outdoors reviews dataset)

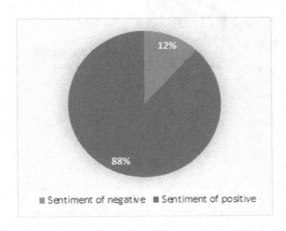

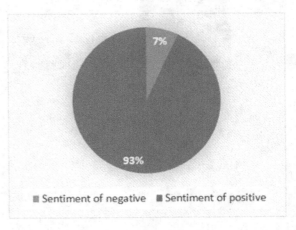

4.3 Reputation Scores after Cleaning

After we cleaned and preprocessed the datasets of products reviews and used sentiment analysis, we obtained Real Positive Reviews and Real Negative Review as show in Table 7a and Figure 11a on dataset of Baby reviews and Table 7b and Figure 11b on dataset of Sports and Outdoors reviews.

We have calculated Reputation scores after cleaning as the following:

1-   On dataset of Baby reviews

Reputation scores = (PFP * 5scores) / 100

PFP = Positives / (Positives + Negatives)

PFP = 125348 / (125348 + 34079) = 78.62

Reputation scores = (78.62 * 5) / 100 = 3.9scores

2-   On dataset of Sports and Outdoors reviews

Reputation scores = (PFP * 5scores) / 100.

PFP = Positives / (Positives + Negatives)

Reputation scores = (85.38 * 5) / 100 = 4.2scores

Figure 11. Distribution of ratings on datasets (Figure a. On Baby reviews dataset; Figure b. On Sports and Outdoors reviews dataset)

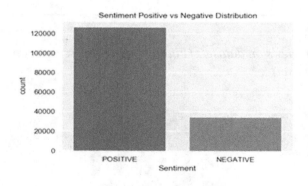
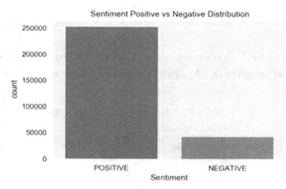

Table 7. Sentiment and number of reviews

a: On Baby reviews dataset		b: On Sports and Outdoors reviews dataset	
Sentiment	**No. of Reviews**	**Sentiment**	**No. of Reviews**
NEGATIVE	34079	NEGATIVE	43320
POSITIVE	125348	POSITIVE	253017

4.4 Training and Testing Sets

To build our model a training set is carried out in the dataset and for validation of our model a test set is built. We list the statistics of the data set in Table 8a and Table 8b. The dataset of Baby reviews was randomly divided into training set and test set. Training data contains 120594 reviews and the testing set contains 40198 reviews. Dataset of Sports and Outdoors reviews was randomly divided into training set and test set. Training data contains 222252 reviews and the testing set contains 74085 reviews.

Table 8. Training and testing on datasets

a: On Baby reviews dataset		b: On Sports and Outdoors reviews dataset	
Training	**Testing**	**Training**	**Testing**
120594	40198	222252	74085

4.5 Reputation Scores after Cleaning and after Using Logistic Regression Algorithm

Building a sentiment classifier to identify whether the review has positive or negative sentiment, the Logistic Classifier model will use the CountVectorizer Selection and TfidfVectorizer Selection from the training data to develop a model to predict True positive reviews, False positive reviews, True negative reviews, and True negative reviews. In this study, through Confusion matrix as shown in Figure 12a, 12b, 12c, and 12d we use True positive reviews as positive sentiment and True negative reviews as negative sentiment as show in Table 9 and Table 10 and Table 11 and Table 12 Then we calculate Reputation scores with CountVectorizer and TfidfVectorizer Selection on Baby reviews dataset, and Sports and Outdoors dataset, as explained in next steps.

1- CountVectorizer on Baby reviews dataset

Table 9. Sentiment and number of reviews

Sentiment	No. of Reviews
NEGATIVE	4935
POSITIVE	30128

Reputation scores = (PFP * 5scores) / 100

PFP = Positives / (Positives + Negatives)

PFP = 30128 / (30128 + 4935) = 60.18

Reputation scores = (60.18 * 5) / 100 = 3.0scores

2-   TfidfVectorizer on Baby reviews dataset

Table 10. Sentiment and number of reviews

Sentiment	No. of Reviews
NEGATIVE	3314
POSITIVE	30907

Reputation scores = (PFP * 5scores) / 100

PFP = Positives / (Positives + Negatives)

PFP = 30907 / (30907 + 3314) = 90.31

Reputation scores = (60.18 * 5) / 100 = 4.5scores

3-   CountVectorizer on Sports and Outdoors reviews dataset

Table 11. Sentiment and number of reviews

Sentiment	No. of Reviews
NEGATIVE	8121
POSITIVE	65964

Reputation scores = (PFP* 5 scores) / 100

PFP = Positives / (Positives + Negatives)

PFP = 65964 / (65964 + 8121) = 89.03

Reputation scores = (89.03 * 5) / 100 = 4.4scores

4-   TfidfVectorizer on Sports and Outdoors reviews dataset

Table 12. Sentiment and number of reviews

Sentiment	No. of Reviews
NEGATIVE	8963
POSITIVE	65122

Reputation scores = (PFP* 5 scores) / 100

PFP = Positives / (Positives + negatives)

PFP = 65122/(65122+8963) = 87.90

Reputation scores = (87.90 * 5) / 100 = 4.3 Scores

4.6 Unfair Reviews Detection Methods

The main goal of opinion unfair reviews Detection is to identify each unfair review. So there are mainly two methods to detect unfair reviews: unfair Positive Reviews value and unfair Negative Reviews value. One method using logistic regression algorithm with CountVectorizer Selection, and the second method using TfidfVectorizer Selection.

Table 13 displays the results of evaluation parameters for two different features selection and provides a summary of recordings of unfair reviews rate and fair reviews rate obtained from the experiment. The graph in Figures 13 and Figure 17 show the percentage of evaluation parameters with two features selection, CountVectorizer Selection and TfidfVectorizer Selection and we identfied a rate of unfair Negative Reviews,unfair Positive Reviews, fair Negative Reviews, fair Positive Reviews for comparative analysis of logistic regression algorithm.

Table 13. Evaluation parameters for two different methods

Logistic regression algorithm (on Baby dataset)				
Features	Unfair Positive Reviews Rate	Unfair negative Reviews Rate	Fair Positive Reviews Rate	Fair negative Reviews Rate
CountVectorizer	42.41	4.74	95.25	57.58
TfidfVectorizer	61.33	2.27	97.72	38.66

Figure 12. Confusion matrix on datasets (Figure a. On Baby reviews dataset with CountVectorizer Selection; Figure b. On Baby reviews dataset with TfidfVectorizer Selection; Figure c. On Sports and Outdoors dataset with CountVectorizer S; Figure d. On Sports and Outdoors dataset with TfidfVectorizer S)

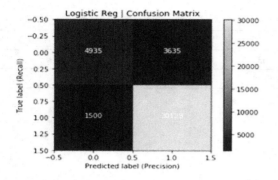

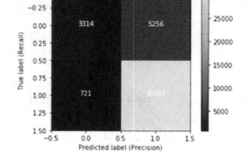

Figure a. On Baby reviews dataset with CountVectorizer Selection
Selection

Figure b. On Baby reviews dataset with TfidfVectorizer

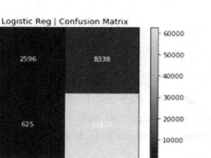

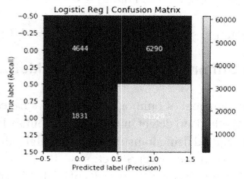

Figure c. On Sports and Outdoors dataset with CountVectorizer S
S

Figure c. On Sports and Outdoors dataset with TfidfVectorizer

Figure 13. Percentage of evaluation parameters with two features selection on baby dataset

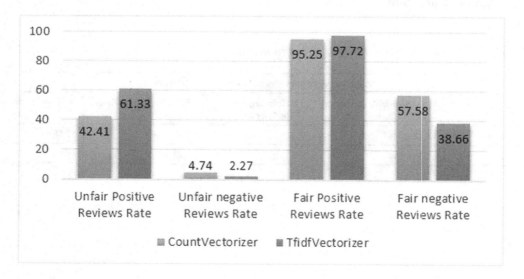

We have used CountVectorizer Selection for detection processes because, throughout our implementation, we have compared between CountVectorizer Selection and TfidfVectorizer Selection with Logistic Regression algorithm and we found more accuracy and less time with CountVectorizer Selection, and applied it for Baby and Sports and Outdoors datasets, as shown in Table 14 and Table 15 and Figures 14 and 15. In the Table 16a, Table 16b, Figure 16 and Figure 17 present the percentage of comparison result of Precision, Recall on Baby and Sports and Outdoors datasets, and all of these metrics are calculated for each Features selection of CountVectorize and TfidfVectorizer.

Table 14. A Comparison of the accuracy and time taken to the build model on baby reviews dataset

Logistic regression algorithm (on Sports and Outdoors dataset)		
Features	Accuracy %	Time taken to build model (seconds)
CountVectorizer	87.22	44.2
TfidfVectorizer	85.13	45.6

Table 15. A Comparison of the accuracy and time taken to the build model on sports and outdoors reviews dataset

Logistic regression algorithm (on Sports and Outdoors dataset)		
Features	Accuracy %	Time taken to build model (seconds)
CountVectorizer	89.03	87
TfidfVectorizer	87.90	96

Figure 14. Accuracy and time taken to the build model (seconds) on baby reviews dataset

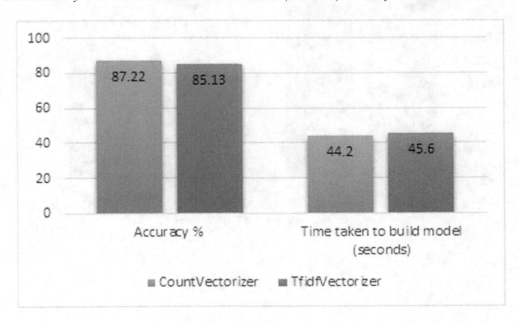

Figure 15. Accuracy and time taken to the build model (seconds) on sports and outdoors reviews dataset

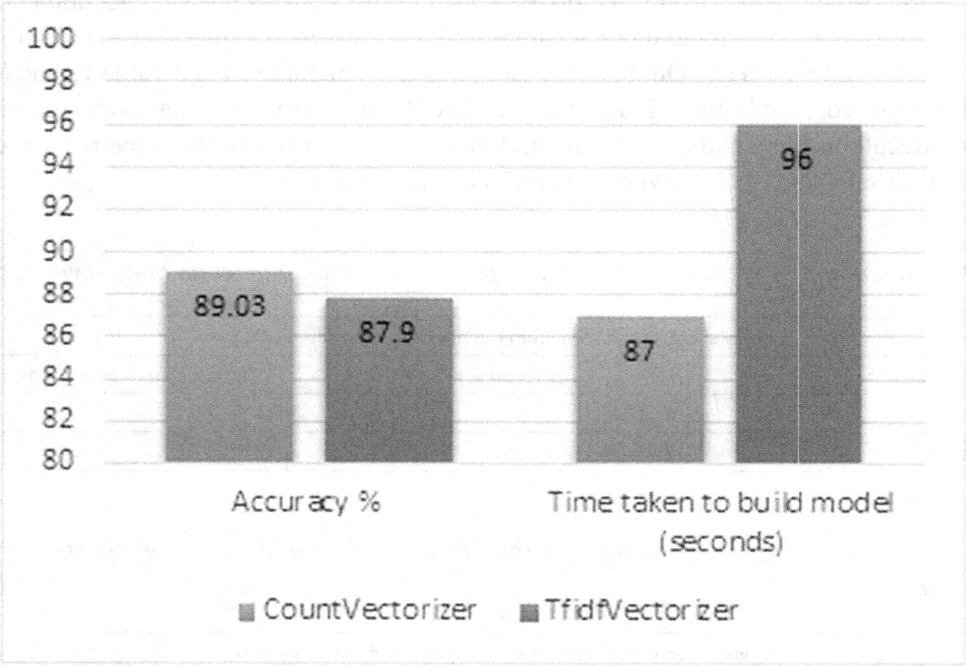

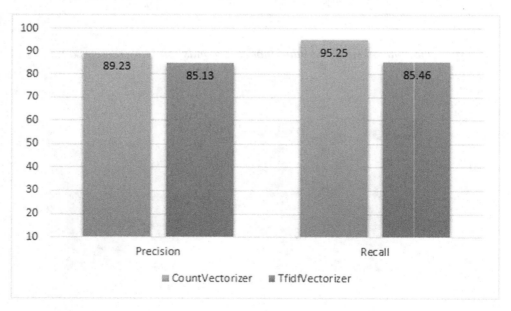

Figure 16. Percentage of comparison result of precision, recall on baby reviews dataset

Figure 17. Percentage of comparison result of precision, recall on sports and outdoors reviews dataset

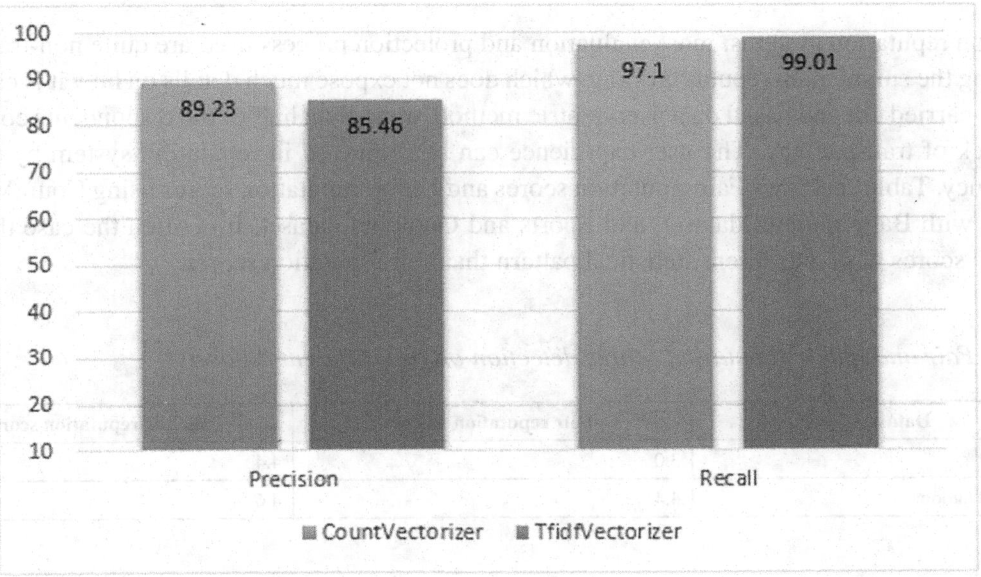

Table 16. Comparison result of precision and recall

a) On Baby reviews dataset			b) On Sports and Outdoors reviews dataset		
Features	**Precision**	**Recall**	**Features**	**Precision**	**Recall**
CountVectorizer	89.23	95.25	CountVectorizer	89.23	97.10
TfidfVectorizer	85.13	85.46	TfidfVectorizer	85.46	99.01

Table 17. Evaluation parameters for two different methods

Logistic regression algorithm (on Sports and Outdoors dataset)				
Features	**Unfair Positive Reviews Rate**	**Fair negative Reviews Rate**	**Unfair Positive Reviews Rate**	**Fair negative Reviews Rate**
CountVectorizer	57.52	42.47	2.89	97.10
TfidfVectorizer	76.25	23.74	0.98	99.01

Table 18. Positive feedback percentage before and after cleaning on two different datasets

Datasets	The positive feedback percentage before cleaning	The positive feedback percentage after cleaning
Baby	88.14	60.18
Sports and Outdoors	92.93	89.03

4.7. Unfair Reputation Scores Detection with Countvectorizer Selection

In common reputation systems, most evaluation and protection process used are quite non-transparent, only giving the summed up reputation value which does not expose much details on how it is calculated. In a study carried out and based on a user-centric method, more than half of the respondents complained of this lack of transparency. The user experience can be improved in reputation system by enhanced transparency. Table 19 shows Fair reputation scores and Unfair reputation scores using CountVectorizer Selection with Baby reviews dataset, and Sports and Outdoors dataset. It is often the case that unfair reputation scores have a different statistical pattern than fair reputation scores.

Table 19. Fair and unfair reputation scores detection on two different datasets

Datasets	Fair reputation scores	Unfair reputation scores
Baby	3.0	4.4
Sports and Outdoors	4.4	4.6

4.8. Collusion and Manipulation Detection with Countvectorizer Selection

Collusion and manipulation are illegal cooperation between seller and customer in order to cheat or deceive others. The seller may try to collude with the customer in order to increase his/her reputation likewise the seller may try to collude with the customer in order to decrease the reputation of another seller.

Our detection of collusion and manipulation depended on the best feature selection that was used with Logistic regression algorithm in this study. Through the Table 19, and after detecting Fair reputation scores and Unfair reputation scores through our methods for Reputation scores calculation, before cleaning and after using Logistic regression algorithm, we found on Baby and Sports and Outdoors datasets with CountVectorizer Selection, that there was collusion and manipulation between the seller and customer, and we have calculated Collusion and manipulation Percentage (CMP), as shown in equation 10.

CMP = Fair reputation scores – Unfair reputation scores / Total scores * 100   (10)

CMP on baby dataset = (4.4 – 3.0) / 5 * 100 = 2.8

CMP on Sports and Outdoors dataset = (4.6 – 4.4) / 5 * 100 = 4

The percentage of Collusion and manipulation on baby dataset is 28, the percentage of Collusion and manipulation on Sports and Outdoors dataset is 4.

Figure 18. Percentage of evaluation parameters with two features selection on sports and outdoors dataset

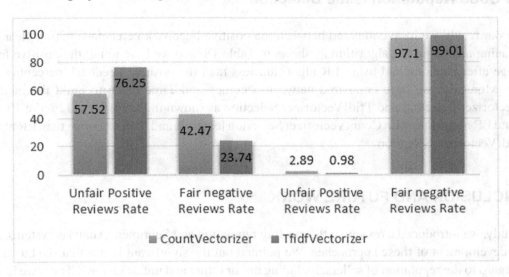

Figure 19. Comparison between the positive feedback percentage before cleaning and after cleaning

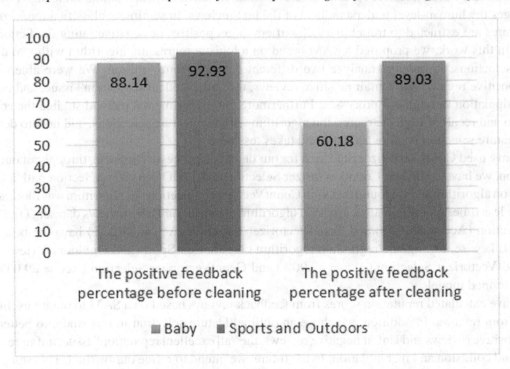

4.9. All Good Reputation Issue Detection

Through our result, we have compared between the positive Feedback percentage before cleaning and after cleaning and using LR algorithm as shows in Table 18, and we have found the positive feedback percentage after cleaning and using LR algorithm less than the positive Feedback percentage before cleaning. Moreover, we have compared between accuracy and Time taken to build the model with CountVectorizer Selection and TfidfVectorizer Selection as shown in Figure 18 and Figure 19, and we have found LR algorithm with CountVectorizer Selection less time and more accurate than LR algorithm with TfidfVectorizer Selection

5. CONCLUSION AND FUTURE WORK

In this study, we introduced a review of the existing reputation and Sentiment Analysis systems, and the relevant development of these approaches. We pointed out the significant issues that the buyers might face in regard to the reputation of sellers, including unfair rating and unfair reviews. Then, we illustrated some potential solutions that are capable of computing reputation scores without including Unfair positive reviews and Unfair negative reviews in an E-Commerce environment. Natural Language Processing encourages the human-level understandings of the text reviews. In sentiment classification, significant text features are extracted to train binary classifiers to get positive or negative rating predictions Qiao (2019). In this work, we proposed a SAM based on a logistic regression algorithm with two different feature selections, in order to analyze two different datasets from Amazon. We were able to detect Unfair positive reviews and Unfair negative reviews, the "all excellent reputation" issue, and collusion and manipulation through our processes. Furthermore, our experimental method studied the accuracy, precision and recall of Logistic regression algorithm with two feature selections, and how to determine which feature selection is more accurate and takes less time.

We have used CountVectorizer Selection for our detection processes because, throughout our implementation, we have compared CountVectorizer Selection and TfidfVectorizer Selection with a Logistic Regression algorithm and we found that with CountVectorizer Selection our algorithm was more accurate and took less time. As for logistic regression algorithm classifier on Baby reviews dataset, TfidfVectorizer Selection (Acc = 85.13%) and CountVectorizer Selection (Acc = 87.22%) have the best-trained models. Likewise, for logistic regression algorithm classifier on Sports and Outdoors reviews dataset with TfidfVectorizer Selection (Acc = 87.90%) and CountVectorizer Selection (Acc = 89.03%) have the best-trained models.

We have calculated reputation scores from feedback reviews based on a SAM to obtain useful information from reviews. In addition, we chose an optimal feature selection in this study, to better detect Unfair positive reviews and Unfair negative reviews, the "all excellent reputation" issue, unfair reputation scores, and collusion and manipulation. In the future, we intend to refine our method. This study can be extended by improving some aspects and subtasks of our approach. In the following, we propose some suggestions and future extensions to our work:

- Add more and different feature selections to our approach, instead of CountVectorizer and TfidfVectorizer Selections. For example, Hofmann and Chisholm (2016) performed an initial basic analysis; a more sophisticated approach using word n-grams is adopted to yield improvements in performance.

- Try to combine our classifier with a stronger supervised learning method such as Support-Vector Machines (SVMs) to have better accuracy with sentiment analysis.
- Apply sentiment classification algorithms in social commerce environments, such as Facebook or Twitter, to detect Unfair reviews, the "all excellent reputation" issue, unfair reputation scores, and collusion and manipulation.
- Use various tools such as R studio, Statistical Analysis System (SAS) to implement and evaluate the performance of our work.

ACKNOWLEDGMENT

The first author would like to thank the Libyan Ministry of Education and Canadian Bureau for International Education (CBIE).

REFERENCES

Abdel-Hafez, A., & Xu, Y. (2013). A survey of user modelling in social media websites. *Computer and Information Science*, 6(4), 59–71. doi:10.5539/cis.v6n4p59

Abdel-Hafez, A., Xu, Y., & Tjondronegoro, D. (2012). Product reputation model: An opinion mining based approach. In Sdad@ ecml/pkdd (pp. 16–27). Academic Press.

Adler, B. T., de Alfaro, L., Kulshreshtha, A., & Pye, I. (2011). Reputation systems for open collaboration. *Communications of the ACM*, 54(8), 81. doi:10.1145/1978542.1978560 PMID:23564961

Agarwal, B., & Mittal, N. (2016). Prominent feature extraction for review analysis: An empirical study. *Journal of Experimental & Theoretical Artificial Intelligence*, 28(3), 485–498. doi:10.1080/095281 3X.2014.977830

Aggarwal, A. (2016). Detecting and mitigating the effect of manipulated reputation on online social networks. *Proceedings of the 25th international conference companion on world wide web* (pp. 293–297). Academic Press. 10.1145/2872518.2888601

Barbado, R., Araque, O., & Iglesias, C. A. (2019). A framework for fake review detection in online consumer electronics retailers. *Information Processing & Management*, 56(4), 1234–1244. doi:10.1016/j. ipm.2019.03.002

Breure, E. (2013). hotel reviews- can we trust them? Brown, J., & Morgan, J. (2006). Reputation in online auctions: The market for trust. *California Management Review*, 49(1), 61–81.

Brunner, R. J., & Kim, E. J. (2016). Teaching data science. *Procedia Computer Science*, 80, 1947–1956.

Catherine, R., & Cohen, W. (2017). Transnets: Learning to transform for recommendation. *Proceedings of the eleventh ACM conference on recommender systems* (pp. 288–296). ACM. 10.1145/3109859.3109878

Chang, V. (2018). A proposed social network analysis platform for big data analytics. *Technological Forecasting and Social Change*, *130*, 57–68. doi:10.1016/j.techfore.2017.11.002

Chen, Y., Chai, Y., Liu, Y., & Xu, Y. (2015). Analysis of review helpfulness based on consumer perspective. *Tsinghua Science and Technology*, *20*(3), 293–305.

Dashtipour, K., Poria, S., Hussain, A., Cambria, E., Hawalah, A. Y., Gelbukh, A., & Zhou, Q. (2016). Multilingual sentiment analysis: State of the art and independent comparison of techniques. *Cognitive Computation*, *8*(4), 757–771.

Elmurngi, E., & Gherbi, A. (2017a). Detecting fake reviews through sentiment analysis using machine learning techniques. *IARIA/data analytics*, 65-72.

Elmurngi, E., & Gherbi, A. (2017b). An empirical study on detecting fake reviews using machine learning techniques. *Proceedings of the 2017 seventh international conference on innovative computing technology (INTECH)* (pp. 107–114). Academic Press. 10.1109/INTECH.2017.8102442

Elmurngi, E. I., & Gherbi, A. (2018). Unfair reviews detection on amazon reviews using sentiment analysis with supervised learning techniques. *JCS*, *14*(5), 714–726.

Engonopoulos, N., Lazaridou, A., Paliouras, G., & Chandrinos, K. (2011). Els: a word-level method for entity-level sentiment analysis. *Proceedings of the international conference on web intelligence, mining and semantics* (p. 12). Academic Press. 10.1145/1988688.1988703

Ert, E., Fleischer, A., & Magen, N. (2016). Trust and reputation in the sharing economy: The role of personal photos in Airbnb. *Tourism Management*, *55*, 62–73. doi:10.1016/j.tourman.2016.01.013

Farmer, R., & Glass, B. (2010). *Building web reputation systems*. O'Reilly Media, Inc.

Fattah, M. A. (2017). A novel statistical feature selection approach for text categorization. *Journal of Information Processing Systems*, *13*(5).

Feng, S., Xing, L., Gogar, A., & Choi, Y. (2012). Distributional footprints of deceptive product reviews. *Proceedings of the Sixth international AAAI conference on weblogs and social media*. Academic Press.

Gamal, D., Alfonse, M., & El-Horbaty, E.-S., & M Salem, A.-B. (2019). Analysis of machine learning algorithms for opinion mining in different domains. *Machine Learning and Knowledge Extraction*, *1*(1), 224–234. doi:10.3390/make1010014

Gutowska, A., & Sloane, A. (2009). Modelling the b2c marketplace: Evaluation of a reputation metric for e-commerce. *Proceedings of the International conference on web information systems and technologies* (pp. 212–226). Academic Press.

Guyon, I., & Elisseeff, A. (2003). An introduction to variable and feature selection. *Journal of Machine Learning Research*, *3*(March), 1157–1182.

Hammer, S., Kiefhaber, R., Redlin, M., Andre, E., & Ungerer, T. (2013). A user-centric study of reputation metrics in online communities. In Umap workshops. Academic Press.

Harmon, A. (2004). Amazon glitch unmasks war of reviewers. *New York Times*.

Hinton, G., Vinyals, O., & Dean, J. (2015). Distilling the knowledge in a neural network.

Hoffman, K., Zage, D., & Nita-Rotaru, C. (2009). A survey of attack and defense techniques for reputation systems. *ACM Computing Surveys*, *42*(1), 1–31. doi:10.1145/1592451.1592452

Hofmann, M., & Chisholm, A. (2016). *Text mining and visualization: case studies using open-source tools* (Vol. 40). CRC Press. doi:10.1201/b19007

Iqbal, S., Zulqurnain, A., Wani, Y., & Hussain, K. (2015). The survey of sentiment and opinion mining for behavior analysis of social media.

Jha, V., Ramu, S., Shenoy, P. D., & Venugopal, K. (2017). Reputation systems: Evaluating reputation among all good sellers. *Data-Enabled Discovery and Applications*, *1*(1), 8. doi:10.100741688-017-0008-8

Jøsang, A. (2012). Robustness of trust and reputation systems: Does it matter? Proceedings of the Ifip international conference on trust management (pp. 253–262). Academic Press.

Karyotis, C., Doctor, F., Iqbal, R., James, A., & Chang, V. (2018). A fuzzy computational model of emotion for cloud based sentiment analysis. *Information Sciences*, *433*, 448–463. doi:10.1016/j.ins.2017.02.004

Koncz, P., & Paralic, J. (2011). An approach to feature selection for sentiment analysis. *Proceedings of the 2011 15th IEEE international conference on intelligent engineering systems* (pp. 357–362). IEEE Press. 10.1109/INES.2011.5954773

Lin, Y., Lei, H., Wu, J., & Li, X. (2015). An empirical study on sentiment classification of Chinese review using word embedding.

Ling, G., Lyu, M. R., & King, I. (2014). Ratings meet reviews, a combined approach to recommend. *Proceedings of the 8th ACM conference on recommender systems* (pp. 105–112). ACM. 10.1145/2645710.2645728

Malik, Z., & Bouguettaya, A. (2009). Rater credibility assessment in web services interactions. *World Wide Web (Bussum)*, *12*(1), 3–25. doi:10.100711280-008-0056-y

McAuley, J., & Leskovec, J. (2013). Hidden factors and hidden topics: understanding rating dimensions with review text. *Proceedings of the 7th ACM conference on recommender systems* (pp. 165–172). ACM. 10.1145/2507157.2507163

Moraes, R., Valiati, J. F., & Neto, W. P. G. (2013). Document-level sentiment classification: An empirical comparison between svm and ann. *Expert Systems with Applications*, *40*(2), 621–633. doi:10.1016/j.eswa.2012.07.059

Mukherjee, A., Liu, B., & Glance, N. (2012). Spotting fake reviewer groups in consumer reviews. *Proceedings of the 21st international conference on world wide web* (pp. 191–200). Academic Press. 10.1145/2187836.2187863

Noorian, Z., & Ulieru, M. (2010). The state of the art in trust and reputation systems: A framework for comparison. *Journal of Theoretical and Applied Electronic Commerce Research, 5*(2), 97–117. doi:10.4067/S0718-18762010000200007

Pang, B., & Lee, L. (2008). Opinion mining and sentiment analysis. *Foundations and Trends R in Information Retrieval, 2*(1–2), 1-135.

Qiao, R. (2019). Yelp review rating prediction: Sentiment analysis and the neighborhood-based recommender. Unpublished doctoral dissertation, UCLA.

Resnick, P., Kuwabara, K., Zeckhauser, R., & Friedman, E. (2000, December). Reputation systems. *Communications of the ACM, 43*(12), 45–48. doi:10.1145/355112.355122

Resnick, P., & Zeckhauser, R. (2002). Trust among strangers in internet transactions: Empirical analysis of ebay's reputation system. In *The economics of the internet and e-commerce* (pp. 127–157). Emerald Group Publishing Limited. doi:10.1016/S0278-0984(02)11030-3

Resnick, P., Zeckhauser, R., Friedman, E., & Kuwabara, K. (2000). Reputation systems. *Communications of the ACM, 43*(12), 45–45. doi:10.1145/355112.355122

Reyes-Menendez, A., Saura, J. R., & Martinez-Navalon, J. G. (2019). The impact of e-wom on hotels management reputation: Exploring tripadvisor review credibility with the elm model. *IEEE Access, 7*, 68868–68877. doi:10.1109/ACCESS.2019.2919030

Saini, N. K., Sihag, V. K., & Yadav, R. C. (2014). A reactive approach for detection of collusion attacks in p2p trust and reputation systems. Proceedings of the 2014 IEEE international advance computing conference (IACC) (pp. 312–317). doi:10.1109/IAdCC.2014.6779340

Shoukry, A., & Rafea, A. (2012). Sentence-level Arabic sentiment analysis. Proceedings of the 2012 international conference on collaboration technologies and systems (CTS) (pp. 546–550). doi:10.1109/CTS.2012.6261103

Sun, Y., & Liu, Y. (2012). Security of online reputation systems: The evolution of attacks and defenses. *IEEE Signal Processing Magazine, 29*(2), 87–97. doi:10.1109/MSP.2011.942344

Sussin, J., & Thompson, E. (2012). The consequences of fake fans, 'likes' and reviews on social networks. Gartner Research.

Swamynathan, G., Almeroth, K. C., & Zhao, B. Y. (2010). The design of a reliable reputation system. *Electronic Commerce Research, 10*(3-4), 239–270. doi:10.100710660-010-9064-y

Tan, Y., Zhang, M., Liu, Y., & Ma, S. (2016). Rating-boosted latent topics: Understanding users and items with ratings and reviews. *IJCAI (United States), 16*, 2640–2646.

Tavakolifard, M., & Almeroth, K. C. (2012). A taxonomy to express open challenges in trust and reputation systems. *Journal of Communication, 7*(7), 538–551.

Tian, N., Xu, Y., Li, Y., Abdel-Hafez, A., & Josang, A. (2014). Generating product feature hierarchy from product reviews. *Proceedings of the International conference on web information systems and technologies* (pp. 264–278). Academic Press.

Tian, N., Xu, Y., Li, Y., Abdel-Hafez, A., & Jøsang, A. (2014). Product feature taxonomy learning based on user reviews. Webist, (2), 184–192.

Xu, G., Cao, Y., Zhang, Y., Zhang, G., Li, X., & Feng, Z. (2016). Trm: computing reputation score by mining reviews. *Proceedings of the Workshops at the thirtieth AAAI conference on artificial intelligence.* Academic Press.

Zhou, H., & Song, F. (2015). Aspect-level sentiment analysis based on a generalized probabilistic topic and syntax model. *Proceedings of the twenty-eighth international flairs conference.* Academic Press.

This research was previously published in the International Journal of Organizational and Collective Intelligence (IJOCI), 10(1); pages 32-62, copyright year 2020 by IGI Publishing (an imprint of IGI Global).

Chapter 53
Hybrid Approach for Sentiment Analysis of Twitter Posts Using a Dictionary–Based Approach and Fuzzy Logic Methods:
Study Case on Cloud Service Providers

Jamilah Rabeh Alharbi

Department of Computer Science, King Abdulaziz University, Jeddah, Saudi Arabia

Wadee S. Alhalabi

Department of Computer Science, King Abdulaziz University, Jeddah, Saudi Arabia

ABSTRACT

Recently, sentiment analysis of social media has become a hot topic because of the huge amount of information that is provided in these networks. Twitter is a popular social media application offers businesses and government the opportunities to share and acquire information. This article proposes a technique that aims at measuring customers' satisfaction with cloud service providers, based on their tweets. Existing techniques focused on classifying sentimental text as either positive or negative, while the proposed technique classifies the tweets into five categories to provide better information. A hybrid approach of dictionary-based and Fuzzy Inference Process (FIP) is developed for this purpose. This direction was selected for its advantages and flexibility in addressing complex problems, using terms that reflect on human behaviors and experiences. The proposed hybrid-based technique used fuzzy systems in order to accurately identify the sentiment of the input text while addressing the challenges that are facing sentiment analysis using various fuzzy parameters.

DOI: 10.4018/978-1-6684-6303-1.ch053

INTRODUCTION

Social media are considered as a huge corpus for extracting information of various types. One of the 'hot topics' in social media usage is the sentiment analysis. A group's opinions and feelings about any mentioned topic, serve as a valuable source of marketing for companies and consumers alike. Companies may utilize this information to measure customers' satisfaction about the product and it helps facilitate the decision-making process of the consumer. Consumers may seek both positive and/or negative feedback prior to make a decision, which is known as 'opinion mining'. Twitter, which has over 600 million users and nearly 330 million active users worldwide (Statista, 2017), rapidly becomes a 'golden astrologer' in the corporate universe, as it allows companies to elicit and analyze the sentiment of users' tweets and employ the result of the analysis to grow their own image and trademark. There are two key parameters that directing any research on sentiment analysis, these are: the target field and the study sample. In this study, the study sample will be the consumer reviews that are collected from Twitter and Cloud Service Providers will serve as the target field in this study.

Several approaches were developed to enhance the accuracy of the sentiment analysis in social networks. The most accurate results were obtained using a hybrid technique of machine learning approaches (e.g. support vector machine, Naïve-Bayes and K-mean Fuzzy) and lexicon-based approaches, like a dictionary-based and corpus-based approaches. A dictionary-based approach is based on utilizing dictionaries that include words and their sentiments, which is a robust and straight-forward approach as most dictionaries list synonyms and antonyms for each term. While there are various such dictionaries available online, according to Islam Zibran (2017) and Jhaveri et al. (2011) SentiWordNet and SentiStrength are the best among other online dictionaries. Different techniques addressed different challenges of sentiment analysis. These challenges have been addressed in the previous work, but separately. Some techniques focused on increasing the accuracy using a hybrid approach, but did not address the challenges of intensity, wsd and comparative words. Accordingly, a new technique that solved the expected forms of sentimental text, these are word sense, comparative word, compound words, negative, intensity, sarcasm and big data, is required.

The aim of this study is to measure user satisfaction about the Cloud services provided by Google, Microsoft and Amazon. Tracking the users' replies will present a general view on the satisfaction level and customers' opinions, which give the providers information about possible improvements. The proposed approach is built using these well-known dictionaries that are mentioned above and using fuzzy logic classification. Fuzzy logic is a computational model that mimics human decision-making process. Fuzzy logic represents the domain of interest using fuzzy terms, similar to how the human brain absorbs information (e.g. a temperature is hot, a speed is slow). The ability of the human brain to reason with uncertainties, inspired researchers to develop a fuzzy logic model (Liu & Cocea, 2017). Fuzzy allows to create general rules for decision making with uncertainty (Mary & Arockiam, 2017; Serguieva et al., 2017). Tweet classification, similar to other classification systems, is implemented based on a set of extracted features and using a classification procedure/algorithm. Fuzzy Inference Process (FIP) is used for the classification process because of its flexibility in addressing complex problems. Moreover, FIP allows for incorporating various feature forms, such as those extracted directly from the input or using a dictionary-based approach.

The proposed approach accurately classifies tweets based on their sentiment content. Accordingly, the tweets will be categorized into five categories: Very Positive, Positive, Neutral, Negative, Very Negative. The proposed model is built to achieve a set of goals: 1) To collect cloud services' relevant tweets and analyzes them in real time. 2) To provide cloud services with reports about customers' feedback. 3) To assist consumers in decision making within in a brief time span. 4) To gain analysis results that closely matched with human analysis. 5) To obtain accurate sentiment analysis results. The contribution of this paper is to propose a hybrid technique that uses the available resources, a set of rules, a fuzzy classification in order to accurately identify the sentiment of the input text while facing the challenges that are facing sentiment analysis.

The proposed approach is validated using precision, recall and F-score. The results showed that the proposed approach achieved precision of 83%, recall of 89% and F-score at 83%, compared with the human review. The rest of the paper gives an overview of the state-of-art. Then, the research methodology will be demonstrated. The architectural diagram and the main model(s) of the system will be discussed in detail. Then, a showcase is presented that demonstrated how the proposed approach processes tweets, besides the experimental design. Then, the obtained results are presented. Finally, the performance evaluation, comparative analysis and conclusion are presented.

LITERATURE REVIEW

Sentiment analysis employed language processing, text and biometrics to understand users' intention. It is heavily used in feedback analysis, decision-making and social media examination. Sentiment analysis involves opinion and feeling mining. The basis of opinion mining is to identify the polarity of a text as being either positive, negative or neutral. While feelings or emotions in the text can be identified as angry, happy, sad or etc. Subjectivity and objectivity identification are common classification tasks in sentiment analysis (Bhonde et al., 2015); while subjectivity depends on context, objectivity depends on the meaning, which is often harder to detect (Pang & Lee, 2004). Knowledge of the domain is key to obtain meaningful results; this is often referred to as 'Feature Identification Topic Modeling' (Hu & Liu, 2004).

Sentiment Analysis Approaches

Existing sentiment analysis techniques are classified into the lexicon-based approach, machine learning approach and hybrid approach. Lexicon-based approach obtains the text orientation from the semantic point of view. It is based on the idea that the polarity the text is identified by the polarity of its word components (Taboada et al., 2011). Lexicon-based approach uses a specific pool of 'lexis' to classify the semantic orientation of a text (Mac, 2011; Musto et al., 2014). There are three approaches to sentiment analysis via lexicon, these are: manual construction, dictionary-based and corpus-based. The manual approach relay on manual construction of sentiments and its corresponding features, thus, it is hard and time consuming. A dictionary-based approach depends on examining the polarities of the words using lexical databases, like WordNet. The dictionary construction starts with a seed, which is a small set of words with negative and positive polarities that are gathered manually. Then, the dictionary grows by performing online searches for antonyms and synonyms, which are added to the 'seed' list. These iterations continue till no newer words can be found. When the process is completed, a manual check is used to clean up the list (Mestry et al., 2016). A well-known dictionary for polarity mapping is the SentiWordNet and SentiStrength. The SentiWordNet contains a big list of English terms (17,660 terms), along with positive and negative scores ranging from 0 to 1for each, meanings, part of speech. According to (vJhaveri et al., 2011), SentiwordNet is the most reliable sentimental dictionary. SentiStrength is a part of the CyberEmotions project, which aimed at detecting the strength of sentiments that are expressed in social media by using a lexical approach. SentiStrength provides an indicator from [-5 to 5], according to word strength (Islam & Zibran, 2017). A corpus-based approach is based on pattern mining in a corpus; thus, the advantage of this approach is in discovering sentimental terms within a specific context.

Machine learning is an inductive procedure that learns to classify data (Sebastiani, 2002). Machine learning can be supervised or unsupervised; both are used to classify sentimental expressions in text. Supervised learning uses a set of classified examples and mapping between inputs and outputs to classify new examples. Supervised learning can be either a classification or a regression task (Kotsiantis et al., 2007; Mac Kim, 2011). Unsupervised learning is developed by providing a set of items that need to be grouped into classes without prior knowledge or pre-classified data (Mac, 2011). Semi-supervised learning is defined by combining the two forms (Pedrycz & Chen, 2016). In sentiment analysis, machine learning approach uses existing classification algorithms, such as decision tree, support vector machine and neural networks with features extracted from the input text, such as word's vector, part of speech and identified a topic to implement opinion mining.

The hybrid approach depends on both lexicon and machine learning and it provides accurate results and a better way for addressing the challenges of sentiment analysis. Lexicon-based approach is unsupervised, thus, does not require training data and it is domain independent, one lexicon could be built for all domains (Vaghela & Jadav, 2016). However, relying on individual words makes dictionary-based approach is subject to error as the context of the words are ignored. Machine learning is easier to be conducted and takes context into consideration, however, it is domain dependent and required a training data, which might not be available for a specific domain. Hybrid approach combined the advantages of both dictionary and machine learning approaches. However, it is more challenging to combine these approaches and construct coherent processes that do not conflict with each other.

LITERATURE REVIEW

In dictionary-based approach, Jhaveri et al. (2011) proposed a model that assigned values in the ranges of [-5,-1], [0] and [1-5] for negative words that are identified in the dictionary, words that are not present in the dictionary and positive word in the dictionary, respectively. Then, the sum of all words in the input text is used to classify the input into negative, neutral or positive. Although, part of speech (POS) affected the polarity of the words, Jhaveri et al. (2011) ignore this effect by choosing the least polarity of any POS. Moreover, word sense disambiguation was not implemented. Jhaveri et al. (2011) compared the performance of Afinn dictionary with SentiWordNet and machine learning approaches and it was found that SentiWordNet-based model produced the best results. Sheeba Vivekanandan (2014) classified inputs text by matching its word components with lists of negative and positive words. The words are identified as positive, negative or neutral. Then, these words are filtered out with reference to their polarity in SentiWordNet and using fuzzy logic. A filtered negative, positive and neutral words are used as input to a clustering process, which finds the best cluster (positive, negative and neutral cluster) for the refined text. Liu et al. (2016) used a list of positive and negative words and word matching to categorize the words in the input text. Moreover, the adverb effects, such as intensity and negative are combined with the words' polarity. The final output can be either positive, if the sum of the positive words is greater than negative, or negative if the negative words are greater in sum or neutral if the sum of the positive and negative words are equal. Similarly, Bidulya Brunova (2016) used lists of positive and negative words, add the effect of the intensity words and the effect of the negative words using a set of rules to classify input into either positive or negative class. Singh et al. (2017) used a lexical and dictionaries with a set of rules to classify tweets into five categories, these are: very negative, negative, neutral, positive and highly positive.

Using machine learning, Gamon (2004) used support vector machine (SVM) classifier with word's vector and part of speech tags to classify tweets of product review into four categories ranging from bad to good. Rohini et al. (2016) used decision tree classification with term frequency inverse document frequency (tf-idf) to classify input text into positive and negative classes. Similarly, Shakeel Karwal (2016) used random forest with the term frequency to classify comments about financial budget into positive, negative and neural classes. A similar technique for classifying text into positive and negative classes using random forest and based on term frequency was presented by Nurwidyantoro (2016). Hegde Padma (2017) increased the ranged of the output by adding some feelings into the output classes. Accordingly, random forest is used to output of the following labels: negative, neutral, positive and very positive. Chachra et al. (2017) used neural network with word's vector to classify sarcastic from non-sarcastic tweets. Chiong et al. (2018) used a set of binary features that is extracted from a list that included subjective descriptions of the financial related terms and polarities with SVM of positive or negative classes. Cambria et al. (2018) used a network of related words to extract the context of the word and then applied deep learning to classify inputs into positive and negative classes.

In hybrid category, Mishra et al. (2016) used classification algorithm and the polarity identified using SentiWordNet, POS, term frequency and co-occurrence to classify the input text into: negative, neutral, positive. Ray Chakrabarti (2017) used deep learning neural network with a list of negative words to classify tweets on mobile products into three categories, positive, negative and neutral. The classification is implemented from different perspectives, such as general, battery life, service, size, etc. Appel et al. (2018) used the polarity identified using SentiWordNet, rules to reflect the effect of negative words and compound sentences with Naïve Bayesian and maximum entropy classification techniques to classify input text into positive and negative opinion.

In summary, various sentiment analysis techniques are presented in the literature. These techniques differ by the utilized resources, field, and target output. A summary of the reviewed literature is given in Table 1.

CHALLENGES AND REQUIREMENTS OF THE SENTIMENTAL ANALYSIS

According to the literature review conducted in the previous section. A set of requirements and challenges facing sentimental analysis can be concluded, which will be highlighted in this section.

Table 1. Comparative studies

Reference	Dictionary-based	Machine Learning	Opinion and Feelings	Domain	Compared To	Concept
Jhaveri et al. (2011)	✓	✗	✗	E-commerce	Bag-of-Word Classification & Afinn- Dictionary	Compared Multiple Dictionary
Sheeba Vivekanandan (2014)	✓	Clustering	✗	Product review	NA	Dictionary based and Clustering
Liu et al. (2016)	✓	✗	✗	Social Media Review Text for Micro-Video	NA	Multi dictionaries
Bidulya Brunova (2016)	✓	✗	✗	Bank Service Quality	NA	Dictionary based approach
Singh et al. (2017)	✓	✗	✓	Economy	NA	Lexicon + Corpus
Gamon (2004)	✗	Classification	✓	Product Review	NA	Support Vector Machine
Rohini et al. (2016)	✗	Classification	✗	Movie Review	Other Classifiers	decision tree with tf-idf
Shakeel Karwal (2016)	✗	Classification	✗	Financial Indian Union Budget	NA	Random Forest
Nurwidyantoro (2016)	✗	Classification	✗	Economic News in Bahasa Indonesia	NA	Naïve Bayes Multinomial
Hegde Padma (2017)	✗	Classification	✓	Mobile Product Reviews	Machine Translated	Decision tree
Chachra et al. (2017)	✗	Classification	✓	General Tweets	NA	Neural Network for Sarcastic Identification
Chiong et al. (2018)	✗	Classification	✗	Finance	Deep Learning	Support Vector Machine
Cambria et al. (2018)	✗	Classification	✗	General	Baseline results in competition	Deep Learning
Mishra et al. (2016)	✓	Classification	✗	Smart City Reviews	NA	SentiWordNet, POS, Frequency
Ray Chakrabarti (2017)	✓	Classification	✗	Product Review	-	Deep Learning Neural Network
Appel et al. (2018)	✓	Classification	✗	Movies Review	NA	SentiWordNet, Negative and Compound

SENTIMENTAL ANALYSIS CHALLENGES

While it has enormous benefits, sentiment analysis is a complex task and there are numerous challenges when considering sentiment analysis:

1. Languages: applying sentiment analysis on non-English languages is challenging because online sentiment dictionaries are mainly in English language. Furthermore, writing in mixing languages with identical alphabet may be more challenging.

2. Word sense disambiguation: identifying the sense of a word for a word that carries multiple meanings is challenging in sentiment analysis, which often depends on context and field. Moreover, the polarity of the word depends on the context, for instance: the word 'big', which refers to size, is considered as a negative adjective for computer devices but a positive adjective for cars (Balaji et al., 2017).

3. Comparative sentences: computing the polarity of comparison sentences is hard. For instance: "iPhone X is more beautiful than iPhone 8", indicates that the word 'beautiful' is associated with "iPhone X."

4. Negation words: ignoring the handling of negation words is a main cause for a completely incorrect result. For example, a statement "the weather was not bad last week" contains negative polarity for the word "bad" but the attendance of negation changes the meaning entirely.

5. Intensity: distinguish the strength of the opinion (positive vs. extremely positive) and identifying classes that are exceedingly positive or negative is one of the sentiment analysis challenges.

6. Sarcasm: Some writers include ironic comments to form a positive meaning, while the intended opinion is negative or vice versa. For example, the use of icons in improper context or duplication of punctuation as ironic style, which required complicated analysis (Balaji et al., 2017).

7. Grammatically incorrect words: errors, abbreviations, poor spelling, punctuation and grammar that may be included in short 'microblogs', such as Twitter 'tweets' are hard to be identified and analyzed.

8. Improving accuracy of algorithms: developing and adapting algorithms and techniques that enhance the classification accuracy is challenging as there is no clear way to identify such algorithms (Vohra & Teraiya, 2013).

9. Real-time opinion mining: opinions are subjective expressions that express people appraisals, feelings or sentiments toward objects. Recently, there has been an enormous growth in the use of social networking websites, like Twitter and Facebook, in real-time. Processing these opinions required real-time technique.

10. Real-time data collection: encouraged by this growth, businesses, the media and review groups progressively looks for ways to mine Twitter. This is done in hopes of gathering insight into shared thoughts and experiences about a particular item or service. Thus, for the collection and analysis of tweets or reviews in a near to real-time environment, it is vital to have an automated system.

11. Variations in opinions over time: another challenge lies in being able to observe opinions as they change over time. Opinions are dynamic in nature and vary over time, which is useful for many applications. For example, monitoring if a certain product satisfaction improved over time (Vohra & Teraiya, 2013).

Sentimental Analysis Gap

In order to situate the state-of-the-art sentiment analysis according to the challenges that are identified previously, a comparison study between the reviewed literature according to the identified challenges is conducted as given in Table 2.

Table 2. Comparative studies between the existing systems according to the identified challenges

Reference	Non-English	WSD	Comparative	Negative	Intensity	Sarcasm	Grammatical Error	Accuracy	Real-Time	Automatic Collection	Time-Dependent
Jhaveri et al. (2011)	✗	✗	✗	✓	✗	✗	✗	✗	✗	✗	✗
Vivekanandan (2014)	✗	✓	✗	✗	✗	✗	✗	✗	✗	✗	✗
Liu et al. (2016)	✗	✗	✗	✓	✓	✗	✗	✗	✗	✗	✗
Bidulya Brunova (2016)	✗	✗	✗	✓	✓	✗	✗	✗	✗	✗	✗
Singh et al. (2017)	✗	✗	✗	✓	✓	✗	✗	✗	✗	✗	✗
Gamon (2004)	✗	✗	✗	✗	✗	✗	✗	✓	✓	✗	✗
Rohini et al. (2016)	✗	✗	✗	✗	✗	✗	✗	✓	✗	✗	✗
Karwal (2016)	✗	✗	✗	✗	✗	✗	✗	✓	✓	✗	✗
Nurwidyantoro (2016)	✓	✗	✗	✗	✗	✗	✗	✓	✓	✗	✗
Hegde Padma (2017)	✓	✗	✗	✗	✗	✗	✗	✓	✓	✗	✗
Chachra et al. (2017)	✓	✗	✗	✗	✗	✓	✗	✓	✓	✗	✗
Chiong et al. (2018)	✗	✗	✗	✗	✗	✗	✗	✓	✓	✗	✗
Cambria et al. (2018)	✗	✓	✗	✗	✗	✗	✗	✓	✓	✗	✗
Mishra et al. (2016)	✗	✗	✗	✗	✗	✗	✗	✓	✓	✗	✗
Chakrabarti (2017)	✗	✗	✗	✓	✗	✗	✗	✓	✓	✗	✗
Appel et al. (2018)	✗	✗	✓	✓	✗	✗	✗	✓	✓	✗	✗

As given in Table 2, different techniques addressed different challenges of sentiment analysis. By excluding the syntactic features of non-English and errors, the remaining challenges have been addressed in the previous work, but separately. Some techniques focused on increasing the accuracy using the hybrid approach, but did not address the challenges of intensity, wsd and comparative words. Accordingly, a new technique that solved the expected challenges in the sentimental text, these are word sense, comparative word, compound words, negative, intensity, sarcasm and automatic data collection, is required. Although, the literature on hybrid approach is limited, this approach showed capabilities in solving the limitation of the other approaches. Accordingly, the proposed hybrid technique used available resources, a set of rules, a fuzzy classification in order to accurately identify the sentiment of the input text while addressing the challenges that are facing sentiment analysis.

METHODOLOGY

A hybrid-based technique is proposed with the aim of addressing the following challenges: comparative, intensity, negative words, accuracy, real-time and automatic collection of the data. The proposed technique is built, as illustrated in Figure 1, in four phases, these are: data collection, pre-processing, feature extraction and model construction. These phases will be discussed in the following sections.

Figure 1. Basic structure of the proposed technique

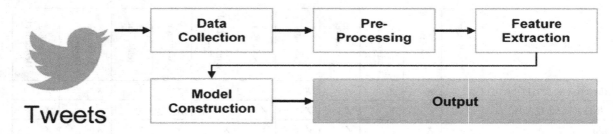

Data Collection

A dataset of tweets about cloud service providers is collected automatically. These tweets are intended to measure customers' satisfaction. The dataset is collected by implementing the following steps:

1. Businesses selection: three companies are selected, as listed in Table 3.
2. Hashtags selection: the hashtags that are related to the chosen companies are selected, allowing for a more central focus, as listed in Table 4.
3. Tweets collection: Tweets of the selected hashtag are collected accordingly. The collected dataset is composed of 9263 tweets. The collected tweets are directly delivered to the database and made available for further processing.

Table 3. Hashtags source

No	Companies	Official Page on twitter
1	Amazon	Amazon web service @awscloud
2	Microsoft	Microsoft Azure @azure
3	Google	GoogleCloud @googlecloud

Table 4. Active hashtags

Amazon Web Service	Microsoft Azure	Google Cloud
#aws	#Azure	#Googlecloud
#awssummit	#Azuresummit	#googlecloudsummit
#awscloud	#Azurecloud	#GoogleCloudPlatform
-	-	#GCP

Pre-Processing

The pre-processing phase is implemented over the collected tweets, as illustrated in Figure 2. The pre-processing phase is responsible for reshaping the collected tweets and making them ready for the feature extraction step. The aim of the pre-processing phase is to remove unwanted parts, such as: URLs, stop words, punctuation, non-English words, symbols and to highlight significant parts. These steps are outlined below:

1. **Punctuation Removal**: involves the detection and removal of any punctuation mark, with the exception of the exclamation mark (!). Punctuation removal is specially used to detect and remove all tweets with question marks, because questions are considered to be an example of subjective text, as opposed to sentimental text.
2. **Tokenizer**: dividing the tweet's text into tokens based on the white spaces. This process also in-cludes removing duplicated spaces to normalize the text.
3. **Disjunction Processor**: removal of the textual part of the tweet that comes before disjunction words, such as: "but", "however" and "otherwise". The presence of these words in a tweet increases the probability of having two reverse opinions. Often, the opinion holder expresses his opinion after these words as given in the example illustrated in Figure 3.
4. **Stop Words Removal:** Stop words are words that are sentiment-less. Accordingly, a list is used to remove stop words in the input text. A snapshot of this list is provided in Table 5.
5. **URL Removal:** detection and removal of URLs by applying regular expression matching.
6. **Number Removal:** detection and removal of numbers by applying regular expression matching.
7. **Non-English Removal:** detection and removal of any non-English letters by applying regular expression matching.
8. **Twitter Terms Removal:** used in the detection and removal of particular terms that refer to related entities. Two specific terms are detected and removed: the "Mention" term, which is a word started with (@) symbol that is used to "tag" somebody in a tweet and "RT", which is signifed a 're-tweet'.
9. **Hashtag Detector:** detecting hashtags (#) and removing terms starting that follow such hashtags.
10. **Emoticons Detector:** detection and separation of emoticons.
11. **Negation, Adverb:** detection and separation of negation words and adverbs (intensive and excla-mation detector).

Figure 2. Pre-processing phase in tweet analysis

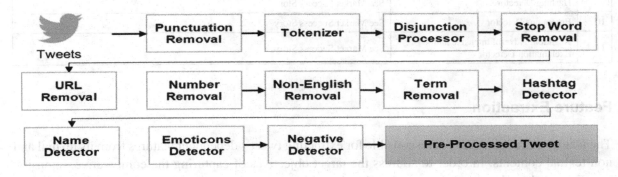

The pre-processing steps are implemented sequentially, and the output of each step is formed the input of the next one. An example of the output from each processing step is given in Table 6.

Figure 3. Example of disjunction detector

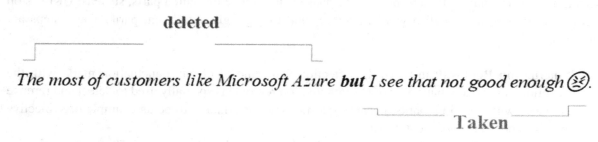

Table 5. Stop-words example

a's	Able	About	Above
according	accordingly	actually	she

Table 6. Pre-processing phase output

No	Phase	Output
	Input: See our @Microsoft Go-To Market Success Story @Azure #Azure http://t.co/K2sw5w8qcv	
1	Punctuations Removal	See our @Microsoft Go To Market Success Story @Azure#Azure http://t.co/K2sw5w8qcv
2	Tokenizer	See our @Microsoft Go To Market Success Story @Azure #Azure http://t.co/K2sw5w8qcv
3	Disjunction Processor	See our @Microsoft Go To Market Success Story @Azure #Azure http://t.co/K2sw5w8qcv
4	StopWords Removal	See @Microsoft Market Success Story@Azur#Azure http://t.co/K2sw5w8qcv
5	URL Removal	See @Microsoft Market Success Story @Azure #Azure
6	Numbers Removal	See @Microsoft Market Success Story @Azure #Azure
7	Non-English Removal	See @Microsoft Market Success Story @Azure #Azure
8	Twitter Terms Removal	See Market Success Story # Azure
9	Hashtag Detector	See Market Success Story
10	Emoticons Detector	See Market Success Story
11	Negation, Adverb, Intensive and Exclamation Detector	See Market Success Story

Feature Extraction

The feature extraction phase is responsible for extracting tweet's dependent features from its textual and non-textual contents. In order to address the target objectives of capturing the comparative, intensity, negative words, enhance accuracy and enable domain-independent and big data processing, the involved features address almost all the aspects of the textual and non-textual components of the tweets. The input to the feature extraction phase is, the dictionaries and the extracted elements in the pre-processing phase. As outlined in Table 7, five groups of features are used in the proposed technique: the polarity of words with reference to two dictionaries, the influence of emoticons, ontology, hashtags and likes/retweets.

Model Construction

Successful tweet classification depends on a set of variables that identify its demonstrative category: the polarity of its terms, associated emoticons, ontological effect, retweets or likes and the hashtag effect. The values of these variables are either numerical, (in the case of gauging polarity, retweets or likes and hashtags) or categorical (in the case of emoticons and ontological effect). The values of these variables have a fuzzy influence on the final classification of the tweet. Accordingly, a fuzzy controller system is proposed for classification purposes.

Takagi-Sugeno-Kang (TSK) Fuzzy Logic controller is favored among other fuzzy controllers when the developed system requires more freedom to incorporate linear systems into one fuzzy system, as in the case of developed sentiment analysis. Accordingly, a TSK-based sentiment analysis is developed, illuminating the 'de-fuzzification' step as the final output required. In this step, the output needs to be one linguistic term rather than a crisp value, as illustrated in Figure 4.

Figure 4. Fuzzy system formation for sentiment analysis

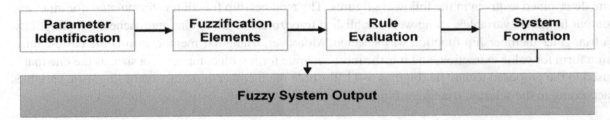

Parameter Identification

Based on the selected features, a set of parameters for the constructed model is identified, these parameters, are described in Table 7 and its values and effects are given in Table 8.

Table 7. Utilized features in tweet analysis

No	Feature	Description
1	Textual Polarity	Polarity of the words that are presented in the tweet
2	Emoticons effect	Sentimental effects of the presented emoticons
3	Ontology effect	Sentimental effects of some words, negative, adverbs, etc.
4	Hashtag effect	Sentimental effects of the hashtags mentioned in the Tweet
5	Likes or Retweets	Sentimental effects of the number of likes &readers that support tweet

Table 8. Utilized features in tweet analysis

Parameter	Shortcut	Values	Effect
Terms Polarity 1	TP1	Numerical [-1-1]	Linear
Terms Polarity 2	TP2	Numerical [-5-5]	Linear
Emoji	Em	Categorical	Associative
Ontological Effect	Ont	Categorical	Associative
Hashtag Influence	HIP, HIN	Numerical	Linear
Likes-Retweet number	Likes, RT	Numerical	Linear

Fuzzification Elements

The Fuzzification step involves converting the crisp values of the input parameters into linguistic terms based on the membership function. For categorical-type parameters, there is no fuzzification step, however, the fuzzy sets and membership function for these parameters are identified. The fuzzy sets are determined as given in the following figures. The membership function is formulated, for input and output linguistic variables, using well-established trapezoidal or triangular approaches. For simplicity, a triangular membership function was selected. Moreover, triangular membership is the easiest function form for value extraction, and it is the most accurate form with compact data size, as the one that is used in the proposed technique. Figures 5–11 illustrate the membership function of linguistic variables according to the selected triangular function.

Figure 5. Initial membership function for TP1

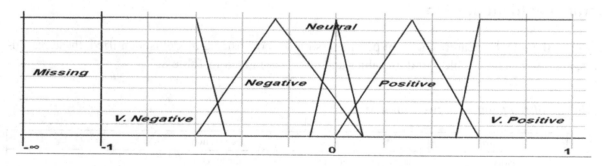

Figure 6. Initial membership function for TP2

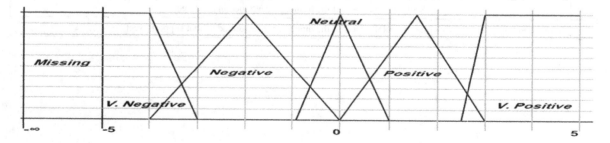

Figure 7. Initial membership function for Em

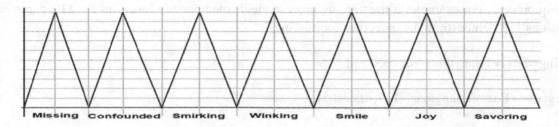

Figure 8. Initial membership function for Ont

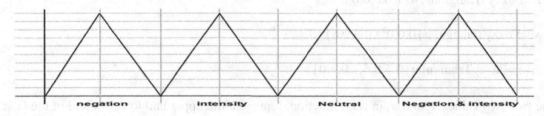

Figure 9. Initial membership function for HI

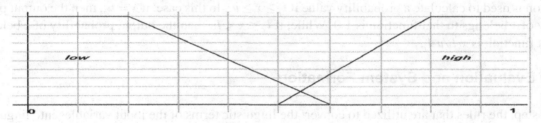

Figure 10. Initial membership function for likrs-RT

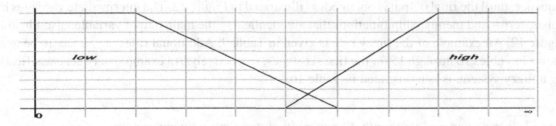

Figure 11. Initial membership function for Output

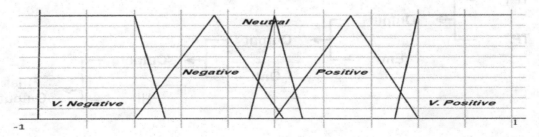

The boundary and slope of each linguistic term in the membership function are determined in the training process. For example: if the training process yields membership functions for TP1 parameter, Equations 1–6 demonstrate the outcomes for missing 'v'.

$$\text{missing} = \text{FuzzyTriangular}\{-\infty, -\infty, -1, -1\} \tag{1}$$

$$\text{V.Negative} = \text{FuzzyTriangular}\{-1, -1, -0.6, -0.5\} \tag{2}$$

$$\text{Negative} = \text{FuzzyTriangular}\{-0.6, -0.3, -0.3, 0.1\} \tag{3}$$

$$\text{Neutral} = \text{FuzzyTriangular}\{-0.1, 0.0, 0.0, 0.1\} \tag{4}$$

$$\text{Positive} = \text{FuzzyTriangular}\{0.0, 0.3, 0.3, 0.6\} \tag{5}$$

$$\text{V.Positive} = \text{FuzzyTriangular}\{0.5, 0.6, 1.0, 1.0\} \tag{6}$$

The first two values, l_1 and u_1 in each function, represent the upper and lower-bound of the first line in the triangle. The third and fourth values, u_2 and l_2, represent the upper and lower-bound of the second line. The fuzzification process is implemented by anticipating each input value, x, in each function. The function is used to calculate a probability value if $l_1 \geq x \geq u_2$. In this case, if $x = u_2$, then the output probability of x belongs to that function is 1.0. While, if $l_1 < x < l_2$, then the output probability of x belongs to that function is $x - l_1 / u - l_1$.

Rule Evaluation and System Formation

In the step, the rules that are utilized to convert the linguistic terms of the input variables into linguistic terms of output variables are identified. As the proposed technique is essentially a 'system of systems', using these rules generates intermediate outputs that are used as inputs in the next system. This continues in sequence, until the final output is obtained, as illustrated in Figure 12. The intermediate variables have linguistic terms and membership functions that are identical to the main output variable, also illustrated in Figure 12. An example of the fuzzy rule is given in Table 9. Additional rules are added, to be tested, as shown in Tables 10 through 15 for the first six stages, respectively. An example of tweet classification, using a fuzzy system, is demonstrated in Table 16.

Figure 12. Parameters and rule evaluation of multi-systems in sentiment analysis

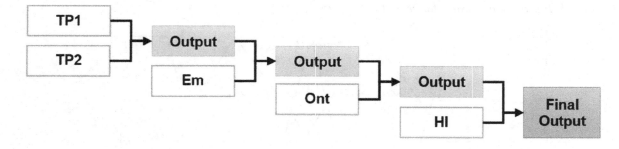

Table 9. Examples of the set of fuzzy logic rules for the first stage

Rules
IF *TP1* is missing AND *TP2* is missing THEN *Out*is Neutral
IF *TP1* is missing AND *TP2* is V. Negative THEN *Out*is V. Negative
IF *TP1* is missing AND *TP2* is Negative THEN *Out*is Negative

Table 10. Complete set of fuzzy logic rules for the first stage

		TP1					
		Missing	VN	NG	N	P	VP
TP2	**missing**	N	VN	NG	N	P	VP
	VN	VN	VN	VN	NG	NG	N
	NG	NG	VN	NG	NG	N	P
	N	N	NG	NG	N	P	VP
	P	P	NG	N	P	P	VP
	VP	V.P	N	P	VP	VP	VP

Table 11. Complete set of fuzzy logic rules for the second stage

		Em						
		missing	confound	smirking	winking	smile	joy	savoring
Out	**VN**	VN	VN	VN	VN	VN	NG	NG
	NG	NG	VN	NG	NG	NG	NG	NG
	N	N	NG	NG	P	P	P	P
	P	P	NG	NG	P	P	P	VP
	VP	VP	P	P	VP	VP	VP	VP

Table 12. Complete set of fuzzy logic rules for the third stage

		Ont			
		Negation	Intensity	neutral	Intensity with negation
Out	**VN**	VP	VN	VN	NG
	NG	P	VN	NG	NG
	N	N	N	N	N
	P	NG	VP	P	P
	VP	VN	VP	VP	P

Table 13. Complete set of fuzzy logic rules for the fourth stage

		HI for positive tweets	
		low	high
Out	VN	VN	NG
	NG	NG	NG
	N	N	N
	P	P	VP
	VP	VP	VP

Table 14. Complete set of fuzzy logic rules for the fifth stage

		HI for negative tweets	
		Low	high
Out	VN	VN	VN
	NG	NG	VN
	N	N	N
	P	P	P
	VP	VP	VP

Table 15. Complete set of fuzzy logic rules for the sixth stage

		Likes number – Retweets number	
		low	high
Out	VN	VN	VN
	NG	NG	VN
	N	N	N
	P	P	VP
	VP	VP	VP

Crisp-Based Sentiment Classification

In order to ease the implementation of the proposed technique, a linear model is proposed by assigning a range of values for each category in the output and categorical variables (ontology and emoticon effect). Accordingly, a simple linear equation is used to calculate the value of the output, based on the values of the input variables, as given in Equation 7. Each category of input variables, then gives crisp value, fitting with the rules implemented in the fuzzy system; this is to ensure that the output is identical in both systems.

Polarity= (TP+Em+HIP+HIN+Likes or RT)*Ont (7)

Equation 7 is formed, according to the determined effects of each feature, as discussed previously and listed in Table 8.

TERM AND SENTENCE POLARITY

To assign a polarity of a word, according to the rules evolved in the proposed fuzzy system, the polarities of the word in the online dictionaries are located, categorized, normalized and combined to produce a single polarity value. In the categorization step, the assigned category reflects the desired final output category of. These categories are illustrated in Table 17.

Table 16. Example tweet classification using fuzzy system

Process	Results
Input Tweet Collection	*RT @SalemaRice: #AWScloud is very interesting, and it provide a lot of amazing features 😋 😍.*
Preprocessing	*Very/interesting/provide/lot/amazing/features/😋/😍*
Fuzzification	Ont(positive)/ TP1(positive)- TP2(positive)/ TP1(neutral)- TP2(positive)/ Ont(positive)/ TP1(positive)-TP1(positive)/ Em(smile)/ Em(smile)
Combine Polarities (Sentence polarity)	TP1(positive) Average TP2(positive) Average Em(smile) Largest Ont(positive) Largest HI(high)
RuleEvolution	TP1(positive) & TP2(positive) → Out(positive) Out(positive) & Em(smile) → Out(positive) Out(positive) & Ont(positive) → Out(v.positive) Out(v.positive) & HI(high) → Out(v.positive)
Output Classification	Very positive

Table 17. Polarity categories and values according to the dictionaries

Category	SentiWordNet	SentiStrength
Very positive	0.5 or higher	5,4
Positive	Higher than 0 and less than 0.5	3,2
Neutral	0	0, 1, -1
Negative	Less than 0 and more than -0.5	-2, -3
Very negative	-0.5 or less	-5 or -4

A normalization step applied because the two dictionaries use different value ranges. This normalization is simply implemented by modifying the values of SentiStrength to match the values of SentiWordNet. Finally, combining the two polarities is implemented according to the rules developed in the fuzzy system, as follows:

1. If the word exists in both dictionaries, then the combined polarity is calculated as the average value of the two polarities.
2. If the word does not exist in SentiWordNet, then the combined polarity is the polarity value that is obtained from SentiStrength.
3. If the word does not exist in SentiStrength, then the combined polarity is the polarity value that is obtained from SentiWordNet.
4. If the word does not appear in either dictionary, it is given neutral polarity, which is zero.

Emoticon Polarity

To calculate the emoticon influence within the crisp system, a crisp value is assigned to each emoticon. The polarity value of each emoticon is assigned based on two factors: the polarity of the emoticon's description and its category in the developed fuzzy system, as outlined in Table 18.

Table 18. Emoticon polarity

Emo.	Description	Fuzzy Group	Dictionary Look-up term	Total Polarity
😂	face with tears of joy	joy	joy polarity	0.333
😄	smiling face with open mouth and smiling eyes	smile	smile polarity + 0.02	0.145
👌	Ok	smile	ok polarity	0.14
😋	face savoring delicious food	savoring	delicious polarity	0.666
😍	smiling face with heart-shaped eyes	smile	smile + heart polarities	0.214
😏	smirking face	smirking	smirk polarity	- 0.375
😖	confounded face	confound	confounded polarity	- 0.5
😘	face throwing a kiss	winking	kiss polarity	0.03

ONTOLOGY POLARITY

Similar to emoticons, to calculate the ontological influence in the crisp system, a crisp value is assigned to each ontological category. Table 19 lists the polarity values assigned to the involved categories and Table 20 presents examples of assigning polarity values for ontology components and combination of multiple components (e.g.: 'late' = -0.02582, 'well' = 0.693181 and 'clever' 0.5227).

Table 19. Ontology influences example tweets

Category	Purpose	Polarity Assigned
Negation word	Reverse Influence	-1
Intensity word	Duplicate Influence	2
Intensity with Negation word	Reduction of effecting negation words	-0.2

Table 20. Ontology influences example words

Negation		Intensity		Negation & Intensity	
String	**Polarity**	**String**	**Polarity**	**String**	**Polarity**
Not easy	-0.1347	very easy	0.2695	Not very easy	-0.026
Not late	0.025	Too late	-0.0516	Not too late	0.0051
Not well	-0.693	very well	1.3863	Not very well	-0.138

HASHTAG EFFECT

The hashtag influence is calculated based on the ratio between the tweets linked by a specific hashtag to the total number of tweets. This indicator represents a real-time public opinion about the topic that is represented by the hashtag. In order to add firm influence, a threshold at value 0.6 is selected and confirmed empirically. Accordingly, if at least 60% of the tweets are positive, the indicator will be positive and vice versa. Empirically, a positive hashtag is assigned a value of 0.15 and -0.15 if the hashtag is negative. Moreover, tweets polarity, by which the influence is calculated should be firmed positive or negative. Empirically, the polarity of positive tweets is greater than or equal to 0.35 and the polarity of the negative tweets is equal or less than -0.35. Thus, the hashtag effect is calculated using Equation 8 and followed by a set of rules that are described in the following.

Hashtag indicator = (Majority count / Hashtag tweets count)   (8)

Rules:

- If the hashtag indicator for positive is equal or greater than 60% and total polarity of tweet is equal or greater than 0.35 then add 0.15 to the tweet polarity.
- If the hashtag indicator for negative is equal or greater than 60% and total polarity of tweet is equal or less than -0.35 then add – 0.15 to the tweet polarity.

LIKES OR RETWEET EFFECT

The influence of likes or retweets is calculated once a tweet received at least 200 of either one. In order to add firm influence, a threshold at value 200 is selected and confirmed empirically. Accordingly, if at least 200 likes or retweets occurred, then, the indicator will be positive or negative, based on the rules of adding this effect, which are as follows:

- If the numbers of likes or retweets is equal or greater than 200 and total polarity of the tweet is equal or greater than 0.35 then add 0.15 to tweet polarity.
- If the number of likes or retweets is equal or greater than 200 and total polarity of the tweet is equal or less than -0.35 then add – 0.15 to tweet polarity.
- Otherwise add zero.

TWEET CLASSIFICATION

After the polarity of the tweet is calculated, using Equation 7 and according to the values of the involved features, the tweet is classified into one of the following categories:

1. If polarity is greater than or equal to 0.5, then the tweet isclassified as Very Positive.
2. If polarity is less than 0.5 and greater than 0.0, then the tweet is classified as Positive.
3. If polarity is equal to 0.0, then the tweet is classified as Neutral.
4. If polarity is less than 0.0 and greater than -0.5, then the tweet is classified as Negative.
5. If polarity is less than or equal to -0.5, then the tweet is classified as Very Negative.

An example of tweet classification using the proposed model in crisp form is provided in Table 21.

IMPLEMENTATION AND EXAMPLE

The proposed technique is implemented using ASP.Net and based on the MVC model. Various libraries were used to obtain maximum possible performance and reliability in the system, including: LinqToTwitter, LinqToSQL and Entity Framework. Figure 13 illustrates the flowchart of the proposed technique and Table 21 illustrates an example of how the proposed technique is implemented.

Table 21. Example tweet classification using crisp system

Process	Results
Input Tweet Collection	*RT @SalemaRice: #AWScloud is very interesting, and it provide a lot of amazing features* 🖐️ 😍.
Preprocessing	*Very/interesting/provide/lot/amazing/features/*🖐️*/*😍
Fuzzification	Ont(2)/ TP1(0.375)- TP2(0.4)/ TP1(0.03)- TP2(0.0)/ Ont(2)/ TP1(0.41)- TP2(0.4)/ TP1(0.3)-TP2(0.4)/ Em(0.214)/ Em(0.14)
Combine Polarities (Sentence polarity)	TP1 =0.28, TP2 =0.3 TP = 0.29 Average Em = 0.214 Largest Ont =2 Largest HIP= 0.15, HIN=0 Like or RT= 17 likes and 40 retweets
Total Polarity Calculation	(0.29+0.2+0.15+0+0) *2= 1.2
Output Classification	Very positive

EXPERIMENT AND RESULTS

In the data acquisition step, it was noted that some hashtags are more active than others. Azure and Amazon Web Service hashtags are more active than the hashtags of Google Cloud. As a sample, 1500 tweets for each company were obtained. Upon application of the sentiment analysis technique, the results for each service provider are calculated independently. The results for each company are displayed in Table 22.

Figure 13. The implementation of the proposed technique

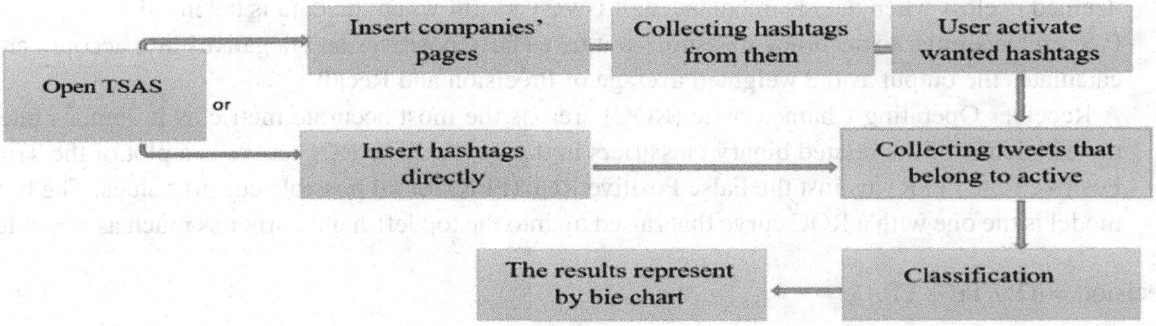

Table 22. Satisfaction customers' satisfaction ratio

Company	Very Positive	Positive	Neutral	Negative	Very Negative
AWS	27%	30%	23%	9%	11%
Google	20%	27%	30%	17%	6%
Azure	32%	36%	21%	7%	7%

As noted, Google Cloud has a higher neutral and unsatisfactory (negative and very negative) ratio. Microsoft has a higher satisfaction (positive and very positive) ratio and lower unsatisfactory ratio. The differences between Microsoft and Amazon are insignificant, which reflects that both providers are providing satisfactory services for their customers. According to BobEvan (2017), Forbes Magazine's Top 10 Cloud-Computing Vendors for 2017 placed Microsoft at the top spot, Amazon 2nd and Google 6th.

Table 23. Confusion matrix

	True Matches	True Non-Matches
Model Predicted Matches	True Positive (TP)	False Negative (FN)
Model Predicted Non- Matches	False Positive (FP)	True Negative (TN)

PERFORMANCE EVALUATIONS

There are many ways to measure and evaluate the performance of a classification task, among those the confusion matrix for multi–class gives a clear insight into the output results. Results are calculated based on the number of true and false tweet classification, as shown in Table 23. As given in Equations 9-12, the most popular criteria used are:

1. Precision: indicates whether the predictions of the positive class are valid.
2. Recall: indicates how often the predictions actually pick up a positive classification, also known as the sensitivity and true positive rate.

3. Accuracy: is usually the first metric employed when evaluating a model. Although, accuracy is deemed useless when data is imbalanced, it is very useful when the data is balanced.
4. F-Score: is similar to accuracy measure, as it takes false positives and negatives into account and calculates the output as the weighted average of Precision and Recall.
5. A Receiver Operating Characteristic (ROC) area: is the most accurate metric as it demonstrates the efficiency of the related binary classifiers in the system. The ROC curve is a plot of the True Positive Rate (TPR) against the False Positive Rate (FPR) for all possible cut-off values. The best model is the one with a ROC curve that raised up into the top left-hand corner as much as possible.

$$\text{Precision} = TP / TF + FP \qquad (9)$$

$$\text{Recall (TPR)} = \qquad (10)$$

$$\text{F- score} = 2 \text{ x} \qquad (11)$$

$$FPR = FP / FP + TN \qquad (12)$$

Table 24. Confusion matrix for system

	VP	P	N	NG	VN	HR	Recall
VP	85	0	0	0	0	85	100%
P	4	94	2	2	4	106	88%
N	11	6	97	26	27	167	58%
NG	0	0	1	72	0	73	98%
VN	0	0	0	0	69	69	100%
System predicted	100	100	100	100	100	Sample=500	-
precision	85%	94%	79%	72%	69%	-	-
F-sore	91%	90%	72%	83%	81%	-	-

The final step is evaluating the proposed technique is to calculate the performance measure of the output in comparison to the human review. Human review was conducted manually, by asking three experts in the linguistic field at the department of linguistics to annotate the sample tweets with one of the five labels, very negative, negative, neutral, positive and very positive. Only samples that receive the same annotation class from all the expert are considered. Accordingly, a sample of 500 tweets (100 for each class) out of the 4500 tweets collected for the three providers are selected.

Table 24 illustrates the confusion matrix of the proposed technique. Besides, the average Precision, Recall and F score measures are given in the same table. Firmed values of these measures are given in Table 25. As shown in Table 25, precision, recall and f score were calculated and the results conclude:

- The proposed technique achieved precision of 83% on the constructed dataset, which reflects that the proposed technique is highly accurate.

- The proposed technique achieved recall of 89% on the constructed dataset, which reflects that the proposed technique has very good convergence.
- The proposed technique achieved fscore of 83%, which is a good indicator for the accuracy of the proposed technique.

Table 25. Metrics results

Categories	Precision	Recall	F-score
Very Positive	85%	100%	91%
Positive	94%	88%	90%
Natural	97%	58%	72%
Negative	72%	98%	83%
Very Negative	69%	100%	81%
average	83%	89%	83%

According to the ROC curves that are illustrated in Figure 14 and Figure15, the proposed technique gives excellent classifications for Very Positive and Positive categories. The curves of the Very Negative and Negative categories are very decent, as shown in Figure 17 and Figure 18. On the other hand, an unstable curve detected in the natural category, as shown in Figure 16, which represents the unsatisfactory accuracy that were illustrated also in the confusion matrix.

Figure14. ROC curve for very positive category

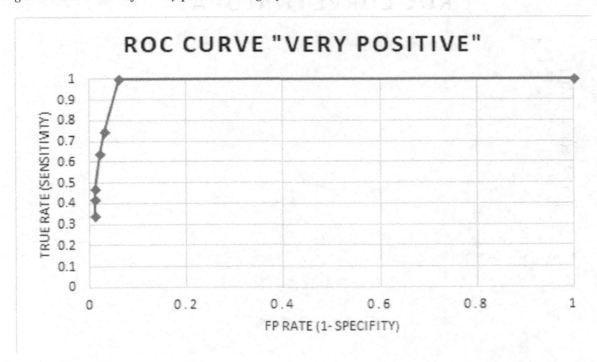

Figure 15. ROC curve for positive category

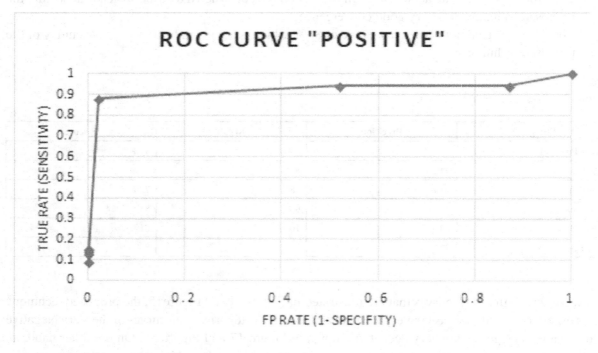

Figure 16.ROC curve for natural category

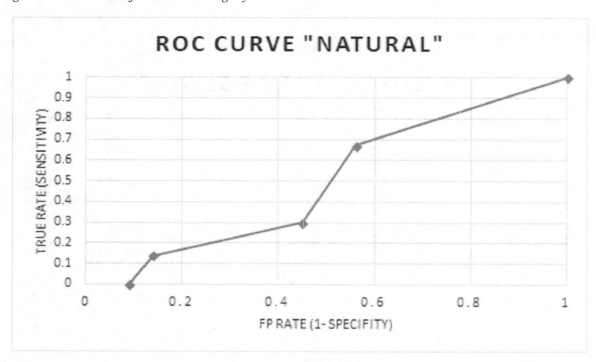

Figure 17. ROC curve for negative category

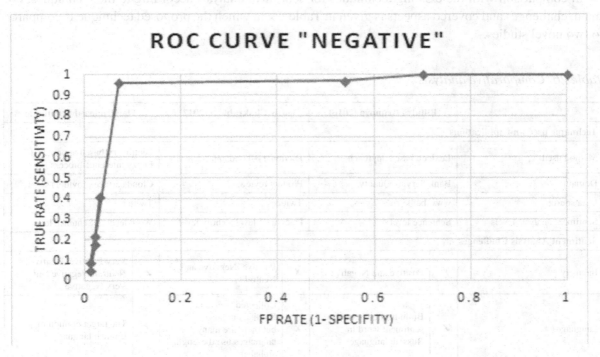

Figure 18. ROC curve for very negative category

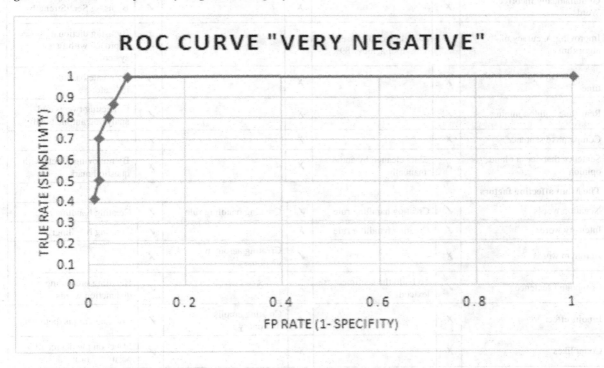

In comparison with the existing techniques for sentiment analysis according to the techniques, domain, challenges and covered aspects is given in Table 26, in which the proposed technique is compared to two novel studies.

Table 26. Comparative analysis

	Bidulya Brunova (2016)		Ray Chakrabarti (2017)		The Proposed Technique
Technique used and applications					
Method used		Lexicon based approach.		Dictionary-based approach	Dictionary-based approach + Fuzzy inference process
Domain		Bank Service Quality		Product review	Cloud service providers
Data source		www.banki.ru		Twitter	Twitter
Sentiment analysis levels		Sentence level		Document level+ entity level	Word level & Sentence level
Sentiment Analysis Challenges					
Intensity	✗	Positive and Negative	✗	Positive, Negative and Neutral	✓	Very Positive, Positive, Neutral, Negative and Very Negative
Languages	✓	Build limited lexicon sentiment word in Russian language	✗	Collected tweets in English language but there are many languages use the English alphabet	✓	The target opinion in English language.
Sarcasm	✗	-	✗	-	✓	-
Grammatically Incorrect Words	✗	-	✗	-	✓	By using SentiStrength
Improving Accuracy of algorithm	✓	Develop a rule-based classifier achieve 89%	✗	-	✓	By using dictionary based approach with fuzzy system
Variations in Opinions with time	✗	-	✗	-	✓	By create hashtags indicator
Real-time opinion mining	✗	-	✗	-	✓	Collecting tweets and analyzing automatically
Comparative sentence	✗	-	✗	-	✓	-
Sentence that doesn't hold opinion	✗	Data cleaned by authors manually	✗	-	✗	By removing tweets with question mark
The Main affecting factors					
Negation words	✓	Creating handling rule	✓	Creating handling rule	✓	Creating handling rule
Intensity words	✓	Creating handling rule	✗	-	✓	Creating handlingrule
Acronym words	✗	-	✓	Creating acronym dictionary	✗	-
Compound sentence	✓	To build the sentiment lexicon	✗	-	✓	Handling presenting disjunction words
Emojis effect	✗	-	✓	Creating emojis dictionary	✓	Creating emojis dictionary
Count likes	✗	-	✗	-	✓	Effect on the degree of positivity or negativity
Count retweets	–	NA	✗	-	✓	Effect on the degree of positivity or negativity

Bidulya Brunova (2016) proposed a technique that is time consuming for the filtering reviews manually. This technique used a costume lexicon that contains a limited number of words and for this reason, this technique have averted a few issues. Moreover, it is limited to evaluating the quality of banking services. Yet, it obtained a high accuracy rating when compared with Naïve Bayes. This technique was the best when considering accuracy improvement, however, used limited words. A total number of 671 positive and negative words are given by reviews and applied on 200 client reviews. On the other hand, the proposed technique uses two dictionaries, each of which contains tens of thousands of words that are related to enormous fields.

Ray Chakrabarti (2017) proposed a technique that depends on the entity level among various aspects. This technique is similar to the proposed technique in using dictionaries to handle negation words and emoticons. One of the advantages of this technique is using a large dataset of 3000 tweets. However, this model did not address most of the challenges that facing sentiment analysis.

Generally, the proposed technique classifies tweets into five categories in order to provide an output of more gradual scale. Sarcasm is not covered in the proposed technique because it is devoted to Cloud Service Providers customer opinions regarding a company and/or its representatives, individuals interested in cloud marketing and consumers. Accordingly, the probability of sarcasm is weak, in comparison to mobile phone reviews, for example, or many other commonly used products. Grammatically incorrect words were also not covered because Twitter, as a user-friendly microblog, allows for the heavily informal speech. Utilizing online dictionaries, like SentiStrength, can help to reduce this issue, as it was built based on analyzing social web text and informal language. In the aim of accuracy improvement, we used two dictionaries and generated fuzzy rules. To cover variations and changes in opinions over time, the proposed technique uses the hashtag indicator, which reflect the public opinion in a real-time manner about the hashtag topic. The proposed technique is implemented in real-time to reflect the current semantic status of the tweets that are related to the hashtag. The proposed technique collects the underlying tweets and analyzed them automatically, which make it able to implement real-time opinion mining. The comparative sentence was not covered in our system. Tweets were collected based on hashtags that contained the service name, rather than a public field name, so the probability of a comparison between two products is unlikely. As for the opinion-less expressions, the proposed technique, in the pre-processing phase all tweets that contain a question mark (?) are removed. Although, some questions contain positive and negative opinion and some has sarcasm expressions, the proposed model did not address this issue and it is left for future research. For the compound sentences, the proposed technique processes the section that started after the disjunction words only.

CONCLUSION

This paper proposed a new sentiment analysis technique for measuring customers' satisfaction about different Cloud Service Providers. The results concluded that Microsoft and Amazon are better according to customers' satisfaction compared to Google Cloud. Generally, the analyzed hashtags for Microsoft and Amazon reflects high customer satisfaction and low satisfaction for Google Cloud. In the experimental results, the proposed technique that is evaluated on 500 input text, gave precision of 83%, recall of 89% and F Score of 83% when compared to human reviews on the test samples. The results showed that the proposed technique is very accurate in classifying the classes of Very Positive and Positive. Moreover, the proposed technique gave good results in classifying Negative and Very Negative samples. The neutral category carries some confusion, as an unstable curve was detected, which represented poor accuracy via ROC curve. In closing, it was noted that applying the proposed technique to Stock Market analysis may aid in predicting daily movement of stocks, based on expert economic tweets.

Generally, the proposed hybrid-based technique used the available resources, a set of rules, a fuzzy classification in order to accurately identify the sentiment of the input text while addressing the challenges that are facing sentiment analysis, which are: comparative, intensity, negative words, accuracy, real-time and automatic collection of the data. These challenges were not collectively addressed in the existing techniques as each of these challenges required different resources, rules and classification approach. Accordingly, these challenges were addressed as parameters in the developed fuzzy-system and combined together to implement sentimental analysis process.

Although the proposed technique addressed most of the sentimental analysis challenges, some challenges, such as processing acronym words, questions with opinions and words in non-English language were not addressed. Thus, future work will focus on representing these challenges via new fuzzy parameters, incorporating these parameters into the proposed system and implement a comprehensive sentimental analysis. Moreover, future work will be devoted to increase accuracy, by including more dictionaries with additional technological terms. This will, in turn, assist in making analysis more accurate for technological tweets.

ACKNOWLEDGMENT

This Project was funded by King Abdulaziz City for Science and Technology (KACST) under grant number (1-17-02-009-0014). The authors, therefore acknowledge with thanks KACST technical and financial support.

REFERENCES

Appel, O., Chiclana, F., Carter, J., & Fujita, H. (2018). Successes and challenges in developing a hybrid approach to sentiment analysis. *Applied Intelligence*, *48*(5), 1176–1188.

Balaji, P., Nagaraju, O., & Haritha, D. (2017). Levels of sentiment analysis and its challenges: A literature review. *Paper presented at the 2017 International Conference on Big Data Analytics and Computational Intelligence (ICBDAC)*. Academic Press. 10.1109/ICBDACI.2017.8070879

Bhonde, R., Bhagwat, B., Ingulkar, S., & Pande, A. (2015). Sentiment Analysis Based on Dictionary Approach. *International Journal of Emerging Engineering Research and Technology*, *3*(1), 51–55.

Bidulya, Y., & Brunova, E. (2016). Sentiment analysis for bank service quality: A rule-based classifier. *Paper presented at the 2016 IEEE 10th International Conference on Application of Information and Communication Technologies (AICT)*. IEEE Press. 10.1109/ICAICT.2016.7991688

Evans, B. (2017). The Top 5 Cloud-Computing Vendors: #1 Microsoft, #2 Amazon, #3 IBM, #4 Salesforce, #5 SAP. Forbes. Retrieved from https://www.forbes.com/sites/bobevans1/2017/11/07/the-top-5-cloud-computing-vendors-1-microsoft-2-amazon-3-ibm-4-salesforce-5-sap/#75cd88c56f2e

Cambria, E., Poria, S., Hazarika, D., & Kwok, K. (2018). SenticNet 5: discovering conceptual primitives for sentiment analysis by means of context embeddings. *Paper presented at the Proceedings of AAAI.* AAAI Press.

Chachra, A., Mehndiratta, P., & Gupta, M. (2017). Sentiment analysis of text using deep convolution neural networks. *Paper presented at the 2017 Tenth International Conference on Contemporary Computing (IC3).* Academic Press. 10.1109/IC3.2017.8284327

Chiong, R., Fan, Z., Hu, Z., Adam, M. T., Lutz, B., & Neumann, D. (2018). A sentiment analysis-based machine learning approach for financial market prediction via news disclosures. *Paper presented at the Genetic and Evolutionary Computation Conference Companion.* Academic Press. 10.1145/3205651.3205682

Gamon, M. (2004). Sentiment classification on customer feedback data: noisy data, large feature vectors, and the role of linguistic analysis. *Paper presented at the 20th international conference on Computational Linguistics.* Academic Press. 10.3115/1220355.1220476

Hegde, Y., & Padma, S. (2017). Sentiment Analysis Using Random Forest Ensemble for Mobile Product Reviews in Kannada. *Paper presented at the 2017 IEEE 7th International Advance Computing Conference (IACC).* IEEE Press. 10.1109/IACC.2017.0160

Hu, M., & Liu, B. (2004). Mining and summarizing customer reviews. *Paper presented at the tenth ACM SIGKDD international conference on Knowledge discovery and data mining.* ACM.

Islam, M. R., & Zibran, M. F. (2017). A Comparison of Dictionary Building Methods for Sentiment Analysis in Software Engineering Text. *Paper presented at the 2017 ACM/IEEE International Symposium on Empirical Software Engineering and Measurement (ESEM).* Academic Press. 10.1109/ESEM.2017.67

Jhaveri, D., Chaudhari, A., & Kurup, L. (2011). Twitter sentiment analysis on e-commerce websites in India. *International Journal of Computers and Applications.*

Kotsiantis, S. B., Zaharakis, I., & Pintelas, P. (2007). Supervised machine learning: A review of classification techniques. *Emerging artificial intelligence applications in computer engineering, 160,* 3-24.

Liu, H., & Cocea, M. (2017). Fuzzy rule based systems for interpretable sentiment analysis. *Paper presented at the 2017 Ninth International Conference on Advanced Computational Intelligence (ICACI).* Academic Press. 10.1109/ICACI.2017.7974497

Liu, Z., Yang, N., & Cao, S. (2016). Sentiment-analysis of review text for micro-video. *Paper presented at the 2016 2nd IEEE International Conference on Computer and Communications (ICCC).* IEEE Press.

Mac Kim, S. (2011). *Recognising emotions and sentiments in text.* University of Sydney.

Mary, A. J. J., & Arockiam, L. (2017). ASFuL: Aspect based sentiment summarization using fuzzy logic. *Paper presented at the 2017 International Conference on Algorithms, Methodology, Models and Applications in Emerging Technologies (ICAMMAET).* Academic Press. 10.1109/ICAMMAET.2017.8186681

Mestry, P., Joshi, S., Mehta, S., & Save, A. (●●●). A Survey on Twitter Sentiment Analysis with Various Algorithms. *International Journal of Computers and Applications, 975,* 8887.

Statista. (2017). Twitter: number of active users 2010-2017. Retrieved from http://www.statista.com/statistics/282087/number-of-monthlyactive-twitter-users/

Mishra, P., Rajnish, R., & Kumar, P. (2016, October). Sentiment analysis of Twitter data: Case study on digital India. *Proceedings of the 2016 International Conference on Information Technology (InCITe)-The Next Generation IT Summit on the Theme-Internet of Things: Connect your Worlds* (pp. 148-153). IEEE. 10.1109/INCITE.2016.7857607

Musto, C., Semeraro, G., & Polignano, M. (2014, December). A comparison of lexicon-based approaches for sentiment analysis of microblog posts. *Proceedings of DART@ AI* IA* (pp. 59-68). Academic Press.

Nurwidyantoro, A. (2016). Sentiment analysis of economic news in Bahasa Indonesia using majority vote classifier. *Paper presented at the 2016 International Conference on Data and Software Engineering (ICoDSE)*. Academic Press.

Pang, B., & Lee, L. (2004). A sentimental education: Sentiment analysis using subjectivity summarization based on minimum cuts. Paper presented at the 42nd annual meeting on Association for Computational Linguistics. Academic Press. 10.3115/1218955.1218990

Pedrycz, W. & Chen, S.-M. (2016). *Sentiment Analysis and Ontology Engineering*. Springer.

Ray, P., & Chakrabarti, A. (2017). Twitter sentiment analysis for product review using lexicon method. *Paper presented at the 2017 International Conference on Data Management, Analytics and Innovation (ICDMAI)*. Academic Press. 10.1109/ICDMAI.2017.8073512

Rohini, V., Thomas, M., & Latha, C. A. (2016). Domain based sentiment analysis in regional Language-Kannada using machine learning algorithm. *Paper presented at the IEEE International Conference on Recent Trends in Electronics, Information & Communication Technology (RTEICT)*. IEEE Press. 10.1109/RTEICT.2016.7807872

Sebastiani, F. (2002). Machine learning in automated text categorization. *ACM computing surveys, 34*(1), 1-47.

Serguieva, A., Ishibuchi, H., Yager, R. R., & Alade, V. P. (2017). Guest Editorial Special Issue on Fuzzy Techniques in Financial Modeling and Simulation. *IEEE Transactions on Fuzzy Systems, 25*(2), 245–248. doi:10.1109/TFUZZ.2017.2682542

Shakeel, M., & Karwal, V. (2016). Lexicon-based sentiment analysis of Indian Union Budget 2016–17. *Paper presented at the 2016 International Conference on Signal Processing and Communication (ICSC)*. Academic Press.

Sheeba, J., & Vivekanandan, K. (2014). A fuzzy logic based on sentiment classification. *International Journal of Data Mining & Knowledge Management Process, 4*(4), 27. doi:10.5121/ijdkp.2014.4403

Singh, P., Sawhney, R. S., & Kahlon, K. S. (2018). Sentiment analysis of demonetization of 500 & 1000 rupee banknotes by Indian government. *ICT Express, 4*(3), 124–129.

Taboada, M., Brooke, J., Tofiloski, M., Voll, K., & Stede, M. (2011). Lexicon-based methods for sentiment analysis. *Computational Linguistics, 37*(2), 267–307. doi:10.1162/COLI_a_00049

Vaghela, V. B., & Jadav, B. M. (2016). Analysis of various sentiment classification techniques. *International Journal of Computers and Applications, 140*(3).

Vohra, M. S. & Teraiya, J. (2013). Applications and challenges for sentiment analysis: A survey. *International journal of engineering research and technology, 2*(2).

This research was previously published in the International Journal on Semantic Web and Information Systems (IJSWIS), 16(1); pages 116-145, copyright year 2020 by IGI Publishing (an imprint of IGI Global).

Chapter 54
Sentiment Analysis as a Restricted NLP Problem

Akshi Kumar
Delhi Technological University, India

Divya Gupta
https://orcid.org/0000-0003-1214-635X
Galgotias University, India

ABSTRACT

With the accelerated evolution of social networks, there is a tremendous increase in opinions by the people about products or services. While this user-generated content in natural language is intended to be valuable, its large amounts require use of content mining methods and NLP to uncover the knowledge for various tasks. In this study, sentiment analysis is used to analyze and understand the opinions of users using statistical approaches, knowledge-based approaches, hybrid approaches, and concept-based ontologies. Unfortunately, sentiment analysis also experiences a range of difficulties like colloquial words, negation handling, ambiguity in word sense, coreference resolution, which highlight another perspective emphasizing that sentiment analysis is certainly a restricted NLP problem. The purpose of this chapter is to discover how sentiment analysis is a restricted NLP problem. Thus, this chapter discussed the concept of sentiment analysis in the field of NLP and explored that sentiment analysis is a restricted NLP problem due to the sophisticated nature of natural language.

INTRODUCTION

With the emergence of WWW and the Internet, the interest of social media has increased tremendously over the past few years. This new wave of social media has generated a boundless amount of data which contains the emotions, feelings, sentiments or opinions of the users. This abundant data on the web is in the form of micro-blogs, web journals, posts, comments, audits and reviews in the Natural Language. The scientific communities and business world are utilizing this user opinionated data accessible on various social media sites to gather, process and extract the learning through natural language processing.

DOI: 10.4018/978-1-6684-6303-1.ch054

In this way, there is a need to detect and distinguish the sentiments, attitudes, emotions and opinions of the users from the user's generated content. Sentiment Analysis is the process which aids to recognize and classify the emotions and opinions of users in the communicated information, in order to determine whether the opinion of the user towards a specific service or product is positive, negative or neutral through NLP, computational linguistics and text analysis. While this user opinionated data is intended to be useful, the bulk of this data requires preprocessing and text mining techniques for the evaluation of sentiments from the text written in natural language. Sentiment Analysis permits organizations to trace their brand reception and popularity, enquire about new product perception and anticipation by the consumers, improve customer relation models, enquire company reputation in the eyes of customers and to track the stock market. According to the Local consumer review survey (Bloem, 2017), 84 percent of the total people trust online reviews as much as a personal recommendation given to them. Thus, it is important to mine online reviews to determine the hidden sentiments behind them.

According to Techopedia (2014), Sentiment Analysis is defined as "*a type of data mining that measures the inclination of people's opinions through NLP, computational linguistics and text analysis, which are used to extract and analyze subjective information from the Web- mostly social media and similar sources*". The analyzed data measures the consumer's experiences and opinions towards the products, services or proposed schemes and discloses the contextual orientation of the content. Sentiment analysis encounters many challenges due to its analysis process. These challenges become hindrances in examining the precise significance of sentiments and identifying the sentiment polarity. Some of the common challenges faced by sentiment analysis include difficulties in feature extraction, increased complexity in analyzing label opinionated data, the complication in analysis of other regional languages, requirements of world knowledge, increased domain dependency etc. Unfortunately, sentiment analysis also experiences various difficulties due to the sophisticated nature of the natural language that is being used in the user opinionated data. Some of these issues are generated by NLP overheads like colloquial words, coreference resolution, word sense disambiguation and so on. These issues add more difficulty to the process of sentiment analysis and emphasize that sentiment analysis is a restricted NLP problem. Different algorithms have been applied to analyze the sentiments of the user-generated data. The techniques applied to the user-generated data ranges from statistical to knowledge-based techniques. Even hybrid techniques have been used for the sentiment analysis. Various algorithms, as discussed above, have been employed by sentiment analysis to provide good results, but they have their own limitations in providing high accuracy. It is found from the literature that deep learning methodologies are being used for extracting knowledge from huge amounts of content to reveal useful information and hidden sentiments. Many researchers have explored sentiment analysis from various perspectives but none of the work has focused on explaining sentiment analysis as a restricted NLP problem.

Thus, this chapter presents an overview of Sentiment analysis, which is followed by the related work in section 2, then the detailed description of generally employed methodologies and techniques in Sentiment analysis are discussed in Section 3. Section 4 explains the applications of Sentiment Analysis. Section 5 describes the challenges faced by the Sentiment Analysis and then the challenges relevant to NLP are discussed in Section 6. Section 7 explores the solutions and recommendations to resolve the challenges and in the next section, some future research directions have been explored.

RELATED WORK

As sentiment analysis is a progressing field of research, thus a lot of research has been done and still going on in this field. Cambria (2016) have discussed the sentiment analysis and its basic process as sentiment detection and its polarity classification. Zhang et al. (2018) examined the sentiment analysis from three perspectives, i.e. sentence level, document level and feature-based level. Ainur et al. (2006), Noura et al. (2010), Nikos et al. (2011), Thomas (2013), Haochen & Fei (2015) have examined sentiment analysis at various levels such as document, sentence and feature-based level. Patel et al. (2015) have also studied sentiment analysis on various levels. The researchers have also discussed various methods of sentiment analysis, like SVM and Naive Bayes. Tsytsarau et al. (2012) reviewed the various sentiment analysis techniques such as machine learning, corpus-based, semantic-based and statistical-based techniques. The researchers have also examined the document-level sentiment analysis. Pang & Lee (2008) have also provided a wide overview of the various methodologies and techniques used in the process of sentiment analysis. The researchers were encouraged to resolve the difficulties in the sentiment analysis. Kharde et al. (2016) have reviewed the process of sentiment analysis on the twitter dataset. The researchers have also compared the sentiment analysis techniques that incorporate machine learning as well as lexicon-based techniques. The issues and challenges associated with the process of sentiment analysis, as well as the various applications where sentiment analysis can be employed were also investigated by the researchers. Kalchbrenner et al. (2014) have also employed machine learning techniques like dynamic CNN for sentiment analysis and achieved great outcomes. Similarly, the machine learning techniques were discussed by Tang et al. (2009) for customer survey for analyzing the sentiments at the document level.

Yanyan et al. (2017) presented a strategy to develop an enormous sentiment word reference for microblog data to elevate the performance of sentiment analysis. Li et al. (2015) have explored different highlights of an SVM classifier for analyzing the sentiments. Turney et al. (2003) and Yang et al. (2013) have discussed vocabulary-based techniques. Researchers, Turney et al. (2003) have also proffered an algorithm to investigate the inclination of the text towards sentiments extremity. Hu and Liu (2004) produced a lexicon consisting of both positive and negative sentiment keywords through seed words in WordNet. Bravo-Marquez et al. (2016) presented a strategy of enlarging the dictionary in a supervised way for better sentiment analysis. Yang et al. (2013) introduced an improved method for emotional dictionary modelling.

Pang & Lee (2008) have reviewed the different methods and applications of sentiment analysis. The researchers have discussed sentiment analysis of document level by focusing primarily on the machine learning techniques of sentiment analysis. Zhang et al. (2018) have employed deep learning techniques for sentiment analysis whereas Kim (2014) proposed an improved strategy which is based on CNN to identify the sentiments from English language text at the sentence level by utilizing dynamic and static keywords embeddings. Liu et al. (2016) proposed a hybrid technique for bilingual context incorporating deep learning attributes. Many researchers have studied sentiment analysis on languages other than English. Al-Azani & El-Alfy (2018) have classified sentiments of non-verbal features, i.e. emojis in Arabic language microblogs by employing the deep recurrent neural networks techniques. In the research article, the researchers have also compared the performance of baseline traditional learning methods and deep neural networks to reveal that the best results are attained when using bidirectional GRU. Dahou et al. (2016) have also worked on Arabic language tweets and audits for sentiment classification. Alayba et al. (2017) discussed the analysis of sentiments of Arabic health issues. Sallab et al. (2015) discussed

Arabic sentiment analysis by employing deep learning. Similarly, Abbes et al. (2017) employed deep neural networks to discover sentiments from reviews written in the Arabic language. Aziz & Tao (2016) have utilized machine learning techniques such as SVMs, Naive Bayesian, random forests and decision trees to identify the sentiments from multiple datasets of Arabic languages.

Many researchers like Ling et al. (2014), Chalothom et al. (2015), Matthew et al. (2015) have presented and discussed various applications of sentiment analysis. Kharde et al. (2016) have investigated the different approaches, including machine learning as well as vocabulary-based approaches that are used for sentiment analysis. The researchers have additionally examined the issues in extracting sentiments from unstructured and heterogeneous context. Issues like sarcasm detection, thwarted expression, entity recognition are studied by the researchers. Kharde et al. (2016) also suggested that the sentiments are classified precisely if the data in consideration is clean and less noisy. Varghese et al. (2013) have investigated the challenges involved with the sentiment analysis.

METHODOLOGY OF SENTIMENT ANALYSIS

Types of Sentiment Analysis

Analyzing the sentiments of the user from the user-generated content is generally classified into two types, as described in Figure 1:

1. **Polarity based Sentiment Analysis:** In polarity-based sentiment analysis, the expressed sentiments of the user in a document, sentence or an entity feature are grouped into three polarities, i.e. positive, negative and neutral. It implies that the consumer's opinion about the product or service in consideration could be at any one of the extremities, i.e. it could be either positive, negative or neutral. If the review by a user is, "The customer service provided by your organization is so poor, that it is killing me!", then the polarity-based sentiment classification can predict that the polarity of review is negative.

Figure 1. Types of Sentiment Analysis

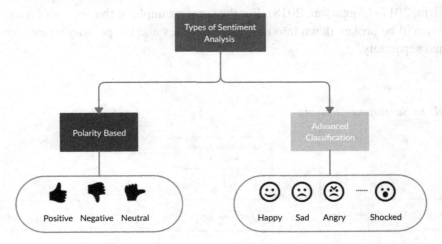

2. **Advanced classification-based sentiment analysis:** In the advanced classification-based sentiment analysis, the sentiments of the user are beyond the above-mentioned extremities. The sentiments are classified into further classification states. For instance, the user expressed sentiment can be considered on the basis of emotional states such as anger, happiness, sadness and excitement. If the review by a user is, "The customer service provided by your organization is so poor, that it is killing me!", then the advanced sentiment classification can predict that the review expresses anger of the user.

An alternative technique for evaluating the sentiments of the user in the user-generated data is the use of scaling framework. In this technique, the user's sentiments are grouped in the ranks on the scale of -10 to +10.

Levels of Sentiment Analysis

The primary aim of Sentiment Mining is to process the sentence and analyze the sentiments of a given expression and to determine the polarity of the sentiments. Sentiment analysis has been explored from various perspectives. The most prominent perspective is to classify the sentiment analysis at three levels, described as follows in Figure 2:

1. Document-level: At document-level, the overall sentiment of the whole document is determined. For the small data set, the document level sentiment analysis shows great accuracy. This stage treats the document as an individual entity. For example: If a document is written about a particular element, the aim is to evaluate the sentiment polarity for that element i.e. whether the document conveys positive, negative or neutral sentiment about the entity in consideration (Khaled et al., 2015) (Aggarwal, 2018). For instance, the reviews of a particular laptop is that it has amazing resolution and the size is sleek. The processor seems good but one can get better configurations in the said price. Thus, at document level, the overall sentiment of the customer review is evaluated to be negative.
2. Sentence-level: At the Sentence-level, the degree of examination is nearly a subjective arrangement, and the analysis at this level is restricted to the sentences and their communicated sentiments. In particular, this stage decides if each sentence communicates a positive, negative or neutral sentiment (Safrin, 2017) (Aggarwal, 2018). For the same example of the review of a particular laptop. The review will be broken down into multiple sentences and the polarity of each sentence will be determined separately.

Figure 2. Levels of Sentiment Analysis

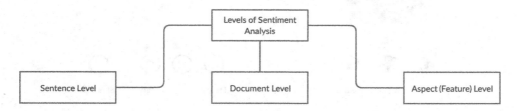

3. Aspect (feature) level: Aspect-level sentiment analysis is more complex than the other two levels. At aspect level, instead of inspecting language constructs (like sentences, passages or documents), a finer-grained inspection of different aspects of each product is performed. Aspect level sentiment analysis first extracts the different features for a product in consideration and then discerns the polarity for the various features of that particular product. For example, different characters like size, memory, price, camera etc. of mobile will be distinguished at the first stage, and then the polarity of each of these characteristics will be determined at the second stage (Beigi et al., 2016).

Process of Sentiment Analysis

The process of perceiving and classifying the sentiments in the opinionated text, so as to find out whether the frame of mind of the user about a particular item is positive, negative or neutral, principally contains five phases: Collection of Data, Preprocessing and Text Preparation, Subjectivity Detection, Sentiment Classification and Presentation of Output.

The graphical representation of the methodology of the sentiment analysis is described in Figure 3:

A. Collection of Data

The first phase of the sentiment analysis process is Collecting data, which is the most significant phase of sentiment analysis. If the amount of the information is inadequate or the quality of the gathered information is poor, then the general performance of the model is impeded. Administration clients or product users post their emotions, opinions and experience about the products online via web-based networking media like web journals, blogs, reviews etc. Collection of data from a wide range of data sources such as blogs, micro-blogging sites, review sites and social media platforms is the primary job.

B. Preprocessing Data and Text Preparation

The second phase of the sentiment analysis process is preprocessing data and text preparation. As the opinions and emotions are communicated in various ways, with various settings of composing, technical words, utilization of short structures and slang due to which the information becomes tremendous and complicated. Manual examination of this user-generated data is basically incomprehensible. Thus, unique programming languages and strategies are utilized to process and investigate the user-generated content (Seerat & Azam, 2012). Preprocessing is the process of removal of stopwords, punctuation, numbers, emoticons, hashtags; stemming and lemmatization. In the task of text preparation, the user-generated opinionated context is filtered. It incorporates recognizing and eliminating non-literary and non-relevant data (i.e. the data which is not important to the field or subject of concentrate) from the user-generated content (Chandni et al., 2015).

Figure 3. Process of sentiment analysis

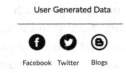

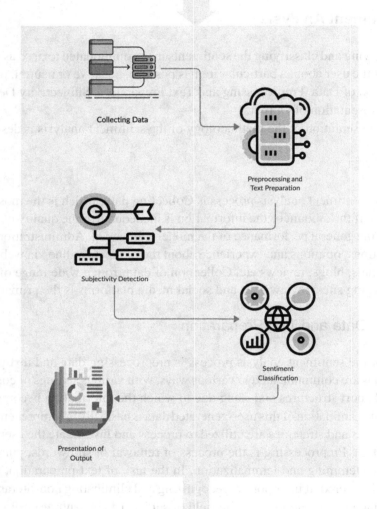

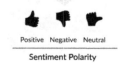

C. Subjectivity Detection

The third phase of the sentiment analysis process is the subjectivity detection phase. In this phase, all the sentences of the user-generated data are reviewed for subjectivity. The sentences that convey subjective expressions are kept, whereas the sentences with objective articulations are discarded. Sentiment analysis is performed at various levels of language such as at the lexical, morphological, discourse, semantic and pragmatic levels, using prevalent computational procedures like Unigrams, Frequency count, lemmas and negation.

D. Sentiment Classification

The next stage of the sentiment analysis process is classifying the sentiments from the opinionated data into various categories. Sentiments are commonly categorized into three classes, i.e. positive, negative and neutral. In this stage of the sentiment analysis process, all subjective sentences are classified into the sentiment classes such as positive, negative, neutral, bad, good, like, dislike.

E. Presentation of Output

Presentation of output is the last phase of the process of sentiment analysis. In this phase, the orientation of the unstructured user opinionated data is presented into meaningful information, which is displayed in the form of diagrams and graphs such as a bar chart, pie charts and line graphs.

Techniques of Sentiment Analysis

Sentiment investigation is an extremely worthwhile field due to immense measure of information accessible on the web. Thus, multiple techniques are applied to extract and express the sentiments of a product or service. The techniques of sentiment analysis can be classified into four key categories such as statistical approach, knowledge-based approach, hybrid approach and concept-based approaches, as shown in Figure 4.

Statistical Approaches / Machine Learning Techniques

Statistical approaches exploit basic components of machine learning from Artificial Intelligent systems, for example, semantic inspection, support vector machines, semantic inclination and bag of words (Aggarwal, 2018). Many experiments have been performed utilizing the increasingly advanced strategies that attempt to distinguish the individual who has communicated the feeling and the objective of the user-generated data. Machine learning strategy essentially operates by training a large data set and learning from its experience. Machine learning is the logical examination of computation and factual models that computer frameworks utilize to play out a specific task without using explicit guidelines, relying on patterns and inference. Machine learning approaches can be categorized into three classes: supervised learning, unsupervised learning and semi-supervised learning.

Figure 4. Techniques of Sentiment Analysis

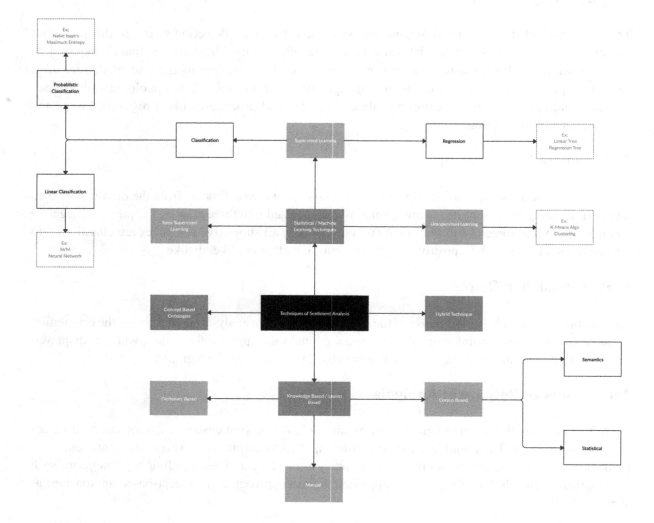

Supervised Techniques

Supervised learning relies on the presence of marked data. The two datasets are utilized in this methodology. The first set of input data is also known as training data and has a known label value or result, for example, valid/invalid or value of any commodity at a time. This data is utilized for training on the selected classifier. A model is set up through a preparation procedure wherein it is required to make predictions and is adjusted when those predictions are not right. The process continues until the desired level of accuracy is not achieved on the training data. The prime reason is that the algorithm can learn by analyzing and comparing the actual values with the instructed values to discover the extremity of the sentiments. The second set of data is the unlabeled test data on which this learnt ability is applied to predict the label values known as classes (Kamble & Itkikar, 2018) (Yadlapalli et al., 2019).

Thus, it can be implied that in supervised learning, all data is marked and the machine is trained for every input with a particular target. The input variable (X) and the output variable (Y) is known. Y

=f(X) The machine has to predict the function f that maps X to Y. The common problems of supervised learning are further categorized into two methodologies: classification and regression (Ahmad et al., 2017). If the output variable is a category, like 'costly' or 'cheap', then the problem is called a classification problem. If the output variable is a real value, like 'price', then the problem is a regression problem (Medhat et al., 2014) (Samal et al., 2017) (Sharma et al., 2019).

1. Classification problem:

The classification problem is generally about identifying or predicting a label. It filters the data in different classes, e.g. when given some comment; the data can be filtered out as 'positive' or 'negative'. Classification can be linear as well as probabilistic (Medhat et al., 2014) (Kamble & Itkikar, 2018).

    a.   Linear classification: A linear classifier identifies the class of an object based on the value of the linear combination of characteristics. A linear classifier can represent any mapping that is linearly separable. There are various types of linear classifiers, among which the most popular are Support Vector Machine and Neural Network (Medhat et al., 2014) (Kamble & Itkikar, 2018).

        i.   Support Vector Machine (SVM): A Support Vector Machine (SVM) is a type of supervised machine learning, that is also known as high edge classifiers. This technique is mainly used to segregate (or classify) multiple types of inputs. Each individual input can be hypothetically represented on a plane as a single coordinate. SVMs are used to create a hypothetical plane separating different types of inputs into different classes (Medhat et al., 2014) (Kamble & Itkikar, 2018) (Sharma et al., 2019).

In sentiment analysis, the text is divided by a hyperplane as per the sentiments where the margin between the different sentiment classes is as high as possible (Bhuta et al., 2014). This technique can deal with enormous feature spaces with a large number of dimensions. The learning capability of support vector machines is not dependent on the dimensions of the feature space as it does not compute the complexity of the hypothesis by the number of features (Bhuta et al., 2014). In spite of the fact that SVM outflanks all the conventional techniques for sentiment classification, it is a black box strategy. It is hard to examine the type of classification and to distinguish which sentiment terms are increasingly significant for classification (Sharma & Dey, 2012). This is one of the weaknesses of utilizing SVM as a technique for sentiment classification (Bhuta et al., 2014). There are various possibilities in SVM. It can take off some outlier samples and still result in better classification. It can be used to classify more than two types of inputs as well (Chandni et al., 2015).

        ii.   Neural Network: A neural network can be defined as a complex architecture with numerous layers of interconnected units. Every unit is a complicated function of the input data. From the previous unit, input is taken and processed to provide an outcome which is utilized by the next connected unit. All these connected units are individually known as the neuron, and the whole combined architecture is known as a Neural Network. The values processed to the functions of each unit are acquired as the training of the neural network. The neural system replicates the above behaviour to learn about gathered information and to predict the outcomes (Ouyang et al., 2015).

All the neural networks consist of one input and one output layer whose design is application-specific. For instance, in the process of sentiment analysis, the sentences that need to be analyzed can be considered as the input, and the classifier which would yield the sentiment to be positive, negative or neutral can be the output.

The inner layers of the neural network are known as hidden layers. A neural network can have a number of hidden layers, and each hidden layer can have several units. Every unit (which is also known as a neuron) influences the overall outcome. As every unit can only influence the overall result just marginally, the impact is magnified when that result goes through a few layers of neurons and provides extremely precise outcomes (Aggarwal et al., 2019).

b. Probabilistic classification: Probabilistic classifier is a classifier which works on probability and is able to estimate a probabilistic distribution over a set of classes rather than giving a class to which an object belongs to. Probability classification can be done using Naïve Bayes or Maximum Entropy Techniques.

    i. Naïve Bayes: Naive Bayes algorithm is a supervised machine learning technique in the family of sample probabilistic classifiers which is based on the probabilistic methodology. This algorithm is primarily utilized for training the classifiers, which are then employed to classify the sentiments in a text. The main principle behind this methodology is the assumption that the features are independent of each other as it is based on BOWs and does not take the position of features in the text into consideration (Sharma et al., 2019). This technique is one of the least complex and common techniques for the training of the classifier. It is based on the likelihood of occurrence of feature words in the document. It utilizes Bayes Theorem to foresee the likelihood that a given list of features has a place with a specific label (Kamble & Itkikar, 2018). The probability that a sentiment (ST) occurs in a given sentence (SN) is determined by the rule: "P(ST/SN) =P(ST)P(SN/ST)/P(SN)" (Ahmad et al., 2017) (Kamble & Itkikar, 2018).

The prime advantage of this methodology is that this technique is easy to interpret, and the outcomes are determined proficiently (Ahmad et al., 2017). One of the major disadvantages is the presumption that the features are independent of each other in the feature space (Desai & Mehta, 2016) (Ahmad et al., 2017).

    ii. Maximum entropy classifier: The maximum entropy classifier is also a probabilistic classifier like Naïve Bayes except that it doesn't assume that features act independently. It is associated with the category of exponential models. It is employed mainly when very little information is available about the prior distributions. The distribution of the feature should be as uniform as possible, which implies that it should have the highest possible entropy. The distribution is constrained to be the least non-uniform (Bhuta et al., 2014).

It is normally used in sentiment analysis for text classification where the words are not independent. The time required for training is more in Maximum entropy as compared to Naïve Bayes (Sharef et al.,2016). The major advantage of this methodology is that it does not experience the ill effects of the independence assumption (Bhuta et al., 2014). Whereas, due to the evaluation of constraints from the labelled data, the data could be inadequate and dispersed, which may cause the technique to experience the issues of overfitting. To enhance the performance remarkably a prior for all the features can be introduced.

2.   Regression Problem

Unlike classification problems, where output is a discrete value, regression problems have continuous values. The different regression algorithms are linear regression, regression trees etc. Predicting the temperature in a city is a regression problem because it is a real value whereas predicting the trend in the stock market is not a regression problem because it is a discrete value(rise/fall).

Unsupervised Techniques

Supervised learning techniques employ labelled information which is difficult to produce and gather the labelled data for training. Whereas collecting the unlabeled user-generated data is simpler and is possible in great quantity from web-based sources. It can be gathered either by utilizing a few of the prevailing tools or by building custom tools to capture the user-generated data. As the unsupervised techniques do not employ the usage of the labelled data, thus, the limitation of labelled training data can be controlled by utilizing unsupervised methods for sentiment analysis. Unsupervised techniques need enormous amounts of training data. This is the primary issue of employing unsupervised techniques. Regardless of the issues, this methodology tenders an approach to get information from the unannotated user-generated data (Pang & Lee, 2008).

Unsupervised techniques include K- means technique. K-means clustering is one of the fundamental and popular approaches for data clustering. It is an iterative algorithm and is based on partition of data into clusters. The input to this algorithm is the count of vital clusters and it yields the centroids of the clusters as the outputs. In the initial step of this algorithm, "n" arbitrary data entries are selected as the centroids and in every successive step, all other data entries are allotted to their nearest centroid on the basis of the euclidean distance. In the next progression, the centroid is recalibrated as the average of all the data entries that are assigned to the particular cluster. These steps are repeated until the desired distance value is achieved or they have no modification. The sentiment score is awarded on the basis of the cluster they belong to. The k-means approach is a simple and fast technique. The small and noisy data can induce high sparseness in the dataset, which inturn reduces the efficiency of the approach (Zul et al., 2018) (Orkphol et al., 2019) (Wu et al., 2019).

Semi-Supervised Techniques

This model uses both supervised and unsupervised approaches. It uses both unlabeled as well as labelled data to gain knowledge, which is not there in Supervised or Unsupervised learning.

This approach was proposed because of the absence of volume of labelled data. In the semi-supervised techniques, unlabeled data is used to gain information about the knowledge about joint distribution over classification attributes as this data does not include information about the different categories of sentiments in the user-generated data. Due to the absence of volume of labelled data, employing the semi-supervised approaches would yield better outcomes as compared to the supervised approaches. Semi-supervised approaches also have an advantage over the non-supervised approaches as the semi-supervised approaches include some prior knowledge into the unsupervised models. Most commonly used semi-supervised learning algorithms are generative models, multi-view learning, graph-based methods, and self-training (Gieseke et al., 2012) (Shahnawaj & Astya, 2017).

Knowledge-Based (Rule/lexicon) Approach

Knowledge-based Approaches for sentiment analysis utilizes the sentiment dictionaries with sentiment reflecting words and compare it with data under consideration to determine the polarity of the sentiments (Andrea et al., 2017). This technique classifies the opinionated data on the occurrence of unequivocal influence expressions, for example, tragic, cheerful, exhausted, and terrified. Few knowledge bases additionally allot abstract words a presumably liking to certain feelings along with the record of evident influence terms. The task of creating a sentiment lexicon can be accomplished in three ways as follows (Vohra & Teraiya, 2013):

1. **Manual Construction Approach:** It is a very monotonous, wearying and time-consuming process and thus is rarely used nowadays.
2. **Dictionary Based Approach:** In the dictionary-based approach, the words that reflect the sentiments of the users are gathered manually. The orientation of these words is known apriori. Then the collection of words are developed gradually via looking through words in Corpora or thesaurus for their opposites and equivalent words. This cycle is terminated when there are no more words left to explore. The limitation of the dictionary-based approach is that it is not reliable to discover the sentiments of the user corresponding to the domain specification (Kumar & Sebastian, 2012).
3. **Corpus-Based Approach:** Corpus-based methodology eliminates the issues of dictionary-based approach. It acquires the sentiment labels as well as the context which is generally utilized in machine learning techniques. The accuracy of this method is also relatively high. But this methodology is not as proficient as a dictionary-based methodology as it requires an enormous corpus to enclose the terms of English language, which is a very tedious process. Regardless of this drawback, this approach is commonly employed as a result of its huge preferred function of furnishing the sentiment terms with domain-specific polarities. This approach uses two different techniques, namely, Statistical and Semantic.

The main advantage of knowledge-based approaches general knowledge sentiment lexicons has more extensive term inclusion. One of the major limitations of this technique is the finite count of phrases and terms in the lexicons, which might cause difficulty in determining sentiments from dynamic environments. Another challenge with this technique is that dictionaries allocate a fixed sentiment polarity and score to the opinion terms without considering the utilization of these opinion terms in the data under consideration (Andrea et al., 2017).

Hybrid Approaches

This methodology utilizes statistical as well as the lexicon-based techniques. It incorporates the advantages of both the approaches – stability and readability of knowledge-based approach and high performance and accuracy from a supervised machine learning approach. Implementing the statistical and knowledge-based techniques combined helps in enhancing the performance and accuracy of the process of sentiment analysis. The advantages of hybrid techniques include lexicon-learning symbiosis, detection and analysis of sentiments at the concept level and lesser sensitivity to modifications in the subject domain. The disadvantage of this technique is that the data with noise (i.e. data that contains superfluous and unrelated terms for the topic of the review) are generally associated with unbiased tags as this approach is unsuccessful in identifying any sentiment (Andrea et al., 2017).

Concept-Based Ontologies

Ontologies can be described as "explicit, machine-readable specification of a shared conceptualization" (Studer et al., 1998). Ontologies are utilized for exhibiting the expressions in a domain of interest as well as to represent the association between these expressions. Ontologies can be implemented in and are now applied in different fields such as Sentimental analysis. Ontologies are employed as the principal mode of knowledge presented in the Semantic Web. This approach uses a huge knowledge-base, and with this, we can analyze the conceptual information of natural language opinion behind multiword expressions. Sentimental analysis often uses web ontologies for semantic networks. In Concept-based Ontologies techniques, the primary task is to create an ontology that comprises features, their attributes and components, that were discussed by individuals who are vigorously offering their opinions on the social web. The ontology can be generated in Web Ontology Language (OWL). After developing an ontology, the created ontology is then utilized for extraction of the object-features and attributes from the specified domain. The data collected is preprocessed, and then the input vector for classification is created. The output is the data categorized into three categories of sentiments, i.e. positive, negative or neutral. In the event of determining the sentiments via concept-based ontologies techniques, the feature extraction is a simple and time-efficient process (Kumar & Joshi, 2017).

APPLICATIONS OF SENTIMENT ANALYSIS

With the evolution of the Internet, an individual's lifestyle has been changed to being highly revealing of their perspectives and expressions. This inclination assisted the researchers in receiving consumer-produced data. The user-generated content can be utilized by sentiment analysis for various tasks. The major application tasks of sentiment analysis are shown in Figure 5:

1. **Purchasing Product or Service:** Buying an item or service is no longer a troublesome errand. Using sentiment analysis, one can assess another's conclusion and experience about any item or administration without much difficulty. Thus, making the comparison of the items with the contending brands easier. At present, individuals would not prefer to depend on an external expert. Sentiment Analysis is employed to obtain consumer's opinions and sentiments from the web content and analyze it to present them in a highly structured and understandable manner.
2. **Quality Improvement in Product or service:** The producers can gather the public's sentiments and opinions of products and services through sentiment analysis and thus one can improve the quality of the products with respect to the criticism and favourable opinions received. The online product reviews can be collected from websites like Amazon, Rotten Tomatoes and IMDb.
3. **Marketing research:** Sentiment Analysis techniques can be used for marketing research. The recent trends of the buyers about some products and services or the ongoing frame of mind of the overall

population towards some new government strategy can be investigated by the process of sentiment analysis. In this way, sentiment analysis can contribute to the collective intelligent research.

4. **Recommendation Systems:** Sentiment analysis can be employed in recommendation systems. The sentiments and opinions of the individuals can be assessed as positive, negative and neutral. The framework can suggest individuals, the products with positive sentiments and avoid those with negative responses of the user.

5. **Detection of "flame":** Analyzing the user-generated content of social media can be done effectively by the process of sentiment analysis. Arrogant expressions, over warmed words or contempt language utilized in messages, discussion passages or tweets on different web sources, can be detected automatically in sentiment analysis.

6. **Spam Review Detection:** Since the web can be accessed by everyone, anyone can post anything on the web; this enhanced the probability of spam data on the web. In the world of online reviews, where there are genuine reviews, there exists a lot of spam reviews also which can be given by some individuals or maybe the organizations themselves for their advertisement. Detection of spam reviews is a big application in sentiment analysis, e.g. an e-mail may be considered as 'spam' or 'not spam'. This task has a great impact on industrial communities also.

7. **Policy-Making:** Sentiment analysis techniques are used by the policymakers to take people's perspective towards policies into consideration and to utilize this data to make new policies.

8. **Decision Making:** User's sentiments and opinions are extremely valuable components in the decision-making process. Sentiment analysis provides analyzed sentiments of the users, which can be viably utilized in the process of decision making.

Figure 5. Application tasks of Sentiment Analysis

As discussed above, it is contemplated that sentiment analysis is a fast-growing tool used in the world of Natural Language Processing in order to detect and evaluate the user's emotions, feelings, views and different perspectives about a certain product or service, and can be utilized to perform various tasks. Sentiment analysis is an advanced stage of data mining which utilizes different processes to extract the information from a certain unstructured text, and it has gained a lot of popularity because of the implementation of these tasks in versatile applications in the various fields. Some of the applications are as displayed by Figure 6:

1. **Social Media:** People use social networking sites nowadays to express their views in many contexts. The media may be Facebook, Twitter, etc. The current issues are discussed on social networking websites through blogs or different forums, which gives researchers an opportunity to analyze the text in various forms and come up with even better algorithms.

2. **Industries or business organization:** Sentiment analysis plays a significant role in the business world. Industries can take the survey of their products or services from their consumers and hence improve the same. Different customers will have different views about some product and service. And the data set is quite large to manually deal with. Hence a sentiment analysis or opinion mining tool will prove to be very helpful in understanding the average customer reviews.

3. **Education:** In the education field also, sentiment analysis plays a significant role. Since the feedback is taken by the students or parents at the end of the session, the analysis of this feedback will give way out to improve the teaching-learning process. The faculty will come to know the expectations of the students and the limitations of self. This analysis may help the faculty to improve his teaching methods. Not only this, it can be quite helpful for the management also like if they get the summarized feedback of faculty through an automated analysis tool, thus the appraisal process can be done in an efficient manner.

4. **E-Commerce:** Purchasing and selling of products and services online are known as e-commerce. Sentiment analysis is very helpful in this context. If a person wants to buy something online, he can take a survey of the reviews given by other persons who bought the same product, before buying one. If all the reviews are analyzed and summarized, it will save a great deal of time and effort of the buyer. Sentiment analysis can assist in summarizing the different reviews. Similarly, if a user wants to sell something, he can take a survey of the market before actually quoting the price of his product.

5. **Finance Sector:** Sentiment analysis plays a significant role in the finance sector. A user can look at the market trends before investing in the stock market. Monitoring of financial news on the web can be done with the help of automatic sentiment detection tools.

6. **Hospitality industry:** People share their experiences about their travels like hotels or travel providers. Many sites which are very popular for this are TripAdvisor, Trivago etc. Before getting the bookings done, people look for reviews of other users and analyze them manually to reach any conclusion. If some automated analysis tool is available for analyzing the reviews, the task becomes much easier. Not only the customers are benefited from this, but also the hotel management authorities and travel providers can improve their services by looking at the analysis of feedback given by customers.

7. **Politics:** The views of voters about various issues can be analyzed by politicians in order to work in a better way. During elections, various surveys take place, which, when analyzed, can help a common man in deciding the right candidate.

8. **Entertainment:** In the field of entertainment, sentiment analysis plays an essential role. People look at the reviews of a movie or play or any other event before watching them. From the several reviews, if the feature-based extraction is done like the story of a movie is good, the direction is bad, casting is good, the music is very good, and so on, then a user can easily decide whether to go for that movie or not based on his preferences about different features of a movie.

9.   **Medical sector:** The views of doctors and patients about a particular treatment or medicine can help the authorities to work in a particular direction, e.g. if a particular procedure is reviewed as costly by many patients, then the price factor may be reconsidered for future perspectives.

Figure 6. Application areas of Sentiment Analysis

CHALLENGES OF SENTIMENT ANALYSIS

The principal purpose of the sentiment analysis is to acquire the expressed sentiments from the unstructured user opinionated data and to categorize the sentiment into three classes of sentiment orientation, i.e. positive, negative or neutral. But recognizing the polarity words is a strenuous and complex procedure, and it faces many difficulties as users rarely express their sentiments in the same way. Thus, there are numerous aspects due to which sentiment analysis is considered complicated and difficult. Some of these challenges are exhibited in Figure 7, are:

• **Spam review detection:**

Social web networks are represented by obscurity and anonymity of their clients, which might be utilized to misguide different clients on web networks. On the one hand, the surveys and reviews on a specific service or product are exceptionally useful, but on the other hand, there are many fake and phoney reviews too. These fake reviews mislead the users by presenting undeserving positive assessments and untruthful negative assessments. An individual or some association to promote or ruin the overall rating of a specific product or service in political aspects as well as in other areas where the posted reviews can influence user's evaluation of the product or service in consideration might publish the spam reviews and surveys. These spams and fake reviews make sentiment analysis worthless in many application areas. Identifying these phoney (spam) reviews from non-spam sentiments is a major test in the field of sentiment analysis. The issue for sentiment analysis is to build up the appropriate systems and advanced techniques for recognizing and filtering non-spam reviews from the spams in the user opinionated data. Despite the fact that numerous researches have been done in this area in order to overcome this challenge, yet it still is a major concern in the process of sentiment analysis (Seerat & Azam, 2012).

Figure 7. Challenges of Sentiment Analysis

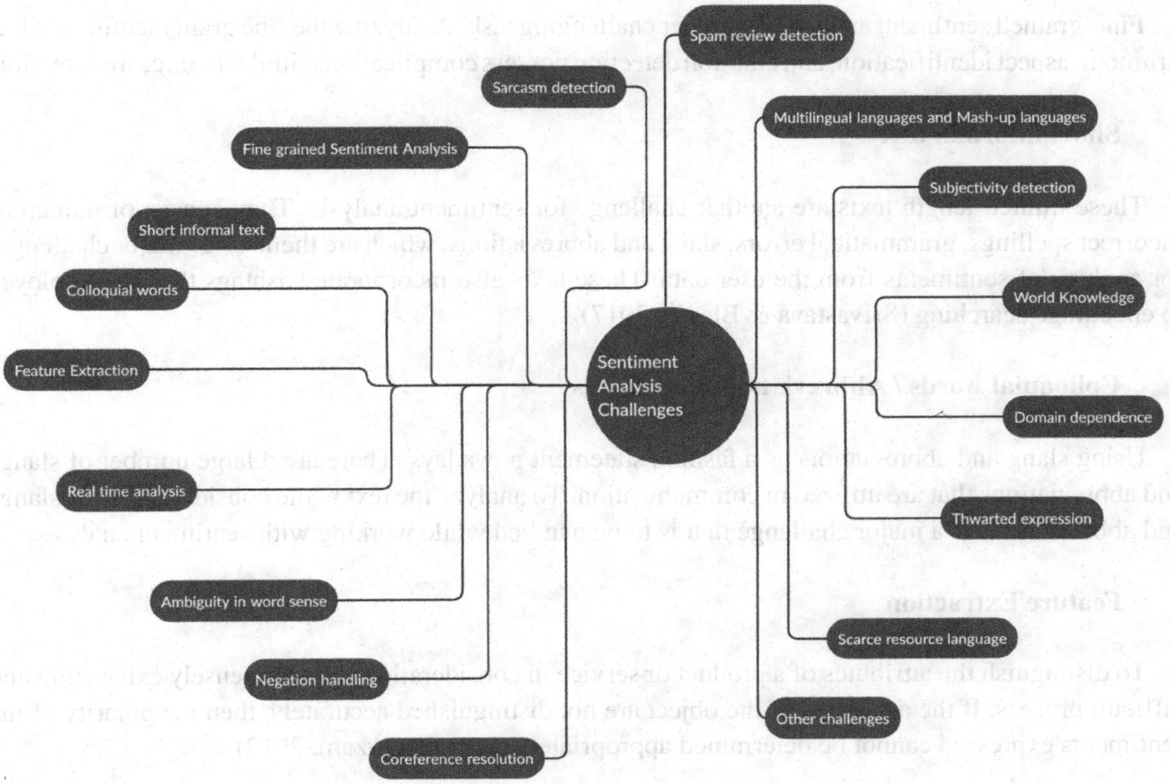

- **Sarcasm detection:**

According to Wikipedia (2020), Sarcasm can be characterized as *"a sharp, bitter, or cutting expression or remark; a bitter gibe or taunt"*. Sentences in a text might be straight forward as well as sarcastic sentences. Sarcastic sentences are an extraordinary kind of sentences which characterize the converse of the expressed feeling of the user. It is constantly indicated utilizing strengthened positive or positive words. Posting sarcastic messages via web-based networking media turns into another fashion to stay away from negative words. Mockery is an exceptional sort of sentiment expression that, for the most part, reverses the direction of the view in the user opinionated text into consideration. These sentences commonly look positive; however, the overall orientation demonstrates negative due to the presence of sarcasm. These sentences convey negative opinions by employing positive words. For instance: a sentence appears to be a compliment; however, it is an insult. At the end of the day, the extremity of a sentence can be a false positive. Recognizing irony and finding the right opinions in a sentence is one of the greatest tests for sentiment analysis (Mohammad, 2017) (Soman et al., 2018).

- **Fine-grained Sentiment Analysis**

Fine-grained sentiment analysis is another challenging task. Analyzing the fine grains sentiments like a rumour, aspect identification, and emotion detection possess complications similar to sarcasm detection.

- **Short informal text**

These limited length texts are another challenge for sentiment analysis. They consist of numerous incorrect spellings, grammatical errors, slang and abbreviations, which are themselves major challenges for analysis of sentiments from the user data. These texts also incorporate hashtags that are employed to encourage searching (Srivastava & Bhatia, 2017).

- **Colloquial words / Abbreviations and slangs**

Using slang and abbreviations is a fashion statement nowadays. There are a large number of slangs and abbreviations that are utilized in communication. To analyze the text while considering these slangs and abbreviations is a major challenge that is to be handled while working with sentiment analysis.

- **Feature Extraction**

To distinguish the attributes of a product or service in consideration is an immensely exhausting and difficult process. If the attributes of the object are not distinguished accurately, then the polarity of the sentiments expressed cannot be determined appropriately (Seerat & Azam, 2012).

- **Real-time analysis**

Static information can be analyzed effectively with contrast to the real-time dynamic data (Ebrahimi et al., 2017). With the expansion in the utilization of social media websites, enormous information is accessible for sentiment mining that increases the requirement for an automated system.

- **Sentiment analysis on audio and video**

Numerous explorers are continuing for content examination in the field of sentiment mining. Along with the text documents, user opinions about a particular product and service can be as audio and video data. Thus the information obtained in the form of audio and video data should be analyzed additionally. But analyzing and determining sentiments from the audio and video content is a very strenuous task.

- **Ambiguity in word sense**

This problem arises when the same term can have diverse interpretations in various contexts. It increases the efforts to develop language-oriented vocabularies and lexicons. In some situations, it also reduces the precision of interpretation of different dialects into the English language. For example, Smaller size would be considered as a positive opinion for laptop chargers, but the same phrase would be regarded as negative if the object in consideration is the cinema multiplex. Thus, to investigate the significance and accurate context of a word is a challenging task.

- **Negation handling**

Negations in a sentence are used to inverse the extremity of that sentence. Negation words like no, not, never etc. are used to reverse the polarity of the sentiments. For instance: "The novel is boring", is a negative polarity sentence whereas "the novel is not boring", is a positive polarity sentence due to the utilization of the negation keyword "not". Negation handling is thus one of the largest challenges, and if not handled properly, the results would be disastrous (Soman et al., 2018).

- **Coreference resolution**

Coreference resolution is the process of discovering all expressions that are concerned with the same object in the given text. In sentences that contain two or more expressions that indicate the same entity then one expression is usually an antecedent and the other expressions are an anaphor (i.e. a truncated structure) (Sonagi & Gore, 2013). For instance: We went to the picnic and had lunch; it was terrible. In this sentence, one needs to determine the reference of "it" in relation to the picnic and dinner. Coreference resolution improves the precision of sentiment analysis as it provides detailed information (Vohra & Teraiya, 2013). If the expressions and phrases referring to the same entity are not identified accurately, then it makes it difficult to understand the sentiments, and it also impacts the accuracy of the sentiment analysis (Vohra & Teraiya, 2013).

- **Multilingual languages and Mashup languages**

Most of the research has been performed in the English language. Thus, most of the tools, libraries and resources have been generated and are available only for the English language. As a large percentage of people around the world are non-native English speakers, thus there is a need to analyze the sentiments from other languages. But due to the different characteristics of the languages (like Arabic, Chinese, German) and limited available resources (El-beltagy & Ali 2013), it is difficult to process the sentiments of the text of these languages. Employing the resources of English to analyze the sentiments from other languages is very cumbersome, and the results are mainly unreliable. Along with other languages, analyzing the mashup languages like Hinglish, which is a combination of Hindi and English, is critical for the analyzers (Soman et al., 2018).

- **Scarce resource language (Sentiment Analysis of data in mother tongue)**

Analysis of sentiments for scarce resource language is a challenge. Those languages and dialects whose annotated corpus, resources and tools are limited or unavailable; their reviews need to be translated into other languages like English for sentiment analysis (Soman et al., 2018).

- **Thwarted expression**

Sometimes, there are sentences where a small number of contents determines the overall polarity (Nasukawa & Yi, 2003) (Vohra & Teraiya, 2013) (Collomb et al., 2014) (Soman et al., 2018). For instance, the cinematography was admirable, the acting was decent, and songs were nice, but the movie is crappy. In such cases, an easy bag of words approach is not suitable as the majority of terms used are positive, but the principal sentiment is negative due to the critical final sentence. In traditional sentiment analysis, the sentence would have been classified as positive due to the greater importance to the word frequency than the word presence.

- **Domain dependence**

Sentiment analysis profoundly relies on the domain. If the domain from where the training data is obtained and classifier are prepared differently from the domain of the test data, then it performs ineffectively. In general, the words that are utilized for communicating the sentiments have different orientations in different domains, which makes it a very challenging task (Vohra & Teraiya, 2013) (Soman et al., 2018).

- **World Knowledge**

To analyze the sentiments of the user from the user opinionated data, sometimes it is important to have the information about the new trends, facts and history of the world. For instance: to analyze the sentence and predict its polarity, "There is no difference between the character of him and Hitler", the system must have the knowledge about the character of Hitler, else the sentence will not be classified into the appropriate sentiment polarity category (Vohra & Teraiya 2013).

- **Subjectivity detection**

Subjectivity detection is also one of the major challenges that are encountered by sentiment analysis (Pang & Lee, 2008) (Soman et al., 2018). Subjectivity detection is the process of differentiating between opinionated and non-opinionated phrases. In sentiment analysis, the strategy of determining subjectivity is one of the crucial activities and is utilized to predict objective phrases. Subjectivity detection is an extremely challenging task for humans as well as for machines with limited emotional potential as the exhibited sentiment can be associated with the same entity as well as with the overall objective of the sentiment analysis (Soman et al., 2018). In real-life applications, the user needs to comprehend the sentiments accurately, thus demands exhaustive and elaborate sentiment analysis of text, which necessitates the characterization of subjective and objective phrases (Liu, 2010). If the subjectivity is determined accurately, it can enhance the system performance (Soman et al., 2018).

- **Other challenges**

Some of the other challenges that are faced by the sentiment analysis are due to the Bipolar words (Ghaleb & Vijendran, 2017) and Grammatical Errors. When a huge amount of data is considered for sentiment analysis, some of the data might be grammatically wrong. To discover the sentiment polarity of a sentence, the grammatical mistakes are to be managed. Sometimes, the data to be analyzed contains noise along with the relevant required data. This noise needs to be filtered before analyzing the data that makes the sentiment analysis task complicated. Thus, noise removal is another challenge that sentiment analysis deals with.

ISSUES RELATED TO SENTIMENT ANALYSIS AND NLP

Natural language processing deals with the manipulation of natural language (i.e. language used by humans) by utilizing computers and artificial intelligence to process and analyze vast amounts of natural language data for various applications like automatic summarization to disease prediction.

It is evident that despite the wide range of applications of Natural language processing, it faces various challenges which are briefly described below:

- **Ambiguity:** One of the major challenges of NLP is the ambiguity of expressions in a text that has variable context. In natural language, many phrases have various interpretations depending on the context in which they are being assessed. The same expression in the sentence can have various implications depending on the manner of interpretation. The ambiguity in a text can be Lexical ambiguity, Syntactic ambiguity or Semantic ambiguity.
- **Personality, intention and style:** An idea can be communicated in various styles depending on the goal or intention in a particular situation. Some of the opinions have contrary polarities than the actual one. These expressions could be ironic or sarcastic and thus would have different inclination from the original sentence. Sarcasm and irony detection in natural language is a major challenge.
- **Grammatical and spelling errors:** The detection and recovery of grammatical and spelling mistakes is a highly demanding and challenging task. Sometimes, accurate words are mapped as mistakes and erroneously used phrases such as homophones are distinguished as correct ones causing a lot of trouble in natural language processing.
- **Named Entity Recognition:** Named Entity recognition is one of the tasks of Natural language processing. In this task, explicit words and expressions are distinguished and classified for different entities like people, area or qualities (Aronson, 2011). This task is made difficult by word order variation, derivation by the usage of suffixes and prefixes, synonymy and polysemy (Nadkarni et al., 2011).
- **Negations:** Some words in natural language are used to inverse the polarity of the intended meaning.
- **Colloquial words:** Abbreviations and slangs used in natural language made the processing difficult and a challenging task. Most of these words are not present in the dictionary of the original language.

As sentiment analysis is considered as a branch of Natural Language Processing intended to mine various sources of data for opinions and sentiment extraction and classification. But there are several issues which pose a barrier in carrying out the fair evaluation of sentiments and makes it unrealistic and difficult to detect and analyze the sentiments. As shown, some of those issues are Colloquial words, negation handling, ambiguity in word sense, coreference resolution, sarcasm detection and bipolar words.

Most of these challenges are due to NLP constructs which restrict in-depth investigation of sentiments in a given text, thus impacting the process of sentiment analysis and making this a formidable task. Therefore, it is concluded that Sentiment analysis is a restricted Natural Language Processing (NLP) problem.

SOLUTIONS AND RECOMMENDATIONS

- RNN for ambiguity: The advanced deep learning methodology for analyzing sentiments is employed for morphology, language syntax and semantics. Recursive neural networks (RNN) is considered the best one for this purpose. The advancements of Recursive neural networks are valuable for eliminating ambiguity and for tasks that employ grammatical tree structure. It is also supportive of tasks that refer to certain specified phrases. For situations that involve nested hierarchy and an intrinsic recursive structure, Recursive neural networks are considered ideal for them. The syntactic principles of language are exceptionally recursive. Thus, the recursive structure is exploited through a model that regards it. An additional advantage of designing sentences with RNN is that the phrases and sentences with variable length can be taken as an input. Moreover, the RNN works more efficiently than the other methodologies for semantic segmentation.

- Deep learning for sarcasm detection: Sarcasm detection is one of the crucial challenges of Natural Language Processing (NLP) as well as sentiment analysis. Deep learning methodologies prove to be very effective and accurate in analyzing the polarity of the sentiments from the sarcastic text. Kumar et al. (2017) proposed a specified deep learning-based model which is based on CNN-LSTM-FF architecture. This technique which is known as deep neural networks (DNNs) performed better than all the previous techniques, and it exhibits the most significant level of accuracy for numerical sarcasm identification. DNN was not just the best for numerical sarcasm; it was better than all other sarcasm detection approaches as well. Ghosh & Veale (2016) proposed another model which is a fusion of a convolutional neural network, a long short-term memory (LSTM) network, and a DNN. This integrated model was an improvement over the previous models like recursive support vector machines (SVMs).

- Another researcher, Al-kabi et al. (2014), has applied lexicon-based methods that depend on POS tagging. The technique is applied to the dataset that deals with the emoticons, chat data and Arabizi. This technique overcame the issues related to domain dependence and multilingual challenges and determined the polarity of the sentiments from the dataset with an accuracy of 93.9% (Hussein, 2018).

- Languages other than English, for instance: Japanese, Arabic and Chinese generally do not possess definite word boundary markers, and thus tokenization is not a necessity. Instead, it requires word segmentation, which is a critical issue for languages other than English. Conditional Random Fields (CRFs) (Lafferty et al., 2001) have been applied that proved to be a success to resolve this complication. CRFs have exhibited better results than hidden Markov models and maximum- entropy Markov models (Kudo et al., 2004) (Peng et al., 2004) (Tseng et al., 2005). In another attempt, word embeddings and deep learning-based methodologies have been applied to the Chinese word segmentation (Chen et al., 2015) (Ma et al., 2015) (Sun et al., 2017).

FUTURE RESEARCH DIRECTIONS

In the past few years, deep learning and soft computing techniques have progressed due to its practical and promising application in the field of sentiment analysis. Deep learning is an advancement over the traditional methods due to the machine's capacity to learn on its own and develop. Deep learning algorithms employing neural networks are immensely powerful and understand sentiments better than the traditional approaches. Recursive and Recurrent Neural Networks specifically LSTMs and GRUs can be further explored to overcome the challenges faced by sentiment analysis.

Hybrid techniques have performed satisfactorily but their utilization for implicit sentiment analysis can be investigated further. As shown that deep learning techniques can resolve and limit the challenges faced by the sentiment analysis due to NLP constructs. An interesting progression to pursue in this regard is to move towards deep learning and soft computing techniques along with their integrated techniques in the field of natural language to resolve restricted issues of sentiment analysis. This endeavour will be very rewarding and will attempt in uncovering the useful hidden information from the user generated data. Deep learning and soft computing will be key for stepping forward in the process of improving the accuracy of the tasks of sentiment analysis as well as it can be employed to solve the open problems discussed in the chapter. The solutions to many such problems have been provided in the chapter. However, many challenges in this field of study remain unsolved. More future research could be dedicated to these challenges. The chapter has uncovered many interesting open challenges that can be promising directions for future research.

CONCLUSION

With the tremendous increase in the online reviews, opinions, recommendations, ratings, and feedback by the people, in the past decade, the focus on the content generated by the user has also proliferated. This wealth of information is thus rewarding for organizations and individuals for various purposes. In this chapter, an overview of sentiment analysis has been presented. The sentiment analysis can be applied on various levels and thus different levels of sentiment analysis as well as the process of sentiment analysis has been explained in detail. The various methodology and techniques, i.e. statistical approach, knowledge-based approach, hybrid approach and concept-based approaches, employed for analyzing the sentiments have been explored and described. This newly produced knowledge from analyzing the sentiments can be successfully employed in the various application domains, as explained in the chapter.

The focus of the chapter has been on the challenges faced by the Sentiment analysis. The major challenges of sentiment analysis like spam review detection, sarcasm detection, colloquial words, multimodal data analysis, negation handling, real-time analysis, multilingual and mashup languages; that still needs to be overcome have been discussed. Despite the numerous researches being done in the field of sentiment analysis, there are some Natural Language Processing (NLP) related issues being faced by sentiment analysis. Most of the issues that are faced by the sentiment analysis are due to the natural language constructs. Some of these issues are colloquial words, negation keywords, ambiguity, coreference resolution. It is evident that these challenges impact the process of Sentiment Analysis and makes it difficult to understand the sentiments. Few of the issues have been resolved using deep learning and advanced integration techniques that have been discussed in the chapter. The basic constructs of the natural language impose restrictions on the analyzing of the sentiments from the user-generated data and making this a formidable task. It acts as a barrier to the advancements in this area. Thus, it can be inferred that the sentiment analysis is a restricted Natural Language Processing (NLP) problem.

ACKNOWLEDGMENT

We would like to thank the scholars of Web Research Group, Department of Computer Science and Engineering, Delhi Technological University for their constant support during the preparation of this manuscript. We would also like to thank "www.flaticon.com" to provide the icons for our figures.

REFERENCES

Abbes, M., Kechaou, Z., & Alimi, A. M. (2017). Enhanced deep learning models for sentiment analysis in Arab social media. *International Conference on Neural Information Processing*. 667-676. 10.1007/978-3-319-70139-4_68

Aggarwal, D., Bali, V., & Mittal, S. (2019). An insight into machine learning techniques for Predictive Analysis and Feature Selection. *International Journal of Innovative Technology and Exploring Engineering*, 8(9S), 342–349. doi:10.35940/ijitee.I1055.0789S19

Aggarwal, D. G. (2018). *Review Paper Sentiment Analysis: An Insight into Techniques, Application and Challenges*. Academic Press.

Ahmad, M., Aftab, S., Muhammad, S. S., & Ahmad, S. (2017). Machine Learning Techniques for Sentiment Analysis: A Review. *International Journal of Multidisciplinary Sciences and Engineering.*, 8(3), 27–32.

Ainur, Y., Yisong, Y., & Claire, C. (2010). Multi-level structured models for document-level sentiment classification. *Proceedings of the 2010 Conference on Empirical Methods in Natural Language Processing*, 1046–1056.

Al-Azani, S., & El-Alfy, E. (2018). Emojis-Based Sentiment Classification of Arabic Microblogs Using Deep Recurrent Neural Networks. *2018 International Conference on Computing Sciences and Engineering (ICCSE)*, 1-6. 10.1109/ICCSE1.2018.8374211

Al-kabi, Gigieh, Alsmadi, & Wahsheh. (2014). *Opinion Mining and Analysis for Arabic Language*. Academic Press.

Alayba, A. M., Palade, V., England, M., & Iqbal, R. (2017). Arabic language sentiment analysis on health services. *2017 1st International Workshop on Arabic Script Analysis and Recognition (ASAR)*, 114-118.

Andrea, A. D., Ferri, F., Grifoni, P., Guzzo, T. (2015). Approaches, Tools and Applications for Sentiment Analysis Implementation. *International Journal of Computer Applications, 125*(3), 26-33.

Aronson, A. R. (2001). Effective mapping of biomedical text to the UMLS Metathesaurus: the MetaMap program. *Proceedings. AMIA Symposium*, 17–21.

Aziz, A. A., & Tao, L. (2016). Word embeddings for Arabic sentiment analysis. *IEEE International Conference on Big Data*, 7, 3820-3825.

Beigi, G., Hu, X., Maciejewski, R., & Liu, H. (2016). An overview of sentiment analysis in social media and its applications in disaster relief. Sentiment analysis and ontology engineering, 313-340.

Bhuta, S., Doshi, A., Doshi, U., & Narvekar, M. (2014). A Review of Techniques for Sentiment Analysis Of Twitter Data. *2014 International Conference on Issues and Challenges in Intelligent Computing Techniques (ICICT)*, 583-591. 10.1109/ICICICT.2014.6781346

Bloem, C. (2017, July 31). *84 Percent of People Trust Online Reviews As Much As Friends. Here's How to Manage What They See*. Retrieved from https://www.inc.com/craig-bloem/84-percent-of-people-trust-online-reviews-as-much-.html

Bravo-Marquez, F., Frank, E., & Pfahringer, B. (2016). Building a Twitter opinion lexicon from automatically-annotated tweets. *Knowledge-Based Systems*, *108*, 65–78. doi:10.1016/j.knosys.2016.05.018

Cambria, E. (2016). Affective computing and sentiment analysis. *IEEE Intelligent Systems*, *31*(2), 102–107. doi:10.1109/MIS.2016.31

Chalothom, T., & Ellman, J. (2015). Simple approaches of sentiment analysis via ensemble learning. Information Science and Applications, 631-639.

Chandni, Chandra, N., Gupta, S., & Pahade, R. (2015). Sentiment analysis and its challenges. *International Journal of Engineering Research & Technology (Ahmedabad)*, *4*(3), 968–970.

Chen, X., Qiu, X., Zhu, C., & Huang, X. J. (2015). Gated recursive neural network for Chinese word segmentation. *Proceedings of the 53rd Annual Meeting of the Association for Computational Linguistics and the 7th International Joint Conference on Natural Language Processing*, 1, 1744-1753. 10.3115/v1/P15-1168

Collomb, A., Costea, C., Joyeux, D., Hasan, O., & Brunie, L. (2014). A study and comparison of sentiment analysis methods for reputation evaluation. *Rapport de recherche RR-LIRIS-2014-002*.

Dahou, A., Xiong, S., Zhou, J., Haddoud, M. H., & Duan, P. (2016). Word embeddings and convolutional neural network for Arabic sentiment classification. *The 26th International Conference on Computational Linguistics (COLING 2016)*, 2418-2427.

Desai, M., & Mehta, M. A. (2016). Techniques for Sentiment Analysis of Twitter Data: A Comprehensive Survey. *International Conference on Computing, Communication and Automation (ICCCA2016)*, 149-154. 10.1109/CCAA.2016.7813707

Ebrahimi, M., Yazdavar, A. H., & Sheth, A. (2017). Challenges of sentiment analysis for dynamic events. *IEEE Intelligent Systems*, *32*(5), 70–75. doi:10.1109/MIS.2017.3711649

El-Beltagy, S. R., & Ali, A. (2013). Open issues in the sentiment analysis of Arabic social media: A case study. *2013 9th International Conference on Innovations in Information Technology (IIT)*, 215-220. 10.1109/Innovations.2013.6544421

Ghaleb, O. A. M., & Vijendran, A. S. (2017). The Challenges of Sentiment Analysis on Social Web Communities. *International Journal of Advance Research in Science and Engineering.*, *6*(12), 117–125.

Ghosh, A., & Veale, T. (2016). Fracking sarcasm using neural network. *Proceedings of the 7th workshop on computational approaches to subjectivity, sentiment and social media analysis*, 161-169. 10.18653/v1/W16-0425

Gieseke, F., Kramer, O. I., Airola, A., & Pahikkala, T. (2012). Efficient recurrent local search strategies for semi- and unsupervised regularized least-squares classification. *Evolutionary Intelligence, 2012*(5), 189–205. doi:10.100712065-012-0068-5

Haochen, Z., & Fei, S. (2015). Aspect-level sentiment analysis based on a generalized probabilistic topic and syntax model. In *Proceedings of the Twenty-Eighth International Florida Artificial Intelligence Research Society Conference*. Association for the Advancement of Artificial Intelligence.

Hu, M., & Liu, B. (2004). Mining and summarizing customer reviews. *Proceedings of the tenth ACM SIGKDD international conference on Knowledge discovery and data mining*, 168-177.

Hussein, D. M. E. D. M. (2018). A survey on sentiment analysis challenges. *Journal of King Saud University-Engineering Sciences., 30*(4), 330–338. doi:10.1016/j.jksues.2016.04.002

Kalchbrenner, N., Grefenstette, E., & Blunsom, P. (2014). A Convolutional Neural Network for Modelling Sentences. *Computation and Language., 655–665. doi:10.3115/v1/P14-1062

Kamble, S. S., & Itkikar, A. R. (2018). Study of supervised machine learning approaches for sentiment analysis. *International Research Journal of Engineering and Technology, 5*(4), 3045–3047.

Khaled, A., Tazi, N. E., & Hossny, A. H. (2015). Sentiment Analysis over Social Networks: An Overview. *2015 IEEE International Conference on Systems, Man, and Cybernetics*, 2174-2179.

Kharde, V., & Sonawane, P. (2016). *Sentiment analysis of twitter data: A survey of techniques.* arXiv preprint arXiv:1601.06971

Kim, Y. (2014). *Convolutional neural networks for sentence classification.* Academic Press.

Kudo, T., Yamamoto, K., & Matsumoto, Y. (2004). Applying conditional random fields to Japanese morphological analysis. *Proceedings of the 2004 Conference on Empirical Methods in Natural Language Processing*, 230–237.

Kumar, A., & Joshi, A. (2017). Ontology-Driven Sentiment Analysis on Social Web for Government Intelligence. *ICEGOV '17: Proceedings of the Special Collection on eGovernment Innovations in India*, 134–139. 10.1145/3055219.3055229

Kumar, A., & Sebastian, T. M. (2012). Sentiment Analysis: A Perspective on Its Past, Present and Future. *International Journal of Intelligent Systems and Applications,* 1–14.

Kumar, L., Somani, A., Bhattacharyya, P. (2017). *"Having 2 Hours to Write a Paper Is Fun!": Detecting Sarcasm in Numerical Portions of Text.* ArXiv, abs/1709.01950

Lafferty, J., McCallum, A., & Pereira, F. C. (2001). Conditional random fields: Probabilistic models for segmenting and labeling sequence data. *Proceedings of the 8th International Conference on Machine Learning*, 282–289.

Li, P., Xu, W., Ma, C., Sun, J., & Yan, Y. (2015). IOA: Improving SVM based sentiment classification through post processing. *Proc. 9th Int. Workshop Semantic Evaluation*, 545–550. 10.18653/v1/S15-2091

Lincy, W., & Kumar, N. M. (2016). A survey on challenges in sentiment analysis. *International Journal of Emerging Technology in Computer Science & Electronics*, *21*(3), 409–412.

Ling, P., Geng, C., Menghou, Z., & Chunya, L. (2014). *What Do Seller Manipulations of Online Product Reviews Mean to Consumers?* (HKIBS Working Paper Series 070-1314) Hong Kong Institute of Business Studies, Lingnan University, Hong Kong.

Liu, B. (2010). Sentiment Analysis: A Multi-Faceted Problem. *IEEE Intelligent Systems*.

Liu, G., Xu, X., Deng, B., Chen, S., & Li, L. (n.d.). A hybrid method for bilingual text sentiment classification based on deep learning. *17th IEEE/ACIS International Conference on Software Engineering Artificial Intelligence Networking and Parallel/Distributed Computing (SNPD)*, 93-98. 10.1109/SNPD.2016.7515884

Ma, J., & Hinrichs, E. (2015). Accurate linear-time Chinese word segmentation via embedding matching. *Proceedings of the 53rd Annual Meeting of the Association for Computational Linguistics and the 7th International Joint Conference on Natural Language Processing*, 1, 1733–1743. 10.3115/v1/P15-1167

Matthew, J. K., Spencer, G., & Andrea, Z. (2015). Potential applications of sentiment analysis in educational research and practice – Is SITE the friendliest conference? In *Proceedings of Society for Information Technology & Teacher Education International Conference 2015*. Association for the Advancement of Computing in Education (AACE).

Medhat, W., Hassan, A., & Korashy, H. (2014). Sentiment analysis algorithms and applications: A survey. *Ain Shams Engineering Journal. Elsevier.*, *5*(4), 1093–1113. doi:10.1016/j.asej.2014.04.011

Mohammad, S. M. (2017). Challenges in sentiment analysis. In A practical guide to sentiment analysis. Springer.

Nadkarni, P. M., Ohno-Machado, L., & Chapman, W. W. (2011). Natural language processing: An introduction. *Journal of the American Medical Informatics Association*, *18*(5), 544–551. doi:10.1136/amiajnl-2011-000464 PMID:21846786

Nasukawa, T., & Yi, J. (2003). Sentiment analysis: Capturing favorability using natural language processing. *Proceedings of the 2nd international conference on Knowledge capture*, 70-77. 10.1145/945645.945658

Nikos, E., Angeliki, L., Georgios, P., & Konstantinos, C. 2011. ELS: a word-level method for entity-level sentiment analysis. *WIMS '11 Proceedings of the International Conference on Web Intelligence, Mining and Semantics*.

Noura, F., Elie, C., Rawad, A. A., & Hazem, H. 2010. Sentence-level and document-level sentiment mining for Arabic texts. *Proceeding IEEE International Conference on Data Mining Workshops*.

Orkphol, K., Yang, W. (2019). Sentiment Analysis on Microblogging with K-Means Clustering and Artificial Bee Colony. *International Journal of Computational Intelligence and Applications, 18*(3).

Osimo & Mureddu. (2011). *Research Challenge on Opinion Mining and Sentiment Analysis*. Academic Press.

Ouyang, X., Zhou, P., Li, C. H., & Liu, L. (2015). Sentiment Analysis using Convolutional Neural Network. *2015 IEEE International Conference on Computer and Information Technology; Ubiquitous Computing and Communications; Dependable, Autonomic and Secure Computing; Pervasive Intelligence and Computing*, 2359-2364.

Pang, B., & Lee, L. (2008). Opinion Mining and Sentiment Analysis. *Foundations and Trends in Information Retrieval.*, *2*(1), 1–135. doi:10.1561/1500000011

Patel, V., Prabhu, G., & Bhowmick, K. (2015). A Survey of Opinion Mining and Sentiment Analysis. *International Journal of Computers and Applications*, *131*(1), 24–27. doi:10.5120/ijca2015907218

Peng, F., Feng, F., & McCallum, A. (2004). Chinese segmentation and new word detection using conditional random fields. *Proceedings of the 20th International Conference on Computational Linguistics*, 562– 568. 10.3115/1220355.1220436

Safrin, R. (2017). *Sentiment Analysis on Online Product Review*. Academic Press.

Sallab, A. A. A., Baly, R., Badaro, G., Hajj, H., Hajj, W. E., & Shaban, K. B. (2015). Deep learning models for sentiment analysis in Arabic. *Proceedings of the Second Workshop on Arabic Natural Language Processing*, 9–17. 10.18653/v1/W15-3202

Samal, B. R., Behera, A. K., & Panda, M. (2017). Performance Analysis of Supervised Machine Learning Techniques for Sentiment Analysis. *2017 IEEE 3rd International Conference on Sensing, Signal Processing and Security (ICSSS)*, 128-133.

Seerat, B., & Azam, F. (2012). Opinion mining: Issues and challenges (A Survey). *International Journal of Computers and Applications*, *49*(9), 42–51. doi:10.5120/7658-0762

Shahnawaz, A. P. (2017). Sentiment Analysis: Approaches and Open Issues. *International Conference on Computing, Communication and Automation (ICCCA2017)*, 154-158.

Sharef, N. M., Zin, H. M., & Nadali, S. (2016). Overview and Future Opportunities of Sentiment Analysis Approaches for Big Data. *Journal of Computational Science*, *12*(3), 153–168. doi:10.3844/jcssp.2016.153.168

Sharma, A., & Dey, S. (2012). A comparative study of feature selection and machine learning techniques for sentiment analysis. *Proceedings of the 2012 ACM Research in Applied Computation Symposium*, 1-7. 10.1145/2401603.2401605

Sharma, D., Sabharwal, M., Goyal, V., & Vij, M. (2019). Sentiment Analysis Techniques for Social Media Data: A Review. *First International Conference on Sustainable Technologies for Computational Intelligence. Proceedings of ICTSCI 2019*, 75-90.

Soman, S. J., Swaminathan, P., Anandan, R., Kalaivani, K. (2018). A comparative review of the challenges encountered in sentiment analysis of Indian regional language tweets vs English language tweets. *International Journal of Engineering & Technology, 7*(2), 319-322.

Sonagi, A., & Gore, D. (2013). Sentiment Analysis and Challenges Involved: A Survey. *International Journal of Scientific Research (Ahmedabad, India)*, *4*(1), 1928–1932.

Srivastava, R., & Bhatia, M. P. S. (2017). Challenges with sentiment analysis of on-line micro-texts. *International Journal of Intelligent Systems and Applications*, *9*(7), 31–40. doi:10.5815/ijisa.2017.07.04

Studer, R., Benjamins, R., & Fensel, D. (1998). Knowledge engineering: Principles and methods. *Data & Knowledge Engineering*, *25*(1–2), 161–198. doi:10.1016/S0169-023X(97)00056-6

Sun, S., Luo, C., & Chen, J. (2017). A Review of Natural Language Processing Techniques for Opinion Mining Systems. *Information Fusion*, *36*, 10–25. doi:10.1016/j.inffus.2016.10.004

Tang, H., Tan, S., & Cheng, X. (2009). A survey on sentiment detection of reviews. *Expert Systems with Applications*, *36*(7), 10760–10773. doi:10.1016/j.eswa.2009.02.063

Tawunrat, C., Jeremy, E., 2015. Chapter Information Science and Applications, Simple Approaches of Sentiment Analysis via Ensemble Learning. *Lecture Notes in Electrical Engineering, 339*.

Techopedia. (2014, January 21). *Sentiment Analysis*. Retrieved from https://www.techopedia.com/definition/29695/sentiment-analysis

Thomas, B. (2013). *What Consumers Think About Brands on Social Media, and What Businesses Need to do About it Report*. Keep Social Honest.

Tseng, H., Chang, P. C., Andrew, G., Jurafsky, D., & Manning, C. D. (2005). A conditional random field word segmenter for sighan bakeoff 2005. *Proceedings of the fourth SIGHAN workshop on Chinese language Processing*, 168–171.

Tsytsarau, M., & Palpanas, T. (2012). Survey on mining subjective data on the web. *Data Mining and Knowledge Discovery*, *24*(3), 478–514. doi:10.100710618-011-0238-6

Turney, P. D., & Littman, M. L. (2003). Measuring praise and criticism: Inference of semantic orientation from association. *ACM Transactions on Information Systems*, *21*(4), 315–346. doi:10.1145/944012.944013

Varghese, R., & Jayasree, M. (2013). A Survey on Sentiment Analysis and Opinion Mining. *IJRET: International Journal of Research in Engineering and Technology.*, *2*(11), 312–317. doi:10.15623/ijret.2013.0211048

Vohra, S., & Teraiya, J. (2013). Applications and Challenges for Sentiment Analysis: A Survey. *International Journal of Engineering Research & Technology (Ahmedabad)*, *2*(2), 1–5.

Wikipedia. (2020, May 29). *Sarcasm*. Retrieved from https://en.wikipedia.org/wiki/Sarcasm#:~:text=From%20Wikipedia%2C%20the%20free%20encyclopedia,sarcasm%20is%20not%20necessarily%20ironic

Wu, S., Liu, Y., Wang, J., & Li, Q. (2019). Sentiment Analysis Method Based on K-means and On-line Transfer Learning. *CMC-Computers Materials & Continua*, *60*(3), 1207–1222. doi:10.32604/cmc.2019.05835

Yadlapalli, S. S., Reddy, R. R., & Sasikala, T. (2019). Advanced Twitter sentiment analysis using supervised techniques and minimalistic features. Ambient Communications and Computer Systems, RACCCS 2019, 91-104.

Yang, A. M., Lin, J. H., Zhou, Y. M., & Chen, J. (2013). Research on building a Chinese sentiment lexicon based on SO-PMI. Applied Mechanics and Materials, 263, 1688-1693.

Yanyan, Z., Bing, Q., & Qiuhui, S., & Ting, L. (2017). Large-scale sentiment lexicon collection and its application in sentiment classification. *Journal of Chinese Information Processing.*, *31*(2), 187–193.

Zhang, L., Wang, S., & Liu, B. (2018). Deep learning for sentiment analysis: A survey. *Wiley Interdisciplinary Reviews. Data Mining and Knowledge Discovery*, *8*(4), e1253. doi:10.1002/widm.1253

Zul, M. I., Yulia, F., & Nurmalasari, D. (2018). Social Media Sentiment Analysis Using K-Means and Naïve Bayes Algorithm. *2nd International Conference on Electrical Engineering and Informatics (ICon EEI)*, 24-29. 10.1109/ICon-EEI.2018.8784326

ADDITIONAL READING

Cambria, E., Das, D., Bandyopadhyay, S., & Feraco, A. (2017). *A Practical Guide to Sentiment Analysis*. Springer. doi:10.1007/978-3-319-55394-8

Cambria, E., Poria, S., Gelbukh, A., & Thelwall, M. (2017). Sentiment Analysis is a Big Suitcase. *IEEE Intelligent Systems*, *32*(6), 74–80. doi:10.1109/MIS.2017.4531228

Chaturvedi, I., Poria, S., & Cambria, E. (2017). Basic tasks of sentiment analysis. Encyclopedia of Social Network Analysis and Mining. 1-28.

Khaled, A., Tazi, N. E., & Hossny, A. H. (2015). Sentiment Analysis over Social Networks: An Overview. *2015 IEEE International Conference on Systems, Man, and Cybernetics*. 2174-2179.

Kumar, A., & Sebastian, T. M. (2012). Sentiment Analysis on Twitter. *IJCSI International Journal of Computer Science Issues*. 9(4,3). 372-378.

Kumar, A., & Sebastian, T. M. (2012). Sentiment Analysis: A Perspective on Its Past, Present and Future. *International Journal of Intelligent Systems and Applications*. 1–14.

Montoyo, A., Martínez-Barco, P., & Balahur, A. (2012). Subjectivity and sentiment analysis: An overview of the current state of the area and envisaged developments. *Decision Support Systems. Elsevier.*, *53*(4), 675–679. doi:10.1016/j.dss.2012.05.022

Taboada, M. (2016). Sentiment Analysis: An Overview from Linguistics. *Annual Review of Linguistics*, *2*(1), 325–347. doi:10.1146/annurev-linguistics-011415-040518

KEY TERMS AND DEFINITIONS

Natural Language Processing: Natural language processing is a process that deals with the manipulation of natural language (i.e., language used by humans) by utilizing computers and artificial intelligence to process and analyze huge amounts of natural language data for various applications ranging from automatic summarization to disease prediction.

Opinionated Text: Opinionated text can be defined as the text acquired from blogs, social networking sites or any other online portal in which the users have expressed their disposition and point of view towards any particular product or service.

Scarce Resource language: Scarce resource languages are those languages that lack text processing resources and only have basic dictionaries. The sentiment analysis of these languages is difficult due to the absence of developed processing tools and resources for these languages.

Sentiment Analysis: Sentiment Analysis is the technique that aids to recognize and classify the emotions and opinions of users in the communicated information, so that the opinion of the user for a certain utility or commodity can be determined as being positive, negative or neutral through NLP and content analysis.

Sentiment Polarity: Sentiment polarity for an element defines the orientation of the expressed sentiment, i.e., it determines if the text expresses the positive, negative or neutral sentiment of the user about the entity in consideration.

Subjectivity Detection: Subjectivity detection is the process of differentiating between opinionated and non-opinionated phrases.

Word Sense Disambiguation: Word sense disambiguation is described as a process of recognizing the implication of a term with respect to the context of the sentence. This problem arises when the same word can have diverse meanings in various contexts.

Chapter 55
Automatic Human Emotion Classification in Web Document Using Fuzzy Inference System (FIS):
Human Emotion Classification

P Mohamed Shakeel

Faculty of Information and Communication Technology, Universiti Teknikal Malaysia Melaka, Malaysia

S Baskar

Department of Electronics and Communication Engineering, Karpagam Academy of Higher Education, Coimbatore, India

ABSTRACT

Textual information mining deals with various information extraction methods that can be evolved from the rapid growth of textual information through human machine interface for analyzing emotions which are taken by a facial expression. The problem of emotions in text is concerned with the fast development of web 2.0 documents that are assigned by users with emotion labels, namely: sadness, surprise, happiness, empathy, anger, warmness, boredom, and amusement. Such emotions can give a new characteristic for document categorization. Textual information mining deals with various information extraction methods that can evolved from the rapid growth of textual information through a human machine interface for analyzing emotions, which are taken by a facial expression. The problem of emotions from text is concerned with the fast development of web 2.0 documents that are assigned by users with emotion labels. Such emotions can give a new characteristic for document categorization.

DOI: 10.4018/978-1-6684-6303-1.ch055

INTRODUCTION

Knowledge discovery and data mining is an iterative process,which is implemented using numerous procedure steps. The mining process will be employed to the huge corpus to extract meaningful information from raw data. The web mining data repository contains semi structured or unstructured text documents. Nowadays, web documents and their On-line libraries, search engines and other huge web document repositories are growing rapidly as because software and hardware integration in the entire domain plays a significant role and ease user interface. In that manual categorizing of every documents using a web mining process become difficult and costly.So as to deal with these issues, automatic mining process is considered for organizing and easily browsing by use of catalogs and minimal human intervention through machine interaction.

The machine supported analysis are dealing with the knowledge discovery process (Asha & Devi. 2012). It utilizes different types of techniques from information extraction, information retrieval and also natural language processing and links them with the methods and algorithms of data mining, KDD, statistics, and machine learning. Nowadays, everyone can express their emotions and options easily through blogs, microblogs, news portals, and they become both the speakers and listeners. Focusing on these huge amount information, public emotions can be detected automaticallyfrom online documents based on the suggestion is emerging recently. Most of the studies on emotion analysis first focus on the writer's perspective. Classified movie reviews into positive and negative emotions, the subjectivity of adjective phrases with emotional categories Kavita (2012). Beyond binary classification, classified blog posts into 37 emotion classes.

From these data modeling perspective,the proposed work focuses on the issues of the unstructured P. Ananthi and R. Manivannan (2015) data sets and deliberated a method which employs the data mining approach to the domain of the textual information. The main aim is to effectively extract the emotional content of texts in huge amount of web content and documents collected from online content and classifies the emotional content of text information using Fuzzy Inference System (FIS) and the emotions are taken by a facial expression through machine interface. Support Vector Machine (SVM) is used to reduced features for the classification process. This process may be help of online users to get their related documents based on their emotional preferences.

RELATED WORK

Nowadays, people are very much aware with online communication and incline to express their feelings on the web. Considering this situation, the author Tim Li (2008) present a hybrid system based on efficiently mining emotional distress inclinations from publicly availableblogs.This blog is used to identify required people so as to give timely promote and intervention better public health. In this proposed system also describe a handcrafted model which includes human judgment and facilitates the adjustment of the forecast in machine learning on blog content.

To present the written text we acquire varied writing styles like informal and formal. Generally a small bit of text can express lots of emotional conditions,spirits or thoughts by means of linguistic and words.In order to extract the text emotions different techniques and approaches are utilized in the meadow of Opinion Mining and Sentiment Analysis.In paper Jasleen Kaur, Jatinderkumar Saini (2009) author analyzed the Formal and Informal text pieces in the meadow of Opinion Mining and Sentiment Analysis in universal languages. To analyze author considered 8 universal languages (English, Chinese, Arabic, Malaysian, Spanish, Turkish, Persian, Korean) formal and informal text from the poetry,poems,thesis and documents, etc., and also 4 feature selection parameters (IG, TF-IDF, n-gram, MI and MMI).The results showed that Arabian language has maximum performance and accuracy in the field of opinion Mining. From the experimented results between the IG and TF-IDF, parameters, IG performance is higher than all others.

In Bao et al. (2012) author concerned with the issue of mining social emotions from text. In recent times, the fast growth of web 2.0 websites and documents is assigned by social website users with emotion labels like sadness, surprise and happiness through machine interface. These emotions can give a novel characteristic for document classification, and so help online users to predict related documents based on their emotional preferences. The main goal of this paper is to discover the links between affective terms and social emotions on which predict the social emotion from the text content. Particularly, a joint emotion topic model by expanding Latent Dirichlet Allocation is used for emotion modeling. Initially, create a set of latent topics from emotion, then it trailed by creating sentimental terms from each topic.

Estimating the speaker's emotion is one of the challenging tasks in speech technology. Most of the existing methods concentrate either on text features or audio. Thus, in Jasmine Bhaskar (2015) author proposes a novel method for emotion classification of audio conversation depend on both text and speech. The novelty in this method is in creating the single feature vector for classification and feature selection. The main contributing on this paper is to enhance the accuracy of emotion classification of speech in light of both text and audio features. The typical methods, for example Support Vector Machines, Natural Language Processing, SentiWordNe and WordNet Affect are used in this approach. The Semval 2007 and eNTERFACE '05 emotion databases are taken in this proposed work.

Text sentiment analysis, also stated to as emotional polarity calculation, has become a successfully developing extreme in the text mining community. Thus, in Nan Li, Desheng Dash Wu (2010) author proposes online forums, hotspot forecast and detection utilizing text mining and sentiment analysis methods. Initially, generate an algorithm to examine the emotional polarity of a text and acquire a value for each bit of text. Then, the algorithm joined with Support Vector Machine (SVM) and K-means clustering to progress the unsupervised text mining method. This proposed text mining approach initially form the different types of clusters, signifying a each center of a hotspot forum in the current time interval. The Sina sports forums dataset is used in this proposed work which spans a range of 31 various forums and 220,053 posts. The experimental results achieves the promising results of SVM prediction resembles 80% of K-means clustering.

E-learning is becoming well-liked and influential standard for web based education system. It is very significant to cluster the online opinion (feedback) of the learners emotion in the e-learning framework. Identifying the learner's emotional state is very difficult task, whether they are satisfied with the one-learning environment. Recently, the twitter R. C. Balabantaray (2012) has become more popular with their micro blogging and the millions of users are habitually shared their emotion or opinion on the blogs. Thus, in M.Ravichandran, G. Kulanthaivel (2014) author proposes a new approach for sentiment mining in twitter based messages. Twitter is one of the best sources for performing sentiment mining. Initially, the information is extracted from blog data. Learners sentiment polarity (positive and negative) information is used in this model. Naïve Bayesian approach is used for analyzing the sentimental behaviors of the training data. During the testing phase, to e-learner emotional states are discovered based on the testing phase data. Finally, the maxentropy techniques and Support Vector Machines (SVM) are compared with the proposed system.

EMOTION ANALYSIS

The emotion mining by takes advantage of the words in a text, and especially their co-occurrence with words that have categorical emotional meaning. To differentiate between words directly denoting to emotional states for example "cheerful," "fear" and those having only an indirect reference that its means of context, for example words that specifies emotional sources for instance "killer" or emotional replies such as "cry". But, the emotion mining from text based content is not a simple task. Thus, The problem is defined as follows

Given N training web contents, a word-emotion mapping dictionary is created. The dictionary is define as $W \times E$ matrix, (i,j) is defined as items in this matrix, emotion e_i define as the probability of emotion on word w_j. For each webdocument $d_i(i=1,2,3,...,N)$, the document content, the jth word in content is represented by $w_j(j=1,2,...,W)$ and the emotions are represented by $e=(e_1,e_2,...,e_E)$. Probability of emotion is defined as follows

$$P(w/e) = \frac{|w,e|}{\sum_{w' \in W}|(w',e)|} \tag{1}$$

Where $|(w,e)|$ is the co-occurrence count between emotion $e \in E$ and word $w \in W$ for all the web documents.

FUZZY INFERENCE SYSTEM (FIS)

The text classification has been utilized in numerous application such as topic identification, E-mail filtering, automatic meta-data organization, documents's organization for web pages and databases and text filtering Dr. Shilpa Dang and Peerzada Hamid Ahmad (2015). In this study, used two types of emotion categories, positive and negative, and different types of emotions are included such as "anger," "frustration," and "boredom," "neutral," "happiness," etc. However, the morphological vagueness in the description of emotion categories denotes that they can overlap each other in their vector information spaces.To tackle this problem, the proposed system employed two machine learning algorithms.

The proposed system as shown in Figure 1 is structured into two phases, namely emotional classification based on text-mining approach utilizing Support Vector Machine (SVM) and fuzzy rule based emotion mining controlled by FIS. The main aim of Fuzzy Inference System (FIS) is to accurately model the links between emotions and words, and progress the performance of its related tasks such as emotion prediction. Different types of basic emotion and their textural description as shown in Table 1.

In this proposed approach, rules are simplified, the total rules are 50 and contains seven emotions controls, comprised of BrowPosition, EyesDirection, BrowEmotions, BrowWrinkle, EyeOpen, Sneer, MouthOpen and MouthSmiles analysed through machine interface with face expressions.

The fuzzy input comprises six emotion classeswith their probability values. Each emotion has three variables such as Low (L), Medium (M), High (H), implemented utilizing triangle Membership Functions (MF). The inputs are classified as low when the input is between -0.3 and 0.3; medium when input value is between 0.1 and 0.9 and high, when input is between 0.7 and 1.5 as shown in Figure 2.

Figure 1. Fuzzy inference system based emotion mining

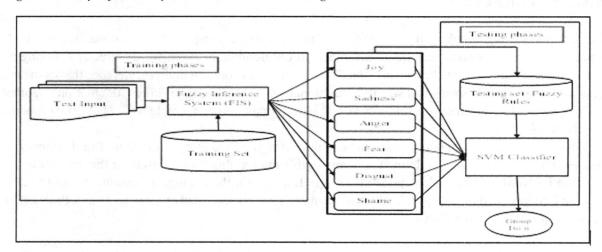

Table 1. Expressions of basic emotions

No	Basic Emotions	Textual description of Emotions
1	Joy	The mouth is open and near the ears, the mouth corner or corners of the mouth are pulled back. The eyebrows are relaxed.
2	Sadness	The eyebrows which are inside are bent upward. The mouth is relaxed and The eyes are slightly closed.
3	Fear	The eyebrows are stretched and pulled simultaneously. The inner eyebrows are bent upward and the eyes are nervous and alert.
4	Anger	The inner eyebrows are pulled together and downward. The eyes are opened wide. The lips are closed without a gap or exposing the teeth while opening the lips.
5	Disgust	The eyelids and eyebrows are relaxed. The upper lip is stretched and curled, often unevenly.
6	Surprise	The eyebrows are up-stretched. The upper eyelids are open, the lower eyelids are relaxed. The jaw is opened.

Figure 2. Membership function of input

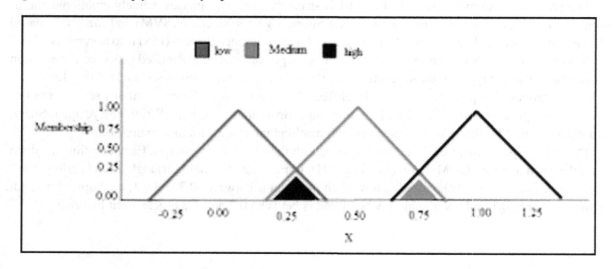

Fuzzy inference systems (FIS), which are also named as fuzzy rule-based systems, are consist four blocks such as Fuzzifier, Rules, Inference, Defuzzifier Shalini Puri (2011). Fuzzifier transforms the crisp inputs into fuzzy inputs by MFs that characterize fuzzy sets of input vectors. Rules are comprised fuzzy IF-THEN rules, Inference engine is used for fuzzy rules and Defuzzifier which transforms the fuzzy output into crisp output. Defuzzification progression requires the most computational complexity in FIS, and height Defuzzification process or Center-Of-Gravity (COG) is common. The major element in an FIS is "Rules," and rules are communicated in term of IF-THEN statements. All of morphological variables of outputs and inputs need to be related utilizing rules. Example fuzzy rules are shown in Table 2.

Table 2. Fuzzy rules

Rule 1	If (anger is H) OR (fear is H)THENEyeOpen low is angerfear
Rule 2	IF(fear IS L) AND (disgust IS L) AND (sadness IS L) AND (joy IS L) AND (shame IS L) AND (anger IS L) THEN EyeOpen Low IS shamejoyneutral;
Rule 3	IF (shame IS H) OR (joy IS H) THEN EyeOpen L IS shamejoyneutral;
Rule 4	IF (disgust IS H) THEN EyeOpen L IS disgust;
Rule 5	IF (sadness IS H) THEN EyeOpen L IS sadness;

FIS employes simple EyesDirection control, there are only two rules such as the intensity of shame is high, the shame will be chosen and when the intensity of shame is medium the same rule is employed. However, the weight is decreased by half such as 0.5. But these two conditions, output are setting default value 0 which denotes a neutral emotion. Triangle MF implies that intensity reduces the value of Eyesdirection control utilizing COG defuzzification. Similar methods using triangle MF employ to the rest of the emotions.

SUPPORT VECTOR MACHINE

Support Vector Machine (SVM) is one of the machine learning system which uses vector space model (VSM) to separate the sample into various classes which is accomplished by learning process of SVM. In SVM three different types of learning processes are used such as supervised, semi supervised and unsupervised learning. VSM is widely utilized in information retrieval where each document is characterized as a vector, and each dimension relates to a separate terms.The basic idea of SVM is to separate two classes with the huge data from pre-classified data by using an optimal hyperplane. In SVM, the nonlinearly separable issue are often resolved by mapping the input data samples Sandip S (2011).

Let us assume that an arbitrary document vector, $\vec{d_i}$, is define as follows

$$\vec{d_i} = w_{1i}, w_{2i}, \ldots, w_{ni} \qquad (2)$$

Where w_{ki} denotes the weigh of kth word in document i. One of the best known schemes such as Term Frequency-Inverse Document Frequency (TF-IDF) Kranti Ghag and Ketan Shah(2014) weighting is used in this system.An arbitrary normalized (TF-IDF) weighting w_{ki} is defined as follows

$$w_{ki} = c(t_k, d_i) = \frac{tf_{ik} \log(N / n_k)}{\sqrt{\sum_{k=1}^{n} (tf_{ik})^2 \left[\log(N / n_k)\right]^2}} \tag{3}$$

Where $t_k = k$th is defined as word in web document d_i, $idf_k = \log(N/n_k)$ is defined as inverse web document frequency of the word in entire data set, tf_{ik} is define as frequency of the word t_k in web document d_i, n_k is defined as the number of web documents comprising the word t_k and N is defined as the total number of web document in the dataset.

The each emotion class e is signified by a set of web documents $d_i (i=1,2,3,\ldots,N)$. Then, generated a model veor for an arbitrary emotion, E by using $\overrightarrow{d_j}$ an arbitrary emotion class vector. More formally, each E calculated as follows:

$$E = \frac{1}{|M_j|} \sum_{\overrightarrow{d_i} \in M_j}^{|M_j|} \overrightarrow{d_i} \tag{4}$$

Where $|M_j|$ is characterizes the number of documents in d_i. After organizing the vector model for each and every emotion class, the entire system is signified with a set of vector model $D=E_1,E_2,\ldots,E_s$, where sdenotes the number of separate emotional classes to be predictable.

In VSM, queries and documents are signified as vectors, and cosine angle between the two vectors utilized as similarity of them. The similarity between an emotional class, E and query text Q, is defined as follows

$$sim(Q,E) = \sum_{k=1}^{n} w_{kq} * E_k \tag{5}$$

So as to measure the similarity between the $W \times E$ matrix with the size of $s \times n$. and a query text, initially,convert the query text into new $n \times 1$ matrix similar to $W \times E$ matrix. Where n is the size of the word and s defined as the number of emotions. For each row of $W \times E$ matrix(emotion), make multiplication opetion beeen one row of $W \times E$ matrix and query matrix Q. After these process, the m scalar values is signifying the cosine similarity. The final emotional class is selected by using the maximum value from this index. The final classification results is as follows

$$VSM(Q) = \arg \max_j (sim(Q,E)) \tag{6}$$

The SVM hyperplane in utilizing the VSM for classification is the closeness hyperplane line where web documents in the same class form a closeness region, and regions of various classes do not overlap.

The final SVM classification results hope us to use TF-IDF values for emotion classification because the FIS value has very low term frequency (-0.3 and 0.3) but it has high inverse document frequency values (0.7 and 1.5) and also use medium level values (0.1 and 0.9). Therefore, in this proposed work selected to use VSM for emotion classification in the text (web document).

RESULTS AND DISCUSSION

Training and Test Datasets

For training, ISEAR dataset is utilized for conducting the experiment.So as to predict the emotions which limited in the text, thus the FIS system have to learn. In this proposed work six different various emotions are used such as Joy, Sadness, Fear, Anger, Disgust, Surprise. This proposed system used 200 training dataset from ISEAR. Testing is performed on WPARD datasets Mukesh(2014).

Metrics

F-Measure

The F-measure is defined by using the recall (R) and precision (P).This is also named as the F1 measure, since precision and recall are evenly weighted.

$$F = \frac{2.precision.recall}{(precision + recall)} \tag{7}$$

Precision

Precision is defined as a fraction of the web documents retrieved that are related to the user's information required.Precision denotes to the closeness among document measurements to each other.

$$precision = \frac{\left|\{relevant\ web\ document\} \cap \{retrieved\ web\ documents\}\right|}{\{retrieved\ web\ documents\}} \tag{8}$$

Recall

Recall is defined as the fraction of the web documents that are significant to the query that are fruitfully retrieved.

$$recall = \frac{\left|\{relevant\ web\ document\} \cap \{retrieved\ web\ documents\}\right|}{\{relevant\ web\ document\}} \tag{9}$$

Accuracy

Accuracy is defined as the closeness of a measurement to the positive value, i.e., a highly accurate measuring system will provide very close to the positive value.

Results

The Table 3 contain of Precision, F1 score, Accuracy Recall, result's values for Joy, Sadness, Fear, Anger, Disgust, Surprise respectively.

Figure 3 shows the text classification results in terms of precision and recall values. The highest precision and recall value for Text Classification are attained with 0.6 data ratio, the values are 94.21% and 79.35%.

Table 3. Results for ISEAR testing dataset

No.	Emotions	F1	Precision	Recall	Accuracy
1	Joy	74.07	65.12	82.33	85.8
2	Sadness	63.35	76.60	86.40	80.83
3	Fear	82.47	72.90	85.75	88.9
4	Anger	80.62	74.14	88.55	82.83
5	Disgust	84.51	78.14	82.22	89.86
6	Surprise	82.36	79.35	84.21	83.26

Figure 3. Result of text classification

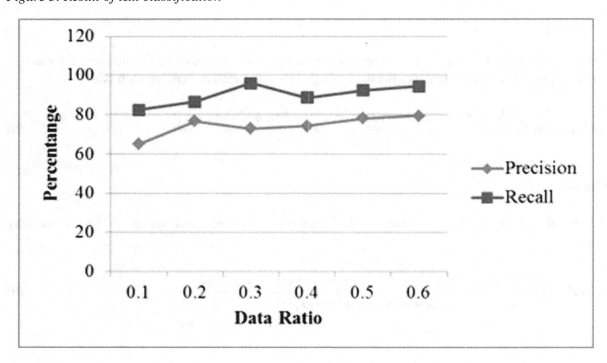

Figure 4. Prediction accuracy

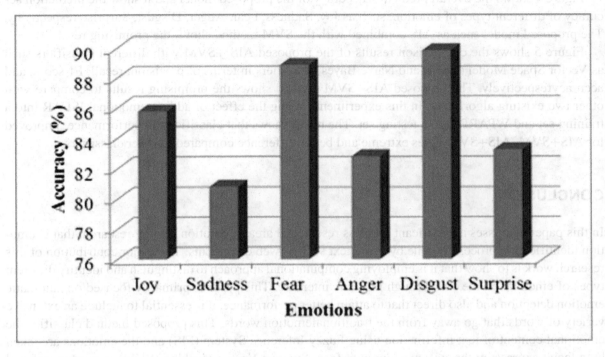

Figure 5. Comparison of the AIS +SVM with different classifiers

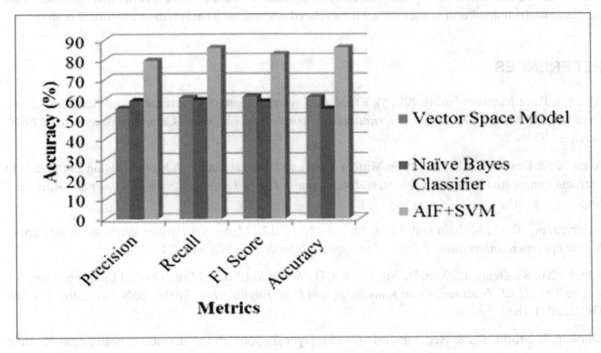

Figure 4 shows the overall prediction accuracy of the proposed model and it show the prediction accuracy of different types of emotion, such as Joy, Sadness, Fear, Anger, Disgust, Surprise respectively. The proposed model such as AIS combined with the SVM method shows the promising result.

Figure 5 shows the comparison results of the proposed AIS +SVM with different classifiers such as Vector Space Model (VSM) and Naïve Bayes Classifiers in terms of precision, recall, F1 score, and accuracyrespectively. The proposed AIS+SVM method shows the promising results to compare with other two existing algorithms. In this experiment, seeing the effect of adding emotional ISEAR into a training set and WPARD into a testing set. The result shows that classification performance, improved for AIS+SVM. AIS+SVM gives extreme and better difference compared to other classifiers.

CONCLUSION

In this paper addresses a significant and less researched area of emotion mining research, that is emotion identification process is done by using text such as web documents. The major contribution of this research work is to show that it is employing computational approach to distinguish and identify different types of emotions in the text through machine interface. This paper is primarily focused on automatic emotion detection and also direct that to attain better performance, it is essential to include an extensive variety of words that go away from the traditionalemotion words. This proposed method classifies the emotional content of text information using Fuzzy Inference System (FIS) and the emotions are taken by a facial expression through machine interface. Support Vector Machine (SVM) is used to reduced features for the classification process. In this process, a variety of emotion related words were trained and also tested and their usability established by their effectiveness in VSM classification approach. This process may be help of online users to get their related documents based on their emotional preferences.

REFERENCES

Ananthi, P., & Manivannan, R. (2015). Efficient Keyword Search on Structured and Semi-Structured Data from Relational Databases. *International Journal of Inventions in Computer Science and Engineering*, 2(3).

Asha, K., & Devi, T. (2012). Study on Mining Emotions from Literature: A Method Using Computers to Extract Opinionated Knowledge Nuggets. *International Journal of Emerging Technology and Advanced Engineering*, 2(8).

Balabantaray, R. C., Mohammad, M., & Sharma, N. (2012). Multi-class twitter emotion classification: A new approach. *International Journal of Applied Information Systems*, 4(1), 48–53.

Bao, S., Xu, S., Zhang, L., Yan, R., Su, Z., Han, D., & Yu, Y. (2012). Mining Social Emotions from Affective Text. *IEEE Transactions on Knowledge and Data Engineering*, 24(9), 1658–1670. doi:10.1109/TKDE.2011.188

Bhaskar, J., Sruthi, K., & Nedungadi, P. (2015). Hybrid approach for emotion classification of audio conversation based on text and speech mining. *Procedia Computer Science*, 46, 635–643. doi:10.1016/j.procs.2015.02.112

Dang, S., & Ahmad, P. H. (2015). A Review of Text Mining Techniques Associated with Various Application Areas. *International Journal of Science and Research, 4*(2).

Ganesan, K. A., Sundaresan, N., & Deo, H. (2008). Mining tag clouds and emoticons behind community feedback. *WWW, 8,* 1181–1182.

Ghag, K., & Shah, K. (2014). SentiTFIDF – Sentiment Classification using Relative Term Frequency Inverse Document Frequency. *International Journal of Advanced Computer Science and Applications, 5*(2). doi:10.14569/IJACSA.2014.050206

Jain, M. C., & Kulkarni, V. Y. (2014). TexEmo: Conveying emotion from text-the study. *International Journal of Computers and Applications, 86*(4).

Kaur, J., & Saini, J. R. (2009). An analysis of opinion mining research works based on language, writing style and feature selection parameters. *International Journal of Advanced Networking Applications, 1*(1).

Li, N., & Wu, D. D. (2010). Using text mining and sentiment analysis for online forums hotspot detection and forecast. *Decision Support Systems, 48*(2), 354–368.

Li, T. M., Chau, M., Wong, P. W., & Yip, P. S. (2012, May). A hybrid system for online detection of emotional distress. In *Pacific-Asia Workshop on Intelligence and Security Informatics* (pp. 73-80). Springer.

Patil, S. S., & Chaudhari, A. P. (2012). Classification of Emotions from Text using SVM based opinion mining. *International Journal of Computer Engineering & Technology, 3*(1), 330–338.

Puri, S. (2011). A Fuzzy Similarity Based Concept Mining Model for Text Classification. *International Journal of Advanced Computer Science and Applications, 2*(11). doi:10.14569/IJACSA.2011.021119

Ravichandran, M., & Kulanthaivel, G. (2014). Twitter sentiment mining (Tsm) framework based learners emotional state classification and visualization for e-learning system. *Journal of Theoretical and Applied Information Technology, 69*(1).

This research was previously published in the International Journal of Technology and Human Interaction (IJTHI), 16(1); pages 94-104, copyright year 2020 by IGI Publishing (an imprint of IGI Global).

Chapter 56
Hybrid Recommender System Using Emotional Fingerprints Model

Anthony Nosshi

Mansoura University, Mansoura, Egypt

Aziza Saad Asem

Mansoura University, Mansoura, Egypt

Mohammed Badr Senousy

Sadat Academy for Management Sciences, Cairo, Egypt

ABSTRACT

With today's information overload, recommender systems are important to help users in finding needed information. In the movies domain, finding a good movie to watch is not an easy task. Emotions play an important role in deciding which movie to watch. People usually express their emotions in reviews or comments about the movies. In this article, an emotional fingerprint-based model (EFBM) for movies recommendation is proposed. The model is based on grouping movies by emotional patterns of some key factors changing in time and forming fingerprints or emotional tracks, which are the heart of the proposed recommender. Then, it is incorporated into collaborative filtering to detect the interest connected with topics. Experimental simulation is conducted to understand the behavior of the proposed approach. Results are represented to evaluate the proposed recommender.

1. INTRODUCTION

Nowadays, People are using the internet in their everyday tasks more than ever (Borg & Smith, 2018). Thus, users get a large volume of information every time they search for something online. Accordingly, this big amount of information overwhelmed users (Mezni & Fayala, 2018), (Kunaver & Požrl, 2017). Therefore recommender systems are important to suggest the most suitable items for users (Lacerda,

DOI: 10.4018/978-1-6684-6303-1.ch056

2017). The recommender systems intended to automatically understand the user's inclinations and provide them with an item list that they will mostly like (Karimi, Jannach, & Jugovac, 2018). There are three approaches to the recommender systems: Collaborative Filtering (CF) (Nalmpantis & Tjortjis, 2017), Content Based (CB) (Frolov & Oseledets, 2017) and hybrid (Sulikowski, Zdziebko, & Turzyński, 2017) as on (Figure 1).

Figure 1. Recommender systems approaches (Batchakui, 2017)

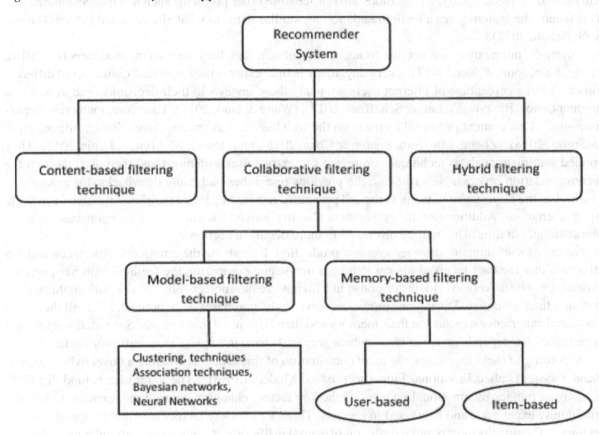

CF goal is to give the users a customized recommendation based on "votes" made by others in form of ratings (Fu, Qu, Moges, & Lu, 2018), (Pang et al., 2018), (F. Wang et al., 2017). It is remarked by the ability to provide new recommendations to users that vary from what they have already chosen or seen before (Xie, Chen, Shang, Huang, & Li, 2015), (Valcarce, Parapar, & Barreiro, 2018), (Pang, Jin, Zhang, & Zhu, 2017). Whereas in CB systems, a user can receive recommendation without any assistance from others. It is suitable for finding different user's interests (Champiri, Shahamiri, & Salim, 2015), (Xu, Dutta, Datta, & Ge, 2017), (Mezni & Fayala, 2018), (Jang, Yang, Kim, & Park, 2018). It relies on finding item features, and create a user profile based on her preferences (Shu, Shen, Liu, Yi, & Zhang, 2018).

Traditional recommendation systems suffer from multiple limitations. For example, to enable the CF making a good recommendation, there should be enough set of ratings, which usually does not happen

(Parvin, Moradi, & Esmaeili, 2018), (Ha & Lee, 2017). This sparsity problem leads to poor recommendation (Chu & Lee, 2017). Further, most of similarity metrics use the user ratings only without taking into account any other source of information (Parvin et al., 2018). Additionally, traditional CF suffers from the cold start problem (Gonzalez Camacho & Alves-Souza, 2018). This affects the newly added users or items to the system because there is no previous information about either users or items. Therefore, it cannot find or use any past preferences. The recommendation can be poor as it will not give her any dissimilar but relevant products (Zhao, Wang, Wang, Zhou, & Jiang, 2018), (Minkov, Kahanov, & Kuflik, 2017). Additionally, CB methods also suffer from other problems such as Over-Specialization. This means the system gives a recommendation for similar items to what already rated before (Hariadi & Nurjanah, 2017).

Currently, online users are not just content consumers, rather, they are content producers (Li, 2018), (Yang, Shin, Joun, & Koo, 2017). Every day, many people express their opinions online about different topics. A large percentage of internet users are using these reviews in their decisions such as to buy a product or not (Brazytė, Weber, & Schaffner, 2017), (Wang & Guo, 2017). Therefore, many researchers have studied the content produced by users on the web like on (Contratres, Alves-Souza, Filgueiras, & DeSouza, 2018), (Zheng, Luo, Sun, Zhang, & Chen, 2018), and (Bader, Mokryn, & Lanir, 2017). They applied sentiment analysis techniques on reviews to extract user's opinions and then used them in the recommendation process. Nevertheless, the previous researches had many drawbacks, for example, it overlooked the importance of using verbs and pronouns; rather, they based their investigation on a single word or emotion. Additionally, the researchers also overlooked tracking emotions connected to some object/subject in time. This will be discussed in more details in section 2.

On the movies domain, the user's review production depends on the emotional experience and the aftertaste that the user received after watching a movie and comparing the feelings with her previous experience. The drivers to criticize or praise in a review are the subjects/objects, the philosophical context, and their emotions. During our movies reviews study, two bases were noticed. First, all the user's emotional experience depends on their memory and their individual impressions. Second, the emotional experience also depends on some ideas, which scenarists tried to express to specific auditoria.

According to these two bases, the main contribution of this article is creating a novel hybrid recommender system called Emotional Fingerprint based Model "EFBM". The main idea behind "EFBM" is to group movies by emotional patterns of the key factors changing across time, extracted from the community experience and expressed in reviews. Those movies key factors are what people discuss in reviews, reflecting the most popular problems of everyday life, objects, philosophical concepts, and ideas. These individual patterns in time form fingerprints or emotional tracks, which are the heart of the proposed recommender. This research also tries to forward the emotional pattern tracking, as an individual experience, into CF like model to detect the interest connected with topics and build a recommender. Further, this research assumes that the decomposition of the subject domain into its components allows considering the changes happening in time to that domain. In other words, it is not possible to directly compare movies made 20 years ago with movies made 1 year ago. Because the newer movies have newer imaging technologies, newer effects, etc. Thus, the knowledge of both the structure of the subject area and the changes in that structure over time is essential for constructing the model of the recommender. In turn, the method of comparing movies with each other is to compare the viewer's emotions in each direction in the structure of the domain, and in dynamics over a certain period.

The way EFBM works is illustrated in the following example. Supposing there is a corpus of 3 movies M1, M2 and M3. Six features [f1, f2, …, f6] for each movie were extracted. The corpus covers the time of nine weeks [w1, w2, ..., w9]. For every week, reviews that have references to a feature are countered and the total amount is added to the movie watch table (Figure 2. A). Eventually, based on that table, a diagram for each movie feature in a period of 4 weeks, starting from rolling in cinemas, is drawn. The timeline, in that case, plays a role independently for every movie. For illustration simplicity, the diagrams for only two features were drawn: f1 and f3 (Figure 2. B). Then, how movies are similar by features are discovered via graphs matching. As shown in the diagrams, the left group M1 and M2 are similar by f1, and the right group M2 and M3 are similar by f3.

The remainder of this article is organized as follows: section 2 discusses the state of Art. Section 3 shows the proposed recommender. Section 4 discusses the recommender implementation. Section 5 represents the experiment and discussion of the proposed recommender. Section 6 discusses the conclusion and future work.

Figure 2. Illustration of EFBM

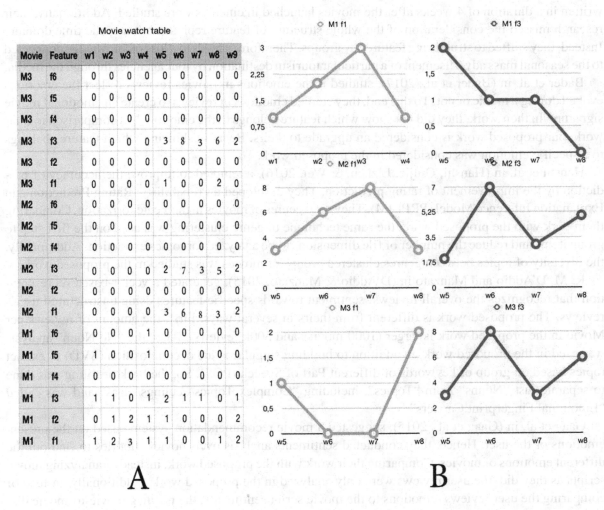

Movie watch table

Movie	Feature	w1	w2	w3	w4	w5	w6	w7	w8	w9
M3	f6	0	0	0	0	0	0	0	0	0
M3	f5	0	0	0	0	0	0	0	0	0
M3	f4	0	0	0	0	0	0	0	0	0
M3	f3	0	0	0	0	3	8	3	6	2
M3	f2	0	0	0	0	0	0	0	0	0
M3	f1	0	0	0	0	1	0	0	2	0
M2	f6	0	0	0	0	0	0	0	0	0
M2	f5	0	0	0	0	0	0	0	0	0
M2	f4	0	0	0	0	0	0	0	0	0
M2	f3	0	0	0	0	2	7	3	5	2
M2	f2	0	0	0	0	0	0	0	0	0
M2	f1	0	0	0	0	3	6	8	3	2
M1	f6	0	0	0	1	0	0	0	0	0
M1	f5	1	0	0	1	0	0	0	0	0
M1	f4	0	0	0	0	0	0	0	0	0
M1	f3	1	1	0	1	2	1	1	0	1
M1	f2	0	1	2	1	1	0	0	0	2
M1	f1	1	2	3	1	1	0	0	1	2

A

B

2. CURRENT STATE OF ART

In an attempt to mitigate the recommendation problems, many studies were conducted to utilize the user's produced content in recommender systems as follows:

Contratres et al. in (Contratres et al., 2018), proposed a recommender system that considered the sentiments extracted from user's social media accounts like Facebook. Still, the Bag of Words (BOW) approach they followed missed the representation of subject domain and weights of every review according to the completeness of knowledge in the domain (by direction: sound, translation, actors play, directors work, special effects, etc.). Additionally, they missed the impact of temporal factors.

Zheng et al. in (Zheng et al., 2018), developed a recommender system using opinion mining that considered the temporal factors in the tourism domain. Moreover, they used the SVD++ to combine the sentiment with the time effect. However, movies have different nature than tourism destination domain. During our research, it was noticed that people usually like/dislike and review movies after a few weeks from its start in cinemas because they get fresh emotions and share them actively. Therefore, the reviews written in a duration of 4 weeks after the movies launched in cinemas were studied. Additionally, their research missed the consideration of the whole structure of feature representation in the time domain. Instead, they shifted to structuring features by groups. Therefore, it leads to a loss of knowledge connected to the seasonal mass advertisement of a particular tourism destination by tour agencies through the media.

Bader et al. in (Bader et al., 2017), studied if the emotions in movies reviews reflect the emotions evoked during a movie or not. To this end, they studied emotions in reviews to create an emotional movie signature. In their work, they did not show which feature belongs to the emotion. In a comparison to their work, our proposed work is considered an upgrade to theirs. Because showing which features belongs to a specific emotion was considered in the proposed work.

Hanshi et al. in (Hanshi, Qiujie, Lizhen, & Wei, 2016), attempted to improve the accuracy of prediction by the improvement of rating prediction. They developed a Probabilistic Rating Prediction and Explanation Inference Model (PRPEIM). They used genres of movies in their categorization. Comparing their work with the proposed work, the same technique of genre clustering was used on the first step to group items and reduce the number of file dimensions to be analyzed for topics extraction. Additionally, the diversity of topics between genres clustered groups of movies was studied in the proposed work.

R. M. D'Addio and Manzato in (D'Addio & Manzato, 2015), generated a vector-based representation that recognizes the overall reviews' sentiment towards specific features using unstructured user's reviews. The proposed work is different from theirs in several ways. First, the amount of reviews per Movie in the proposed work is larger (1000 movies and 500k reviews). Also, the "No Noun" analysis was used in the proposed work, in addition to building singular value decomposition (SVD) to extract topics based on group of keywords of different Part of Speech (POS). So, the back profiling was done to separate just "Nouns" from "Topics", including "Complex Topics/Feelings/Ideas" and was called "Emotional Fingerprint Carriers"

Gaag et al. in (Gaag et al., 2015), suggested a movie recommendation system based on the present emotions of the user. Hence, they conducted sentiments analysis over movies subtitles to find out the different emotions of movies. Comparing their work with the proposed work, instead of analyzing movie scripts as they did, the user reviews were only analyzed in the proposed work. Additionally, instead of comparing the user reviews' emotions to the movie script sentiments, the pos/neg movie-to-movie distance matrices were calculated by comparing vectors of shapes for every emotion/topic curve (formed by count of emotion/topic in 4 weeks' period, compressed with SAX as it will be discussed in section 3).

Xu et al. in (Xu, Datta, & Dutta, 2012), created a recommender system that focuses on adjective features. They adapted the Regularized Singular Value Decomposition (RSVD) concept to build the vectors of user features and item features for prediction accuracy. Whereas in the proposed work, the RSVD was used to extract keywords forming topics that were converted to features. Additionally, words were not used. Rather, the words were aggregated manually into concepts/features. The keywords become part of the rules to find a feature in reviews. They are not only consisting of Adjectives linked as in mentioned work but also Nouns, Adjectives, and Pronouns.

Fernández-Tobías et al. in (Fernández-Tobías, Cantador, & Plaza, 2013), introduced a model for emotion computation depending on social tags. They utilized the cross-domain folksonomies to create multiple methods that transformed item profiles from tag-based to emotion-oriented based profiles. Whereas in the proposed work, the "tags/emotion domain" space was formed on the preparation step from a group of reviews clustered by genres (using two metrics: classical and custom). Therefore, the proposed work's approach uses only text, and no matter if the social tags are wrong or do not exist. Additionally, the compressing technique was applied using the SAX algorithm on the "curves" of emotions count in the time domain.

Orellana-Rodriguez et al. in (Orellana-Rodriguez, Diaz-Aviles, & Nejdl, 2015), introduced a method for the automatic affective context extraction from short films' comments on YouTube. Nevertheless, their idea regarding trying to understand the role of emotions and affect of content still misses the time domain.

Colace et al. in (Colace, De Santo, Greco, Moscato, & Picariello, 2015), introduced a recommender system that used several aspects of online social networks and integrated them together with the context information and items' features. Still, their approach needs recalculating the matrix every time as new content appears. But in the proposed work, a distance matrix was built and used for K-nearest neighbors recommender.

2.1. Drawbacks and Limitations of the Previous Studies

1. In the aforementioned studies, the sentiment analysis was based on either nouns or adjectives only. Whereas the topic analysis based on adjectives, nouns, verbs, and pronouns can form a similarity based on some concept/idea, but not just based on a single word or emotion.
2. The presented concept of understanding the role of emotions and affect of content still misses feature representation in the time domain.
3. Despite the need of recalculating the matrix every time as new content appears as in (Colace et al., 2015), it is more convenient to build a distance matrix and use it for K-nearest neighbors recommender.
4. Although using genre as input for movies clustering gives very weak results, it can divide the comments' corpus into smaller groups to start the analysis in the proposed work.
5. User's emotions cannot be compared with the effect of a movie. Because the emotional reviews cannot be counterposed with emotions in a script. The visual picture is very different from written movie's script and the subjectivity of user can be very different depending on the movies visual picture and other factors like location, mood, previously seen movie, etc. Conversely, the script can give us a kind of emotional fingerprint of a movie. Thus, it is better to figure out the emotional fingerprint of a movie through collaborative filtering of emotions distributed in time and forming time patterns.

3. THE PROPOSED RECOMMENDER

To build the proposed recommender, a dataset from IMDB[1] was used. The first step is to analyze the customers' reviews to find features of movies and group the movies according to the features (Chakraborty, Pagolu, & Garla, 2014). The proposed methodology follows the three strategies discussed below in Table 1.

Table 1. Description of the strategies for data analysis

Details	Strategy 1	Strategy 2	Strategy 3
Strategy Goals	What is inside a data set?	Which products and features are discussed?	What are the feelings and motivations behind the review's author?
Example	Some specific discussion problems are common in both movies and books such as plot, which actor is the most frightening, who is most liked girlfriend among actress, how a popular actor doesn't get the main role in a movie.	Traditional subjects like effects, plot, play, ...	Very subjective reviews or paragraphs where opinion is described in a very personal way or in form of likes or dislikes.
Techniques	Clustering before splitting into pos/neg/neu to see what is discussed in the dataset	Splitting by sentiment/ product/features, then train some model	Discover opinion spamming, focusing on discovering the real intention of the review, regardless who wrote it depending on "the power of negative impact"

Then, the algorithm in (Figure 3) was applied. Firstly, there is a need to reduce the data dimensions to build a couple of smaller models and to aggregate them later. On the first step (Block 1, Figure 3), genres were combined using a dimension expanding technique.

They were combined pair by pair and a matrix was formed for each movie, where 1 is set when a movie belongs to genres pair and 0 if not, as shown in Figure 4.

Then (Block 2, Figure 3) a distance matrix was developed and applied using the Jaccard distance (Bouchard, Jousselme, & Doré, 2013). The Jaccard distance was modified with a complementary weight, to calculate the value of information given in genres field. The weight was calculated as follows:

$$w^{wgh}_{ij} = -\log(w_i) * -\log(w_j) \tag{1}$$

Where

w^{wgh}_{ij}:: is the complementary weight.
$w_{j:}$ is the complementary weight of movie by genre

and

$$w_i = \frac{N^{movie\_id_i}_{genres}}{\sum_{movie_{id}=0}^{|movie\_id|} N^{movie\_id_i}_{genres}} \tag{2}$$

Where N: is the movie count by all genres.

Figure 3. Proposed recommendation algorithm workflow

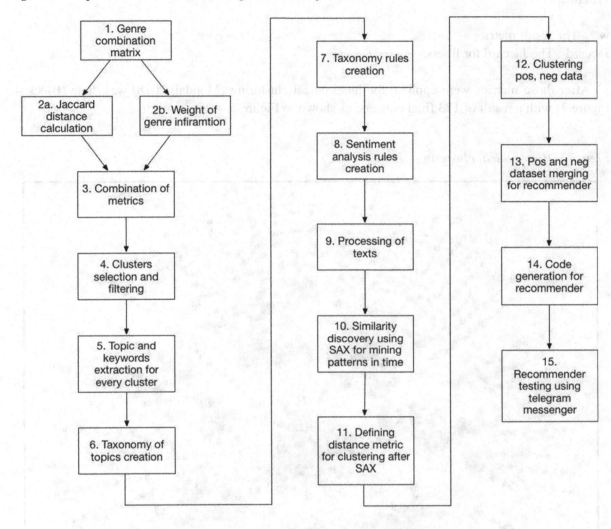

Figure 4. Sample of generation combination

	movie_url	movie_title	Source	Link	Action-Adventure	Action-Comedy	Adventure-Comedy	Drama-R
1	tt0017925	The General	genre_present	genre_present	1	1	1	
2	tt0018455	Sunrise: A Song of	genre_present	genre_present	0	0	0	
3	tt0018578	Wings	genre_present	genre_present	0	0	0	
4	tt0019729	The Broadway	genre_present	genre_present	0	0	0	
5	tt0020629	All Quiet on the	genre_present	genre_present	0	0	0	

Afterwards, the resulting metric for every movie is (Block 3, Figure 3):

$$w^{res}_{ij} = Jaccard_{ij} * w^{wgh}_{ij} \tag{3}$$

Where

w^{res}_{ij}: The result metrics
$Jaccard_{ij}$: The Jaccard for ij sets.

After those metrics were applied, the hierarchical clustering (Mondal, 2018) was done (Block 4, Figure 3) with a result of 173 final clusters, as shown in Figure 5.

Figure 5. Hierarchical clustering

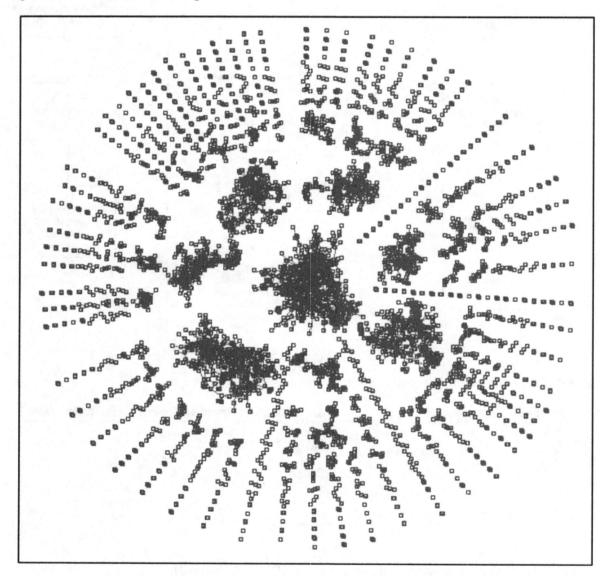

At the fifth step (Block 5, Figure 3), a topic extraction was applied using SAS[2] Enterprise Miner for every cluster to discover the cluster' topics and words that can define features of objects or emotions mentioned. Text Topic and Text Cluster nodes were applied. Figure 6 shows an example of cluster processing: The Text cluster was set up with following settings (Z. Zhao, Albright, Cox, & Bieringer, 2013):

- SVD resolution: high
- Max SVD dimensions 250 (chosen after several rub with step 50)
- Descriptive terms: 15
- Algorithm: Expectation Maximization.

Figure 6. Example of cluster processing

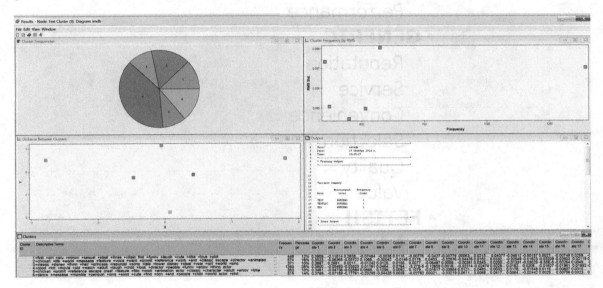

Where SVD resolution "indicates the resolution to be used when computing the SVD dimensions. The software has the capability to automatically determine the number of SVD dimensions to compute. When the value of Max SVD Dimensions is fixed, a higher resolution will lead to more SVD dimensions being calculated." (Zhao et al., 2013) And where Max SVD dimensions "specifies the maximum number of SVD dimensions to be calculated and needs to be defined as greater than or equal to two dimensions." (Zhao et al., 2013)

Then, the products and features taxonomy (Block 6 and 7, Figure 3) was created manually after the topic extraction. The following algorithm was applied to complete a list of topics and words for features:

1. Read movie names in every cluster.
2. If there were more than 60% of movies seen in a cluster, then the overall description of the cluster was possible to write.
3. If movies were unseen, the description of movies on IMDB links has been read.
4. If movies in a set were significantly different, in that case, the general ideas what about this cluster is noted down.

5. If nothing helps, the keywords were selected from the cluster description with an attempt to suggest what people are concerned about and describe a film.

Figure 7. The structure of sentiment model after applying the algorithm sample

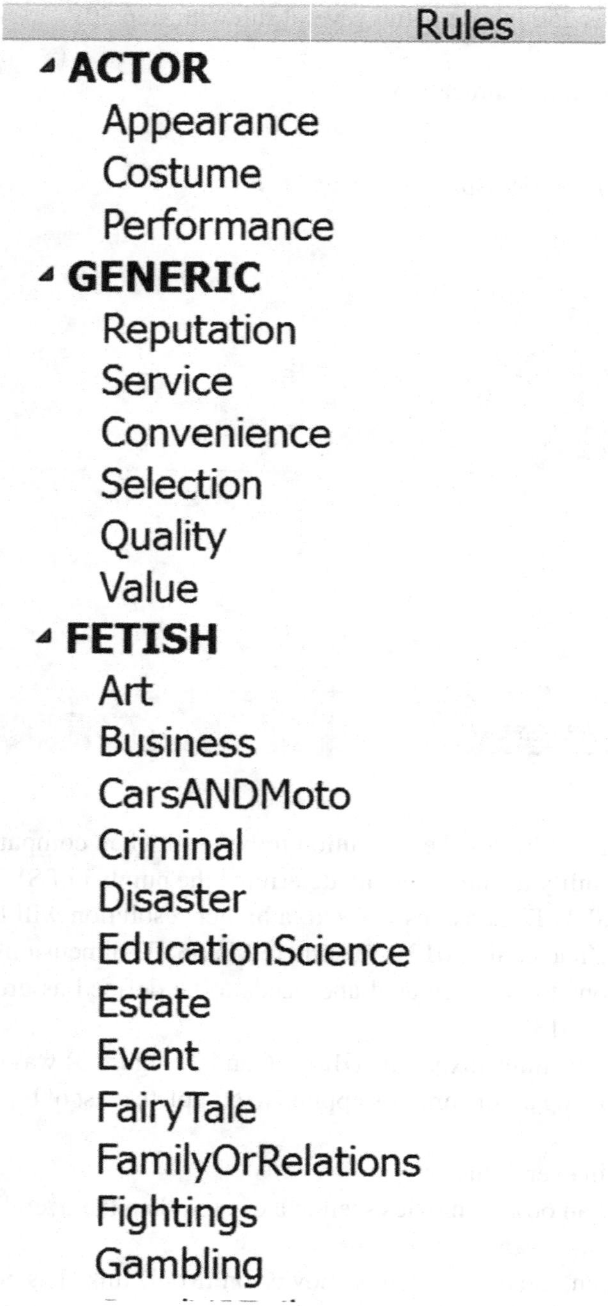

	Rules
▲ **ACTOR**	
Appearance	
Costume	
Performance	
▲ **GENERIC**	
Reputation	
Service	
Convenience	
Selection	
Quality	
Value	
▲ **FETISH**	
Art	
Business	
CarsANDMoto	
Criminal	
Disaster	
EducationScience	
Estate	
Event	
FairyTale	
FamilyOrRelations	
Fightings	
Gambling	

Additional keywords from 25 rows (25 topics people are talking about) were also added to the cluster description. The rule was: sometimes it is better to select some words from all topics than to guess which problem describes each topic. Figure 7 shows a structure sample of sentiment analysis model (Block 8, Figure 3) after the aforementioned algorithm was applied.

Afterwards, (Block 9–15, Figure 3) a sentiment analysis model was applied to every cluster separately to look visually how the data was different after the analysis. Figure 8 shows the statistics of two sample clusters (A for cluster_id = 83, B for cluster_id = 97) after sentiment analysis model was applied. Still, this is an intermediate result. The real post-analysis was applied to the merged text corpus using other principles as will be described later. Accordingly, we tried to formulate what is an emotional/sentimental fingerprint in sentiment mining based on the analysis of movies reviews, i.e. the similar state when one person's feelings change according to the same patterns in time regarding a movie topic, actor or director to the feelings of another person.

Figure 8. The statistics of two sample clusters after sentiment analysis model applied

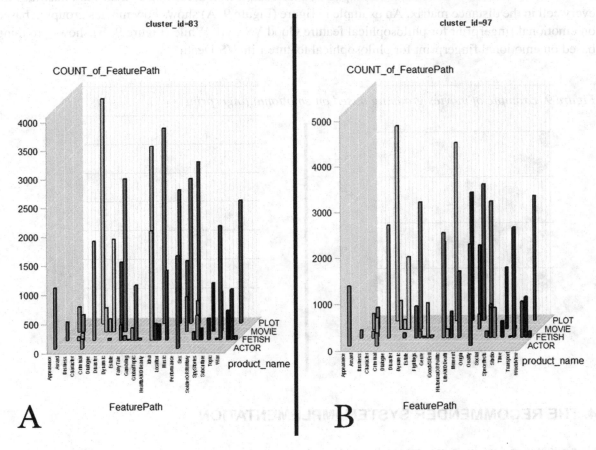

The duration period when a pattern is detected was set to 25 days. The similarity of patterns is discovered with SAX[3] approach. SAX is a symbolic representation for time series that is characterized by its ability of dimensionality reduction, in addition to a lower-bounding distance measure indexing. The

SAX approach was applied with a window of 25 days and intersection of 20%. Size of the alphabet is 5, the number of levels is 7. The similarity was detected per feature of sentiment polarity. The 25 days period was chosen after the analysis of movie reviews for new movies. The movies were played in theaters for about 3-4 weeks and most of fresh feelings and emotions are observed in that period. The SAX symbolic sequences were decoded as {"a":-2,"b":-1,"c":0,"d":1,"e":2}. After the application of SAX, every pair of symbolic vectors were compared through calculation of distances by the formula:

$$min([(vec\_cos(i,j)) \; for \; i,j \; in \; b]) \tag{4}$$

Where variables are as follows: for every vector i (From set a which describes the first movie) and every vector j (From set b which describes the second movie), and b is the set of SAX symbolic sequences. The resulting vector consists of minimal distance or empirically taken distance of 100000 if the length of any initial vector after SAX for some sentiment is zero. As a result, a distance matrix was formed for every feature of every polarity of sentiments. In the final step, the neutral sentiments were dropped, and the final distance was calculated as a pair by pair comparison according to a formula max(a,b) for every cell in the distance matrix. An example in figure (Figure 9. A) shows how movies grouping based on emotional fingerprint for philosophical feature Good VS Evil. While (Figure 9. B) shows grouping based on emotional fingerprint for philosophical feature Life VS Death.

Figure 9. Example of movies grouping based on emotional fingerprint

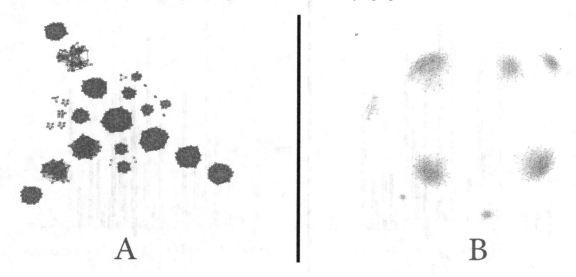

4. THE RECOMMENDER SYSTEM IMPLEMENTATION

Using distance matrix, a recommender system was built using Telegram messenger (Telegram bot[4]). The bot is a simple engine that allows to add buttons and send messages to the client. The recommender system (Figure 10) has a simple dialog bot that navigates in movies collections according to the closest neighbor technique.

Figure 10. Recommender app workflow

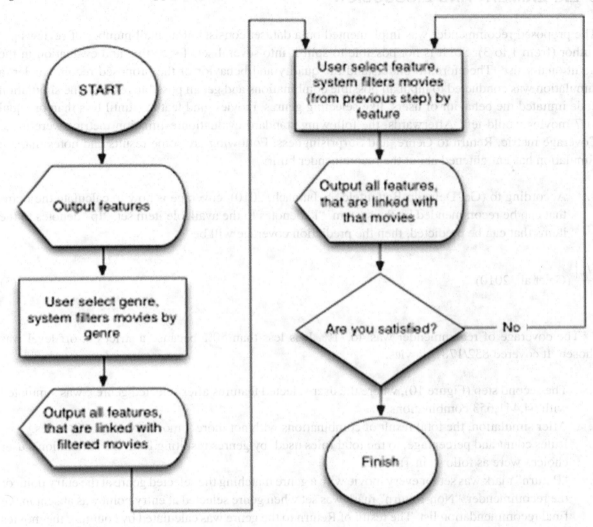

In the recommender system, the distance matrices for all features were calculated. Every movie is 1:n features. So, after picking up genre, N movies with M features were obtained. User select first feature and the system moves inside this feature distance matrix, getting only movies with selected parameters. At the realization part, the system picks up all neighbors and shows features in this filtered set of movies to the users. Thus, they can choose the second feature. Then, do filtering based on features. The output is the nearest neighbors with their features. Accordingly, the processes are repeated until there are no more features to be filtered.

5. EXPERIMENT AND DISCUSSION

The proposed recommender was implemented on a dataset consists of a small number of reviews per author (from 1 to 3). So, it is not possible to split it into several sets for testing and evaluation in the traditional sense. Therefore, to understand the quality and behavior of the proposed recommender, a simulation was conducted to input all possible combinations and get all possible results. The simulation code imitated the behavior of users, like selecting genres, movies, and features until less than or equal to 7 movies would left. Afterwards, the following standard evaluation estimation metrics were used: Coverage metric, Return to Genre, and Surprisingness. Following are some results and notes that the simulation has enlightened about the recommender built:

1. According to (Ge, Delgado-Battenfeld, & Jannach, 2010), coverage is how to calculate the items that can be recommended by the system. "I" denotes to the available item set, "Ip" denotes to the items that can be predicted, then the prediction coverage will be

$$\frac{|I_P|}{|I|} \text{ (Ge et al., 2010)} \tag{5}$$

The coverage of recommender was 46,71%. It is less than 50% because a strict cut-off level was chosen. It covered 832/1781 movies.

2. The second step (Figure 10), where the user selected features after selected genres, was simulated with 64,441,653 combinations.
3. After simulation, the total result of combinations with not more 7 movies was 39,362 cases.
4. Rules count and percentage, to the total rules used, by genres resulting from the simulation's user choices were as follows in Table 2:
5. "Return" mark was set for every movie with a genre matching the selected genre at the entry point of the recommender. "Non-Return" mark was set when genre selected at entry point was absent in the final recommendation list. The result of Return to the genre was calculated by counting the movies in the recommended set. In the simulation, the results to a user who follows the recommendation would return her to Comedy, Crime, Drama, Adventure, and Action with a high probability. In the other case, the recommender would not recommend returning to the genre to get the same shape of emotional experience concerning the selected features. Table 3 shows the Return & Non-Return of some genres:
6. The complexity of recommender was estimated by considering how long the list of movies is in every final recommendation. The estimation was aggregated by genres with an average length of movies list metric applied to each of "return" and "non return" groups. Noting that, the output can belong to the initial genre or not. Therefore, the criteria were:

$$\text{avg(len\_of\_movies\_in\_recommender) by "return/non\_return" by "genre"} \tag{6}$$

Table 2. Rules count and percentage

Genre	Rules Total	Percentage
Mystery	980	2.50%
Romance	2186	5.60%
Comedy	5688	14.50%
Sci-Fi	1124	2.90%
Family	641	1.60%
Horror	899	2.30%
Thriller	2170	5.50%
Film-Noir	278	0.70%
Crime	5310	13.50%
Drama	5698	14.50%
Fantasy	726	1.80%
Animation	2045	5.20%
Adventure	4068	10.30%
Action	5340	13.60%
Sport	362	0.90%
War	96	0.20%
Biography	1557	4.00%
History	194	0.50%

Table 3. Return % vs non-return%

Genre	Return %	Non-Return %
Mystery	22	78
Romance	34	66
Comedy	73	27
Sci-Fi	28	72
Family	21	79
Horror	22	78
Thriller	40	60
Film-Noir	11	89
Crime	67	33
Drama	79	21
Fantasy	14	86
Animation	46	54
Adventure	64	36
Action	71	29
Sport	11	89
War	2	98
Biography	34	66
History	6	94

This was called "Surprisingness". The basic idea behind it is that: for a user, it is easier and natural to select from a short list, than from a long one. So, the shorter the list is (denoted here as value), the more the user tends to choose the movie. If a user was not returned, then this was a surprise for her. The result was as follows in Table 4.

A user's choice, between the recommended items, influenced by how the output items represented and visualized in the recommended list. The length and design of the recommendation list affect the probability to choose a movie. It is intuitional and natural that people select items from shorter lists than a longer one. For illustration, movies that are out of genre are denoted with S (Surprisingness), and those are in genre are denoted with NS (Non-Surprisingness). The user's choice depends on the design and the length of the recommendation list. Therefore, the user might choose from the shorter list. Following are some examples of how the recommender can produce the output list to the user:

1. Form 1: By separating items according to the genre: Out of genre: [S1, S2, S3] VS In genre [NS1, NS2, NS3, NS4, NS5].
2. Form 2: By mixing both In genre and Out of genre: [NS1, NS2, S1, S2, NS5, S3, NS3, NS4].
3. Form 3: By features contained inside the "in and out" of genres: Feature 1: [NS5, S3, NS3, NS4], Feature 2: [NS1, NS2, S1], Feature 3: [S1, S2, NS5].

Table 4. Surprisingness vs non-surprisingness

Genre	Surprisingness	Non-Surprisingness
Mystery	4.05	3.47
Romance	3.47	3.03
Comedy	3.62	2.45
Sci-Fi	3.74	3.37
Family	3.8	3.99
Horror	4.03	3.17
Thriller	4.11	2.47
Film-Noir	5.01	0
Crime	3.97	2.27
Drama	3.31	2.56
Fantasy	3.83	3.31
Animation	4.4	3.27
Adventure	4.12	2.76
Action	3.34	2.21
Sport	4.89	2.73
War	6.71	0
Biography	3.8	2.99
History	5.42	7.43

Different designs can affect the user's selection. The hypothesis with "Surprisingness/Non-Surprisingness" is that: the less the value is, the more the user tends to choose the movie in Form 1. In other cases, the choice would depend on the distribution of S and NS. The recommender represented the output as in Form 1. For illustration, the following is an example applied to the Comedy genre (Figure 11). When recommender presented in Form 1, a user might tend to choose from the shorter list with avg length of 2.45 movies. Whereas in Forms 2 and 3, the probability to choose an item from the longer list is higher. The final recommendation if a user started from Comedy genre would consist of 3-4 movies in "out of genre" list, and 2-3 movies in "In genre" list. Figure 11 shows features selected under simulation. It also shows what options could also affect the user under navigating.

From the list above, if people were interested in ('Gambling', 'LifeANDDeath'), ('Idea', 'Social'), ('Art', 'Moment'), ('Appearance', 'Sex'), ('Character', 'Gambling'), ('Moment', 'Subculture'), etc. - there was no surprise that they would return to Genre. But if user preferred ('Appearance', 'HealthANDBeauty'), ('Dialogue', 'Idea'), ('SoldierORMilitary', 'SpyStories'), ('Fightings', 'HistoricalORPolitic'), ('Estate', 'WorldView'), ('GoodVSEvil', 'SoldierORMilitary'), etc. - user would switch to another genre. Though, the results are not absolute and still need further research. The table below (Table 5) shows the coefficient of Surprisingness/Non-Surprisingness for every genre and its ratio. It was calculated by the formula:

coef=1-Non-Surprisingness/Surprisingness (7)

Figure 11. Screenshot of final surprisingness vs Non-surprisingness log file

```
File  Edit  Format  View  Help


Genre: Comedy. Surprisingness: 3.62. Non-Surprisingness:
2.45
Genre: Comedy. Surprisingness: [('Dubbing'. 'Event').
('Idea'. 'Sex'). ('Gambling'. 'SpyStories').
('Appearance'. 'HealthANDBeauty'). ('Dialogue'. 'Idea').
('SoldierORMilitary'. 'SpyStories'). ('Fightings'.
'HistoricalORPolitic'). ('Character'. 'Topic').
('GlobalTopic'. 'Social'). ('GlobalTopic'. 'Performance').
('FairyTale'. 'Transport'). ('Idea'. 'Moment'). ('Estate'.
'WorldView'). ('GoodVSEvil'. 'SoldierORMilitary').
('Business'. 'Criminal'). ('Art'. 'Estate'). ('FairyTale'.
'Gambling')]
 Non-Surprisingness: [('Critic'. 'Music'). ('Gambling'.
'LifeANDDeath'). ('Award'. 'Subculture'). ('Business'.
'CarsANDMoto'). ('Director'. 'Dynamic'). ('Genre'.
'WorldView'). ('Idea'. 'Social'). ('Art'. 'Moment').
('Appearance'. 'Sex'). ('Character'. 'Gambling').
('Appearance'. 'Topic'). ('Criminal'. 'Event').
('Dubbing'. 'Social'). ('Budget'. 'Time'). ('Dialogue'.
'Estate'). ('Performance'. 'WorldView'). ('Criminal'.
'Subculture'). ('Disaster'. 'Moment'). ('Character'.
'LifeANDDeath'). ('Moment'. 'Subculture'). ('Moment'.
'Time'). ('Dynamic'. 'LifeANDDeath'). ('Appearance'.
'Performance'). ('Dynamic'. 'Gambling'). ('Costume'.
'Idea'). ('Business'. 'Moment'). ('GlobalTopic'.
'WorldView'). ('Director'. 'Idea'). ('Director'.
'EducationScience'). ('HistoricalORPolitic'. 'Topic').
('Award'. 'SpyStories'). ('Origin'. 'War').
('CarsANDMoto'. 'Performance'). ('Criminal'. 'Origin').
('Costume'. 'Location'). ('Performance'.
'SoldierORMilitary'). ('Appearance'. 'Transport').
('HealthANDBeauty'. 'Time'). ('Criminal'. 'Quality').
('Moment'. 'SoldierORMilitary'). ('Budget'. 'Location')]
```

The color shows possible preference of the user to switch the genre depending on the length of choice and preferable features. The less the value (the redder is the color), the more preferable is for the user to switch.

Table 5. Coefficient of surprisingness/non-surprisingness

Genre	Coef, S/N-S
Mystery	0,14
Romance	0,13
Comedy	0,32
Sci-Fi	0,10
Family	-0,05
Horror	0,21
Thriller	0,40
Film-Noir	1,00
Crime	0,43
Drama	0,23
Fantasy	0,14
Animation	0,26
Adventure	0,33
Action	0,34
Sport	0,44
War	1,00
Biography	0,21
History	-0,37

6. CONCLUSION

The main objective of this paper is to create a new hybrid recommender system using Emotional Fingerprints Based Model "EFBM". The proposed recommender groups movies by emotional patterns of the key factors written by the community in reviews and changing across time. These key factors are what people usually discuss in reviews and reflect their every day's life problems. The emotional patterns in time form fingerprints that are used to match similar movies. The proposed recommender was implemented using Telegram Messenger (Telegram Bot).

An experiment was conducted to understand the quality and behavior of the recommender. The simulation imitated the user's behavior to make all possible selections until there was less than or equal to 7 movies left. Afterwards, some metrics were applied to the simulation results such as coverage, return vs non-return to genre and surprisingness vs non-surprisingness. The complexity of the recommender was estimated via the estimation of the recommendation list length.

The model has mainly three constraints. The first is the predefined structure of topics based on the idea of big text corpus of reviews. The second is the methodology of movie recommendation based on clustering. The third is the static choice of cut-off level for movie similarity. The predefined structure might bring very new ideas or topics which can appear during the development of a society, new forms of social relations, new inventions and so on. Clustering of movies does not allow the model to work in real-time with the current algorithm. Static choice of cut-off level for movie similarity in all clusters leads to the risk of dropping some movies. That is why the coverage metric result is relatively low.

Figure 12. IMDB proposal "Coffee and Cigarettes", "Broken Flowers", "Dead Man", "Ghost Dog", "Night on Earth", "Limits of control"

For future work, in order to improve the current work, a new dataset, where there would be a relation of 1 user to n reviews, should be created to validate the model. Currently, there still too few data to test the recommender. The dataset used in the experiment was mostly consisting of 1 user - 1 review relations, so this adds a limitation on evaluation too. The philosophical concept of the emotional fingerprint in movies is about the state of the collective mind during a period of time, which is impacted by the detected feature. So, supposing the dataset is with the proper relation of one person to many movies, the evaluation of recommender effectiveness still has the following open questions: Can the user change his mind to watch a different movie than the suggested in the recommender list because of an advertising? Is it enough for a user to prefer a movie if it has a feature she loves? Is it enough for the user to watch a movie if she is impacted by reviews about some features? Is the mass "euphoria" based on some topic is the reason why a group of people would watch a particular movie or switch their preferences to other movies about a chosen topic? For example, when people like the vampire movie "Only Lovers Left Alive" with strong "life and death" topic, will people look for another "life and death" movie such as "Bicentennial Man"? Or just go by tag "movie with vampires" or "Movies by Jim Jarmusch" as it is shown on Figure 12?

Additionally, the absence of subjectivity should be handled, because currently, the current dataset has a random sample of unique users. Also, the model of movie watching used in this work should be improved. The hypothesis was that the movie popularity is lasting for 4 weeks only (A cinema-oriented approach). Thus, it is possible to lose people who watch movies outside the cinema, for example at home. Therefore, comments should be split to "Cinema watchers" and "Home watchers" depending on the movie release date. In addition, what happens if the user like/dislike the movie or only a feature should be studied. i.e. can the user dislike a movie, at the same time she likes some features and that would be the reason to watch it? Also, other metrics for the synthesis of recommender from "emotional fingerprint" patterns shall be applied. Moreover, adding additional criteria, for example, study the behavior of the recommender users depending on location, weather, mood and time of day.

REFERENCES

Bader, N., Mokryn, O., & Lanir, J. (2017). Exploring Emotions in Online Movie Reviews for Online Browsing. In *Proceedings of the 22nd International Conference on Intelligent User Interfaces Companion*, Limassol, Cyprus. ACM. 10.1145/3030024.3040982

Borg, K., & Smith, L. (2018). Digital inclusion and online behaviour: Five typologies of Australian internet users. *Behaviour & Information Technology*, *37*(4), 367–380. doi:10.1080/0144929X.2018.1436593

Bouchard, M., Jousselme, A.-L., & Doré, P.-E. (2013). A proof for the positive definiteness of the Jaccard index matrix. *International Journal of Approximate Reasoning*, *54*(5), 615–626. doi:10.1016/j.ijar.2013.01.006

Brazytė, K., Weber, F., & Schaffner, D. (2017). Sustainability Management of Hotels: How Do Customers Respond in Online Reviews? *Journal of Quality Assurance in Hospitality & Tourism*, *18*(3), 282–307. doi:10.1080/1528008X.2016.1230033

Chakraborty, G., Pagolu, M., & Garla, S. (2014). *Text mining and analysis: practical methods, examples, and case studies using SAS*. SAS Institute.

Champiri, Z. D., Shahamiri, S. R., & Salim, S. S. B. (2015). A systematic review of scholar context-aware recommender systems. *Expert Systems with Applications, 42*(3), 1743–1758. doi:10.1016/j.eswa.2014.09.017

Chu, P. M., & Lee, S. J. (2017). A novel recommender system for E-commerce. In *2017 10th International Congress on Image and Signal Processing, BioMedical Engineering and Informatics (CISP-BMEI)* (pp. 1–5). 10.1109/CISP-BMEI.2017.8302310

Colace, F., De Santo, M., Greco, L., Moscato, V., & Picariello, A. (2015). A collaborative user-centered framework for recommending items in Online Social Networks. *Computers in Human Behavior, 51*, 694–704. doi:10.1016/j.chb.2014.12.011

Contratres, F. G., Alves-Souza, S. N., Filgueiras, L. V. L., & DeSouza, L. S. (2018). Sentiment Analysis of Social Network Data for Cold-Start Relief in Recommender Systems. In Á. Rocha, H. Adeli, L. P. Reis, & S. Costanzo (Eds.), *Trends and Advances in Information Systems and Technologies* (pp. 122–132). Cham: Springer International Publishing. doi:10.1007/978-3-319-77712-2_12

D'Addio, R. M., & Manzato, M. G. (2015). A sentiment-based item description approach for kNN collaborative filtering. In *Proceedings of the 30th Annual ACM Symposium on Applied Computing* (pp. 1060–1065). ACM. 10.1145/2695664.2695747

Betru, B. T., Onana, C. A., & Batchakui, B. (2017, March). Deep Learning Methods on Recommender System: A Survey of State-of-the-art. *International Journal of Computers and Applications, 162*, 17–22. doi:10.5120/ijca2017913361

Fernández-Tobías, I., Cantador, I., & Plaza, L. (2013). An emotion dimensional model based on social tags: Crossing folksonomies and enhancing recommendations. In *International Conference on Electronic Commerce and Web Technologies* (pp. 88–100). Springer. 10.1007/978-3-642-39878-0_9

Frolov, E., & Oseledets, I. (2017). Tensor methods and recommender systems. *Wiley Interdisciplinary Reviews. Data Mining and Knowledge Discovery, 7*(3), e1201. doi:10.1002/widm.1201

Fu, M., Qu, H., Moges, D., & Lu, L. (2018). Attention based collaborative filtering. *Neurocomputing, 311*, 88–98. doi:10.1016/j.neucom.2018.05.049

Gaag, P., Granvogl, D., Jackermeier, R., Ludwig, F., Rosenlöhner, J., & Uitz, A. (2015). FROY: exploring sentiment-based movie recommendations. In *Proceedings of the 14th International Conference on Mobile and Ubiquitous Multimedia* (pp. 345–349). ACM. 10.1145/2836041.2841205

Ge, M., Delgado-Battenfeld, C., & Jannach, D. (2010). Beyond accuracy: evaluating recommender systems by coverage and serendipity. *Proceedings of the Fourth ACM Conference on Recommender Systems*. Barcelona, Spain: ACM. 10.1145/1864708.1864761

Gonzalez Camacho, L. A., & Alves-Souza, S. N. (2018). Social network data to alleviate cold-start in recommender system: A systematic review. *Information Processing & Management, 54*(4), 529–544. doi:10.1016/j.ipm.2018.03.004

Ha, T., & Lee, S. (2017). Item-network-based collaborative filtering: A personalized recommendation method based on a user's item network. *Information Processing & Management*, *53*(5), 1171–1184. doi:10.1016/j.ipm.2017.05.003

Hanshi, W., Qiujie, F., Lizhen, L., & Wei, S. (2016). A probabilistic rating prediction and explanation inference model for recommender systems. *China Communications*, *13*(2), 79–94.

Hariadi, I, & Nurjanah, D. (2017). Hybrid attribute and personality based recommender system for book recommendation. In *2017 International Conference on Data and Software Engineering (ICoDSE)* (pp. 1–5). doi:10.1109/ICODSE.2017.8285874

Jang, Y. H., Yang, S. S., Kim, H. J., & Park, S. C. (2017). Design of Nonlinear Data-Based Wellness Content Recommendation Algorithm. In *Advances in Computer Science and Ubiquitous Computing* (pp. 766–771). Springer Singapore.

Karimi, M., Jannach, D., & Jugovac, M. (2018). News recommender systems – Survey and roads ahead. In *Information Processing & Management*.

Kunaver, M., & Požrl, T. (2017). Diversity in recommender systems – A survey. *Knowledge-Based Systems*, *123*, 154–162. doi:10.1016/j.knosys.2017.02.009

Lacerda, A. (2017). Multi-Objective Ranked Bandits for Recommender Systems. *Neurocomputing*, *246*, 12–24. doi:10.1016/j.neucom.2016.12.076

Li, M. (2018). Computer-mediated collaborative writing in L2 contexts: An analysis of empirical research. *Computer Assisted Language Learning*, *31*(8), 1–23. doi:10.1080/09588221.2018.1465981

Mezni, H., & Fayala, M. (2018). Time-aware service recommendation: Taxonomy, review, and challenges. *Software, Practice & Experience*, *0*(0). doi:10.1002pe.2605

Minkov, E., Kahanov, K., & Kuflik, T. (2017). Graph-based recommendation integrating rating history and domain knowledge: Application to on-site guidance of museum visitors. *Journal of the Association for Information Science and Technology*, *68*(8), 1911–1924. doi:10.1002/asi.23837

Mondal, S. A. (2018). An improved approximation algorithm for hierarchical clustering. *Pattern Recognition Letters*, *104*, 23–28. doi:10.1016/j.patrec.2018.01.015

Nalmpantis, O., & Tjortjis, C. (2017). The 50/50 Recommender: A Method Incorporating Personality into Movie Recommender Systems BT - Engineering Applications of Neural Networks. In G. Boracchi, L. Iliadis, C. Jayne, & A. Likas (Eds.), (pp. 498–507). Cham: Springer International Publishing.

Orellana-Rodriguez, C., Diaz-Aviles, E., & Nejdl, W. (2015). Mining Affective Context in Short Films for Emotion-Aware Recommendation. In *Proceedings of the 26th ACM Conference on Hypertext & Social Media* (pp. 185–194). ACM. 10.1145/2700171.2791042

Pang, Y., Jin, Y., Zhang, Y., & Zhu, T. (2017). Collaborative filtering recommendation for MOOC application. *Computer Applications in Engineering Education*, *25*(1), 120–128. doi:10.1002/cae.21785

Pang, Y., Liu, W., Jin, Y., Peng, H., Xia, T., & Wu, Y. (2018). Adaptive recommendation for MOOC with collaborative filtering and time series. *Computer Applications in Engineering Education, 0*(0). doi:10.1002/cae.21995

Parvin, H., Moradi, P., & Esmaeili, S. (2018). A collaborative filtering method based on genetic algorithm and trust statements. In *2018 6th Iranian Joint Congress on Fuzzy and Intelligent Systems (CFIS)* (pp. 13–16). 10.1109/CFIS.2018.8336613

Shu, J., Shen, X., Liu, H., Yi, B., & Zhang, Z. (2018). A content-based recommendation algorithm for learning resources. *Multimedia Systems, 24*(2), 163–173. doi:10.100700530-017-0539-8

Sulikowski, P., Zdziebko, T., & Turzyński, D. (2017). Modeling online user product interest for recommender systems and ergonomics studies. *Concurrency and Computation, 0*(0), e4301. doi:10.1002/cpe.4301

Valcarce, D., Parapar, J., & Barreiro, Á. (2018). Finding and analysing good neighbourhoods to improve collaborative filtering. *Knowledge-Based Systems, 159*, 193–202.

Wang, F., Lin, S., Luo, X., Wu, H., Wang, R., & Zhou, F. (2017). A Data-Driven Approach for Sketch-Based 3D Shape Retrieval via Similar Drawing-Style Recommendation. *Computer Graphics Forum, 36*(7), 157–166. doi:10.1111/cgf.13281

Wang, H., & Guo, K. (2017). The impact of online reviews on exhibitor behaviour: Evidence from movie industry. *Enterprise Information Systems, 11*(10), 1518–1534. doi:10.1080/17517575.2016.1233458

Xie, F., Chen, Z., Shang, J., Huang, W., & Li, J. (2015). Item Similarity Learning Methods for Collaborative Filtering Recommender Systems. In *2015 IEEE 29th International Conference on Advanced Information Networking and Applications* (pp. 896–903). 10.1109/AINA.2015.285

Xu, X., Datta, A., & Dutta, K. (2012). Using adjective features from user reviews to generate higher quality and explainable recommendations. In Shaping the Future of ICT Research. Methods and Approaches (pp. 18–34). Springer. doi:10.1007/978-3-642-35142-6_2

Xu, X., Dutta, K., Datta, A., & Ge, C. (2017). Identifying functional aspects from user reviews for functionality-based mobile app recommendation. *Journal of the Association for Information Science and Technology, 69*(2), 242–255. doi:10.1002/asi.23932

Yang, S.-B., Shin, S.-H., Joun, Y., & Koo, C. (2017). Exploring the comparative importance of online hotel reviews' heuristic attributes in review helpfulness: A conjoint analysis approach. *Journal of Travel & Tourism Marketing, 34*(7), 963–985. doi:10.1080/10548408.2016.1251872

Zhao, Q., Wang, C., Wang, P., Zhou, M., & Jiang, C. (2018). A Novel Method on Information Recommendation via Hybrid Similarity. *IEEE Transactions on Systems, Man, and Cybernetics. Systems, 48*(3), 448–459. doi:10.1109/TSMC.2016.2633573

Zhao, Z., Albright, R., Cox, J., & Bieringer, A. (2013). *Text mine your big data: What high performance really means. White Paper, SAS Institute Inc.* Retrieved from https://www.sas.com/content/dam/SAS/en_us/doc/whitepaper1/text-mine-your-big-data-106554.pdf

Zheng, X., Luo, Y., Sun, L., Zhang, J., & Chen, F. (2018). A tourism destination recommender system using users' sentiment and temporal dynamics. *Journal of Intelligent Information Systems, 51*(3), 557–578. doi:10.100710844-018-0496-5

ENDNOTES

[1] https://www.imdb.com/
[2] https://www.sas.com/en_us/home.html
[3] http://www.cs.ucr.edu/~eamonn/SAX.htm
[4] https://core.telegram.org/bots/api

This research was previously published in the International Journal of Information Retrieval Research (IJIRR), 9(3); pages 48-70, copyright year 2019 by IGI Publishing (an imprint of IGI Global).

Chapter 57
Using Intelligent Text Analysis of Online Reviews to Determine the Main Factors of Restaurant Value Propositions

Elizaveta Fainshtein

iD https://orcid.org/0000-0002-6503-7248

National Research University Higher School of Economics, Russia

Elena Serova

iD https://orcid.org/0000-0002-9510-3496

National Research University Higher School of Economics, Russia

ABSTRACT

This chapter discusses the sentiment classification of text messages containing customer reviews of an online restaurant service system using machine-learning methods, in particular text mining and multivariate text sentiment analysis. The study determines the structure of value proposition factors based on online restaurant reviews on TripAdvisor, collecting information on consumer preferences and the restaurant services in St. Petersburg (Russia) quality assessment and examines the influence of service format and reviews tonality on ratings restaurants factors. The service format context is proposed as the main attribute influencing the formation of the restaurant business value proposition and of relevance for online reviews. The results showed the key factors in the study of the sentiment were cuisine and dishes, reviews and ratings, and targeted search. MANOVA analysis represented that for special offers and features, reviews and ratings, factors and quantitative star ratings influenced the negative and positive sentiment of online reviews significantly.

DOI: 10.4018/978-1-6684-6303-1.ch057

INTRODUCTION

Nowadays, according to the increasing availability and popularity of e-commerce, social media, information portals, and media service platforms to gauge the opinions of restaurant consumers, online restaurant reviews are emerging as a new market phenomenon that plays an increasingly important role in value proposition decisions (Sheng et al., 2017; Ordanini & Pasini, 2008). Online reviews provide consumers with a wealth of information about service and product quality, which can reduce their uncertainty about ordering through restaurant systems. These reviews have a significant impact on restaurant service sales. With the ease of accessibility of mobile technology, online access through media service platforms to the experiences of consumers is accelerating and replacing more traditional forms of company brand assessment. The most popular online review platforms include sources such as Afisha Restaurants, Restoclub, TripAdvisor, Allcafe, and Restorating. The large volume of online restaurant reviews is also an indispensable resource for restaurants. Companies can analyze their customer experiences of service and food quality in more detail and in a timely manner, and understand potential growth points in relationship marketing and business modeling, whether there is a need to improve customer loyalty through online interaction, delivery systems, quality of service, or the menu, to determine the structure of significant factors in the value proposition.

The period of the pandemic served as a strong motivating aspect for the restructuring of commercial business and forced the transition to an online business format, and building and / or optimizing e-commerce systems and the delivery service, in a large number of commercial enterprises in the service sector, including the restaurant industry. With this in mind, it is important to understand what drives customers to come back or not to a restaurant, what motivates them to recommend a restaurant to their friends and family or not, what brand image is, and what factors create value for customers. In this regard, it is possible to track the growing popularity and importance of analytics for online restaurant service reviews, and the amount of relevant research using text mining and machine learning tools. A review of previous research related to online restaurant reviews published in academic research has shown an emerging reliance on Internet resources as sources of information for decision-making about restaurant products (e.g. Vásquez & Chik, 2015; Kaviya et al., 2017; Berezina et al., 2019), which heightens the need for more research on online restaurant reviews. It is important for a restaurant management system to use the information available from online customer reviews to better understand the needs of the target audience and improve the efficiency of the business. However, the online environment generates so much information that it can be difficult for managers to collect it all and analyze it manually. For this reason, this article uses text mining methods and systems that allow to extract meaningful patterns from large amounts of text information and demonstrate a possible way to process the data using machine learning (e.g. Hossain et al., 2017; Gogolev & Ozhegov, 2019; English & Fleischman, 2019; Ramos et al., 2020). The current study uses online customer testimonials, which are external evaluations of the restaurant business as part of e-commerce, a strong indicator of service quality. Detailed ratings provide more information about consumer preferences than individual overall ratings, and allow the timely modification of the restaurant's value proposition to increase the competitiveness of the service provided (Jannach et al., 2014). Multivariate analysis of the sentiment of the text allows to capture the subjectivity of online customer reviews in terms of semantic orientation associated with the constituents of the text.

In theory, identifying structured information from a free-form review text is difficult and time-consuming, so research on the main attributes of online restaurant reviews is rare. The field of research focused on understanding how factors specific to consumer inquiries in restaurants, as described in online customer reviews, reflecting their food experience, can influence a company's overall brand and brand ratings. Value proposition remains one of the topical areas where the amount of scientific research is only gaining momentum. Methodologically, most of the empirical research on online restaurant reviews typically uses only uninformative metadata, such as numerical ratings assigned by consumers, to avoid diving into the essential factors to improve restaurant business models. Previous research by the authors has shown that the semantic analysis of consumer requests provides richer and more extensive information for the restaurant industry and is a more informative indicator of consumer attitudes than the statistical processing of numerical ratings (Fainshtein & Serova, 2020). However, the format of the free text content of reviews in online reviews, in contrast to search queries, requires a separate study in the understanding of the authors.

Therefore, this study aims to close the knowledge gap by examining the underlying drivers of consumer demand for restaurant service, as described in online customer reviews, using machine learning. In particular, the research finds empirical answers to the following questions: What factors do consumers consider in online reviews when describing their experience of a restaurant? How do consumers' online attitudes about these factors affect overall restaurant ratings? This is achieved by comparing online restaurant reviews from satisfied customers who are willing to recommend the service to other consumers and dissatisfied reviews who discourage others from using a restaurant where they had a negative experience. The results of the study make it possible to understand which aspects of the food and service offered by restaurants generate positive and negative reviews in the online environment, which form the key factors of a competitive value proposition in the restaurant industry.

BACKGROUND: LITERATURE REVIEW

Customer Satisfaction With Online Restaurant Service and Behavioral Intentions

An online restaurant review includes describing and assessing the personal experience of a particular restaurant or purchasing meals or takeaways (Lane, 2013). Defining satisfied and dissatisfied customers is an important research issue among scholars of various disciplines, including management and marketing, which are actively used in the restaurant business (Titz et al., 2004; Parikh et al., 2014; Yang et al., 2017). The concept of measuring customer satisfaction and consumer behavior has been extensively studied by marketing researchers. The impact of social media on business transformation is recognized as important as it drives relationship marketing, brand sustainability and competitiveness. Repeat purchases and positive "electronic word of mouth" (EWOM) recommendations that encourage the use of a restaurant service directly depend on customer loyalty when writing online restaurant reviews. In other words, customer satisfaction reinforces a positive attitude towards a restaurant's online service brand and increases the likelihood of repeat purchases. On the other hand, dissatisfaction can lead to negative attitudes towards the brand and reduce the likelihood of repeat purchases.

At the moment, all online data about restaurants, their dishes and the service provided can be divided into two main groups: content created and posted directly by the producer of products and services (Producer Generated Content, PGC) and content created and posted directly by users (User Generated Content, UGC) independently of the restaurant (e.g. Salehi-Esfahani et al., 2016; Oliveira, & Casais, 2019; Cassar et al., 2020). The first group includes various marketing and advertising materials about the brand, products and services of the restaurant. The second group includes such types of social online content as forums, blogs, sites that systematize reviews, which may contain comments and consumer ratings, reviews, a collection of popular questions and answers (FAQ), user photo and video reports. The restaurant is able to independently influence the first type of content, choose the published information and form a personal brand, and then the second type directly depends on the influence of consumers, their assessments and the manifestation of loyalty to the restaurant, where the company is able to exert only an indirect influence.

One of the key approaches to answering the question of customer satisfaction and predicting a potential behavior strategy, which allows to form a high-quality value proposition, is measuring the service format (quality of service) and analyzing the key factors by which users make a choice when ordering online from a particular restaurant (Jensen & Hansen, 2007; Jin et al., 2012; Beuscart et al., 2016; Li et al., 2020). The service format is the level of service provision based on the perception of the client, which includes solving customer problems, satisfying the desires for a certain lifestyle, analyzing and controlling measures to create value for products, forming a competitive strategy, expressed in the initiation of emotions when selling goods and services for long-term customer support, stimulation of repeat purchases through a positive brand image. Elements of this definition have already been encountered in the papers of marketing and management researchers (Grönroos, 2011; Randhawa & Scerri, 2015). The perceived quality of service is part of a broader concept of customer satisfaction and behavioral intentions, which includes customer loyalty, which is key in shaping the value proposition.

Customers of online restaurant services use various elements to measure the quality of service they receive. The authors' research shows that in search queries, customer satisfaction is influenced by both the tangible and intangible aspects of service quality. In the previous study, after processing keyword data obtained in the Google KeyWord Planner system, keywords for the number of requests for restaurant service from restaurants in St. Petersburg (Russia) were broken down into seven main criteria for the most popular requests that can affect the attractiveness of the value proposition. Elements directly related to the service - geographic ((1) geolocation), psychographic ((2) reviews and ratings, including customer experience; (3) targeted search), behavioral ((4) promotions and discounts; (5) special offers and features), socio-demographic factors ((6) menu; (7) price). It has been argued that a denial of service or system failure that provokes less-than-full service can affect perceptions of service quality, satisfaction, and future behavioral intentions. Therefore, it is important for the restaurant business to recognize the factors that increase customer satisfaction and ensure their loyalty, on the basis of which a competitive value proposition can be formed.

The growth of e-commerce integration and the transition of the restaurant service system to online service increases the referral effect from regular customers. Dissatisfied online customer reviews can also be useful for restaurant management systems. First, comments like these can help restaurants by pointing out problem areas that may require careful attention and performance improvement (Harrison-Walker, 2019). Second, the impact of the service recovery paradox is also a significant factor when evaluating online reviews. The paradox of the restoration of services draws attention to the fact that the degree of satisfaction with customer service will be higher for those customers who, after specifying the defects in the service, received compensation for damage from the restaurant management than for those customers who immediately received the purchased services and products (Harrison-Walker, 2019; Żyminkowska, 2019; Mostert et al., 2012; Mejia et al., 2012). A review of scientific studies confirms that the service recovery paradox strategies increase customer loyalty as the company is attentive to feedback (Roggeveen et al., 2012; Liu et al., 2019). However, if the remarks are ignored or noticed but not addressed, this can lead to customer dissatisfaction with the service of the restaurant, and, consequently, to a low level of repeat purchases and negative EWOM (Yoo, 2020). A negative EWOM score causes significant damage to companies in the restaurant business, since most of the customers tend to leave and search for negative online reviews, considering negative comments to be more diagnostic, sincere and informative than positive or neutral ones.

In the decision-making process, reviews containing negative information are more important than positive information. A negative EWOM can deter potential customers from considering a particular product, service, or the restaurant brand itself, thereby damaging a company's reputation and financial strength. It can also very quickly go viral in online e-commerce systems and, spreading through all information channels, possibly reducing capital and brand image, reducing sales, and in extreme cases, completely shutting down the restaurant business, since the hospitality industry depends a lot on consumer loyalty.

Evaluating Customer Satisfaction With Online Restaurant Services in Web 3.0

The proliferation of electronic data collection systems, EWOM, and the development of e-commerce and the transition of most commercial brands to online sales during the pandemic, forever changed the status of customer opinion about food in online restaurant reviews. Based on Web 3.0 semantic technology, EWOM enables users to massively disseminate customer experiences of goods and services, as well as exchange and track content, which fosters a collective intelligence (Nayar, 2015). The semantic network in innovation for the exchange of data about EWOM services is manifested as the evolution of the value of consumer opinion, by taking into account the network interactions of users. Consumer-generated online reviews can be much more easily, systematically and widely disseminated than verbal, informal exchange of information between a small closed group of acquaintances or friends. More than ever, there is a trend that customers increasingly rely on online reviews to make decisions about which restaurant to order lunch from and which dish to choose (Ulker-Demirel, 2019). Therefore, it is not surprising that new paradigms of the technological possibilities of using the Semantic Web 3.0 allow a large number of customers to influence the value proposition of a restaurant. This makes it possible to make strategic managerial decisions, based on data analysis on the principle: the more users are involved, the more objective data can be collected and processed about the information material, products or services of the restaurant.

A survey of more than 5,500 online customers found that 59% of survey respondents considered consumer reviews to be more valuable than expert reviews (Piller, 1999; Kim et al., 2017). Online restaurant reviews have a broader impact on consumers, influencing demand, engagement marketing, and brand loyalty, both online and offline. In particular, online reviews focus managers on new opportunities for quality development and areas that need to be addressed through marketing innovation.

There are two forms of customer experience data analysis. The most popular form of online restaurant reviews is quantitative. A 1 to 5 star review system, is the most readily available to query. Moreover, such a form of input can be easily saved and processed by computer technology. In this way, a large dataset of customer testimonials can be collected over a long period of time, which can then be standardized and analyzed (Mustak et al., 2016).

Textual comments of online reviews are qualitative in nature. Descriptive data of customer experiences is a more complex and informative method requiring intelligent and multivariate analysis of the sentiment of the text. It reveals in detail what exactly had a positive or negative effect on the customer. Because online text reviews allow reviewers to substantiate the reasons and context, in which they rated a product the way they did. This is one of the reasons why online text reviews usually complement numerical ratings. In other words, the contextual information contained in online text reviews can help potential customers make intelligent interpretations of the ratings from other users and therefore potentially make EWOM more useful and informative. Several websites, such as the online review service TripAdvisor, have been very successful in encouraging consumers to submit large numbers of text comments, reviews and ratings.

Online reviews of consumer experiences empower potential customers by enabling them to access more accurate and up-to-date information about the products and services of restaurants. In addition to customer interests, restaurant managers also benefit from working with information in online customer surveys, as they provide information on the strengths and weaknesses of the services provided, which makes text processing very useful in customer relationship marketing. Research suggests that customer feedback is increasingly important and influences consumer decision-making when choosing a restaurant (e.g. Yang et al., 2017; Kaviya et al., 2017; Chkoniya & Mateus, 2019; Li et al., 2020). Online customer reviews of products and services are becoming an increasingly important type of EWOM content. They are a valuable source of information to help customers make the right purchase decisions and help companies shape their value proposition in a service format more intelligently.

Factors That Affect Online Restaurant Review Rankings

Star ratings in online customer reviews play an important role in building consumer confidence in restaurant companies and are an important factor in business success. A number of research reviews have identified various factors that influence online rankings, such as post-transaction services (English & Fleischman, 2019), consumer experiences (Beuscart et al., 2016), relationship services (Berezina et al., 2019) and the use of reviewing media sites (Fan et al., 2017). However, there has been limited research on the factors that influence the ratings consumers give to restaurants through the use of text mining, and how consumer attitudes at the factor level affect their overall restaurant ratings.

Of particular note is the study by Zhang, Zhang, and Law (2014) showing the high impact of EWOM for restaurants, depending on four factors of restaurant service - food, physical environment, employee service, and cost. These factors greatly contribute to customer satisfaction in restaurants. Research has shown that one factor can replace another in the process of describing the value of a customer's use of a service. This research also confirms five criteria affect restaurant ratings in online reviews: food, service, atmosphere, price and context.

Therefore, the hypothesis for the study is that consumers' opinions of food, service, atmosphere, price and context have a significant impact on their overall positive or negative sentiment in restaurant rating text, as evidenced by the overall ratings in quantitative star values in online reviews of restaurant service.

METHODOLOGY

Data Collection

The data were taken from online restaurant reviews on TripAdvisor, which collects information on consumer preferences and the assessment of the quality of restaurants, St. Petersburg, Russia. The dataset consists of 201 customer reviews from 16 chain restaurants in St. Petersburg, Russia, including 242 restaurants. Seven main factors were included in the data analysis: factors based on value segments of consumer demand for restaurants in accordance with the classical segmentation structure: geographic (geolocation), psychographic (reviews and ratings, including impressions customers; targeted search), behavioral (promotions and discounts; specials and features), socio-demographic factors (menu; price) analyzed by the authors in a previous study (Fainshtein & Serova, 2020). Other categories in the data have been excluded to eliminate potential outliers.

Since the depth and granularity of an online review can affect the quality and quantity of information, and longer reviews include more data about products and services, how and where they were obtained, and in what context, the authors include in the analysis of each restaurant the 1 most recent review of at least 50 words. As a result, the dataset included 201 reviews from 242 restaurants in the 16 largest restaurant chains in St. Petersburg.

Predictive Analysis and Multivariate Analysis of the Text Sentiment

The growth of business information volumes means there is a need to analyze and automate different kinds of textual information.

Intelligent text analysis or text mining can be defined as automated extracting knowledge process from text data. Its peculiarity (in contrast to the analysis of other data) is that the initial information is not structured and formalized and it cannot be described by simple mathematical functions. The authors highlight three areas of the successful use of text mining applications and systems:

- supporting the decision making processes on the all levels of management;
- knowledge management;
- marketing research.

The main purpose of text mining is to extract information that is necessary for effective decision-making. Text mining allows not only the extraction of useful insights from unstructured data management projects, but also an expectation of higher ROI (return on investment) from them. For businesses, this means the ability to benefit from the use of big data, avoiding costly manual processing: to set aside irrelevant data and information and just get answers. With the growth of the volume of textual information to reduce the cost of its processing, there is a need for automation.

Intellectual capital is considered now as one of the main assets of an organization. It can generate up 50% of profit. As an organization grows, it accumulates a significant amount of intellectual assets. However, as a rule, their storage is not always well structured and standardized, different departments may use different tools for storing documents or even perform without storage. This makes it difficult or impossible to find information. The problem is especially real during mergers and acquisitions. To effectively use of intellectual capital, text-mining systems can:

- automatically collect and select information from various sources and compile it in a single format;
- provide an interface for searching documents by user-specified parameters;
- supplement documents with metadata (for example: source of documents, date of its creation, authors, etc.);
- pre-index and cluster documents;
- customize the levels of access to information based on security requirements.

Intelligent Text Analysis can be extremely useful in the sphere of marketing research. Text mining systems help to better understand the information field in which the company operates and how the customers (current and potential) relate to and cooperate with the company. Text mining systems can sort incoming customer's orders and provide more complete information about the customers and their needs at the output. The processing time of orders is reduced, saving money for the company.

To build a development strategy, companies need feedback and objective assessments of the use of their and competing products. Due to the large number of sources of information (scientific publications, product reviews, marketing research, conference proceedings, business news, etc.), automatic processing is also required here.

A very important task of text mining is sentiment analysis. The emotional attitude of the author needs to be evaluated. This is used, for example, to classify reviews of products or the assessment of the company itself.

Recent research in the field of marketing actively uses the technologies of intelligent and multivariate analysis of the sentiment of the text for analytics of marketing interactions and working with statistical data on consumer requests. Thanks to the methods of machine learning in information processing, the availability and efficiency of working with data from commercial organizations, including in restaurants, has increased.

The service format assumes that high-quality descriptive data of customer experiences in the text comments of online reviews are emotionally viewed as negative or positive, when certain factors in a certain tonal color encourage the client to leave comments about the strengths or weaknesses of the service. Therefore, in this study, the tonality of the text is understood as the attitude towards something described as a factor, negative or positive.

Intellectual and multidimensional analysis of the sentiment of the text (Kaviya et al., 2017; Hossain et al., 2017; Fan et al., 2017) is used to understand the attitude and opinion about the interaction with the company and customer's emotions about the product and service.

Sentiment analysis in the study was divided into two sequential stages: first, determining which text segments in the reviews contain dimensions and second, determining the polarity and strength of the tonality of each of these dimensions.

In the first phase of identifying attributes in online restaurant reviews, the study used factors from a previous study by the authors (Fainshtein & Serova, 2020) and developed a semi-supervised machine learning approach that included topic identification and mood classification. This approach identified seven attributes in online restaurant reviews that correlate strongly with positive and negative customer opinions, and helped determine both the overall scale of sentiment and the driving forces that restaurants need to consider when shaping their value proposition.

First, a set of keywords was proposed for each factor, for the initial loading of the classifier. The study used factors based on value segments of consumer demand for restaurants in St. Petersburg (Russia) in accordance with the classic segmentation structure. The authors build on their previous work (Fainshtein & Serova, 2020), where, using semantic analysis of keywords of consumer searches, the seven factors of the service format were identified, which potential customers pay attention to based on their requests for industry data. Each of the factor categories has fixed keyword attributes corresponding to the factor's topic.

Second, 201 online reviews from TripAdvisor's online review service were selected for analysis, each of which were the most recent text review containing at least 50 words, belonging to one of 242 restaurants in the 16 largest restaurant chains.

The seven factors were used to determine which of them were contained in the online survey. If the sentence contained any word that was included in one of the seven factor word lists, the sentence was considered to have the corresponding factor. A sentence could contain more than one word, and the words in a sentence could fall into more than one word list. Thus, the frequency of words that fell into the same list for each sentence was calculated. The list with the most words was identified as the main factor.

At the second stage of determining the polarity of emotional moods in the text (positive or negative sentiment), the study used sentiment lexicons in the QDA Miner Lite program and an extended list of 89 words compiled from the results of the CHAID analysis of consumer keywords (Fainshtein & Serova, 2020). The words were rated between most negative and most positive. The resulting QDA Miner Lite scores and sentiment scores are the sum of the scores for positive and negative words in a sentence. For multivariate analysis of the sentiment of the text, MANOVA was carried out using the SPSS 24.0 software package to check the influence of the seven factors and the quantitative assessments on the negative and positive sentiment of online reviews.

EMPIRICAL RESULTS

The sentiment analysis yielded negative and positive sentiments of online reviews (Table 1), and the seven indicators (Table 2) that measure the focus and depth of customer opinion on geolocation, reviews and ratings, targeted search, promotions and discounts, special offers, and features, menu, and prices of restaurants. To account for the different number of words in the reviews, the sentiment scores of the text (Table 2, Figure 1) were weighted in proportion to the number of sentences of each factor, based on the following calculations:

$$Sentiment_{ij} = Sentiment\ Score_{ij} \times \frac{Amount\ of\ words\ of\ the\ Factor_{ij}}{\sum Amount\ of\ words\ of\ the\ Factors_{ij}} \tag{1}$$

where
  $i = 1 \dots N$ online overview
  j = geolocation, reviews and ratings, targeted search, promotions and discounts, special offers and features, menu, restaurant prices

Table 1. Sentiment of online reviews of restaurants in St. Petersburg, 2020

The sentiment of online reviews	Number of words	% of words	Tonality
Positive	17091	53.4	1.06
Negative	14895	46.6	0.93

This study took into account two control variables related to online customer reviews. Reviewing behavior is related to the emotional color of the review, which is posted on TripAdvisor, which shows the direction of the sentiment of online reviews (Table 1). Of great importance is the number of stars (from 1 to 5), which the client marked in the column for evaluating the restaurant's service on the site. The popularity of a restaurant chain is measured by the number of extreme positive and negative reviews received about individual restaurants within the chain. The sentiment targeting of online reviews was based on a binary approach: "1" for a restaurant with extreme positive reviews and "0" for negative reviews. The weighted ratings of the seven factors were used as explanatory variables, and the overall star ratings of each review and their sentiment direction were the dependent variable.

Next, were used the MANOVA model to test the relationship between the seven factors that measure the directionality of the sentiment of customers' opinions and the quantitative star ratings, accompanying text feedback on negative or positive sentiment of online reviews. Multilevel analysis allows to take into account in detail the hierarchical structure of the reviews and their settings, and to carry out a multidimensional analysis of the sentiment of the text.

Table 2. Significant factors in the value proposition of restaurants in online customer reviews in St. Petersburg, 2020

Factors	Number of words	% of words	Tonality
Geolocation	662	2.1	0.14
Reviews and ratings	8581	26.8	1.88
Targeted search	5817	18.2	1.27
Promotions and discounts	1873	5.9	0.41
Special offers and features	3920	12.2	0.86
Menu	9970	31.2	2.18
Price	1163	3.6	0.25

The MANOVA analysis (Table 3) shows that for special offers and features, reviews and ratings, factors and quantitative star ratings influenced the negative and positive sentiment of online reviews. Special offers and features (F = 14.931, p ‹0.05) and the criterion of reviews and ratings (F = 8.530, p‹ 0.05) have an impact on the value proposition within their group and confirm the hypothesis that consumers' opinions about food, service, atmosphere, price, and context have a significant impact on their overall positive or negative sentiment in the restaurant review text, as evidenced by overall quantitative star ratings in online restaurant reviews. However, the criterion of geolocation, targeted search, promotions and discounts, menu, prices are not independent significant variables.

For online reviews from TripAdvisor, sentiment lexicons in the QDA Miner Lite program revealed the most influential factors in menu, reviews and ratings, and targeted restaurant search. For the subsequent MANOVA, the significant factors were special offers, reviews and ratings. This means that the majority of customers who reviewed on TripAdvisor visited the analyzed restaurants based on the reviews and ratings from other users, rather than responding to any other of the seven factors. In the first case, a study of the lexicons of sentiment shows that one group of respondents choose a restaurant based on the emotional component, where the review was most emotional, vivid and detailed (the number of words in the review, which accounted for one of seven factors (Figure 1)), while another group made their choice based on a practical component, as shown by multivariate analysis of variance.

Table 3. MANOVA analysis: testing the influence of seven factors and quantitative star ratings on negative and positive sentiment of online reviews

Multivariate results				
Factors	df	Wilks's λ	F	Sig.
Geolocation	25	0,220	0,048*	0,827
Reviews and ratings	103	0,219	8,530*	0,004
Targeted search	82	0,221	0,406*	0,525
Promotions and discounts	38	0,221	0,026*	0,871
Special conditions and features	69	0,220	14,931*	0,001
Menu	134	0,219	0,080*	0,777
Price	40	0,220	1,035*	0,310
* p<0.05				

Note: the analysis uses the following values: df - degrees of freedom; Wilks's λ - Wilks lambda; F is the value of the F-criterion; Sig. - significance.

Figure 1. Distribution of words in online customer reviews of a St. Petersburg restaurant chain on TripAdvisor review platform, 2020

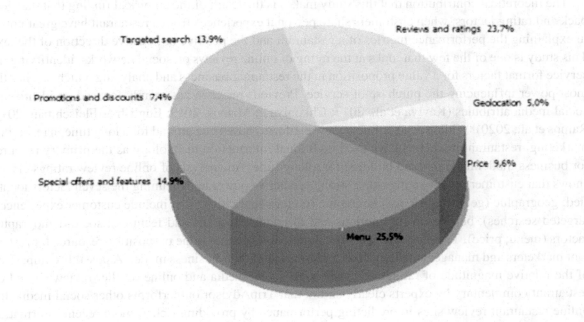

Distribution of codes (Frequency)

Targeted search 13,9%
Reviews and ratings 23,7%
Promotions and discounts 7,4%
Geolocation 5,0%
Price 9,6%
Special offers and features 14,9%
Menu 25,5%

SOLUTIONS AND RECOMMENDATIONS

Theoretical Implications

This study used text mining to explain consumer behavior when writing online restaurant reviews and the factors that matter to them that restaurant managers could use in shaping the value proposition to increase competitiveness. The theory of text mining clearly substantiates the statistical significance of certain factors among online consumer reviews and shows that potential customers pay attention to positive and negative reviews when they evaluate information about the experiences of other consumers to avoid potential risks and reap the possible benefits of a restaurant visit. The theory also shows how to work with sentiment analysis tools to maximize restaurant visits by incorporating in-demand factors from online customer reviews into value propositions, thereby increasing demand for restaurant services.

This study demonstrates that a statistically significant positive relationship between positive or negative sentiment in restaurant rating text, seven service factors and quantitative star ratings in the restaurant business.

Previous scholars have conducted empirical research to test the impact of social media or traditional information technology ratings on restaurant performance by evaluating a focus on company performance. In terms of the key contribution, this study is the first to empirically identify key service format factors for value propositions and test the impact of online reviews that will help improve the future performance of restaurants.

In addition, with regard to considering the sentiment direction and ratings of online reviews on social media, this study collected online review information for each member of the largest restaurant chains in St. Petersburg (Russia) on TripAdvisor to improve reliability, as opposed to forming a variety of empirical findings from local websites or survey-based studies.

The theoretical contribution that this study makes is the result of the empirical finding that the feedback and rating factors, when customers share personal experiences from a restaurant have great power in explaining the performance metrics of a restaurant and the positive or negative direction of the text. This study is one of the few that looks at the rating of online reviews on social networks, identifying the service format factors for a value proposition in the restaurant business and analyzing which one has the most power influencing the purchase of service. Previous research has mainly focused on identifying social media attributes (Kaviya et al., 2017; Chkoniya & Mateus, 2019; English & Fleischman, 2019; Ramos et al., 2020). While social online review platforms have been around for a long time in restaurant marketing, restaurant marketers have used traditional information technology as the primary resource for business modeling and brand building for a long time. An analysis of online review ratings clearly shows that customer review ratings have strong predictive power in explaining the seven factors identified: geographic (geolocation), psychographic (reviews and ratings that include customer experiences; targeted searches), behavioral (promotions and discounts; specials and features), socio-demographic factors (menu; price). These results may offer a more informative value proposition resource for restaurant marketers and managers to predict the performance of their business model. A possible comparison of the relative magnitude of ratings across popular social media and online reseller reviews based on restaurant commentary by experts clearly shows that TripAdvisor outperforms other social media and online restaurant review sites in predicting performance by providing richer, more recent information from users. This study also provides a comprehensive literature review of restaurant research, identifying the most popular and effective methods used for industry analytics.

Management Implications

The practical contributions of this study will help restaurant marketers understand the role of social media marketing and the potential application of online customer reviews. Restaurant marketers must consider both traditional customer satisfaction and the star rating of online reviews to maintain a competitive edge.

Social media can help restaurants by increasing the likelihood of table reservations by boosting EWOM promotion (Nayar, 2015). Restaurant managers can use social media platforms as an important brand building and engagement channel for developing customer relationships (Ulker-Demirel, 2019). Marketers should also track and use social media online review ratings as the dominant internal data to drive service and optimize value propositions. In addition, managers can expect to improve their overall financial performance by increasing their social media ratings. Getting higher online rankings leads to stronger brand awareness and more referrals from customers. Higher online review ratings, and working with the seven in-demand factors, can help reduce the cost of traditional promotion.

This study suggests that restaurant marketing strategists should continue to use online customer review tools to make management decisions. This will lead to better service, increased profitability, lower costs and increased customer loyalty.

Thanks to technological convergence, including the ability to collect a large amount of information about consumers, the analysis of data from online reviews is faster and more efficient. What's more, restaurants can now reach out to its customers in a more personalized way, which leads to an increase in the conversion of visits to sites with online reviews to offline sales. The restaurant must calculate its benefit from the existing business structure and value proposition by examining the potential costs and revenues, taking into account the factors important to the customer, by which he determines whether to visit a particular restaurant, and then make a decision to obtain the optimal combination of factors in his value proposition. This research helps marketers and restaurant managers better allocate marketing budgets and suggests a method to optimize the factors to include in the value proposition.

LIMITATIONS AND FUTURE RESEARCH DIRECTIONS

While this study provides a comprehensive view of the positive or negative directionality of restaurant rating texts and star ratings for customer satisfaction, and identifies seven factors and their impact on restaurant value propositions, there are limitations. First, the use of predictive and multivariate analysis of the sentiment of the text may not be fully accurate. Second, future research can develop this theory and apply other analytical tools to study the relationship between customer satisfaction and their ratings on online social media reviews.

Further research could investigate whether the results of customer satisfaction reviews, social media ratings for the current period are more reliable than the results of the analysis of customer satisfaction in previous years. Researchers could also confirm the results of this study in hotel restaurants, in further research.

In addition, this study only included one of the most popular online review websites: TripAdvisor. Since there is the possibility that some new online intermediary or social media site could become a more significant influencer in the market, it is imperative that future research reflects newly emerging sites. Future research should expand the list of review sources to better understand the sentiment ratings of online reviews and their impact on restaurant value propositions.

CONCLUSION

This study examined the influence of consumers' opinions on food, service, atmosphere, price and context. The impact of seven factors typical for consumer inquiries in the field of restaurant services - geographic (geolocation), psychographic (reviews and ratings, including customer experience; targeted search), behavioral (promotions and discounts; special offers and features), socio-demographic factors (menu; price) on the positive or negative orientation of the sentiment of the restaurant rating text, and how quantitative star ratings in online restaurant service reviews are interconnected with them, which restaurant customers evaluate in their reviews.

According to the findings, ratings based on online restaurant reviews on TripAdvisor, which collects information on consumer preferences and the assessment of restaurants in St. Petersburg (Russia), are an informative source and allow to check the influence of seven factors and quantitative star ratings on the negative and positive tone of online reviews. The results confirm a direct link between the reviews and ratings factor, when customers describe their personal experience of interaction with the restaurant, the most significant thing to consider when forming a relevant, competitive value proposition for a restaurant business and focus on relationship marketing, customer focus and increasing the loyalty of potential clients.

This research can be useful for marketers, restaurateurs and their managers to quickly respond to consumer requests and modernize their value proposition based on which of the seven factors is their priority. The results of this study can directly increase the competitiveness of a restaurant and can improve marketers and managers' understanding of how to improve the quality of service for customers in general.

REFERENCES

Berezina, K., Ciftci, O., & Cobanoglu, C. (2019). Robots, artificial intelligence, and service automation in restaurants. In *Robots, Artificial Intelligence, and Service Automation in Travel, Tourism and Hospitality*. Emerald Publishing Limited. doi:10.1108/978-1-78756-687-320191010

Beuscart, J. S., Mellet, K., & Trespeuch, M. (2016). Reactivity without legitimacy? Online consumer reviews in the restaurant industry. *Journal of Cultural Economics*, 9(5), 458–475. doi:10.1080/175303 50.2016.1210534

Cassar, M. L., Caruana, A., & Konietzny, J. (2020). Wine and satisfaction with fine dining restaurants: An analysis of tourist experiences from user generated content on TripAdvisor. *Journal of Wine Research*, 1–16.

Chkoniya, V., & Mateus, A. (2019). Digital Category Management: How Technology Can Enable the Supplier-Retailer Relationship. In Smart Marketing With the Internet of Things (pp. 139-163). IGI Global.

English, P., & Fleischman, D. (2019). Food for thought in restaurant reviews: Lifestyle journalism or an extension of marketing in UK and Australian newspapers. *Journalism Practice*, 13(1), 90–104. doi: 10.1080/17512786.2017.1397530

Fainshtein, E., & Serova, E. (2020). Value Proposition of Network Companies Providing Restaurant Services in Russia: Analysis and Evaluation. In Anthropological Approaches to Understanding Consumption Patterns and Consumer Behavior (pp. 137-158). IGI Global.

Fan, Z. P., Che, Y. J., & Chen, Z. Y. (2017). Product sales forecasting using online reviews and historical sales data: A method combining the Bass model and sentiment analysis. *Journal of Business Research*, *74*, 90–100. doi:10.1016/j.jbusres.2017.01.010

Gogolev, S., & Ozhegov, E. M. (2019). Comparison of Machine Learning Algorithms in Restaurant Revenue Prediction. In *International Conference on Analysis of Images, Social Networks and Texts* (pp. 27-36). Springer.

Grönroos, C. (2011). A service perspective on business relationships: The value creation, interaction and marketing interface. *Industrial Marketing Management*, *40*(2), 240–247. doi:10.1016/j.indmarman.2010.06.036

Harrison-Walker, L. J. (2019). The effect of consumer emotions on outcome behaviors following service failure. *Journal of Services Marketing*, *33*(3), 285–302. doi:10.1108/JSM-04-2018-0124

Hossain, F. T., Hossain, M. I., & Nawshin, S. (2017). *Machine learning based class level prediction of restaurant reviews. In 2017 IEEE Region 10 Humanitarian Technology Conference (R10-HTC)*. IEEE.

Jannach, D., Zanker, M., & Fuchs, M. (2014). Leveraging multi-criteria customer feedback for satisfaction analysis and improved recommendations. *Information Technology & Tourism*, *14*(2), 119–149. doi:10.100740558-014-0010-z

Jensen, Ø., & Hansen, K. V. (2007). Consumer values among restaurant customers. *International Journal of Hospitality Management*, *26*(3), 603–622. doi:10.1016/j.ijhm.2006.05.004

Jin, N., Lee, S., & Huffman, L. (2012). Impact of restaurant experience on brand image and customer loyalty: Moderating role of dining motivation. *Journal of Travel & Tourism Marketing*, *29*(6), 532–551. doi:10.1080/10548408.2012.701552

Kaviya, K., Roshini, C., Vaidhehi, V., & Sweetlin, J. D. (2017). Sentiment analysis for restaurant rating. In *2017 IEEE International Conference on Smart Technologies and Management for Computing, Communication, Controls, Energy and Materials (ICSTM)* (pp. 140-145). IEEE.

Kim, W. G., & Park, S. A. (2017). Social media review rating versus traditional customer satisfaction. *International Journal of Contemporary Hospitality Management*, *29*(2), 784–802. doi:10.1108/IJCHM-11-2015-0627

Lane, C. (2013). Taste makers in the "fine-dining" restaurant industry: The attribution of aesthetic and economic value by gastronomic guides. *Poetics*, *41*(4), 342–365. doi:10.1016/j.poetic.2013.05.003

Li, H., Xie, K. L., & Zhang, Z. (2020). The effects of consumer experience and disconfirmation on the timing of online review: Field evidence from the restaurant business. *International Journal of Hospitality Management*, *84*, 102344. doi:10.1016/j.ijhm.2019.102344

Liu, H., Jayawardhena, C., Dibb, S., & Ranaweera, C. (2019). Examining the trade-off between compensation and promptness in eWOM-triggered service recovery: A restorative justice perspective. *Tourism Management, 75*, 381–392. doi:10.1016/j.tourman.2019.05.008

Mejia, J., Mankad, S., & Gopal, A. (2020). Service Quality Using Text Mining: Measurement and Consequences. *Manufacturing & Service Operations Management*, 1–19. doi:10.1287/msom.2020.0883

Mostert, P., Petzer, D., & De Meyer, C. (2012). A theoretical and empirical investigation into service failure and service recovery in the restaurant Industry. In Service Science Research, Strategy and Innovation: Dynamic Knowledge Management Methods (pp. 86-99). IGI Global. doi:10.4018/978-1-4666-0077-5.ch005

Mustak, M., Jaakkola, E., Halinen, A., & Kaartemo, V. (2016). Customer participation management. *Journal of Service Management, 27*(3), 250–275. doi:10.1108/JOSM-01-2015-0014

Nayar, R. (2015). Role of Web 3.0 in Service Innovation. In *The Handbook of Service Innovation* (pp. 253–280). Springer. doi:10.1007/978-1-4471-6590-3_13

Oliveira, B., & Casais, B. (2019). The importance of user-generated photos in restaurant selection. *Journal of Hospitality and Tourism Technology, 10*(1), 2–14. doi:10.1108/JHTT-11-2017-0130

Ordanini, A., & Pasini, P. (2008). Service co-production and value co-creation: The case for a service-oriented architecture (SOA). *European Management Journal, 26*(5), 289–297. doi:10.1016/j.emj.2008.04.005

Parikh, A., Behnke, C., Vorvoreanu, M., Almanza, B., & Nelson, D. (2014). Motives for reading and articulating user-generated restaurant reviews on Yelp. com. *Journal of Hospitality and Tourism Technology, 5*(2), 160–176. doi:10.1108/JHTT-04-2013-0011

Piller, C. (1999). Everyone is a critic in cyberspace. *Los Angeles Times, 3*(12), A1.

Ramos, K., Cuamea, O., Morgan, J., & Estrada, A. (2020). Social Networks' Factors Driving Consumer Restaurant Choice: *An Exploratory Analysis. In International Conference on Applied Human Factors and Ergonomics* (pp. 158-164). Springer.

Randhawa, K., & Scerri, M. (2015). Service innovation: A review of the literature. In *The handbook of service innovation* (pp. 27–51). Springer. doi:10.1007/978-1-4471-6590-3_2

Roggeveen, A. L., Tsiros, M., & Grewal, D. (2012). Understanding the co-creation effect: When does collaborating with customers provide a lift to service recovery? *Journal of the Academy of Marketing Science, 40*(6), 771–790. doi:10.100711747-011-0274-1

Salehi-Esfahani, S., Ravichandran, S., Israeli, A., & Bolden, E. III. (2016). Investigating information adoption tendencies based on restaurants' user-generated content utilizing a modified information adoption model. *Journal of Hospitality Marketing & Management, 25*(8), 925–953. doi:10.1080/19368623 .2016.1171190

Sheng, J., Amankwah-Amoah, J., & Wang, X. (2017). A multidisciplinary perspective of big data in management research. *International Journal of Production Economics, 191*, 97–112. doi:10.1016/j. ijpe.2017.06.006

Titz, K., Lanza-Abbott, J. A., & Cruz, G. C. Y. (2004). The anatomy of restaurant reviews: An exploratory study. *International Journal of Hospitality & Tourism Administration, 5*(1), 49–65. doi:10.1300/J149v05n01_03

Ulker-Demirel, E. (2019). The Features of New Communication Channels and Digital Marketing. In *Handbook of Research on Narrative Advertising* (pp. 302–313). IGI Global. doi:10.4018/978-1-5225-9790-2.ch026

Vásquez, C., & Chik, A. (2015). "I am not a foodie…": Culinary capital in online reviews of Michelin restaurants. *Food & Foodways, 23*(4), 231–250. doi:10.1080/07409710.2015.1102483

Yang, S. B., Hlee, S., Lee, J., & Koo, C. (2017). An empirical examination of online restaurant reviews on Yelp. com. *International Journal of Contemporary Hospitality Management, 29*(2), 817–839. doi:10.1108/IJCHM-11-2015-0643

Yoo, C. W. (2020). An Exploration of the Role of Service Recovery in Negative Electronic Word-of-Mouth Management. *Information Systems Frontiers, 22*(3), 719–734. doi:10.100710796-018-9880-5

Zhang, Z., Zhang, Z., & Law, R. (2014). Relative importance and combined effects of attributes on customer satisfaction. *Service Industries Journal, 34*(6), 550–566. doi:10.1080/02642069.2014.871537

Żyminkowska, K. (2019). Concepts of Customer Activism. In *Customer Engagement in Theory and Practice* (pp. 1–22). Palgrave Pivot. doi:10.1007/978-3-030-11677-4_1

KEY TERMS AND DEFINITIONS

EWOM (Electronic Word-of-Mouth): Any positive or negative review made by potential, current or former customers about a company's product that is available to many potential customers and is shared through social networks.

Multivariate Analysis of Variance (MANOVA): This is a type of multivariate analysis used for analyzing data that includes more than one dependent variable at a time.

Sentiment Analysis of the Text (Direction of the Review): Is the computer identification and clustering of the opinions expressed in a piece of text to determine what the author's attitude to a particular topic, product or service is (positive, negative, or neutral).

Service Format: The level of service provision based on the perception of the client, which includes solving the problems of the buyer of services, satisfying the desires for a certain lifestyle, analyzing, and controlling measures to create value for products, forming a competitive strategy, expressed in the emotions when selling goods and services for long-term customers, stimulating repeat purchases through a positive brand image.

Text Mining: An automated analytic tool for understanding and sorting unstructured text that makes it easier to manage the data it describes. Text analysis tools are often used to gain valuable insights in e-commerce and digital marketing, for example, when analyzing social media discussions, survey responses, and online reviews.

Text Mining Technologies: An artificial intelligence tool used by companies to transform raw data into useful information. By using software to find patterns in big data sets, businesses can learn more about their customers to develop better marketing strategies, increase sales, and reduce costs.

Value Proposition: A strategic tool for positioning a product or service related to the exceptional properties of the products, which, through its unique characteristics, helps the company differentiate itself from competitors in the market.

This research was previously published in the Handbook of Research on Applied Data Science and Artificial Intelligence in Business and Industry; pages 223-240, copyright year 2021 by Engineering Science Reference (an imprint of IGI Global).

Chapter 58
A Novel Algorithm for Sentiment Analysis of Online Movie Reviews

Bisma Shah
Jamia Hamdard, India

Farheen Siddiqui
Jamia Hamdard, India

ABSTRACT

Others' opinions can be decisive while choosing among various options, especially when those choices involve worthy resources like spending time and money buying products or services. Customers relying on their peers' past reviews on e-commerce websites or social media have drawn a considerable interest to sentiment analysis due to realization of its commercial and business benefits. Sentiment analysis can be exercised on movie reviews, blogs, customer feedback, etc. This chapter presents a novel approach to perform sentiment analysis of movie reviews given by users on different websites. Also, challenges like presence of thwarted words, world knowledge, and subjectivity detection in sentiments are addressed in this chapter. The results are validated by using two supervised machine learning approaches, k-nearest neighbor and naive Bayes, both on method of sentiment analysis without addressing aforementioned challenges and on proposed method of sentiment analysis with all challenges addressed. Empirical results show that proposed method outperformed the one that left challenges unaddressed.

INTRODUCTION

Sentiment Analysis (SA) is an on-going field of research in text mining field and is used for the computational treatment of opinions, sentiments and subjectivity of text. It is used to understand the mind-sets, opinions and sentiments of people in general in regards to a specific product or a movie or an occasion. It helps in identifying and extracting subjective information in source materials and categorizes them as positive, negative, or neutral. Decision making process has always been influenced by the huge data

DOI: 10.4018/978-1-6684-6303-1.ch058

available and the human nature to always rely on opinion of other people regarding a particular product or an event. This unique feature has a significant impact on deciding matters that have financial, medical, social, business or other ramifications. Keeping in view the large amount of comments or reviews for a particular product and the colossal advancement in web users, there arises a dire need to build up a framework that gathers, constructs, analyzes and characterizes the remarks or reviews present online. A review is usually written by a person who has used a particular product or a service. The nature of review is immensely affected by an individual's interests, opinions and viewpoints. People who give biased reviews consequently impact the reputation of a forum or an organization to which the review is being contributed. Increase in the number of such people has posed a huge challenge to characterize and sort out the real issues and prospects of the product by virtue of which a user questions the authenticity of the content. In view of improving the scope of a particular product, huge organizations depend on individual reviews of clients and consider it to be of incredible significance in putting content construct advertisements on websites that effectively help a forthcoming buyer. Also movie enthusiasts and voters employ the same approach for analysis of certain information as an ever increasing number of individuals are utilizing social networking sites, online shopping and trend analysts who in the wake of scrutinizing the reviews available settle on different issues. For instance putting the promotion of a Kitchen Aid Mixer on a food blog impacts purchase choices as well as goes far in altering the advertising technique. Reviewers are being enthusiastically promoted by the advertising division of an organization by sending samples of product to be assessed or supporting discounts in blogs or in social networking locales like Facebook and Twitter. This has prompted the expansion in the volume of information accessible and the need to characterize the accessible data effectively as these have a larger impact on the reputation of a particular organization.

Large amount of data generated online by reviews can be processed so as to extract useful information from them, using suitable methods and approaches of Sentiment analysis, thereby supporting operational, managerial, and strategic decision making (Liu, 2010). But it is not sufficient to consider just the subjective nature of opinion for decision making (Buche, Chandak, & Zadgaonkar, 2013). Additionally, the written work aptitudes and selection of words by benefactors to a great extent rely on upon the proficiency of language and the demeanor of the author. There exist different kinds of opinions of users like regular, implicit, direct, indirect and comparative. The flexibility of expression and anonymity also accompanies a cost. Individuals with concealed plans effortlessly game the framework to give people the impression that they are independent members from the general population and post fake sentiments to promote or defame some targeted products, services, affiliations, or individuals without revealing their actual intentions, or the individual or affiliation that they are secretly working for. People with these intentions are popularly known as *opinion spammers* and their exercises are called *opinion spamming* (Abbasi, Chen, Thoms, & Fu, 2008). Moreover, online reviews are composed by the customers from their edge of interests and inclinations, they can be a mix of a positive and negative opinion and that may not necessarily help in categorizing reviews as positive or negative. For instance, consider the sentence "The Chinese dishes of this restaurant are not as good as their Thai dishes". Relative opinions like these are different in natural language processing. When a positive word "good" is negated like "not as good as", readers find it challenging to assimilate even how good the Thai dishes were, because this decides the taste of the Chinese dishes too. So while handling negation, it must be properly figured out that the presence of negation updates which part of the meaning expressed (Liu, 2012; Abbasi, France, Zhang, & Chen, 2011).

In today's web world, textual information which is available can be basically categorized into two broad categories, facts and opinions. Facts present the objective statements about the events and objects. The subjective statements that reflect the sentiments and perception of a person about an event or an object are called Opinions or sentiments. Extracting subjective information from text and determining the overall contextual polarity or opinion of the writer of the text is called Sentiment Analysis. According to Liu (2012), " Suppose given is an arrangement of judgemental text documents D in which sentiments or opinions related to a particular object are given, the role of sentiment analysis (also called opinion mining) is to find out those features and attributes of the object that have been commented on in each document d belonging to D and to determine the polarity of the comments (that is, whether the comments are positive, negative or neutral) ". Sentiment Analysis is technically very challenging but also practically very useful. For instance, for businesses it is always useful to know public or consumer opinions about their product and services so as to know the reasons of their profits or losses. Also, the customer who wants to buy a product would like to know the opinions about that product from the existing users.

This chapter aims to characterize the polarity of an opinion in a movie dataset comprising of movie reviews given by the users by adopting text classification approach. The MATLAB R2014a serial update 2 (version 8.3.0.532) classification tool is used to train a classifier for the purpose of data classification. In this chapter, k-Nearest neighbor (kNN) and Naive Bayes classifier is used and then comparisons have been made between the proposed method addressing the challenges faced and the method where challenges are not addressed on the basis of analysis of various evaluation measures like accuracy, precision, recall and Fscore. Besides introduction, this chapter throws light on need of Sentiment analysis, gives the statement of existing problem, lays down the criteria for categorization of various methods of Sentiment analysis, gives various applications of Sentiment analysis, surveys the previous researches done in the field of Sentiment analysis, discusses the challenges faced while analyzing sentiments, presents the proposed solutions and recommendations to the existing problems, depicts the results obtained, highlights the future scope of current research work and at last concludes the discussion.

Need of Sentiment Analysis

Social media has turned into a fundamental part of social life. It influences the convictions, values, and demeanors of individuals, and also their aims and practices. Social media, besides acting as a personal communication media, has emerged as a platform to impart feelings about items and services or even political and general occasions among its users. Moreover, it empowers governments and organizations to connect with individuals while enabling users to make informed decisions. Because of its widespread prevalence, a gigantic amount of user opinions or reviews are being produced and shared daily. Therefore, extracting information, key ideas, and thoughts from social media content is essential for generating knowledge and formulation of strategies, and hence the need for Sentiment Analysis.

Problem Statement

Methods used to analyze data in the past included surveys, interviews, questionnaires etc. But these traditional methods were time consuming, limited in scale and required more manpower. Analyzing the information manually for sentiments does not make sense, especially when the information is huge in volume and having various Internet slangs. Thus the concept of Sentiment Analysis or Opinion Mining came into being. Sentiment classification has gained a lot of attention in recent years (Pang, Lee, &

Vaithyanathan, 2002). The main aim of Sentiment analysis is to identify and extract opinions and attitudes from a given piece of text towards a particular subject (Pang, & Lee, 2008).

With time, a lot of approaches for Sentiment analysis came into existence. As an example, one method of Sentiment Analysis involved finding the sentiments by first searching for opinion words in the text and then on the basis of count of positive and negative words in the text, evaluated the final sentiment of text. But still these methods including the one just mentioned lagged behind in one way or the other. Some possible reasons include inefficiency to handle the challenges like presence of thwarted words in reviews, finding sentiments in reviews having occurrence of world knowledge words in them, subjectivity detection in sentiments, etc. So the authors have proposed a solution that will serve as a method of solving these problems faced in sentiment analysis. This chapter proposes a novel algorithm to handle all the aforementioned challenges while determining the overall sentiment of reviews and then compares various performance metrics of the proposed algorithm and the already existing method of Sentiment Analysis mentioned above in which these challenges are not handled.

The objective of this chapter is to recognize and classify sentiments expressed in a piece of text in movie reviews given by users, particularly so as to decide whether the writer's attitude towards a particular topic (or theme), product, etc. is positive, negative or neutral.

The scope of this chapter is to analyse the sentiments expressed by the users or the reviews given by users on movies. A particular movie review is scanned for the presence of positive, negative or neutral sentiment using the proposed algorithm. Moreover, different challenges are addressed while analyzing the sentiments. The ability to handle these challenges enables the proposed research method to analyze sentiments more accurately.

Criterion for Categorization of Different Methods of Sentiment Analysis

Different methods of Sentiment analysis can be categorized based on certain criterion or from different points of views. These include: technique used, view of text, level of detail of text analysis, rating level, etc.

1. **Technical Point of View:** Sentiment Analysis methods fall into four categories from a technical point of view: machine learning, lexicon-based, statistical and rule-based approaches. These are discussed below:
    a. **Machine Learning Approach:** The machine learning approach involves training a known dataset by using several learning algorithms so as to determine the sentiment in a given piece of text.
    b. **Lexicon-Based Approach:** In lexicon-based approach, semantic orientation of words or sentences is used for estimating the polarity of sentiments expressed by the users in a review. The "semantic orientation" can be thought of as a measure of subjectivity and opinion in text.
    c. **Rule-Based Approach:** In rule-based approach, opinion words are searched in a text and then classification is done on the basis of the number of positive and negative words. Different **rules** are being considered here for classification such as dictionary polarity, booster words, negation words, *idioms*, mixed opinions, emoticons etc.
    d. **Statistical Approach:** In statistical models, each review is represented as a blend of latent aspects and ratings. Aspects and their ratings are assumed to be represented by multinomial distributions and attempts are made to group head terms into aspects and sentiments into ratings.

2. **Global or Specific Point of View:** Distinctions can be made between methods which rate a review keeping in view the sentiment strength for different aspects of a product and methods which endeavor to rate a review on a global level. A large proportion of techniques that focus on global review classification consider just the polarity of reviews (positive/negative) and are dependent on machine learning techniques. But the techniques that perform a more detailed classification of reviews (e.g., three or five star ratings) utilize more linguistic features like intensification, negation, modality and discourse structure (Carrillo de Albornoz, Plaza, Gervás, & Díaz, 2011).

3. **Different Classes of Sentiment Analysis:** Sentiments of reviews can be categorized into three classes, that is, positive, negative and neutral sentiments (Bholane Savita, & Gore, 2016):

    a. **Positive Sentiments:** This alludes to positive state of mind of speaker or reviewer about the text. Happiness, joy, smile, etc. are the emotions reflected with positive sentiments. For example, in case of political reviews, presence of more positive reviews/sentiments about the politician indicate that people are happy with his work.

    b. **Negative Sentiments:** This alludes to negative state of mind of speaker or reviewer about the text. Sadness, jealousy, hate, etc. are the emotions reflected with negative sentiments. As an example, in case of political reviews, presence of more negative reviews/sentiments about the politician indicate that people are not happy with his work.

    c. **Neutral Sentiments:** Neutral sentiments reflect no emotions or opinion about the text. These are neither preferred nor neglected. In spite of the fact that this class suggests nothing, it plays a crucial role in distinguishing positive and negative classes in a better way.

4. **Levels of Sentiment Classification:** Based on levels of classification, there exist three classes of sentiments: phrase level, document level and aspect level.

    a. **Phrase Level Classification:** Two or more than two words constitute a Phrase. In Phrase level classification, sentiments are classified by taking whole phrase into consideration. Also called Sentence level or Word-level classification, it determines polarity of sentiments for each sentence of a review and even for each word of a sentence. Initially it decides if the phrase is neutral or polar; in case the phrase comes out to be polar, then it is categorized into positive and negative classes. Drawback of phrase level classification is that presence of refuted or negation words sometimes leads to inaccurate results.

    b. **Document Level Classification:** Document level classification intends to determine the polarity of sentiments for the entire review. A single theme or topic is taken into consideration to categorize the sentiments as positive, negative, or neutral. Drawback of document level classification is that it is not useful for comparison of two products having similar features.

    c. **Aspect Level Classification:** Aspect level classification deals with finding if the opinion expressed about a particular feature or aspect is positive, negative or neutral. An aspect can be thought of as some component of an entity. The opinion information obtained from this classification level is very fine grained and that can be helpful in various domains of sentiment analysis. In this classification, the overall opinion is related to the feature of the entity. An example of entity is Apple iPhone and aspect can be its battery, camera, screen etc.

Applications of Sentiment Analysis

Reputation of the product, which is derived from the opinion of others is an important information when consumers have to make a decision or a choice regarding a product or service. Sentiment analysis is a field of research that can be used to reveal this information about a product or service. Sentiment analysis finds its applications in the following:

1. Helping customers in the choice of products or services by providing recommendations based on the intelligence of the crowd. People usually get attracted to certain specific aspects while choosing a product or service. A single global rating could not help as it could be deceiving. Ratings on certain aspects of the product or a service can be estimated by reorganizing reviewer's opinions using Sentiment analysis.
2. Companies can enhance the aspects that are discovered unsuitable by the customers after knowing customer's opinion on their products or services. Also priority in importance of aspects for the customers can be determined.
3. Various other technologies incorporate Sentiment analysis as a component. One thought could be to bar the most subjective area of a document and hence enhance data mining in text analysis or proposing web advertisements for products or services according to opinion of viewers (and expelling the others).
4. Various potential outcomes are possible in the Human/Machine interface area if we can recognize what individuals think regarding a particular product or service or an event.
5. Sentiment analysis can be also used in business for competitive advantage. Analyzing how much positive or negative customer's reviews on a certain product are does not serve sufficient. Sentiment analysis can help businesses to analyse the reviews of their competitors' products or services and hence provides them the opportunity to perk up their performance.
6. Sentiment analysis can be used in politics as well. Campaign managers are able to monitor the opinion of different voters on different issues and can be used to find out how voters relate to the speeches and actions of the candidates running for various positions in elections.

Background

This section exemplifies the related works in the field of sentiment analysis done so far to determine the polarity of sentiments in texts by employing various methods of text mining like text classification, text clustering and natural language processing. Pang, Lee, & Vaithyanathan (2002) employed three machine learning techniques-Naive Bayes, Maximum entropy classification and Support vector Machine (SVM) on the data of movie reviews; and identified various factors that make sentiment classification more complex as compared to topic based categorization. Turney (2002) classified reviews of four different domains (reviews of automobiles, books, movies and travel destinations) by designing an unsupervised learning algorithm. A data-driven method for automatically learning the content selection rules from a corpus and its associated database was introduced by Barzilay and Lapata (2005) for a concept-to-text generation system in which a content selection component was utilized for deciding which information should be produced as output by a natural language generation system. Emotional estimations for natural-language texts was presented by Ma, Prendinger, & Ishizuka (2005) in a method which was based on a keyword spotting technique. By dividing a text into words, this system estimates emotions for each of these words and performs a sentence-level processing technique. A new method was proposed by Wilson, Wiebe, & Hoffmann (2005) for analyzing the sentiments of phrases that worked in two stages: firstly, it checks for the presence of facts or sentiments in an expression and then elucidates the polarity of sentiments present in that expression.

The foundation of the research area of sentiment classification was laid down by the work of Ortony, Clore, & Foss (1987). They developed a taxonomy of affective lexicon and paid special attention to isolate the terms having an emotional connotation. A keyword based approach was introduced by Rimon (2005) for classifying sentiments. This approach used terms, mainly adjectives (e.g. awesome, awful) as sentiment indicators. Sources such as WordNet or machine learning algorithms that infer the best indicators from tagged samples in the domain of interest, can be used to manually prepare and semi automatically compose the list of indicators. To perform document wise sentiment polarity classification, Matsumoto, Takamura, & Okumura (2005) used syntactic relations between words in sentences. Frequent word sub-sequences and dependency sub-trees were extracted from sentences in a document dataset by using text mining techniques, which were then used as features of support vector machines. Dave, Lawrence, & Pennock (2003) examined several kinds of products and proposed a method that automatically distinguished positive and negative reviews on these products. Information retrieval techniques for feature extraction and scoring are drawn by the classifier used, and various metrics results and heuristics change as per the testing situation. Unlike the research of Pang, Lee, & Vaithyanathan (2002), this method achieved best accuracy rate by using word bigram-based classifier on the dataset. From the results, they concluded that the unigram-based model does not always produce best results and that data or information used determines the best settings of the classifier. Sentiment Analysis can be thought of as the process in which subjective information is identified in source materials (Pang, & Lee, 2008; Liu, 2012).

A comparative study on sentimental analysis and its application in recommendation system was provided by Chidananda, Sagnika, & Sahoo (2017). The study of various methods for predicting the stock market was given by Jadhav and Wakode (2017) by using the sentiment score of financial news on Twitter data.

Deng, Sinha, & Zhao (2017) proposed domain-dependent lexicons to deal with the fact that some words can reveal different sentiments, positive or negative, on the basis of the domain being used. Developments in the kinds and uses of online networking sites such as forums, blogs, etc. have enabled users to impart their insights on different domains (Moslmi, Albared, Al-Shabi, Omar, & Abdullah, 2017). Aydogan and Akcayol (2016), after carrying out an exhaustive study on Sentiment analysis employing different Machine learning algorithms found that SVM and Naïve Bayes have higher estimation capability and hence are most commonly used. A survey presented by Brindha, Prabha, & Sukumaran (2016) on different classification approaches (KNN, Naive Bayes, SVM, Decision Tree and Regression) revealed that almost all classification approaches were suited to the characteristics of text data. They further inferred that better quality of text results and exact information can be obtained in addition to reduced access time by further study on classification development.

The performance of Sentiment analysis is heavily dependent on how effectively a training set is defined. For accurate analysis of text, quality of dataset plays an important part. Likewise, syntax analysis of sentence helps in increasing accuracy and means of the results (Hussein, 2016). Gathering people's sentiments, opinions, emotions and attitudes, etc. regarding certain products, topics, individuals, associations and services is referred to as Sentiment Analysis (Pradhan, Vala, & Balani, 2016). Pagolu, Challa, Panda, & Majhi (2016) examined sentiments of people in tweets by employing two different textual representations, namely, Word2vec and N-gram. Moreover, relationship between stock market movement of company and sentiments in tweets was analyzed by applying Sentiment analysis and various machine learning approaches like logistic regression, SMO and Random Forest to extracted tweets. The emotions identified in the text were used by Rangel and Rosso (2016) for author profiling, especially detecting the age and gender of author. The opinions extracted from user reviews are important not only for users but also for companies in the sense that this information can help users in making decisions regarding purchasing different products and hence this forms the basis for enhancing the quality of services and products offered by various companies (Zarate, García, Martínez, & Palacios, 2016).

Positive and negative sentiments of cancer patients were detected by a tool, namely SentiHealth (SCH-pt), developed by (Rodrigues, Dores, Camilo-Junior, & Rosa, 2016) in Portuguese language. A method for detecting the sentiment of Twitter and DailyStrength post was proposed by Korkontzelos, Nikfarjam, Shardlow, Sarker, Ananiadou, & Gonzalez (2016).

Major tasks of Sentiment Analysis include:

1. Categorization of textual documents into positive and negative polarity classes, (Dave et al., 2003; Kim, & Hovy, 2004);
2. Identification of textual topics and the opinions associated with them (Wang, Lu, & Zhai, 2010; Jo, & Oh, 2011); and
3. Summarization of opinions (Hu, & Liu, 2004; Ku, Liang, & Chen, 2006).

MAIN FOCUS OF THE CHAPTER

Challenges in Sentiment Analysis

Opinion mining, unlike traditional text mining which concentrates on analysis of facts, deals with attitudes (Pang, Lee, & Vaithyanathan, 2002). Categorization of sentiments, sentiment classification based on features and summarization of opinions are the fundamental fields of research. Analysis of the opinions on a certain object comes under the process of Sentiment categorization. Feature based classification is concerned with the process of analyzing and classifying based on the features of a particular object. Opinion summarizing deals with mining only the features of the product for which customers have expressed their opinions, and this feature makes it unique from the classic text summarizing where a subset of a review is considered and some of the original statements are rewritten to catch the fundamental idea.

Some challenges in analyzing sentiments in reviews include:

1. **Implicit Sentiment and Sarcasm:** At times, an implicit sentiment may be incorporated in a sentence, that is, a sentence may not have presence of opinion deciding keywords but still an opinion may be inferred from it. Consider the following illustration.

I bought shirt a week ago, and it became fade after one wash.

The above sentence is a negative one although there is no occurrence of any negative sentiment bearing words in it. Thus what is more important in Sentiment analysis is identifying semantics than detecting syntax.

2. **Thwarted Expectations:** Sometimes the author intentionally sets up context just to invalidate it towards the end. Consider the following example:

I decided to watch movie after I heard claims that it is best film, the actors and the supporting cast is good as well. However, it can't hold up.

Despite the fact that the above sentence contains more positive words, it is considered to be a negative sentence on account of the pivotal last sentence.

3. **World Knowledge:** Sometimes the text contains another entity to refer to one entity. In that case, the knowledge of the entity which is used to refer another is required to identify the sentiment. For detecting sentiments, world knowledge needs to be included in the system. Consider the following example:

She is as beautiful as Snow White.

Here, to identify the sentiment orientation of the text, one has to know about 'Snow White'. Consider another example:

He is a Doctor Zhivago.

Although this sentence delineates a positive sentiment, but one still needs to know about Doctor Zhivago to find out the correct sentiment.

4. **Subjectivity Detection:** Subjectivity classification aims to find if a review sentence is opinionated or non-opinionated (subjective or objective), usually in the presence of an opinion expression in a sentence. A sentence is considered an objective sentence if it has some factual information and is considered subjective if it expresses personal feelings, views, emotions, or beliefs. Subjectivity detection aims at enhancing the performance of the system by filtering out the impact of subjective words on the overall sentiment. But this is not an easy task to do.

Consider the following examples:

I hate drama movies.

I hate the movie "I love stories".

In the former example, an objective fact is presented whereas in the latter example opinion about a particular movie is depicted.

5. **Grammar and Spellings:** Users tend to commit a ton of mistakes in the semantics of the language and even the spellings of words because of being too causal when posting online. This can be handled generally by checking for them in the pre-processing stage.
6. **Trustworthiness:** The perspectives of various clients on different subjects is the most imperative property of social information, yet there are many fake accounts being made that give fake perspectives and reviews to either push or draw an entity on the stage. This poses a great challenge during analyzing sentiments.

7. **Language:** Another challenge that emerges while analyzing the sentiments is the flexibility that social media sites provide its users for posting reviews in different languages. This makes the task of sentiment analysis a lot more difficult. This problem can be handled by either using translation mechanisms or constructing different engines for dealing with different languages.

Some of these challenges like presence of thwarted words in reviews, occurrence of world knowledge words and subjectivity detection in reviews have been addressed in this chapter.

SOLUTIONS AND RECOMMENDATIONS

This section describes the approach that the authors have proposed for analyzing the sentiments of online movie reviews as well as presenting solutions to tackle the various challenges faced in Sentiment analysis.

Dataset

The dataset used in this chapter for analysing sentiments is Kaggle movie review corpora, which contains reviews given by the users about movies. The proposed sentiment analysis method is then employed for further polarizing these reviews. This dataset contains 156060 entries of users' reviews about movies and is available at https://www.kaggle.com/c/sentiment-analysis-on-movie-reviews/data ("Sentiment Analysis on Movie Reviews | Kaggle", 2015).

Pseudo-Code

8. **Input:** Movie Review dataset.
9. **Output:** Final sentiment/polarity of a normal review as well as a review having presence of thwarted words, world knowledge words and subjective words.
10. **Pre-Processing:**
    a. **Sub-Phrase Removal:** [*Uid,pos*]=*unique*(*sentence id*); where *Uid* and *pos* denote id and position of unique phrases found using *unique*() respectively. Thus only unique phrases are selected, thereby eliminating sub-phrases.
    b. **Conversion to Lower-Case:** *lower*(*phrase*); where *lower*() function is used to convert the *phrase* written in any case to lowercase.
11. **Top n Opinion Words Selection:** Opinion words are selected based on their contribution to the overall sentiment of phrases.
12. **Feature Extraction:**
    a. **Frequency (Count) of Opinion Words:**
        Check for the presence of opinion words in a review phrase
        Evaluate count of positive opinion words (finalcountpos)
        Evaluate count of negative opinion words (finalcountneg)
if finalcountpos> finalcountneg

$$finalsentiment = \left(\frac{finalcountpos}{finalcountpos + finalcountneg}\right) else\ if\ finalcountneg > finalcountpos$$

$$finalsentiment = -\left(\frac{finalcountneg}{finalcountpos + finalcountneg}\right) else$$

final sentiment = neutral feature_1 = [final count pos; final count neg; final sentiment]

Thwarted Words:

Check for the presence or absence of thwarted words in a review phrase
Evaluate count of presence of thwarted words (finalcount_presence)
Evaluate count of absence of thwarted words (finalcount_absence)
if finalcount_presence > finalcount_absence

$$finalsentiment = -\left(\frac{finalcount\_presence}{finalcount\_presence + finalcount\_absence}\right) else$$

final sentiment = neutral feature_2 = [final count_presence; final count_absence; final sentiment]

World knowledge:

Check for the presence or absence of world knowledge words in a review phrase
Evaluate count of presence of world knowledge words (finalcount_presence)
Evaluate count of absence of world knowledge words (finalcount_absence)
if finalcount_presence > finalcount_absence
Check weight of world knowledge word (world_weight)
if world_weight == -1

$$finalsentiment = -\left(\frac{finalcount\_presence}{finalcount\_presence + finalcount\_absence}\right) if\ world\_weight == 1$$

$$finalsentiment = \left(\frac{finalcount\_presence}{finalcount\_presence + finalcount\_absence}\right) else$$

final sentiment = neutral feature_3 = [final count_presence; final count_absence; final sentiment]

Subjectivity Detection:

Check for the presence of subjective words in a review phrase
if subjective word is present
Remove subjective word from phrase
Find count of positive opinion words (finalcount_pos), count of negative opinion words (finalcount_neg)
    and final sentiment (finalsentiment) as found in feature_1
else
Find count of positive opinion words (finalcount_pos), count of negative opinion words (finalcount_neg)
    and final sentiment (finalsentiment) as found in feature_1

Feature_4 = [final count_pos; final count_neg; final sentiment]

Thus,

Overall_feature = [feature_1; feature_2; feature_3; feature_4].

This *Overal_feature* feature set is used for training the classifier.

13. **Classification:** k Nearest Neighbor (kNN) and Naive Bayes classifiers are used to classify the sentiments and to evaluate various performance metrics of classification.

Detailed Methodology

An outline of the steps and techniques followed for sentiment analysis are depicted in Figure 1.

Figure 1. Proposed framework for sentiment analysis

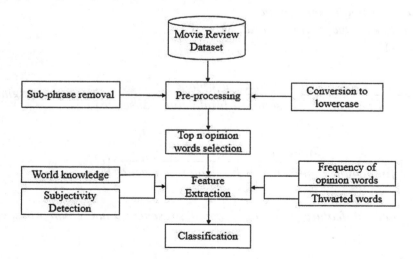

At first movie reviews dataset files are read thoroughly, afterwards the further process begins as follows:

14. **Pre-Processing:** Pre-processing is a process where undesirable data is removed from the whole dataset, thereby preparing desired data for classification. Preprocessing is exercised to reduce noise in text, which further helps the classifier to improve its performance, and accelerating classification process, thus aiding in analyzing sentiments in real time. Some pre-processing methods employed are:

    a. **Sub-Phrase Removal:** The dataset from Kaggle movie review corpora being used here consists of phrases as well as the sub-phrases of movie reviews. These sub-phrases are of no use in analyzing sentiments since the polarity of opinion words that occur in sub-phrases are already considered in the original phrase. Hence removal of sub-phrases should be done to minimize the overhead for estimating the polarity of opinion words over and over again. A dataset containing only original phrases is thus obtained for analysis of sentiments.

    b. **Conversion to Lowercase:** This is done to avoid distinction between words simply on case and to ensure proper matching of words. Figure 2 and 3 show respectively the movie review dataset containing sub-phrases and the dataset with sub-phrases removed.

15. **Top *n* Opinion Words Selection:** After pre-processing, the authors choose from the dataset opinion words, which contribute to the overall sentiment of a phrase. Weights are assigned to these selected words as per their polarity. These frequent words amount to the interesting features that need to be analysed and further leads to more accurate results while polarizing sentiments of the whole phrase.

Figure 2. Dataset containing sub-phrases

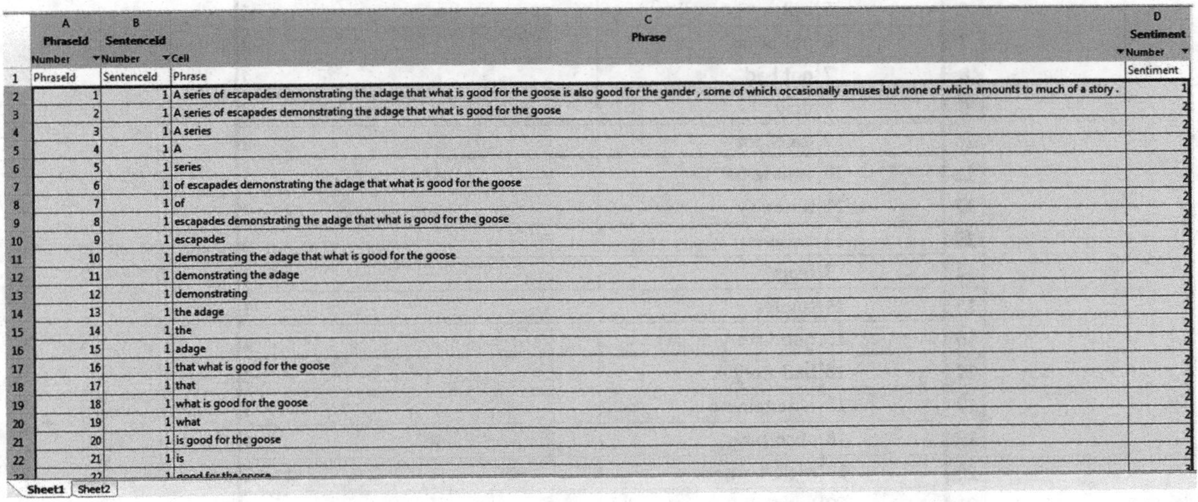

Figure 3. Dataset with sub-phrases removed

	1
1	'''A series of escapades demonstrating the adage that what is good for the goose is also good for the gander , some of which occ...
2	'This quiet , introspective and entertaining independent is worth seeking .'
3	'Even fans of Ismail Merchant ''s work , I suspect , would have a hard time sitting through this one .'
4	'''A positively thrilling combination of ethnography and all the intrigue , betrayal , deceit and murder of a Shakespearean tragedy...
5	'Aggressive self-glorification and a manipulative whitewash .'
6	'A comedy-drama of nearly epic proportions rooted in a sincere performance by the title character undergoing midlife crisis .'
7	'Narratively , Trouble Every Day is a plodding mess .'
8	'The Importance of Being Earnest , so thick with wit it plays like a reading from Bartlett ''s Familiar Quotations'
9	'But it does n''t leave you with much .'
10	'You could hate it for the same reason .'
11	'There ''s little to recommend Snow Dogs , unless one considers cliched dialogue and perverse escapism a source of high hilarity .'
12	'''Kung Pow is Oedekerk ''s realization of his childhood dream to be in a martial-arts flick , and proves that sometimes the dream...

Figure 4. Selected opinion words and their weights

	A SequenceNo Number	B FeaturesWords Cell	C Weight0neutral1pos1neg Number
1	Sequence ...	Features/Words	Weight(0-neutral,1-pos,-1-neg)
2	1	lunatic	-1
3	2	good	1
4	3	bad	-1
5	4	sanguine	1
6	5	evil	-1
7	6	not good	-1
8	7	not bad	1
9	8	ugly	-1
10	9	excellent	1
11	10	wonderful	1
12	11	furiously	-1
13	12	amuses	1
14	13	fears	-1
15	14	foibles	-1
16	15	good story	1
17	16	bad story	-1
18	17	entertaining	1
19	18	absorbing	1
20	19	melodramatic	-1
21	20	heartfelt	1
22	21	proud	1
23	22	betrayal	-1

Sheet1 | Sheet2 | Sheet3 | Sheet4 | Sheet5

Figure 4 shows the selected opinion words and their corresponding weights.

16. **Feature Extraction:** Feature extraction is the process of generating set of features or appropriate characteristics of target object by transforming input data. It finds its applications in decreasing the dimensions of the feature space (Kummer, & Savoy, 2012), that is, feature extraction techniques reduce a high dimensional input to a lower dimension while preserving the desired characteristics and removing the unwanted ones. Decreased feature space imply less amount of data to be investigated, thus making the classifiers more effective as well as helping to identify relevant features to be considered in classification process. Some of the features extracted from the movie dataset are:

   a. **Frequency (Count) of Occurrence of Opinion Words:** The basic approach of statistical feature extraction is to use recurring words in the corpus as feature values. Frequency of occurrence of each of top *n* selected opinion words is counted for each review phrase of the corpora; an overall positive and negative score for the phrase text is counted and hence the overall sentiment of the phrase is calculated. If the reviews contain more positive than negative terms, it is assumed as positive review; if the reviews contain more negative than positive terms, it is assumed as negative review; otherwise it is neutral. The sentiment thus obtained is counted as first feature for the proposed algorithm. Frequency (count of occurrence) of positive opinion words, negative opinion words and hence the overall sentiment is illustrated in Figure 5.

Figure 5. Frequency (count) of opinion words

Fields	📼	phrase	⊞ finalcountpos	⊞ finalcountneg	⊞ finalsentiment
1		'A series of escapades demonstrating the adage that what is good for the goose is also good for the gander , some of which ...	3	0	1
2		'This quiet , introspective and entertaining independent is worth seeking .'	2	0	1
3		'Even fans of Ismail Merchant "s work , I suspect , would have a hard time sitting through this one .'	0	0	2
4		'A positively thrilling combination of ethnography and all the intrigue , betrayal , deceit and murder of a Shakespearean trag...	1	2	-0.6667
5		'Aggressive self-glorification and a manipulative whitewash .'	0	0	2
6		'A comedy-drama of nearly epic proportions rooted in a sincere performance by the title character undergoing midlife crisis .'	2	0	1
7		'Narratively , Trouble Every Day is a plodding mess .'	0	0	2
8		'The Importance of Being Earnest , so thick with wit it plays like a reading from Bartlett "s Familiar Quotations'	5	0	1
9		'But it does "t leave you with much .'	1	0	1
10		'You could hate it for the same reason .'	0	1	-1
11		'There "s little to recommend Snow Dogs , unless one considers cliched dialogue and perverse escapism a source of high hil...	1	2	-0.6667
12		'Kung Pow is Oedekerk "s realization of his childhood dream to be in a martial-arts flick , and proves that sometimes the dre...	0	0	2

   b. **Thwarted Words:** This is one of the challenges of Sentiment Analysis that has been addressed in this chapter. Sometimes the user intentionally sets up context just to invalidate it towards the end. Consider the following example*: I decided to watch movie after I heard claims that it is best film, the actors and the supporting cast is good as well. However, it can't hold up.* Despite the fact that the above sentence contains more positive words, it is considered to be a negative sentence on account of the pivotal last sentence. Thus the impact of presence of thwarted words on overall sentiment of review phrases can be computed as:

   i. **Step 1:** Create a knowledge base of thwarted words and assign weight to each thwarted word according to its polarity.

   ii. **Step 2:** Check for the presence of thwarted words in reviews.

   iii.   **Step 3:** On the occurrence of a thwarted word, compute its corresponding weight from the knowledge base.

   iv.   **Step 4:** Update the polarity (sentiment) of review depending on the polarity of thwarted word to get the final sentiment of review.

   v.   **Step 5:** The sentiment thus obtained becomes another feature for the proposed algorithm.

Figure 6 and 7 shows the sentiments of movie review dataset without handling the presence of thwarted word challenge (already existing method) and with challenge handled (proposed method) respectively.

Figure 6. Sentiment of thwarted word feature before addressing challenge

Fields	phrase	finalcountpos	finalcountneg	finalsentiment
1749	'The way the roundelay of partners functions , and the interplay within partnerships and among partnerships and the general air of Gator-bashi...	1	0	1
1750	'But while the highly predictable narrative falls short , Treasure Planet is truly gorgeous to behold .'	1	0	1
1751	'Directed with purpose and finesse by England "s Roger Mitchell , who handily makes the move from pleasing , relatively lightweight commerci...	2	0	1
1752	'I hate the movie "I love stories"'	1	1	2
1753	'I like the movie "I hate stories"'	1	1	2
1754	'I decided to watch movie after I heard claims that it is best film, the actors and the supporting cast is good as well. However, it can't hold up.'	2	0	1
1755	'He is a Doctor Zhivago. '	0	0	2
1756	'The story was monstrous. '	0	0	2

Figure 7. Sentiment of thwarted word feature after addressing challenge

Fields	phrase	finalcount_presence	finalcount_absence	finalsentiment
1748	'A muddle splashed with bloody beauty as vivid as any Scorsese has ever given us .'	0	0	2
1749	'The way the roundelay of partners functions , and the interplay within partnerships and among partnerships and the general air of Gator-bas...	0	0	2
1750	'But while the highly predictable narrative falls short , Treasure Planet is truly gorgeous to behold .'	1	0	-1
1751	'Directed with purpose and finesse by England "s Roger Mitchell , who handily makes the move from pleasing , relatively lightweight comme...	1	0	-1
1752	'I hate the movie "I love stories"'	0	0	2
1753	'I like the movie "I hate stories"'	0	0	2
1754	'I decided to watch movie after I heard claims that it is best film, the actors and the supporting cast is good as well. However, it can't hold up.'	1	0	-1
1755	'He is a Doctor Zhivago. '	0	0	2
1756	'The story was monstrous. '	0	0	2

   c.   **World Knowledge:** Another challenge of Sentiment Analysis handled in this chapter is world knowledge. Sometimes the text contains another entity to refer to one entity. In that case, the knowledge of the entity which is used to refer another is required to identify the sentiment. For detecting sentiments, world knowledge needs to be included in the system. Consider the following example:

She is as beautiful as Snow White.

Here, to identify the sentiment orientation of the text, one has to know about 'Snow White'. Consider another example:

He is a Doctor Zhivago.

Although this sentence delineates a positive sentiment, but one still needs to know about Doctor Zhivago to find out the correct sentiment.

This challenge is handled as:

i.   **Step 1:** Create a knowledge base of world knowledge words and assign weight to each world knowledge word according to its polarity.

ii. **Step 2:** Check for the presence of world knowledge words in reviews.

iii. **Step 3:** On the occurrence of a world knowledge word, check its corresponding weight from the knowledge base.

iv. **Step 4:** Update the polarity (sentiment) of the review depending on the polarity of the world knowledge word.

v.   **Step 5:** The sentiment thus obtained becomes another feature for the algorithm.

Figure 8 and 9 shows the sentiments of movie review dataset without handling the World knowledge challenge (already existing method) and with challenge handled (proposed method) respectively.

Figure 8. Sentiment of world knowledge feature before addressing challenge

Fields	phrase	finalcountpos	finalcountneg	finalsentiment
1749	'The way the roundelay of partners functions , and the interplay within partnerships and among partnerships and the general air of Gator-bashi...	1	0	1
1750	'But while the highly predictable narrative falls short , Treasure Planet is truly gorgeous to behold .'	1	0	1
1751	'Directed with purpose and finesse by England ''s Roger Mitchell , who handily makes the move from pleasing , relatively lightweight commerci...	2	0	1
1752	'I hate the movie "I love stories"'	1	1	2
1753	'I like the movie "I hate stories"'	1	1	2
1754	'I decided to watch movie after I heard claims that it is best film, the actors and the supporting cast is good as well. However, it can't hold up.'	2	0	1
1755	'He is a Doctor Zhivago. '	0	0	2
1756	'The story was monstrous. '	0	0	2

Figure 9. Sentiment of world knowledge feature after addressing challenge

Fields	phrase	finalcount_presence	finalcount_absence	finalsentiment
1748	'A muddle splashed with bloody beauty ...	0	0	2
1749	'The way the roundelay of partners funct...	0	0	2
1750	'But while the highly predictable narrativ...	0	0	2
1751	'Directed with purpose and finesse by En...	0	0	2
1752	'I hate the movie "I love stories"'	0	0	2
1753	'I like the movie "I hate stories"'	0	0	2
1754	'I decided to watch movie after I heard cl...	0	0	2
1755	'He is a Doctor Zhivago. '	1	0	1
1756	'The story was monstrous. '	0	0	2

d.   **Subjectivity Detection:** Next challenge addressed is Subjectivity detection in sentiments. Subjectivity classification aims to find if a review sentence is opinionated or non-opinionated (subjective or objective), usually in the presence of an opinion expression in a sentence. A sentence is considered an objective sentence if it has some factual information and is considered subjective if it expresses personal feelings, views, emotions, or beliefs. Subjectivity detection aims at enhancing the performance of the system by filtering out the impact of subjective words on the overall sentiment. But this is not an easy task to do.

Consider the following examples:

I hate drama movies.

I hate the movie "I love stories".

I like the movie "I hate stories".

In the former example, an objective fact is presented whereas in the latter examples, opinion about a particular movie is depicted.

This challenge is addressed as:

    i.   **Step 1:** Create a knowledge base of subjectivity words.

    ii.   **Step 2:** Check for the presence of subjective words in a review.

    iii.   **Step 3:** On the occurrence of a subjective word, the effect of subjective word in the review is discarded by removing it from the review phrase.

    iv.   **Step 4:** Polarity (sentiment) of the updated review phrase is calculated based on the frequency (count) of positive or negative words in the phrase.

    v.   **Step 5:** The sentiment thus obtained becomes another feature for the algorithm.

Figure 10 and 11 shows the sentiments of movie review dataset without handling the Subjectivity detection challenge (already existing method) and with challenge handled (proposed method) respectively.

Figure 10. Sentiment of subjectivity detection feature before addressing challenge

Fields	⊡ phrase	⊞ finalcountpos	⊞ finalcountneg	⊞ finalsentiment
1749	'The way the roundelay of partners functions , and the interplay within partnerships and among partnerships and the general air of Gator-bashi...	1	0	1
1750	'But while the highly predictable narrative falls short , Treasure Planet is truly gorgeous to behold .'	1	0	1
1751	'Directed with purpose and finesse by England ''s Roger Mitchell, who handily makes the move from pleasing , relatively lightweight commerci...	2	0	1
1752	'I hate the movie "I love stories"'	1	1	2
1753	'I like the movie "I hate stories"'	1	1	2
1754	'I decided to watch movie after I heard claims that it is best film, the actors and the supporting cast is good as well. However, it can't hold up.'	2	0	1
1755	'He is a Doctor Zhivago. '	0	0	2
1756	'The story was monstrous. '	0	0	2

Figure 11. Sentiment of subjectivity detection feature after addressing challenge

Fields	⊡ phrase	⊞ finalcount_pos	⊞ finalcount_neg	⊞ finalsentiment
1748	'A muddle splashed with bloody beauty as vivid as any Scors...	1	0	1
1749	'The way the roundelay of partners functions , and the interpl...	1	0	1
1750	'But while the highly predictable narrative falls short , Treasur...	1	0	1
1751	'Directed with purpose and finesse by England ''s Roger Mitc...	2	0	1
1752	'I hate the movie "I love stories"'	0	1	-1
1753	'I like the movie "I hate stories"'	1	0	1
1754	'I decided to watch movie after I heard claims that it is best fil...	2	0	1
1755	'He is a Doctor Zhivago. '	0	0	2
1756	'The story was monstrous. '	0	0	2

Thus, to find the overall sentiment of an object (here review phrases), first the sentiment words (or opinion words) about the features of the said object are identified. Various features are extracted and then assigned weight on the basis of their polarity. Finally, the polarity weights of all the features of the object are aggregated in a feature set *overall_feature* in order to get the overall opinion about the given object. This *overall_feature* feature set is used for training the classifier.

17. **Classification:** Classification is the process of assigning documents to suitable categories. Here, the movie reviews are assigned to suitable pre-defined classes/categories on the basis of their overall sentiment. Classifiers like kNN, SVM, Naive Bayes, Logistic Regression, Stochastic Gradient Descent (SGD), Random Forest and many more can be used for this purpose. In this chapter, the authors have used two supervised machine learning models to validate the results for both the methods of Sentiment Analysis – one with challenges unhandled and the other with challenges handled (proposed method). These models are Naive Bayes classifier and k Nearest Neighbor classifier.

a. **Naive Bayes Classifier:** Naive Bayes classifier is based on a probabilistic learning method and the assumption that terms occur independently of each other. The foundation Naive Bayesian was built so as to include unlabelled data. The undertaking of learning of a generative model is to appraise the parameters using labelled training data only. Using estimated parameters, the algorithm classifies new documents by ascertaining the given document belongs to which generated class. The working of Naive Bayes classifier (Govindarajan, & M., 2013) is as follows:

i. **Step 1:** Consider a training set of samples having k classes $C_1, C_2, ..., C_k$ ith the label of each class being T. An n-dimensional vector, $X = \{x_1, x_2, ..., x_n\}$, which represents n measured values of the n attributes, $A_1, A_2, ..., A_n$ respectively is associated with every sample.

ii. **Step 2:** The given sample X is classified by the classifier in such a way that it belongs to the highest posterior probability containing class. This implies X is anticipated to be grouped to the class C_i if and only if $P(C_i|X) > P(C_j|X)$ for $1 \leq j \leq m$, $j \neq i$. Thus the class that maximizes $P(C_i|X)$ is found; this maximized value of $P(C_i|X)$ for class C_i is referred to as maximum posterior hypothesis.

In Naive Bayes technique, the basic idea to find the probabilities of categories given a text document by using the joint probabilities of words and categories. It is based on the assumption of word independence. In case of movie reviews, Naive Bayes classifier attempts to evaluate the probability of a document (review) being positive or negative, given its contents.

Bayes theorem for conditional probability is used as the initial point in this classifier, stating that, for a given data point x and class C.

$$P(C \,/\, x) = \frac{P(x \,/\, C).P(C)}{P(x)}$$

Now assuming that the probability of each of the attributes of a data point $x = \{x_1, x_2, ..., x_j\}$, occurring in a given class is independent, we can estimate the probability of x as follows:

$$P(C / x) = P(C)\Pi P(x_j / C)$$

Thus, the conditional probabilities of each attributes occurring on the predicted classes are required to be estimated from the training data set to train a Naive Bayes classifier.

b. **k Nearest Neighbor (kNN) Classifier:** k Nearest Neighbor (kNN) is the simplest and the oldest classifier that can be employed for classifying text (Cover, & Hart, 1967). It is an interpretation of example-based method in which the decision on how to generalize beyond the training data is deferred as long as a new query instance comes across (Sebastiani, 2002). The principle on which kNN classifier works is that the closest points (reviews) in space, found by calculating a similarity measure between test review and each neighbor, are grouped to the same class (Patel, & Mistry, 2015). A reasonable distance or similarity measure, for example, Euclidean distance is selected for finding k-nearest neighbors of a new instance that needs to be classified. In other words, the k-Nearest Neighbor algorithm classifies a new occurrence by checking for its k closest instances called neighbors in the data set, and predicting the class of a new instance (Kalaivani, & Shunmuganathan, 2013) depending on classes that belong to the majority of its k neighbors.

Reasons for Choosing kNN and Naive Bayes Classifiers Over Random Forest, SGD and Logistic Regression:

i. KNN and Naive Bayes results are more interpretable than Logistic Regression and Random Forests.
ii. KNN is easier to explain than Logistic Regression, Naive Bayes is somewhat easier but Random Forests are very difficult to explain/interpret (since they are black boxes).
iii. Training speed of KNN and Naive Bayes is fast as compared to Random Forests. Whereas Logistic Regression has an average training speed.
iv. A Naive Bayes converges quicker than discriminative models like Logistic Regression, if conditional independence assumption holds, and hence minimum training data is required.
v. The speed at which Naïve Bayes perform prediction is fast as compared to Random Forests (owing to large number of trees).
vi. Lesser amount of parameter tuning is required for KNN than Random Forests.
vii. Naive Bayes performs well even with small number of observations as compared to Random Forests.
viii. Though both Naive Bayes and Random Forests perform well in separating noise from sound, Random Forests fail if noise ratio is very high. Logistic Regression has no such ability.
ix. KNN gives calibrated probabilities of class membership whereas Random Forests may have some possibility.
x. A large number of hyper parameters like the regularization parameter and a number of iterations are required in SGD.
xi. SGD is sensitive to feature scaling.
xii. Random Forests and Logistic Regression are highly biased.

c. **Cross Validation:** The predictive evaluation of the classifier is done by using a technique called Cross validation in which the original dataset is partitioned into a training set to train the model and a test set to access it. A 10-fold cross validation have been used with a sample size of 156060 and the ratio of training data to testing data being 80/20.

EXPERIMENTAL SETUP

This research work has been implemented in MATLAB R2014a serial update 2 (version 8.3.0.532).

Evaluation Criteria

Various standard evaluation measures have been used in this chapter to calculate the effectiveness of proposed method such as accuracy, precision, recall and Fscore. These metrics were estimated by making use of features like True Positive (t_p), True Negative (t_n), False Positive (f_p), and False Negative (f_n) (Khan, Baharudin, & Khan, 2013) defined as:

- **True Positive (t_p):** A test result is said to be true positive if it detects the condition when the condition is actually present. In other words, all extracted features that correctly match with the features annotated positive manually are known as true positive (t_p) features.
- **True Negative (t_n):** A test result is said to be true negative if it does not detect the condition when the condition is absent. In other words, all non-positive features that the proposed method does not extract are called true negative (t_n) features.
- **False Positive (f_p):** A test result can be called as false positive if it detects the condition when actually the condition is absent. In other words, all non-positive features that the proposed method includes in positive features are known as false positive (f_p) features.
- **False Negative (f_n):** A test result can be called as false negative if it does not detect the condition when actually the condition is present. In other words, all positive features that the proposed method includes in non-positive features are called false negative (f_n) features.

These features are shown in Table 1.

Table 1. Various features for estimating evaluation measures of classification (Owais, Nafis, & Khanna, 2015)

Predicted Class (Observation)	Actual Class (Expectation)	
	Present	Absent
Positive	True Positive(t_p)	False Positive(f_p)
Negative	False Negative(f_n)	True Negative(t_n)

Results

The results of various performance metrics (parameters) of classification using Naive Bayes and kNN classifiers, of the method of Sentiment analysis without addressing the challenges like presence of Thwarted words, World knowledge and Subjectivity detection in sentiments and the novel proposed method of Sentiment analysis with all these challenges addressed, are given below:

18. **Accuracy:** Accuracy is a parameter of test that describes the proportion of true results (both true positives and true negatives) present in the total population. It can be used to estimate the efficiency of the framework employed and is defined as:

$$Accuracy = \frac{t_p + t_n}{t_p + f_p + t_n + f_n}$$

Comparison between accuracy in results of the two methods is shown in Figure 12 and 13.

Figure 12. Accuracy without challenges addressed

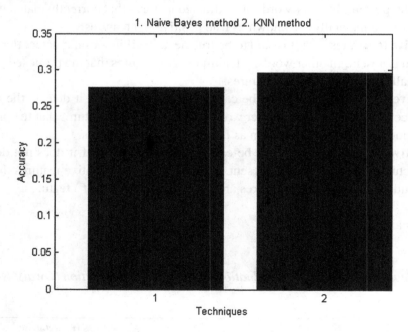

19. **Precision:** Precision is a parameter of test that represents the ratio of true positives to all the positive results (both true positives and false positives) present in the total population. The exactness of a classifier can be measured by this parameter and is defined as:

$$Precision = \frac{t_p}{t_p + f_p}$$

Figure 13. Accuracy with challenges addressed

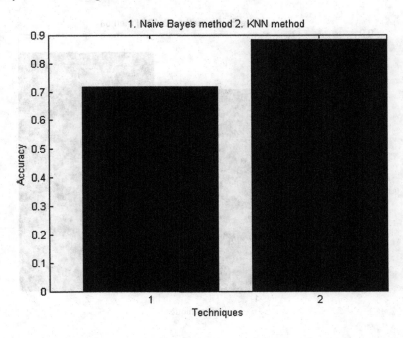

Precision in results given by the two methods is depicted in Figure 14 and 15.

Figure 14. Precision without challenges addressed

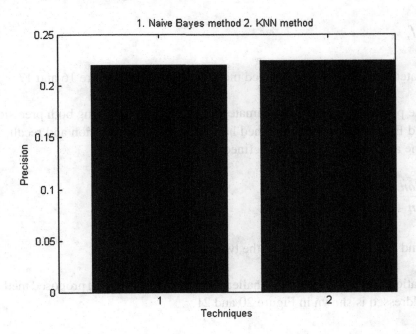

Figure 15. Precision with challenges addressed

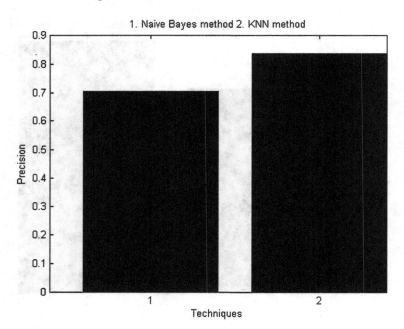

20. **Recall:** Recall can be referred to as the parameter of test that describes the proportion of the true positives against both true positives and false negatives present in the total population. It is used to measure the sensitivity of a classifier and is defined as:

$$Recall = \frac{t_p}{t_p + f_n}.$$

Recall calculated using the two mentioned methods is shown in Figure 16 and 17.

21. **Fscore:** The parameter of test that estimates the score by considering both precision and recall of test is called Fscore. Fscore is a weighed harmonic mean of precision and recall. This parameter measures the accuracy of test and is defined as:

$$F = 2.\frac{Precision.Recall}{Precision + Recall}$$

Figure 18 and 19 compares Fscore of the two methods.

Overall evaluation of the method where challenges are unaddressed and proposed methodology where challenges are addressed is shown in Figure 20 and 21.

Figure 16. Recall without challenges addressed

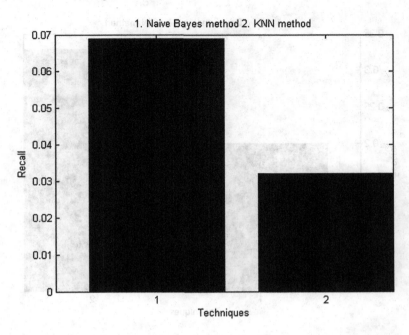

Figure 17. Recall with challenges addressed

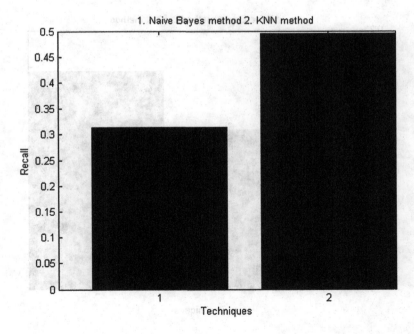

Figure 18. Fscore without challenges addressed

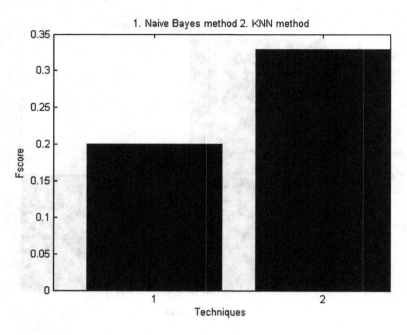

Figure 19. Fscore with challenges addressed

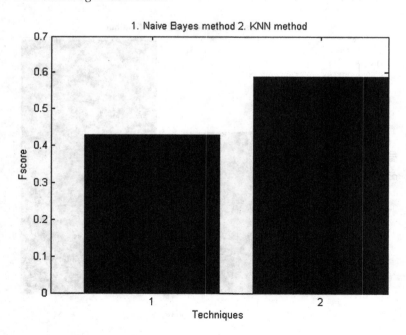

Figure 20. Results of method where challenges are unaddressed

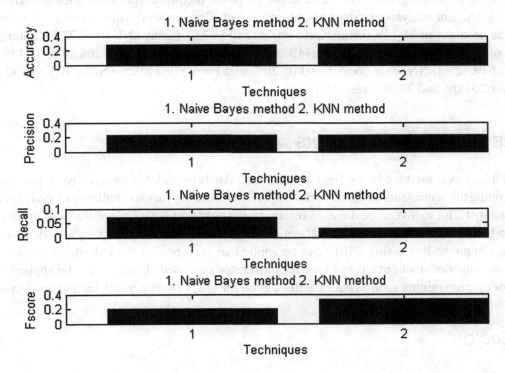

Figure 21. Results of method where challenges are addressed

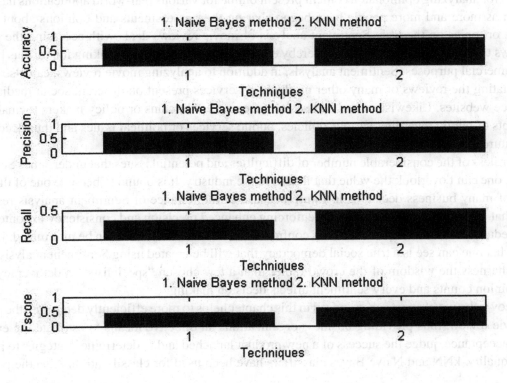

It can be seen from Figures 20 and 21 that the proposed method outperformed the already existing method of sentiment analysis that does not address the challenges faced while analyzing sentiments. It achieved an accuracy of 71.75% (using Naive Bayes) and 88.38% (using kNN) over 27.56% and 29.61%, precision of 70.33% (Naive Bayes) and 83.44% (kNN) over 21.95% and 22.40%, recall of 31.43% (Naive Bayes) and 49.42% (kNN) over 06.88% and 03.20%, and Fscore of 42.92% (Naive Bayes) and 58.75% (kNN) over 20.00% and 32.88% respectively.

FUTURE RESEARCH DIRECTIONS

Although a lot has been done in the field of Sentiment Analysis and this research work presents novel ways of finding the sentiments of movie reviews as well as handling various challenges faced in analyzing sentiments, still a lot more can be done. In future, classifiers like Genetic algorithm and fuzzy classification can be applied on movie reviews dataset or reviews on any other subject area. In-depth concepts of Natural Language Processing (NLP) can be applied so as to predict the polarity of reviews posted online or of some document in a better way. Moreover, the proposed algorithm can be applied on other domains of opinion mining such as political discussion forums, newspaper articles and product reviews.

CONCLUSION

The field of sentiment analysis has emerged as an exciting new research direction since an ample number of real-world applications exist that rely on determining people's opinion for better decision-making. The need for analyzing opinionated content present online for various real-world applications has gained attention as more and more people have begun sharing their assessments and opinions about various products or topics on the web. Sentiment analysis of movie reviews deals with accessing the polarity of reviews that the users communicate, thereby enabling strategic decision-making for various business and commercial purposes. Sentiment analysis, in addition to analyzing movie reviews, can also be used for evaluating the reviews of many other products or services present on different social media and e-commerce websites. Likewise, it can be used to encourage politicians or policy makers to analyze the sentiments of public regarding various policies, public services or political issues and thus accordingly frame future policies.

Regardless of the considerable number of difficulties and potential issues that undermines Sentiment analysis, one can't overlook the value that it adds to the industry. It is bound to become one of the major drivers of many business decisions in future because of the reliance of Sentiment analysis results on factors that are so inherently humane. By enforcing enhanced precision and consistency in content mining procedures, some of the present issues confronted in Sentiment analysis can be minimized. Looking ahead, what one can see is a true social democracy that will be created using Sentiment analysis, where one can harness the wisdom of the crowd rather than a few chosen "specialists"- a democracy where every opinion counts and every sentiment affects decision making.

Moreover the novel approach proposed in this chapter helps to more efficiently determine the polarity of a movie review, thus providing business organizations an effective means to estimate the extent of product acceptance, judge the success of a new product launched and to determine strategies to improve product quality. kNN and Naive Bayes classifiers have been used for classification. Also the proposed algorithm addressed challenges like presence of thwarted words, world knowledge words, and Subjectivity detection while analysing the sentiment and it outperformed the already existing method where challenges are not addressed.

ACKNOWLEDGMENT

All praise be to Allah, Lord of the Worlds, and may the peace and blessings be on the most noble of Prophets and Messengers, our Prophet Muhammad, and on his family and all of his Companions. I offer to Him all praise and gratitude, and seek His assistance and forgiveness. I seek refuge in Allah from the evils of our souls and the wickedness of our deeds. Whomsoever Allah guides, none can misguide, and whomsoever Allah misguides, none can guide. I thank Allah, the Exalted, for the completion of this chapter. Alhamdulillah, Allah gave me enough strength and patience to tackle every problem with calm and ease.

I would like to express my profound gratitude to my research guide Dr. Farheen Siddiqui, Assistant Professor, School of Engineering Sciences and Technology (SEST), Jamia Hamdard, for her good guidance and direction, advice, strong support, highly-valued criticisms, deep insights and for providing resourceful information that contributed to the quality of this research.

I am highly thankful to my family for their love and support throughout my life and my studies. My parents, Mrs. & Mr. Mohammad Ismail Shah, raised me to believe that I could achieve anything I set my mind to. Thank you for your love, prayers, caring and sacrifices for educating and preparing me for my future.

Finally, my thanks go to all the people who have supported me to complete my research work directly or indirectly.

This research received no specific grant from any funding agency in the public, commercial, or not-for-profit sectors.

REFERENCES

Abbasi, A., Chen, H., Thoms, S., & Fu, T. (2008). Affect Analysis of Web Forums and Blogs Using Correlation Ensembles. *IEEE Transactions on Knowledge and Data Engineering*, *20*(9), 1168–1180. doi:10.1109/TKDE.2008.51

Abbasi, A., France, S., Zhang, Z., & Chen, H. (2011). Selecting Attributes for Sentiment Classification Using Feature Relation Networks. *IEEE Transactions on Knowledge and Data Engineering*, *23*(2), 447–462. doi:10.1109/TKDE.2010.110

Al-Moslmi, T., Albared, M., Al-Shabi, A., Omar, N., & Abdullah, S. (n.d.). Arabic senti-lexicon: Constructing publicly available language resources for Arabic sentiment analysis. Journal of Information Science, 1–18.

Aydoğan, E., & Akcayol, M. (2016). A comprehensive survey for sentiment analysis tasks using machine learning techniques. In *INnovations in Intelligent SysTems and Applications (INISTA), 2016 International Symposium on*. Sinaia, Romania: IEEE. 10.1109/INISTA.2016.7571856

Barzilay, R., & Lapata, M. (2005). Collective content selection for concept-to-text generation. In *Proceedings of the conference on Human Language Technology and Empirical Methods in Natural Language Processing* (pp. 331-338). Stroudsburg, PA: Association for computational linguistics.

Bholane Savita, D., & Gore, D. (2016). Sentiment Analysis on Twitter Data Using Support Vector Machine. *International Journal of Computer Science Trends and Technology, 4*(3), 365–370.

Brindha, S., Prabha, K., & Sukumaran, S. (2016). A Survey on Classification Techniques for Text Mining. In *Advanced Computing and Communication Systems (ICACCS), 2016 3rd International Conference on*. Coimbatore, India: IEEE. 10.1109/ICACCS.2016.7586371

Buche, A., Chandak, M. B., & Zadgaonkar, A. (2013, June). Opinion mining and Analysis: A survey. *International Journal on Natural Language Computing, 2*(3).

Carrillo de Albornoz, J., Plaza, L., Gervás, P., & Díaz, A. (2011). A joint model of feature mining and sentiment analysis for product review rating. In *ECIR'11 Proceedings of the 33rd European conference on Advances in information retrieval* (pp. 55-66). Berlin: Springer. 10.1007/978-3-642-20161-5_8

Chidananda, H. T., Sagnika, S., & Sahoo, L. (2017, February). Survey on Sentiment Analysis: A Comparative Study. *International Journal of Computers and Applications, 159*(6), 4–7. doi:10.5120/ijca2017912952

Cover, T., & Hart, P. (1967). Nearest neighbour pattern classification. *IEEE Transactions on Information Theory, 13*(1), 21–27. doi:10.1109/TIT.1967.1053964

Dave, K., Lawrence, S., & Pennock, D. (2003). Mining the peanut gallery: opinion extraction and semantic classification of product reviews. In *Proceedings of the 12th international conference on World Wide Web* (pp. 519-528). Budapest, Hungary: ACM. 10.1145/775152.775226

Deng, S., Sinha, A. P., & Zhao, H. (2017, February). Adapting sentiment lexicons to domain-specific social media texts. *Decision Support Systems, 94*(C), 65–76.

Govindarajan, M., & M., R. (2013). A Survey of Classification Methods and Applications for Sentiment Analysis. *International Journal of Engineering Science, 2*(12), 11–15.

Hu, M., & Liu, B. (2004). Mining and summarizing customer reviews. In *KDD '04 Proceedings of the tenth ACM SIGKDD international conference on Knowledge discovery and data mining* (pp. 168-177). New York, NY: ACM. 10.1145/1014052.1014073

Hussein, D. (2016). A survey on sentiment analysis challenges. *Journal Of King Saud University -. Engineering and Science.* doi:10.1016/j.jksues.2016.04.002

Jadhav, R., & Wakode, M. S. (2017, March). Survey: Sentiment Analysis of Twitter Data for Stock Market Prediction. *International Journal of Advanced Research in Computer and Communication Engineering, 6*(3), 558–562. doi:10.17148/IJARCCE.2017.63129

Jo, Y., & Oh, A. (2011). Aspect and sentiment unification model for online review analysis. In *WSDM '11 Proceedings of the fourth ACM international conference on Web search and data mining* (pp. 815-824). New York, NY: ACM. 10.1145/1935826.1935932

Kalaivani, P., & Shunmuganathan, D. (2013). Sentiment classification of movie reviews by supervised machine learning approaches. *Indian Journal of Computer Science and Engineering*, *4*(4), 285–292.

Khan, K., Baharudin, B., & Khan, A. (2014). Identifying Product Features from Customer Reviews Using Hybrid Patterns. *The International Arab Journal of Information Technology*, *11*(3), 281–286.

Kim, S., & Hovy, E. (2004). Determining the sentiment of opinions. In *COLING '04 Proceedings of the 20th international conference on Computational Linguistics*. Stroudsburg, PA: Association for Computational Linguistics. 10.3115/1220355.1220555

Korkontzelos, I., Nikfarjam, A., Shardlow, M., Sarker, A., Ananiadou, S., & Gonzalez, G. H. (2016, August). Analysis of the effect of sentiment analysis on extracting adverse drug reactions from tweets and forum posts. *Journal of Biomedical Informatics*, *62*(C), 148–158. doi:10.1016/j.jbi.2016.06.007 PMID:27363901

Ku, L., Liang, Y., & Chen, H. (2006). Opinion Extraction, Summarization and Tracking in News and Blog Corpora. *AAAI Spring Symposium: Computational Approaches to Analyzing Weblogs*, 100-107.

Kummer, O., & Savoy, J. (2012). Feature Selection in Sentiment Analysis. In *CORIA 2012 Proceedings of the 9th Conference on Information Retrieval and Applications* (pp. 273-284). Bordeaux.

Liu, B. (2010). Sentiment analysis and subjectivity. In N. Indurkhya & F. Damerau (Eds.), *Handbook of Natural Language Processing* (2nd ed., pp. 627–661). CRC Press.

Liu, B. (2012). *Sentiment analysis and opinion mining*. San Rafael, CA: Morgan & Claypool.

Ma, C., Prendinger, H., & Ishizuka, M. (2005). Emotion estimation and reasoning based on affective textual interaction. In *Affective Computing and Intelligent Interaction* (Vol. 3784, pp. 622–628). Berlin: Springer. doi:10.1007/11573548_80

Matsumoto, S., Takamura, H., & Okumura, M. (2005). Sentiment classification using word sub-sequences and dependency sub-trees. In *PAKDD'05 Proceedings of the 9th Pacific-Asia conference on Advances in Knowledge Discovery and Data Mining* (pp. 301-311). Berlin: Springer. 10.1007/11430919_37

Ortony, A., Clore, G. L., & Foss, M. A. (1987). The referential structure of the affective lexicon. *Cognitive Science*, *11*(3), 341–364. doi:10.120715516709cog1103_4

Owais, S., Nafis, P., & Khanna, S. (2015). An Improved Method for Detection of Satire from User-Generated Content. *(IJCSIT). International Journal of Computer Science and Information Technologies*, *6*(3), 2084–2088.

Pagolu, V., Reddy, K., & Panda, G. (2016). Sentiment analysis of Twitter data for predicting stock market movements. In *International Conference on Signal Processing, Communication, Power and Embedded System (SCOPES)*, 2016 (pp. 1345-1350). Paralakhemundi, India: IEEE. 10.1109/SCOPES.2016.7955659

Pang, B., Lee, L., & Vaithyanathan, S. (2002). Thumbs up? Sentiment classification using machine learning techniques. *Proceeding of the conference on empirical methods in natural language processing*, 79-86.

Pang, B., & Lee, L. (2008). Opinion mining and sentiment analysis. *Foundations and Trends in Information Retrieval*, *2*(1-2), 1-135.

Patel, M., & Mistry, M. (2015). A Review: Text Classification on Social Media Data. *IOSR Journal of Computer Engineering, 17*(1), 80-84.

Pradhan, V. M., Vala, J., & Balani, P. (2016, January). A Survey on Sentiment Analysis Algorithms for Opinion Mining. *International Journal of Computers and Applications, 133*(9), 7–11. doi:10.5120/ijca2016907977

Rangel, F., & Rosso, P. (2016). On the impact of emotions on author profiling. *Information Processing & Management, 52*(1), 73–92. doi:10.1016/j.ipm.2015.06.003

Rimon, M. (2005). Sentiment classification: Linguistic and non-linguistic issues. *Proceedings of Israel Association for Theoretical Linguistics, 21*.

Rodrigues, R. G., Dores, R. M., & Camilo-Junior, C. G. (2016, January). SentiHealth-Cancer: A sentiment analysis tool to help detecting mood of patients in online social networks. *International Journal of Medical Informatics, 85*(1), 80–95. doi:10.1016/j.ijmedinf.2015.09.007 PMID:26514078

Salas-Zárate, M. P., Valencia-García, R., Ruiz-Martínez, A., & Colomo-Palacios, R. (2017, August 1). Feature-based opinion mining in financial news: An ontology-driven approach. *Journal of Information Science, 43*(4), 458–479. doi:10.1177/0165551516645528

Sebastiani, F. (2002). Machine learning in automated text categorization. *ACM Computing Surveys, 34*(1), 1–47. doi:10.1145/505282.505283

Sentiment Analysis on Movie Reviews. (2015). Retrieved February 09, 2017, from https://www.kaggle.com/c/sentiment-analysis-on-movie-reviews/data

Turney, P. (2002). Thumbs up or thumbs down? Semantic orientation applied to unsupervised classification of reviews. In *Proceedings of the 40th annual meeting of the association for computational linguistics* (pp. 417-424). Stroudsburg, PA: Association for Computational Linguistics.

Wang, H., Lu, Y., & Zhai, C. (2010). Latent aspect rating analysis on review text data: a rating regression approach. In *KDD '10 Proceedings of the 16th ACM SIGKDD international conference on Knowledge discovery and data mining* (pp. 783-792). New York, NY: ACM. 10.1145/1835804.1835903

Wilson, T., Wiebe, J., & Hoffmann, P. (2005). Recognizing contextual polarity in phrase level sentiment analysis. In *Proceedings of the conference on Human Language Technology and Empirical Methods in Natural Language Processing* (pp. 347-354). Stroudsburg, PA: Association for Computational Linguistics. 10.3115/1220575.1220619

KEY TERMS AND DEFINITIONS

Efficiency: Maximum productivity achieved with minimum waste of efforts or expense is called efficiency.

Euclidean Distance: Euclidean distance gives the measurement of length of a segment that joins two points, that is, distance between two points in a plane or three-dimensional space.

Feature Space: A hypothetical space which uses a point to represent each pattern sample in n-dimensional space is called feature space in pattern recognition. Dimensions of a feature space can be specified by the number of features utilized in portraying the patterns.

Harmonic Mean: The ratio of "number of the given values" and "sum of the reciprocals of the given values" is called harmonic mean.

Natural Language Processing (NLP): A branch of artificial intelligence that examines, understands, and creates languages used naturally by humans, thereby interacting with computers using natural languages of humans instead of computer languages in both written and spoken contexts is referred to as natural language processing (NLP). In other words, NLP is concerned with programming computers so that it can process large corpora of natural languages in an effective manner.

Opinion Mining: A sub-discipline of computational linguistics concerned with extraction of opinions, demeanors, and emotions expressed by users on the web towards different individuals, products, services, topics, and their features is called opinion mining.

Performance Metrics of Classification: The various measures that can be employed in assessment of performance or quality of classifiers or different learning methods and learned models are called performance metrics of classification.

Positive Predictive Value: In statistics and diagnostic tests, the proportion of positive results that are true positive results is called positive predictive value (PPV). Also called precision, it can be used to evaluate performance of a test.

Semantic Orientation: Classifying words as positive, negative, or neutral to identify the polarity of an opinion on a feature f is called semantic orientation.

Sensitivity: The measurement of proportion of correctly identified positives is called Sensitivity. In other words, it measures how good a test is at detecting the positives. It is also called true positive rate, recall, or probability of detection in some fields.

Supervised Learning: The machine learning task of analyzing labelled training data and hence inferring a function is called supervised learning. It can then be employed to map new examples.

This research was previously published in Social Network Analytics for Contemporary Business Organizations; pages 106-140, copyright year 2018 by Business Science Reference (an imprint of IGI Global).

APPENDIX 1

Accuracy, Precision, Recall and Fscore Results of Existing Method Using Naive Bayes Classifier

- Accuracy: 27.56%
- Precision: 21.95%
- Recall: 06.88%
- Fscore: 20.00%

APPENDIX 2

Accuracy, Precision, Recall and Fscore Results of Proposed Method Using Naive Bayes Classifier

- Accuracy: 71.75%
- Precision: 70.33%
- Recall: 31.43%
- Fscore: 42.92%

APPENDIX 3

Accuracy, Precision, Recall and Fscore Results of Existing Method Using kNN Classifier

- Accuracy: 29.61%
- Precision: 22.40%
- Recall: 03.20%
- Fscore: 32.88%

APPENDIX 4

Accuracy, Precision, Recall and Fscore Results of Proposed Method Using kNN Classifier

- Accuracy: 88.38%
- Precision: 83.44%
- Recall: 49.42%
- Fscore: 58.75%

Chapter 59
Discovery of Sustainable Transport Modes Underlying TripAdvisor Reviews With Sentiment Analysis:
Transport Domain Adaptation of Sentiment Labelled Data Set

Ainhoa Serna

iD https://orcid.org/0000-0003-4750-3222
University of the Basque Country, Spain

Jon Kepa Gerrikagoitia
BRTA Basque Research and Technology Alliance, Spain

ABSTRACT

In recent years, digital technology and research methods have developed natural language processing for better understanding consumers and what they share in social media. There are hardly any studies in transportation analysis with TripAdvisor, and moreover, there is not a complete analysis from the point of view of sentiment analysis. The aim of study is to investigate and discover the presence of sustainable transport modes underlying in non-categorized TripAdvisor texts, such as walking mobility in order to impact positively in public services and businesses. The methodology follows a quantitative and qualitative approach based on knowledge discovery techniques. Thus, data gathering, normalization, classification, polarity analysis, and labelling tasks have been carried out to obtain sentiment labelled training data set in the transport domain as a valuable contribution for predictive analytics. This research has allowed the authors to discover sustainable transport modes underlying the texts, focused on walking mobility but extensible to other means of transport and social media sources.

DOI: 10.4018/978-1-6684-6303-1.ch059

INTRODUCTION

Mobility with motor vehicles has a negative environmental impact. Over time, means of transportation have emerged as an alternative to the use of motor vehicles. Examples of sustainable transport are bicycle, public transport (subway, tram, bus), electric car, and so on. Conforming to the EU Transport Council in 2001, *"a sustainable transport system is one that allows individuals and societies to meet their needs for access to areas of activity with total safely, in a manner consistent with human and ecosystem health, and that is also balanced equally between different generations"* (European Commission - Mobility and Transport, 2018).

Additionally, tourist activity generates wealth in the receiving place and is an excellent great source of employment. However, as a counterpart, it can also be a destructive activity. It is estimated that tourism activity produces up to 8% of global greenhouse gas emissions from 2009 to 2013 (Lenzen, Sun, Faturay et al., 2018). Even if we take into account the energy used in hotels, transport or hygiene products, it represents up to 12.5% (Sánchez, 2018). Moreover, cities across Europe have adopted or strengthened Low Emission Zones (LEZ) in response to the growing air pollution crisis. These measures have been taken by more than 250 EU cities. A study shows that 67% of interviewees favour the adoption of LEZ either strongly or slightly. LEZ should move forward to zero-emission mobility zones (ZEZ), that will eventually be turned into policies to promote transitioning to healthier alternatives like walking, cycling jointly with the electrification of all forms of transport like taxis, public transport and private vehicles (Müller and Le Petit, 2019).

Furthermore, tourism produces large quantities of the content generated by users (User Generated Content) that is rapidly growing. There is a wide variety of subjects in this type of content, and one of them is mobility. On the other hand, the different languages and contexts are relevant to react when consumers around the world are speaking various languages and as digital platforms increase the range of users on these platforms, such as Social Media data of TripAdvisor platform. Being platforms worldwide that include users from different countries, the variety and richness of the data that can be extracted and the knowledge that can be created with them can be very relevant for different companies, both public and private.

In recent years, in particular, digital technology and research methods have developed the concept of Natural Language Processing that has become a preferred means for better understanding consumers and what they share in. Regarding the economic and business relevance of NLP, forecasts that Global NLP Market is projected to rise to $26.4 billion by 2024 and the CAGR (Compound Annual Growth Rate) of 21% from 2019 (MarketsandMarkets, 2019) will continue to increase. Given the current importance of this area and future forecasts, this research will focus on the application of NLP in the field of transport, since the contribution of this research can be relevant both at the level of global and local business. For this reason, this investigation analyses the different transport modes, focus on sustainable transports. In this research, natural language processing techniques are applied to Social Media data (UGC), to evaluate the impressions of visitors regarding success factors that can be used as planning aid tools. The study has been developed according to transport mode used and languages.

Regarding the novelty of this research, it should be noted that there are numerous TripAdvisor articles but mainly focused on tourism, such as monuments, hotels, restaurants, attractions…etc. There are hardly any studies in transportation analysis with TripAdvisor, and moreover, there is no a complete analysis of sentiment analysis. This article proposes TripAdvisor as a data source for the study of modes of transport, user ratings and automated sentiment-detection algorithms.

Study aims to investigate and discover the presence of sustainable transport modes underlying in non-categorized TripAdvisor texts, such as walking mobility in order to impact positively in public services and businesses. The research is based on a qualitative and quantitative method following (KDD) Knowledge discovery in databases techniques. Thus, data gathering, normalization, classification, polarity analysis and labelling tasks have been carried out to obtain sentiment labelled training data set, in the transport domain as a valuable contribution for predictive analytics.

For this purpose, the use case is focused in Croatia. It includes essential information about activities and travels of UGC from TripAdvisor in Spanish and English languages, aiming to demonstrate the value of Social Media-related data as a valuable data source to get a better understanding of tourism mobility (easy mobility across all transport) and transport modes to enhance the tourism destination management.

The chapter is structured according to the following: section 2 lays out the background, analysis of the Social Media research in the transport area and the progress of one of the most sustainable means of transport, the bicycle, also, the contributions of the authors. The key focus of this chapter is defined in section 3, describing the research methodology and phases. Afterwards, section 4 details the solutions and recommendations with the main results of the phases. Finally, the paper presents future lines and the conclusions of the research. Additionally, after the references section, the suggestions on additional readings and key terms defined by the authors are added.

BACKGROUND

The literature review is divided into two parts. The first part reviews the literature on the study of Social Media in the transport sector in general. The second part shows the progress of one of the most sustainable means of transport, the bicycle.

Social Media Analysis in the Urban Transport Area

TripAdvisor is a database for travel analysis for recent work in the field of sentiment analysis. Gal-Tzur (2018) focuses on TripAdvisor's Q&A forums section and offers a framework for automatically categorizing transportation-related issues addressed in those forums and collecting travel-related questions. Ali et al. (2019) propose a latent Dirichlet allocation (LDA) model based on topics and an ontology, with embedding words approach for the classification of sentiment. The proposed framework collects transport content from social networks, eliminates irrelevant content to extract meaningful information, and uses LDA to create topics and features from the data collected.

Recent researches regarding Social Media in urban transport (Kuflik, Minkov, Nocera et al., 2017; Serna, Gerrikagoitia, Bernabe and Ruiz, 2017a) are worthy of note in order to explore urban mobility from another viewpoint. Newly, there has been a substantial increase in research in this field. A system for collecting, processing and mining Geo-located tweets has been designed and developed by Pereira (2017). More specifically, the program provides functionality for the parallel selection of geo-located tweets, preprocessing of English or Portuguese tweets, thematic modelling, transport-specific text classifications, and aggregation and data visualizers, from several predefined areas or cities. Furthermore, there are numerous possible sources of transport data, which are differentiated by the vast quantity of available material, the speed at which it is accessed and the diversity of formats to be delivered (Ruiz, Mars, Arroyo and Serna, 2016). The application of this knowledge on Transport Planning is a task involving advanced techniques of data mining. The authors identified plausible applicable Social Media data sources that could be utilized in planning of transport and discussed their benefits and disadvantages. A summary of incipient developments for planning of transport is then addressed. Besides, several opportunities to use Big Data related to social networks, in particular, are emphasized.

Others researches discuss probable Social Media activities for providers of transport services and makers of transport policy suggesting that substantial transport policy knowledge can be obtained from UGC (Gal-Tzur et al., 2014). Information on technology challenges linked to social network data mining in transport are presented in Grant-Muller (2014). A text mining method is provided, which provides the foundation for novel investigation in this field, to obtain significant transportation sector data, including taxonomy, polarity analysis, and measuring accuracy. In 2015, Grant-Muller (2015) confirmed the alternative of adding data from content produced by users can complement, improve and even replace conventional data gathering and highlight the need to develop automated methods to gathering and analyzing transport-related Social Media data.

Conforming to Serna, Gerrikagoitia, Bernabe & Ruiz (2017b) empirically evidence the viability of the automated identification of the difficulties in in the field of sustainable urban mobility using the user generated-content reviews. The methodology improves knowledge in conventional surveys and expands quantitative research by using big data approaches. Gu, Qian & Chen (2016) propose that Twitter posts provide an accurate and cost-effective option to classify incident data on both arterials and highways. Moreover, they present a method for crawling, processing and filtering tweets which are accessible openly.

Social Media Analysis Focus on the Bicycle Transport Mode

The public bicycle shared (PBS) systems research area has drawn the attention of researchers who in recent years have published their findings from a variety of viewpoints. Several studies have investigated the area of study on PBS transport modes (Serna & Gasparovic, 2018; Nickkar et al., 2019; Serna, Ruiz, Gerrikagoitia & Arroyo, 2019). For example, according to Serna et al., (2019), so far, the literature has overlooked the effect of Social Media on public bicycle shared systems alongside official statistics data that include following data: populations, the quantity of docking stations and weather information such as temperature, raininess, humidity, pressure, etc. Their research filled this gap and led to a novel investigation source to supplement current information with knowledge derived from Social Media in order to understand the conduct of travel and establish predictive models for the use of the mode of travel.

In 2019, Serna et al. (2019) also provide a comprehensive literature review on PBS systems, showing, for example, that some researchers, such as Shaheen, Guzman, and Zhang (2010) researched PBS systems as a feasible choice for mobility, demonstrating the progress of 3 generations of public bicycle shared systems in three continents (Asia, America and Europe) from 1965 until 2010. Other research works have concentrated on the facilities of the network, and the operational features that are strongly associated to the utilization of PBS systems, such as convenient sign-up procedures, 24/7 opening hours or sign-up opportunities (Buck & Buehler, 2013; El-Assi, Mahmoud & Habib, 2017). Also, researchers considered the socio-demographic features, including population, employment, mixed-use and retail density as well as riders' educational rates were related to increased public use of bicycles (Hampshire & Marla, 2012; Buck and Buehler, 2012; Rixey 2013; El-Assi et al.,2017). Moreover, the environment was also analyzed to show that storm, strong wind, rain and low temperatures negatively affect the use of bike shares (Gebhart, and Noland, 2014). Furthermore, users' digital footprint was an essential source of data to fill the demand-supply gap for bike-sharing (Zhao, Wang and Deng, 2015; Bordagaray, dell'Olio, Fonzone, Ibeas, 2016).

RESEARCH METHODOLOGY

The methodology follows a qualitative and quantitative approach that consists of two main phases (see Figure 1). The first phase consists of identifying, obtaining, capturing, normalizing, analyzing, classifying and discovering the different modes of transport in the TripAdvisor reviews, also applying the sentiment analysis to assign polarity (positivity, negativity, neutrality). Besides, a dashboard is developed to understand and manage the results easily. The second phase developed involves the process of collecting a set of data automatically labelled with sentiment based on the reviews rated with 5 and 1 stars and measuring their accuracy.

Figure 1. Research methodology and general process

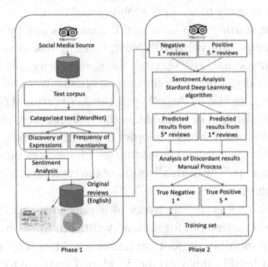

Case Study

The case study is focused in Croatia and includes UGC from TripAdvisor in Spanish and English languages, demonstrating the value of Social Media data as a valuable data source to get a better understanding of tourism, mobility and transport modes. English and Spanish are the top two languages. One fact to emphasize is that about 91 per cent of reviews were posted in English.

Regarding the methodology, the first phase comprises the following steps: source identification, Social Media source acquisition, data preparation for the analysis, sentiment analysis, storage and data visualization (Serna & Gasparovic, 2018).

Phase 1

Step 1: Source Identification

TripAdvisor includes impressions of travellers for different purposes: business, leisure, and so on. The information-gathering was implemented with reviews that include data about mobility in different sections of transportation (taxis & shuttles, ferries, bus transportation, tramways, funicular railway...etc.) within TripAdvisor.

Step 2: Social Media Source Acquisition

This technique involves the processing of raw and unstructured data, consists of data acquisition, normalization and cleaning. Web scraper software has been implemented to acquire information from TripAdvisor.

Step 3: Data Preparation for the Analysis

The discovery of expressions relating to walking mobility and the morph-syntactic analysis is realized in two distinct processes. The starting step is to load the reviews one by one to identify the language with the Shuyo language detector (Shuyo, 2010). Next, Freeling that is an Open Source library which offers a broad range of linguistic analysis services for several languages for automatic multilingual processing (Padró and Stanilovsky, 2012) with the corresponding WordNet lexicons version 3.1 (2012) (Miller, 1995; Fellbaum, 1998), and GNU Aspell spell checker version 0.60.8 (2019) (Atkinson, 2003) for specific languages are established. For example, in the spell checker, some improvements to be able to detect localism and abbreviation are added. In order to correct the texts, the spell checker is applied. The normalization of the reviews is a crucial procedure which involves the management and adaptation of the emoticons and abbreviations. The normalization of the reviews is a crucial procedure which covers both abbreviations and emoticons

After this process, the next task is the discovery of expressions and synonyms related to walking mobility. This process has been carried out for reviews written in Spanish. Words and expressions that are synonymous with walking mobility on foot are identified. Then they are added in the category of mobility on foot to avoid their loss. In this way, the developed software tool can identify and add them automatically, improving these shortcomings.

Next, Freeling Analyzer including WordNet database integration and an ad-hoc software is used, each word being labelled morph-syntactically within a transport classification as a result of this method. Furthermore, numerous nouns are described by transport modes with their adjectives, and common nouns have been categorized by the number of occurrences in order to obtain exhaustive details.

Step 4: Sentiment Analysis

In this step, the polarity is calculated with the SentiWordNet polarity lexicon (Baccianella, Esuli & Sebastiani, 2010; Esuli & Sebastiani, 2006). In order to select the correct meaning depending on the context, the UKB Word Sense Disambiguation program (Agirre & Soroa, 2009), has been used.

Step 5: Storage

For the scalable data storage and management, it is necessary this process. The downloaded reviews are homogenized and stored in the Apache Solr search Engine in JSON, a standard format (Smiley & Pugh, 2011).

Step 6: Data Visualization

The previous steps are implemented in a software workflow that provides data to be shown in a visual (dashboard) interface to monitor and interpret information quickly. The dashboard has been developed with a robust and versatile UI (user interface), customizable pie charts and histogram and so on, based on the Solr Apache Foundation (open source). The data provided by the workflow has been indexed to provide efficient response time to queries.

Phase 2: Sentiment Labelled Data Set

This phase consists of the creation of a "*Sentiment Labelled Data Set*" as a training dataset for supervised learning algorithms.

Step 1: Filtered

First, the reviews written in English have been filtered (rated on 1 to 5 stars scale). The process consisted of selecting only the reviews rated with 1 and 5 stars in order to get the extremes in both positivities (5 *) and negativity (1 *).

Step 2: Stanford Deep Learning Algorithm

In this step, sentiment analysis is applied using Stanford Deep learning algorithm (Socher et al., 2013). Many sentiment prediction systems (polarity orientation) only work with terms/concepts isolating that offer positive and negative scores for positive and negative terms respectively and summarize these scores. Therefore, the order of terms is overlooked, and essential knowledge is lost. In comparison, this deep learning model constructs a illustration of whole phrases based on the form of the sentence. It calculates the sentiment based on how the terms constitute the meaning of longer sentences.

To order to achieve a better precision in the transport domain, a random manual review will then be carried out of the 10 per cent of the overall evaluations listed as positive or negative. Later, during the selection process, two files were created, one containing the positive reviews and the other with the negative ones, respectively.

Step 3: Analysis of Discordant Results

Therefore, these two files (positive and negative) have to be cleaned manually, which ensures that the reviews are positive or negative with total certainty. This step is crucial, otherwise, the results of both, the training set and the created model would be inconsistent and invalid in order to predict reliably.

SOLUTIONS AND RECOMMENDATIONS

Phase 1

A dashboard with dynamic graphics was created to analyze TripAdvisor's Social Media reviews data which recognizes positive and negative factors and their potential impacts on sustainable tourism and transportation. Also, different means of transport are classified and selected according to day/month/year, term/word, mode of transport, place, ranking, language, city, adjective, adverb, transport company…etc. Besides, the original review and its corresponding title are obtained.

This dashboard allows different visual representations with dymanic graphics (tabular, historical data evolution, word cloud, and pie chart) to interpret the results. Beginning from Figure 2 (upper part) on the top left, the first block helps to choose by date. The next block enables to search and filter by a concept or term. Afterward, there is a cloud tag showing the diverse means of transport that were discovered. Following, a dymanic pie chart containing the top languages. Lastly, a description of the dates information is given in the last block of the upper part of the section.

In the central division of Figure 2, the first findings are defined in a timeline diagram with the number of TripAdvisor's observations (reviews), and it is showed as an example filtering from 12/12/2007 to 03/07/2018. The years on the x-axis are shown and the number of the reviews y-axis. Additionally, Figure 2 illustrates that the topic of research is becoming more and more important in Social Media year after year. This histogram is also a dynamic graph, which allows you to choose different time frames and update the graph automatically.

The bottom section allows filtering by word (nouns), adverb and adjective, city and review rating.

Figure 2. Visual Analytics Dashboard

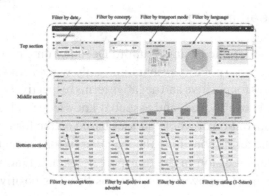

In TripAdvisor, the different transport modes are grouped and represented as follows: *cable car* 36% (called Tramway), *taxis and shuttles* with 22.4% of reviews; *funicular railway* 2.9% (called Mass Transportation Systems), *ferries* with 2.5%, and *bus* transportation with 0.4%.

Sustainable transport such as a bicycle or walking mobility are not included in the Transportation section of TripAdvisor, but it is possible to find these modes of transportation in "Walking & Biking

Tours" section that encompasses two subsections, "Walking Tours" and "Bike & Mountain Bike Tours" (walking 32.6%, bike 3.1%).

It should be noted that 74.7% of transport is sustainable transport such as bicycle, walking, public transport (cable car, funicular railway), and that walking is the 2nd most reviewed mode of transport after the cable car.

Table 1. Top 7 Transport modes in the reviews.

Transport Mode	Sustainable Transport ranking	# Reviews
Cable car	2	10,352
Walking	1	9,354
Taxi and shuttles	4	6,437
Bicycle	1	882
Funicular Railway	2	845
Ferry	3	717
Bus	3	112

Furthermore, 86% of the reviews rate the *cable car* and 73% the *funicular railway* with the two highest scores (excellent and very good) and only 4% and 3% respectively, with the worst scores (poor and terrible). 96% and 89% of the reviews about *walking* and *bicycles* respectively are rated with the maximum rate (excellent). In *ferries* transport modes 69% of the reviews are rated with the two highest scores (excellent and very good) and 18% with the worst scores (poor and terrible).

The *cable car* is rated good (2494 times), great (2240), nice (1118), spectacular (860), beautiful (859), short (769), stunning (757). The number of occurrences of negative ratings is much smaller than positive ones, specifically, negatively rated with these attributes are expensive (1015), Long queues (16), bad information/ service (5), disappointment (3), mistake (5), overpriced (3), dangerous (2), regretful (1). *Taxis & shuttles* are qualified with the maximum number of occurrences with these adjectives friendly (1592), good (1771), excellent (1123), great (1624), helpful (835), clean (827), professional (790) and comfortable (757). Negatively rated attributes are bad taxi driver (4), official complaint (1), a thief (2). *Private Buses* are rated with good (2897), great (2727), friendly (1635), excellent (1337), nice (1187), clean (899), beautiful (880), easy (856) and helpful (838). Negatively rated attributes are waste of money and waste of day (4), rushed and hurried (2), mediocre (2), not pleasant (8), late (16), rude (7), stressful (5).

Ferries are positively rated with special experience, friendly, kind, excellent, well organized, the best way, fantastic, clean, brilliant, gorgeous. Negatively rated are disappointed (10), guide rude (4), rushed (4), racist (1), abusive (1). *Walking* is positively rated with great, best, fantastic, terrific, vibrant, guide passionate, amazing guide, knowledgeable, caring. Negatively rated attributes are almost inexistent, one example would be the expression "too long to walk". *Bicycle* is positively rated with amazing, excellent customer service, great bikes, strongly recommend, great quality, very good condition and perfectly maintained, stunning, Friendly helpful service. There are very few negative reviews, with these adjectives: unsuccessfully (10), disappointed (12).

Discovery of Expression Related to "Walking Mobility" Results

In this task, reviews written in Spanish on walking mobility that was not identified are discovered in the reviews. This manages to discover 59% of occurrences concerning to the number of reviews with the automatic categorization of the walking mobility as a mode of transport.

The results of the task about the discovery of expressions and disambiguation in the walking mobility are shown in the following tables (tables 2 and 3). For this, expressions or words that refer to walking mobility are added and those in different context does not mean the same are disambiguated. As an example, part of these expressions is shown in table 2:

Table 2. Discovery of synonymous expressions related to walking mobility (in Spanish)

Synonymous expressions of walking mobility		
"andar"	"ir a pie"	"desplazarse a pie"
"pasear"	"rondar"	"corretear"
"deambular"	"atravesar"	"correr"
"transitar"	"caminar"	"trotar"
"vagar"	"circular"	"marchar a pie"
"zanquear"	"avanzar"	"visitar a pie"
"recorrer"	"venir a pie"	"trasladarse a pie"
"patear"	"callejear"	"moverse a pie"
"acceder a pie"		

Besides, the Spanish expression "a pie" (on foot) depending on the context has different meanings. In one case, it means that the mode of mobility is walking, but in another case, it means close, that it is close to a place.

In Table 3, as an example, original sentences of the reviews are shown, with synonymous expressions that indicate walking mobility. Also, examples of the different meaning of the expression "a pie" (on foot) are shown depending on the context.

Phase 2: Sentiment Labelled Data Set Results

This process uses reviews written in English, it is described in phase 2 of the "Research methodology" section (graphically represented in Figure 3), and this section shows the obtained results.

Figure 3. Phase 2: Sentiment Labelled Data Set process

Table 3. Original sentences with the discovered expressions related to walking mobility (in Spanish)

Original sentence	Meaning
"Muy bien ubicado para **acceder a pie** a varias de las atracciones."	walking transport mode
"También dispones de un tranvía **a pie de** la plaza Ban Jelačić."	near
"… nos permitió **recorrer a pie** las mejores zonas de Zagreb."	walking transport mode
"… para conocer la ciudad **a pie** y disfrutarla."	walking transport mode
",….. a 5 minutos **a pie** de la plaza Ban Jelačić"	walking transport mode
"Muy bien situado cerca de la plaza Ban Jelačić **a pie del** hotel."	near
"…., ofrece un **paseo a pie** inmejorable."	walking transport mode
"Nos ha encantado, la ubicación perfecta para **ir a pie** a un montón de sitios. "	walking transport mode
"Se puede ir **pateando** a los sitios más representativos de la ciudad."	walking transport mode
"… ideal para **visitar a pie** ….."	walking transport mode
"… la verdad es q en 15-20 min **andando** se llega perfectamente."	walking transport mode
"..unos cinco o diez minutos **andando** y bien comunicado con el centro de la ciudad"	walking transport mode
"..con una parada de tranvía al lado y **andando** a 20 minutos"	walking transport mode
"que te permite llegar al centro **paseando** un cuarto de hora o coger directamente el tranvía."	walking transport mode
"…. **caminando** 10 minutos llegas a la calle ….."	walking transport mode

* discovered expressions are highlighted in bold in the sentence (first column).

The results corroborated the hypothesis that users rate reviews with five stars, that is, the maximum score, but each sentence that makes up that review can have different polarity orientation, we can find positive, negative and neutral sentences. In the same way, it happens with the very negative reviews, those scored with one star.

Furthermore, the results of analyzing the 5 * reviews sentence by sentence with the Stanford Sentiment algorithm, were that 25% of the sentences in the positive reviews file are classified as neutral and, or negative. As for the negative reviews, 23% of the reviews scored with 1 * are considered neutral and, or positive. The accuracy, according to the following formula is 76%.

$$Accuracy = \frac{TP + TN}{TP + FP + FN + TN}$$

Where True Positive, True Negative, False Positive and False Negative are represented by TP, TN, FP and FN, respectively.

Analyzing the results manually, it is observed that some of the sentences are valued as negative due to the word "war" although they are really neutral sentences, as can be seen in the following table, in the sentences of the reviews made to the means of transport "cable car" (in English).

Next, in Figure 4, a tree-shaped sentiment of the sentence *"There is evidence of the war and a museum explains what happened to Dubrovnik and the role of the fort during the war in 80s/90s."* is shown. The calculus of the orientation is wrong predicted (negative) since it is a neutral sentence. Negative nodes are marked with x in the figure.

Table 4. Prediction and True sentiment related to cable car mobility (rated with five stars)

Original sentence	Sentiment Prediction	True Sentiment
"Loved the War museum, spent ages there."	positive	positive
"There is evidence of the war and a museum explains what happened to Dubrovnik and the role of the fort during the war in 80s/90s."	negative	neutral
"There is an old fort there that now has a display showing pictures of the recent war in Croatia."	negative	neutral
"The fort has interesting history going back to Napoleon and was used extensively by Croatians during the 1991-1995 war."	negative	positive
"Be sure while you are on the top of the mountain to visit the fortress, where you will see the shell holes from the Serb bombardment during the siege of Dubrovnik."	negative	neutral
"Have lunch at the top and be sure to visit the fortress to learn about the 90s Balkan war (from a decidedly Croatian perspective)."	negative	positive
"If you go to the war museum at Fort Imperial and go up the steps to the roof then you get even better views than the cable car observation deck."	negative	neutral

Figure 4. Example of negative prediction for neutral sentiment

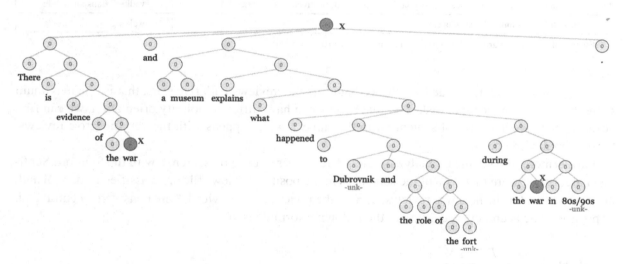

Analyzing the predictions of the negative reviews manually, it is observed that one of the sentences is valued as positive due to the word "*cheaper*", although it is a negative sentence. Also, it is observed that some sentences with the expression "*would not recommend*", despite being identified as negative, the adverbial particle "*not*", when evaluated separately from the verb "*recommend*" to which it is linked, the algorithm is wrong and assigns a positive value to the sentence. Besides, some very negative sentences (such as the first three sentences and the fifth in Table 5) are predicted as neutral.

Next, in Figure 5, a tree-shaped sentiment of the "*I definitely would not recommend this taxi service to anyone*" sentence is shown. The calculus of the orientation is wrong predicted (positive) since it is a negative sentence.

Table 5. Prediction and true sentiment related to cable car mobility (rated 1 star)

Original sentence	Sentiment Prediction	True Sentiment
"False information ! ! !"	neutral	negative
"It was scary."	neutral	negative
"Tourist trap."	neutral	negative
"Consider booking a return trip in a taxi it would be alot cheaper ! !"	positive	negative
"Please look at alternatives before you book with these thieves."	neutral	negative
"I definitely would not recommend this taxi service to anyone."	positive	negative
"Would NOT recommend this Company."	positive	negative

Figure 5. Example of positive prediction for negative sentiment

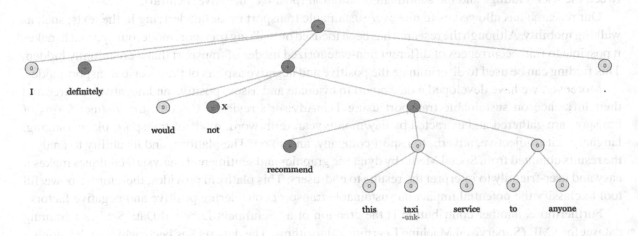

FUTURE RESEARCH DIRECTIONS

First of all, as future research, it is proposed to develop a new phase that consists of the development of models using machine learning (ML) techniques, taking advantage of the labelled data set (positive and negative reviews). Thus, for the purpose of predictive analysis, this investigation provides sentiment labelled data collection. With these two classifications (positive and negative reviews), algorithms can be trained with a supervised learning approach using the previously analyzed data model. In order to improve labelling precision, an ensemble agreement (consensus) approach can be used. Ensemble agreement means that many algorithms predicted the same class of an occurrence (Jurka et al., 2013).

Another future line can focus on testing the data valued with 5 and 1 star related to the transport domain with different algorithms to see the accuracy achieved in the automatic labelling of the data set, making a detailed analysis of the wrong predictions.

Moreover, it would be convenient to feed the training set with a more extensive data set, adding transport data from other data sources such as Twitter, Facebook, transport forums, etc. and analyze how it affects the models and their accuracy.

Besides, considering the energy model transition that is taking place nowadays, it would be relevant to analyze the presence of electric mobility electric bicycles, electric scooters, electric cars, electric buses, electric Tuk Tuk, etc. On the other hand, it would be beneficial to extend the search for synonymous expressions of mobility "on foot" to other languages besides Spanish.

CONCLUSION

Regarding the main findings of the research, first, the reference social network in trips/travels (TripAdvisor) has been characterized by modes of transport, analyzing reviews within categorized transport sections and reviews that are published in any other section such as Hotels, Things to do, Restaurants, Shopping, etc. Second, the sentiment of the characteristics of the different modes of transport has been identified, beyond the rating of the reviews, since it has been shown that there is not always a correspondence between the user's ratings and the sentiment orientation (positive, negative, neutral).

Our research has allowed us to discover sustainable transport modes underlying in the texts, such as walking mobility. Although the research has been focused on walking transport mode, our approach makes it possible to find occurrences of different non-categorized modes of transport that were initially hidden. This finding can be used to discriminate the positive and negative aspects of the diverse transport modes.

Moreover, we have developed a dashboard to evaluate and assess positive and negative features and their influence on sustainable transport using TripAdvisor's reviews. Besides, the distinct forms of transport are gathered and extracted by day/month/year, term/word, mode of transport, place, ranking, language, city, adjective, adverb, transport company, and so on. The platform and its ability to analyze the results obtained from Social Media by dynamic graphics and sentimental analysis techniques makes it easy and user-friendly to interpret the results to end-users. This platform provides, therefore, a powerful tool to classify the potential impact on sustainable transport considering positive and negative factors.

Furthermore, another contribution is the creation of a "Sentiment Labelled Data Set" as a training dataset for SML (Supervised Machine Learning) algorithms. The data set has been achieved developing models for ML taking advantage of the available labelled data set (positive and negative reviews) of the research. Thus, this sentiment labelled data set can be used for predictive analytics.

There may be inconsistencies between user ratings and Sentiment Analysis methods because users sometimes write negative sentences with positive opinions and vice versa as has been demonstrated. Therefore, new approaches must be used to assess positivity, negativity and neutrality employing consensus among Sentiment Analysis methods. Users in TripAdvisor can describe their experiences openly and influence impacting the viability of a business. To identify the weaknesses and strengths of public and private transport, it is therefore essential to apply Sentiment Analysis techniques to reviews, such as TripAdvisor. Furthermore, because of a large number of applications in the tourism sector, the quality enhancement of mobility aspects in the various transport modes through Sentiment Analysis techniques has great potential and impact.

Regarding the results, the exceptionally high presence of the means of sustainable transport should be noted very positively. In fact, 74.7% of transport is sustainable transport such as a bicycle, walking, public transport (cable car, funicular railway). Walking is the second most reviewed mode of transport after the cable car. 68% of reviews are rated with the highest score, and only 1.4% are rated with the worst score. As we can conclude, that there is a positive assessment about overall results.

Besides, knowing the users' opinions about the different modes of transport, as well as the characteristics that they value positively and negatively, is crucial to improve the service.

About the data we can extract from TripAdvisor, UGC presents the lack of socio-demographic data in the Social Media in most cases, and it is not generalizable to the entire population. Nowadays, TripAdvisor 's data quality is good as there are abundant and wide-ranging data, several languages, etc. Moreover, visitors that write reviews in TripAdvisor also explain the positive and poor characteristics of the different modes of transportation. Depending on the language to be analyzed, the difficulties are not the same. On the one hand, languages such as English are the first to benefit from advances in PLN, and yet, for other languages with few speakers such as Maltese, there is little progress and development. On the other hand, Spanish language is a vibrant language in synonymous. That characteristic that makes it such a rich language, with a wide range of expressive possibilities, is also a problem for PLN techniques, since it hinders the accuracy of automatic analysis, even having PLN resources.

Social Media provides basic features of data (variables) that can be acquired such as the language, mode of transport, date, country, town, city, state of transportation, punctuality, pricing, route, service, polarity analysis (neutral-positive), etc. Comparing to conventional surveys, the gaps and, or supplementary data you need and can be obtained from daily surveys mainly include demographic data, area (location), age, gender; occupation, personal data on education level, living arrangements, for example on your own, with children, with parents; the main motivations for visiting, the flight scheduling, when they plan to make a journey, what is the first airport of departure, the airline used, etc. Moreover, the Croatian Tourism Authority was conscious that travelers from other countries are hesitant to respond to surveys, but interestingly they write reviews in TripAdvisor and, thanks to the system and method developed, their feedback can be taken into account.

Regarding limitations, the automatic data gathering process has important shortcomings. TripAdvisor, frequently changes the structure of its content, making it difficult to search and download content automatically. Thus, it is necessary to verify the data manually and update the URL's (uniform resource locator). Also, the information on the different means of transport even having a category for it, does not combine all the means of transport that are scattered in different sections. Therefore, for proper data capture, the platform needs to be updated and tested with relative frequency. Another problem is that TripAdvisor uses automatic translations of different languages, so in this investigation the data analysis has been carried out discarding such translations, capturing only the original reviews to avoid mistakes related to wrong translations.

REFERENCES

Agirre, E., & Soroa, A. (2009). Personalizing pagerank for word sense disambiguation. *Proceedings of the 12th Conference of the European Chapter of the Association for Computational Linguistics (EACL 2009)*, 33–41. 10.3115/1609067.1609070

Ali, F., Kwak, D., Khan, P., El-Sappagh, S., Ali, A., Ullah, S., Kim, K. H., & Kwak, K. S. (2019). Transportation sentiment analysis using word embedding and ontology-based topic modeling. *Knowledge-Based Systems*, *174*, 27–42. doi:10.1016/j.knosys.2019.02.033

Atkinson, K. (2003). *GNU Aspell*. Retrieved from http://aspell.sourceforge.net/

Baccianella, S., Esuli, A., & Sebastiani, F. (2010). SentiWordNet 3.0: An enhanced lexical resource for sentiment analysis and opinion mining. *LREC, 10*, 2200–2204.

Bordagaray, M., dell'Olio, L., Fonzone, A., & Ibeas, Á. (2016). Capturing the conditions that introduce systematic variation in bike-sharing travel behavior using data mining techniques. *Transportation Research Part C, Emerging Technologies, 71*, 231–248. doi:10.1016/j.trc.2016.07.009

Buck, D., & Buehler, R. (2012). Bike lanes and other determinants of capital bikeshare trips. *Proceedings of the 91st Transportation Research Board Annual Meeting.*

Buck, D., Buehler, R., Happ, P., Rawls, B., Chung, P., & Borecki, N. (2013). Are bikeshare users different from regular cyclists? A first look at short-term users, annual members, and area cyclists in the Washington, DC, region. *Transportation Research Record: Journal of the Transportation Research Board, 2387*(1), 112–119. doi:10.3141/2387-13

El-Assi, W., Mahmoud, M. S., & Habib, K. N. (2017). Effects of built environment and weather on bike sharing demand: A station level analysis of commercial bike sharing in Toronto. *Transportation, 44*(3), 589–613. doi:10.100711116-015-9669-z

Esuli, A., & Sebastiani, F. (2006). Sentiwordnet: A publicly available lexical resource for opinion mining. *LREC, 6*, 417–422.

European Commission. (2018). *Mobility and Transport*. Retrieved from https://ec.europa.eu/transport/themes/sustainable_en

Fellbaum, C. (Ed.). (1998). WordNet: An Electronic Lexical Database. Cambridge, MA: MIT Press.

Gal-Tzur, A., Grant-Muller, S. M., Kuflik, T., Minkov, E., Nocera, S., & Shoor, I. (2014). The potential of Social Media in delivering transport policy goals. *Transport Policy, 32*, 115–123. doi:10.1016/j.tranpol.2014.01.007

Gal-Tzur, A., Rechavi, A., Beimel, D., & Freund, S. (2018). An improved methodology for extracting information required for transport-related decisions from Q&A forums: A case study of TripAdvisor. *Travel Behaviour & Society, 10*, 1–9. doi:10.1016/j.tbs.2017.08.001

Gebhart, K., & Noland, R. B. (2014). The impact of weather conditions on capital bikeshare trips. *Transportation, 41*, 1205–1225. doi:10.100711116-014-9540-7

Grant-Muller, S. M., Gal-Tzur, A., Minkov, E., Nocera, S., Kuflik, T., & Shoor, I. (2014). Enhancing transport data collection through Social Media sources: Methods, challenges and opportunities for textual data. *IET Intelligent Transport Systems, 9*(4), 407–417. doi:10.1049/iet-its.2013.0214

Gu, Y., Qian, Z. S., & Chen, F. (2016). From Twitter to detector: Real-time traffic incident detection using Social Media data. *Transportation Research Part C, Emerging Technologies, 67*, 321–342. doi:10.1016/j.trc.2016.02.011

Hampshire, R. C., & Marla, L. (2012). An analysis of bike sharing usage: Explaining trip generation and attraction from observed demand. *Proceedings of the 91st Annual Meeting of the Transportation Research Board*, 22–26.

Jurka, T. P., Collingwood, L., Boydstun, A. E., Grossman, E., & van Atteveldt, W. (2013). RTextTools: A Supervised Learning Package for Text Classification. *The R Journal*, *5*(1), 6. doi:10.32614/RJ-2013-001

Kuflik, T., Minkov, E., Nocera, S., Grant-Muller, S., Gal-Tzur, A., & Shoor, I. (2017). Automating a framework to extract and analyse transport related Social Media content: The potential and the challenges. *Transportation Research Part C: Emerging Technologies, 77*, 275-291.

Lenzen, M., Sun, Y., Faturay, F., Ting, Y.-P., Geschke, A., & Malik, A. (2018). The carbon footprint of global tourism. *Nature Climate Change*, *8*(6), 522–528. doi:10.103841558-018-0141-x

MarketsandMarkets. (2019). *Natural Language Processing Market by Component, Deployment Mode, Organization Size, Type, Application, Vertical And Region - Global Forecast to 2024*. Retrieved from https://www.reportlinker.com/p05834031/Natural-Language-Processing-Market-by-Component-Deployment-Mode-Organization-Size-Type-Application-Vertical-And-Region-Global-Forecast-to.html

Miller, G. A. (1995). WordNet: A Lexical Database for English. *Communications of the ACM*, *38*(11), 39–41. doi:10.1145/219717.219748

Müller, J., & Le Petit, Y. (2019). *Transport & Environment*. Retrieved from https://www.transportenvironment.org/sites/te/files/publications/2019_09_Briefing_LEZ-ZEZ_final.pdf

Nickkar, A., Banerjee, S., Chavis, C., Bhuyan, I. A., & Barnes, P. (2019). A spatial-temporal gender and land use analysis of bikeshare ridership: The case study of Baltimore City. *City Cult. Soc*, *18*, 100291. doi:10.1016/j.ccs.2019.100291

Padró, L., & Stanilovsky, E. (2012). Freeling 3.0: Towards Wider Multilinguality. *Proceedings of the Eight International Conference on Language Resources and Evaluation (LREC'12)*.

Pereira, J. F. F. (2017). *Social Media Text Processing and Semantic Analysis for Smart Cities*. arXiv preprint arXiv:1709.03406

Rixey, R. A. (2013). Station-level forecasting of bikesharing ridership: Station network effects in three US systems. *Transportation Research Record: Journal of the Transportation Research Board*, *2387*(1), 46–55. doi:10.3141/2387-06

Ruiz, T., Mars, L., Arroyo, R., & Serna, A. (2016). Social Networks, Big Data and Transport Planning. *Transportation Research Procedia, 18*, 446-452.

Sánchez, J. (2018). *Cómo hacer turismo sostenible*. Retrieved from: https://www.ecologiaverde.com/como-hacer-turismo-sostenible-1216.html

Serna, A., & Gasparovic, S. (2018). Transport analysis approach based on big data and text mining analysis from social media. *Transportation Research Procedia, 33*, 291–298. doi:10.1016/j.trpro.2018.10.105

Serna, A., Gerrikagoitia, J. K., Bernabé, U., & Ruiz, T. (2017a). Sustainability analysis on Urban Mobility based on Social Media content. *Transportation Research Procedia*, *24*, 1–8. doi:10.1016/j.trpro.2017.05.059

Serna, A., Gerrikagoitia, J. K., Bernabe, U., & Ruiz, T. (2017b). A method to assess sustainable mobility for sustainable tourism: The case of the public bike systems. In *Information and Communication Technologies in Tourism 2017* (pp. 727–739). Springer. doi:10.1007/978-3-319-51168-9_52

Serna, A., Ruiz, T., Gerrikagoitia, J. K., & Arroyo, R. (2019). Identification of Enablers and Barriers for Public Bike Share System Adoption using Social Media and Statistical Models. *Sustainability*, *11*(22), 6259. doi:10.3390u11226259

Shaheen, S. A., Guzman, S., & Zhang, H. (2010). Bikesharing in Europe, the Americas, and Asia: Past, present, and future. *Transportation Research Record: Journal of the Transportation Research Board*, *2143*(1), 159–167. doi:10.3141/2143-20

Shuyo, N. (2010). *Language Detection Library for Java*. Retrieved from https://github.com/shuyo/language-detection/

Smiley, D., & Pugh, D. E. (2011). *Apache Solr 3 Enterprise Search Server*. Packt Publishing Ltd.

Socher, R., Perelygin, A., Wu, J., Chuang, J., Manning, C. D., Ng, A. Y., & Potts, C. (2013, October). Recursive deep models for semantic compositionality over a sentiment treebank. In *Proceedings of the 2013 conference on empirical methods in natural language processing* (pp. 1631-1642). Academic Press.

Zhao, J., Wang, J., & Deng, W. (2015). Exploring bikesharing travel time and trip chain by gender and day of the week. *Transportation Research Part C, Emerging Technologies*, *58*, 251–264. doi:10.1016/j.trc.2015.01.030

ADDITIONAL READING

Gräbner, D., Zanker, M., Fliedl, G., & Fuchs, M. (2012, January). Classification of customer reviews based on sentiment analysis. In *Information and Comm. Technologies in Tourism* (pp. 460–470). Springer. doi:10.1007/978-3-7091-1142-0_40

Guzman, E., & Maalej, W. (2014, August). How do users like this feature? a fine grained sentiment analysis of app reviews. In *2014 IEEE 22nd international requirements engineering conference (RE)* (pp. 153-162). IEEE.

Ivo Cré, P. (2019). *European Platform on sustainable urban mobility plans*. Retrieved from https://www.eltis.org/sites/default/files/urban_vehicle_access_regulations_and_sustainable_urban_mo bility_planning.pdf

Kadriu, A., Abazi, L., & Abazi, H. (2019). Albanian Text Classification: Bag of Words Model and Word Analogies. *Business Systems Research Journal*, *10*(1), 74–87. doi:10.2478/bsrj-2019-0006

Klopotan, I., Zoroja, J., & Meško, M. (2018). Early warning system in business, finance, and economics: Bibliometric and topic analysis. *International Journal of Engineering Business Management*, *10*, 1847979018797013. doi:10.1177/1847979018797013

Palakvangsa-Na-Ayudhya, S., Sriarunrungreung, V., Thongprasan, P., & Porcharoen, S. (2011, May). Nebular: A sentiment classification system for the tourism business. In *2011 eighth international joint conference on computer science and software engineering (JCSSE)* (pp. 293-298). IEEE. 10.1109/JCSSE.2011.5930137

Pejic-Bach, M., Bertoncel, T., Meško, M., & Krstic, Ž. (2020). Text mining of industry 4.0 job advertisements. *International Journal of Information Management*, *50*, 416–431. doi:10.1016/j.ijinfomgt.2019.07.014

Pejic Bach, M., Krstic, Ž., Seljan, S., & Turulja, L. (2019). Text mining for big data analysis in financial sector: A literature review. *Sustainability*, *11*(5), 1277. doi:10.3390u11051277

Pejic Bach, M., Pivar, J., & Dumicic, K. (2017). Data anonymization patent landscape. *Croatian Operational Research Review*, *8*(1), 265–281. doi:10.17535/crorr.2017.0017

Rashidi, T. H., Abbasi, A., Maghrebi, M., Hasan, S., & Waller, T. S. (2017). Exploring the capacity of social media data for modelling travel behaviour: Opportunities and challenges. *Transportation Research Part C, Emerging Technologies*, *75*, 197–211. doi:10.1016/j.trc.2016.12.008

KEY TERMS AND DEFINITIONS

Natural Language: Language created as a mode of communication between people.

Natural Language Processing or NLP: It is a subset of Artificial Intelligence that makes possible through different computer algorithms to process digital content generated by people (natural language). NLP aims to simulate the interpretation of humans.

Sentiment Analysis: It is a natural language processing technique (NLP), which describes the sentiment orientation (positive, negative, neutral) underlying into the information.

Sentiment Labelled Data Set: They are sets of data, composed of sentences taken from real reviews of people, to which polarity (sentiment orientation) is added, so these sentences are labelled with a positive or negative or neutral sentiment.

Supervised Learning: It is an algorithm that uses labelled data and analyses the training data and accordingly produces an inferred model, which can be used to classify new data.

Sustainable Transport: Are those modes of transport that reduce environmental pollution impacting collective well-being and besides, some of them even reduce traffic congestion and promote health.

Unsupervised Learning: It is an algorithm that uses unlabelled data, where the model works on its own to discover information.

Chapter 60
An Approach to Opinion Mining in Community Graph Using Graph Mining Techniques

Bapuji Rao

iD https://orcid.org/0000-0002-2781-9708

Indira Gandhi Institute of Technology, Sarang, India

ABSTRACT

Opinions are the central theme to almost all human activities, as well the key influencers of our behaviours. Opinions related to sentiments, evaluations, attitudes, and emotions are the features of studying of opinion mining. It is important to study peoples of various communities sentiments about the schemes implemented by the government agencies as well as NGOs. The opinion mining is about the opinions of various communities of villages of a Panchayat about various social schemes implemented by the government of India. This article proposes an algorithm for opinion mining in a community graph for various social schemes run by the Panchayat using graph mining techniques. The algorithm has been implemented in C++ programming language.

INTRODUCTION

Sentiment analysis is to study and analyzes people's attitudes, evaluations, and opinions for topics, services, individuals, issues, products, organizations, events, and etc. The other name of sentiment analysis is opinion mining. Some other alternate names with slightly different tasks are emotion analysis, subjectivity analysis, opinion mining, opinion extraction, review mining, sentiment analysis, sentiment mining, and affect analysis. However, the above all analysis comes under sentiment analysis or opinion mining. Sentiment analysis is commonly used in industry, whereas opinion mining and sentiment analysis are frequently used in academia according to the author (Bing Liu, 2012). Opinion mining attracts some selected groups of people. Generally, the government, the lawmakers, and politicians are interested in knowing the response of the special people to the government policies. Since opinion mining focuses

DOI: 10.4018/978-1-6684-6303-1.ch060

on the features level mining. So, it is easy mine the commented features as well as the sentiment mining. These comments could be used to generate various types of opinion summaries as well as in depth analysis of general attitudes. Generally, most of the researches are interested in product features identification, opinions identification of the products, and determining the sentiment process of the opinions which comes under the feature level opinion mining.

LITERATURE REVIEW

Many companies create their opinion mining systems to automatically maintaining of review and opinion of websites. These systems gather a large volume of information from the web continuously. The gathered information's are review of products, brand value, and different political issues. Sometimes the opinion mining and sentiment analysis are used as sub-component technology to get into the depth of customer relationship management and recommendation systems through their feedbacks i.e. either positive or negative. Sometimes opinion mining and sentiment analysis are used to detect and exclude bias language in social communication proposed by the authors (Cambria, Schuller, Xia, & Havasi, 2013).

Opinion Mining mainly extracts the subjective statements from texts, which actually identifies the opinions, the orientation opinion and the extraction of actual arguments from the opinions. The authors (Helander, Lawrence, & Liu, 2007) represented an online discussion as a graph. The entities vertices are such as messages, users etc. and the edges among the entities are considered as relationships.

Social Network Analysis which analyze the relationships between the existing entities in a social network. So, in a social network, analysis of people may consist of detection of various friend groups, detection of influence group of people, and so on. For the social network analysis of people, the authors (Stavrianou, Velcin, & Chauchat, 2010) proposed a new framework for discussion analysis is the combination of Opinion Mining Techniques and Social Network Techniques. It studies the structure of online debate and analyzes all the user's reactions, preferences, and opinions related to a particular subject. The authors have proposed the model based on graph representation. Generally, in a graph representation, the users are considered as vertices of the graph. The authors have proposed message objects are the vertices in the graph. Similarly, the authors have represented a directed graph i.e. G = (M, R) for the online discussions, where M is the message objects and R is the set of edges which shows the relationship between two message objects. Hence this graph is termed as opinion-based graph.

The authors (Fisher, Smith, & Welser, 2006) applied social network techniques to analyze newsgroups and interpret the members of the groups with the assigned roles. It was achieved by the way the people related to each other upon post reply relations in a graph-based model. The authors (Java, Song, Finin, & Tseng, 2007) analyzed the Twitter's social network. The authors have tried to know the intentions of the associated users and the reason of using such networks by the user. The authors have tried to identify the community formation. They categorized these community formations into three groups. These three groups are: information created by the communities, information received by the communities and communities which is responsible for creation of friendship. The authors (Scripps, Tan, & Esfahanian, 2007) introduced a new technique to define the number of communities to be attached to a node. Based on this, the authors have assigned the roles of nodes based upon the community structure.

The authors (Zhang, Xia, Meng, & Yu, 2009) proposed a graph with two sets i.e. F is the product features and W is the opinion words. Then a bi-partite link is created by using all the elements of F and O. Finally, a graph is defined as G = (F, O, R), where, R is the weight of the link between product feature F and opinion word W. The authors have hypothesized all the opinion words available in the product features. The bi-partite link is created based on the occurrence of opinion word in a sentence having the product feature.

The authors (Rashid & Quigley, 2009) proposed the study for ambient displays in indoor academic environments. The authors (Shannon, Kenny, & Quigley, 2009) discussed the opportunities of effectiveness of ambient information technology to know the user's social connectedness. The authors (Quinn, Chen, & Mulvenna, 2012) examined the social networking's real concepts and ingredients, the trend and related research, and the models with tie formation approaches. The authors (Bryson & Tanguy, 2010) proposed a model; the Dynamic Emotion Representation (DER) is to maintain the interaction of set of incomplete states to bring under emotional control. The author (Wiberg, 2011) proposed to develop architectural and computational concepts and theories which facilitate a new form of cooperation among architects, engineers, and the users. This leads to explore the architectural informatics as an opportunity.

The author proposes a new method of opinion mining in a village community graph using graph mining techniques which makes the result easy and understandable since the result is considered as one sub-graph. The author's proposed approach is completely different from the above referred approaches by different authors.

BASIC DEFINITIONS

Social Community Graph

The authors (Rao, Mitra, & Narayana, 2014) have proposed a social community graph, $G = (V, E)$, where V is considered as set of villages i.e. $V = \{V_1, V_2, ..., V_n\}$ and E is considered as set of links or connectivity or edges i.e. $E = \{E_1, E_2, ..., E_n\}$ between the villages. Each village has a set of communities and forms a sub-community graph by means of connectivity among communities.

Directed and Undirected Graph

A graph $G = (V, E)$ which consist of two sets i.e., a set $V=\{V_1, V_2, ..., V_n\}$, called a set of all nodes or vertices and a set $E=\{E_1, E_2, ..., E_n\}$, called a set of all arcs or edges. The set E is the set of pair of elements from V. Between pair of nodes the edge is created. When the edge has a specific direction, then such edge is considered as directed edge. Such graph is termed as directed graph or digraph. Similarly, when the edge has no specific direction, then such edge is considered as undirected edge and such graph is known as undirected graph (Horowitz, Sahani, & Mehta, 2013).

Bi-Partite Graph

A bi-partite graph $G = (X \cup Y, E)$, where X and Y are sets of vertices and every edge $\{e_1, e_2\} \in E$ such that $e_1 \in X$ and $e_2 \in Y$, but there is no edge that connects any two vertices in X or any two vertices in Y. That is, edges only form between X and Y (Horowitz, Sahani, & Mehta, 2013).

Graph Mining

To extract the useful and meaningful knowledge from data represented as graph is known as mining graph data. Sometimes it is also known as graph-based data mining (Cook & Holder, 2007). Mostly the kind of knowledge extracted from graphs is considered as a graph. Hence, sometimes the knowledge is referred to as sequences or patterns, which are mined from the data, and generally termed as sub-graphs of the graphical data.

PROPOSED MODEL

Figure 1. Village community graph

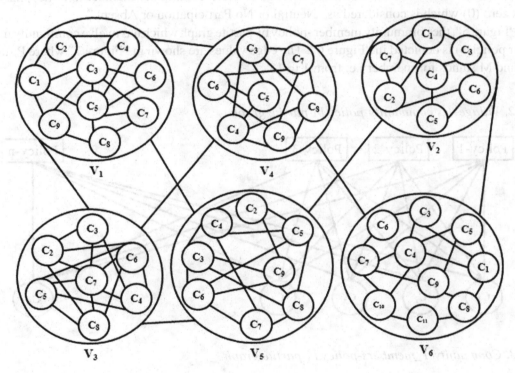

The author propose an undirected village community graph $G = (V, E)$ where V is considered as vertices i.e. $\{V_1, V_2, V_3, ..., V_n\}$ and E is the edges i.e. the connectivity among the villages depicted in "Figure 1" (Rao, Mitra, & Narayana, 2014); (Rao & Mishra, 2016). Each village has m-communities and each community has x-members. The proposed model consists of six villages $\{V_1, V_2, V_3, V_4, V_5, V_6\}$ and their total communities are $\{9, 7, 7, 7, 8, 10\}$. Further, the villages community members are $\{1, 2, 3, 4, 5, 6, 7, 8, 9\}$, $\{1, 2, 3, 4, 5, 6, 7\}$, $\{2, 3, 4, 5, 6, 7, 8\}$, $\{3, 4, 5, 6, 7, 8, 9\}$, $\{2, 3, 4, 5, 6, 7, 8, 9\}$, and $\{1, 3, 4, 5, 6, 7, 8, 9, 10, 11\}$ respectively. The above community graph has 48 number of underlying community members' graphs. Village V_1's community C_1's underlying community member graph is depicted in "Figure 5". When there are n-policies to be taken into consideration for opinion of m-communities of a village, then there exists a bi-partite graph between the m-communities and n-policies. Since community and policy are considered as two types of nodes, hence it is called as community-policy bi-partite graph which is depicted in "Figure 2". The community-policy bi-partite graph has m-number of underlying community members-policy bi-partite graphs which is depicted in "Figure 3" and "Figure 4" respectively. Since the community-policy bi-partite graph has m-communities. So, in the above "Figure 1", there are 48 number of underlying community members-policy bi-partite graphs.

The community members-policy bi-partite graph has two types of edges i.e. directed and undirected. Further the directed edge again divided into two types. Based on the type of edges, the opinions are neutral or good or average or bad and accordingly the values are fixed from 0-3. The directed edge from community member to policy, the opinion value is one (1) which is considered as "Good". The directed edge from Policy to community member, the opinion value is two (2) which is considered as "Average". Similarly, for the undirected edge between community members to policy, the opinion value is three (3) which is considered as "Poor or Bad". For no edge between community member to Policy, the opinion value is zero (0) which is considered as "Neutral or No Participation or Absent."

For "Figure 5", the community member -policy bi-partite graph which has twelve community members and four policies) is depicted in "Figure 6". The edge values are shown in "Figure 7" where P stands for policy and M stands for member i.e. from 1 to 12.

Figure 2. Village-1's community-policy bi-partite graph

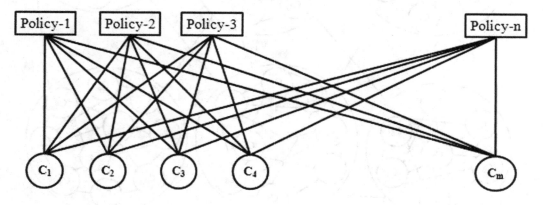

Figure 3. Community-1_members-policy bi-partite graph

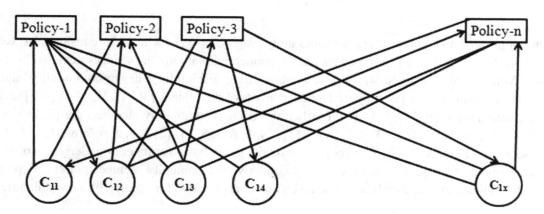

Figure 4. Community-m_members-policy bi-partite graph

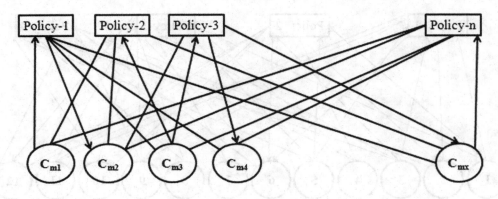

Figure 5. Community C_1's underlying community member graph of village V_1

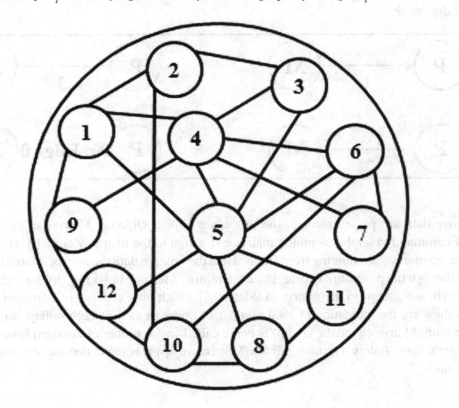

The proposed algorithm OmComm(), is to read number of villages and assign to 'nv'. Then for 'nv' villages, it starts reading every village dataset file name and assign to 'vdata'. This 'vdata' contains details of village data based on the template shown in "Figure 8". The details of village data are read from 'vdata' and assigns to 'vn', 'np', 'nc', and cn[ ][2] which assigns only community number and number community members. cdata[nc] is the array used to read and assign 'nc' number of community members opinion dataset files for every village since a village comprising of m-communities.

Figure 6. Community C_1 members-policy bi-partite graph

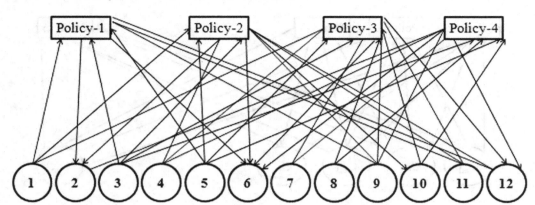

Figure 7. Edge values

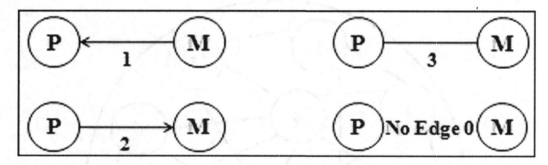

The above data are passed through the procedure Create_Opinion_Matrix(cn, cdata, nc, np) for creation of community members opinion matrix and assign to the matrix Matrix[][] which exclusively contains the opinion values ranging from 0 to 3. Then the opinion data the matrix, Matrix[][], cn, and np are passed through the procedure Create_Policy_Opinion_Matrix(Matrix, cn, np) for creation of policy opinion matrix and assign to the matrix POMatrix[][] which only consists of non-zero values. These non-zero values are the indication of total number of opinions against each policy. So the procedure Create_Opinion_Matrix(cn, cdata, nc, np) is being called 'nv' (number of villages) times and in return the procedure Create_Policy_Opinion_Matrix(Matrix, cn, np) is being called for 'nc' (number of communities) times.

EXPERIMENTAL RESULTS

The dataset for villages can be created by following the template of village dataset depicted in "Figure 8". Every community has a set of community members. These community members opinion dataset can be created by following the template of community members opinion dataset depicted in "Figure 9". The proposed community graph depicted in "Figure 1" consists of six villages namely V_1, V_2, V_3, V_4, V_5, and V_6. Hence six number of village datasets were created. Village V_1 and V_6 dataset are depicted in Figure 10 and Figure 13. Village V_1 consists of nine communities ranging from 1 to 9 and the total community members for these nine communities are 12, 10, 7, 6, 11, 8, 13, 15, and 8 respectively and depicted in Figure 10. For theses nine communities, the community member opinion dataset were created. For village V_1's, community C_1 and C_9's opinion dataset files are depicted in Figure 11 and Figure 12, which only consist of opinion values for the four policies ranging from 0 to 3. Similarly remaining five villages' dataset and community members' opinion dataset were created. Village V_6 which consists of ten communities i.e. 1 and 3 through 11 and the total number of community members are 9, 10, 11, 12, 14, 13, 9, 7, 8, and 6 respectively and depicted in "Figure 13". For theses ten communities, the community member opinion dataset was created. For village V_6's, community C_1 and C_{11}'s opinion dataset files are depicted in "Figure 14" and "Figure 15".

Algorithm 1. Proposed algorithm

```
Algorithm OmComm()
Algorithm convention is based on text book (Horowitz, Sahani, & Mehta, 2013).
// global declarations
nv: To assign number of villages.
vdata: To assign village dataset file name.
vn: To assign village number.
nc: To assign number of communities in a village.
np:To assign number of policies.
cdata[nc]: To assign 'nc' number of community members opinion dataset file names.
cn[nc][2]: To assign community number and total community members.
Matrix[ncm][np]: To assign member's opinion (1-good, 2-Average, 3-Bad/Poor, 0-Absent/Neutral) on policies.
POMatrix[np][4]: To assign the counting of opinions for 'np' policies.
{
read(nv); // read number of villages
for i:=1 to nv do
{
read(vdata); // read i^th village dataset file name
open(vdata); // open vdata file for reading
read(vn);
read(np);
read(nc);
for j:=1 to nc do
{
// to read community number and toyal community members from file and assign
// to cn[][]
read(cn[j][1]);
read(cn[j][2]);
// to read j^th community members opinion dataset file name
read(cdata[j]);
}
close(vdata);
Create_Opinion_Matrix(cn[ ][2], cdata[ ], nc, np);
}
}
```

Algorithm 2. Procedure to create opinion matrix

```
Procedure Create_Opinion_Matrix(cn[ ][2], cdata[ ], nc, np)
Matrix[][]: To store the opinion matrix.
{
for i:=1 to nc do
{
open(cdata[i]); // open iᵗʰ community members opinion dataset file for reading
for j:=1 to cn[1][2] do
{
for k:=1 to np do
{
read(opinion); // read the opinion value from cdata[] file and assign to opinion
Matrix[j][k]:= opinion;
}
}
close(cdata[i]); // close iᵗʰ community members opinion dataset file
Create_Policy_Opinion_Matrix(Matrix[][], cn[i][2], np);
}
}
```

Algorithm 3. Procedure to create policy opinion matrix

```
Procedure Create_Policy_Opinion_Matrix(Matrix[ ][ ], tcm, np)
POMatrix[][]: To store the policy opinion matrix.
{
for i:=1 to np do
for j:=1 to 4 do // four opinion values are 1(good), 2(average), 3(poor/bad), and
// 0(absent/neutral)
POMatrix[i][j]:=0;
// to count opinions for 'np' policies
for i:=1 to np do
for j:=1 to tcm do
{
if(Matrix[j][i]=1) then POMatrix[i][1]:=POMatrix[i][1]+1;
if(Matrix[j][i]=2) then POMatrix[i][2]:=POMatrix[i][2]+1;
if(Matrix[j][i]=3) then POMatrix[i][3]:=POMatrix[i][3]+1;
if(Matrix[j][i]=0) then POMatrix[i][4]:=POMatrix[i][4]+1;
}
}
```

The author has implemented the proposed algorithm using C++ programming language by creating six village dataset files namely v-1.txt (depicted in "Figure 10"), v-2.txt, v-3.txt, v-4.txt, v-5.txt, and v-6.txt (depicted in "Figure 13"), respectively. Similarly, the author has created forty-eight community member opinion dataset files. For village V_1, the dataset files were {c-11.txt (depicted in "Figure 11"), c-12.txt, c-13.txt, c-14.txt, c-15.txt, c-16.txt, c-17.txt, c-18.txt, c-19.txt (depicted in "Figure 12")}, village V_2, the dataset files are {{c-21.txt, c-22.txt, c-23.txt, c-24.txt, c-25.txt, c-26.txt, c-27.txt}, village V_3, the dataset files were {c-32.txt, c-33.txt, c-34.txt, c-35.txt, c-36.txt, c-37.txt, c-38.txt}, village V_4, the dataset files were {c-43.txt, c-44.txt, c-45.txt, c-46.txt, c-47.txt, c-48.txt, c-49.txt}, village V_5, the dataset files were {c-52.txt, c-53.txt, c-54.txt, c-55.txt, c-56.txt, c-57.txt, c-58.txt, c-59.txt}, and village V_6, the dataset files were {c-61.txt (depicted in "Figure 14"), c-63.txt, c-64.txt, c-65.txt, c-66.txt, c-67.txt, c-68.txt, c-69.txt, c-610.txt, c-611.txt (depicted in "Figure 15")} created.

Figure 8. Templates of village dataset

Village Code or Number (vn)	
Number of Policies (np)	
Number of Communities (nc)	
Community Code-1	**Number of Community Members (ncm)**
Community Code-2	**Number of Community Members (ncm)**
Community Code-3	**Number of Community Members (ncm)**
....	....
....	....
Community Code- nc	**Number of Community Members (ncm)**

Figure 9. Templates of community members' opinion dataset

	Policy-1	Policy-2	—	—	—	Policy-np
Member-1	OC	OC	----	----	----	OC
Member-2	OC	OC	----	----	----	OC
------------	OC	OC	----	----	----	OC
------------	OC	OC	----	----	----	OC
------------	OC	OC	----	----	----	OC
Member-ncm	OC	OC	----	----	----	OC

Figure 10. Village V₁ dataset

1	
4	
9	
1	12
2	10
3	7
4	6
5	11
6	8
7	13
8	15
9	8

Figure 11. Community C₁ members opinion dataset file of V₁

1	1	3	0
2	2	0	3
1	1	1	1
0	3	3	3
1	1	1	1
2	2	2	2
0	0	3	3
0	0	1	1
3	3	3	3
1	1	2	0
3	3	3	0
3	3	2	2

Figure 12. Community C_9 members opinion dataset file of V_1

1	1	1	1
2	3	2	3
2	0	3	0
2	2	2	2
1	0	0	2
1	3	1	3
3	1	2	1
1	0	1	0

Figure 13. Village V_6 dataset

6	
4	
10	
1	9
3	10
4	11
5	12
6	14
	13
8	9
9	7
10	8
11	6

Figure 14. Community C_1 members opinion dataset file of V_6

2	2	0	3
1	1	1	1
0	3	3	3
1	1	1	1
2	2	2	2
3	3	3	3
1	1	2	0
3	3	3	0
3	3	2	2

Figure 15. Community C_{11} members opinion dataset file of V_6

1	1	3	1
1	2	1	0
2	1	2	1
0	0	3	1
0	0	1	1
3	3	3	3

Upon inputting the above six village dataset files v-1.txt, v-2.txt, v-3.txt, v-4.txt, v-5.txt, and v-6.txt and forty-eight opinion dataset files to the experiment, the algorithm starts reading village dataset one by one and assign to the variable 'vdata'. For every village's dataset, the details such as community number and total community members are assigned to the matrix, cn[][]. For every community, the corresponding community member opinion dataset file name is assigned to the array, cdata[]. These two datasets are passed by calling the procedure Create_Opinion_Matrix(cn[][2], cdata[], nc, np), which represents the opinion matrix in memory using Matrix[][]. Then the matrix, Matrix[][] is being passed by calling the procedure Create_Policy_Opinion_Matrix(Matrix[][], cn[][2], np), which finally represents the policy opinion matrix in the memory using POMatrix[][].

The algorithm was written and compiled in C++. The experiment was run on Intel Core I5-3230M CPU + 2.60 GHz Laptop having 4GB of memory in MS-Windows 7. After successful run, total forty-eight community members opinion matrices and the corresponding forty-eight community policy-opinion matrices were created and the related output are depicted from "Figure 16" to "Figure 19".

Figure 16. Community C_1 members-opinion and policy-opinion matrices of village V_1

```
Village V1's Community Member - Opinion, Policy - Opinion Matrices

[ Community C1 Members-Opinion Matrix ]
      C1     P-1     P-2     P-3     P-4
      M1      1       1       3       0
      M2      2       2       0       3
      M3      1       1       1       1
      M4      0       3       3       3
      M5      1       1       1       1
      M6      2       2       2       2
      M7      0       0       3       3
      M8      0       0       1       1
      M9      3       3       3       3
      M10     1       1       2       0
      M11     3       3       3       0
      M12     3       3       2       2


[ Community C1 Policy-Opinion Matrix ]
Members=12    Good(1)      Avg(2)      Bad(3) Neutral(0)
   Policy-1      4            2           3        3
   Policy-2      4            2           4        2
   Policy-3      3            3           5        1
   Policy-4      3            2           4        3
```

Figure 17. Community C_9 members-opinion and policy-opinion matrices of village V_1

```
[ Community C9 Members-Opinion Matrix ]
      C9     P-1     P-2     P-3     P-4
      M1      1       1       1       1
      M2      2       3       2       3
      M3      2       0       3       0
      M4      2       2       2       2
      M5      1       0       0       2
      M6      1       3       1       3
      M7      3       1       2       1
      M8      1       0       1       0

[ Community C9 Policy-Opinion Matrix ]
Members= 8    Good(1)      Avg(2)      Bad(3) Neutral(0)
   Policy-1      4            3           1        0
   Policy-2      2            1           2        3
   Policy-3      3            3           1        1
   Policy-4      2            2           2        2
```

Figure 18. Community C₁ members-opinion and policy-opinion matrices of village V₆

Figure 18. Community C_1 members-opinion and policy-opinion matrices of village V_6

```
Village V6's Community Member - Opinion, Policy - Opinion Matrices

[ Community C1 Members-Opinion Matrix ]
    C1      P-1     P-2     P-3     P-4
    M1       2       2       0       3
    M2       1       1       1       1
    M3       0       3       3       3
    M4       1       1       1       1
    M5       2       2       2       2
    M6       3       3       3       3
    M7       1       1       2       0
    M8       3       3       3       0
    M9       3       3       2       2

[ Community C1 Policy-Opinion Matrix ]
Members= 9     Good(1)     Avg(2)      Bad(3) Neutral(0)
   Policy-1       3           2           3          1
   Policy-2       3           2           4          0
   Policy-3       2           3           3          1
   Policy-4       2           2           3          2
```

Figure 19. Community C_{11} members-opinion and policy-opinion matrices of village V_6

```
[ Community C11 Members-Opinion Matrix ]
    C11     P-1     P-2     P-3     P-4
    M1       1       1       3       1
    M2       1       2       1       0
    M3       2       1       2       1
    M4       0       0       3       1
    M5       0       0       1       1
    M6       3       3       3       3

[ Community C11 Policy-Opinion Matrix ]
Members= 6     Good(1)     Avg(2)      Bad(3) Neutral(0)
   Policy-1       2           1           1          2
   Policy-2       2           1           1          2
   Policy-3       2           1           3          0
   Policy-4       4           0           1          1
```

CONCLUSION

This paper is a kind of approach of opinion mining about the opinions of various communities of villages of a Panchayat about various social schemes implemented by the Government. The author has proposed an algorithm for opinion mining in a community graph for various social schemes implemented by the Panchayat using graph mining techniques. Graph mining technique has been incorporated because of the result in a form of sub-graph which make understands in a simpler and easier way. An example was considered and the same used for the proposed algorithm. The required numbers of datasets were created and input to the proposed algorithm and implemented using C++ programming language. The observed results were satisfactory.

REFERENCES

Liu, B. (2012). Sentiment Analysis and Opinion Mining, Morgan & Claypool Publishers.

Bryson, J. J., & Tanguy, E. (2010). Simplifying the design of human-like behaviour: Emotions as durative dynamic state for action selection. *International Journal of Synthetic Emotions*, *1*(1), 30–50. doi:10.4018/jse.2010101603

Cambria, E., Schuller, B., Xia, Y., & Havasi, C. (2013). *New Avenues in Opinion Mining and Sentiment Analysis*. IEEE.

Cook, D. J., & Holder, L. B. (2007). Mining Graph Data. John Wiley & Sons, Inc.

Fisher, D., Smith, M., & Welser, H. (2006). You are who you talk to: Detecting roles in usenet news-groups. In *Proceedings of the 39th Annual HICSS,* Washington, DC. IEEE. 10.1109/HICSS.2006.536

Helander, M., Lawrence, R., & Liu, Y. (2007). Looking for great ideas: Analyzing the innovation jam. In *Proceedings of the ACM SIGKDD International Conference on Knowledge Discovery and Data Mining*. 10.1145/1348549.1348557

Horowitz, E., Sahni, S., & Mehta, D. (2013). Fundamentals of Data Structures in C++ (2nd ed.). Hyderabad, India: Universities Press Private Limited.

Java, A., Song, X., Finin, T., & Tseng, B. (2007). Why we twitter: understanding microblogging usage and communities. In *Proceedings of 9th WebKDD and 1st SNA-KDD 2007 workshop on Web Mining and Social Network Analysis* (pp. 56–66). ACM. 10.1145/1348549.1348556

Quinn, D., Chen, L., & Mulvenna, M. (2012). Social network analysis: A survey. *International Journal of Ambient Computing and Intelligence*, *4*(3), 46-58.

Rao, B., Mitra, A., & Narayana, U. (2014). An approach to Study Properties and Behaviour of Social Network Using Graph Mining Techniques. In *Proceedings of DIGNATE 2014: ETEECT 2014*, India (pp. 13-17).

Rao, Bapuji., & Mishra, S. N. (2016). Detection of influential communities and members in a community graph of villages using graph mining techniques. *International Journal of Computer Science and Information Security*, *14*(5), 85-94. Retrieved from https://sites.google.com/site/ijcsis/

Rashid, U., & Quigley, A. (2009). Ambient Displays in Academic Settings: Avoiding their Underutilization. *International Journal of Ambient Computing and Intelligence*, *1*(2), 31–38. doi:10.4018/jaci.2009040104

Scripps, J., Tan, P.-N., & Esfahanian, A.-H. (2007). Node roles and community structure in networks. In *Proceedings of 9th WebKDD and 1st SNA-KDD 2007 workshop on Web Mining and Social Network Analysis* (pp. 26–35). ACM. 10.1145/1348549.1348553

Shannon, R., Kenny, E., & Quigley, A. (2009). Using ambient social reminders to stay in touch with friends. *International Journal of Ambient Computing and Intelligence*, *1*(2), 70–78. doi:10.4018/jaci.2009040109

Stavrianou, A., Velcin, J., & Chauchat, J.-H. (2010). A combination of opinion mining and social network techniques for discussion analysis. In *From Sociology to Computing in Social Networks* (pp. 59–79). Springer Vienna; doi:10.1007/978-3-7091-0294-7_4

Wiberg, M. (2011). Making the Case for "Architectural Informatics": A New Research Horizon for Ambient Computing? *International Journal of Ambient Computing and Intelligence*, 3(3), 1–7. doi:10.4018/jaci.2011070101

Zhang, S., Xia, Y., Meng, Y., & Yu, H. (2009). A Bootstrapping Method for Finer-Grained Opinion Mining Using Graph Model. In *Proceedings of 23rd Pacific Asia Conference on Language, Information and Computation, PACLIC 23*, Hong Kong, China (pp. 589–595).

This research was previously published in the International Journal of Synthetic Emotions (IJSE), 9(2); pages 94-110, copyright year 2018 by IGI Publishing (an imprint of IGI Global).

Chapter 61
The Concept of Big Data in Bureaucratic Service Using Sentiment Analysis

Lia Muliawaty
Universitas Pasundan, Bandung, Indonesia

Kamal Alamsyah
Universitas Pasundan, Bandung, Indonesia

Ummu Salamah
Universitas Pasundan, Bandung, Indonesia

Dian Sa'adillah Maylawati
UIN Sunan Gunung Djati Bandung, Bandung, Indonesia & Universiti Teknikal Malaysia Melaka, Melaka, Malaysia

ABSTRACT

The implementation of bureaucratic reform in Indonesia is not optimal and faces various obstacles. At present, public services demand excellent service and meet public satisfaction. The obstacles are rigid bureaucracy, incompetent bureaucrats or apparatuses, not professional, and there are technological gaps. Rapid technological development, such as digital technology and big data, has not been responded to positively by most bureaucrats. Big Data has a great potential for improving bureaucratic and public services. With a qualitative method and a waterfall software development life cycle, this article provides the design of a bureaucracy sentiment analysis application which implements Big Data technology for analyzing the opinions about bureaucratic service in Indonesia. This is for the purpose that the bureaucratic services can be improved based on societal opinion. The results of the experiment using RapidMiner showed that sentiment analysis as a Big Data technique for bureaucratic service based on societal opinion can be used to evaluate performance better.

DOI: 10.4018/978-1-6684-6303-1.ch061

INTRODUCTION

Until today, there has been a stigma regarding the performance of bureaucrats and bureaucracy in various governments in the world, especially governments in developing countries such as Indonesia. Bureaucracy in many developing countries is rigid, slow, inefficient, ineffective and so on. In the midst of society, a "bad" stigma develops about bureaucracy, related to the services provided because it is still far from the expectations of society, there are "bacterial" pathologies in the body of the bureaucracy, making the image of the bureaucracy in the public eye "bad."

Therefore, the negative stigma needs to be eliminated. One way is to do bureaucratic reform. The Indonesian government carried out reforms since 1998, together with the formation of the Reform Order. Reformation is a systematic, integrated and comprehensive effort aimed at realizing good governance, including good public governance, and good corporate governance (Damanhuri, 2017). The demands of bureaucratic reform in Indonesia occur as a result of public pressure on past government dissatisfaction (Mariana, 2017).

The fact is that bureaucratic reform in Indonesia has not been optimally implemented because of various obstacles, especially in the bureaucrats or apparatus as implementers of the policy. For example, the quality of public services that have not been optimal, is not in accordance with the criteria of the New Public Service (NPS) model. So that the level of community satisfaction is still low on services provided by the government. Some bureaucratic reforms in the aspect of public services that are the focus of attention are issues of corruption and public service and public information disclosure.

The essence of bureaucracy is its Human Resources (HR), namely bureaucrats or apparatus. HR factors that are incompetent, unprofessional, and do not master modern technology, are the weaknesses of bureaucratic reform in Indonesia. This has led to a gap between technological advances, such as digital technology and big data, with slow and less responsive bureaucracy. According to Kaloh, that work begins to change into knowledge-based work and human resource needs also change towards knowledge workers.

Figure 1. Percentage of social media user in Indonesia

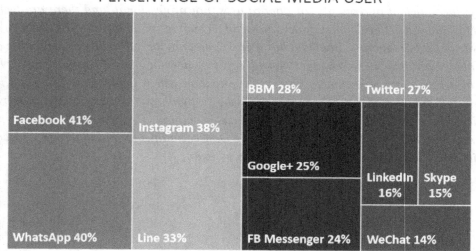

To improve the quality of HR in serving the community, big data technology can be used optimally, one of which is opinion mining from social media (Jumadi, Maylawati, Subaeki, & Ridwan, 2016). Where data from social media and analyzed so as to get an analysis of community sentiment on the quality of service bureaucracy in Indonesia. Until January 2018, social media users in Indonesia reached 132.7 million out of a total population of 265.4 million (Laksana, 2018). This figure is relatively fantastic, where around 50% of Indonesia's population owns and becomes an active social media user, starting from Twitter, Facebook, Instagram, Youtube, and so on. The smartphone is the main choice (90%) that is used as a device to run social media applications. Based on survey results that described in Figure 1, YouTube is the most widely used social media reaching 43%, followed by Facebook 41%, WhatsApp 40%, Instagram 38%, Line 33%, BBM 28%, Twitter 27%, Google+ 25%, FB Messenger 24%, LinkedIn 16%, Skype 15%, and WeChat 14% (Haryanto, 2018). Social media users in Indonesia have a unique pattern, one of which is based on gender, men are more active using social media such as Facebook and Instagram than women for users in the age range of 18 to 24 years. Therefore, this article utilizes social media and big data technology to analyze people's sentiments and opinions about bureaucratic services in Indonesia.

RESEARCH METHOD

This research used a qualitative method. The qualitative research method is used in the following conditions (Tracy, 2016): (a) when there is rarely any information available about the topic (b) when the researcher's variables are unclear and unknown, and (c) when a relevant theory base is missing in any sense (Tavallaei & Abu Talib, 2010). Qualitative research can be used to examine topics such as contextual conditions-the social, institutional, and environmental conditions. Qualitative research is an inductive process which builds concepts, hypotheses, or theories rather than testing hypotheses. One of the uses of the research method delineates the process (rather than the outcome or product) of meaning-making. Qualitative research is focusing on the emergence of situations. The research methodology is a case study that has the following characteristics: particularistic, descriptive, and heuristic. A qualitative research is an inductive process which builds concepts, hypotheses, or theories rather than testing hypotheses. One of the uses of the research method delineates the process (rather than the outcome or product) of meaning-making (Sharan B. Merriam, 2009). Qualitative research is focusing on the emergence of situations. Qualitative researchers are concerned primarily with the process, rather than outcomes or products, qualitative researchers are interested in meaning how people make sense of their lives, experiences, and their structures of the world, the qualitative researcher is the primary instrument for data collection and analysis, qualitative research involves fieldwork.

Technology is developed rapidly today, so that utilizing the technology for social science will be very useful and current research (Hernandez, 2017; Moses, 2015; Nielsen, Lene Hansen, Kira Storgaard, Stage, & Billestrup, 2015; Yeo, Zaman, & Kulathuramaiyer, 2013). Besides the qualitative method, this research used Waterfall as the Software Development Life Cycle (SDLC). The waterfall is the basic and simple software development method that begins from requirement elicitation, analysis, design, implementation, testing, deployment, and maintenance (Ruparelia, 2010; Pressman, 2011; Sommerville, 2010). In requirement elicitation, the needs of stakeholder and system are collected (Ramdhani, Maylawati, Amin, & Aulawi, 2018). Then, in analysis and design, we create a system model, among others architecture model and software model using Unified Modelling Language (Booch, 2005, 1998; Maylawati, Darmalaksana, & Ramdhani, 2018; Maylawati, Ramdhani, & Amin, 2018). In the implementing and testing phase, we used RapidMiners for analyzing the sentiment of bureaucratic service. Sentiment analysis in RapidMiners uses Deep Learning method is the development of Artificial Neural Network (ANN) method with add multiple hidden layers between input and output layer (Ahmad, Farman, & Jan, 2019; Schmidhuber, 2015). Moreover, Deep Learning is a popular method with a various algorithm in text analytics research today.

Figure 2. Research methodology activity flow

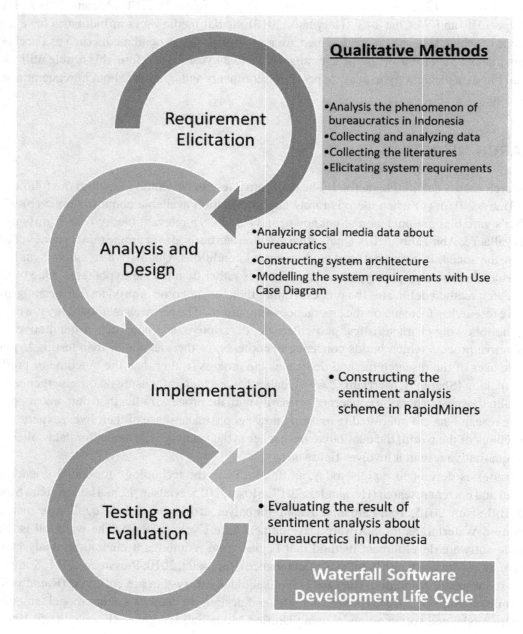

From the explanation above, in this research, qualitative methods are combined with SDLC and Big Data Technology for sentiment analysis from social media. Figure 2 describes about flow activity of research methodology. In requirement, elicitation is implemented a qualitative method with analyzing the phenomena, facts, and condition of bureaucracy in Indonesia. Then, besides collecting the related literature studies, the data from social media are also collected and analyzed that used as an input requirement of sentiment analysis system. Therefore, this is one of the differences with the research before combining information technology techniques and social science.

RESULT AND DISCUSSION

The Performance of Bureaucrats in the Digital Age

Bureaucracy is a device/ institution of employees/ HR and a system of government administration carried out by civil servants based on legislation (Damanhuri., 2017). Bureaucracy is a storage place for typical and unique public trust. "In general, the term 'bureaucracy' is regarded as having a negative connotation, although there have been anarchists that enjoyed the excess of formalism and rigor" (Liviora, 2018). There are three bureaucratic concepts, namely (Mariana, 2017) 2) The Concept of Parkinson Law; and 3) Ovulation Concept (2017, p. 93). Bureaucracy is characterized by hierarchy, specialization, formalization, and impersonality (Widiyastuti, Andretti Abdillah, & Kurniawan, 2014). Bureaucracy only emphasizes how the bureaucratic machine should be professionally and rationally run. Furthermore, bureaucracy shows a lot about how government organizations are adopted by means of official kingdoms. The bureaucratic model currently being implemented does not show a system that represents the nature of justice, transparency, and efficiency (Sanrego Nz & Muhammad, 2013).

Social media is one of the characteristics of technological development in the era of Industry 4.0. In the Industrial 4.0 era, where everything is connected to internet technology (internet of things) (Kemeristekdikti, 2018; Nizam, 2018; Sadiyoko, 2017). Where industry 4.0 is characterized by internet usage in each sector, both in the economy, social, education, and other sectors. The entire process and production utilizes internet technology and utilizes digital technology, artificial intelligence, big data, robotics, etc. which are also known as the disruptive innovation phenomenon (Office of Chief Economist Bank Mandiri, 2018; Sumber Daya: Iptek & Dikti, 2018). Big data is a very large set of data that can be computationally analyzed to find patterns, trends, associations, and specifically, those related to habits and human interactions (Chen & Zhang, 2014; Sagiroglu & Sinanc, 2013; Wu, Zhu, Wu, & Ding, 2014). In analyzing social media, of course, big data technology is needed, considering that data in the media has big data characteristics. At the beginning of its appearance, big data only has 3V characteristics, including volume, variety, and velocity (Sagiroglu & Sinanc, 2013; Tan, Blake, Saleh, & Dustdar, 2013). However, there are currently at least 10V, 17V, up to more, including volume, velocity, variety, veracity, value, validity, variability, venue, vocabulary, vagueness, visualization, etc. (Arockia, Varnekha, & Veneshia, 2017; Borne, 2014). Social media that has various types of data such as text, images and videos is very suitable if processed with big data technology. Various big data applications are ready to use to process and analyze data from social media to reveal insight knowledge from the data (Panatula, Kumar, & Geetha, 2019; Vinutha & Raju, 2018).

The discovery of computer technology is a big leap of human civilization on earth that drives other discoveries, such as digital technology. The digital age is a new paradigm in the government bureaucracy in Indonesia, including the public service sector. This paradigm is an important and radical transition from New Public Management (NPM) towards a digital governance model (Kosorukov, 2017). Most governments in the regions have not been able to implement bureaucratic digitalization because of various factors, including large costs and qualifications of human resources who master technology are still minimal. Although there are exceptions to the cities of Bandung and Banyuwangi which are considered capable of applying modern technology.

Through the use of digital devices (e-government), public services are more efficient, effective, fast, and accurate (Pamoragung, Suryadi, & Ramdhani, 2006). So that bureaucratic procedures are more practical and brief. Similarly, through digitalization, the number of operational officers can be reduced but the number of services can be increased (Ramdhani, Aulawi, & Gojali, 2018). Previously, the process of public services such as health services, education, licensing, etc., took a long time/ took a long time. Besides that, direct interaction between bureaucrats or apparatus can encourage acts of corruption and the like.

Rapid technological developments have caused previous technologies to become unused or obsolete, such as hardware or computer software. In addition, it has a direct impact on its users, namely the bureaucrats and apparatus must improve their knowledge and skills with these new devices. If not done it can cause their performance to be unproductive and the level of community satisfaction low. Public services require the involvement of many actors because their implementation is related to many actors. Faulkner also explained the need for cooperation in implementing public services. Government Leadership and Public Services can be generated and sustained a sense of shared purpose and responsibility.

Big Data: A New Paradigm, Challenges, and Constraints

Big Data can be used by all parties and sectors, including government. For example, for the provision of health services, education, and improving the quality of the bureaucracy and its bureaucrats. The use of big data is important for improving the quality of public services, especially associated with modern developments that require many aspects, including excellent service quality and speed of service processes. At present, the public policy model adopts many services provided by the private sector in order to fulfill public satisfaction as service users. Through big data, policies or programs can be designed appropriately, efficiently and effectively. So far, Big Data has been used by large private companies in improving product quality, developing markets, and choosing the right marketing techniques. Big Data provides accurate data so that programs designed using big data have high accuracy and are economical. Big Data has a variety of data and large so that it is just how to process and use these data for interest.

But Big Data cannot be accessed or processed with traditional devices because of the huge amount of data and many variants. So to access it requires the latest technology. This is an obstacle for some companies and governments in utilizing the potential of Big Data. As is known, most governments are held in a limited and less optimal manner. The limitations of technology-based work devices have caused the minimal quality of public services, low bureaucrat work productivity, rigid bureaucratic procedures, and non-optimal results.

This is caused by a variety of factors, including the quality of human resources (HR) and their working devices. Only a few local governments are able to provide the latest technology-based work tools because these facilities are expensive and require professional HR. Knowledge-based works require knowledge of workers. The change in work orientation is a new paradigm and challenges and obstacles for bureaucrats in carrying out efficient and effective bureaucracy. The criteria for efficient and effective bureaucracy is the absolute demand in modern government, namely in order to provide quality and optimal public services.

Sentiment Analysis Architecture as Big Data Technology for Bureaucratic

The data from social media that is the easiest to process is text. Text is the unstructured data, so that it must be conducted the pre-process until the text data ready to be processed in mining process (Maylawati, Sugilar, & Yudhiantara, 2018; Maylawati, Ramdhani, Rahman, & Darmalaksana, 2017; Maylawati & Saptawati, 2017; Slamet et al., 2018). In the requirement elicitation phase, we defined several requirements of bureaucracy sentiment analyzer application, among others:

1. The application can read the corpus that contains document from social media, such as Twitter, Facebook, or blog and news website;
2. The application can do text pre-processing, such as lowercase, tokenizing, emoticon handling, abbreviation handling, a regular expression (regex) removal, stopwords removal, and stemming;
3. The application can conduct feature extraction, either bag of words or multiple words (n-gram);
4. The application can conduct feature selection, such as removing redundant;
5. The application can do the mining process with a classification technique for sentiment analysis using a specific algorithm, such as the Naive Bayes algorithm, Decision Tree, Artificial Neural Network, and so on. Where in the mining process there are two main processes in classification, among others training process and testing process;
6. The application provides the result of bureaucracy sentiment analysis.

Figure 3 describes the bureaucracy sentiment analyzer architecture, while Figure 4 describes the use case diagram of bureaucracy sentiment analyzer which is representation model of analysis in Waterfall SDLC after requirement elicitation.

Figure 3. Bureaucracy sentiment analyzer architecture

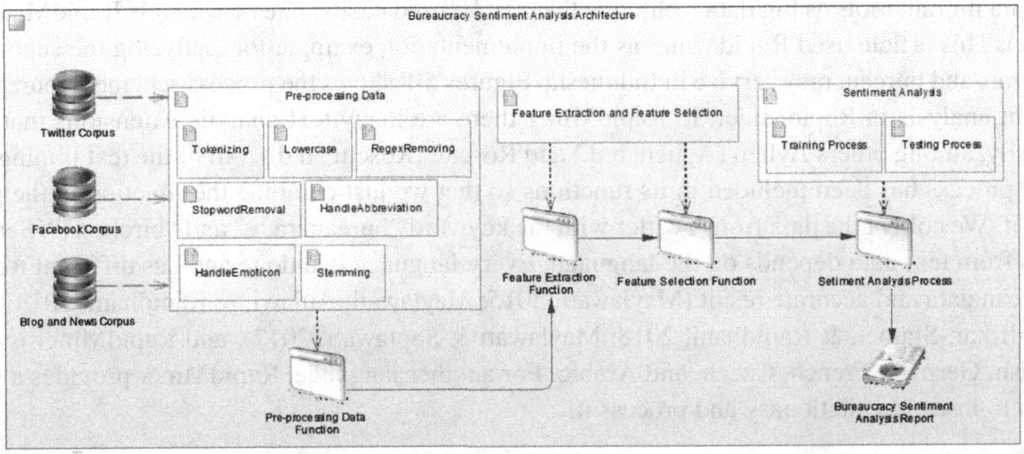

Figure 4. Use case diagram of bureaucracy sentiment analyzer

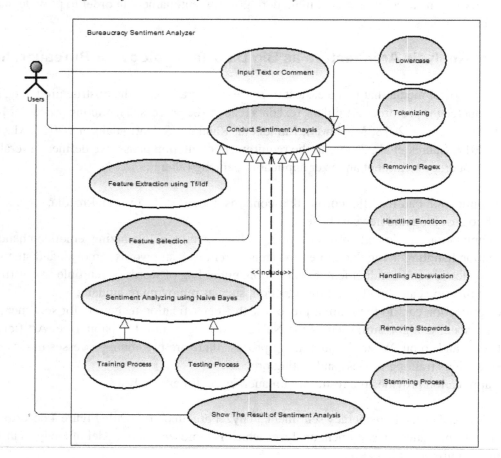

The Example of Sentiment Analysis Application

Many data mining tools as big data technique that can be used easily, one of which is RapidMiner (Studio, n.d.). This article used RapidMiner as the implementation example for analyzing the sentiment of bureaucrats and bureaucracy service in Indonesia. Figures 5-8 shows the process scheme of bureaucracy sentiment analysis in RapidMiner. In RapidMiner there are many text analytic extensions that can be used easily, among others Aylien (Aylien, n.d.) and Rosette (Rosette, n.d.). All of the text mining or text analytic process has been included in its functions so that we just combine the function in the process and run it. We collect the data from Twitter with the keyword "bureaucracy" and "birokrasi". Sentiment analysis from text data depends on the language. Every language is unique and has different treatment to get clean data and accurate result (Maylawati, 2015; Maylawati, Aulawi, & Ramdhani, 2019; Maylawati, Zulfikar, Slamet, & Ramdhani, 2018; Maylawati & Saptawati, 2017), and RapidMiner is limited to English, German, French, Czech, and Arabic. For another language, RapidMiner provides a general function to insert the dictionary and process it.

Figure 5-8 also describes the result of bureaucracy sentiment analysis from Twitter directly. Figure 5 shows the result of bureaucracy sentiment analysis using Aylien, from 100 tweets from Twitter, 62 tweets have a positive opinion, 32 tweets are negative, and 6 tweets are neutral. While, the result using Rosette quite different (with the same data collection and illustrated in Figure 6), where positive tweets are 21, 40 tweets are negative, and 39 tweets are neutral-. Even though there are different in classifying the sentiment, but the important thing is from that experiment (with 100 tweets) around 41.5% the opinions about bureaucratic service are positive, around 36% are negative opinion, and around 22.5% are neutral opinion. It means that the community feels quite satisfied with bureaucratic services, although those who have a positive and neutral opinion are not too much different. However, it remains to be noted that there are also many who think negatively about the existing bureaucratic services. This result can be used as an evaluation material for things that are not suitable, not good so that the community is not satisfied and has a negative opinion on bureaucratic services.

We also collect 200 tweets with the Indonesian language for analyzing the sentiment about bureaucracy in Indonesia. The result of Aylien in Figure 7 shows that only 3 tweets that have a positive opinion, 1 tweet is negative, and 196 tweets are neutral. While the result using Rosette in Figure 8 shows that 1 tweet is detected has a positive opinion, 0 for the negative tweet, 5 for neutral tweets and 194 tweets for unsupported language. The results of sentiment analysis with Indonesian text in RapidMiner have not been capable yet to be used to analyze the public opinion about bureaucracy in Indonesia, because-it is constrained by language processing that has not been supported by RapidMiner. Those result can be used as an illustration of how the public opinion about bureaucracy. Besides that, the process in RapidMiner is an implementation illustration of sentiment analysis process as big data technique that has been provided in architecture and use case diagram above (in Figure 3 and 4). The main idea is big data technology can be used to improve bureaucracy service based on society or public opinions.

Figure 5. The result of Aylien for bureaucracy sentiment analysis

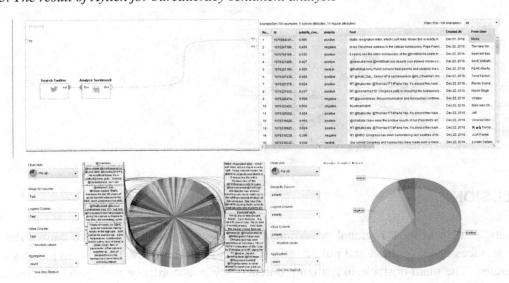

Figure 6. The result of Rosette for bureaucracy sentiment analysis

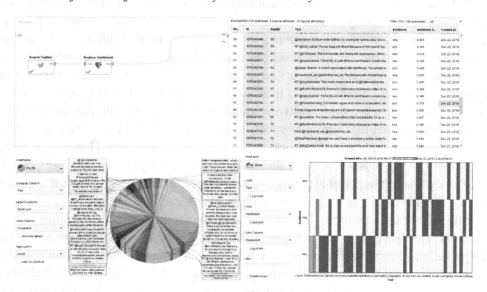

Figure 7. The result of Aylien for bureaucracy sentiment analysis with Indonesian text

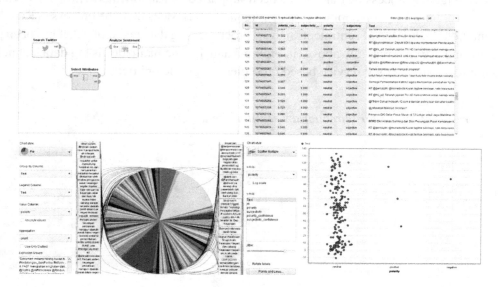

CONCLUSION

Bureaucratic reform in most regional governments has not yet materialized. This causes the quality of public services is not optimal and public satisfaction is low. Therefore, the reform process needs to be accelerated. The main obstacle in realizing bureaucracy in accordance with good governance is its human resources, namely bureaucrats. Most bureaucrats are unprofessional, do not have the expertise that is in accordance with the field and work responsibilities. So that the performance of bureaucrats is not optimal. Another obstacle is the factor of working facilities or working devices that are limited and simple. While, the demands of the modern bureaucracy are work devices based on modern technology, such as digital technology. Big data can be utilized by regional government bureaucracies because of the two main factors above, namely bureaucrats and modern technological devices. So that the potential for big data can be used optimally. This article success to design a sentiment analysis architecture and functional model as big data technology for bureaucracy opinion in social media. The experiment proved that the result of sentiment can be used as information to evaluate, to make a decision, and to improve bureaucracy service quality.

Figure 8. The result of Rosette for bureaucracy sentiment analysis with Indonesian text

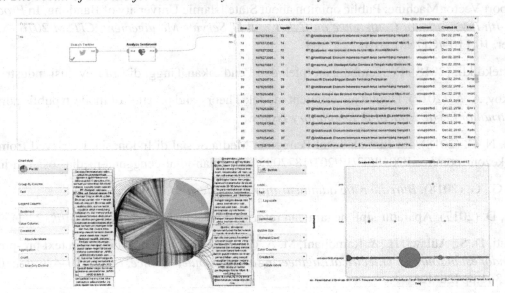

REFERENCES

Ahmad, J., Farman, H., & Jan, Z. (2019). Deep Learning Methods and Applications. In Deep Learning: Convergence to Big Data Analytics (pp. 31-42). Springer. doi:10.1007/978-981-13-3459-7_3

Arockia, P. S., Varnekha, S. S., & Veneshia, K. A. (2017). The 17 V's of Big Data. *International Research Journal of Engineering and Technology, 4*(9), 3–6. Retrieved from https://irjet.net/archives/V4/i9/IRJET-V4I957.pdf

Aylien. (n.d.). Aylien Text Analytics. Retrieved from https://aylien.com/

Booch, G. (1998). *Object-Oriented Analysis and Design* (2nd ed.). Santa Clara, CA: Addison-Wesley.

Booch. (2005). *The Unified Modeling Language User Guide*. Addison-Wesley. Retrieved from http://books.google.com/books?id=xfQ8JCbxDK8C&pgis=1

Borne, K. (2014). Top 10 List – The V's of Big Data. *Data Science Central*. Retrieved from https://www.datasciencecentral.com/profiles/blogs/top-10-list-the-v-s-of-big-data

Damanhuri, J. R. (2017). Reaktualisasi reformasi birokrasi menuju good governance. In Prosiding Seminar Nasional Pendidikan FKIP (pp. 297–304).

Haryanto, A. T. (2018). 130 Juta Orang Indonesia Tercatat Aktif di Medsos. Retrieved from https://inet. detik.com/cyberlife/d-3912429/130-juta-orang-indonesia-tercatat-aktif-di-medsos

Hernandez, A. A. (2017). Green IT Adoption Practices in Education Sector : A Developing Country Perspective. *International Journal of Sociotechnology and Knowledge Development (IJSKD)*. doi:10.4018/IJSKD.2017070101

Jumadi, M., D. S. A., Subaeki, B., & Ridwan, T. (2016). Opinion mining on Twitter microblogging using Support Vector Machine: Public opinion about State Islamic University of Bandung. In *Proceedings of 2016 4th International Conference on Cyber and IT Service Management, CITSM 2016*. Academic Publisher. 10.1109/CITSM.2016.7577569

Kemeristekdikti. (2018). Pengembangan Iptek dan Pendidikan Tinggi di Era Revolusi Industri 4.0.

Kosorukov, A. A. (2017). Digital government model: Theory and practice of modern public administration. *Journal of Legal, Ethical & Regulatory Issues*.

Laksana, N. C. (2018). Ini Jumlah Total Pengguna Media Sosial di Indonesia. Retrieved from https://techno.okezone.com/read/2018/03/13/207/1872093/ini-jumlah-total-pengguna-media-sosial-di-indonesia

Liviora, G., G. (2018). *Bureaucratic administration in modern society*.

Mariana, D. (2017). Aparatur sipil negara dan reformasi birokrasi. *Jurnal Ilmu Politik*, *22*(1), 91–104.

Maylawati, D. S., Aulawi, H., & Ramdhani, M. A. (2019). Flexibility of Indonesian text pre-processing library. *Indonesian Journal of Electrical Engineering and Computer Science*, *13*(1), 420–426. doi:10.11591/ijeecs.v13.i1.pp420-426

Maylawati, D. S., Darmalaksana, W., & Ramdhani, M. A. (2018). Systematic Design of Expert System Using Unified Modelling Language. *IOP Conference Series. Materials Science and Engineering*, *288*(1), 012047. doi:10.1088/1757-899X/288/1/012047

Maylawati, D. S., Ramdhani, M. A., & Amin, A. S. (2018). Tracing the Linkage of Several Unified Modelling Language Diagrams in Software Modelling Based on Best Practices. *International Journal of Engineering & Technology*, *7*(2.29), 776–780. doi:10.14419/ijet.v7i2.29.14255

Maylawati, D. S., Ramdhani, M. A., Rahman, A., & Darmalaksana, W. (2017). Incremental technique with set of frequent word item sets for mining large Indonesian text data. In *Proceedings of the 2017 5th International Conference on Cyber and IT Service Management CITSM 2017* (pp. 1–6). Academic Publisher. doi:10.1109/CITSM.2017.8089224

Maylawati, D. S., Sugilar, H., & Yudhiantara, R. A. (2018). Kualitas perangkat lunak: Modularitas pustaka text pre-processing. *Jurnal Perspektif*, *1*(2).

Maylawati, D. S., Zulfikar, W. B., Slamet, C., & Ramdhani, M. A. (2018). An Improved of Stemming Algorithm for Mining Indonesian Text with Slang on Social Media. In *Proceedings of the 6th International Conference on Cyber and IT Service Management (CITSM 2018)*. Academic Publisher. 10.1109/CITSM.2018.8674054

Maylawati, D. S. A. (2015). Pembangunan Library pre-processing untuk text mining dengan representasi himpunan frequent word itemset (HFWI) Studi Kasus: Bahasa Gaul Indonesia. Bandung.

Merriam, S. B. (2009). *Qualitative Research: A Guide to Design and Implementation.* Wiley. doi:10.1017/CBO9781107415324.004

Moses, J. A. (2015). A project management approach to learning. International Journal of Sociotechnology and Knowledge Development.

Muhammad Nizam, S. (2018). *Revolusi industri 4.0: Suatu Pengenalan.* Seranta FELDA Jabatan Perdana Menteri.

Nielsen, L. H., & Storgaard, K., Stage, J., & Billestrup, J. (2015). A Template for Design Personas: Analysis of 47 Persona Descriptions from Danish Industries and Organizations. *International Journal of Sociotechnology and Knowledge Development.* doi:10.4018/ijskd.2015010104

Office of Chief Economist Bank Mandiri. (2018). Menghadapi Era RI 4.0.

Pamoragung, A., Suryadi, K., & Ramdhani, M. A. (2006). Enhancing the Implementation of E-Government in Indonesia through the High-Quality of Virtual Community and Knowledge Portal Design. In *Proceedings of the European Conference on e-Government* (pp. 341–348).

Panatula, K., G., Kumar, D., S., Geetha, T. V. S. K., & E. (2019). Performance evaluation of cloud service with hadoop for twitter data. *Indonesian Journal of Electrical Engineering and Computer Science, 13*(1).

Philip Chen, C. L., & Zhang, C. Y. (2014). Data-intensive applications, challenges, techniques and technologies: A survey on Big Data. *Information Sciences, 275,* 314–347. doi:10.1016/j.ins.2014.01.015

Pressman, R. S. (2011). *Software Engineering: A Practitioner's Approach* (7th ed.). New York: McGraw-Hill.

Ramdhani, M. A., Aulawi, H., & Gojali, D. (2018). Analysis of determinant factors of e-Government implementation. *IOP Conference Series. Materials Science and Engineering, 434,* 12049. doi:10.1088/1757-899X/434/1/012049

Ramdhani, M. A., Sa'adillah Maylawati, D., Amin, A. S., & Aulawi, H. (2018). Requirements Elicitation in Software Engineering. *IACSIT International Journal of Engineering and Technology.* doi:10.14419/ijet.v7i2.29.14254

Rosette. (n.d.). Rosette Text Analytics. Retrieved from https://www.rosette.com/

Ruparelia, N. B. (2010). Software Development Lifecycle Models. *Software Engineering Notes, 35*(3), 8. doi:10.1145/1764810.1764814

Sa'Adillah Maylawati, D., & Putri Saptawati, G. A. (2017). Set of Frequent Word Item sets as Feature Representation for Text with Indonesian Slang. In *Journal of Physics* (Vol. 801). Conference Series; doi:10.1088/1742-6596/801/1/012066

Sa'Adillah Maylawati, D., & Putri Saptawati, G. A. (2017). Set of Frequent Word Item sets as Feature Representation for Text with Indonesian Slang. *Journal of Physics: Conference Series, 801*(1). doi:10.1088/1742-6596/801/1/012066

Sadiyoko, A. (2017). *Industry 4.0 Ancaman, Tantangan atau Kesempatan*. Oratio Dies XXIV FTI UNPAR.

Sagiroglu, S., & Sinanc, D. (2013). Big data: A review. In *Proceedings of the 2013 International Conference on Collaboration Technologies and Systems, CTS 2013*. Academic Press. 10.1109/CTS.2013.6567202

Sanrego Nz, Y. D., & Muhammad, R. (2013). Analisa perbandingan model birokrasi Indonesia: Model modern David Osborne, Ted Gaebler dan pendekatan konsep Islam perspektif Umer Chapra. *Jurnal Al-Muzara'ah*, *1*(1), 18–38.

Schmidhuber, J. (2015). Deep Learning in neural networks: An overview. *Neural Networks*, *61*, 85–117. doi:10.1016/j.neunet.2014.09.003 PMID:25462637

Slamet, C., Atmadja, A. R., Maylawati, D. S., Lestari, R. S., Darmalaksana, W., & Ramdhani, M. A. (2018). Automated Text Summarization for Indonesian Article Using Vector Space Model. In *Proceedings of the IOP Conference Series: Materials Science and Engineering*. 10.1088/1757-899X/288/1/012037

Sommerville, I. (2010). Software Engineering. In *Software Engineering*. doi:10.1111/j.1365-2362.2005.01463.x

Rapidminer Studio. (n.d.). RapidMiner. Retrieved from https://rapidminer.com/

Sumber Daya: Iptek & Dikti. (2018). Era Revolusi Industri 4.0 Saatnya Generasi Millenial Menjadi Dosen Masa Depan.

Tan, W., Blake, M. B., Saleh, I., & Dustdar, S. (2013). Social-network-sourced big data analytics. *IEEE Internet Computing*, *17*(5), 62–69. doi:10.1109/MIC.2013.100

Tavallaei, M., & Talib, M. A. (2010). A general perspective on role of theory in qualitative research. *Journal of International Social Research*, *3*(11).

Tracy, J. S. (2016). *Qualitative Research Methods*. United Kingdom: Wiley-Blackwell.

Vinutha, D. & Raju, G.T. (18AD). An Accurate and Efficient Scheduler for Hadoop MapReduce Framework. *Indonesian Journal of Electrical Engineering and Computer Science 2, 12*(3).

Widiyastuti, S., Abdillah, L.A., & Kurniawan. (2014). Sistem Informasi Eksekutif Bagian Kepegawaian Pada Pt. Pelindo Ii (Persero) Palembang. *Seminar Nasional Teknologi Informasi, Komunikasi Dan Manajemen*.

Wu, X., Zhu, X., Wu, G. Q., & Ding, W. (2014). Data mining with big data. *IEEE Transactions on Knowledge and Data Engineering*. doi:10.1109/TKDE.2013.109

Yeo, A. W., Zaman, T., & Kulathuramaiyer, N. (2013). Indigenous Knowledge Management in the Kelabit Community in Eastern Malaysia: Insights and Reflections for Contemporary KM Design. *International Journal of Sociotechnology and Knowledge Development*, *5*(1), 23–36. doi:10.4018/jskd.2013010103

This research was previously published in the International Journal of Sociotechnology and Knowledge Development (IJSKD), 11(3); pages 1-13, copyright year 2019 by IGI Publishing (an imprint of IGI Global).

Chapter 62
Sentiment Analysis Using Cuckoo Search for Optimized Feature Selection on Kaggle Tweets

Akshi Kumar
Delhi Technological University, Delhi, India

Shikhar Garg
Delhi Technological University, Delhi, India

Arunima Jaiswal
Indira Gandhi Delhi Technical University for Women, Delhi, India

Shobhit Verma
Delhi Technological University, Delhi, India

Siddhant Kumar
Delhi Technological University, Delhi, India

ABSTRACT

Selecting the optimal set of features to determine sentiment in online textual content is imperative for superior classification results. Optimal feature selection is computationally hard task and fosters the need for devising novel techniques to improve the classifier performance. In this work, the binary adaptation of cuckoo search (nature inspired, meta-heuristic algorithm) known as the Binary Cuckoo Search is proposed for the optimum feature selection for a sentiment analysis of textual online content. The baseline supervised learning techniques such as SVM, etc., have been firstly implemented with the traditional tf-idf model and then with the novel feature optimization model. Benchmark Kaggle dataset, which includes a collection of tweets is considered to report the results. The results are assessed on the basis of performance accuracy. Empirical analysis validates that the proposed implementation of a binary cuckoo search for feature selection optimization in a sentiment analysis task outperforms the elementary supervised algorithms based on the conventional tf-idf score.

DOI: 10.4018/978-1-6684-6303-1.ch062

INTRODUCTION

The increasing traction of social media avenues to verbalize personal notions & beliefs has created a need to put in place a paradigm which can analyse the humongous amount of data involved, the task is typically referred to as sentiment analysis (Kumar & Sharma, 2016). Formally, Sentiment Analysis is defined as the study, and subsequent categorization, of an individual's feelings and opinions, communicated through text, with respect to a certain context (Kumar & Abraham, 2017; Kumar & Teeja, 2012). The categorization is carried out along the lines of polarities, such as positive and negative, etc. (Kumar & Sebastian, 2012; Kumar & Sharma, 2017).

Sentiment analysis, also known as opinion mining, is the means of recognizing and designating opinions communicated through a written piece to ascertain the author's connotation (positive, objective or negative) of that piece using a combination of statistical and computational techniques (Kumar & Jaiswal, 2017).

The core module of the Sentiment Analysis process employs feature extraction, a process used to convert input data, consisting of text indicating opinions, into an array of features, which can represent the input data very well (Kumar & Khorwal, 2017). Feature Selection is a technique used to select a subset of relevant features, discarding nonessential attributes (Kumar & Rani, 2016). Effective and efficient feature selection affects the quality of sentiments extracted and hence the classifier performance. But it has been observed that many features exist which don't contribute to accuracy, and thus can be removed without causing much loss. Fewer features reduce the complexity of the analysis, facilitating optimization.

Many researchers have adopted metaheuristic or stochastic methods for employing efficacious feature selection (Kumar, Khorwal, & Chaudhary, 2017). Metaheuristic methods exploit the trade-off which exists between a relatively robust solution and computational effort. Swarm intelligence-based stochastic methods are distinctly attractive for feature selection. Swarm Intelligence is the area of artificial intelligence that deals with systems composed of multiple entities called agents that correlate using self-organization and localized control. Agents are governed by simple rules and their behaviours are governed by their actual roles they play in their natural habitat. Movement of individual agents is decentralized, however, interaction between agents' results in a universal intelligent behaviour.

Cuckoo Search (CS) algorithm is a nature inspired, metaheuristic *optimization algorithm* which belongs to a group of swarm intelligence algorithms (Yang & Deb, 2009). The algorithm takes its inspiration from the cuckoo birds' parasitic practice of laying their eggs in the nests of hosts. The primary objective is to combine a set of binary coordinates for each solution, signifying if a particular feature belongs to the subsequent group of features or not. A classifier is trained with the selected features, encoded by the significance of the eggs. The solution's quality is then determined by evaluating each nest (Yang & Deb, 2009).

Recent literature has shown that CS algorithm has been surveyed as being more computationally efficient than PSO (Adnan & Razzaque, 2013).

Pereira et al. (2014) have developed a binary adaptation of CS algorithm, named Binary Cuckoo Search (Bcs). BCS is designed specifically to achieve optimum feature selection. It is the modified variant of the generic Cuckoo Search (CS) algorithm, which outputs the subset of features that are most efficient in classification.

In this paper, the authors present the application of Binary Cuckoo Search for sentiment analysis on tweets. Our approximation is based on the model given by Pereira et al. (2014). The author had applied binary cuckoo search on publicly available datasets on diabetes (768 samples, 8 features 2 classes), DNA (2000 samples, 180 features, 3classes), Heart (270 samples, 13 features, 2 classes), Mushrooms (8124 samples, 112 features, 2 classes). This study demonstrates the working of the model when applied on Kaggle dataset for sentiment analysis using optimized feature selection. Within the scope of our knowledge, this work involves the novel implementation of binary cuckoo search for employing optimized feature selection for enhanced sentiment classification task.

The Sentiment analysis task consists of four subtasks namely: (1) Pre-processing of tweets, (2) Feature extraction using Term Frequency – Inverse Document Frequency (TF-IDF) (Roelleke & Wang, 2008), (3) Feature Selection using Binary Cuckoo Search (BCS) Algorithm and (4) Classification using five supervised classification techniques namely K-Nearest Neighbours (k-NN), Decision Tree, Support Vector Machine (SVM), Multilayer Perceptron (MLP), and Naïve Bayesian (NB). The results are evaluated on the basis of accuracy.

The remainder of the paper has been organised as follows: Section 2 reviews the already existing studies and the related work. Section 3 gives an insight into the system architecture and the proposed optimised approach. Section 4 illustrates the implementation details such as tools used by the authors. Section 5 provides results of the experiment along with its analysis. Section 6 concludes the paper and presents the future scope of this study.

RELATED WORK

Sentiment Analysis is getting a lot of attention from researchers in recent times. This is mainly due to the business significance of mining user opinions (Kumar & Joshi, 2017). Social network has become a major source of such user opinions. Users express their opinion on myriad topics ranging from product reviews to government performance reviews. For example, Medhat, Hassan and Korashy (2014) discussed about the various primary and advanced algorithms for sentiment analysis like Decision Tree Classifiers, Support Vector Machines, Maximum Entropy, Neural Network, Bayesian Network etc. It has also used some Lexicon-based Approach like Dictionary based approach and Corpus based approach. Fields related to Sentiment Analysis like transfer learning, emotion detection and so on were also discussed in this study. Kumar et al. (2012) presented a survey of the vast extent and volume of work that had been carried out in the field of opinion mining. This paper covered both lexicon based as well as machine learning based method used for analysis. Work done on different granularity level like document level, sentence level and phrase level had also been surveyed. Chaudhari et al. (2015) had also presented a survey of the various machine learning techniques applied to the domain of sentiment analysis. It provided a comprehensive view of machine learning in sentiment analysis. SVM, Naïve Bayesian and multilayer perceptron are some of the classification algorithms that had been surveyed in the paper. These algorithms are baseline supervised machine learning algorithms that have found significant applications in many classification tasks. Kumar and Jaiswal (2017) briefly explained about the empirical comparison between Twitter and Tumblr for sentiment analysis employing techniques like SVM, KNN, MLP etc. The results were evaluated based on the key performance indicators like accuracy, precision, recall and F score.

Recently a lot of research is being done in the field of swarm intelligence algorithms. These algorithms have become a natural choice for finding solutions to optimisation and NP hard problems (Yu, Wang, Han, Liu, & Zhang, 2015). For example, Sumathi et al (2014) proposed Artificial Bee Colony algorithm for selecting an optimal feature sub-set. The dataset used was IMDB movie reviews. Inverse document Frequency technique was used for creating feature vector. The classification algorithms used were Naïve Bayesian, Ripple Down Rule Learner (RIDOR), and Fuzzy Unordered Rule Induction Algorithm (FURIA) Their model had shown the increased accuracy by 1.63% to 3.81%, reduced the root mean square error (RMSE) by 5.35% to 17.56% and improved the precision by 1.3% to 3.99%. Basari, Hussin, Ananta and Zeniarja (2013) used a PSO-SVM hybrid model for classifying sentiments on Twitter data set. TF and TF-IDF was used for feature weighting. Particle swarm optimisation was used to select an optimum set of features. SVM algorithm was used for classification. The model showed improvement in accuracy from 71.87% to 77%. Gupta, Reddy and Ekbal (2015) used the particle swarm optimisation on SemEval-2014 benchmarks. PSO was used for selecting the most optimal features. Conditional Random Field (CRF) was used as learning model. The accuracy had decreased from 81.91% to 71.25% for laptop domain. This accuracy when compared with benchmarks was still promising and had been achieved with a substantial reduction in feature set.

Cuckoo search is the metaheuristic algorithm that had been initially introduced by Yang et al. (2009). It is inspired by the patristic behaviour of cuckoo birds with levy flights operation of some fruit flies and birds. This algorithm uses a continuous variation of cuckoo search. Douglas Rodrigues et al. (2013) introduced a binary cuckoo search algorithm for feature selection. The paper examined the BCS algorithm on theft detection in power distribution (Brazilian electrical company). BCS treats the feature vector as corners of hypercube having integral coordinated. Gunavathi and Premalatha (2015) had employed cuckoo search for feature selection optimization in cancer classification. The datasets used were Ovarian Cancer, Lung Michigan, Diffuse large B-cell lymphoma (DLBCL) Harvard, Lung Harvard2 and Acute myeloid leukaemia (AML-ALL) datasets. KNN was employed as a fitness method for the cuckoo search algorithm. It yielded an average of 100% accuracy. Pandey, Rajpoot and Saraswat (2017) had accomplished the task of sentiment classification using a hybrid Cuckoo Search method. This hybrid method was based on k-means and the meta-heuristic algorithm (Cuckoo Search).

SYSTEM ARCHITECTURE

The primary step includes gathering of the required data from Kaggle. This dataset consists of 7086 tweets labelled as either positive (1) or negative (0). It is then followed by pre-processing the dataset by removing any inconsistency, noise and incompleteness within it as the next step. The data is first converted to lower case and then cleaned by removing repeated characters, #tags, @symbols, punctuations, and then transformed using stemming. The features were extracted from the pre-processed tweets using tf-idf technique. Binary Cuckoo Search was then employed on the resulting feature matrix to yield an optimal set of features which would then be used to train over the classifier using the supervised learning techniques. The implementation was carried out in python. The flowchart in Figure 1 summarizes the process.

This section is divided into three sub-sections. Section 3.1 describes the dataset used in the study. Section 3.2 gives details about the supervised classification techniques used in this study. Section 3.3 outlines the optimised approach taken by this research for feature-selection and also includes the pseudo-code.

Figure 1. Framework of the system

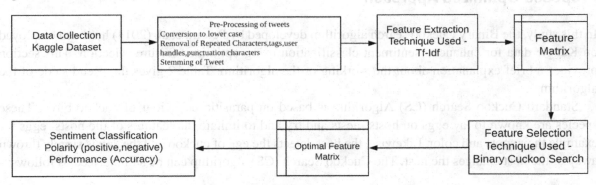

Dataset

For sentiment classification, the data has been taken from the data science website Kaggle (2011). Kaggle is a data science competition platform. Competitors are given a stage to build efficient and innovative models to solve machine learning problems. These problems could involve prediction of a value or classifying the data into different classes or generation of new data. The source of Kaggle dataset is the data provided by real world companies, giving everyone involved a hands-on experience of the complexity that could be encountered while dealing with real world data. Cross validation is required on the supervised learning algorithms to avoid the dreaded problem of over-fitting which in turn increases the generalisation of the results obtained.

The training data contains 7086 tweets labelled as positive (1) or negative (0). The data was split in the ratio of 80:20 (training: testing) with *10-fold cross validation.*

Supervised Techniques

Table 1 shows a description of the supervised algorithms that are used.

Table 1. Description of supervised algorithms used

Techniques	Details
Support Vector Machine (SVM)	Support Vector Machine is a classifier that is discriminative in nature. It differentiates the classes within the data by a separating hyperplane. The labelled training set is modelled as points in the hyperspace. For *n* classes in the labelled training data set, there are *n-1* hyperplanes calculated. These planes are calculated as optimally as possible (Tian, Shi, & Liu, 2012).
K-Nearest Neighbours (k-NN)	k - Nearest Neighbours algorithm models the labelled training set as points in the parametric space. Any new input (set of parameters) is assigned the class to which the majority of the k nearest neighbours belong. Thus, the training step is simple and quick.
Decision Trees (DT)	The decision tree classifier employs a straightforward technique. It employs a tree like data structure to divide the labelled data repeatedly into sub-areas. Each division is done on the basis of one or a set of parameters (Song & Ying, 2015).
Naïve Bayesian classifier (NB)	NB classifiers are simple probabilistic classifiers, based on the Bayes' theorem. It makes a few independence assumptions between the features (Rish, 2001).
Multilayer Perceptron (MLP)	ANNs are computational models, motivated by the biological model of the brain (Ramchoun, Amine, Idrissi, Ghanou, & Ettaouil, 2016). MLPs are a class of feed-forward ANN. It comprises at least 3 layers of nodes (neurons), wherein each neuron uses a nonlinear activation function. Supervised learning in such a model employs the back-propagation technique.

Proposed Optimized Approach

In this study, the Binary Cuckoo search algorithm developed by Pereira et al. (2014) has been employed on Kaggle data for enhanced sentiment classification using optimized feature selection. This section provides a brief explanation about the working of the algorithm. Table 2 gives the pseudocode of the algorithm.

Standard Cuckoo Search (CS) Algorithm is based on parasitic behaviour of cuckoo birds. These species are known to lay eggs on hosts' nests and try and to imitate the features of the hosts' eggs for example their spots and color. Likewise, the host detects the egg of cuckoo and the egg is simply thrown away or the host changes the nest. The Cuckoo Search (CS) algorithm can be summarized as follows: -

1. Each cuckoo randomly selects a host (nest) to lay eggs.
2. The number of nests does not change over time and can be considered fixed. The nests which are fitter (high quality) will have more chances of being present in the following generation.
3. If the host detects the egg laid by cuckoo, the egg can be discarded or the nest itself can be abandoned, in which case the host will build a new one. P_a [0, 1] represents the probability of host detecting the egg (laid by cuckoo).

Cuckoo Search explores the search space using combinations of local and global random walks. The local random walk is used to update the value of eggs in continuous manner. The global random walk is implemented employing Levy Flights. Levy flight employs a random stride length drawn from a Levy Arrangement. The major reason of CS being more efficient in exploration of the search space is that the step size gradually becomes longer.

Standard Cuckoo Search updates a continuous search space. The feature selection requires the search space to be discrete. Binary Cuckoo Search (BCS), a variant of CS, models the search space as n-dimensional Boolean lattice, wherein the updates of solution are carried out across the corners of this hypercube. A binary vector, where 1 represents feature selected and 0 represents otherwise, is used to represent the set of features. Sigmoid function is used to convert the value of new egg at time step (continuous) in the region of [0, 1]. Then a threshold is applied to convert it to either 0 or 1, in other words to discretise it.

Here, it is considered that each nest has 1 egg, and an egg is an n-dimensional binary vector. A zero at the ith position corresponds to rejection of the ith parameter, and a one at the ith position corresponds to selection of the ith parameter.

The algorithm as mentioned in Table 2 depicts the pseudo-code of the algorithm. It starts with the first loop as shown by steps 1–4, initialize each nest with a binary vector (step 3), and steps 8–42 marks the actual implementation of the said algorithm. Z'_1 and Z'_2 are the training and evaluation batches individually, which is acquired by selecting the features from the egg (feature selection vector) in each nest. Z'_1 is then used to train the classifier, and Z'_2 is used to measure the accuracy of this classifier. The accuracy is used as the objective function and defines the fitness of the egg. Steps 14-15 obtain the best solution and stores that solution in g'. The loop in steps 26-30 is responsible to replace the least fit eggs with new eggs, using the probability p. Finally, steps 31-41 employ Levy flights to update the binary vector for each nest and Sigmoid function to restrict the solutions, as explained above.

Each feature in the classification process is a distinct word in the grammar of the corpus. Every word has a non-zero Tf-Idf score for the tweets it occurs in and a score of 0 in tweets where it is absent. Every tweet is now mathematically modelled as a d dimensional vector, where d is the number of distinct words in the corpus. These make up the d features on which feature selection is applied.

Standard CS updates the search space towards continuous valued coordinates. In this work, a minor modification has been done to the basic BCS algorithm. The said change has been done for employing the creation of the new eggs that eventually aided in effective feature selection task. The proposed equation for the same has been given below:

$$x_i(t+1) = \begin{cases} 1, & S(x_i(t)) > \sigma \\ 0, & otherwise \end{cases} \tag{1}$$

$$S(x_i(t)) = \frac{1}{1 + e^{-x_i(t)}} \tag{2}$$

where, $\sigma \sim U(0,1)$

IMPLEMENTATION DETAILS

This section is divided into two sub-sections. Section 4.1 describes various tools used to accomplish the task of classification using BCS. Section 4.2 illustrates a working example of the model adopted by this paper.

Tools

For implementation of the proposed model python was used. Python provides support of many libraries. These libraries are not only powerful but also very easy to install and use. Table 3 briefs about the various libraries that were used in this study.

Working Example

This section illustrates the pre-processing, feature selection and classification process being employed in this study. The example is chosen to be of a smaller scale than the tweets in our dataset for illustration purpose only.

The sample tweet taken is: *"I am very very veryyy happy for Leonardo, finallyyyy, Oscar! #oscars #yay"*.

The above sample tweet will be pre-processed as follows:

1. Conversion of tweet to lowercase

The tweet is first converted into a uniform lowercase, so that same words are not distinguished by variation in cases of letters. After conversion, the following is obtained:

"i am very very veryyy happy for leonardo, finallyyyy, oscar! #oscars #yay @leonardodicaprio"

Table 2. Pseudo code of Binary Cuckoo Search

BCS-Feature selection algorithm	
Input	Labelled training set Z_1, evaluating set Z_2, loss parameter p, α value, number of nests n, dimension d, number of generations(iterations) T, c_1 and C_2 values
Output	Global best position g'

1. for each nest n_i (i = 1, ..., m)**do:**
2. for each dimension j (j = 1, ..., d) **do:**
3. $x_i^j(0) \leftarrow$ Random{0, 1}
4. end
5. $f_i \leftarrow -\infty$
6. end
7. *global_fit* $\leftarrow -\infty$
8. for each iteration t (t = 1, ..., T) **do:**
9. for each nest n_i (i = 1, ..., m) **do:**
10. Create Z'$_1$ and Z'$_2$ from Z$_1$, Z$_2$ respectively, such that
         both contains only features in n_i in which $x_i^j(t)$ is not 0
11. Train SVM over Z'$_1$, evaluate over Z'$_2$ store accuracy in
         acc
12. if(acc > f_i) **then:**
13. $f_2 \leftarrow$ acc
14. for each dimension j (j = 1, ..., d) **do:**
15. $x'^j_i \leftarrow x_i^j(t)$
16. end
17. end
18. end
19. [*max_fit, max_index*] $\leftarrow$ max(*f*)
20. if(*max_fit* > *global_fit*) **then:**
21. *global_fit* $\leftarrow$ *max_fit*
22. for each dimension j (j = 1, ..., d) **do:**
23. $g'^j \leftarrow x_{max\_index\,(t)}^j$
24. end
25. end

26. for each nest n_i (i = 1, ..., m) **do:**
27. for each dimension j (j = 1, ..., d) **do:**
28. Select the worst nests with p $\in$ [0,1] and replace
             them with new random solutions;
29. end
30. end
31. for each nest n_i (i = 1, ..., m)**do:**
32. for each dimension j (j = 1, ..., d) **do:**
33. $x_i\left(t+1\right) = x_i\left(t\right) + \alpha \oplus Levy\left(\lambda\right)$
34. if ($S\left(x_i^j\left(t\right)\right) > \sigma$) **then:**
35. $x_i^j\left(t\right) \leftarrow 1$
36. else
37. $x_i^j\left(t\right) \leftarrow 0$
38. end
39. end
40. end
41. end

Table 3. Description of Python packages used

Package	Description
Scikit-learn	This library has many classification, regression and clustering algorithms. It can be easily used along with other python libraries like numpy and scipy. It has been used to implement various supervised classification algorithms on which the accuracy is determined after feature selection ("Documentation of scikit-learn 0.19.1.", n.d.).
Numpy	This library has support to work with large arrays and matrices. It also has mathematical functions that can be applied on these structures. It is optimised to reduce the computation time required to work with large matrices (Walt, Colbert, & Varoquaux, 2011). It provides the ability to operate on various elements of matrices in parallel whenever it is possible. This implementation involves large matrices when extracting features using tf-idf and also when feature selection is done on these matrices. It is further used when the position of the agent has to be updated as the position is encoded as a binary 1 D array.
Scipy	It is the library which is used for scientific computing. It has modules for linear algebra, FFT, optimisation, image processing, etc. ("SciPy", 2015). Some of the available packages include stats (statistical functions), optimise (optimization algorithms including linear programming), sparse (sparse matrix and related functions) and so on.
Nltk	Nltk is a very comprehensive collection of programs and libraries aimed at statistical and symbolic natural language processing for English Language. It has lot of inbuilt functions like Stemmers, Lemantiser, and Tokeniser etc. (Bird & Loper, 2004). Different variations of these inbuilt functions are also present. In this paper Porter Stemmer has been used for pre-processing of tweets.

2.   Removal of repeated characters

The repeated characters in a word signify emphasis in an informal communication medium like twitter. These are removed to extract the actual word. After this step, the following is obtained:

"i am very very very happy for leonardo, finally, oscar! #oscars #yay @leonardodicaprio"

3.   Removal of tags and user handles

We consider that hash tags and tags to other accounts do not hold any information about the emotion of the tweet. Thus, these are removed in the final stage of pre-processing. After this, the following is obtained:

"i am very very very happy for leonardo, finally, oscar!"

4.   Removal of punctuation characters

The punctuation symbols like '!', '.', ',' are removed as well. After this step, the tweet will be: "i am very very very happy for Leonardo finally oscar"

5.   Stemming the Tweet

It is the process of reducing the word to its root form. Most Stemming algorithms are based on suffix stripping rules. Porter Stemmer, which is one of the most famous stemmers, has been used in this paper. After Stemming, the following is obtained: "veri veri veri happi for leonardo final oscar"

After pre-processing, the resultant tweet appears to be as follows:

"veri veri veri happi for leonardo final oscar"

Next explanation of the procedure of allocating the *tf-idf score vectors* for all the input parameters is presented. The tf-idf technique is used to calculate scores of the words in the corpus, and subsequently use them as input parameters for classification. So, the *tf-idf score vector* for every input parameter is calculated by the procedure explained in section 3. Table 4 shows the tf-idf scores for the tweet(various words in the tweets).

Table 4. Tf-idf scores of the sample tweet

Veri	happi	for	leonardo	final	oscar
0.102	0.0201	0.169	0.015	0.000	0.069

The vector X_t is an n dimensional vector, (n is the no. of words in the corpus), where $X_t[d]$ is the score of the dth word. For words not occurring in the tweet, the corresponding value in the vector is 0.

The Cuckoo search algorithm finds the optimal proper subset of the features for which the accuracy is maximum. This search involves training the model using a given subset of the features. In certain iteration, the feature selection vector is a binary vector, where the ith element being 0 means the ith feature is not selected, and 1 means the ith element is selected.

Let us understand with the help of an example as explained below, where feature selection vector, X, have the following values for the words in the sample tweet:

$X[i]=1$

$X[am]=0$

$X[very]=0$

$X[happy]=1$

$X[for]=1$

$X[Leonardo]=0$

$X[finally]=0$

$X[Oscar]=1$

The columns corresponding to the words for which X[t] is 0 will be removed from the training dataset matrix and the input vector. The number of features is thus reduced. In another permutation, a different subset of the words may be chosen for training and classification processes. The 'fitness' of an egg (a solution) is proportional to the accuracy of the classification yielded from the corresponding subset of words.

RESULTS AND ANALYSIS

In this section the performance of the proposed model is evaluated using accuracy. For discussing the results, the empirical analysis has been broadly divided into three parts, they are: (i) The variation of accuracy with respect to population size, (ii) variation of accuracy with respect to alpha and a (iii) comparison in terms of accuracy and features selected between non-optimised and optimised approaches.

Effect of Population Size on Accuracy

Population size is one of the most important hyper parameters. The size decides whether the initial search space was explored "enough" or not. It makes the search insensitive to the initial stage. There is no explicit relationship between the size and accuracy, but it is generally seen that the accuracy increases with size up to a certain value after which it shows inconsistent behaviour. Aim was to select "right" size for the analysis so that the training time is minimised and good probability of finding an optimal subset can be obtained.

For understanding the effect of the size of the population on accuracy, the following parameters are kept as constant; T = 100, alpha = 1, p = 0.35, algorithm used is SVM (Linear Kernel). Accuracy has been expressed in percentages. The line graph in Figure 2 shows that the population size of 100 yields the highest accuracy in the model proposed.

Figure 2. Variation of accuracy with population size

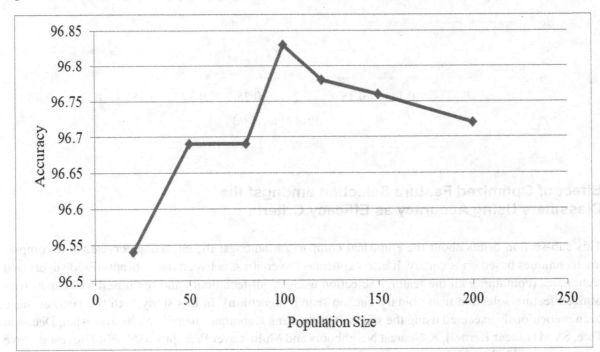

Effect of Loss Probability on Accuracy

For understanding the effect of loss probability on accuracy, the following parameters have been kept constant, T = 100, population size = 100, algorithm used is SVM (Liner Kernel). Figure 3 depicts that the value of loss probability doesn't affect the accuracy to a greater extent. From this, it can be inferred that CS algorithm can be applied to many problems without fine tuning these parameters and this makes the algorithm more robust. The graph in Figure 3 shows the variation of accuracy with loss probability parameter.

Figure 3. Variation of accuracy with loss probability parameter

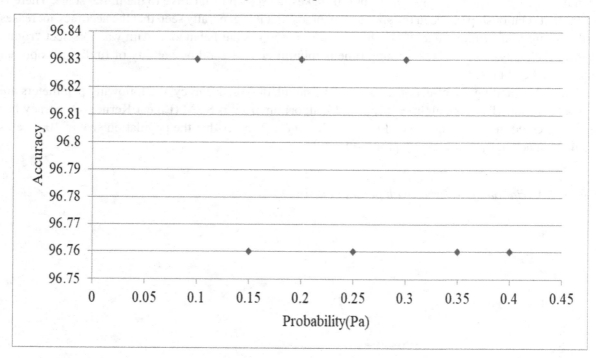

Effect of Optimized Feature Selection amongst the Classifiers Using Accuracy as Efficacy Criteria

This sub-section briefs about the empirical comparison amongst the chosen supervised soft computing techniques based on accuracy. It also explicates the contrast between the non-optimised supervised techniques (containing all the features selection using tf-idf technique) and optimised techniques (optimized feature selection using binary cuckoo search algorithm). In this study both the versions have been meticulously executed using the said soft computing techniques namely Naïve Bayesian, Decision Tree, SVM (Linear Kernel), K-Nearest Neighbours and Multi-Layer Perceptron (MLP). The results have been illustrated below.

Table 5 depicts that the accuracy yielded by the said supervised soft computing techniques. The results of this study indicate that the best accuracy without optimisation is achieved by Decision Tree (DT) algorithm on Kaggle dataset, i.e. 89.90%. DT outperformed every other supervised classification algorithm in terms of Accuracy, followed by Support Vector Machines (SVM), Multi-Layer Perceptron (MLP) techniques. Then comes K-Nearest Neighbours (k-NN), followed by Naïve Bayesian (NB). Amongst all, NB showed the lowest accuracy of around 87.71%. The maximum accuracy gain was obtained by NB (9.15%) while SVM, MLP, k-NN showed an appreciable gain in accuracy (approximately 7%). The average accuracy gain was of 7.45%.

Table 5. Accuracy obtained using optimised and non-optimised approach

Algorithm	Non-Optimized Approach (TF-IDF) Accuracy (%)	Optimized Approach (TF-IDF + BCS) Accuracy (%)	Increase In Accuracy (%)
Naïve Bayesian	**87.71**	**96.26**	**9.15**
Decision Tree	**89.90**	96.26	6.36
SVM	89.12	**96.54**	7.42
k-NN	88.42	95.56	7.14
MLP	89.11	96.30	7.19

Table 6 displays the number of features selected in the two approaches. In Non –Optimised approach all the classification algorithms used the same number of features (856). After applying BCS for feature selection the minimum number of features selected was 379 (KNN) which is 44.27% selection and maximum was 580 (SVM) which is 67.75% selection. The table shows that on an average 53.17% features were selected.

Table 6. Number of features selected in optimised and non-optimised approach

Algorithm	Non-Optimized Approach (TF-IDF) #Features	Optimized Approach (TF-IDF + BCS) #Features	Features Selected (%)
Naïve Bayesian	856	395	46.14
Decision Tree	856	497	58.06
SVM	856	**580**	**67.75**
k-NN	856	**379**	**44.27**
MLP	856	425	49.64

CONCLUSION

This paper empirically contrasted the supervised soft computing such as SVM, multilayer perceptron, Decision Tree, Naïve Bayesian and k Nearest Neighbour on Kaggle dataset. 7086 tweets were analysed based on accuracy as efficacy criteria. This study also demonstrates the implementation of aforesaid techniques via employing optimization of features using binary cuckoo search algorithm.

The study shows that Binary cuckoo search with levy flights is found to be a very efficient algorithm for feature selection. It depicts that with only 53.17% of the features selected on an average, the average accuracy gain is of 7.45%. This shows that out of the features selected through tf-idf technique, 47% of features were redundant and were acting as a noise to the function that determines accuracy. Removal of such features increases the accuracy and also increases generalisation of these features. It is natural method to reduce the problem of over-fitting. The optimum sentiment accuracy is realized by Support Vector Machine (SVM) utilizing feature selection optimization via Binary Cuckoo Search algorithm on the Kaggle dataset, followed by Multi-Layer Perceptron (MLP), Naïve Bayesian (NB), Decision Tree (DT) and K-Nearest Neighbour (KNN) which yielded the lowest accuracy.

This paper has successfully tackled the age-old problem of trade-off between optimum feature selection and performance as the approach has been able to yield a significant reduction in the feature set and an increase in performance at the same time. The results denote that the application of BCS on Kaggle dataset for optimized feature selection using the said supervised soft computing techniques has produced enhanced sentiment classification accuracy.

The analysis and results of this algorithm has opened the avenue of exploring other nature inspired optimization algorithms, such as the BAT algorithm, moth flame algorithm, flower pollination etc. for the optimized feature selection. The accuracy of the sentiment categorization task may be tested by employing other soft computing and evolutionary techniques like fuzzy logic, genetic algorithm etc. Literature shows that majority of the work has been done for textual sentiment analysis; hence other multimedia data can also be explored.

REFERENCES

Kumar, A., & Sharma, A. (2016). Paradigm Shifts from E-Governance to S-Governance. *The Human Element of Big Data: Issues, Analytics, and Performance*, 213.

Kumar, A., & Abraham, A. (2017). Opinion Mining to Assist User Acceptance Testing for Open-Beta Versions. *Journal of Information Assurance & Security*, *12*(4), 146–153.

Kumar, A., & Teeja, M. S. (2012). Sentiment analysis: A perspective on its past, present and future. *International Journal of Intelligent Systems and Applications*, *4*(10), 1–14. doi:10.5815/ijisa.2012.10.01

Kumar, A., & Sebastian, T. M. (2012). Machine learning assisted sentiment analysis. In *Proceedings of International Conference on Computer Science & Engineering (ICCSE'2012)* (pp. 123-130).

Kumar, A., & Sharma, A. (2017). Systematic Literature Review on Opinion Mining of Big Data for Government Intelligence. *Webology, 14*(2).

Pang, B., & Lee, L. (2008). Opinion mining and sentiment analysis. Foundations and Trends in Information Retrieval, 2(1–2), 1–135. doi:10.1561/1500000011

Kumar, A., & Sebastian, T. M. (2012). Sentiment analysis on twitter. *International Journal of Computer Science Issues*, *9*(3), 372–378.

Kumar, A., Dogra, P., & Dabas, V. (2015, August). Emotion analysis of Twitter using opinion mining. *2015 Eighth International Conference on Contemporary Computing IC3* (pp. 285-290). IEEE.

Kumar, A., & Jaiswal, A. (2017). Empirical Study of Twitter and Tumblr for Sentiment Analysis using Soft Computing Techniques. In *Proceedings of the World Congress on Engineering and Computer Science* (Vol. 1).

Kumar, A., & Jaiswal, A. (2017). *Image sentiment analysis using convolution neural network*. Springer.

Kumar, A., & Khorwal, R. (2017). *Firefly algorithm for feature selection in sentiment analysis. Computational Intelligence in Data Mining* (pp. 693–703). Singapore: Springer.

Kumar, A., & Rani, R. (2016, October). Sentiment analysis using neural network. *2nd International Conference on Next Generation Computing Technologies NGCT* (pp. 262-267). IEEE.

Kumar, A., Khorwal, R., & Chaudhary, S. (2016). A Survey on Sentiment Analysis using Swarm Intelligence. *Indian Journal of Science and Technology*, *9*(39), 1–7. doi:10.17485/ijst/2016/v9i39/100766

Yang, X. S., & Deb, S. (2009, December). Cuckoo search via Lévy flights. In *World Congress on Nature & Biologically Inspired Computing NaBIC 2009* (pp. 210-214). IEEE.

Adnan, M. A., & Razzaque, M. A. (2013, March). A comparative study of particle swarm optimization and Cuckoo search techniques through problem-specific distance function. In *2013 International Conference of Information and Communication Technology (ICoICT)* (pp. 88-92). IEEE.

Pereira, L. A. M., Rodrigues, D., Almeida, T. N. S., Ramos, C. C. O., Souza, A. N., Yang, X. S., & Papa, J. P. (2014). A binary cuckoo search and its application for feature selection. In *Cuckoo Search and Firefly Algorithm* (pp. 141–154). Cham: Springer; . doi:10.1007/978-3-319-02141-6_7

Roelleke, T., & Wang, J. (2008, July). TF-IDF uncovered: a study of theories and probabilities. In *Proceedings of the 31st annual international ACM SIGIR conference on Research and development in information retrieval* (pp. 435-442). ACM.

Kumar, A., & Joshi, A. (2017, March). Ontology Driven Sentiment Analysis on Social Web for Government Intelligence. In *Proceedings of the Special Collection on eGovernment Innovations in India* (pp. 134-139). ACM.

Medhat, W., Hassan, A., & Korashy, H. (2014). Sentiment analysis algorithms and applications: A survey. Ain Shams Engineering Journal, *5*(4), 1093–1113. doi:10.1016/j.asej.2014.04.011

Kumar, A., & Sebastian, T. M. (2012). Sentiment analysis: A perspective on its past, present and future. *International Journal of Intelligent Systems and Applications*, *4*(10), 1–14. doi:10.5815/ijisa.2012.10.01

Chaudhari, M., & Govilkar, S. (2015). A survey of machine learning techniques for sentiment classification. *International Journal of Computational Science & Applications*, *5*(3), 13–23. doi:10.5121/ijcsa.2015.5302

Yu, T., Wang, L., Han, X., Liu, Y., & Zhang, L. (2015). Swarm intelligence optimization algorithms and their application.

Sumathi, T., Karthik, S., & Marikkannan, M. (2014). Artificial bee colony optimization for feature selection in opinion mining. *Journal of Theoretical and Applied Information Technology, 66*(1).

Basari, A. S. H., Hussin, B., Ananta, I. G. P., & Zeniarja, J. (2013). Opinion mining of movie review using hybrid method of support vector machine and particle swarm optimization. *Procedia Engineering, 53*, 453–462. doi:10.1016/j.proeng.2013.02.059

Gupta, D. K., Reddy, K. S., & Ekbal, A. (2015, June). Pso-asent: Feature selection using particle swarm optimization for aspect based sentiment analysis. In *International conference on applications of natural language to information systems* (pp. 220-233). Cham: Springer.

Gunavathi, C., & Premalatha, K. (2015). Cuckoo search optimisation for feature selection in cancer classification: A new approach. *International Journal of Data Mining and Bioinformatics, 13*(3), 248–265. doi:10.1504/IJDMB.2015.072092

Pandey, A. C., Rajpoot, D. S., & Saraswat, M. (2017). Twitter sentiment analysis using hybrid cuckoo search method. *Information Processing & Management, 53*(4), 764–779. doi:10.1016/j.ipm.2017.02.004

Tian, Y., Shi, Y., & Liu, X. (2012). Recent advances on support vector machines research. *Technological and Economic Development of Economy, 18*(1), 5–33. doi:10.3846/20294913.2012.661205

Tesileanu, R. (2017). Introduction to Statistical Computing in Scala-an Implementation of the K-Nearest Neighbors classifier [technical report].

Song, Y. Y., & Ying, L. U. (2015). Decision tree methods: Applications for classification and prediction. *Shanghai Jingshen Yixue, 27*(2), 130.

Rish, I. (2001, August). An empirical study of the naive Bayes classifier. In IJCAI 2001 workshop on empirical methods in artificial intelligence (Vol. 3, No. 22, pp. 41-46). IBM.

Ramchoun, H., Amine, M., Idrissi, J., Ghanou, Y., & Ettaouil, M. (2016). Multilayer Perceptron: Architecture Optimization and Training. IJIMAI, 4(1), 26–30. doi:10.9781/ijimai.2016.415

Sentiment Classification. (2011). Retrieved from https://www.kaggle.com/c/si650winter11/data

Documentation of scikit-learn 0.19.1. (n.d.). Retrieved from http://scikit-learn.org

Walt, S. V. D., Colbert, S. C., & Varoquaux, G. (2011). The NumPy array: A structure for efficient numerical computation. *Computing in Science & Engineering, 13*(2), 22–30. doi:10.1109/MCSE.2011.37

SciPy. (2015, October 25). Retrieved from https://docs.scipy.org/doc/scipy/reference/

Bird, S., & Loper, E. (2004, July). NLTK: the natural language toolkit. In *Proceedings of the ACL 2004 on Interactive poster and demonstration sessions* (p. 31). Association for Computational Linguistics. doi:10.3115/1219044.1219075

This research was previously published in the International Journal of Information Retrieval Research (IJIRR), 9(1); pages 1-15, copyright year 2019 by IGI Publishing (an imprint of IGI Global).

Chapter 63
Parallel Hybrid BBO Search Method for Twitter Sentiment Analysis of Large Scale Datasets Using MapReduce

Ashish Kumar Tripathi
Delhi Technological University, New Delhi, India

Kapil Sharma
Delhi Technological University, New Delhi, India

Manju Bala
Indraprastha College of Women, New Delhi, India

Abstract

Sentiment analysis is an eminent part of data mining for the investigation of user perception. Twitter is one of the popular social platforms for expressing thoughts in the form of tweets. Nowadays, tweets are widely used for analyzing the sentiments of the users, and utilized for decision making purposes. Though clustering and classification methods are used for the twitter sentiment analysis, meta-heuristic based clustering methods has witnessed better performance due to subjective nature of tweets. However, sequential meta-heuristic based clustering methods are computation intensive for large scale datasets. Therefore, in this paper, a novel MapReduce based K-means biogeography based optimizer(MR-KBBO) is proposed to leverage the strength of biogeography based optimizer with MapReduce model to efficiently cluster the large scale data. The proposed method is validated against four state-of-the-art MapReduce based clustering methods namely; parallel K-means, parallel K-means particle swarm optimization, MapReduce based artificial bee colony optimization, dynamic frequency based parallel k-bat algorithm on four large scale twitter datasets. Further, speedup measure is used to illustrate the computation performance on varying number of nodes. Experimental results demonstrate that the proposed method is efficient in sentiment mining for the large scale twitter datasets.

DOI: 10.4018/978-1-6684-6303-1.ch063

INTRODUCTION

From last one decade, enormous growth of the digital data has been observed (Gantz J, 2018). The social sites such as Instagram, Face-book, Twitter etc., are the major source of the digital data. Such huge availability of data has attracted the user based industries to analyze the sentiments of users for making business strategies. Thus, efficient data mining methods are required for the sentiment analysis of the social media. Twitter, one of the popular social media, provides a prodigious platform for the sentiment analysis. Twitter database has approximately 200 millions of users and nearby 400 million tweets are posted every day. Often, user shares their personal experiences about products or companies. Since, the maximum length of the tweet is 140 characters. Therefore, some short symbols like emoji are available for expressing the sentiments. The study of the tweets can deliver profound viewpoints and emotions about any subject (Asur, S., & Huberman, B. A. 2010). Sentiment analysis methods are mainly classified into three categories: machine learning based methods, hybrid methods and lexicon based methods (Medhat, W., Hassan, A., & Korashy, H. 2014). The methods based on lexicon require prior knowledge of sentiment lexicon to predict the sentiment. However, for the short-hand and emoji based texts, lexicon-based methods fail to perform well (Khan, A. Z., Atique, M., & Thakare, V. M. 2015). Pandey et al. (Pandey, A. C., Rajpoot, D. S., & Saraswat, M. 2017) proposed a hybrid cuckoo search based method for Twitter sentiment analysis and concluded that emoticons are good predictors of the sentiments for short texts. Further, Canuto et al. (Canuto, S., Gonçalves, M. A., & Benevenuto, F. 2016) used the meta level features for prediction of sentiments. Bravo et al. (Bravo-Marquez, F., Mendoza, M., & Poblete, B. 2013) proposed a supervised approach to amalgamate the strengths of emotions and polarities for revamping the twitter opinion prediction. Furthermore, Mohammad et al. (Mohammad, S. M., Zhu, X., Kiritchenko, S., & Martin, J. 2015) employed the supervised classifier to analyze emotion stimulus, emotion state, and intent of tweets for the US election. An ontology-based method was introduced for sentiment analysis of tweets by Kontopoulos et al. (Kontopoulos, E., Berberidis, C., Dergiades, T., & Bassiliades, N. 2013) where a sentiment grade was allocated to each different perception in the tweet. Agarwal et al. (Agarwal, B., Mittal, N., Bansal, P., & Garg, S. 2015) presented a novel approach using common sense information taken from ConceptNet based ontology method for the sentiment analysis. Furthermore, SentiCircle method was introduced by Saif, et al. (Saif, H., He, Y., Fernandez, M., & Alani, H. 2016), in which context specific polarity of words was determined. Qiu et al. (Qiu, G., Liu, B., Bu, J., & Chen, C. 2009, July) proposed a semi-supervised algorithm for sentiment mining. Furthermore, Pandarachalil et al. (Pandarachalil, R., Sendhilkumar, S., & Mahalakshmi, G. S. 2015) introduced a distributed unsupervised approach for extraction of the lexicons. Likewise, Fernndez et al. (Fernández-Gavilanes, M., Álvarez-López, T., Juncal-Martínez, J., Costa-Montenegro, E., & González-Castaño, F. J. 2016) proposed an unsupervised algorithm to predict the sentiment polarity of the informal texts using linguistic sentiment propagation model.

Recently, natural language processing (NLP) is used to study the semantics in the features for improving the efficiency of the methods (Kanakaraj, M., & Guddeti, R. M. R. 2015, March). Altnel et al. (Altınel, B., & Ganiz, M. C. 2016) introduced semantic smoothing kernels for extracting class specific semantics using vector space models (VSM). Muhammad et al. (Muhammad, A., Wiratunga, N., & Lothian, R. 2016) proposed a lexicon based method using textual neighborhood for social media opinion mining. Further, Appel et al. (Appel, O., Chiclana, F., Carter, J., & Fujita, H. 2016) introduced hybridized approach based on NLP and fuzzy for the semantic polarity classification. Chen et al. (Chen, T., Xu, R., He, Y., Xia, Y., & Wang, X. (2016)) used the sequence modeling based neural network for the text document sentiment prediction. Sulis et al. (Sulis, E., Farías, D. I. H., Rosso, P., Patti, V., & Ruffo, G. (2016)) studied the influence of figurative linguistic phenomena for distinguishing the tweets with the tags like irony, sarcasm using psycholinguistic and emotional features. Basari et al. (Basari, A. S. H., Hussin, B., Ananta, I. G. P., & Zeniarja, J. 2013) introduced hybrid particle swarm optimization (PSO) with support vector machine (SVM) for classification of the movies. Likewise, Gupta et al. (Gupta, D. K., Reddy, K. S., & Ekbal, A. 2015, June) performed aspect-based sentiment analysis using PSO-Asent method. However, the accuracy of PSO-Asent method on the unlabeled data was quite low. Further, Zhu et al. (Zhu, J., Wang, H., & Mao, J. 2010, April) introduced a hybrid approach using conditional random forest (CRF) and genetic algorithm (GA) for the prediction of sentiment. Meta-heuristic methods have shown good potential for clustering the sentiments of the twitter dataset (Pandey, A. C., Rajpoot, D. S., & Saraswat, M. 2017). However, on large scale datasets, these methods fail to perform in reasonable amount of time due to the sequential execution. For handling the computational complexities of large scale datasets, parallel and distributed computation is highly advantageous. With the years of progress, Apache hadoop is used by the researchers for the parallelization of the algorithms. Hadoop [31 (hadoop wiki)], an open source platform by Apache, handles the large datasets by using distributed processing. Hadoop is capable in processing gigabytes of data with commodity hardware and has its own file system, termed as hadoop distributed file system (HDFS) (Shvachko, K., Kuang, H., Radia, S., & Chansler, R. 2010). MapReduce (Dean, J., & Ghemawat, S. 2008) is a programming model for the parallelization of algorithms [34, 35](Khezr, S. N., & Navimipour, N. J. (2015), Anitha, M. A., & Nazeer, K. A. 2017, March). Zhao et al. (Zhao, W., Ma, H., & He, Q. 2009, December) introduced parallel version of K-Means algorithm. Though K-means is an efficient unsupervised mining method (Boiy, E., Hens, P., Deschacht, K., & Moens, M. F. 2007, June), but it is sensitive towards initial cluster centroids and data shape. Meta-heuristics methods are widely used in association with K-means for finding the optimal set of centroids. Wang et al. (Wang, J., Yuan, D., & Jiang, M. 2012, November) proposed a hybrid method using K-means and particle swarm optimization (K-PSO) to cluster massive datasets. A MapReduce based parallel artificial bee colony algorithm (MR-ABC) was presented by Banharnsakun et al. (Banharnsakun, A. 2017) for clustering large scale datasets. An efficient method for handling large datasets was presented by Tripathi et al. (Tripathi, A. K., Sharma, K., & Bala, 2017) and termed as dynamic frequency based K-Bat algorithm (DFBPKBA). As No free lunch theorem (Wolpert, D. H., & Macready, W. G. 1997) states that there exists no meta-heuristic method for all set of optimization problems, this paper introduces a novel hybrid method based on K-means and biogeography based optimizer (MR-KBBO). Biogeography based optimizer, proposed by Samon (Simon, D. 2008), is an evolutionary based meta-heuristic algorithm based on theory of island biogeography. This algorithm has outperformed the existing meta-heuristics on various benchmark and real world optimization problems (Pandey, A. C., Pal, R., & Kulhari 2017, Pal, R., & Saraswat, M. 2017). The proposed method (MR-KBBO) is used for the sentiment analysis of large sized twitter dataset. The MR-KBBO method utilizes the strengths of BBO for finding the optimal cluster centroids and MapReduce programming model to handle the large scale datasets. Moreover, the performance of MR-KBBO is compared with four state-of-the-art MapReduce based parallel methods namely; parallel K-means, parallel K-PSO, MR-ABC, DFBPKBA in terms of accuracy and computation time. The parallel computation efficiency of the MR-KBBO has been analyzed through speedup graphs with different number of machines in the cluster.

BACKGROUND

In this section, first Mapreduce architecture is described which is used for the parallelization of the proposed method, followed by the K-Means and biogeography based optimization algorithm.

Hadoop MapReduce

Hadoop (Banharnsakun, A. 2017) is a framework which provides distributed processing platform for large scale data processing. It distributes giant datasets across a set of computers which are connected in the hadoop cluster. Hadoop cluster is a collection of computers interconnected through local area network. It can easily scale up from single server to hundreds of machines for handling large datasets, concurrency control and failure recovery. Hadoop works on its own file system known as hadoop distributed file system (HDFS), to process the zeta-bytes of data. Furthermore, hadoop uses MapReduce (Anitha, M. A., & Nazeer, K. A. 2017, March) parallel programming model, which is used for processing large data on multiple machines. Figure 1 depicts the architecture of the MapReduce programming model for the parallel computation. As shown in the Figure 1, MapReduce splits the data into equal size small chunks called input splits. Further, MapReduce processes the data in the form of key/value pairs. The complete cycle of MapReduce consists of two main phases, namely Map and Reduce. In the map phase, Map function works on each key/value pair, processes it, and produces output again on the form of key/value pair. Reduce phase, starts followed by the Map phase in which Reduce function is invoked on the output generated by the Map phase. The Map phase is basically designed for task decomposition while Reduce is responsible for the amalgamation of final results.

K-Means Algorithm

K-means (Kogan, J., Teboulle, M., & Nicholas, C. 2005) is a popular data clustering algorithm which divides N data objects into in K clusters with the aim of minimizing the distance of each data object from its cluster centroid. The distance of each data object from its centroid can be calculate by using a distance metric such as Euclidean distance (Danielsson, P. E. 1980) or cosine measure (Wilkinson, R., & Hingston, P. 1991, September). Further, the main motivation of the K-means algorithm is to partition the data in such a way that minimizes the squared error between data objects and their centroid. K-means clustering works with prior known number of clusters. However, if the numbers of clusters are not known, elbow method (Nugent, R., Dean, N., & Ayers, E. 2010), information criterion method (Jain, A. K. 2010), silhouette method (Chiang, M. M. T., & Mirkin, B. 2010), etc. can be used to find the number of centroids. The steps of K-means algorithm are presented in Algorithm 1.

Algorithm 1. K-Means
1. Initialize the k cluster-heads by randomly chosen data points
2. Compute the distance of each data point with the centre heads and assign it to the closest cluster
3. Update the cluster-heads C_i defined by the following formula:

$$Ci = \frac{1}{n_i} \sum_{\forall di \in ci} di = 1,2,2 \dots k \ .$$

where d_i denotes the data objects that belong to cluster C_i and n_i is the sum of data objects in cluster c_i

4.   Repeat steps 2 and 3 for maximum iterations or while convergence is not reached

Figure 1. MapReduce parallel programming model

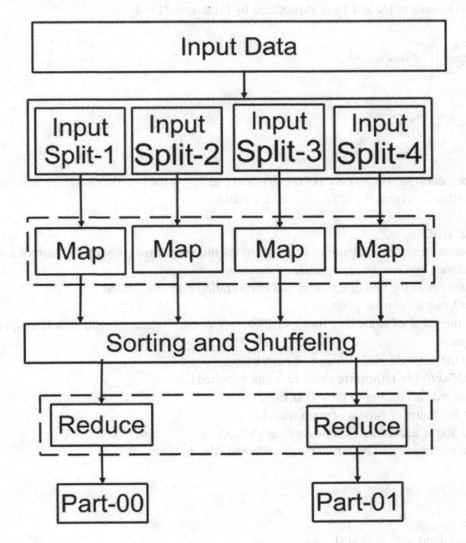

BBO

Biogeography based optimization (BBO) is a meta-heuristic algorithm inspired by theory of island biogeography and proposed by (Dan simon Simon, D. 2008) in 2008. The proposed algorithm is based on the distribution and equilibrium of species in different islands. The species move between various islands in the search of better one. In BBO, the quality of island is mathematically represented by habitat suitability index (HSI) which depends on the various factors called suitability index variables (SIVs). The islands with high *HSI* value share the information of their features with low *HSI* islands and the species migrate from low *HSI* island to high *HSI* island to attain equilibrium. The emigration (μ_i and immigration (λ_i rates of the ith island are defined by Equations (1)-(2).

$$\lambda_i = I^*\left(1 - \frac{S_i}{S_{max}}\right); \quad i=1,2,3,\ldots,m \tag{1}$$

$$\mu_i = E^*\left(\frac{S_i}{S_{max}}\right); \quad i=1,2,3,\ldots \tag{2}$$

Where S_i represents the species count of the ith island and S_{max} is the population size or maximum species count. Algorithm 2 defines the main steps of the BBO.

Algorithm 2. BBO

  Input: parameters *Pmig*, *Pmut*, *N* and *MaxItr* as the migration probability, mutation probability, number of Islands and maximum number of iteration.

  μ_i and λ_i are set as the and emigration and immigration rate of ith island

  Output: Optimal centroid position

  Initialize the value of suitability Index variable SIV of each island (candidate solution) randomly in the search space

  Calculate the value of HSI (fitness) of each island

  while (*i<MaxItr*) or **(stopping criteria is not reached)** do

  Sort the islands according to their HSI value

  Calculate the value of fitness of each island

  Update λi and μ_i according to fitness of each island

  Apply the migration and mutation on the selected islands

i=i+1;

  end while

  Return the island with best HSI

PROPOSED METHOD

MR-KBBO method starts the process of clustering the tweets in three phases;

In the first phase Tweets are pre-processed, in the second phase feature are extracted, and in the third phase, clustering is performed using MR-KBBO.

Pre-Processing

Before extracting the features, the raw tweets are pre-processed to remove useless and noisy words such as stop words, URLs, fuzzy words etc. The proposed method used the following steps for the pre-processing:

- Remove URLS from the tweets by using regular expression. A regular expression elucidates a search pattern for the text or string. It is used to search any specific textual or string pattern such as email address, URLs etc.
- "@Username" is replaced with "usr".
- Multiple spaces are replaced with single space.
- Forward slash (/), backward slash (n) and all parentheses are removed.
- # is removed from the hashtags(#), for example #ashish is replaced with ashish and "@" is removed from the user name i.e @Username is replaced with usr.
- All the stop words such as the, a, is, as etc are removed. For this comparing them with stop word dictionary is used.
- All the words are converted to lower case.
- Sequence of repeated characters is removed for example "hiiiiiiiiiii" is re-placed with "hi".
- The words not starting with alphabet are removed.

Feature Extraction

In this phase, the features are extracted from the pre-processed twitter dataset. The tweets are transformed into feature vector matrix by extracting the 11 features given below.

1. **Word Length:** It is defined as the total word count of the tweet.
2. **Number of Positive Emoji:** It represents the count of symbols, such as:), ;),: D, etc., which are used to express positive emotions. For this, positive emoticon dictionary is used (Emoticon dictionary, 2015).
3. **Number of Negative Emoji:** It represents the count of symbols such as >: (,: (,: (, etc. These symbols are used by the users for expressing the negative emotions. For this negative emoticon dictionary is used (Emoticon dictionary, 2015).
4. **Number of Neutral Emoji:** It is straight faced emoji which do not deliver any type of emotion. This feature is computed using neutral emoticon dictionary (Emoticon dictionary, 2015).
5. **Positive Exclamation:** The words, such as hurrah!, wow! etc., are known as exclamatory words, these words are used to carry a very strong opinion/feeling about the message. Positive exclamation dictionary is used for computing this feature (Exclamation word dictionary, 2015).
6. **Negative Exclamation:** These are the words, which express negative emotions of the users. This feature is counted by using negative exclamation dictionary (Exclamation word dictionary, 2015).

7. **Negation:** Negation words such as no, not are used to express negative opinion.
8. **Positive word count:** The positive words such as confidence, achieve are counted using positive word dictionary (jeffreybreen, 2015).
9. **Negative word count:** This feature counts the sum of negative words such as guilt, sadness, shame etc., and it is found using dictionary (jeffreybreen, 2015)
10. **Neutral word count:** The words such as 'rarely, ok' are treated as the neutral word and they does not provide any information about the emotion or opinion (psy, 2015).
11. **Intense word count:** Intense words are used to make tweet more effective/intense, such as very, like or much. Intense word count is determined by matching the word with intense word dictionary (psy, 2015).

The above mentioned features are good predictor for the sentiment of the tweets and used by Pandey et al. (Pandey, A. C., Rajpoot, D. S., & Saraswat, M. 2017). However, sarcastic or irony present in tweets may affect their value. To overcome the effect of sarcasm or irony, hyperbole features (interjection, quotes, punctuation, etc.) (Bharti, S. K., Babu, K. S., & Jena, S. K. 2015), pragmatic feature (smilies, emoticons, etc.) (Bharti, S. K., Vachha, B., Pradhan, R. K., Babu, K. S., & Jena, S. K. 2016), explicit incongruity (Joshi, A., Bhattacharyya, P., & Carman, M. J. 2017), implicit congruity (Joshi, A., Sharma, V., & Bhattacharyya, P. 2015), are used. Hyperbole (Bharti, S. K., Vachha, B., Pradhan, R. K., Babu, K. S., & Jena, S. K. 2016) in tweets is the amalgamation of features such as punctuation marks, quotes, interjection and intensifier. The proposed method increases the negative count word if interjection appears in the beginning and intensifier comes in the rest of the tweet. For example "wow, that's a great sale, I am not going shop anything!!", begins with wow and not is appearing at the rest part. Therefore, this represents sarcasm. In a tweet, implicit incongruity (Joshi, A., Sharma, V., & Bhattacharyya, P. 2015) is evident with the appearance of an implied phrase contradicting a positive polarity word. In the tweet, "i like science so so much that i scored minimum marks in it". In this tweet, love is the polar word and, "i scored least marks", contains incongruous attached with the polar word i.e love. In such cases, the feature value of negative count is updated. Explicit incongruity indicates the presence of polar words, mostly in the cases when the tweet has a prior positive sentiment (Joshi, A., Bhattacharyya, P., & Carman, M. J. 2017). In the tweet "I love being annoyed", love has positive polarity and annoyed has negative polarity. For identifying such type of tweets, the value of negative word count is increased. Moreover, tweets such as, "I hate Kohli, since he always makes hundred", consists of negative sentiment word before the positive polarity word. These tweets are actually positive but look like negative. For such cases, positive word count feature is increased. Further, pragmatic features are identified by the presence smiles, emoticons. These features have prime role in identifying sarcasm in the tweets. In the tweet "I study 20 hours daily to be such poor student:)" contains positive word, negative word and positive emoji as well. In such cases, negative word count is incremented.

Hybrid Clustering Based on K-Means and BBO

The proposed clustering method (MR-KBBO) leverages the strength of BBO for improving the quality of clustering and K-means algorithm for finding the initial cluster heads. K-means is a simple and popular clustering method, but it often fall into local optimum in the presence of noise. In the proposed method, first K-means algorithm is run for 10 iteration to get some near by solution and then BBO is used to optimize the clustering process. For any meta-heuristic algorithm, the results are highly dependent on the quality of initial candidate solution. Since in BBO, population is initialized randomly, which may cause increase the convergence time stagnation in local optima. Therefore, this method utilizes the K-means for generating good candidate solution of BBO which gives precise solution and better convergence rate. Further, in the clustering process each tweet represents a vector of F where, F denotes the number of features. The value of each feature is scaled in the range [0, 1] to standardize the range feature variables. In MR-KBBO based clustering, the position *SIV* of each island represents a set of cluster centroids (C_1, C_2, C_3... C_K), where K represents the number of clusters. The minimization of intra-cluster distance is considered as *HSI* (fitness) of each island and it is calculated using Equation (3). Where $|Z_l - C_j|$ denotes the Euclidean distance between centroid C_j and tweet Z_l and w_{lj} is the weight associated with l[th] tweet which has value 1 if the belongs to cluster C_j else it is 0. The optimal clusters corresponds *SIV* value of the island having the best *HSI*.

MAPREDUCE MODEL OF MR-KBBO FOR PARALLEL PROCESSING

In the MR-KBBO method, the main computation intensive task is the calculation of the distance between each data point from their center heads. For the data set of N tweets with F features and K clusters, $K \times N$ distances have to be calculated at each iteration. Therefore, traditional sequential algorithm are not able provide the results in the given time, when the data size becomes large. In the MapReduce programming model this task of distance computation can be executed in parallel by distributing the task over multiple machines. As a whole the procedure of MR-KBBO is described in Figure 2. It can be depicted from the Figure 2, that for the first iteration, center heads are computed by running the K-means algorithm for 10 iterations and in the rest of iterations they are updated using BBO as described in Algorithm 2. The intra cluster variance, is evaluated at the end of each MapReduce cycle, which represent

Figure 2. Complete flow of MR-KBBO for large scale twitter sentiment analysis

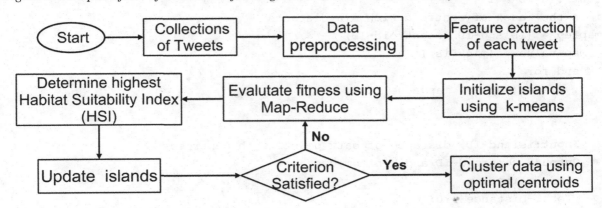

HSI of islands (candidate solution). The value of emigration rate (μ_i) and immigration (λ_i) is calculate using the *HSI* value. Further, the islands (center heads) are updated according to (μ_i) and (λ_i), by applying mutation and migration operation. This process is repeated till the maximum number of iterations are reached or desired solution is not found. The complete MR-KBBO cycle consists of two phases namely;

MR-KBBO-map and MR-KBBO-reduce. The MR-KBBO Map phase starts with retrieving the initial cluster centroids and the tweet data set from the HDFS. In this phase, the map function is invoked for each tweet which is inputted to it in the form of key/value pair as described in section hadoop section. The map function than computes the distance of a feature vector (tweet) from each centeroid and returns the minimum distance with its centroid-ID. Thereafter, map functions emit the output in the form of key/value pair. The output key contains island-ID with the centroid-ID of cluster having minimum distance and the output value contains the distance of data point with the centroid-ID. The complete pseudo code of the map function is shown in Algorithm 3.

Further, MR-KBBO-reduce phase starts followed by the MR-KBBO-map phase. The Reduce function of this phase gets the input data, which is produced by the map phase and grouped by the key. The reduce function key contains the island-ID (candidate solution) and the centroid-ID while the value contains the corresponding minimum distance. The reduce function aggregates all the values with same key and calculates the total distance which serves as the HSI value of the island. The pseudo code of the reduce phase is shown in Algorithm 4.

Algorithm 3. MR-KBBO Map
   Input: Data sample and population
   Output: centroid-ID and *HSI*

```
read (biogeography)          // this file contains population
 Map (key: tweet-ID, value: tweet)
  for each island in biogeography do;
          island-ID = extract-island-ID(biogeography)
          centroidsArray = extract-centroids(biogeography) //          the
SIV of Islands
          min-Dist = get-minDistance(record; centroid-Array)
centroid-ID = i                                                       //
i is the index of centroid with min distance
mapkey = (island-ID + centroid-ID)
  map-value = (min-Dist)
   end for
     write (mapkey, mapvalue);


  Input:island-ID, distance of data points with centroids
  Output: centroid-ID and Minimum distance
   Initialization
   Total-Distance = 0;
     Reduce (Key:(island-ID, centroid-ID), value-list: min-Distance
       for each value in value-list do
           Min-Distance=retrieve (min-Distance (value))
           Total-Distance=Total-Distance + min-Distance
       end for
     write(key, Total-Distance)
```

EXPERIMENTAL RESULTS

In this section, the accuracy and parallel performance of the proposed method has been discussed. Four baseline datasets of the tweeter are used for testing the accuracy of the proposed method which is described as follows.

Testdata.manual.2009.06.14: This dataset is publicly available on Stanford Twitter corpus (Testdata. manual.2009.06.14, 2015) and it has 498 total tweets out of which 182 are positive, 177 negative, and 139 neutral. The dataset is generated by collecting tweets based on topics like Obama, China, Iran, north Korea, Google, Nike, Kindle and San Francisco, in the duration from May 11, 2009 to Jul 14, 2009. The dataset is labeled as 0 for negative, 2 for neutral and 4 for positive sentiment.

Twitter-sanders-apple: This dataset have been collected from Oct 15, 2011 to Oct 20, 2011 by Sander Analytics (Twitter-sanders-apple,(2015)on topics Apple, Google, Microsoft, and Twitter. The tweets were labeled by Niek Sanders in positive, negative or neutral polarity. In this dataset, positive tweets are labeled by pos, negative by neg, and neutral tweets were represented by neut. The complete dataset was divided into two parts as given below.

Twitter-sanders-apple2: This dataset consists of 479 tweets out of which 163 tweets are positive, 509 tweets are neutral and 316 tweets are negative.

Twitter-sanders-apple3: This dataset have 988 total tweets out of which 163 are positive, 509 are neutral and 316 are the negative tweets.

Twitter avsh: This dataset is collected and labeled by Pandey et al. (Pandey, A. C., Rajpoot, D. S., & Saraswat, M. 2017) and has 2000 tweets posted from No. 17, 2014 to Dec 10, 2014. The dataset has 1000 positive tweets and 1000 negative tweets. The positive tweets were labeled by 0, while negative tweets were labeled by 1(Twitter dataset, 2014).

To evaluate the performance of MR-KBBO on large scale data, synthetic datasets sets are formed by duplicating each data instance of the baseline dataset by 10,000 times. Table 1 summarizes the synthetic dataset used for the experiments. The parameter values of all the methods taken for comparison have been elucidated in Table 2. All the methods were programmed in java and experiments were run on a Hadoop cluster of 5 computers. The master computer was a laptop with Intel Core i5, 2.30GHz frequency, 8 GB RAM and 500 GB hard disk. The slave computers were desktop each having a configuration Intel Corei3, 3.40GHz, 4 GB RAM, and 500 GB hard disk. To implement all the methods hadoop 2.6.0 is used with java 1.7.0 and the operating system was Ubuntu version 14.04.

Further, the performance of the proposed method (MR-KBBO) is compared with four other MapReduce based state-of-the-art methods namely parallel K-Means, parallel K-PSO parallel MR-ABC, DFBPKBA in terms of mean ac-curacy and mean computation time. Table 3 shows the mean of accuracy and computation time (MCT) obtained by running each method 30 times. The mean computation time is determined by running each method on cluster with 5 nodes. It can be depicted from the table, that the proposed method has outperformed all the considered methods in terms of accuracy. However, the mean computation of the k-means algorithm is less as compared to meta-heuristic based method. Further, a statistical comparison is performed to test the significant difference of the MR-KBBO and the other compared methods. For this, a non parametric statistical test, named Wilcoxon rank sum test is conducted with 5% significance level. The p value has been computed for all the considered datasets using the fitness value of the proposed and compared methods. In Wilcoxon rank sum test, if the value of $p < 0.5$(for 95% confidence), the NULL hypothesis is rejected and symbolized by `+' or `-' otherwise it is accepted and represented as `=`. However, the `+` symbol indicates superiority and `-` indicate that inferiority of the proposed method with the considered methods. Table 4 demonstrates pair wise comparison of the significant levels (SGFT) of MR-KBBO with other compared methods. The value of *SGFT* is `+` if $p < 0.5$ and mean fitness of the proposed method is better than the compared method. However, if $p < 0.5$ and mean fitness of the MR-KBBO is poor than the considered algorithm, the value of *SGFT* is represented by `-`. It can be depicted from the Table 4 that the p value <0.5 on all the four considered datasets. Thus, it is concluded that the proposed method is significantly different from the considered methods on all the datasets.

Furthermore, the speedup performance of the MR-KBBO is also studied on all the considered large scale synthetic datasets. The speedup measure of a method is defined by Equation (4).

$$S = \frac{T_1}{T_n} \tag{4}$$

where, T_1 is the running time when a method is run on 1 computer(node) and T_N is the running time on a cluster with N nodes. The speedup performance of MR-KBBO, is analyzed by incrementing one node on each run. Figure 3 depict the running time performance of MR-KBBO with varying number of nodes and the corresponding speedup measure are presented in table 5. It can be concluded from the Figure 3, that the running time of MR-KBBO decreases gradually with the increase of nodes in the hadoop cluster. Also table 5 shows a significant speedup of the proposed method with the increasing number of nodes. Thus, it is concluded that the proposed MR-KBBO method can be efficiently used for the twitter sentiment analysis of the large scale datasets.

CONCLUSION

In this paper, a novel parallel and hybrid clustering method (MR-KBBO) has been proposed for the sentiment analysis of large-scale twitter datasets. The proposed method leverages the strengths of the BBO for optimizing the clustering task and MapReduce model to handle large scale datasets. The random initialization process of BBO has been modified by the solutions obtained from 10 iterations of K-means to speed up the convergence. The accuracy of the proposed method has been validated on four large Twitter datasets and compared with four MapReduce based state-of-the-art namely; parallel K-means, parallel K-PSO, MR-ABC, DFBPKBA. Further, Wilcoxon rank sum test witnessed that the proposed method is significantly different and better than all other considered methods. Moreover, the parallel performance of the proposed method is analyzed using the speedup measure by testing it on different number of nodes in the cluster. From the experimental and statistical results, it can be concluded that the proposed method can be efficiently used as better alternative for twitter sentiment analysis of the large scale datasets. In future, the proposed method may be tested on some more parallel platforms such as spark to improve the computation time.

Table 1. Dataset description

S.No	Dataset	NOC	NOI	Positive	Negative	Neutral
1	Twitter-avsh	2	20,000,000	1,000,000	1,000,000	-
2	Twitter-apple2	2	4,790,000	163,000	316,000	-
3	Twitter-apple3	3	9,880,000	163,000	316,000	509,000
5	Testdata-manual	6	4,980,000	182,000	182,000	139,000

Table 2. Considered methods parameter values

Parameter Name	K-Means	parallel K-PSO	DFBPKBA	MR-ABC	MR-KBBO
Population size (pop)	--	40	40	40	40
Number of Iterations(itr)	500	500	500	500	500
Inertial Constant (w)	--	0.5	--	--	--
Cognitive Constant (c1)	--	1	--	--	--
Social Constant (c2)	--	1	--	--	--
Alpha (α)	--	.09	--	--	--
fmin	--	--	0	--	--
fmax	--	--	10	--	--
gamma (γ)	--	--	0.01	--	--
emission rate (r0)	--	--	0.5	--	--
Crossover rate(CR)	--	--	--	--	.01
Mutation Rate (M)	--	--	--	--	0.1

Table 3. Mean Accuracy and mean computation time over 30 runs

S.No	Dataset	Criteria	Parallel K-means	Parallel K-PSO	MR-ABC	DFBPKA	MR-KBBO
1	Twitter avsh	Mean Accuracy	55.16	59.16	63.45	65.85	68.21
		Mean time	2.05E+04	2.27E+04	2.25E+04	2.26E+04	2.25E+04
2	Twitter sander-2	Mean Accuracy	59.31	69.683	74.79	78.79	90.50
		Mean Time	1.14E+E04	1.54E+E04	1.53E+04	1.52E+04	1.52E+04
3	Twitter sander-3	MeanAccuracy	67.75	78.45	82.75	80.70	91.44
		Mean Time	1.80E+04	2.14E+04	2.13E+04	2.14E+04	2.13E+04
4	Testdata-manual	Mean Accuracy	62.21	72.55	72.45	74.75	88.80
		Mean Time	1.04E+04	1.28E+04	1.26E+04	1.25E+04	1.24E+04

Table 4. Results of Wilcoxon test for statistically significance level of 0:05

S.No	Dataset Name	MR-KBBO-PK-Means		MR-KBBO-parallel KPSO		MR-KBBO-DBBPKBA		MR-KBBO-MR-ABC	
		P-Value	SGFT	P-Value	SGFT	P-Value	SGFT	P-Value	SGFT
1	Twitter avsh	3.35E-05	+	7.67E-05	+	3.40E-08	+	4.11E-06	+
2	Twitter sander-2	1.45E-07	+	2.24E-11	+	2.24E-11	+	3.01E-09	+
3	Twitter sander-3	5.45E-06	+	4.45E-65	+	4.03E-07	+	1.36E-07	+
4	Testdata-manual	8.60E-09	+	7.09E-45	+	8.02E-05	+	6.08E-09	+

Table 5. Speedup Measure of MR-KBBO obtained by varying number of nodes

Dataset Name	2 Node cluster	3 Node Cluster	4 Node Cluster	5 Node Cluster
Twitter avsh	1.6825	2.3274	3.3245	4.3802
Twitter sander2	1.6898	2.4075	3.0650	4.1991
Twitter sander3	1.6615	2.3615	3.0348	4.0449
Twitter Manual	1.6699	2.3366	3.1589	4.0398

Figure 3. The speedup graph of (a) Twitter Manual (b) Twitter sander 2 (c) Twitter sander 3 (d) Twitter avsh

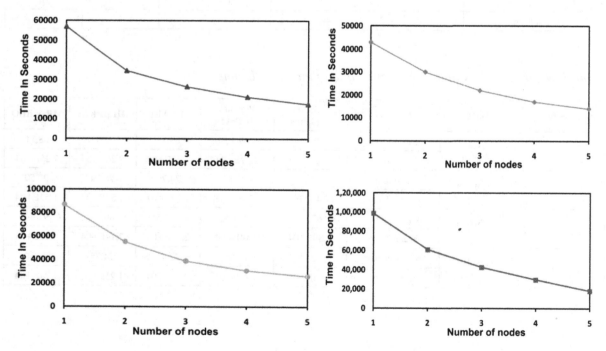

REFERENCES

Agarwal, B., Mittal, N., Bansal, P., & Garg, S. (2015). Sentiment analysis using common-sense and context information. *Computational Intelligence and Neuroscience, 2015*, 30. doi:10.1155/2015/715730 PMID:25866505

Altınel, B., & Ganiz, M. C. (2016). A new hybrid semi-supervised algorithm for text classification with class-based semantics. *Knowledge-Based Systems, 108*, 50–64. doi:10.1016/j.knosys.2016.06.021

Anitha, M. A., & Nazeer, K. A. (2017, March). Improved Parallel Clustering with Optimal Initial Centroids. In Recent Advances in Electronics and Communication Technology (ICRAECT), 2017 International Conference on (pp. 114-120). IEEE.

Appel, O., Chiclana, F., Carter, J., & Fujita, H. (2016). A hybrid approach to the sentiment analysis problem at the sentence level. *Knowledge-Based Systems, 108*, 110–124. doi:10.1016/j.knosys.2016.05.040

Asur, S., & Huberman, B. A. (2010, August). Predicting the future with social media. In Proceedings of the 2010 IEEE/WIC/ACM International Conference on Web Intelligence and Intelligent Agent Technology-Volume 01 (pp. 492-499). IEEE Computer Society. 10.1109/WI-IAT.2010.63

Banharnsakun, A. (2017). A MapReduce-based artificial bee colony for large-scale data clustering. *Pattern Recognition Letters, 93*, 78–84. doi:10.1016/j.patrec.2016.07.027

Basari, A. S. H., Hussin, B., Ananta, I. G. P., & Zeniarja, J. (2013). Opinion mining of movie review using hybrid method of support vector machine and particle swarm optimization. *Procedia Engineering, 53*, 453–462. doi:10.1016/j.proeng.2013.02.059

Bharti, S. K., Babu, K. S., & Jena, S. K. (2015, August). Parsing-based sarcasm sentiment recognition in twitter data. In Proceedings of the 2015 IEEE/ACM International Conference on Advances in Social Networks Analysis and Mining 2015 (pp. 1373-1380). ACM. 10.1145/2808797.2808910

Bharti, S. K., Vachha, B., Pradhan, R. K., Babu, K. S., & Jena, S. K. (2016). Sarcastic sentiment detection in tweets streamed in real time: A big data approach. *Digital Communications and Networks, 2*(3), 108–121. doi:10.1016/j.dcan.2016.06.002

Boiy, E., Hens, P., Deschacht, K., & Moens, M. F. (2007, June). Automatic Sentiment Analysis in Online Text. In ELPUB (pp. 349-360).

Bravo-Marquez, F., Mendoza, M., & Poblete, B. (2013, August). Combining strengths, emotions and polarities for boosting Twitter sentiment analysis. In *Proceedings of the Second International Workshop on Issues of Sentiment Discovery and Opinion Mining* (p. 2). ACM. 10.1145/2502069.2502071

Cambria, E. (2016). Affective computing and sentiment analysis. *IEEE Intelligent Systems, 31*(2), 102–107. doi:10.1109/MIS.2016.31

Canuto, S., Gonçalves, M. A., & Benevenuto, F. (2016, February). Exploiting new sentiment-based meta-level features for effective sentiment analysis. In *Proceedings of the ninth ACM international conference on web search and data mining* (pp. 53-62). ACM. 10.1145/2835776.2835821

Chen, T., Xu, R., He, Y., Xia, Y., & Wang, X. (2016). Learning user and product distributed representations using a sequence model for sentiment analysis. *IEEE Computational Intelligence Magazine, 11*(3), 34–44. doi:10.1109/MCI.2016.2572539

Chiang, M. M. T., & Mirkin, B. (2010). Intelligent choice of the number of clusters in k-means clustering: An experimental study with different cluster spreads. *Journal of Classification, 27*(1), 3–40. doi:10.100700357-010-9049-5

Coletta, L. F. S., da Silva, N. F. F., Hruschka, E. R., & Hruschka, E. R. (2014, October). Combining classification and clustering for tweet sentiment analysis. In Intelligent Systems (BRACIS), 2014 Brazilian Conference on (pp. 210-215). IEEE. 10.1109/BRACIS.2014.46

Danielsson, P. E. (1980). Euclidean distance mapping. *Computer Graphics and Image Processing, 14*(3), 227–248. doi:10.1016/0146-664X(80)90054-4

Dean, J., & Ghemawat, S. (2008). MapReduce: Simplified data processing on large clusters. *Communications of the ACM, 51*(1), 107–113. doi:10.1145/1327452.1327492

Emoticon dictionary, (2015), http://www.netlingo.com/smileys.php

Fernández-Gavilanes, M., Álvarez-López, T., Juncal-Martínez, J., Costa-Montenegro, E., & González-Castaño, F. J. (2016). Unsupervised method for sentiment analysis in online texts. *Expert Systems with Applications, 58*, 57–75. doi:10.1016/j.eswa.2016.03.031

Frontpage - hadoop wiki, https://wiki.apache.org/hadoop/, (Accessed on 02/27/2018).

Gupta, D. K., Reddy, K. S., & Ekbal, A. (2015, June). Pso-asent: Feature selection using particle swarm optimization for aspect based sentiment analysis. In International conference on applications of natural language to information systems (pp. 220-233). Springer, Cham.

Hu, X., Tang, L., Tang, J., & Liu, H. (2013, February). Exploiting social relations for sentiment analysis in microblogging. In *Proceedings of the sixth ACM international conference on Web search and data mining* (pp. 537-546). ACM. 10.1145/2433396.2433465

Jain, A. K. (2010). Data clustering: 50 years beyond K-means. *Pattern Recognition Letters, 31*(8), 651–666. doi:10.1016/j.patrec.2009.09.011

jeffreybreen (2015). Negative word dictionary. twitter-sentiment-analysis-tutorial-201107/data/opinion-lexicon-English/Negative-words.txt

jeffreybreen (2015). Positive word dictionary. twitter-sentiment-analysis-tutorial-201107/data/opinion-lexicon-English/positive-words.txt.

Joshi, A., Bhattacharyya, P., & Carman, M. J. (2017). Automatic sarcasm detection: A survey. [CSUR]. *ACM Computing Surveys, 50*(5), 73. doi:10.1145/3124420

Joshi, A., Sharma, V., & Bhattacharyya, P. (2015). Harnessing context incongruity for sarcasm detection. In *Proceedings of the 53rd Annual Meeting of the Association for Computational Linguistics and the 7th International Joint Conference on Natural Language Processing* (Volume 2: Short Papers) (Vol. 2, pp. 757-762).

Kanakaraj, M., & Guddeti, R. M. R. (2015, March). NLP based sentiment analysis on Twitter data using ensemble classifiers. In Signal processing, communication and networking (ICSCN), 2015 3rd international conference on (pp. 1-5). IEEE. 10.1109/ICSCN.2015.7219856

Kanungoy, T., Mountz, D. M., Netanyahux, N. S., Piatko, C., Silvermank, R., & Wu, A. Y. (2000). An E cient k-Means Clustering Algorithm: Analysis and Implementation.

Khan, A. Z., Atique, M., & Thakare, V. M. (2015). Combining lexicon-based and learning-based methods for Twitter sentiment analysis. International Journal of Electronics, Communication and Soft Computing Science & Engineering (IJECSCSE), 89.

Khezr, S. N., & Navimipour, N. J. (2015). MapReduce and its application in optimization algorithms: A comprehensive study. Majlesi Journal of Multimedia Processing, 4(3).

Kogan, J., Teboulle, M., & Nicholas, C. (2005). Data driven similarity measures for k-means like clustering algorithms. *Information Retrieval, 8*(2), 331–349. doi:10.100710791-005-5666-8

Kontopoulos, E., Berberidis, C., Dergiades, T., & Bassiliades, N. (2013). Ontology-based sentiment analysis of twitter posts. *Expert Systems with Applications, 40*(10), 4065–4074. doi:10.1016/j.eswa.2013.01.001

Medhat, W., Hassan, A., & Korashy, H. (2014). Sentiment analysis algorithms and applications: A survey. *Ain Shams Engineering Journal, 5*(4), 1093–1113. doi:10.1016/j.asej.2014.04.011

Mohammad, S. M., Zhu, X., Kiritchenko, S., & Martin, J. (2015). Sentiment, emotion, purpose, and style in electoral tweets. *Information Processing & Management, 51*(4), 480–499. doi:10.1016/j.ipm.2014.09.003

Muhammad, A., Wiratunga, N., & Lothian, R. (2016). Contextual sentiment analysis for social media genres. *Knowledge-Based Systems, 108*, 92–101. doi:10.1016/j.knosys.2016.05.032

Nugent, R., Dean, N., & Ayers, E. (2010). Skill set profile clustering: the empty K-means algorithm with automatic specification of starting cluster centers.

Pal, R., & Saraswat, M. (2017, August). Data clustering using enhanced biogeography-based optimization. In Contemporary Computing (IC3), 2017 Tenth International Conference on (pp. 1-6). IEEE. 10.1109/IC3.2017.8284305

Pandarachalil, R., Sendhilkumar, S., & Mahalakshmi, G. S. (2015). Twitter sentiment analysis for large-scale data: An unsupervised approach. *Cognitive Computation, 7*(2), 254–262. doi:10.100712559-014-9310-z

Pandey, A. C., Pal, R., & Kulhari, A. Unsupervised data classification using improved biogeography based optimization. International Journal of System Assurance Engineering and Management, 1-9.

Pandey, A. C., Rajpoot, D. S., & Saraswat, M. (2017). Twitter sentiment analysis using hybrid cuckoo search method. *Information Processing & Management, 53*(4), 764–779. doi:10.1016/j.ipm.2017.02.004

Psychological feelings, (2015). http://www.psychpage.com/learning/library/assess/feelings.html

Qiu, G., Liu, B., Bu, J., & Chen, C. (2009, July). Expanding domain sentiment lexicon through double propagation. In IJCAI (Vol. 9, pp. 1199-1204).

R. D. Gantz J. The digital universe in 2020: Big data, bigger digital shadows, https://www.emc.com/leadership/digitaluniverse/2012iview/executive-summary-a-universe-of.html

Saif, H., He, Y., Fernandez, M., & Alani, H. (2016). Contextual semantics for sentiment analysis of Twitter. *Information Processing & Management, 52*(1), 5–19. doi:10.1016/j.ipm.2015.01.005

Shvachko, K., Kuang, H., Radia, S., & Chansler, R. (2010). Mass Storage Systems and Technologies (MSST). In 2010 IEEE 26th Symposium on. IEEE (pp. 1-10).

Simon, D. (2008). Biogeography-based optimization. *IEEE Transactions on Evolutionary Computation, 12*(6), 702–713. doi:10.1109/TEVC.2008.919004

Stopwords. https://www.ranks.nl/stopwords

Sulis, E., Farías, D. I. H., Rosso, P., Patti, V., & Ruffo, G. (2016). Figurative messages and affect in Twitter: Differences between# irony, # sarcasm and# not. *Knowledge-Based Systems, 108*, 132–143. doi:10.1016/j.knosys.2016.05.035

Testdata.manual.2009.06.14, (2015), http://help.sentiment140.com/for-students/

Tripathi, A. K., Sharma, K., & Bala, M. Dynamic frequency based parallel k-bat algorithm for massive data clustering (DFBPKBA). International Journal of System Assurance Engineering and Management, 1-9.

Twitte dataset, (2014). https://drive.google.com/file/d/0BwPSGZHAP%20%20yoN2pZcVl1Qmp1OEU/view?usp=sharing%20

Twitter-sanders-apple. (2015),http://boston.lti.cs.cmu.edu/classes/95-%20865m %20K/HW/HW3/

Wilkinson, R., & Hingston, P. (1991, September). Using the cosine measure in a neural network for document retrieval. In *Proceedings of the 14th annual international ACM SIGIR conference on Research and development in information retrieval* (pp. 202-210). ACM. 10.1145/122860.122880

Wolpert, D. H., & Macready, W. G. (1997). No Free Lunch Theorems for Optimization IEEE TRANSACTIONS ON. *Evolutionary Computation*, E997.

Zhao, W., Ma, H., & He, Q. (2009, December). Parallel k-means clustering based on mapreduce. In *IEEE International Conference on Cloud Computing* (pp. 674-679). Springer, Berlin, Heidelberg. 10.1007/978-3-642-10665-1_71

Zhu, J., Wang, H., & Mao, J. (2010, April). Sentiment classification using genetic algorithm and conditional random fields. In Information Management and Engineering (ICIME), 2010 The 2nd IEEE International Conference on (pp. 193-196). IEEE. 10.1109/ICIME.2010.5478084

This research was previously published in the International Journal of Information Security and Privacy (IJISP), 13(3); pages 106-122, copyright year 2019 by IGI Publishing (an imprint of IGI Global).

Chapter 64
Sentiment Analysis of Arabic Documents:
Main Challenges and Recent Advances

Hichem Rahab

(iD) https://orcid.org/0000-0002-4411-0901

ICISI Laboratory, University of Khenchela, Algeria

Mahieddine Djoudi

(iD) https://orcid.org/0000-0002-2998-5574

TechNE Laboratory, University of Poitiers, France

Abdelhafid Zitouni

(iD) https://orcid.org/0000-0003-2498-4967

LIRE Laboratory, University of Constantine 2, Algeria

ABSTRACT

Today, it is usual that a consumer seeks for others' feelings about their purchasing experience on the web before a simple decision of buying a product or a service. Sentiment analysis intends to help people in taking profit from the available opinionated texts on the web for their decision making, and business is one of its challenging areas. Considerable work of sentiment analysis has been achieved in English and other Indo-European languages. Despite the important number of Arabic speakers and internet users, studies in Arabic sentiment analysis are still insufficient. The current chapter vocation is to give the main challenges of Arabic sentiment together with their recent proposed solutions in the literature. The chapter flowchart is presented in a novel manner that obtains the main challenges from presented literature works. Then it gives the proposed solutions for each challenge. The chapter reaches the finding that the future tendency will be toward rule-based techniques and deep learning, allowing for more dealings with Arabic language inherent characteristics.

DOI: 10.4018/978-1-6684-6303-1.ch064

INTRODUCTION

The evolution of Internet use in today's world is coupled with an important advancement in offering services for users. A tremendous amount of information and data is generated, and more needs emerge to take benefit from it (Liu, 2012). The importance of taking into accounts other opinions and advises in decision-making process (sales, voting, etc.) is a result of the neutrality of this information and its independence from any conflict of interest (Liu, 2015). When someone would sell a new product, ask for a service like a hotel booking or go to a new restaurant, or even take the decision in elections, he is no more limited to advice of family members and near friends. On Internet there are several web sites, discussion forums and social networks allowing their visitors to open debates and giving their comments on subjects, products and services of their interest (Guellil et al., 2019).

Sentiment analysis seeks to discover positive and negative sentiments about objects (ex. Cellular phones) and their attributes (image quality, weight, etc.) through natural language processing NLP, text mining and data-mining techniques (Aggarwal, 2018). Sentiment analysis aims to classify discovered people opinions into well-defined categories to facilitate hidden phenomenon understanding. Sentiment analysis can be seen as an automatic summarization of subjective documents, which allow positive or negative polarity extraction from textual documents (Pang & Lee, 2004). Opinion mining use is not limited to product reviews; it can reach user attitudes, political attitudes etc. (Aggarwal, 2018).

The application of sentiment analysis techniques covers a widespread of domains, such as business, politics, security and healthcare, to cite a few. Using sentiment analysis in healthcare domain can profit from available opinionated data in social media and web forums to help in the improvement of healthcare systems by controlling epidemics and guarantee a better care for patients (Ramírez-Tinoco et al., 2019). In the security domain, opinion mining can be used to control exchanged discussions in e-mails (Danowski, 2012), in social networks or even in phone conversations (Iskra et al., 2004). The available data at low cost in social media can be very beneficial to prevent possible perturbations in different events. This information can provide useful information for authorities and organizations, allowing them to take suitable decisions by understanding their people's mood (Subramaniyaswamy et al., 2017).

An important number of works in data mining and sentiment analysis is achieved in European languages, especially in English. Resources in these languages are available and enough in term of quantity and quality. However, in low resourced languages such as Arabic, the number of dedicated resources in very limited. Arabic is a Semitic language with more than 400 million speakers in 22 countries, and it is the fourth most used language in the Internet by 226 million users (*Internet World Stats*, n.d.). Arabic letters are used to write other languages, such as Person and Urdu. The Arabic language is also important as the language of the Holy Quran the book of 1.5 billion muslins around the world.

The aim of the present chapter is to provide sentiment analysis community, newcomers especially, with the important problematic questions and their last proposed solutions in the literature. The research questions that this chapter intends to answer are: what are the recent problems that sentiment analysis has to solve? What are the important methods used in sentiment analysis for the resolution of each problem? Are these methods sufficient to overcome the new challenges in the domain? And what will be the future tendency of the research in opinion mining and sentiment analysis? Unlike traditional surveys, listing sentiment analysis works according to adopted approaches and used methods and tools, the authors in this chapter extract, from literary works, the main challenges and their corresponding solutions. By the adopted methodology, the authors reach the new tendency in the domain, in order to respond to new challenges.

The chapter is organized as follows. The Second section presents related notions to Arabic language and sentiment analysis. In the third section, a literature review of recent works is included. The main challenges of Arabic sentiment analysis are described in section four. In the fifth section, the solutions and the recommendations, to the given challenges, are depicted. The next section gives future research directions in the domain. The chapter is concluded in the seventh section.

BACKGROUND

Characteristics of the Arabic Language

Arabic is a morphologically rich language characterized by coding, at the word level, a big amount of syntactic units of information (Tsarfaty et al., 2010). Arabic is the most important in the family of Semitic languages with; Amharic, Tigrinya, Hebrew, among others (Djoudi & Harous, 2008). Semitic languages family share a common characteristic of rich and complex morphology with similar syntactic generation rules (Marsi et al., 2005).

Arabic means, in this chapter, Modern Standard Arabic, which is, in our days, the most used form of the Arabic language in administration, education and media. Arabic is written from right to left, and Arabic alphabet is composed of 28 letters, three among them are considered long vowels Alif 'ا', Waw 'و', and Ya 'ي'. In addition, Arabic has a set of short vowels called diacritics. Diacritics are optional is most cases in Arabic texts; they are useful in a text to remove ambiguity and also to guide pronunciation (Boudad et al., 2017).

Arabic Lexicon

A word in Arabic can take one of the three forms; noun /Ăis.m/ (اسم), verb /fiς.l/(فعل) or particle/Har.f/ (حرف). A noun is a word which has a meaning and allows an entity or an object designation regardless any time, example /Alšajaraħ/[1] (الشجرة) (tree), /AltaTaw~ur/(التطور)(development). Nouns can be grouped according to their origins into three categories; static nouns /Al ÂsmaA' AljaAmidaħ/ (الأسماء الجامدة) which are not derived from any others words, derived nouns /Al ÂsmaA' Almuš.taqaħ/ (الأسماء المشتقة) are obtained from other word called roots /jiðr/(جذر) and numbers nouns /ÂsmaA' Al ÂςdaAd/ (أسماء الأعداد). In the difference of nouns, verbs allow designing event or meaning in relation to a well-determined time. In Arabic, there are three times; past, present and imperative. The past, or unaccomplished time / AlmaADiy/ (الماضي), designs an action accomplished before the pronunciation. In the present and the future /AlmuDaAriς/ (المضارع), the verb is not accomplished, and it is related to the present or future times (Saadane, 2015). Imperative designs an order, advice or suggestion to do an act.

Arabic Morphology

The morphological aspect is, perhaps, the most studied in Arabic language (Habash, 2010) as Arabic is a morphologically rich and complex language. Arabic is an agglutinated language in the sense that the same word can be formed by different terms. In this case, a set of clitics are attached to the word; each one represents a part of a sentence (Boudad et al., 2017).

Table 1. the verb /xaraja/ خرج (go out) in past, present and future

Time	انأ ÂnaA 'I'	نحن naH.n 'we'	َتنأ Ânta You (m)²	ِتنأ Ânti You (f)	امتنأ ÂntumaA you (d)	متنأ Ântum You (pm)	نتنأ Ântun~a You (pf)
Past	خرجت	خرجنا	خرجتَ	خرجتِ	خرجتما	خرجتم	خرجتن
Present	أخرُجُ	نخرج	تخرج	تخرجين	تخرجان	تخرجون	تخرجن
Imperative	-	-	أخرج	أخرجي	أخرجا	أخرجوا	أخرجن

Table 2. the verb xaraja خرج (go out) in past, present and future (continued)

وه huwa He	Time	يه hiya She	امه humaA They (dm)	امه humaA They (df)	مه hum they (pm)	نه hun~a They (pf)
خرج	Past	خرجت	خرجا	خرجتا	خرجوا	خرجن
يخرج	Present	تخرج	يخرجان	تخرجان	يخرجون	يخرجن
-	Imperative	-	-	-	-	-

Derivation /Al ĂštiqAq/(قاقتشالا) is related to obtaining a word from another word, the root /Al maSdar/(ردصملا). The root of a word may be different in pronunciation and part of speech category; even it has convenient meaning. Derivation variations in Arabic are seven: the active participle /Ăsm Al faAçil/(لعافلا مسا), the passive participle /Ăsm Al mafaçuwl/ (لوعفملا مسا), the resembling participle / AlSifa Almušabahaħ biAsm Al faAçil/ (لعافلا مساب ةهبشملا ةفصلا), the elative name /Ăsm Al tafDyl/ (ليضفتلا مسا), the time adverbial/Ăsm AlzamAn/(نامزلا مسا), the place adverbial /Ăsm AlmakaAn/ (ناكملا مسا), and the noun of instrument /Ăsm AlÂlaħ/ (ةلآلا مسا).

Inflectional morphology design word variations among different grammatical categories by preserving the same meaning. Inflectional morphology is done according to (Boudad et al., 2017): time (past or present), mood (indicative, subjunctive, imperative, etc.), person (first, second, or third), number (single, dual or plural), genre (feminine or masculine), case (accusative, genitive or nominative), and voice (passive or active).

Sentiment Analysis

Sentiment analysis also known as opinion mining is a field that uses Natural Language Processing NLP, text mining and computational linguistics techniques in order to identify, extract and quantify sentiment and subjective information from text written in natural languages (Rahab et al., 2018). The expressions sentiment analysis and opinion mining are used interchangeably in most works in literature (Liu, 2010, 2012). However, some works may state the difference as in (Medhat et al., 2014) where the sentiment analysis is defined as the extraction and study of sentiments expressed in texts while opinion mining vocation is about analyzing people's opinion about an entity. One of the main applications of opinion mining is texts polarity classification when a document is studied to know whether it expresses a positive, negative, or neutral opinion.

Handling Levels

A sentiment analysis system may deal with opinionated documents, at several levels according to the nature of the study and the type of the document. Three levels are considered in sentiment analysis literature; the document level, the sentence level and the aspect level.

- **Document Level:** At the document level, the whole document is considered as a single unit; the opinion mining becomes a classification task and often a binary classification task (Aggarwal, 2018). This level is appropriate for sentiment analysis from reviews where a single entity is targeted in each document.
- **Sentence Level:** At this level, the document sentences are firstly classified into subjective and objective categories. Here, phrases may be parts of sentences, and a phrase can take the form of an idiom or a proverb (Ibrahim et al., 2015). In the second time subjective sentences will be classified into either positive or negative categories. The final step is the aggregation of individual sentences sentiment to obtain the whole document semantic orientation.
- **Aspect Level:** In the aspect or feature level, opinions toward entity aspects are studied individually. Aspect level is very useful in dealing with product reviews, where the reviewer may like some aspects of the product and dislike others. The task starts by extracting product aspects, for example from pros and cons of a product review (Liu, 2010), then opinions that target these aspects are obtained and calculated, the global review sentiment is calculated from sentiments about all aspects of the product (Ismail et al., 2016).

Classification Approaches

The first and the most used method is a machine learning-based, also called a corpus-based approach. In this approach a corpus of annotated documents is needed to train a classifier, the annotation can be manual (Mountassir et al., 2013; Rahab et al., 2019), automatic (Rushdi-Saleh et al., 2011) or by using a Crowdsourcing system (Abdul-Mageed & Diab, 2012a; Bougrine et al., 2017). In the next step, a set of features is selected to represent documents in the classification stage. In the classification, several methods are used in literature, and the most popular are Support Vector Machines, Naïve Bayes, and Decision trees, among others.

For the lexicon-based approach, a sentiment lexicon of words or phrases of known sentiment orientation is compiled, and sentiment orientation of documents is determined in function of the appearance of sentiment words and/or phrases. Sentiment lexicons creation can be manual, dictionary-based or lexicon-based. The manual technique is the most precise, but it is time-consuming and laborious; thus it is no more used alone, it is generally used in addition to other techniques as first cold start step and/or as final check step. The dictionary-based method starts with a manually created list of seed words with known sentimental orientation, then by propagation of this list using search engine corpora as WordNet or a thesaurus. An important characteristic of such technique is its domain independence.

The hybrid approach constitutes a combination of the aforementioned techniques, lexicon-based and machine learning approaches, at different levels of their implementation (Elshakankery & Ahmed, 2019).

Literature Survey

Sentiment analysis research had rapid growth in recent years; this advancement is due to its application in different domains. Works in Arabic sentiment analysis are still limited when compared with its importance in the world. A lot of effort is made in the last decade to reduce this gap, especially by developing dedicated resources (Abdul-mageed & Sandra, 2012; Al-hussaini & Al-dossari, 2017; Elnagar et al., 2018; Mahyoub et al., 2014; Rahab et al., 2019).

A lexicon of 2500 words from Sudanese dialect is manually collected from Twitter and other Arabic web sites in (Abdelhameed & Hernández, 2019). The collected data is then manually annotated as positive or negative by the authors. Before the classification step, the collected dataset is passed by a set of pre-processing subphases including; tokenization, removing stop words and stemming. The training dataset is formed by 608 positive words and 1246 negative ones. The authors use 646 tweets collected from Twitter as test dataset. The best classification result is obtained in term of F_mesure using support vector machines classifier.

HILATSA is a hybrid approach for dialectal Arabic sentiment analysis (Elshakankery & Ahmed, 2019). The approach is composed of a lexicon, a machine learning classifier, and a word learner. The lexicon is created by dialectal words collected from Twitter and manually annotated where, each word has three counts, the first is the number of times the word appears in positive tweets, the second for the number of times the word appears in negative tweets and the last for the number of times it has appeared in neutral tweets. Additional three lexicons were created for popular emotions, special intensification words, and popular dialectal idioms. Each tweet is preprocessed by a set of steps including detection of emotions from the emotion lexicon, removing numbers and non-Arabic words, removing the diacritical marks, converting letters with different formats in a unique one, using an algorithm to detect negation, stemming and detecting idioms from idioms lexicon. For Arabic people names, the authors use a list prepared by (Zayed & El-Beltagy, 2015) for the detection and elimination of person names in colloquial Arabic.

In order to study the sentiment analysis in Arabic reviews, two different datasets are used in (Rahab et al., 2019). The first dataset, SANA, is collected from Arabic newspaper web sites, while the second dataset is OCA (Opinion Corpus for Arabic) (Rushdi-Saleh et al., 2011) available online for research purposes. The reviews are manually annotated by MApTTER approach developed in the scope of the same work. For experimentation, three machine learning methods; Support Vector Machines, Naïve Bayes, and K-Nearest Neighbors were tested. Obtained performance differs with the used corpus and word vector model. The SANA corpus best results are obtained by application of the light stemming.

For Arabic named entity recognition ANER, a methodology of transfer learning using neural networks is built (Al-smadi et al., 2020). The authors developed a model Pooled-GRU with Multilingual Universal Sentence Encoder USE, in addition to the baseline Bi-LSTM-CRF developed earlier par the same authors. The experimental study is conducted using the WikiFANE$_{Gold}$ dataset, WikiFANE$_{Gold}$ consists of 8 main classes: (1) Person (PER), (2) Location (LOC), (3) Organization (ORG), (4) Vehicle (VEH), (5) Geopolitical (GPE), (6) Facility (FAC),(7) Weapon (WEA), and (8) Product (PRO). The eight main classes span over 50 more fine-grained classes. Both of the proposed models are trained and tested with the same dataset. The proposed model Pooled-GRU achieves 91% of accuracy and 90.25% of F1mesure outperforming the baseline model by around 17% in F1mesure.

ANETAC (Ameur, 2019) is a freely available dataset of English to Arabic named entity transliteration and classification (Hadj Ameur et al., 2019). ANETAC consists of 79,924 named entities divided into three classes: Person by 61.662, Location by 12.679 and Organization by 5.583 named entities. The authors divided their corpus into three subsets; training with 75.898 named entities, development with 1004 named entities and test with 3013 named entities. After a pre-processing step, the system identifies for each English sentence the set of names entities which it contains. Then, each English named entity is associated with a set of Arabic transliteration candidates. Finally, the best Arabic candidate will be selected in function of the obtained score. In the transliteration results, the performance of English-to-Arabic outperforms that of Arabic-to-English, and the authors report the need for more work to improve this later.

In the goal of comparing different methods of opinion spam detection in Arabic reviews, several investigations were carried out by saeed et al. (Saeed et al., 2019). The developed approach is based on three modules; pre-processing, extraction module and spam detection. In the pre-processing module, a set of operations are conducted including; tokenization, removal of non-Arabic content, normalization of words form, stop words removal and light stemming. In the extraction module, different n-gram models are constructed, and their polarity is determined by a sentiment lexicon of 17.000 words/phrases. To handle negation, the authors constructed a list of 50 negation words, and the extracted N-grams are checked to determine whether they are preceded by a negation. When an N-gram is preceded by a negation word, its polarity will be reversed. In the spam detection module, four methods are used: rule-based, machine learning, majority voting and stacking ensemble. In experimentation, two datasets were used: The first dataset is the Deceptive Opinion Spam Corpus (DOSC), it contains 1600 reviews translated from English to Arabic by Arabic expert translators. The second dataset is Hotel Arabic Reviews Dataset (HARD) (Elnagar et al., 2018); it consists of 94.052 reviews. The experimentation results show that spam detection is improved when using negation handling and the rule-based classifier outperforms machine learning classifier.

MAIN CHALLENGES OF ARABIC SENTIMENT ANALYSIS

Arabic Language Complexity

As explained in the background section and literature survey, Arabic has a set of inherent complex characteristics making Arabic sentiment analysis ASA and Arabic Natural Language Processing ANLP in general hard tasks. The Arabic script itself poses real challenges to the automatic process of the language. An Arabic letter may have several forms depending on its position in the word, in the beginning, in the middle, in the end, or alone. For example, the letter 'ب' /b/, in the beginning, takes the form 'بـ', in the middle 'ـبـ', in the end 'ـب', and when it is alone or after letters such 'ا' is written 'ب'as in the word 'باتك' /book/. Some letters may be used interchangeably by users of social media, for example, the letter Alif 'ا' /A/ has three forms 'أ', 'إ', 'آ', and 'ا', the letter yaA 'ي' /y/ can be written as "Alif maqsurah" 'ى' or as it 'ي'and the letter 'ة' can be replaced by haA 'ه' at the end of a word. This problem may produce different writing of the same word in different documents due to authors writing styles or even in the same documents by ignorance of the author.

A very challenging source of ambiguity in Arabic is the omission of diacritics, also known as short vowels. As Arabic is considered a consonantal language, the role of short vowels is handled as a secondary problem compared to consonants (Djoudi et al., 1989). In Arabic, there are eight short vowels, as shown in Table 3, also known as diacritic signs. In today's Arabic writing, diacritics are omitted in almost all Arabic documents, and native speakers can understand the meaning of a word from the context. These diacritic signs are conserved only in the writing of the Holy Quran and in children books and are usually absent in dialectal texts (Fadel et al., 2019). The absence of diacritics, in general, in Arabic texts constitutes a severe problem to face in Arabic Natural Language Processing tasks such as proper nouns extraction and text-to-speech conversion (Farghaly & Shaalan, 2009; Mubarak et al., 2019).

The fragmentation of a text into sentences is an important step in handling the sentiment in documents, and thus unlike Latin languages where a sentence starts with an upper case and is finished with a period, this situation is different in Arabic. Delimiting sentences is a real problem in Arabic documents due to: the absence of capital letters in Arabic, and also the lack in the use of punctuation marks by the Internet and social media users.

Tokenization in some languages such as English is limited to segmenting sequences of letters into words by means of space characters. In agglutinative languages such as Arabic, tokenization needs deep language knowledge, in fact an Arabic word may be segmented on so many tokens, that a set of clitics may be attached to it.

Table 3: Arabic short vowels (diacritics)

Diacritic	Description	Transliteration	Example		
			Arabic	**Transliteration**	**English**
ٷ	فتحة (fatHah)	a	دَهَنَ	dahana	He paints
ٸ	ضمة (Dam~ah)	u	دُهِنَ	duhina	It is painted
ٷ	كسرة (kas.rah)	i	دُهِنَ	duhina	It has been painted
ٸ	فتحتين (fatHatayn)	ā	كتاباً	kitaAbAā	Book (in the accusative)
ٷ	ضمتين (Dam~atayn)	ū	كتابٌ	kitaAbū	Book (in the nominative)
ٷ	كسرتين (kas.ratayn)	i	كتابٍ	kitaAbī	Book (in the genitive)
ٷ	شدة (šad~ah)	~	كسّر	kas~ara	Break
ٷ	سكون (sukuwn)	.	مسجد	mas.jid or masjid	Mosque

Dialectal and Non-Arabic Content (Diglossia)

The Arab world is situated in the middle of the old world; this geographic region is the intersection between nations and civilizations for centuries. This situation influenced Arabic culture, population and language. The colonization movement in the nineteenth and twentieth centuries was the recent and the most influencing contact between the Arab world and the occident. One of the effects of such situation on the Arabic language is the introduction of borrowed words into Arabic daily conversations which contribute to form, in addition to other old languages such as Berber in North Africa, the Arabic Dialects. The coexistence of several forms of Arabic language in the Arab world and the simultaneous use of these varieties in an implicit manner is known as Diglossia (Ferguson, 1959). In the Arab world, there are three varieties of Arabic language which are used simultaneously: Classical Arabic, Modern Standard Arabic and Dialectal Arabic (also known as Colloquial Arabic). Dealing with these three forms is a considerable challenge facing the development of NLP systems; as a consequence, this will alter opinion mining development in Arabic.

Arabizi or Romanized Arabic

Arabizi (Duwairi et al., 2016; Guellil et al., 2020; Guellil, Adeel, et al., 2018; Masmoudi et al., 2019) or Romanized Arabic (Al-badrashiny et al., 2014; Masmoudi et al., 2015; Rushdi-Saleh et al., 2011) is an emergent writing style in the social media sites. Arabizi use is due essentially to the absence of Arabic keyboards in some phones and the speed nature of writing in SMS and Chat discussion. Transliteration is an important step in exploiting the Arabizi content, as most Arabic Natural Language Processing tools are developed for Arabic script (Masmoudi et al., 2019).

Arabizi is different from transliteration in the way that the later has a well-defined rule to transform each character from a source writing system to a destination one (e.g. see (Buckwalter, n.d.; Habash et al., 2007) for Arabic transliteration), while the former is without any standard to be fellowed by the writers. Another difference is that transliteration is a bidirectional function that allows for, in the case of the Arabic language, transforming a text from Latin characters to Arabic characters and the same system can be used to restitute the original Latin text from the transliterated output (Rahab et al., 2019). Another difference which concerns the purpose of each one, namely: Arabizi and transliteration, is that the main transliteration focus in Arabic is to allow non-Arabic speakers to read correctly Arabic texts, while Arabizi has emerged in the social media environment in the luck of Arabic keywords. Arabizi deals with dialectal Arabic in the almost all cases in the difference with transliteration, which is developed especially for MSA and can also deal with any kind of texts due to its well-defined rules.

The main problem in Arabizi transliteration is the absence of a standard of correspondence between Arabic and Latin letters. This problem leads to writing the same word in a very big number of forms, which creates an ambiguity situation to natural language processing systems. The use of abbreviations in Arabizi is another source of ambiguity as these abbreviations are very different from and Arab country to another, or even from one region to another in the same country. Example the use of 'hmd' which mean 'الحمد لله' /Al Hamdu lilah/ (thanks to god) or the use of the English word 'cool' to express the enthusiasm toward a person or an idea. The repetition of letters to express the intension in emotion is another source of difficulty in handling Arabizi content that the number of repetitions is different from a text to another, for example, the word 'jamiiiiiiiil' (nice) which is used to express intension of the Arabic word جميل /jamil/ (nice).

Proper Nouns Translation

Proper nouns translation from/to Arabic to/from foreign languages is a challenging problem in Arabic Natural Language Processing. This problem plays an important role in cross-language Information Retrieval and machine translation (Semmar & Saadane, 2013). In the USA after September 11, 2001, the authorities present a high level of interest to this problem especially in airports where the authorities would be able to well-checking people identity by security reasons (Farghaly & Shaalan, 2009). Sophisticated tools and methods for Arabic person names recognition are subject of interest.

The absence of standard leads to writing the same Arabic person name in a great number of transliteration forms. For example, the Arabic name 'محمد' /muham~ad/ may be transliterated as Mohamed, Muhammed, Muhamed, Mahomet, etc. Also, a Latin noun, English for example, can have a lot of corresponding Arabic nouns. The word 'Washington' can be written in Arabic; 'واشنطغن', 'واشنطن', 'وشنطن', etc.

One factor of difficulty in the person names extraction in the Arabic language is due to the absence of shorts vowels in Arabic texts. In Arabic, diacritics contribute to the determination of grammatical functions of words, for example, the short vowel /Dam~a/ (الضمة) serves to determine the nominative case which distinguishes the subject in Arabic sentences (Farghaly & Shaalan, 2009).

Opinion Spam

The increased amount of user-generated content in the web, especially in last years, leads to the absence of quality control of this content. Manual control of the huge available number of documents is a very difficult task and probably impossible. The importance of reviews opinion as an independent evaluation of products, events, politics etc. attracts spammers to promote their benefiting ideas as independent reviews. Spam content detection is a difficult and complex problem that spammers are usually working to invent new methods allowing them to infiltrate their data in the huge amount of user-generated content. In English language, methods to detect opinion spam are available, but in Arabic, this problem is still without well-established solutions (Abu Hammad & El-Halees, 2015).

Difficulties of spam detection in the Arabic language can be related to a set of factors. The first factor is the Arabic complex morphology compared to other languages such as English. The second factor is related to some Arabic writers whose use Arabic dialects rather than Modern Standard Arabic language in writing their reviews, this means that several Arabic Dialects can be encountered in the same document rather than a single language. The Spelling mistakes is an additional problem to the use of dialectal content, the users in social media products a lot of errors when writing their reviews, and this happens accidentally or by ignorance.

Opinion spam may be categorized in three classes; the untruthful opinion that wants to spread false positive reviews to promote products or viewpoints, or in the other side spreads false negative reviews to harm competitors' reputation of products or viewpoints. A second kind is opinions targeting a brand rather than a product. The non-reviews constitute an additional type of spam opinion content, which diffuses random reviews with irrelevant content (Jindal & Liu, 2008, 2007). A more severe problem is related to spammer groups; when several spammers construct a group in which they coordinate their efforts to control a given object. Spammer groups are damaging due to the fact that they generate more important content and are complicated de detect than spammers working each one alone (Wahsheh et al., 2013b).

Spam web pages are another type of undesirable content on the web. In the goal of increasing their ranking in search engines, such web pages owners use keywords irrelevant to their content to attract people to visit their websites (Wahsheh et al., 2013a).

SOLUTIONS AND RECOMMENDATIONS

Arabic Features Handling (Diacritics Problem Resolution)

Recent works adopt normalization of the input text to deal with problems related to Arabic language characteristics. For example, many works in Arabic sentiment analysis replace all variants of Alif such as 'أ', 'إ' and 'آ' with simple Alif 'ا', the letter 'ة' /ħ/ (TaA marbutah) with 'ه' /h/ (haA marbutah) and the letter 'ى' /ý/ is replaced by'ي'/y/ (Soliman et al., 2017). Even when the normalization resolves a problem, it removes the distinction between several words that may have different meanings and roles in a sentence such as 'أن' and 'إن'or 'على' and 'علي' etc. (Farghaly & Shaalan, 2009). For tatwyl sign '—', it is simply eliminated because the only effect of this sign is the amelioration of the writing style. For diacritic signs, they are removed due to their absence from most documents, and their little impact in the sentiment orientation of texts.

Tokenization in Arabic must be handled while considering Agglutination property. A two-step approach for tokenization is followed in (Attia, 2007), the system distinguishes main tokens from sub-tokens. The first and intuitive step is to extract the main tokens using punctuation marks and white spaces. For sub-tokens, Attia's method consists of combining both morphological analysis and tokenization in different ways. The first method adopts a morphological analyzer and a tokenizer in the same function. The second method uses firstly a tokenizer, then introduces the morphological analyzer. The third method inverses the second; it starts with a morphological analysis which lists the words as possible tokens, then the tokenizer seeks for words in this list.

Automatic diacritization in Arabic is hot research problematic without definitive solutions. The implicit contextual features influence Arabic words meaning and affects diacritization output. A set of automatic diacritization tools such as Farasa (*Farasa*, n.d.) and MADAMIRA (Pasha et al., 2014), and approaches such as the deep learning-based approach Shakkala (Fadel et al., 2019) are developed. The most available methods and tools for automatic diacritization suffer from a high rate of diacritization errors, (Fadel et al., 2019) and this occurs especially at the end of words, this part is very important in Arabic words Part of Speech categorization and proper nouns identification.

Dialectal Content Handling

It is very important to develop suitable resources for each dialect to handle dialectal content in sentiment analysis tasks, thus the varieties in the arabic dialects make the use of resources developed for Modern Standard Arabic insufficient to conduct studies in those dialects (Farghaly & Shaalan, 2009).

Several tools and resources are created to take the Arabic dialectal content into consideration by sentiment analysis applications. Annotated corpora and opinion mining methods are developed for different Arabic dialects to cite a few; Algerian (Guellil, Azouaou, et al., 2018; Meftouh et al., 2012), Tunisian (Masmoudi et al., 2019, 2015; Mulki et al., 2018), Egyptian (El-Beltagy, 2016), Sudanese (Abdelhameed & Hernández, 2019), Palestinian (Jarrar et al., 2017).

Arabizi Transliteration

Arabizi transliteration refers to the process of converting an Arabic text written in Latin script to an equivalent Arabic text in Arabic script. For the fact that Arabizi texts are usually related to Dialectal Arabic DA, the transliteration must take into consideration words of those dialects in any transliteration processes, unless it will confront serious problems with a big number of Arabizi words without Modern Standard Arabic MSA equivalent.

The transliteration of Arabizi texts into Arabic script is done by (Guellil et al., 2020) in a four steps approach.

1. An Arabic corpus for Arabizi is collected from Facebook social media network. The crawled corpus is used to generate a language model for Arabic Algerian Dialect. A pre-processing step is conducted in the goal to filter our non-Arabic words and sentences. The remaining words are used to generate the language model.
2. A set of transliteration rules are established in a way that every letter corresponds to one or several Arabic letters. When several Arabic letters are given, the authors sort them according to the probability of use in a way that the first generated word is the most probable to correspond to the right meaning and it is the word to be used in the case that anyone of the generated words corresponds to the language model. The established words are given in a well-organized table.
3. According to the above-elaborated table, for each word in the Arabizi document, a set of candidate words is generated. For example, the Arabizi word 'kraht' composed of five letters 'k', 'r', 'a'(in the middle), 'h' and 't' each of which has possible corresponding letters, so the result is $2*2*2*2*2=2^5$, i.e. the word has 32 possible candidates.
4. Selection of the best one between obtained candidates from the precedent step. From obtained candidates, the algorithm must select the one that corresponds to an entry in the language model constructed in the first step. In the case when no entry corresponds to the searched word, the first transliteration obtained according to the order of letters in the transliteration table is adopted.

Proper Nouns Recognition and Translation

Proper nouns recognition may be done on the basis of regularities of the Arabic language. For example, many Arabic person names use the word 'بن' /bn/ (son of) written in Latin as 'ben' or 'bin' in the composition of the name. This regularity may help to extract nouns that are not figuring in dictionaries (Farghaly & Shaalan, 2009).

Some recommendations are made to unify Arabic person names writing in Latin scripts. Such recommendations are; the exhaustive use of English letters to have a transliteration which is compatible with available systems, the use of capital and small letters indifferently, the name must be transliterated regardless of its parsing, handling composed names as one unit, for example, Abderrahmane, not Abed Errahmane and the transliteration of definite articles without considering sun versus moon letters. A post-processing phase is proposed, in which the first letter of a name will be capitalized, as in Latin languages (Alghamdi, 2009).

Arabic Sentiment Analysis Resources

Resources creation for morphologically rich languages such as Arabic face difficulties linked to the diversity in adopted labelling approaches (Abdul-Mageed & Diab, 2012a). Three approaches are followed for the creation of Arabic sentiment Analysis resources: manual approach, semi-automatic approach and automatic approach.

Sentiment Lexicon

The manual construction of lexicon is characterized by high precision and efficiency however this method is laborious and time-consuming, thus works adopting this approach are very limited (Abdul-Mageed & Diab, 2012b; Mataoui et al., 2016; Touahri & Mazroui, 2019). For semi-automatic creation, at first step automatic collection of lexicon entries is achieved, then manual checking is done on the obtained lexicon in the goal to limit semantic ambiguity and to ensure the high quality of each entry (El-Beltagy, 2016; Elshakankery & Ahmed, 2019; Guellil, Adeel, et al., 2018). Automatic creation of lexicon have three ways to do with; machine translation based construction, multi-languages based construction and construction merging both above methods (Guellil et al., 2019). Automatic construction is very used thanks to their construction speed and productivity (Altrabsheh et al., 2017; Badaro et al., 2014; ElSahar & El-Beltagy, 2015; Mohammad et al., 2016).

Sentiment Corpora

Collecting documents for corpus creation can be achieved in a manual or automatic manner. The manual collection refers to soliciting different sources such as web sites, discussion forums etc. Automatic creation refers to the use of a web crawler (dedicated script) that allows for the collection of documents from sources such as social networks. The automatic system may use specified queries including the country name, events, person names etc. in the goal of personalizing the desired output (Al-hussaini & Al-dossari, 2017).

An important step in developing sentimental corpora is annotation or labelling. Annotation affects collected documents into predefined categories. Different annotation methods can be found: automatic, manual and Crowdsourcing. Automatic annotation uses the websites rating system, the authors consider the middle point (for example 3 in a rating system of 5 points or 5 in a rating system of 10 points) as representative of the neutral class, above this point the document is considered positive and below this point, the document is labelled as negative (Aly & Atiya, 2013; Rushdi-Saleh et al., 2011). In the manual annotation, a set of human annotators, generally Arabic native speakers with specified skills, are asked to label the corpus with a set of given labels (Abdelhameed & Hernández, 2019; Abdul-Mageed & Diab, 2012a; Alotaibi & Anderson, 2016; Mountassir et al., 2013; Rahab et al., 2018, 2019). Crowdsourcing refers to a collaborative annotation where people are involved in a scientific task by an open call (Bougrine et al., 2017). Different types of Crowdsourcing may occur according to the motivation of driving people to collaborate. The first intuitive manner to incite someone to do something is to pay him, and the share intent is related to the potential motivation to collaboration in a scientific project or the creation of a shared resource. Also, the enjoyment using games-with-a-purpose GWAP may be a motivation to such tasks (Poesio et al., 2017). In the goal to have a high level of homogeneity in the annotation and also a consistency with annotation purpose a set of guidelines are given to annotators in term of advice (Abdul-Mageed & Diab, 2012a; Rahab et al., 2019).

Opinion Spam Detection and Elimination

Opinion spam detection and elimination are crucial as such content may undermine the reputation and credibility of opinion sites. Opinion spam detection in Arabic is done through several approaches. The most used are rule-based approach and machine learning approach.

In their work to detect opinion spam in Arabic economic reviews, the authors in (Abu Hammad & El-Halees, 2015) use TBA dataset collected from three well-known booking websites; TripAdvisor, Booking and Agoda. To annotate their reviews as spam or non-spam the authors use a set of criterion; Reviews about brands only, Non-reviews, Irrelevant review, General review, Hotels that have 100% positive review, The contradiction in the review Body attributes, The contradiction between attributes, duplication and near-duplicate of features and duplicate or near-duplicate reviews. The authors use four machine learning techniques, namely: SVM, NB, ID3 and KNN.

Opinion can be categorized into spam and non-spam classes, and then the spam class may also be divided into low-level opinion spam and high-level opinion spam in (Wahsheh et al., 2013b). The level of opinion spam is determined according to the presence of URL links in the review. The low-level opinion spam is a review containing at least five consecutive numbers or the @ symbol, while the high-level opinion spam is a review with an URL blacklisted in a webspam list.

A web page analyzer is developed by the authors in (Wahsheh et al., 2013a), it allows analyzing web pages in accordance with a set of features. These features can be categorized into content-based and link-based features. Content-based features are features related to the content of the site, such as the duplication of some words or sequences of words in a meaningless manner. For link-based features, they correspond to the method by which the spammers choose the names of their links, like the use of expired domain names or the insertion of links into their pages as comments in many blogs and discussion forums.

FUTURE RESEARCH DIRECTIONS

Due to an urgent need in term of Arabic Natural languages processing tools in recent years, most of these tools and methods are developed following machine learning techniques. These aforementioned methods give rapid results which are not very expensive, and these results don't need deep research in the linguistic background of Arabic language (Farghaly & Shaalan, 2009). The problem of preparing well representative datasets is the main problem in the face of machine learning techniques; thus the future tendency in sentiment analysis in Arabic is the lexicon-based approaches and unsupervised methods (Medhat et al., 2014). These methods are characterized by the time and effort they need, in addition to a strong background in language skills. However, these methods have no need for training data. These methods are also domain-independent, so a system developed at a time may be used in several situations without basically changes.

In the machine learning approach, recent works have a tendency to use deep learning as sub-field in machine learning which is based on the human brain function. Deep learning is based on a set of hidden layer between and input and an output layers (Al-ayyoub et al., 2018). Several techniques are used in deep learning for the Arabic language, namely, Recurrent Neural Networks RNN (Al-smadi et al., 2017), Convolutional Neural networks (CNN)(Alayba et al., 2017), long short- term memory (LSTM) (El-Kilany et al., 2018) and deep neural networks (DNN)(Fadel et al., 2019) among others.

Figure 1. Main challenges and recent solutions to Arabic sentiment analysis

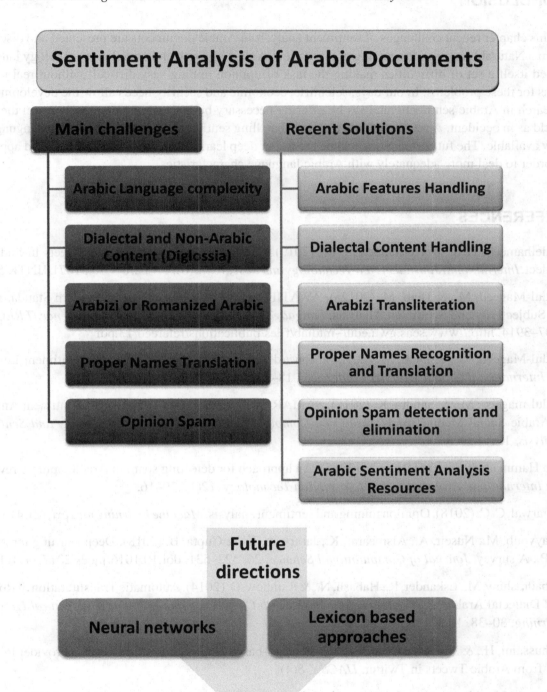

CONCLUSION

In this chapter recent challenges of sentiment analysis in Arabic documents are presented and discussed from a Natural Language Processing point of view. Arabic as a rich and complex morphology language posed itself a set of difficulties making the task of opinion mining very difficult without real resolutions for these problems. In our days, scientific, economic and security needs allow the development of research in Arabic sentiment analysis by offering necessary budgets and human resources in the Arab world as in occident. A set of methods and tools handling sentiment analysis in the Arabic language are now available. The future tendency will be the use of deep learning techniques and rule-based approach in order to deal more adequately with Arabic language characteristics.

REFERENCES

Abdelhameed, H. J., & Hernández, S. M. (2019). Sentiment Analysis of Arabic Tweets in Sudanese Dialect. *International Journal of New Technology and Research*, 5(6), 17–22. doi:10.31871/IJNTR.5.6.20

Abdul-Mageed, M., & Diab, M. (2012a). AWATIF: A Multi-Genre Corpus for Modern Standard Arabic Subjectivity and Sentiment Analysis. *Language Resources and Evaluation Conference (LREC'12)*, 3907–3914. http://www.seas.gwu.edu/~mtdiab/files/publications/refereed/13.pdf

Abdul-Mageed, M., & Diab, M. (2012b). Toward Building a Large-Scale Arabic Sentiment Lexicon. *6th International Global Wordnet Conference*, 18–22.

Abdul-mageed, M., & Sandra, K. (2012). SAMAR : A System for Subjectivity and Sentiment Analysis of Arabic Social Media. *3rd Workshop on Computational Approaches to Subjectivity and Sentiment Analysis,* 19–28.

Abu Hammad, A., & El-Halees, A. (2015). An approach for detecting spam in Arabic opinion reviews. *The International Arab Journal of Information Technology, 12*(1), 10–16.

Aggarwal, C. C. (2018). Opinion mining and sentiment analysis. *Machine Learning for Text*, (2), 413–434.

Al-ayyoub, M., Nuseir, A., Alsmearat, K., Jararweh, Y., & Gupta, B. (2018). Deep learning for Arabic NLP : A survey. *Journal of Computational Science, 26*, 522–531. doi:10.1016/j.jocs.2017.11.011

Al-badrashiny, M., Eskander, R., Habash, N., & Rambow, O. (2014). Automatic Transliteration of Romanized Dialectal Arabic. *Proceedings of the Eighteenth Conference on Computational Natural Language Learning*, 30–38. 10.3115/v1/W14-1604

Al-hussaini, H., & Al-dossari, H. (2017). A Lexicon-based Approach to Build Service Provider Reputation from Arabic Tweets in Twitter. *IJACSA, 8*(4).

Al-smadi, M., Al-zboon, S., Jararweh, Y., & Juola, P. (2020). Transfer Learning for Arabic Named Entity Recognition With Deep Neural Networks. *IEEE Access: Practical Innovations, Open Solutions, 8*, 37736–37745. doi:10.1109/ACCESS.2020.2973319

Al-smadi, M., Qawasmeh, O., Al-ayyoub, M., Jararweh, Y., & Gupta, B. (2017). Deep Recurrent neural network vs. support vector machine for aspect-based sentiment analysis of Arabic hotels' reviews. *Journal of Computational Science*. Advance online publication. doi:10.1016/j.jocs.2017.11.006

Alayba, A. M., Palade, V., England, M., & Iqbal, R. (2017). Arabic Language Sentiment Analysis on Health Services. *1st International Workshop on Arabic Script Analysis and Recognition (ASAR)*, 114–118. 10.1109/ASAR.2017.8067771

Alghamdi, M. (2009). Romanizing Arabic Proper Names : Saudi Arabia Experience. *International Symposium on Arabic Transliteration Standard: Challenges and Solutions.*

Alotaibi, S. S., & Anderson, C. W. (2016). Extending the Knowledge of the Arabic Sentiment Classification Using a Foreign External Lexical Source. *International Journal on Natural Language Computing*, *5*(3), 1–11. doi:10.5121/ijnlc.2016.5301

Altrabsheh, N., El-masri, M., & Mansour, H. (2017). Combining Sentiment Lexicons of Arabic Terms. *Twenty-Third Americas Conference on Information Systems*, 1–10.

Aly, M., & Atiya, A. (2013). LABR: A Large Scale Arabic Book Reviews Dataset. *Proceedings of the 51st Annual Meeting of the Association for Computational Linguistics (*Volume 2*: Short Papers)*, 494–498.

Ameur, M. H. (2019). *ANETAC*. https://github.com/MohamedHadjAmeur/ANETAC

Attia, M. A. (2007). Arabic Tokenization System. *Proceedings of the Association of Computational Linguistics (ACL'07)*, 65–72. 10.3115/1654576.1654588

Badaro, G., Baly, R., & Hajj, H. (2014). *A Large Scale Arabic Sentiment Lexicon for Arabic Opinion Mining*. Arabic Natural Language Processing Workshop Co-Located with EMNLP. doi:10.3115/v1/W14-3623

Boudad, N., Faizi, R., Oulad, R., Thami, H., & Chiheb, R. (2017). Sentiment analysis in Arabic: A review of the literature. *Ain Shams Engineering Journal*, *9*(July), 2479–2490. doi:10.1016/j.asej.2017.04.007

Bougrine, S., Cherroun, H., & Abdelali, A. (2017). Altruistic Crowdsourcing for Arabic Speech Corpus Annotation. *ACLing*, *117*(November), 133–144. doi:10.1016/j.procs.2017.10.102

Buckwalter, T. (n.d.). *Arabic Transliteration*. Retrieved December 18, 2019, from http://www.qamus. org/transliteration.htm

Danowski, J. A. (2012). Sentiment network analysis of taleban and RFE/RL open-source content about Afghanistan. *Open-Source Intelligence and Web Mining Conference [OSINT-WM], August*, 303–310. 10.1109/EISIC.2012.54

Djoudi, M., Fohr, D., & Haton, J.-P. (1989). Phonetic study for automatic recognition of Arabic. *First European Conference on Speech Communication and Technology, EUROSPEECH*, 268–271.

Djoudi, M., & Harous, S. (2008). Text Entry System for Semitic Languages on Mobile Devices. In *Handbook of Research on Mobile Multimedia* (pp. 772–782). IGI Global.

Duwairi, R. M., Alfaqeh, M., Wardat, M., & Alrabadi, A. (2016). Sentiment analysis for Arabizi text. 7th International Conference on Information and Communication Systems, ICICS, 127–132. 10.1109/IACS.2016.7476098

El-Beltagy, S. R. (2016). NileULex: A Phrase and Word Level Sentiment Lexicon for Egyptian and Modern Standard Arabic. *Proceedings of Tenth International Conference on Language Resources and Evaluation (LREC)*, 2900–2905.

El-Kilany, A., Azzam, A., & El-Beltagy, S. R. (2018). Using deep neural networks for extracting sentiment targets in arabic tweets. *Studies in Computational Intelligence*, *740*, 3–15. doi:10.1007/978-3-319-67056-0_1

Elnagar, A., Khalifa, Y. S., & Einea, A. (2018). Hotel Arabic-Reviews Dataset Construction for Sentiment Analysis Applications. *Intelligent Natural Language Processing: Trends and Applications*, 35–52.

ElSahar, H., & El-Beltagy, S. R. (2015). Building Large Arabic Multi-domain Resources for Sentiment Analysis. *International Conference on Intelligent Text Processing and Computational Linguistics*, 23–34. 10.1007/978-3-319-18117-2_2

Elshakankery, K., & Ahmed, M. F. (2019). HILATSA: A hybrid Incremental learning approach for Arabic tweets sentiment analysis. Egyptian Informatics Journal, 1–9. doi:10.1016/j.eij.2019.03.002

Fadel, A., Tuffaha, I., Al-jawarneh, B., & Al-Ayyoub, M. (2019). Arabic Text Diacritization Using Deep Neural Networks. *International Conference on Computer Applications & Information Security,* 2–9. 10.1109/CAIS.2019.8769512

Farasa. (n.d.). http://alt.qcri.org/farasa/

Farghaly, A., & Shaalan, K. (2009). Arabic natural language processing : Challenges and solutions. *ACM Transactions on Asian Language Information Processing*, *8*(4), 1–22. doi:10.1145/1644879.1644881

Ferguson, C. A. (1959). Diglossia. *Word*, *15*(2), 325–340. doi:10.1080/00437956.1959.11659702

Guellil, I., Adeel, A., Azouaou, F., Benali, F., & Hussain, A. (2018). Arabizi sentiment analysis based on transliteration and automatic corpus annotation. *9th Workshop on Computational Approaches to Subjectivity, Sentiment and Social Media Analysis*, 335–341. 10.18653/v1/W18-6249

Guellil, I., Azouaou, F., Benali, F., Hachani, A. E., & Mendoza, M. (2020). The Role of Transliteration in the Process of Arabizi Translation/Sentiment Analysis. In M. Abd Elaziz, M. A. A. Al-qaness, A. A. Ewees, & A. Dahou (Eds.), *Recent Advances in NLP: The Case of Arabic Language* (pp. 101–128). Springer International Publishing. doi:10.1007/978-3-030-34614-0_6

Guellil, I., Azouaou, F., & Hussain, A. (2018). SentiALG : Automated Corpus Annotation for Algerian Sentiment Analysis Introduction. *Proceedings of the International Conference on Brain Inspired Cognitive Systems*, 557–567. 10.1007/978-3-030-00563-4_54

Guellil, I., Azouaou, F., & Mendoza, M. (2019). Arabic sentiment analysis: Studies, resources, and tools. *Social Network Analysis and Mining*, *9*(56), 1–17. doi:10.100713278-019-0602-x

Habash, N. (2010). Introduction to Arabic natural language processing. In G. Hirst (Ed.), Synthesis Lectures on Human Language Technologies (Vol. 3, Issue 1). doi:10.2200/S00277ED1V01Y201008HLT010

Habash, N., Soudi, A., & Buckwalter, T. (2007). On Arabic Transliteration. In Arabic Computational Morphology (Vol. 49, Issue 4, pp. 15–22). doi:10.1007/978-1-4020-6046-5_2

Hadj Ameur, M. S., Meziane, F., & Guessoum, A. (2019). *ANETAC : Arabic named entity transliteration and classification dataset.* ArXiv Preprint ArXiv:1907.03110

Ibrahim, H. S., Abdou, S. M., & Gheith, M. (2015). Idioms-Proverbs Lexicon for Modern Standard Arabic and Colloquial Sentiment Analysis Idioms-Proverbs Lexicon for Modern Standard Arabic and Colloquial Sentiment Analysis. *International Journal of Computers and Applications, 118*(11), 26–31. doi:10.5120/20790-3435

Internet World Stats. (n.d.). https://www.internetworldstats.com/stats7.htm

Iskra, D., Siemund, R., Borno, J., Moreno, A., Emam, O., Choukri, K., Gedge, O., Tropf, H., Nogueiras, A., Zitouni, I., Tsopanoglou, A., & Fakotakis, N. (2004). OrienTel -Telephony databases across Northern Africa and the Middle East Countries and technologies. *LREC*. http://citeseerx.ist.psu.edu/viewdoc/download?doi=10.1.1.360.7554&rep=rep1&type=pdf

Ismail, S., Alsammak, A., & Elshishtawy, T. (2016). A generic approach for extracting aspects and opinions of arabic reviews. *ACM International Conference Proceeding Series, 173*–179. 10.1145/2908446.2908467

Jarrar, M., Habash, N., Alrimawi, F., Akra, D., & Zalmout, N. (2017). Curras: An annotated corpus for the Palestinian Arabic dialect. *Language Resources and Evaluation, 51*(3), 745–775. doi:10.100710579-016-9370-7

Jindal, N., & Liu, B. (2007). Review Spam Detection. *Proceedings of the 16th International Conference on World Wide Web*, 1189–1190. 10.1145/1242572.1242759

Jindal, N., & Liu, B. (2008). Opinion Spam and Analysis. In *Proceedings of the international conference on web search and data mining WSDM'08* (pp. 219–229). ACM. 10.1145/1341531.1341560

Liu, B. (2010). Sentiment Analysis and Subjectivity. In R. Herbrich & T. Graepel (Eds.), Handbook of Natural Language Processing (2nd ed., pp. 627–666). Microsoft Research Ltd.

Liu, B. (2012). Sentiment Analysis and Opinion Mining. *Synthesis Lectures on Human Language Technologies, 5*(1), 1–167. doi:10.2200/S00416ED1V01Y201204HLT016

Liu, B. (2015). *Sentiment Analysis Mining Opinions, Sentiments, and Emotions.* Cambridge University Press. doi:10.1017/CBO9781139084789

Mahyoub, F. H. H., Siddiqui, M. A., & Dahab, M. Y. (2014). Building an Arabic Sentiment Lexicon Using Semi-supervised Learning. Journal of King Saud University - Computer and Information Sciences, 26(4), 417–424. doi:10.1016/j.jksuci.2014.06.003

Marsi, E., Bosch, A. van den, & Soudi, A. (2005). Memory-based morphological analysis generation and part-of-speech tagging of Arabic. *Computational Approaches to Semitic Languages*, 1–8.

Masmoudi, A., Habash, N., Khmekhem, M. E., Estève, Y., & Belguith, L. H. (2015). Arabic Transliteration of Romanized Tunisian Dialect Text: A Preliminary Investigation. *Lecture Notes in Computer Science, 9041*, 608–619. doi:10.1007/978-3-319-18111-0_46

Masmoudi, A., Khmekhem, M. E., Khrouf, M., & Belguith, L. H. (2019). Transliteration of Arabizi into Arabic Script for Tunisian Dialect. *ACM Transactions on Asian and Low-Resource Language Information Processing (TALLIP), 19*(2), Article 32.

Mataoui, M., Zelmati, O., & Boumechache, M. (2016). A Proposed Lexicon-Based Sentiment Analysis Approach for the Vernacular Algerian Arabic. *Res Comput Sci, 110*(1), 55–70. doi:10.13053/rcs-110-1-5

Medhat, W., Hassan, A., & Korashy, H. (2014). Sentiment analysis algorithms and applications : A survey. *Ain Shams Engineering Journal, 5*(4), 1093–1113. doi:10.1016/j.asej.2014.04.011

Meftouh, K., Bouchemal, N., & Smaili, K. (2012). a Study of a Non-Resourced Language : an Algerian Dialect. *Proc. 3td International Workshop on Spoken Languages Technologies for Under-Resourced Languages (SLTU'12).*

Mohammad, S. M., Salameh, M., & Kiritchenko, S. (2016). Sentiment Lexicons for Arabic Social Media. *Tenth International Conference on Language Resources and Evaluation (LREC)*, 33–37.

Mountassir, A., Benbrahim, H., & Berraba, I. (2013). Sentiment classification on arabic corpora. A preliminary cross-study. *International Conference on Innovative Techniques and Applications of Artificial Intelligence, 16*(1), 259–272. 10.3166/dn.16.1.73-96

Mubarak, H., Abdelali, A., Darwish, K., Eldesouki, M., Samih, Y., & Sajjad, H. (2019). A System for Diacritizing Four Varieties of Arabic. *Proceedings of the 2019 Conference on Empirical Methods in Natural Language Processing and the 9th International Joint Conference on Natural Language Processing (EMNLP-IJCNLP)*, 217–222. 10.18653/v1/D19-3037

Mulki, H., Haddad, H., Ali, C. B., & Babao, I. (2018). Tunisian Dialect Sentiment Analysis : A Natural Language Processing-based Approach. *Computación y Sistemas, 22*(4). Advance online publication. doi:10.13053/cys-22-4-3009

Pang, B., & Lee, L. (2004). A Sentimental Education: Sentiment Analysis Using Subjectivity Summarization Based on Minimum Cuts. *42nd Annual Meeting on Association for Computational Linguistics*, 271–278. 10.3115/1218955.1218990

Pasha, A., Al-badrashiny, M., Diab, M., El Kholy, A., Eskander, R., Habash, N., Pooleery, M., Rambow, O., & Roth, M., R. (2014). MADAMIRA : A Fast, Comprehensive Tool for Morphological Analysis and Disambiguation of Arabic. *Proceedings of the Ninth International Conference on Language Resources and Evaluation (LREC'14)*, 1094–1101.

Poesio, M., Chamberlain, J., & Kruschwitz, U. (2017). Crowdsourcing. In Handbook of Linguistic Annotation (pp. 277–295). Academic Press.

Rahab, H., Zitouni, A., & Djoudi, M. (2018). SIAAC: Sentiment Polarity Identification on Arabic Algerian Newspaper Comments. In Applied Computational Intelligence and Mathematical Methods (Vol. 662, pp. 141–149). doi:10.1007/978-3-319-67621-0

Rahab, H., Zitouni, A., & Djoudi, M. (2019). SANA: Sentiment analysis on newspapers comments in Algeria. Journal of King Saud University - Computer and Information Sciences. doi:10.1016/j.jksuci.2019.04.012

Ramírez-Tinoco, F. J., Alor-Hernández, G., Sánchez-Cervantes, J. L., Salas-Zárate, M. del P., & Valencia-García, R. (2019). Use of Sentiment Analysis Techniques in Healthcare Domain. In Current Trends in Semantic Web Technologies: Theory and Practic (pp. 189–212). Springer International Publishing. doi:10.1007/978-3-030-06149-4_8

Rushdi-Saleh, M., Martín-Valdivia, M. T., Ureña-López, L. A., & Perea-Ortega, J. M. (2011). OCA: Opinion corpus for Arabic. *Journal of the American Society for Information Science and Technology*, *62*(10), 2045–2054. doi:10.1002/asi.21598

Saadane, H. (2015). *Le traitement automatique de l'arabe dialectalisé: aspects méthodologiques et algorithmiques* [These de doctorat].

Saeed, R. M. K., Rady, S., & Gharib, T. F. (2019). An ensemble approach for spam detection in Arabic opinion texts. Journal of King Saud University - Computer and Information Sciences. doi:10.1016/j.jksuci.2019.10.002

Semmar, N., & Saadane, H. (2013). Using Transliteration of Proper Names from Arabic to Latin Script to Improve English-Arabic Word Alignment. *International Joint Conference on Natural Language Processing, October*, 1022–1026.

Soliman, A. B., Eissa, K., & El-Beltagy, S. R. (2017). AraVec: A set of Arabic Word Embedding Models for use in Arabic NLP. *Procedia Computer Science*, *117*, 256–265. doi:10.1016/j.procs.2017.10.117

Subramaniyaswamy, V., Logesh, R., Abejith, M., Umasankar, S., & Umamakeswari, A. (2017). Sentiment analysis of tweets for estimating criticality and security of events. *Journal of Organizational and End User Computing*, *29*(4), 51–71. doi:10.4018/JOEUC.2017100103

Touahri, I., & Mazroui, A. (2019). Studying the effect of characteristic vector alteration on Arabic sentiment classification. Journal of King Saud University - Computer and Information Sciences. doi:10.1016/j.jksuci.2019.04.011

Tsarfaty, R., Sandra, K., Candito, M., Rehbein, I., & Foster, J. (2010). Statistical Parsing of Morphologically Rich Languages (SPMRL) What, How and Whither. In *NAACL HLT First Workshop on Statistical Parsing of Morphologically-Rich Languages* (pp. 1–12). ACL.

Wahsheh, H., Al-Kabi, M. N., & Alsmadi, I. (2013a). A link and Content Hybrid Approach for Arabic Web Spam Detection. *International Journal of Intelligent Systems and Applications*, *5*(1), 30–43. doi:10.5815/ijisa.2013.01.03

Wahsheh, H., Al-Kabi, M. N., & Alsmadi, I. (2013b). SPAR: A system to detect spam in Arabic opinions. *IEEE Jordan Conference on Applied Electrical Engineering and Computing Technologies, AEECT 2013*, 1–6. 10.1109/AEECT.2013.6716442

Zayed, O. H., & El-Beltagy, S. R. (2015). Named entity recognition of persons' names in Arabic tweets. *International Conference Recent Advances in Natural Language Processing, RANLP,* 731–738.

ADDITIONAL READING

Aggarwal, C. C. (2018b). Opinion mining and sentiment analysis. In Machine Learning for Text (pp. 413–434). doi:10.1007/978-3-319-73531-3_13

Farghaly, A., & Shaalan, K. (2009). Arabic natural language processing : Challenges and solutions. *ACM Transactions on Asian Language Information Processing*, 8(4), 1–22. doi:10.1145/1644879.1644881

Guellil, I., Azouaou, F., Benali, F., Hachani, A. E., & Mendoza, M. (2020). The Role of Transliteration in the Process of Arabizi Translation/Sentiment Analysis. In M. Abd Elaziz, M. A. A. Al-qaness, A. A. Ewees, & A. Dahou (Eds.), *Recent Advances in NLP: The Case of Arabic Language* (pp. 101–128). Springer International Publishing., doi:10.1007/978-3-030-34614-0_6

Habash, N. (2010). *Introduction to Arabic natural language processing* (G. Hirst, Ed.). Vol. 3). Synthesis Lectures on Human Language Technologies.

Habash, N., Soudi, A., & Buckwalter, T. (2007). On Arabic Transliteration. In Arabic Computational Morphology (Vol. 49, pp. 15–22). doi:10.1007/978-1-4020-6046-5_2

Liu, B. (2012). Sentiment Analysis and Opinion Mining. *Synthesis Lectures on Human Language Technologies*, 5(1), 1–167. doi:10.2200/S00416ED1V01Y201204HLT016

Liu, B. (2015). *Sentiment Analysis Mining Opinions, Sentiments, and Emotions*. Cambridge University Press. doi:10.1017/CBO9781139084789

Rahab, H., Zitouni, A., & Djoudi, M. (2019). SANA: Sentiment analysis on newspapers comments in Algeria. *Journal of King Saud University - Computer and Information Sciences*. . doi:10.1016/j.jksuci.2019.04.012

Wahsheh, H., Al-Kabi, M. N., & Alsmadi, I. (2013a). A link and Content Hybrid Approach for Arabic Web Spam Detection. *International Journal of Intelligent Systems and Applications*, 5(1), 30–43. doi:10.5815/ijisa.2013.01.03

KEY TERMS AND DEFINITIONS

Agglutination: Is the representation of different part-of-speech POS elements in the same word.

Arabizi: Is a writing style that uses Latin script to write Arabic text without any kind of rules which leads to big differences in writing almost all Arabic words. The phenomenon emerged in the space of the Internet and especially by the spreading use of the smartphones without sophisticated Arabic keyboards.

Diacritic: Are signs playing the role of short vowels in the Arabic language, the diacritics signs, even omitted in most of the Arabic texts today, their role is primordial to guide the pronunciation and remove the ambiguity of an important number of Arabic letters.

Diglossia: Is a phenomenon appearing within some populations with a rich cultural heritage; in this situation people use more than one language at the same time.

Opinion: Is someone's viewpoint toward an entity based on their cultural, social and religious background. This point of view may be expressed in review, an article, a tv show or other media they have access to.

Opinion Holder: Is the person or organization claiming an opinion in a document, by an explicit or implicit manner.

Opinion Spam: Opinion that intends to influence the behaviour of Internet users by diffusing commercial, political, or social reviews in the goal to promote or discredit something. Spammers present themselves as independent reviewers without declaring their identity. The spammers may intend to promote their products or viewpoints or discredit the products or viewpoints of their competitors.

Sentiment: Is the positive or negative feeling of a person in response to an instantaneous event without a need to give any motivation. Thus, there is no neutral sentiment, but objectivity can be considered as a no-sentiment.

Transcription: Relays on writing a speech in a script as it is pronounced in the goal to guide the pronunciation of beginners in a language or to convert an audio speech to a text.

Transliteration: Is the process of moving a text from script to another in the goal to allow foreign readers of a language to read texts in this language. Word pronunciation is not considered here.

ENDNOTES

1   For transliteration adopted in this chapter See (Habash et al., 2007)
2   'm' for masculine, 'f' for feminine, 'd' for dual and 'p' for plural.

APPENDIX: ADOPTED TRANSLITERATION SYSTEM

The transliteration system followed in this chapter is the one proposed scheme in (Habash et al., 2007) and presented in the following table.

Table 4. Adopted transliteration system

Arabic Character	Description	Transliteration	Example		
			Arabic	**Transliteration**	**Signification**
ء	همزة	'	سماء	samaA'	Sky
آ	ألف مد	Ā	آمن	Āmana	Secured
أ	ألف بهمزة أعلى	Â	أسأل	saÂala	Ask
ؤ	همزة على الواو	ŵ	مؤتمر	muŵtamar	Conference
إ	ألف بهمزة أسفل	Ă	إنترنت	Ăintarnit	Internet
ئ	همزة على الياء	ŷ	سائل	saAŷil	Liquid
ا	ألف	A	كان	kaAna	It was
ب	باء	b	بريد	bariyd	Post
ة	تاء مربوطة	ħ	مكتبة	maktabaħ or maktabaħū	Library
ت	تاء	t	تنافس	tanaAfus	Concurrence
ث	ثاء	θ	ثالثة	θalaAθaħ or θalaAθaħū	Three
ج	جيم	j	جميل	jamiyl	Beautiful
ح	حاء	H	حاد	HaAd	Prick
خ	خاء	x	خوذة	xawðaħ	Berets
د	دال	d	دليل	daliyl	Guide
ذ	ذال	ð	ذهب	ðahab	Gold
ر	راء	r	رفيع	rafiyσ	Fine
ز	زاي	z	زينة	ziynaħ	Decoration
س	سين	s	سماء	samaA'	Sky
ش	شين	š	شريف	šariyf	Honest
ص	صاد	S	صوت	Sawt	Sound
ض	ضاد	D	ضرير	Dariyr	Blinded
ط	طاد	T	طويل	Tawiyl	Long
ظ	ظاء	Ď	ظلم	Ďulm	Injustice
ع	عين	σ	عمل	σamal	Work
غ	غين	γ	غريب	γariyb	Strange
ف	فاء	f	فيلم	fiylm	Film
ق	قاف	q	قادر	qaAdir	Capable

continues on following page

Table 4. Continued

Arabic Character	Description	Transliteration	Example		
			Arabic	Transliteration	Signification
ك	فاك	k	كريم	kariym	Generous
ل	مال	l	لذيذ	laðiyð	Delicious
م	ميم	m	مدير	mudiyr	Director
ن	نون	n	رون	nuwr	Light
ه	هاء	h	هول	huwl	Devastation
و	واو	w	وصل	waSl	Receive
ى	ألف مقصورة	ý	على	çal ý	On
ي	ياء	y	تين	tiyn	Fig
ˊ	فتحة	a	دَهَنَ	dahana	He hangs
˒	ضمة	u	دُهِنَ	duhina	It is hanged
ˏ	كسرة	i	دُهِنَ	duhina	It is hanged
ˮ	فتحتين	ã	كتابأ	kitaAbAã	Book
˵	ضمتين	ũ	كتابٌ	kitaAbũ	Book
ˏˏ	كسرتين	ī	كتابٍ	kitaAbī	Book
~	شدة (šad~aħ)	~	كسّر	kas~ara	Break
˙	سكون (sukuwn)	.	مسجد	mas.jidou masjid	Mosque
‒	تطويل (taTwiyl) وأ كشيدة (kašiydaħ)	___	مسـجد	mas.___jid ou mas___jid	Mosque
لا	ال التعريف Definition Al	Al	المصلى	AlmuSal~a ý	Small mosque

Chapter 65
Ooredoo Rayek:
A Business Decision Support System Based on Multi–Language Sentiment Analysis of Algerian Operator Telephones

Badia Klouche
LabRI-SBA Laboratory, Ecole Superieure en Informatique, Sidi Bel Abbes, Algeria

Sidi Mohamed Benslimane
https://orcid.org/0000-0002-7008-7434
LabRI-SBA Laboratory, Ecole Superieure en Informatique, Sidi Bel-Abbes, Algeria

Sakina Rim Bennabi
Ecole Superieure en Informatique, Sidi Bel Abbes, Algeria

ABSTRACT

Sentiment analysis is one of the recent areas of emerging research in the classification of sentiment polarity and text mining, particularly with the considerable number of opinions available on social media. The Algerian Operator Telephone Ooredoo, as other operators, deploys in its new strategy to conquer new customers, by exploiting their opinions through a sentiments analysis. The purpose of this work is to set up a system called "Ooredoo Rayek", whose objective is to collect, transliterate, translate and classify the textual data expressed by the Ooredoo operator's customers. This article developed a set of rules allowing the transliteration from Algerian Arabizi to Algerian dialect. Furthermore, the authors used Naïve Bayes (NB) and (Support Vector Machine) SVM classifiers to assign polarity tags to Facebook comments from the official pages of Ooredoo written in multilingual and multi-dialect context. Experimental results show that the system obtains good performance with 83% of accuracy.

DOI: 10.4018/978-1-6684-6303-1.ch065

INTRODUCTION

The Algerian telecommunications business, although in full expansion, is subjecting the various economic actors involved to fierce competitiveness. Operators are therefore called upon to maintain their growth plans and gain new market share. This conquest of new segments is far from being easy and can be envisaged only by new services, providing new experiences to consumers. 5G and even 6G, constitute the bulk of new experiences provided or under development by the three Algerian operators (Mobilis, Djezzy, and Ooredoo), which require significant financial mobilization. However, aggressive investment plans are not enough for them and it is essential to support them with a quality of controlled services and with commercially viable offers. It is easy to admit that streamlined and streamlined development plans, underpinned by strategies to improve the quality of services and attractive rates, are the major issues that will determine the success of any operator in the medium and long term. It is therefore vital that any operator has carefully considered strategies, supported by analyses applied to the existing information assets, for each operator constituted by heterogeneous information (statistics, techniques, quality indicators, customer testimonials, customer complaint archives, etc.) for which operators usually provide for segmented and fully decoupled analyses.

Since the emergence of social networks such as Tweeter, Facebook and Instagram, which have become a vital communication space, Internet users express their sentiments and opinions freely. Consequently, telephone operators took advantage of this situation to provide their offers on the net and evaluate the opinions of their customers.

Nowadays, sentiment analysis (SA) in the various social media has become a topic of great importance for research, industry and development. Thus, sentiment analysis, also called opinion mining, is the field of study that exploits the opinions, sentiments, evaluations, assessments, attitudes and emotions of individuals towards entities, such as these products, services, organizations, individuals, problems, events and subjects (Liu et al., 2012). However, sentiment analysis and the extraction of opinions focus primarily on the opinions of clients who express or imply positive, negative or neutral sentiments. Although Linguistics and Natural Language Processing (NLP) have a long history, there has been little research on opinions and sentiment before the year 2000. The richness of social networks in terms of opinion, emotion and sentiment has led the interest of the research community to focus much more on issues related to the sentiment analysis of Arabic and its dialects, including Arabizi that is a form of online discussion language, where the Latin alphabet is mainly used to write words in Arabic. For example, "internet raw3a" romanized form of "انترنت رائعه" in Arabic that means "wonderful internet". Modern Standard Arabic (MSA) used in newspapers, movie reviews, among others, has been the subject of much research on the sentiment analysis (Abdul-Mageed et al., 2014; Rahab et al., 2018). For this purpose, a large percentage of comments written in Arabic letters in different social networks are shared in Arabic dialect and often mixed with foreign languages (French, English, etc.).

It is in the context of Business Intelligence (BI) that this work is defined, which aims to evaluate the potential of BI as a support for the development and evaluation of strategies mastered before, during and after, promoting a new customer experience.

The main research question that this work is concerned with is, "How to specify the requirements of decision-makers to support and evaluate strategies to improve the quality of operator services based on actionable information to provide a formal, grounded and concise decision?".

As a difference **to** the works related to our theme undertaken in the literature, we brought a decision support for the Ooredoo Algerian Telephone Operator through the implementation of a Sentiment

Analysis system of the comments of its customers in Multi-language. To this end, our research brings several innovative contributions in comparison to other works, including the processing of Arabizi comments from the social network Facebook, the transliteration of Arabizi into Algerian Dialect, the use of a hybrid machine transliteration for the translation of Arabizi and finally applying Machine Learning algorithms for Sentiment Analysis.

In this paper, we use a supervised approach to determine the polarity of the comments of the Ooredoo telephone operator customers, published in different forms (MSA, Arabic dialect, Algerian Dialect, Arabizi, French and English). For that, we started with the phase of transliteration of the comments written in Arabizi and the translation the comments written in dialect. We then used Machine-learning (ML) algorithm such as Support Vector Machines (SVM) and Naive Bayes (NB) to rank customer opinions based on the polarity of the positive, negative and neutral sentiment.

This paper is organized as follows. Section 2 presents related work on sentiment analysis and transliteration to Arabizi. Section 3 explains, in details, our approach. Section 4 highlights the conducted experiments and discusses the obtained results. Finally, Section 5 summarizes the findings of this paper and gives some outlooks of future work.

LITERATURE REVIEW

Many studies have been conducted in the area of SA especially on English texts, while other languages, such as Arabic, received less attention. In this section, we start by presenting a review of related work that targets sentiment analysis for Arabic language. We then summarize works dealing with transliteration of Arabizi.

Sentiment Analysis for Arabic Language

Researchers working on the NLP of Arabic language found difficulties in extracting texts, asArabic is a morphologically rich language (Farghaly & Shaalan, 2009). Recently, there has been a considerable amount of work and effort to collect resources and develop sentiment analysis systems for the Arabic language. However, the number of freely available Arabic datasets and Arabic lexicons for SA are still limited in number, size, availability and dialects coverage.

(Abbasi et al., 2008) examined in their work a binary problem of sentiments analysis of blogs written in Arabic or English. They focused on the extraction and selection of features, the purpose of their study was the detection of hostility on the Web forums. Their results showed that the targeted approach was very successful.

(Elhawary & Elfeky, 2010) developed an engine that explores the Web for financial reviews in Arabic, determining their feelings. The authors' system used an Arabic weighted sentiment lexicon, constructed by taking a set of manually labeled terms while using a similarity graph of Arabic words / expressions, along which the labels are propagated. The evaluation of this approach showed that the classifier of Arab feelings had a similar performance to that of any English sentiment analysis approach.

(Shoukry & Rafea, 2012) used an approach based on a corpus for SA tweets written in MSA and Egyptian dialect. After filtering the tweets, they ended up using standard n-gram functions and experimented with several classifiers (SVM and NB), via the Weka toolkit.

(Khalifa & Omar, 2014) treated the difficulties of ensuring the quality of opinion in Arabic by proposing a hybrid method of approach and classification based on the lexicon using a classifier Naïve Bayes. The proposed method includes pre-processing phases such as transformation, standardization and tokenization, as well as the exploitation of auxiliary information (thesaurus). The lexicon-based approach is executed by replacing certain words with their synonyms using the domain dictionary. The classification task is performed by the NB classifier to rank opinions based on the polarity of the positive or negative sentiment.

(Nabil et al., 2015) presented a classification of four-way feelings that classifies texts into four classes: (objective, subjective negative, subjective positive and mixed subjective). To this end, they applied a wide range of automatic learning algorithms such as Support Vector Machine (SVM), Multinomial Naive Bayes (MNB), Bernoulli Naive Bayes (BNB), K-nearest neighbor (KNN), and stochastic gradient descent to balanced and unbalanced data sets. However, the use of n-grams as unique entities in the multi-channel classification had not worked well.

(Aldayel et al., 2015) proposed a hybrid method of approach and classification based on the lexicon using a classifier Naïve Bayes. The lexicon-based approach is executed by replacing certain words with their synonyms using the domain dictionary. The classification task is performed by the Naïve Bayes classifier to rank opinions based on the polarity of the positive or negative sentiments.

(Kissi et al., 2016) proposed a mathematical approach to classifying message-writing feelings in Arabic Modern Standard Arabic (MSA), based on four decisive functions. The parameters of these functions are the solutions of a linear program, whose objective is to maximize the distance between the negative and positive classes.

(Mataoui et al., 2016) proposed a lexicon-based sentiment analysis approach to determine the vernacular sentiment analysis of the Arab "Algerian Arab". This approach tries to deal with the specific aspects of this very particular Arabic dialect. They proposed an approach composed of four modules classified in: module of calculation of similarity of common sentences; pre-processing module; module stemming and detection of language; polarity calculation module. The experimental results thus obtained show that the system achieves good performance.

(Medhaffar et al., 2017) worked on sentiments analysis of the Tunisian dialect and used machine learning techniques (SVM, NB) to determine the polarity of comments written in Tunisian dialect. They collected and annotated a Tunisian dialect corpus of 17.000 comments from Facebook. This corpus shows a significant improvement compared to the best model trained on other Arabic dialects or MSA data.

(Guellil et al., 2018) presented a tool for sentiment analysis of messages written in Algerian dialect. This tool is based on an approach combining the use of lexicons, as well as a specific treatment of agglutination. They evaluated this approach using two lexicons annotated in feelings and a corpus of tests containing 749 messages. The obtained results are encouraging and show continuous improvement after the execution of each step of their approach.

(Biltawi et al., 2018) used a hybrid approach of sentiment analysis for the Arabic language, which combines lexical and corpus-based techniques. The experimental results showed that the proposed hybrid approach outperforms that based on a corpus.

(Abo et al., 2018) assessed the application of NB and Decision Tree (DT) in sentiment analysis, using a multiple dataset in different languages, in order to understand which of these could yield better results with ML algorithms. Multilingual data sets, such as English, Modern Standard Arabic and dialectal Arabic are collected in their experience where the results obtained are significant.

(Abo et al., 2019) developed a new manual and self-annotated corpus of Sudanese Arabic dialect (SAD) as well as a new lexicon of polarity. Their corpus is a collection of tweeted political tweets annotated by Twitter. They presented a new Subjectivity and Sentiment Analysis (SSA) technique for the Sudanese dialect, which gave a good subjectivity classification result with a score of 83%.

(Alomari et al., 2019) presented a methodology for pre-processing and analysis of tweets related to road traffic in Arabic, especially the Saudi dialect. In addition, they proposed a sentiment classification technique using a lexicon-based approach to understand the sentiment of the Saudi driver.

(Elshakankery & Ahmed, 2019) presented a semi-automatic learning system for the analysis of feelings able to update the lexicon. The proposed approach was tested using different datasets. It reached an accuracy of 73.67% for the 3-class classification problem and 83.73% for the 2-class classification problem. The semiautomatic learning component has been shown to be effective because the accuracy improvement is 17.55%.

(Klouche et al, 2019) presented a general architecture of a sentiment analyzer based on the feedback of Algerian Telephone operator customers, written in Modern Standard Arabic, Arabizi and Algerian dialect. However, the approach is in a preliminary state and no implementation has been carried out.

Table 1 displays a summary of sentiment analysis for Arabic language found in the literature review.

Table 1. Summary of sentiment analysis for Arabic language

Work	Approach	Algorithm	Dataset	Language
Abbasi et al., 2008	Supervised	SVM + L Feature	Web forums	MSA
Elhawary & Elfeky, 2010	Unsupervised	Lexicon based	Reviews	MSA
Shoukry & Rafea, 2012	Supervised	SVM, NB	Twitter	MSA and Egyptian dialect
Khalifa & Omar, 2014	Hybrid	Lexicon based, NB, SVM, KNN	Comments of Jordan hotels	Jordanian dialect
Nabil et al., 2015	Supervised	SVM, KNN, SGD	Twitter	MSA
Aldayel et al., 2015	Hybrid	Lexicon based, SVM	Twitter	MSA and Saudidialect
Mataoui et al, 2016	Unsupervised	Lexiconbased	Social networks	Algerian dialect
Medhafar et al., 2017	Supervised	SVM, NB	Arabic Social networks	Tunisian dialect
Guellil et al., 2018	Unsupervised	Lexiconbased	Social networks	Algerian dialect
Biltawi et al., 2018	Hybrid	Lexiconbased, SVM, NB	OCCA, Twitter	MSA
Abo et al., 2018	Supervised	NB, DT	Social networks	MSA and Arabic dialect
Abo et al., 2019	Supervised	NB, DT	Twitter	Sudanese dialect
Alomari et al., 2019	Unsupervised	lexicon-based	Twitter	Saudi dialect
Elshakankery & Ahmed, 2019	Hybrid	Lexicon based, SVM, Recurrent Neural Network	Twitter	Syrian dialect
Klouche et al, 2019	Hybrid	Lexicon based, SVM, NB	Facebook	Algerian dialect
Our Approach	Supervised	SVM+NB	Facebook	Multi-languages (Arabizi, Algerian dialect, French, English)

It should be noted that the effectiveness of some supervised classifiers, such as SVM and NB, have been applied several times in the literature, giving better results. Previous work by the authors dealt only with the analysis of sentiments in formal language, such as MSA, or dialects.

Our research aims at realizing a decision support system for the Algerian Telephone Operator Ooredoo. We treat the Multi-languages feedback of the customers of the operator to allow it to satisfy at best its targeted customers and to attract new customers from other competing local telephone operators.

Note that there are gaps in the research of the literature on sentiment analysis, as the authors' research does not include the mixing of the Algerian dialect with other informal languages, such as Arabizi. The peculiarity of our work compared to other researchers in this context focuses much more on the transliteration of the Arabizi of the clientele of the Algerian Telephone Operator Ooredoo in all its forms.

Transliteration of Arabizi

The Arabic language has several variants namely: The official language called modern standard Arabic (MSA) and dialectal Arabic (DA) that differs from one Arab country to another. Transliteration is the conversion of one text to another, thus representing words of one language using the approximate equivalent, phonetic or orthographic features of another language. Three approaches are commonly mentioned in the literature to achieve transliteration, namely: based on rules, based on statistics, and those combining the two previous ones (Hybrid).

(Habash et al., 2007) proposed the rule-based approach for transliteration of Arabizi. They used a set of rules that allowed the transition from Arabizi to Arabic and pointed out exceptions and challenges related to vowel processing.

(Darwish, 2014) collected Arabizi words from tweets and trained a character-level language model and a statistical sequence labeling algorithm. They focused on word-level detection. They used word and sequence-level features to identify Arabizi that is mixed with English. The obtained resultachieves an identification accuracy of 98.5%.

(Rosca & Breuel, 2016) presented a model based on neural networks for transliteration between several language pairs, including Arabic and English. The authors describe the application of twoneural-network based sequence-to-sequence models to transliteration that take principled and general-purpose approaches to alignment and one-to-many or many-to-one correspondences.

(Guellil et al., 2017) presented a hybrid approach for the transliteration of Algerian Arabizi. They have developed a set of rules that allow the transition from Arabizi to Arabic script. From these rules, they generated a set of candidates for the transliteration of each word in Arabizi to Arabic. The results obtained show an improvement of the accuracy score that was for the best of the cases of the order of 75.11%.

(Karmani et al., 2019) have proposed a transliteration machine TACA (Tunisian Arabic Chat Alphabet). They used a hybrid method for the transliteration of text written in Tunisian chat. The obtained precision results were 82.8%.

PROPOSED APPROACH

There are many existing researches in the field of Arabic language Sentiment Analysis (SA); however, they are generally restricted to Modern Standard Arabic (MSA) or some dialects of economic or political interest. In this section, we introduce a multi-language sentiment analysis named "Ooredoo Rayek". The sentiment analysis of comments on the official Ooredoo Facebook page requires the implementation of several steps. The proposed prototype has a modular architecture, whose main tasks are: i) collecting comments from the Ooredoo Facebook page, ii) preprocessing of the data, iii) transliteration and translation, and finally iv) determining the polarity of the customer comments.

Figure 1 represents the general architecture of our approach for the extraction of opinions and the sentiments analysis.

Figure 1. Architecture of our approach

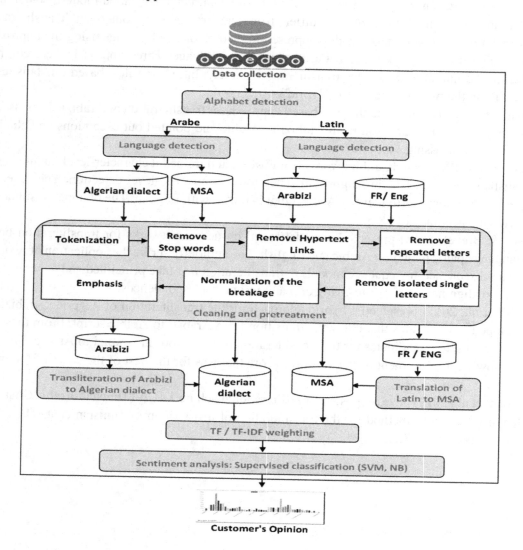

Data Collection

Our sentiment analysis system requires the collection of a large dataset of informal and multi-languages messages with characters in Arabic, Latin and even the combination of Latin and numbers. All the "comments and post" data used are mainly extracted from the Facebook social network, which proves the great use of Algerian Internet users to the Facebook network. All data processed in this work was collected and annotated using the Facepager API. Thus, the corpus used is a set of Facebook comments written in multi-languages and the sources represent comments on the Post published in the official page of the Algerian Telephone Operator Ooredoo during the period between January 15, 2019 and April 24, 2019.

This corpus contains 18141comments with 138803 words. In this dataset, the Algerian dialect is largely used (65% of the data) and the rest is made up of Algerian Arabizi, French, English and MSA.

Language Detection

The Algerian Telephone Operator Ooredoo aimed to know the sentiment of its customersacross the quality of the offered services. However, Ooredoo with its new strategy, conducted surveys on its official Facebook page to the address of its customers to know the craze of Algerian Internet users in their way of communicating with each other on Facebook. Thus, it is determined that local Internet users use a mixture of languages and dialects, which we find for example: French, slang, standard Arabic and especially Arabizi and Algerian dialect. To achieve this goal, it is essential to start first with the detection of the used languages, which is necessary for our sentiment analyzer.

In our study, we wrote a python program that detected the alphabet, in order to group the comments into two corpora: i) Dialect and MSA, ii) Arabizi, French and English. We used the Alphabet Detector 11 python library to detect the Latin and Arabic characters of each comment.

Cleaning and Pretreatment

As we already mentioned in the data collection phase, comments collected from Facebook pages are usually written in informal language. This leads Algerian Internet users to use dialect and slang to express their sentiments. Hence, the need to pre-process comments before moving to the transliteration phase of Arabizi and the translation of French and English languages. The polarity classification phase is finally applied to the newly cleaned corpus. In what follows, we present the pretreatment procedure established in seven phases:

1. **Tokenization:** This first phase requires the decomposition of comments into a set of words called tokens. Each one of them represents a word in the process of our parser, where we simply use spaces between words;
2. **Stop words removal:** In this second phase, we remove the list of stop words, for languages such as English, French or Modern Standard Arabic. For this, lists are available, via tools like NLTK. Concerning the Algerian dialect and Arabizi, there is no resource gathering empty words, such as for example: "*hna*", "*homa*" that are unnecessary personal pronouns in our analysis. We have constructed for this purpose a list of empty words for dialect and Arabizi from the corpus of the collected documents;
3. **Remove Hypertext Links:** This phase consists of deleting all hyperlinks (URLs);

4. **Remove repeated letters:** In this phase, the repeated letters are deleted in the same word, reducing them to a single letter. For example, the word "*bezaaaaaaaaf*" is replaced by the word "*bezaf*";

5. **Remove isolated single letters:** Matching isolated single letters would not provide any useful information for the sentiment analysis phase;

6. **Normalization of the breakage:** In this phase, any comment written in upper case is replaced by its lowercase form. As a result, the words "Strong" and "strong" are reduced to the same instance, which greatly reduces the size of the feature vector;

7. **Emphasis:** In this last phase, it is noted that the substitution of accented letters by their equivalents with respect to non-accented letters makes it possible to unify different words and thus reduce the number of instances in the vocabulary. For example, the sentence "Réseau Téléphonique" is replaced by "Reseau Telephonique".

Transliteration of Arabizi to Algerian Dialect

In the Algerian context, the used language is very often a mixture of Arabic dialect and French or Arabic written in Latin letters mixed with numbers, known as Arabizi.

Arabizi is a "chat" language used by Algerian Internet users to communicate in different social media. It consists of an encoding of Arabic scripts in Latin scripts with the use of numbers and sequences of particular letters to represent Arabic letters, which do not exist in the Latin alphabet.

As examples: the "9" is used to mark the letter "ق" and "9lila" is written to mean "قليلة". "ya-3tikom sa7a connection raha mli7a" which corresponds in Algerian dialect to "يعطيكم الصحة كونيسكسيون راها ماحيح" and which means "Thanks, the connection is good", in English. However, before evaluating the comments written in Arabizi, they were converted from Arabizi to Algerian dialect using our integrated converter, based on a hybrid transliteration machine. In this context, a series of letter and number substitutions are made in the Table 2 to unify this type of terms.

Table 2. Examples of character substitutions in the use of Arabizi

Arabic Letters	Used Numbers	Substitutions
ع	3	a
ح	7	h
ق	9	k

The transliteration function generates all possible cases of writing a transliterated word. In this case, the translation includes words written in anew language other than Arabizi. In our research, we opted for a hybrid approach for transliteration phase, where we designed a converter called to map the comments written in Arabizi into Algerian Dialect. Our converter breaks a comment into a sequence of words or tokens. Each Arabizi word is converted into an Arabic word, by matching the Arabizi letters with the Arabic letters and using the specified correspondences detailed in Table 3.

To extract the best candidate for transliteration of an Arabizi word, we performed the following steps: i) creation of a dictionary of Algerian dialect, ii) realization of a simple search of each candidate within our dictionary and iii) setting up a process based on an applied language model of our corpus.

Table 3. Examples of Arabic letters and their corresponding Latin letters used in Arabizi

Latin Letters	Arabic Correspondence	Latin Letters	Arabic Correspondence	Latin Letters	Arabic Correspondence
A	ى,أ,ة,ع,إ,ا	J	ج	S	س,ص
B	ب	K	ق,ك	T	ت,ط
C	ك,س	L	ل	U	و,أ
D	ظ,ض,د	M	م	V	ف
E	ا	N	ن	W	و
F	ف	O	و,و,أ	X	س ك
G	ق	P	ب	Y	إ,ي
H	ح, ه	Q	ك	Z	ز
I	ع,ي	R	غ,ر	/	/

During this step, we searched each candidate within our set of words, in order to retrieve the number of occurrences. For the search based on our transliteration model, each candidate of our dictionary is searched by extracting the probability of each candidate. If it does not exist in the dictionary, an update is launched for this purpose.

Table 4 shows the results of the words analyzed and transliterated with and without the use of our dictionary. The obtained results demonstrate a good improvement of the execution time.

Table 4. Transliteration results with and without our dictionary

Corpus	Transliterated and Analyzed Word	Elapsed Time
With our dictionary	95.83%	36752 ms
Without our dictionary	89.83%	109076 ms

Translation of the Corpus

Once the preprocessing part has been completed, the transliteration of Arabizi is applied and the corpus in French and English goes into the translation phase to Standard Modern Arabic MSA. We used the Google translation API to perform this phase.

Sentiments Analysis

In this phase, two classifiers of the supervised learning approach (Naive Bayes and SVM) were used in our work to classify the polarity of the data set into positive, negative and neutral classes. Both classifiers are considered by the literature to be the most successful approaches to data mining. The analysis of sentiment by supervised learning requires the preliminary indication of the polarity of the sentiment expressed in the text. Thus, a manual annotation of the collected comments has been made. The input variables are automatically extracted from the corpus formed from the pre-processed comments using the TF / TF-IDF weighting to define the weight of a term in the context of a document.

EXPERIMENTATIONS AND RESULTS ANALYSIS

In this section, we present several experiments related to the application of two algorithms in machine learning, considered to be more efficient in data mining for the polarity classification on the one hand and the transliteration of Arabizi to the Algerian dialect on the other hand.

Training Data

Table 5 presents the training sets of our corpus, composed of multilingual, namely the Algerian dialect, Arabizi, French, English and MSA. In this context, we presented the overall size of our corpus, the number of comments per language, as well as their polarity.

Table 5. Training corpus

Corpus		Train Set	
Dialect +MSA	17778	Positive	3626
Arabizi	276	Negative	9063
French / English	87	Neuter	5784

Experimentations and Evaluation

The obtained results are illustrated using three metrics: precision, recall, and F-measure. Table 6 determines the results of the precision values for the positive, negative and neutral classes for the data set. It is noted in this context that the positive class obtained the highest precision compared to the other two classes.

Table 6. Precision for positives, negatives and neutrals classes

	NB		SVM	
	Filter	**No-Filter**	**Filter**	**No-Filter**
Positives	0.881	0.806	0.780	0.776
Negative	0.750	0.732	0.741	0.753
Neutral	0.676	0.691	0.693	0.688

The data set demonstrated that the classifiers created more accurate models for the three classes. Thus, the accuracy of the positive class is improved with filtering for both the SVM and NB classifiers. In their comparison, the accuracy of the negative class was improved compared to the positive class at the time the NB classifier was used, while it was slightly reduced when using the SVM classifier. Note that the accuracy of the neutral class was also reduced when filtering was applied using the NB classifier.

Figure 2 shows the precision values for the three classes (positive, negative and neutral). It can be seen that the positive class scored the highest in precision compared to the other two classes with a rate of 88.10% for NB and 78% for SVM with filtering, as well as 80.60% for NB and 77.60% for SVM without filtering. When the NB and SVM classifiers have been used without filtering, Recall, Precision and F-measure become lower for negative and neutral classes.

Figure 2. Precision for the positive, negative and neutral classes

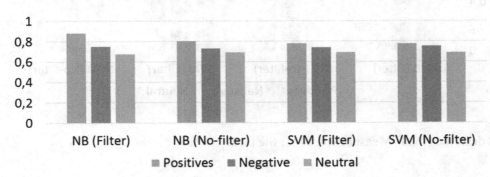

It can then be seen that the classification of the classes with filtering gives better results compared to the classification of the classes without filtering.

Table 7 describes the Recall values for each of the three classes. As noted in this framework, Recall values were improved for the positive class when NB and SVM classifiers were used with filtering. The Recall becomes weaker in the case of negative and neutral classes, when filtering has not been applied for both classifiers.

Table 7. Recall for positives, negatives and neutrals classes

	NB		SVM	
	Filter	**No-Filter**	**Filter**	**No-Filter**
Positives	0.805	0.789	0.798	0.603
Negatives	0.755	0.642	0.702	0.677
Neutrals	0.701	0.663	0.581	0.608

Figure 3 illustrates the Recall values for the three classes, namely positive, negative and neutral.

It can be seen that the recall values have been improved for the positive class with a rate of 80.05% for the NB classifier and 79.80% for the SVM classifier with filtering. On the other hand, a decrease in Recall without filtering was noted with 78.90% for the NB and 60.30% for SVM. Recall becomes lower in the case of negative and neutral classes with successive rates of 75.50% and 70.70% for the

NB classifier and 70.20% and 58.10% for the SVM with filtering, while the unfiltered rates for the two classifiers are lower with rates of 64.20% and 66.30% for the NB and 67.70% and 60.80% for the SVM.

Figure 3. Recall for the positive, negative and neutral classes (add s for negative and neutral)

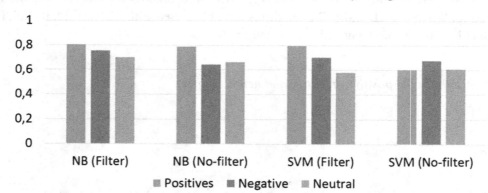

Table 8 describes the F-Measure values for the three classes.

Table 8. F-measure for positives, negatives and neutrals classes.

	NB		SVM	
	Filter	No-Filter	Filter	No-Filter
Positives	0.830	0.772	0.766	0.783
Negative	0.782	0.711	0.712	0.632
Neutrals	0.701	0.569	0.601	0.536

Figure 4 shows the F-measure rates for the three polarity classes. It can be seen that positive polarity obtained the highest score with a rate of 83% for NB and 76.60% for SVM with filtering, but only 77.20% for NB and 78.30% for SVM without filtering. For negative polarity, the rates obtained are 78.20% for NB and 71.20% for SVM with filtering and 71.10% for NB and 63.20% for SVM without filtering.

In addition, we note a decrease in the rates of neutral polarity with respect to positive and negative polarity with a rate of 70.10% for NB and 60.10% for SVM with filtering, as well as 56.90% for NB and 53.60% for SVM.

Our experiments have shown that NB outperforms the SVM algorithm and returns the best scores, in Precision, Recall and F-measure, as shown in Figures 2, 3 and 4, where the NB model reaches 77%.

The transliteration system is evaluated as the rules are created and these are deduced from system errors as a result of each evaluation. We analyze the errors in detail and modify or add rules accordingly in the system, in order to deal with these errors. The final obtained results remain dependent on the errors found in the corpus. Table 9 shows an example of our sentiment analyzer after the transliteration phase.

Figure 4. F- measure for the positive, negative and neutral classes (add s for negative and neutral)

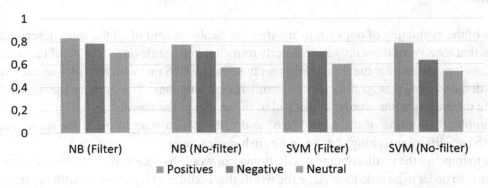

Table 9. Arabizi Comments after converting to Arabic comments using the Arabizi converter

Comments in Arabizi	Comments Converted to Arabic	Polarity
Internet raw3a rebi ibarek	انترنت روعة ربي يبارك	Positive
Ad3af chabaka f dzayer samta rahj	أضعف شبكة في دزايرصامط رهج	Negative
Chkoun li mwalf y activi fi Ooredoo nssa9sih	شكون لي موالف ي اكتيفي اوردو نتقسيه	Neutral
Nbghiha ta3jebni bezzaf Ooredoo	نبغيها تعجبني بزاف اوردو	Positive
Ya3tikom sa7a connexion raha mli7a	يعطيكم صحة كونكسيون راها مليحة	Positive
Dzayer ra7 ttkhallet w ntoumamzl ma dertouvh 3ard chbeb	دزاير راح تتخلط ونتوم مازال ما درتوش عرض شباب	Negative
Internet ta3kom rahameyta fi tiaret	انترنت تاعكم راها ميته في تيارت	Negative

Table 10 shows several outputs from our system with NB and SVM classifiers. In this table, examples are presented for positive, negative and neutral polarities. We cite some examples of our system that generates the correct prediction for some cases, as well as predicting errors for other cases.

For each example, we present the predicted output, the reference and the used classifier.

Table 10. Output examples of Ooredoo Rayek system

Comments	Ooredoo Rayek Output	Reference	Prediction	Classifier
كم من جيغا	Negative	Neuter	Error	NB
كم نطقن تكونون عندي كي افوز؟	Negative	Neuter	Error	NB
برك كنكسيو رديئة شمارات كادبة خرطي	Neuter	Negative	Error	SVM
كنكسيوعانة	Neuter	Negative	Error	NB
كنكسيو	Negative	Neuter	Error	SVM
عندماكلك في جزائر تقف ضعيف داءرة تقرت والية ورقلة	Negative	Negative	Correct	NB
الانترنت جدي احسنتم العمل	Positive	Positive	Correct	NB
فيه اهي15جيغاواودد500مكلمة روعة	Positive	Positive	Correct	SVM
المشكل لشبكة بسبب تاني قولولي مكانش منها الانختابات بسبب لشبكة تاني قولولي مكانش منها ولاو لا الصيانة مكان	Negative	Negative	Correct	NB
معا وريدو	Neutral	Neutral	Correct	SVM

Discussion

The results of the evaluation of our system are after the establishment of all the rules described above. It can be seen that 89.83% of the words are correctly transliterated, while only 10.17% of the words remain in error. The elapsed time for the transliteration phase is 109 076 ms, which is 74% of the overall time used. This demonstrates that Arabizi is not a standardized language. The users of the web in the social media write differently some words, in particular, in the use of the vowels.

For example, the writing of the word "3lah" and "3lh" which want to mean the same meaning but written with two different writings "علاه in English means "why".

In order to improve the results obtained, a dictionary of words has been created with the corresponding transliteration in order to be able to manage the words that could not be processed with the transliteration rules. The dictionary we have designed also contains the words commonly used by Algerian Internet users with their correct transliteration.

The results of the evaluation obtained after the creation of our dictionary are detailed as follows: The elapsed time is 36752 ms, i.e., 42.9%, the words translated and successfully analyzed are 136010 words, i.e., 95.83%.

From this analysis, we deduce a very good improvement in the flow of execution time and an improvement in transliteration results.

The results illustrated in Table 10 show that the NB and SVM classifiers did a very good job, predicting the good examples of the positive class. Only for negative and neutral classes, both NB and SVM classifiers predict incorrect results. This means that the classifiers did not rank the comments well, especially of the neutral class.

We consider that the classification problem of neutral classes does not fall under the NB or SVM classifier type, but rather the distinction of selected comments in objective (neutral) and subjective (positive or negative).

CONCLUSION

Telecom market has become much competitive with a good number of service providers. Hence retaining loyal customers by making them satisfied customers is crucial for the sake of existence of the telecom provider. Business Intelligence derives information or knowledge from huge volumes of business data using a set of machine-learning and analytical techniques to support decision-making and formulating new strategies of an organization.

The objective of this work is to satisfy the concerns of the Algerian Telephone Operator Ooredoo, related to the improvement of the quality of service of its network, vis-à-vis its Algerian clientele. In this paper, we used a supervised approach for the sentiment analysis of multi-language comment, while including the implementation of our integrated converter for transliteration of Arabizi. We have been able to classify the polarity of the comments of the Ooredoo operator's clients written in Algerian dialect, Arabizi, MSA, French and English in their semantic and syntactic complexity. The transliteration and the sentiment analysis thus treated in our work are interdependent subjects implemented in a series of treatments that have for final objective, the detection of the sentiment of the comments.

We have performed different experiments using several ML algorithms such as Naive Bayes classifier, and SVM. A hybrid converter was designed and applied to comments for the transliteration and use of NB and SVM classifiers for Sentiment Analysis.

We reported the obtained results from an evaluation determining the effects of the two classifiers SVM and NB. For this, we obtained an F-measure score using the NB and SVM classifiers respectively of 83% and 76.60% for the positive class, 78.20% and 71.20% for the negative class, as well as 70.10% and 60.10% for the neutral class. We deduce that the design and use of a dictionary for the transliteration phase has significantly improved the results of our polarity classification, as well as a very good improvement in runtime flow.

As future work, we would like to perform a deep analysis of system outputs. In addition, it is important to take into consideration, in our future work, the improvement of our research, while testing our solution with other North African languages, such as the Tunisian, Moroccan, Libyan, and Egyptian dialects.

We also plan to carry out a deep learning approach to Feeling Analysis of our studied system. Thus, we will extrinsically evaluate the quality of our results by integrating them in the context of various tasks, such as the use of a multi-dialect corpus.

ACKNOWLEDGMENT

We acknowledge the Algerian Ministry of Higher Education and Scientific Research, as well as the Directorate General for Scientific Research and Technological Development (DG-RSDT) for funding the Phd project of Badia Klouche.

We also acknowledge the Algerian Telephone Operator Ooredoo and its team for their help in the development of the "Ooredoo Rayek" system.

REFERENCES

Abbasi, A., Chen, H., & Salem, A. (2008). Sentiment Analysis in Multiple Languages: Feature Selection for Opinion Classification in Web Forums. *ACM Transactions on Information Systems*, *26*(3), 1–34. doi:10.1145/1361684.1361685

Abdul-Mageed, M., Diab, M., & Kübler, S. (2014). SAMAR: Subjectivity and sentiment analysis for Arabic social media. *Computer Speech & Language*, *28*(1), 20–37. doi:10.1016/j.csl.2013.03.001

Abo, M. E. M., Ahmad, N., Shah, K., Balakrishnan, V., & Abdelaziz, A. (2018). Sentiment analysis algorithms : evaluation performance of the Arabic and English language. In *Proceedings of the 2018 International Conference on Computer, Control, Electrical, and Electronics Engineering (ICCCEEE)* (pp. 1–5). Academic Press. 10.1109/ICCCEEE.2018.8515844

Abo, M. E. M., Shah, N. A. K., Balakrishnan, V., Kamal, M., Abdelaziz, A., & Haruna, K. (2019). SSA-SDA: Subjectivity and sentiment analysis of Sudanese dialect Arabic. In *Proceedings of the 2019 International Conference on Computer and Information Sciences, ICCIS 2019* (pp. 1–5). Academic Press. 10.1109/ICCISci.2019.8716466

Aldayel, H. K., & Azmi, A. M. (2015). Arabic tweets sentiment analysis – a hybrid scheme. *Journal of Information Science*, 46(6), 782–797. doi:10.1177/0165551515610513

Alomari, E., Mehmood, R., & Katib, I. (2020). Sentiment Analysis of Arabic Tweets for Road Traffic Congestion and Event Detection. In *Smart Infrastructure and Applications* (pp. 37–54). Springer; doi:10.1007/978-3-030-13705-2_2

Biltawi, M., Al-Naymat, G., & Tedmori, S. (2018). Arabic Sentiment Classification: A Hybrid Approach. In *Proceedings of the 2017 International Conference on New Trends in Computing Sciences* (pp. 104–108). Academic Press. doi:10.1109/ICTCS.2017.24

Darwish, K. (2015). Arabizi Detection and Conversion to Arabic.

Elhawary, M., & Elfeky, M. (2010). Mining Arabic Business Reviews. doi:10.1109/ICDMW.2010.24

Elshakankery, K., & Ahmed, M. F. (2019). HILATSA: A hybrid Incremental learning approach for Arabic tweets sentiment analysis. *Egyptian Informatics Journal*, 20(3), 163–171. doi:10.1016/j.eij.2019.03.002

Farghaly, A., & Shaalan, K. (2009). Arabic Natural Language Processing. *Challenges and Solutions*, 8(4), 1–19.

Guellil, I., Azouaou, F., Abbas, M., & Fatiha, S. (2017). Arabizi transliteration of Algerian Arabic dialect into Modern Standard Arabic. In *Social MT 2017/First workshop on Social Media and User Generated Content Machine Translation*. Academic Press.

Guellil, I., Azouaou, F., Saadane, H., Semmar, N., & Commission, A. E. (2018). Une approche fondée sur les lexiques d'analyse de sentiments du dialecte algérien. *TAL Traitement Automatique des Langues*, 58(3), 41-65.

Habash, N., Soudi, A., & Buckwalter, T. (2007). Arabic Computational Morphology. *Arabic Computational Morphology*. doi:. doi:10.1007/978-1-4020-6046-5

Karmani, N., Soussou, H., & Alimi, A. M. (2016). Tunisian Arabic Chat Alphabet Transliteration Using Probabilistic Finite State Transducers. *The International Arab Journal of Information Technology*, 16(2).

Khalifa, K., & Omar, N. (2014). A hybrid method using lexicon-based approach and Naive Bayes classifier for Arabic opinion question answering. *Journal of Computational Science*, 10(10), 1961–1968. doi:10.3844/jcssp.2014.1961.1968

Kissi, M., Madani, A., & Cherif, W. (2016). A hybrid optimal weighting scheme and machine learning for rendering sentiments in tweets. *International Journal of Intelligent Engineering Informatics*, 4(3/4), 322. doi:10.1504/IJIEI.2016.10001302

Klouche, B., & Benslimane, S. (2019). Multilingual sentiments analysis to improve the quality of services provided by Algerian telephone operator. In Proceedings of JERI'2019. Academic Press.

Liu, B. (2012). *Sentiment Analysis (Introduction and Survey) and Opinion Mining*. Morgan &Claypool. doi:10.1162/COLI

Mataoui, M. (2016). A Proposed Lexicon-Based Sentiment Analysis Approach for the Vernacular Algerian Arabic. *Research in Computing Science, 110(April 2016), 55–70. Retrieved* from http://rcs.cic.ipn.mx/2016_110/A

Medhaffar, S., Bougares, F., Estève, Y., & Hadrich-Belguith, L. (2017). Sentiment Analysis of Tunisian Dialects: Linguistic Ressources and Experiments. In *Proceedings of the Third Arabic Natural Language Processing Workshop* (pp. 55–61). Academic Press. 10.18653/v1/W17-1307

Nabil, M., Alaa El-Dien, M., Atiya, A. (2015). ASTD : Arabic Sentiment Tweets Dataset.

Rahab, H., Zitouni, A., & Djoudi, M. (2018). SANA: Sentiment analysis on newspapers comments in Algeria. *Journal of King Saud University - Computer and Information Sciences*, 10–23. doi:10.1016/j.jksuci.2018.04.012

Rosca, M., & Breuel, T. (2016). Sequence-to-sequence neural network models for transliteration.

Shoukry, A., & Rafea, A. (2012). Preprocessing Egyptian Dialect Tweets for Sentiment Mining. In *The Fourth Workshop on Computational* (pp. 47–56). Academic Press.

This research was previously published in the International Journal of Technology Diffusion (IJTD), 11(2); pages 66-81, copyright year 2020 by IGI Publishing (an imprint of IGI Global).

Chapter 66
Opinion Mining for Instructor Evaluations at the Autonomous University of Ciudad Juarez

Rafael Jiménez
https://orcid.org/0000-0001-9904-3059
Universidad Autónoma de Ciudad Juárez, Mexico

Vicente García
https://orcid.org/0000-0003-2820-2918
Universidad Autónoma de Ciudad Juárez, Mexico

Abraham López
Universidad Autónoma de Ciudad Juárez, Mexico

Alejandra Mendoza Carreón
Universidad Autónoma de Ciudad Juárez, Mexico

Alan Ponce
Universidad Autónoma de Ciudad Juárez, Mexico

ABSTRACT

The Autonomous University of Ciudad Juárez performs an instructor evaluation each semester to find strengths, weaknesses, and areas of opportunity during the teaching process. In this chapter, the authors show how opinion mining can be useful for labeling student comments as positives and negatives. For this purpose, a database was created using real opinions obtained from five professors of the UACJ over the last four years, covering a total of 20 subjects. Natural language processing techniques were used on the database to normalize its data. Experimental results using 1-NN and Bagging classifiers shows that it is possible to automatically label positive and negative comments with an accuracy of 80.13%.

DOI: 10.4018/978-1-6684-6303-1.ch066

INTRODUCTION

Opinions are central activities for almost all human beings. When we need to make important decisions, it is essential to know the view of others; therefore, opinions are a valuable source of information. The sentiments analysis or opinion mining is an area that automatically classifies sentiments expressed by a person about a given object, as positive, negative, or neutral (Cortizo, 2019). Opinion mining is used by companies to understand the perceptions that customers have about their products or services and identify areas of opportunity or improve the marketing strategies used (Huddy, 2017).

Teacher evaluations are carried out by the Autonomous University of Ciudad Juárez (UACJ) each semester as a method by which the written opinion of students is recorded to identify strengths, weaknesses, and areas of opportunity in the performance of teachers (Universidad Autonoma de Ciudad Juarez, 2019).

During the period of evaluation, the teaching evaluation office makes available to students a platform in which, in addition to other metrics, two boxes appear where they can freely write positive and negative comments about their teachers during the semester in progress. In this process, a student might mistakenly write negative comments in the positive box and vice versa, as well as a combination of both. It causes the teacher evaluation to not provide easy feedback to teachers as the positive and negative comments are mixed.

During the evaluation process, the student is presented with a series of specific questions about how the teacher leads their class. These questions are answered from bad to excellent, represented with values ranging from 1 to 5. Before finishing the evaluation, the student is allowed to write textual comments about the teacher's performance.

Once the teachers assign a final grade to students, the university's portal allows teacher access to the results of the teacher through the teacher's portal. The results are an average of the grades obtained in each of the specific questions, and positive and negative comments are received. These results help them identify strengths and weaknesses within their teaching model by receiving immediate feedback, which allows them to make relevant changes to their practices to promote better teaching and better learning.

This chapter is an extension of a previous study (Jiménez, García, Florencia-Juárez, Rivera & López-Orozco, 2018). Here, we use sentiment analysis techniques on opinions issued by the students to categorize the comments into positive and negative in their native Spanish language. For this, a comment repository was built with student opinions issued over four years, manually categorized as positive and negative, to build later feature vectors, which were used to train a 1-NN and the Bagging algorithm. Work in the same line was presented by Gutiérrez, Ponce, Ochoa, and Álvarez (2018), in which the performance of teachers was analyzed using reviews written by students of the Polytechnic University of Aguascalientes.

It is important to mine text in Spanish because there is not much work being done in the fields of natural language processing and opinion mining using Spanish language tools and libraries, despite the fact that opinion mining methodologies in English might not fit other languages without making major modifications.

The chapter is organized in the following manner. Section 2 briefly describes related works in opinion mining. In Section 3, the methodology undertaken in the development of research. Section 4 shows the experimental configuration adopted. Subsequently, in Section 5, the results are described and discussed. Finally, Section 6 concludes and proposes future lines of research.

RELATED WORKS

Sentiment analysis, or opinion mining, is the process of automatically extracting opinions using artificial intelligence and natural language processing to understand expressed emotions better, primarily online. Microsoft (2019) states that natural language processing is a tool that aims to design and build software that can analyze, understand, and generate languages that humans can naturally use so that they can eventually communicate with a computer as if it did with another.

An opinion is a "view, judgment, or appraisal formed in mind about a particular matter" (Merriam-Webster, 2019). Liu (2004) classifies opinions into two types:

1. **Direct Opinions:** The opinion is expressed directly at the object or entity. This type of opinion is the one we are interested in mining.
2. **Comparative Opinions:** In which the opinion is expressed by comparing two or more objects or entities in a hierarchical way. This type of opinion aims at giving a reference to which an 'object 1' is better or worse in comparison to 'object 2'.

The role that natural language processing plays in opinion mining is to provide the linguistic information necessary for the extraction of information. This linguistic information is used through the grammatical labeling of words of a sentence to remove stop words and during stemming that allows to reduce a word to its morphological root, discussed in Section 3.

As such, opinion mining has a great field of application. There are large and small companies that only engage in opinion mining to sell analytics to their customers like Revuze (2018), Aspectiva (2019), Brandwatch (2019) and Google (2018); while others use it as an essential tool of their daily operations like Amazon (Amazon Web Services, 2018).

Web Reviews

Opinion mining on the web (Jadhavar & Komarraji, 2018) is used to automate the maintenance of reviews and opinions since social networks are a rich source of large-scale information. Users use them to express their feelings on various topics, many of them, about products. These comments can be classified as positive, negative, or neutral, and from them, valuable information can be extracted for the company's market reports. Some examples of applications in the market are:

- **Meaning cloud:** It is an online application that offers text classification, topic extraction, language identification, thematization, morphosyntactic analysis, corporate reputation, and text clustering (Meaning Cloud, 2019). The application has support for several languages, including English, Spanish, French, Italian, Portuguese, and Catalan. How Meaning Cloud works is through an Excel plugin or through an online service API that contains all the libraries in a single package to perform the extraction of opinions.
- **Vivek Sentiment:** This web application was created using a Naïve Bayes model and utilizes reviews from IMDB.com, a movie database (Narayanan, Arora, & Bhatia, 2016). The system evaluates the comments as positive, negative, or neutral left by registered users in movies and tv shows, in addition to providing the classifier's level of confidence in the result. The application has an

API to use the classifier externally, but only if there is an Internet connection. Another limitation of this application is that its domain only covers the English language.

In Businesses

Companies interested in knowing customers' perceptions of their products or services use opinion mining. The information collected from surveys is classified, making it possible to improve a product, identify areas of opportunity, or improve the marketing strategies used (Smeureanu, 2012). An example of this is Meltwater (2019), which is a consultancy that offers services and packages that help create an analysis of the presence of the brand before consumers and competitors. Among the analyzes that are performed is the sentiment analysis, which monitors how well-received was a message from the company in social networks.

The ability to automatically extract meaningful information from users is of great use for businesses who have or aim to have a great online presence, as they can monitor social networks by analyzing real-time user activity and detecting negative feedback just minutes after the brand issues a new marketing campaign, product or service. Many customer metrics and data analytics are tailor-made for each company by marketing companies using sentiment analysis. An example of this is Brandwatch (2019), who offers brand name analytics for customers looking to track how well they are perceived by users by positive and negative comments and how well users perceive their competitors. One key aspect of Brandwatch is that they offer their customers a way to redefine comment's sentiment if they think it was misclassified. This is because sentiment analysis is an automatic process, which is not completely free of mistakes and primarily because sentiments are subjective, and as such, their perception is influenced by personal feelings.

Government Agencies

Government opinion mining extracts public behavior and opinions on political issues. The use of sentiment analysis helps identify the opinions of voters regarding a candidate before the elections in order to improve campaign strategies (Smeureanu, 2012). An example of this is the National Institute of Statistics, Geography, and Informatics (INEGI), which developed a tool that classified 63 million georeferenced tweets written between 2014 and 2015, with the purpose of generating mobility and tourism statistics, as well as knowing the mood of the population by the state of the country (National Institute of Statistics and Geography, 2017).

METHODOLOGY

The steps that were carried out for the classification of comments of the teacher evaluation were the following:

1) Collection of comments of the teacher evaluation.
2) Preprocessing of the comments.
3) Creation of a feature vector.
4) Validation of our classification model.

These steps are briefly described in the following sections.

Comment Collection

The collection of comments was carried out during the month of January 2017 with the help of the professors of the Multidisciplinary Division of the UACJ in Ciudad Universitaria (CU). The comments collected correspond to four years, 20 subjects, and five professors. Since neither the university nor other teachers have access to other teacher's evaluation results and comments, we had to ask each teacher who was willing to participate in this project to extract their own comments by performing the following steps:

Step 1: Access their teacher evaluation results page, which shows all the courses they have ever imparted. This results page is only available to each teacher and can only be accessed using the credentials issued to them by the university's Information technology (IT) department.

Step 2: Select a subject already evaluated, as current semester courses might be in the process of evaluation.

Step 3: Locate the comments area as featured in Figure 1, where we can find two comment boxes, one for positive comments and one for negative comments.

Step 4: Copy all comments in either the positive comments and paste them into the positive comment's repository, copy all negative comments, and paste them into their corresponding repository.

Figure 1. Positive comments area and negative comments area

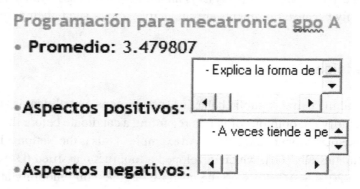

Having all positive and negative comments stored in separate simple text files (.txt) makes it easy to preprocess, as Java can easily read the utf-8 encoding.

Comment Preprocessing

During the preprocessing stage of the project, the sentiment analysis techniques described by Quratulain, Sajjad, and Sayeed (2016) were followed. Below are the steps carried out.

- Validation of comments by reading all comments to find those which had no relevance to teacher evaluation. All comments found to be outside the domain of the teacher evaluation had to be eliminated. It is important since only those comments in which students provide feedback on their experience when taking classes with a professor should be taken into account since comments outside this domain could cause noise to the classifier. For example, the comment shown below was marked as invalid because it does not provide feedback on teacher knowledge, teaching style, or teaching competence, but rather is just a student complaint about something that did.

"Profesor en serio, yo nunca le explique a Yair el método mini, Max el asumió que sí, pero está tonto. Se lo juro."

Translation: "Professor seriously, I never explained Yair the mini max method, assumed that I did, but he is stupid. I swear."

- Identification of comments that were erroneously assigned by the student in the negative comments area, being that the comment is positive and vice versa. Once these comments were identified, they were reassigned to their corresponding repository. This step is necessary to establish what comments represent a positive comment or a negative comment. It is important to consider that tagging comments as positive or negative is a reflection of the personal subjective interpretation of those comments, and therefore, will likely be a difficult endeavor to tag them as a consensus.

- Writing validation was also done manually since all comments had to be read to validate them. All misspelled words were manually edited to correct their spelling. This was done manually as automatically fixing spelling errors lands outside the scope of this project. Example of a spelling correction: "inpuntual" → "impuntual".

Automatic preprocessing with the normalization function was also used, which consisted of:

- Case conversion of characters from uppercase to lowercase to eliminate possible errors when comparing words using Java's toLowerCase() method.

Example:

```
String str = "Hello";
str = str.toLowerCase();
```

- Elimination of accents in some letters since the students do not accentuate the words correctly or simply avoid accents altogether. This caused that the words were being compared correctly. To do this, the replaceAll() method was used. This method takes two parameters x and y. Where parameter x is the character to be replaced by the y character in a string. Example of the method to replace the character 'á' with 'a'.

```
str = str.replaceAll("á", "a");
```

- Elimination of characters, quotes, and underscores. These types of characters contribute nothing. To eliminate these characters, we also used the replaceAll() method explicitly imputing each character to be replaced and its replacement. Example of the elimination of the underscore character, which is then replaced by a no character, shortening the string by one character:

```
str = str.replaceAll("_", "");
```

- Elimination of emojis and other symbols such as ideograms were also removed. An example of this is:

"es una muy buena maestra ❤*"* → *"es una muy buena maestra"*

- Since FreeLing requires all comments to end with a full stop, a period was added at the end of all comments, while also deleting other characters in the comment added automatically by the teacher evaluation system such as the hyphen character ("-") found at the beginning of all comments recollected. Since we know how to remove characters using the replaceAll() method, we use the concatenation operator to add the period character, ".", at the end of the string. Below is an example of the method used:

```
str = str.replaceAll("_", "");
str += ".";
```

The following is an example of the processed comment:

"- Tiene dominio sobre su tema" → *"Tiene dominio sobre su tema."*

- Word tokenization of comments into a list of single words. This process makes it easier to do word matching during the creation of feature vectors in Section 3.3. Word tokenization should be done after the removal of characters and just before stop word removal as it can add punctuations such as ".", "-", "?", "!" to the end of word tokens. Tokenization can be achieved either by utilizing Freeling's tokenizer or Java's StringTokenizer.

Example of Java's StringTokenizer to split a string using its default space delimiter:

```
String message = "Hello Word";
StringTokenizer st = new StringTokenizer(message);
while (st.hasMoreTokens())
{
    System.out.println(st.nextToken());
}
Program output:
Hello
World
```

- Removal of stop words. Stop words are commonly used words like prepositions or articles and do not provide useful information, the stop words list used as a reference to identify words to be removed was printed to a text file from Python's NLTK corpus list of Spanish stop words. This can be done by using the following code in python:

```
import nltk
from nltk.corpus import stopwords
stop_words = set(stopwords.words('spanish'))
with open('Stop Word List.txt', 'w', encoding='utf-8') as f:
    for item in stop_words:
        f.write("\n" + item)
```

Creating a Feature Vector

A feature vector is a vector of *n*-elements or attributes that describe an object. In order to convert a comment to a vector, the attributes that formed it were previously defined. From a list of opinion-indicating words in Spanish independent of the domain, which contain positive and negative words, the feature vector was constructed. The list of words to be used as a dictionary was provided by the Thematic Network on Multilingual and Multimodal Information Treatment (Molina-González, 2013), which consists of 2509 positive words and 5626 negative words. This dictionary is based on Bing Liu's Opinion Lexicon.

To reduce the dimensionality of the vector, we used a package library called FreeLing (2019), which is a morphosyntactic tagger. This library allows to automatically extract the stem of each of the word in the dictionary. By stemming each word, we can reduce the inflected words to their base form, which allows us to remove duplicate stems. By stemming the dictionary words, we saw a decrease of words in the dictionary to 1313 positive and 2949 negative words, or a 47.60% reduction of attributes while still retaining the same value of the dictionary.

To further reduce the dimensionality, an analysis of the stem of the words was performed. During this analysis, a word w was taken and compared to all the words in the same file (positive or negative) were searched to find if the word w was contained within at the start of another word v. That is that a word w can be considered a base for word v, *or* its morphological root. This decreased the number of features to only 584 positive words and 1270 negative words.

Table 1. Example of positive and negative words as characteristics of a vector

List of words					
	Positive	bueno	proactivo	decisivo	mejor
	Negative	impuntual	fastidio	aburrir	inexperto

The creation of a feature vector was carried out from the stem words of positive and negative type as shown in Table 1, where the words "bueno" (good), "proactivo" (proactive), "decisivo" (decisive) and "mejor" (better) are examples of positive word, and "impuntual" (unpunctual), "fastidio" (nuisance), "aburrido" (bored) and "inexperto" (inexperienced) are examples of negative words.

To create a feature vector, the complete 1852 attributes from our dictionary were used to create a list of words vector or attributes vector. This vector is created specifically for the task of word matching the attributes with the words in each instance, and the quantity of words in the dictionary dictates the dimensionality of our vector. After adding all our dictionary words to our attributes vector, a class attribute, called "class", is added at the end of the attribute vector to determine the class value of our vectors.

Table 2. Resulting vector from a comment and the characteristics vector

List of words	bueno	proactivo	decisivo	mejor	impuntual	fastidio	aburrir	inexperto
Vector	1	0	0	1	1	0	0	0

Given a comment "Es un buen professor pero podria ser mejor si no fuera tan imputual", this is preprocessed with the normalization function before being converted to tokens with the help of FreeLing, which would look like {"es", "un", "buen", "profesor", "pero", "podría", "ser", "mejor", "si", "no", "fuera", "tan", "impuntual"}, later the lemma is extracted from the words {"ser", "uno, "bueno", "profesor", "pero", "podria", "ser", "mejor", "si", "no", "ser", "tan", "impuntual"}. Subsequently, the value of 1 is assigned to each attribute if the word exists and 0 in the opposite case. An example of this can be seen in Table 2. At the end of each vector, we added 1 if the comment used to create the vector is positive or cero if the comment used is negative, which corresponds to the class attribute.

After the feature vectors are created, we need to save our vectors and we can either save them to a comma-separated values (CSV) file and use WEKA's built-in ARFF-Viewer to transform our CSV to a relation attribute format file (ARFF) or to write our vectors directly to ARFF.

An ARFF is a text file with an. arff extension and consists of three parts:

1. The relation area is the @Relation header followed by the relation name. The relation name can be given by the user and the name given does not affect the classification product.
   Example: @Relation TeacherEvaluation
2. The attributes area follows after the heading and describes all the characteristics in the attributes vector by listing them with the word: @Attribute followed by the characteristic and the type of values that this attribute can have inside square brackets or NUMERIC if the value it is numerical. To end the attribute area, the Class attribute is included with the possible class values in the relation.
   Attribute example: @ATTRIBUTE triumphant {1,0}
   Example of class attribute: @ATTRIBUTE Class {positive, negative}
3. The data area begins after the word @Data and contains all the vectors created with the values separated by a comma and, at the end, the class to which it belongs or the sign "?" if the feature vector must be evaluated. By using the data shown in Table 2, the following instances must be created:
   For training: 1,0,0,1,1,0,0,0, 1
   For classification: 1,0,0,1,1,0,0, 0,?

The last step we need to do is to determine if any attributes that do not vary at all or that vary too much, and therefore, we can safely remove with the help of the "RemoveUseless" filter in Weka. After applying this filter, our attributes went down from 1852 to only 111, as shown in Table 3.

Table 3. Brief description of the database during the experiments

Number of instances			Number of attributes		
Positive	Negative	Total	Positive	Negative	Total
187	110	297	48	63	111

Validation

Cross-validation is a technique to estimate the performance of a classification model. The main idea of cross-validation is to divide the collected data to estimate the classifier error. One part of the data, the largest, is used to train the classifier, and the remaining part is used for testing the trained classifier with unseen data.

To validate our model, cross-validation using K-folds was performed, where K is the number of iterations used. To carry out the tests, the total set of elements used is divided into K number of equal parts, and during each iteration, one of the K parts is rotated as testing while the remaining parts are used as training until completing K iterations. Table 4 exemplifies the cross-validation algorithm using K = 5 iterations and how test pieces are rotated during each iteration.

Table 4. K-folds example of 5 iterations

Iteration	1	2	3	4	5
	Testing	Training	Training	Training	Training
	Training	**Testing**	Training	Training	Training
Dataset	Training	Training	**Testing**	Training	Training
	Training	Training	Training	**Testing**	Training
	Training	Training	Training	Training	**Testing**

EXPERIMENT CONFIGURATION

All tests were performed with the WEKA software, which is an open-source data mining software that includes machine language algorithms for classification and data preparation (WEKA, 2020). The classification algorithms offered by the WEKA library were analyzed to have a reasonable idea of which of them we should use to classify. The following considerations were taken into account:

- The number of comments used for training.
- The dimensionality of feature vectors.
- The attribute type in the vector, in this case, only a binary value of 0 and 1.

Since we have less than 100,000 comments and the feature vector only contains binary values composed of 0 and 1, it was decided to try the following classifiers:

- Bagging is an ensemble method that feeds base classifiers a random subset of the training set since Bagging resamples the training set with replacement, some instances can be represented multiple times while others might not be. Then it evaluates each classifier's prediction, either by voting or by average, to form a final prediction for a new test instance (Opitz, 1999).
- 1-NN is an algorithm that measures the Euclidean distance from one instance to another (already-classified instance or neighbor) and classifies the new instance as the same class as its nearest neighbor (See, 2016).

WEKA allows users to apply classification algorithms, and to validate using cross-validation of K partitions and the database that is briefly detailed in Table 3. The comments contained in the database went through a preprocessing that was described in Section 3.2., where finally 187 and 110 positive and negative comments could be constructed, respectively.

The dimensionality of the vectors is 111, of which 63 attributes describe positive words and 48 negative words.

For the Bagging and 1-NN classifiers, the default configurations in WEKA were used where the Bagging classifier uses a REPTree for fast decision tree learning, and the 1-NN classifier uses a Euclidean distance kernel and a K = 1.

Table 5. Confusion matrix of two classes

			Predicted Tag	
			Positive	Negative
Real Label		Positive	d	c
		Negative	b	a

As evaluation metrics to measure the performance of the Bagging and 1- NN classifiers, a two-class confusion matrix was used, as shown in Table 5. With this matrix, we can determine the performance of a classifier with the following formulas.

The accuracy of the classification model is a statistical measure of how well the model correctly identifies positive and negative comments, and it is determined by the formula:

$$accuracy = \frac{a+d}{a+b+c+d} \tag{1}$$

The precision is the proportion of correctly classified instances based on the total number of instances classified as belonging to the positive class, and it is determined by the formula:

$$precision = \frac{d}{d+b} \tag{2}$$

The true positive rate (TP) is the proportion of positive instances that were correctly classified, and it is determined by the formula:

$$TP = \frac{d}{c+d} \tag{3}$$

The true negative rate (TN) is the proportion of negative instances that were correctly classified, and it is determined by the formula:

$$TN = \frac{a}{a+b} \tag{4}$$

The false-positive rate (FP) is the proportion of negative instances classified as positive, determined by the formula:

$$FP = \frac{b}{a+b} \tag{5}$$

The false-negative rate (FN) is the proportion of negative instances classified as positive, determined by the formula:

$$FN = \frac{c}{c+d} \tag{6}$$

RESULTS

The overall accuracy results are shown in Table 6. We can observe that the Bagging algorithm obtained the best results of the two classifiers by scoring 3.37% points higher than 1-NN. It indicates a good score for the Bagging algorithm.

Table 7 shows the accuracy by class for each of the classifiers. As can be seen, the negative comments obtain a low classification rate of 59.1% and 62.7% on both algorithms. In contrast, positive comments get results greater than 90%. The low negative results affect the overall classification rate.

Table 6. The global accuracy results table

	Bagging	1-NN
Global Accuracy	80.13%	76.76%

Table 7. Precision table by class

	Bagging	1-NN
Positive	90.4%	90.4%
Negative	62.7%	59.1%

To analyze the behavior by the class of the classifiers, Tables 8 and 9 show the confusion matrix for the Bagging and 1-NN classifiers, respectively.

The confusion matrix M shows that the model correctly classified the elements of the upper left M [1,1] and the lower right M [2,2]. In the lower-left M [2,1] and upper right M [1,2], false positives and negatives are shown, respectively.

Table 8. Confusion matrix for the Bagging classifier

	Bagging	
	Positive	Negative
Positive	169	18
Negative	41	69

Table 9. Confusion matrix for the 1-NN classifier

	1-NN	
	Positive	Negative
Positive	169	18
Negative	45	65

From the confusion matrix for the Bagging classifier in Table 8, a TP of 0.9037, TN of 0.6272, the FP of 0.3727, and the FN of 0.0962 is obtained. Given the rates of FP and FN, we can observe that this classification algorithm has a lower rate of FP than FN, which indicates that there was a lower percentage of negative comments classified as positive than positive comments classified as negative. For the 1- NN classifier in Table 9, a TP of 0.9037, a TN of 0.5909, the FP of 0.4090, and the FN of 0.0962 are obtained.

The Bagging algorithm, unlike the 1-NN algorithm, has a higher TN rate than FP, so fewer negative comments were classified as positive than using 1-NN.

Given the FP and FN of the two classifiers, the Bagging algorithm has the lowest rate of false positives and false negatives. This indicates that with this algorithm had fewer positive comments classified as negative and less negative comments classified as positive.

To give a better idea of how the instances are located in a two-dimensional space and why we get those results, Multidimensional Scaling (MDS) was used to graph the vector database by mapping the instances by their similarities and dissimilarities. It is usually used to visualize data with high dimensionality, in a low dimensions space. In Figure 2, we can see how the positive (red) and negative (cyan) instances are plotted in a cartesian plane. In the figure, it is possible to see how the data gets grouped into three groups marked with the letters A, B, and C. In group A, it is possible to see a convergence of positive instances and does not have the presence in or around that group another class of instances. So, it could be said that the instances that belong to this space will be correctly classified.

The opposite occurs in group C, where there is a slight overlap between positive and negative instances, as some positive instances make their way into a group of negative instances. These positive instances have a minimum effect on the ability classification model.

Group B is precisely the area where the classifier usually makes mistakes. Looking at group C in detail, one could say that positive comments in that area will be classified as negative. In contrast, in group B, negative comments will be classified as positive, given that the nearest instances are all mostly positive.

This overlap that occurs in group B happens since some comments may contain the same particular words in both positive and negative comments. For example, the word "bien" (good). This word is repeated both in negative comments such as:

"realmente la puedo considero como una maestra que enseña del todo bien aunque cumpla con todos los puntos previos, considero que no es su culpa, el salón que nos tocó este semestre se batalla mucho para escuchar (d4-210)." Translation "I can really consider her as a teacher who teaches everything well even though she meets all the previous points, I consider that it is not her fault, the classroom that we had this semester made it hard to listen (d4-210)."

Figure 2. The two-dimensional layout of the instances used for training

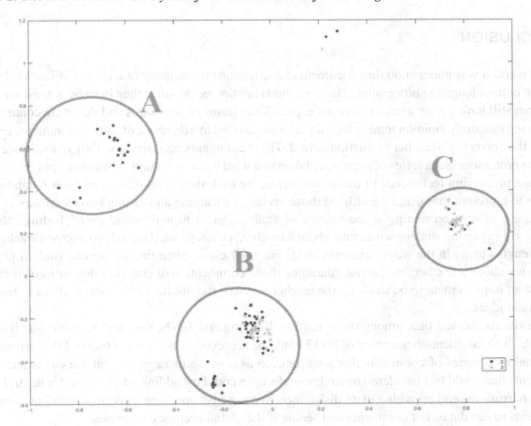

It also occurs in positive comments such as:

"sus grupos casi siempre están vacíos, eso habla bien de él, ya que da la clase bien y les da a los alumnos la calificación que se merecen, no deberían abrir esta materia en veranos, los que no hacen nada buscan como pasar y si se gradúan eso da mala imagen a la UACJ en la industria, a veces se vuelve difícil conseguir un buen trabajo cuando tienen catalogado a los alumnos de la UACJ como inútiles y flojos." Translation: "his groups are almost always empty, that speaks well of him, since he imparts the class well and gives the students the grade they deserve, they should not open this course in summer classes, those who do nothing look for how to pass and if they graduate, that gives the UACJ a bad image in the industry, sometimes it becomes difficult to get a good job when they have classified the UACJ students as useless and lazy"

Having such comments that contain the same amount of positive and negative words and are subjectively ambiguous; therefore, this comment, along with the comments from group B, could be considered neutral. We did not consider making a neutral class as it was not part of the original teacher evaluation, which only has two types of comments. Creating a new class might allow what we call neutral comments from Figure 2 group B to be correctly classified, but it can also lead to misclassifying positive and negative comments as we might introduce noise to those classes by subtraction of Groups A and B's sample size and possibly removing key instances that help correctly classify all instances in Group A.

CONCLUSION

In this work, it was understood that document classification covers many other areas of knowledge, including natural language processing. These methods are not recent since they have been used for many years but still have a long work to be done, especially in terms of semantics and detecting context.

During this study, opinion mining techniques were applied to a database of student comments emitted during the university's teacher evaluation period. These comments correspond to four years, 20 subjects, and five professors. So, a series of steps were taken that went from collecting comments, applying natural language processing techniques to those comments, we took those comments and built a database of vectors to represent them, and we utilized those vectors for training and testing two classifiers.

The use of opinion mining is the science of analyzing text to understand users' feelings about a teacher. By exploring student sentiments about a teacher, a strategy can be made to uncover weaknesses and strengths areas in the way a teacher carries out their class. Even though we can find all positive comments about a teacher, we cannot guarantee those comments will contain relevant information to suggest an improvement to be made by the teacher and will require further human analysis to find improvement ideas.

The results showed that, among the classifiers Bagging and 1-NN, the most accurate was Bagging with which a classification accuracy of 80.13 could be achieved. Also, it was observed that errors were produced by a series of comments that were labeled as positive or negative, but are characterized as comments that could be considered neutral; therefore we could try adding a third class for neutral comments, barring we end up with a class disbalance. We can also continue working on adding more real comments to our dataset of comments and seeing if the global accuracy increases.

Future work will try to integrate the Stanford University CoreNLP library to help with word dependencies and identify entities such as people, places, and organizations. Also, a new comment class label, called neutral, might be added to allow comments shown in their own group to be correctly classified.

REFERENCES

Amazon Web Services. (2018). *Big Data on AWS*. Retrieved from https://aws.amazon.com/big-data/

Aspectiva. (2019). *Aspectiva About Us*. Retrieved from Aspectiva: https://www.aspectiva.com/company/

Brandwatch. (2019). Retrieved from https://www.brandwatch.com/about/

Cortizo, J. C. (2019). *Mineria de Opiniones*. Retrieved from BrainSINS: https://www.brainsins.com/es/blog/mineria-opiniones/3555

Freeling. (2019). *Freeling: FreeLing Home Page*. Retrieved from http://nlp.lsi.upc.edu/freeling/node/1

Google. (2018). *Sentiment Analysis Tutorial*. Retrieved from https://cloud.google.com/natural-language/docs/sentiment-tutorial

Gutiérrez, G., Ponce, J., Ochoa, A., & Álvarez, M. (2018). Analyzing Students Reviews of Teacher Performance Using Support Vector Machines by a Proposed Model. In C. Brito-Loeza & A. Espinosa-Romero (Eds.), *Intelligent Computing Systems*. *820* (pp. 113–122). Springer International Publishing AG. doi:10.1007/978-3-319-76261-6_9

Huddy, G. (2017). *What Is Sentiment Analysis? The importance of understanding how your audience feels about your brand*. Retrieved from https://www.crimsonhexagon.com/blog/what-is-sentiment-analysis/

Jadhavar, R., & Komarraju, A. K. (2018). Sentiment Analysis of Netflix and Competitor Tweets to Classify Customer Opinions. *SAS Global Forum*. Retrieved from https://www.sas.com/content/dam/SAS/support/en/sas-global-forum-proceedings/2018/2708-2018.pdf

Jiménez, R., García, V., Florencia-Juárez, R., Rivera, G., & López-Orozco, F. (2018). Minería de opiniones aplicada a la evaluación docente de la Universidad Autónoma de Ciudad Juárez. *Research in Computing Science*, *147*(6), 167–177. doi:10.13053/rcs-147-6-13

Liu, B., & Hu, M. (2004). *Opinion Mining, Sentiment Analysis, and Opinion Spam Detection*. Retrieved from https://www.cs.uic.edu/~liub/FBS/sentiment-analysis.html

Meaning Cloud. (2019). *General questions*. Retrieved from Meaning Cloud: https://www.meaningcloud.com/

Meltwater. (2019). *About Meltwater*. Retrieved from Meltwater: https://www.meltwater.com/about/

Merriam-Webster. (2019). *Opinion*. Retrieved from Merriam-Webster Dictionary: https://www.merriam-webster.com/dictionary/opinion

Microsoft. (2019). *Natural Language Processing*. Retrieved from https://www.microsoft.com/en-us/research/group/natural-language-processing/

Molina-GonzálezD.Martínez-CámaraE.Martín-ValdiviaM.Perea-OrtegaJ. (2013). *iSOL*. Retrieved from http://timm.ujaen.es/recursos/isol/

Narayanan, V., Arora, I., & Bhatia, A. (2016). *Fast and accurate sentiment classification using an enhanced Naive Bayes model*. Retrieved from http://sentiment.vivekn.com/about/

National Institute of Statistics and Geography. (2017). *State of mind of the tweeters in the United Mexican States*. Retrieved from http://internet.contenidos.inegi.org.mx/contenidos/Productos

Opitz, D. (1999). *Bagging Classifiers*. Retrieved from Popular Ensemble Methods: An Empirical Study: https://www.cs.cmu.edu/afs/cs/project/jair/pub/volume11/opitz99a-html/node3.html

Revuze. (2018). *Revuze Products*. Retrieved from http://revuze.it/product/

See, A. (2016). *Nearest Neighbors.* Retrieved from Stanford Computer Science: https://cs.stanford.edu/people/abisee/nn.pdf

Smeureanu, I., & Bucur, C. (2012). Applying Supervised Opinion Mining Techniques on Online User Reviews. *Informações Econômicas, 16*(2), 81–91.

Universidad Autonoma de Ciudad Juarez. (2019). *Universidad Autonoma de Ciudad Juarez.* Retrieved from https://www.uacj.mx/sa/ed/Paginas/default.aspx

WEKA. (2020). *What is Weka.* Retrieved from University of Auckland School of Computer Science: https://www.cs.auckland.ac.nz/courses/compsci367s1c/tutorials/IntroductionToWeka.pdf

This research was previously published in the Handbook of Research on Natural Language Processing and Smart Service Systems; pages 427-444, copyright year 2021 by Engineering Science Reference (an imprint of IGI Global).

Section 4
Utilization and Applications

Chapter 67
A Survey on Implementation Methods and Applications of Sentiment Analysis

Sudheer Karnam
VIT University, India

Valarmathi B.
VIT University, India

Tulasi Prasad Sariki
VIT University, India

ABSTRACT

Sentiment analysis also called opinion mining, and it studies opinions of people towards products and services. Opinions are very important as the organizations always want to know the public opinions about their products and services. People give their opinions via social media. With the advent of social media like Twitter, Facebook, blogs, forums, etc. sentiment analysis has become important in every field like automobile, medical, film, fashion, stock market, mobile phones, insurance, etc. Analyzing the opinions and predicting the opinion is called sentiment analysis. Sentiment analysis is done using opinion words by classification methods or by sentiment lexicons. This chapter compares different methods of solving sentiment analysis problem, algorithms, its merits and demerits, applications, and also investigates different research problems in sentiment analysis.

INTRODUCTION

The Research of sentiment analysis focused mainly on three methods. 1. *Supervised learning methods 2. Extracting Syntactic relations 3.Sentiment Lexicons* but two other methods were also used to less extent *1.genetic algorithms 2.Neural Networks*. One more classification of research on sentiment analysis *1. Document level 2.Sentence level 3.Aspect level*. Supervised learning mostly works on document level.

DOI: 10.4018/978-1-6684-6303-1.ch067

Sentiment lexicons can be implemented on Aspect as well as sentence level. Document level sentiment analysis dealt with one entity Ex: Movie reviews. Document level sentiment analysis is basically a text classification problem where classifier classifies documents of different topics like politics, sciences, sports, Finance etc. whereas Document level sentiment analysis classifies document into positive or negative. Sentence level sentiment analysis deals with *subjective* and *objective* sentences. Subjective sentences express opinions whereas objective sentence expresses facts. *Aspect level sentiment analysis* deals with multiple entities and their features Ex: In Forums, blogs where different entities are compared on their features, Ex The voice quality of mobile is good, Sony's camera is good compared with Samsung. Lot of Papers has published on the topic of research extracting entity and its aspects (Hu et al., 2004; Kamps et al., 2004). *Supervised learning methods* (Pang et al., 2002) extracts unigram (words) bigram features from the reviews . Features may be sentiments words, Or Parts of speech tag. Many authors discussed about different methods of generation of feature set and applied different machine learning techniques. But many algorithms won't work for cross domains because of language constructs. Yet another area of research in Sentiment analysis is cross language. Kim and Hovy (2006) experimented in translating German e-mails to English and applying English sentiment words to determine semantic orientation. *Sentiment lexicon* uses opinion phrases and words and builds a dictionary based on the synonyms and antonyms of word net. Opinion of the sentence can be found by the number of adjective opinions, verb opinions and their polarity (Kamps et al., 2004). Sentiment analysis finds application in many area like healthcare, automobile, students, feedback analysis, politics, etc (Seki et al., 2016; Ullah, 2016).

Sentiment Analysis Process

Sentiment analysis process includes the steps as shown in Figure 1. Reviews from different sources like blogs, social media, forums etc. are the product reviews. Sentiment identification captures sentiment words like good, great, disaster etc. from product reviews. Feature selection is used to find relevant features like unigrams, bigrams, trigrams etc. Sentiment classification and polarity is a process of classifying the source as positive or negative.

Sentiment Analysis Methods

Different methods for sentiment analysis are given in Figure 2. They are explained in detail in the rest of the paper. Analysis on the methods used in sentiment analysis is depicted in Figure 3.

MACHINE LEARNING TECHNIQUES

Naïve Bayesian Algorithm

Naïve Bayesian is used to fit a model for the data using bayes theorem. Naive Bayesian is based on the formula $P(c|d)=[P(c)P(d|c)]/P(d)$. Given set of Input features ($X=X_1, X_2, X_3,\dots$) the algorithm predicts the class label by finding the value of $p(C_k| X_1, X_2, X_3,\dots X_n)$ for each possible outcome. The outcome which has the maximum value will be the correct prediction p (C k | x 1, …, x n) {\displaystyle p(C_{k}\mid x_{1},\dots, x_{n})\,} p (C k | x 1, …, x n) {\displaystyle p(C_{k}\mid x_{1},\dots, x_{n})\,}

Maximum Entropy

Maximum entropy classification also called as MaxEnt Classifier is generally used in natural language processing and speech processing. In MaxEnt Classifier features are independent unlike in Naïve Bayesian classifier.it is based on the principle of Maximum entropy. Maximum entropy requires more time to train than naïve Bayesian classifier.

Figure 1. Sentiment analysis process

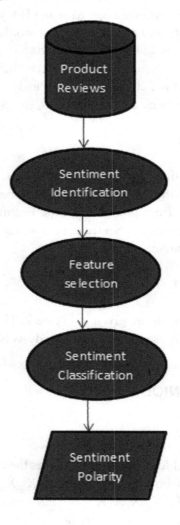

Figure 2. Different methodologies for sentiment analysis

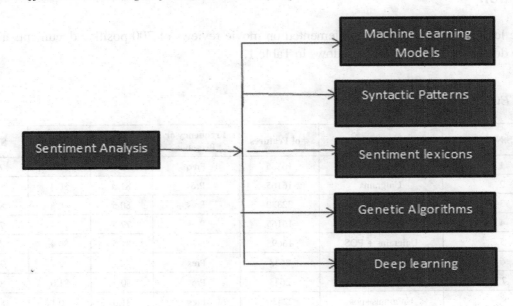

Figure 3. Analysis on different sentiment analysis methods

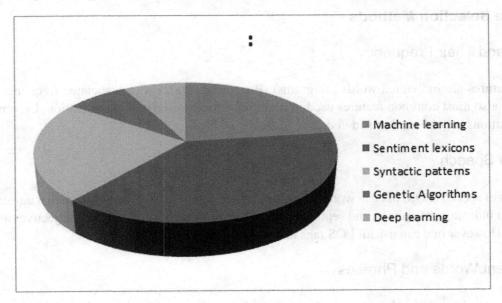

Support Vector Machines

Support vector machine is used to find the best hyper plane the divides the data into two classes. Best Hyper plane is the one in which distance from it to the nearest point is maximised. For nonlinear classifiers we use kernels to find the best hyper plane.

Evaluation

Machine learning algorithms are implemented on movie reviews of 700 positive documents and 700 negative documents. Results are as follows in Table 1.

Table 1. Evaluation results

S.No	Features	# of Features	Frequency or Presence	NB	ME	SVM
1	Unigrams	16165	Freq	78.7	N/A	72.8
2	Unigrams	16165	Pres	81.0	80.4	82.9
3	Unigrams bigrams	32330	Pres	80.6	80.8	82.7
4	Bigrams	16165	Pres	77.3	77.4	77.1
5	Unigrams + POS	16695	Pres	81.5	80.4	81.9
6	Adjectives	2633	Pres	77.-	77.7	75.1
7.	Top 2663 unigrams	2633	Pres	80.3	81.0	81.4
8.	Unigrams+pos	22430	Pres	81.0	80.1	81.6

Feature Selection Methods

Terms and Their Frequency

These features are individual words (unigrams) (Pang et al., 2002) with associated frequency counts. They are also most common features used in traditional, topic based text classification. In some cases, word positions may be also considered.

Parts of Speech

The parts of speech (POS) of each word is another class of features. It has been shown that adjectives are important indicators of opinion and sentiment. Thus some researchers have treated adjectives as special features. However one can use all POS tags and their n-grams as features.

Sentiment Words and Phrases

Sentiment words are natural features as they are words in a language for expressing positive or negative sentiments. Normally adjectives, verbs, will be considered as sentiment words. Other than individual words, there are likewise conclusion expressions and figures of speech for instance cost somebody dearly

Sentiment Shifters

These are expressions that are used to change sentiment orientation.

Ex: I don't like this camera

SENTIMENT LEXICON

Sentiment lexicon uses dictionary of lexical units such as Opinion words, phrases. Sentiment of it can be positive or negative. A limited number of reviewed sets, for example, emphatically positive, somewhat positive, unbiased, somewhat negative, firmly negative can be utilized. Ex: Phrases like excellent phone, good phone.

Methods for Building Lexicons

Manual Creation

Manually a set of adjectives and its polarity can be used as dictionary for sentiment analysis.

Automated Method

Initially a seed list of adjectives can be used and it can be expanded using word net by finding the synonym's and antonyms. While this is mostly used other method of extracting lexicons other ways of creating sentiment lexicons have also been explored such as boot strapping which learns pattern from corpus and doesn't require lexicon.

SentiwordNet

Sentiwordnet is a lexical resource for opinion mining .It assigns three scores positive, negative, neutral to a word. It augments word net with sentiment information.

For instance the scores for the synset superb are:

Pos(superb) = 0.75
Neg(superb) = 0.00
Obj(superb) = 0.25

Related Work in Sentiment Lexicon

Hi and Liu (2004) explained about mining opinion Features, Opinion words and its polarity using Frequent feature generation. First Opinion features are extracted using Noun phrases then Using frequent feature generation we need to find frequent item sets with three words or fewer having a support count of three.Using redundancy pruning redundant features will be removed, Opinion words will be extracted using nearby adjectives of opinion features and its polarity can be known by bootstrapping methods. Experiments have conducted on the Customer review of five electronics product. Human tagger was used to produce a manual list of features to compare with the results of the algorithm used in the paper. Results show that precision and recall at each stage of extraction has improved.

Kamps and Marx (2004) studied about word net to measure semantic orientations of Adjectives. WordNet has Synset which are synonyms of each word. The shortest distance $d(w_i, w_j)$ between any two words w_i and w_j is the length of the shortest path between w_i and w_j. The minimal distance $d(w_i, w_j)$ between words w and w_j says about the similarity.

EVA measures the relative distance of a word to the two reference words good and bad and finds the polarity $EVA(w) = (d(w, bad) - d(w, good)) / d(good, bad)$. Kim and Hovey (2004) finds the people who hold opinion on given topic and sentiment of the opinion. Given a topic and set of texts, the system first selects the sentence that contains topic phrase and holder candidates. Next the holder based region of opinion is delimited. At that point the sentence classifier computes the polarity of all sentiment bearing words separately. At long last the framework joins them to deliver the holder's conclusion for the entire sentence.

Hatzivassilollou (1997) used set of adjectives with known orientations and a corpus to find additional sentiment adjectives in the corpus.one of the rule says that co-joined adjectives usually have the same orientation. For example in the sentence "this mobile phone is beautiful and has good camera features" if beautiful is known to be positive it can be deduced that good camera features is also positive. Rules were also designed for other connectives, namely OR, BUT, EITHER-OR and NEITHER -NOR. This idea is called sentiment consistency

Sentiment Rating Prediction

Classifying opinion documents only as positive or negative may not be sufficient in some applications, where users may need the degree of positivity of negativity. For this purpose, researchers have studied the problem of predicting rating scores (1-5) of reviews (Pang & Lee 2005; Pang et al., 2005). In this case, the problem is typically formulated as regression because the rating scores are ordinal.

Comparative Sentences

Buing Lui (2008) studied about comparative sentences in identifying sentiment of sentence. **Ex** Camera X picture quality is better than camera Y. Clearly the preferable entity is camera X. Key work to be done here is to extract entities, comparatives and feature (Picture quality). Comparative word exists before two entities whereas Superlative word exists before one entity **Ex.** mobile X is the best. For simplicity Comparative words mean both comparative words and superlative words. Sometimes comparative world will not express any opinion **Ex:** Longer. He takes longer time to wake up. However in a particular context it expresses a positive sentiment. **Ex** The batter life of Camera X is longer than that of Camera Y. Program X time is longest than that of program Y. Here Longer is clearly negative. Preferred entity is program Y. So Comparative words are context dependent. Key problem in comparative sentences is finding the context and its polarity. An entity is a noun **Ex:** name of a person a product or company. A feature is adjective or an attribute that is being compared. For example in the sentence Camera X battery life is better than that of Camera Y. Camera X and Y is entities and battery life is the feature

Sarcastic Sentences

Sarcasm is a complex type of discourse act in which the speakers or the essayists say or compose the opposite they mean. Sarcasm is a sophisticated form of speech act in which the speakers or the writers say or write the opposite of what they mean. Tsur et al.(2010), a semi-supervised learning approach was used to identify sarcasms in the given text. The paper gives a number of nice examples of sarcastic titles of reviews for example

1. "I love the cover"(book)
2. Be sure to save your purchase receipt
3. "Great idea, now try again with a real product development team"(e-reader).

Sarcasm detection algorithm was proposed in Tsur et al. (2010)

SYNTACTIC PATTERNS

Each syntactic pattern is a sequence of POS tags with some need constraints Turney (2002).
Patterns of POS Tags for extracting two-word phrases.

Table 2. Syntactic pattern extraction

S.No	First Word	Second Word	Third Word
1	JJ	NN or NNS	Any thing
2	RB,RBR or RBS	JJ	NNS
3	JJ	JJ	Not NN nor NNS
4	NN or NNS	JJ	Not NN nor NNS
5	RB,RBR, or RBS	VB,VBD,VBN or VBG	Anything

The algorithm consists of three steps.

1. Two consecutive words are extracted if their POS tags conform to any of the pattern in above table. For example Pattern 1 means that two consecutive words are extracted if the first word is an adjective and second word is an noun, and the third word is anything. in the example, in the sentence "Ford Icon has superb engine". Superb engine will be extracted because it satisfies the first pattern. The reason these patterns used is that JJ, RB, RBR and RBS words often express opinions or sentiments.
2. The sentiment Orientation of the extracted phrases is estimated using PMI(Point wise mutual Information) measure:

PMI(term1,term2) = $\log_2$(PR(term1^ term2) / PR(term1) PR(term2)) where PR is the probability

PMI measures the statistical dependence between the two terms.

SO(Phrase) = PMI(phrase, "Excellent") – PMI(Phrase, "Poor")

The probabilities are calculated by giving queries to a search engine and collecting the number of hits

3.   Given a review, The Average SO score of all phrases in the given review is computed and the review is classified as positive if the average SO score is positive and negative otherwise.

GENETIC ALGORITHMS

Genetic algorithm works as mimic of human evolution. Initial population is generated by using set of bitstring. Then crossover and mutation is operated to get a new offspring. A fitness function is used to generate new population in which few candidates whose fitness is low will be removed from the population. This process is repeated until you get desired value. In Statistical and Evolutionary Approach to Sentiment Analysis by Carvalho, Prado, and Plastino (2014), a genetic algorithm was proposed for sentiment analysis.

DEEP LEARNING

Deep learning is an extension of neural networks. Neural networks has input layer one or more hidden layers and an output layers. Output is a non-linear function approximation. Each layer is connected to the next neighbouring layer with some weight. During training phase the desired output is compared with the predicted output then the resulting error is propagated backwards, so that weights can be adjusted. This can be done for a few number of iterations until a convergence is achieved, this algorithm is called back propagation. In deep learning we use deep neural network in which each input not only connects to its neighbouring layer but also connected to other layers also. In Hybrid Sentiment Classification method using Neural Network and Fuzzy Logic by Sathe and Mali (2017) back propagation algorithm was used for sentiment analysis.

APPLICATIONS OF SENTIMENT ANALYSIS

Opinion mining on News headlines using SentiWordNet was proposed by Agrawal and Vivk Sharma (Agarwal et al., 2016). SentiWordNet is used to classify each and every word in news headline and finds out total polarity of the sentence. Then total polarity of all the Headlines is calculated. Seki (2017) analysed public sentiment for improvement of local government service by using twitter. Operational test was done with local government officers and found meaningful for the public, such as avoiding full parking lots, finding potholes in the road, suggestions to improve the festivals. Bouazizi and Otsuki (Bouazizi et al., 2016) proposes a pattern based approach for sarcasm detection on twitter. Aroju and Bhargavi (2016) collected the quotations from websites of three popular newspaper dailies of India - The Hindu, The Times of India and Deccan Chronicle on an instance and proposed a methodology to annotate, label and calculate subjectivity and objectivity of quotations.

Generating Subjectivity Lexicons Using Genetic Algorithm for Subjectivity Classification of Big Social Data was proposed by Keshavarz (2016).The aim of this paper is to classify objective tweets and subjective words creating a subjective lexicon, Then the tweets were classified by using these meta features. Genetic algorithm was used for creating subjective words. Guo and Gupta (2018) used twitter to analyse the happiness of people in cities like jobs, children and transport. Natural language processing techniques were used to analyse the tweets in the Greater London area. Park and Kim (2016) have proposed Building Thesaurus Lexicon using Dictionary-Based Approach for Sentiment Classification. Sentiment classification using dictionary based methods will be done using the opinion words present in the dictionary but most of the times opinion words will not be present in the dictionary lexicon, so the lexicon is expanded by looking up the synomnns present in three online dictionaries.

Saini and Kohli (2016), analysed Tweets from twitter and classified into medical domain and non-medical domain, Bayesian classification model was used. In Predicting Movie Trailer Viewer's "Like/ Dislike" via Learned Shot Editing Patterns by Hou, Xiao and Zhang (2016) multiple features were extracted and predicted the feature which is mostly influenced by likes and dislikes of users using SVM and shot length variance is the most influenced feature. Jain, Sharma and Kaushal (2016) detected real time rumours on twitter automatically. Rumour is any information which is circulating in twitter and is not in agreement with the information from credible source. The approach has four steps. First extract live tweets corresponding to twitter trends, identify the topics being talked about in each trend and collect tweets for each topic. Secondly we segregate the tweets whether its tweeter is general user or verified news channel. Thirdly compare the contextual and sentiment mismatch between the tweets comprising of same topic from verified twitter account of news channel and general user. Lastly label the topic as rumour based on mismatch ratio.

Feature Extraction and Opinion Classification Using Class Sequential Rule on Customer Product Review by Nurrahmi and Maharani (2016) extracted the product features by using class Sequential rule and classify the opinion automatically. Movie Review Analysis: Emotion Analysis of IMDb Movie Reviews by Topal and Ozsoyoglu (2016) used IMDB or Amazon for reviews about movie and analysed with respect to their emotion content aggregated and projected onto a movie resulting in an emotional map for movie. One can then make a decision to which movie to watch next by selecting those movies which match his/her emotion pattern. Twitter sentiment analysis in health care using Hadoop and R by Gupta and Kohli (2016) used twitter to know the polarity of reviews of hospitals and the service provided by them, this will be useful for recommendation at the time of ailment.

Security Attack Prediction Based on User Sentiment Analysis of Twitter Data by Hernandez and Sanchez (2016) used twitter to collect the tweets from two sets of users those who use as a platform for expressing views and those who use to present contents related to security attacks on web. The above information can be used to predict whether there is possibility of an attack. Deep learning for Financial sentiment analysis on Finance news Providers by Day and Lee (2016) focuses on investigating the influence of using different financial resources to investment and how to improve the accuracy of forecasting through deep learning. AffinityFinder A System for Deriving Hidden Affinity Relationships on Twitter Utilizing Sentiment Analysis by Abdelmounaam, Daniel, and Smith (2016) developed Affinity finder a System present Affinity Finder, a system for automatically inferring potential friendship relationships (in terms of affinity) amongst Twitter users. The system collects and analyses tweets to derive relationship scores that reflect affinity degrees amongst Twitter users.

Sentiment analysis Twitter data: Case study on digital India by Mishra and Rajnish (2016) Uses dictionary based approach for classifying the tweets as positive or negative and overall polarity is determined. Sentiment analysis of student feedback, A study towards optimal tools by Ullah (2016) analysed the feedbacks of students in Facebook with the use of machine learning algorithms such as Support vector machines, Naive Bayes, and maximum entropy and calculates precision, accuracy. Using trigrams as features gives good precision. In Automatic Sentiment Detection in Naturalistic Audio by Kaushik, Sangwan, and Hansen (2015) explored extracting sentiment from natural audio sources. Generic methods for sentiment extraction generally use transcripts from a speech recognition system and process the transcripts using text based sentiment classifiers.

In Sentiment and Emotion Analysis for Social Multimedia: Methodologies and Applications by You (2016) analyse the social media sentiment analysis of visual and multimedia information analysis. An image is worth of thousand words. Data analysis system for online short video comments by Yang, Cao and Zhang (2016) extracted the short videos comment information from the internet, analyses the fetched information with machine learning techniques and provide results to the video providers for the utilisation of product improvement. Shukri, Yaghi, Aljarah, and Alsawalqah (2015) studied about sentiment analysis in automotive industry. They used Bayesian classification. Results show that BMW has good Positive polarity compared with Mercedes, Audi. Araujo Blaz, and Becker (2016) proposes a method to evaluate the sentiment contained in tickets for IT support.IT tickets involve errors, incidents, requests etc. In twitter sentiment analysis of online transportation service providers by Anastasia and Budi (2016) compared the customer satisfaction of GO-JEK and Grab two important transportation service providers in Indonesia using twitter. In the new eye of smart city: novel citizen sentiment analysis in twitter by Li1 and Ch'ng (2016) tweets from the people were analysed about the smart city monitoring and e-governance. Mutinomial naïve Bayesian classifier is used to build the sentiment classifier. Election Result Prediction Using Twitter sentiment Analysis by Ramteke and Godhia (2016) understands the user's opinion about politics. Thus political entities know their campaigning strategy, so sentiment analysis is used to know the public opinion about politics. Peng, Moh and Moh (2015) used twitter to know the adverse drug events(ADE) of any medicine .ADE may be sentiment about the drug like "this Medicine is terrible". This paper tells a simple method to classify and perform sentiment analysis on ADE's. Twitter sentiment analysis in Healthcare using hadoop and R by Gupta and Kohli (2016) used twitter to know the hospitals selected by the patients at the time of their sufferings and used as a recommendation system for the new patients to select the hospitals. Hadoop was used for the processing of Big data. Sentiment analysis of top India colleges in India using Twitter data by Mamgain, Mehta, and Mittal (2016) analysed the public opinion in twitter about top engineering colleges in India. A probabilistic model based on baye's theorem was used for spell correction and compares the results obtained using different machine learning algorithms like Naïve bayes, support vector machine and artificial neural networks. An ensemble sentiment classification system of twitter data for Airline Service analysis by Wan and Gao (2015) was to know the sentiment of the customers about airlines. Little work has been done on it. In this paper an ensemble sentiment classification strategy was applied.

Analysis on Applications of Sentiment analysis is shown in Figure 4.

Figure 4. Analysis on applications of sentiment analysis

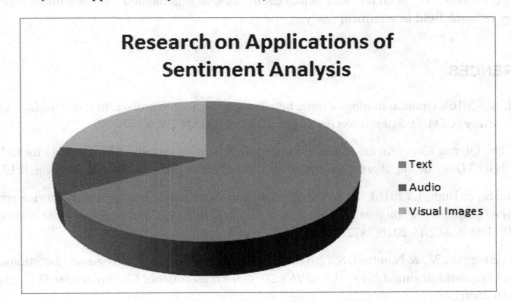

Table 3.Comparison of different methodologies used and applications

Reference	Methodology Used	Application	Data	Year
14,15,16	Lexicon based	Newspaper review	Text	2016
17	Genetic Algorithm	Tweets sentiment	Text	2016
18	Lexicon based	Sentiment of happiness in cities	Text	2016
20	Machine Learning(Naïve Bayesian model)	Health care application	Text	2016
21	Machine learning(SVM)	YouTube videos likes and dislikes	Text	2016
24	Machine learning	Movie trailer reviews	Text	2016
25	Lexicon based	E-health	Text	2016
27	Deep learning	Predicting stocks	Text	2016
30	Machine learning	Students feedback	Text	2016
31	Machine learning	Audio sentiment	Audio	2015
32,33,34	Machine learning	Visual images sentiment	Image	2016
36	Genetic algorithm	Health care	Text	2014

CONCLUSION

The sentiment analysis review was done by focusing the core areas of research, sarcasm, and comparative sentences and explored the different methods of implementing, its merits and demerits. Machine learning techniques and sentiment lexicons are key methods of implementation in sentiment analysis. As sentiment analysis is growing with the advent of social media, increasing the accuracy of the classifiers is still open research field. cross language sentiment analysis, cross domain sentiment analysis, domain dependent words is a key open research field. Feature set selection methods and Sentiment lexicons are also a key research field in sentiment analysis.

REFERENCES

Agarwal, A. (2016). Opinion mining of news headlines using SentiWordNet. In *Colossal Data Analysis and Networking (CDAN), Symposium on*. IEEE. 10.1109/CDAN.2016.7570949

an, Yun, and Qigang Gao. "An ensemble sentiment classification system of Twitter data for airline services analysis." *Data Mining Workshop (ICDMW), 2015 IEEE International Conference on*. IEEE, 2015.

Anastasia, S., & Budi, I. (2016). Twitter sentiment analysis of online transportation service providers. In *Advanced Computer Science and Information Systems (ICACSIS), 2016 International Conference on*. IEEE. 10.1109/ICACSIS.2016.7872807

Aroju, S., Bhargavi, V., & Namburi, S. (2016). Opinion mining on Indian newspaper quotations. In *Signal Processing and Integrated Networks (SPIN), 2016 3rd International Conference on*. IEEE. 10.1109/SPIN.2016.7566797

Blaz, C. C. A., & Becker, K. (2016). Sentiment analysis in tickets for IT support. In *Proceedings of the 13th International Conference on Mining Software Repositories*. ACM. 10.1145/2901739.2901781

Bouazizi, M., & Ohtsuki, T. O. (2016). A Pattern-Based Approach for Sarcasm Detection on Twitter. *IEEE Access: Practical Innovations, Open Solutions, 4*, 5477–5488. doi:10.1109/ACCESS.2016.2594194

Carvalho, J., Prado, A., & Plastino, A. (2014). A statistical and evolutionary approach to sentiment analysis. In *Proceedings of the 2014 IEEE/WIC/ACM International Joint Conferences on Web Intelligence (WI) and Intelligent Agent Technologies (IAT)* (vol. 2). IEEE Computer Society. 10.1109/WI-IAT.2014.87

Davidov, D., Tsur, O., & Rappoport, A. (2010, July). Semi-supervised recognition of sarcastic sentences in twitter and amazon. In *Proceedings of the fourteenth conference on computational natural language learning* (pp. 107-116). Association for Computational Linguistics.

Day, M.-Y., & Lee, C.-C. (2016). Deep learning for financial sentiment analysis on finance news providers. In *Advances in Social Networks Analysis and Mining (ASONAM), 2016 IEEE/ACM International Conference on*. IEEE. 10.1109/ASONAM.2016.7752381

Ganapathibhotla, M., & Liu, B. (2008, August). Mining opinions in comparative sentences. In *Proceedings of the 22nd International Conference on Computational Linguistics* (vol. 1, pp. 241-248). Association for Computational Linguistics.

Guo, W. (2016). Understanding happiness in cities using Twitter: Jobs, children, and transport. In *Smart Cities Conference (ISC2), 2016 IEEE International*. IEEE. 10.1109/ISC2.2016.7580790

Gupta, V. S., & Kohli, S. (2016). Twitter sentiment analysis in healthcare using Hadoop and R. In *Computing for Sustainable Global Development (INDIACom), 2016 3rd International Conference on*. IEEE.

Gupta, V. S., & Kohli, S. (2016). Twitter sentiment analysis in healthcare using Hadoop and R. In *Computing for Sustainable Global Development (INDIACom), 2016 3rd International Conference on*. IEEE.

Hatzivassiloglou, V., & McKeown, K. R. (1997, July). Predicting the semantic orientation of adjectives. In *Proceedings of the eighth conference on European chapter of the Association for Computational Linguistics* (pp. 174-181). Association for Computational Linguistics.

Hernández, A. (2016). Security attack prediction based on user sentiment analysis of Twitter data. In *Industrial Technology (ICIT), 2016 IEEE International Conference on*. IEEE. 10.1109/ICIT.2016.7474819

Hou, Y. (2016). Predicting movie trailer viewer's "like/dislike" via learned shot editing patterns. *IEEE Transactions on Affective Computing*, 7(1), 29–44. doi:10.1109/TAFFC.2015.2444371

Hu, M., & Liu, B. (2004, July). Mining opinion features in customer reviews. AAAI, 4(4), 755-760.

Jain, S., Sharma, V., & Kaushal, R. (2016). Towards automated real-time detection of misinformation on Twitter. In *Advances in Computing, Communications and Informatics (ICACCI), 2016 International Conference on*. IEEE. 10.1109/ICACCI.2016.7732347

Jindal, N., & Liu, B. (2006, July). Mining comparative sentences and relations. *AAAI*, 22, 1331-1336.

Kamps, J., Marx, M.J., Mokken, R.J., & Rijke, M.D. (2004). *Using word net to measure semantic orientations of adjectives*. Academic Press.

Kaushik, Sangwan, & Hansen. (2015). Automatic audio sentiment extraction using keyword spotting. *INTERSPEECH*.

Keshavarz & Abadeh. (2016). SubLex: Generating subjectivity lexicons using genetic algorithm for subjectivity classification of big social data. In *Swarm Intelligence and Evolutionary Computation (CSIEC), 2016 1st Conference on*. IEEE.

Kim, S. M., & Hovy, E. (2004, August). Determining the sentiment of opinions. In *Proceedings of the 20th international conference on Computational Linguistics* (p. 1367). Association for Computational Linguistics.

Ko, E., Yoon, C., & Kim, E. Y. (2016). Discovering visual features for recognizing user's sentiments in social images. In *Big Data and Smart Computing (BigComp), 2016 International Conference on*. IEEE.

Kwon, N., & Hovy, E. (2006, February). Integrating semantic frames from multiple sources. In *International Conference on Intelligent Text Processing and Computational Linguistics* (pp. 1-12). Springer Berlin Heidelberg.

Li, M. (2016). The new eye of smart city: Novel citizen Sentiment Analysis in Twitter. In *Audio, Language and Image Processing (ICALIP), 2016 International Conference on*. IEEE. 10.1109/ICALIP.2016.7846617

Mamgain, N. (2016). Sentiment analysis of top colleges in India using Twitter data. In *Computational Techniques in Information and Communication Technologies (ICCTICT), 2016 International Conference on*. IEEE. 10.1109/ICCTICT.2016.7514636

Medhat, W., Hassan, A., & Korashy, H. (2014). Sentiment analysis algorithms and applications: A survey. *Ain Shams Engineering Journal*, 5(4), 1093–1113. doi:10.1016/j.asej.2014.04.011

Mishra, P., Rajnish, R., & Kumar, P. (2016). Sentiment analysis of Twitter data: Case study on digital India. In *Information Technology (InCITe)-The Next Generation IT Summit on the Theme-Internet of Things: Connect your Worlds, International Conference on*. IEEE. 10.1109/INCITE.2016.7857607

Nurrahmi, H., Maharani, W., & Saadah, S. (2016). Feature extraction and opinion classification using class sequential rule on customer product review. In *Information and Communication Technology (ICoICT), 2016 4th International Conference on*. IEEE. 10.1109/ICoICT.2016.7571891

Pang, B., & Lee, L. (2005, June). Seeing stars: Exploiting class relationships for sentiment categorization with respect to rating scales. In *Proceedings of the 43rd annual meeting on association for computational linguistics* (pp. 115-124). Association for Computational Linguistics. 10.3115/1219840.1219855

Pang, B., Lee, L., & Vaithyanathan, S. (2002, July). Thumbs up? Sentiment classification using machine learning techniques. In *Proceedings of the ACL-02 conference on Empirical methods in natural language processing* (vol. 10, pp. 79-86). Association for Computational Linguistics. 10.3115/1118693.1118704

Park, S., & Kim, Y. (2016). Building thesaurus lexicon using dictionary-based approach for sentiment classification. In *Software Engineering Research, Management and Applications (SERA), 2016 IEEE 14th International Conference on*. IEEE. 10.1109/SERA.2016.7516126

Peng, Y., Moh, M., & Moh, T.-S. (2016). Efficient adverse drug event extraction using Twitter sentiment analysis. In *Advances in Social Networks Analysis and Mining (ASONAM), 2016 IEEE/ACM International Conference on*. IEEE. 10.1109/ASONAM.2016.7752365

Ramteke, J. (2016). Election result prediction using Twitter sentiment analysis. In *Inventive Computation Technologies (ICICT), International Conference on* (vol. 1). IEEE. 10.1109/INVENTIVE.2016.7823280

Ravi, K., & Ravi, V. (2015). A survey on opinion mining and sentiment analysis: Tasks, approaches and applications. *Knowledge-Based Systems*, *89*, 14–46. doi:10.1016/j.knosys.2015.06.015

Rezgui, A., Fahey, D., & Smith, I. (2016). Affinity Finder: A System for Deriving Hidden Affinity Relationships on Twitter Utilizing Sentiment Analysis. In *Future Internet of Things and Cloud Workshops (FiCloudW), IEEE International Conference on*. IEEE.

Saini, S., & Kohli, S. (2016). Machine learning techniques for effective text analysis of social network E-health data. In *Computing for Sustainable Global Development (INDIACom), 2016 3rd International Conference on*. IEEE.

Sathe, J. B., & Mali, M. P. (2017). A hybrid Sentiment Classification method using Neural Network and Fuzzy Logic. In *Intelligent Systems and Control (ISCO), 2017 11th International Conference on*. IEEE. 10.1109/ISCO.2017.7855960

Seki, Y. (2016). Use of Twitter for Analysis of Public Sentiment for Improvement of Local Government Service. In *Smart Computing (SMARTCOMP), 2016 IEEE International Conference on*. IEEE. 10.1109/SMARTCOMP.2016.7501726

Shukri, S. E. (2015). Twitter sentiment analysis: A case study in the automotive industry. In *Applied Electrical Engineering and Computing Technologies (AEECT), 2015 IEEE Jordan Conference on*. IEEE. 10.1109/AEECT.2015.7360594

Topal, K., & Ozsoyoglu, G. (2016). Movie review analysis: Emotion analysis of IMDb movie reviews. In *Advances in Social Networks Analysis and Mining (ASONAM), 2016 IEEE/ACM International Conference on*. IEEE. 10.1109/ASONAM.2016.7752387

Turney, P. D. (2002, July). Thumbs up or thumbs down?: semantic orientation applied to unsupervised classification of reviews. In *Proceedings of the 40th annual meeting on association for computational linguistics* (pp. 417-424). Association for Computational Linguistics.

Ullah, M. A. (2016). Sentiment analysis of students feedback: A study towards optimal tools. In *Computational Intelligence (IWCI), International Workshop on*. IEEE. 10.1109/IWCI.2016.7860361

Wang, Y., & Li, B. (2015). Sentiment analysis for social media images. In *Data Mining Workshop (ICDMW), 2015 IEEE International Conference on*. IEEE.

Yang, N., Cao, S., & Zhang, S. (2016). Data analysis system for online short video comments. In *Computer and Information Science (ICIS), 2016 IEEE/ACIS 15th International Conference on*. IEEE. 10.1109/ICIS.2016.7550946

You, Q. (2016). Sentiment and Emotion Analysis for Social Multimedia: Methodologies and Applications. In *Proceedings of the 2016 ACM on Multimedia Conference*. ACM. 10.1145/2964284.2971475

This research was previously published in Sentiment Analysis and Knowledge Discovery in Contemporary Business; pages 44-58, copyright year 2019 by Business Science Reference (an imprint of IGI Global).

Chapter 68

A Survey on Aspect Extraction Approaches for Sentiment Analysis

Vrps Sastry Yadavilli
National Institute of Technology, Tadepalligudem, India

Karthick Seshadri
ⓘ https://orcid.org/0000-0002-5658-141X
National Institute of Technology, Tadepalligudem, India

ABSTRACT

Aspect-level sentiment analysis gives a detailed view of user opinions expressed towards each feature of a product. Aspect extraction is a challenging task in aspect-level sentiment analysis. Hence, several researchers worked on the problem of aspect extraction during the past decade. The authors begin this chapter with a brief introduction to aspect-level sentimental analysis, which covers the definition of key terms used in this chapter, and the authors also illustrate various subtasks of aspect-level sentiment analysis. The introductory section is followed by an explanation of the various feature learning methods like supervised, unsupervised, semi-supervised, etc. with a discussion regarding their merits and demerits. The authors compare the aspect extraction methods performance with respect to metrics and a detailed discussion on the merits and demerits of the approaches. They conclude the chapter with pointers to the unexplored problems in aspect-level sentiment analysis that may be beneficial to the researchers who wish to pursue work in this challenging and mature domain.

INTRODUCTION

With tremendous growth of world wide web and internet, many users are interested to post reviews about a product in social blogs, merchant web sites and social networking sites. Analyzing and identifying emotions and opinions in this review text can give better insights about a product or service to manufacturers or buyers. Sentiment analysis identifies hidden emotion or opinions in the review text.

DOI: 10.4018/978-1-6684-6303-1.ch068

Sentiment analysis could be applied to each review document (document level sentiment analysis), or to each review sentence (sentence level sentiment analysis) or to each feature phrase (aspect level sentiment analysis). Sentiment analysis at document level deals with mining hidden sentiment in a document about a product. Sentence Level Classification identifies polarity labels such as positive, negative, neutral in each sentence. Aspect level sentiment analysis (ALSA) performs inference of opinions at a fine-grained level i.e., it extracts opinions about a feature of a product. Aspect level sentiment analysis mainly deals with three phases as shown in figure 1. (i) Aspect Extraction, (ii) Aspect Level Sentiment Inference and (iii) Opinion Summarization of extracted aspects.

Figure 1. A generic model for ALSA

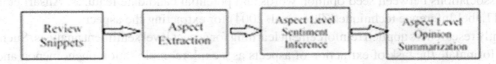

The aspect level sentiment inference refers to identification of opinion words e.g., adjectives, adverbs expressed towards each aspect. Aspect Level Opinion summarization is the process of summarizing opinions expressed towards each aspect as a statistical or textual summary. The following example outlines the phases of aspect level sentiment analysis. From the review snippet "This camera is cheap", extracting "price" is an aspect extraction task; inferring the opinion orientation of the aspect "price" as positive is referred to as the aspect level sentimental inference task; summarizing number of such opinions expressed towards the aspect "price" across all the review snippets is considered as the aspect level opinion summarization task. Out of the three tasks, aspect extraction is important and challenging since aspects can either be explicitly mentioned (explicit aspects) in the text or hidden in the text (implicit aspects). Aspect extraction can be thought of as an imbalanced classification problem because the distribution of product aspects over all sentences is not uniform, the users tend to specify few aspects very frequently, leaving some infrequent but popular aspects in review sentences. It is difficult to prepare enough training data to train a classifier to extract implicit aspects which requires extensive domain knowledge as they are implicitly stated in the text. So, extraction of such aspects can try to address the imbalanced data classification issue. Various approaches for aspect extraction are predominantly classified as follows.

- Unsupervised methods
- Supervised methods
- Semi-supervised methods
- Reinforcement Learning methods
- Soft Computing methods
- Hybrid methods

The unsupervised methods extract aspects based on manually curated rules or heuristics or using some statistical techniques. Hu et al. (2004) adopted association rule mining (Agarwal et al.,1994) to find frequent features in product reviews. Quan et.al. (2014) used a combination of PMI (Bouma et al.

(2009)) and TF-IDF (Salton et al. (1988)) to identify domain specific features. The features with a score above a preset threshold are declared as aspects. These methods are widely applied in sentiment analysis across various domains and languages.

The supervised methods use some predefined dictionary or machine learning or deep learning methods to perform aspect-oriented sentiment analysis. Kobayashi et al. (2007) used a seed opinion lexicon to get opinion words, Syntactic rules are used to find aspects from opinion words. Brychcín et al. (2014) proposed to extract aspects using a supervised machine learning framework called CRF (Lafferty et al. 2001) for extracting aspects.

The semi supervised methods use partially labelled data as a seed input to perform aspect level sentiment analysis. Such methods use bootstrapping, seed lexicon, graph based and word alignment-based techniques to perform aspect extraction. Wang et al. (2008) used bootstrapping to extract aspects by finding associations between seed opinion words and potential candidate features. Ansari et al. (2020) proposed Label Inference technique (Zhou et al. 2004) for extracting the aspects.

Recently researchers applied reinforcement learning for aspect level sentiment analysis. Such research attempts formulate the task of extraction of aspects as a explore-exploitation phenomenon and applied various reinforcement learning techniques like Hierarchal Reinforcement Learning, Deep Reinforcement learning to perform aspect level sentiment analysis. Wang et al. (2019) proposed to integrate LSTM (Hochreiter et al. 1997) and a Policy Network to perform aspect level sentiment classification.

Soft Computing methods consider the task of aspect extraction as an optimization problem and applied techniques like Ant Colony Optimization (J. Handl et al. 2006) and Particle Swarm Optimization (PSO) (Kennedy et al. 2001) to find an optimal subset of aspects. Gupta et al. (2015) adopted a PSO technique to extract noun phrases as an optimal set of aspects which maximizes the F-score of the sentiment classification task. Chifu et al. (2015) proposed to use ant colony optimization to cluster similar sentences and to extract potential aspects associated with the opinion words.

Hybrid approaches integrate two or more of the approaches cited above in hopes of obtaining a better performance. Wu et al. (2018) proposed to train a bi directional GRU (Cho et al. 2004) with dependency rules (Wu et al. 2009) to find dependencies between aspects and other opinion words through parsing. Ray et al. (2020) proposed to train a Convolution Neural Network (Kim Y. et al. 2014) with the dependency rules (Wu et al. 2009) to extract potential aspects from review snippets. In the subsequent sections the chapter outlines the technical details and merits and demerits of each of the approaches mentioned above.

CERTAIN TOOLS

WordNet (Fellbaum et al. 1998)

This dictionary maps the word pairs into their lexical relations such as synonym, hypernym and hyponym.

Senticnet (Cambria et al. 2016)

It is a sentiment polarity identification framework that can be used to assign polarity scores to various sentiment words.

Probase (Wu et al. 2012)

This framework infers various semantic relations between concepts such as cause-effect, hypernym-hyponym relationships.

Stanford Parser (Stanford, 2008)

This parser is used to find syntactic relationships between words such as amod (adjective modifier) and det (determiner).

Tweepy (Tweepy, 2009)

It is a python client library used to fetch tweets into an application.

Nltk (Nltk, 2002.)

This python library is used for performing various language processing tasks such as stemming and lemmatization.

Genism (Genism, 2009)

This python library is used for topic modelling and assorted language preprocessing tasks.

Spacy (Spacy, 2015)

This python library is used for finding syntactic dependencies through dependency parsing and parts of speech tagging.

ASPECT EXTRACTION APPROACHES

This section outlines the seminal aspect extraction approaches found in the literature.

Unsupervised Methods

The Unsupervised Approaches are classified into the following:

- Frequency Based Methods
- Bootstrapping Based Methods
- Statistical Methods.
- Rule Based Methods

Frequency Based Methods

Hu et al. (2004) proposed to extract aspects based on frequent feature identification as shown in Figure 2. Nouns were treated as potential features. Frequent features having frequency greater than a threshold were considered as aspects using association rule mining (Agarwal et al.1994) and discarded those reviews containing infrequent features. Adjectives were considered as opinion words and sentimental inference of each aspect was done by locating nearby adjectives. The sentiment classification of each opinion word (i.e., positive, negative, neutral) was done using Wordnet (Fellbaum et al. 1998), an opinion lexicon dictionary. After identifying opinion identification of sentences containing each aspect, opinion summary corresponding to each aspect was generated. This work operates based on the explicitly mentioned aspects in the reviews.

Moghaddam et al. (2010) proposed an unsupervised opinion miner framework to extract aspects from product reviews. Each word is labelled with its corresponding parts of speech tag and noun phrase stems are extracted using Porter's stemming algorithm (Willett et al. 2006). After pruning stop words, Apriori algorithm (Agarwal et al. 1994) is applied on noun phrases to extract frequent multipart noun phrases. Then for each noun phrase adjectives are extracted as opinion words using K-nearest neighbor (K-NN) algorithm and subsequently the sentiment expressed towards each aspect is inferred. Sentimental inference of each aspect across all the sentences in the review snippet is done and subsequently converted into a rating in the range of 1 to 5.

Figure 2. Aspect extraction using association rule mining

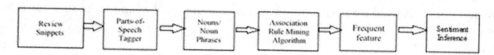

Eirinaki et al. (2012) proposed a High Adjective Count (HAC) algorithm to extract potential features. The algorithm takes review snippets as input, converts the snippets into sentences. Nouns are extracted as features and the nearest adjectives to each feature in a sentence is counted; the features with a high nearest adjective score are regarded as important features. Subsequently, the important features are input to the Max Opinion Score Algorithm, which computes a feature's polarity score as an average opinion score of all nearby adjectives over all the sentences.

Marrese-Taylor et al. (2014) have proposed to use parts of speech tagging and frequent item set mining to extract aspects from sentences. Given review snippets, nouns/noun phrases are extracted from reviews and frequent set mining is adopted (Agrawal et al. 1994) to collect noun phrases with above support threshold as aspects. The opinion orientation of each aspect is inferred as the sum of the opinion scores of nearby adjectives. across all the sentences.

Li et al. (2015) proposed to perform aspect extraction in three phrases namely Frequent Itemset Mining, Order based pruning and Similarity based pruning. Frequent Itemset Mining (Agarwal et al. 1994) is applied on the noun phrases in the review snippet to extract frequent noun phrases with a support greater than a preset threshold as aspects. The term order in each aspect is verified and aspects with irrelevant term order are pruned. Finally, the authors computed the similarity between each aspect and product name, the aspects having high similarity score are retained as final aspects.

Chauhan et al. (2018) prepared a domain specific contextual opinion lexicon, which is a dictionary of opinion words. The noun phrases which are nearer to these opinion words and having frequency greater than threshold are considered as aspects. Subsequently a dependency parser (Stanford, 2008.) and CRF (Lafferty et al. 2001) are used to perform aspect level sentiment classification.

Bootstrapping Based Methods

Bootstrapping based methods consider a seed aspect keyword list to recognize frequently associated opinion words with them. New aspects are also recognized in a similar way with available opinion words as shown in Figure 3.

Bagheri et al. (2013) proposed a bootstrapping algorithm to extract aspects using a seed list of aspect terms. Review snippets are taken as inputs, and multi word terms containing nouns and adjectives are extracted as multi word aspects. FLR score (Nakagawa et al. (2003)) is then calculated to quantify the importance of each multi word aspect term. The top k terms are then extracted as potential aspects. A-Score metric was designed and used to find the correlation between the extracted aspects and product.

Irrelevant aspects with correlation less than a threshold are pruned. Aspects which are invalid (i.e., terms those are not related to the product) are pruned.

Figure 3. Aspect extraction using bootstrapping

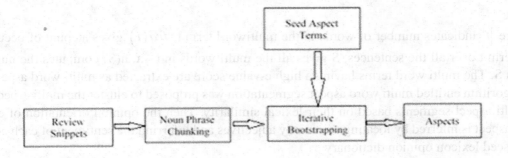

Statistical Methods

These methods use statistical techniques Like PMI, TF-IDF to extract aspects as shown in Figure 4.

Figure 4. Aspect extraction using statistical methods

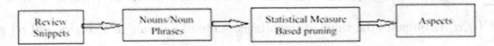

Raju et al. (2009) considered noun phrases from review snippets as aspects and filtered noun phrases that begin with determiner words like "other", "yours", "those" etc. KL divergence (Tomokiyo et al. 2003) between a noun phrase and review corpus to estimate the importance score of each noun phrase is measured. The KL Divergence between two probability distributions P, Q can be computed as given in equation (1) (Tomokiyo et al. 2003).

$$D_{KL}(P \| Q) = \sum_{x \in X} P(x) \log \frac{P(x)}{Q(x)} \dots\dots\dots \tag{1}$$

In equation (1), P, Q are two probability distributions defined on the probability space X.

They clustered the Noun phrases using the Group Average Agglomerative Clustering (GAAC) (Kaufman et al.1999) with the degree of overlap in the number of N-grams as a similarity measure. Finally, those noun phrases with high N-gram overlap scores are extracted as aspects from each cluster.

Zhu et al. (2011) proposed to extract multi word aspect terms using c-value score (Frantzi et al. 2000). The proposed Multi Aspect Bootstrapping algorithm takes review snippets as input, and extracts multi word terms and then it calculates the c-value score (Frantzi et al. 2000) of each multi word term. The c-value score is calculated as given in equation (2) (Frantzi et al. 2000).

$$c-value(t) = \log|t| . frq(t) . - \left(\frac{1}{n(S)}\right) \sum_S freq(S). \ldots\ldots \quad (2)$$

where $|t|$ .indicates number of words in the multiword term t, $frq(t)$ .gives a count of occurrences of the term t over all the sentences, S gives all the multi words in t .t, n(S) computes the number of terms in S. The multi word terms having a high c-value score are extracted as multi word aspects. Another algorithm entitled multi word aspect segmentation was proposed to cluster the multi aspect words into multi aspect segments based on their lexical similarity. Then the opinion orientation of each extracted aspect is inferred by locating the nearby adjectives and inferring the sentiment of each adjective using a seed lexicon opinion dictionary

Quan et.al. (2014) proposed to use PMI-TFIDF measure to measure the correlation between noun phrase and product term as given in equation (3) (Quan et.al. (2014)).

$$PMI\text{-}TFIDF \ (p, q) = \quad . \log \frac{pr(p,q). \sum_k TFIDF(p,d_k) \sum_k TFIDF(q,d_k)}{pr(p).pr(q)} \ . \ldots\ldots \quad (3)$$

$pr(p,q)$ .denotes the probability of both the terms p, q cooccurring with each other in the review corpus. $\sum_k TFIDF(p,d_k)$ .gives the value of significance score of a term p in a corpus. $\sum_k TFIDF(q,d_k)$ .computes the value of importance score of a term q in a corpus, $pr(p)$ .gives frequency estimate of the term p over all terms in a corpus. . $pr(q)$ .denotes frequency estimate of term q over all terms in a corpus The noun phrases with correlation scores greater than a threshold are extracted as domain specific aspects. Each sentence is represented in the form of a dependency tree using a dependency parser. aspect, opinion pairs using Dependency rules are used to extract aspects-opinion pairs. The opinion words with a less PMI-TFIDF score are filtered out from the list of Opinion words.

Rule Based Methods

These methods adopt parser-based dependency rules (Wu et al. 2009) to extract aspects as shown in Figure 5.

Figure 5. Aspect extraction using dependency rules

Poria et.al. (2014) proposed to use dependency rules to extract aspects from reviews. Each sentence is represented in the form of a dependency parse tree using the Stanford parser (Stanford,2008.) and lemmatization is then applied on each sentence. Nouns are then extracted from reviews and considered as explicit aspects. They have clustered aspects which are synonyms of one another provided by wordnet (Fellbaum et al. 1998). Opinion words are identified with the help of a seed opinion lexicon dictionary and the relation between each aspect and opinion word is determined using manually curated rules.

Rana et al. (2017) proposed to take Annotated reviews with parts of speech tags are taken as input and then adjectives, frequent nouns / noun phrases are extracted using manually preset rules. Similarity between two noun phrases is measured using the Normalized Google Distance (NGD) as specified in equation (4) (Cilibrasi et al.2007).

$$NGD(x,y) = \frac{max\{\log f(x),\log f(y)\} - \log f(x,y)}{\log N - \min\{\log f(x),\log f(y)\}} \dots\dots\dots\dots \quad (4)$$

The NGD between two noun phrases x and y is calculated as a function of number of web pages on which both noun phrases occur ($f(x,y)$) and number of web pages on which each noun phrases occur

Table 1. Summary of unsupervised methods

Author Name	Year	Method Used	Dataset	Language	Precision (%)	Recall (%)
Hu, M., & Liu, B.	2004	Frequency based	Product Reviews (Amazon, 1996a.)	English	53	49
Raju, S.	2009	Frequency based	Product Reviews (Amazon, 1996b.)	English	67	61
Moghaddam, S.	2010	Frequency based	Product Reviews (Epinions,1999.)	English	80	87
Zhu, J.	2011	Boot Strapping	Product Reviews (DianPing, 2010.)	English	69	56
Eirinaki, M.	2012	HAC	Product Reviews (Bing et al. 2004)	English	82	85
Bagheri, A.	2013	Bootstrapping	Product Reviews (Amazon, 1996a.)	English	81	68
Marrese-Taylor, E.	2014	Frequency based	Tourism Reviews (Tripadvisor,2000.)	English	90	93
Poria, S.	2014	Rule based	Product Reviews (Bing et al. 2004)	English	89	91
Quan, C.	2014	PMI	Product Reviews (Bing et al. 2004)	English	84	91
Li, Y.	2015	Bootstrapping	Product Reviews (Bing et al. 2004)	English	95	88
Rana, T.	2017	Two-fold rule based	Product Reviews (Bing et al. 2004)	English	87	92
Chauhan, G.S.	2018	Contextual opinion Lexicon + Dependency Parser	Product Reviews (Amazon,1996b.)	English	86	85

(f(x), f(y)) and the total number of web pages searched(N). The noun phrases are grouped using NGD. Each noun cluster is treated as a potential aspect.

Table 1 shows that Bootstrapping approach provides a high precision and moderate recall due to partial supervision in the form of the initial set of seed opinion words. The frequency-based methods achieve a low precision and recall on Product Reviews because less frequent but important terms are ignored by these methods. The rule-based methods achieve moderate precision and a high recall on product reviews since the performance of rule-based methods depends on the quality of the rules chosen.

Supervised Methods

The supervised methods generally adopted for aspect extraction are based on the following methods:

- Sequence labelling
- Machine learning
- Deep learning

Sequence Labelling Based Methods

Kobayashi et al. (2007) used dependency rules for extracting aspects. The opinion words are identified using a predefined seed lexicon dictionary. Subsequently the authors identified strength of association between extracted opinion words and noun phrases to collect aspects using their cooccurrence frequencies.

A lexicalized HMM model (Cutting et al. 1992.) was leveraged by Jin et al. (2009) for extracting aspect-opinion pairs and for performing aspect level sentiment classification. After tagging each word with its part-of-speech, a hybrid tag sequence is used to identify whether it is an opinion word or aspect with the help of HMM (Cutting et al. 1992). Adjectives that are in the vicinity of an aspect are retrieved as opinion words and sentences without any opinion word are pruned. The authors then performed sentimental inference of each opinion word using a seed opinion lexicon dictionary.

In a subsequent research work done by Li et al. (2010), Linear CRF (Lafferty et al. 2001), Skip Chain CRF (Sutton et al. 2006) and Skip tree CRF (Sutton et al. 2006) were employed for the aspect-opinion pair extraction. A CRF (Lafferty et al. 2001) is a probabilistic graphical model based on conditional distribution $p(z|t)$.as given in equation (5) (Lafferty et al. 2001).

$$P(z|t) = \frac{\exp\left(\sum_{k=1}^{l} U(t_k, z_k) . \sum_{k=1}^{l-1} V(z_k, z_{k+1})\right)}{Z(t)} \dots\dots\dots\dots(5).$$

z .gives a vector of random variables over class labels. t .gives observed feature vectors. $Z(t)$ .s a normalization factor. $V(z_k, z_{k+1})$ specifies how likely the label z_{k+1} .can be seen after the label z_k . $U(t_k, z_k)$ denotes the joint likelihood of the variable t_k .and the label z_k .

The authors adopted a Linear CRF to identify the polarity orientation between two continuous words, (i.e., if they are connected by the conjunction" and" the words represent similar sentiment polarity; however, if they are connected by" but" to the words are considered to have opposite polarities). Skip chain

CRF was used to model the semantic relationship between two text sequences which are connected by a conjunction having same parts of speech tag. A sentence is depicted in the form of a dependency tree using tree CRF. Finally, SkipTreeCRF is used to give a combined representation of these two structures Skip chain CRF and tree CRF to extract aspect and opinion pairs that are semantically connected by conjunctions and exhibit syntactic dependencies in a sentence.

Li et al. (2012) proposed to construct parse tree from each sentence using a dependency parser and by supplying opinion words as predicate list. The irrelevant opinion targets are pruned using some heuristic rules. Then the extraction of the potential opinion targets was considered as a binary classification problem to infer aspects.

Brychcín et al. (2014) proposed to extract aspects using CRF ((Lafferty et al. 2001) by labelling each sentence using BIO tagging. and opinion orientation of each aspect is determined by finding out opinion words occurring within a contextual window of ten words in each sentence. Given a predefined set of categories an implementation of maximum entropy binary classifier (Konkol et al. 2014) was used for determining each aspect category. Then aspect category of a sentence is taken as an assembled result of individual classifiers.

Machine Learning Based Methods

Agarwal et al. (2016) adopted information gain (Lerman et al. 1984) and minimum redundancy Maximum Relevance mrMR (Ding et al. 2005) measures for aspect extraction as given in equations (6) -(8) (Ding et al. 2005).

$$A = MI\left(f_m, c\right) = \sum_{f_m, c} p\left(f_m, c\right) \log \frac{p\left(f_m, , c\right)}{p\left(f_m, \right) . p\left(c\right)} \ldots \ldots (6) .$$

$$B = MI\left(f_i, f_j, \right) = \sum_{f_i, f_j} p\left(f_i, f_j, \right) \log \frac{p\left(f_i, f_j, \right)}{p\left(f_i, f_j, \right)} \ldots \ldots \ldots \tag{7}$$

'A' indicates the correlation between a feature f_m .and the class label c. 'B' denotes the correlation between two features namely f_i, f_j. Mutual Information Difference (MID) measure can be computed using equation (8) (Ding et al. 2005).

$$\text{MID (Mutual Information Difference)} = \max\left(A - B\right) \ldots \ldots \tag{8}$$

$$Information\, Gain\left(S, a\right) = H\left(S\right) - H\left(S|a\right) \ldots \ldots (9) .$$

$$H\left(S\right) = \sum_{I=1}^{C} - P_i \log P_i \ldots \ldots \ldots \ldots \ldots \ldots \ldots \ldots \ldots \tag{10}$$

In equation (9) (Lerman et al. 1984) H(S) is the entropy of dataset S before observing any feature. $H(S \mid a)$. denotes the entropy of S after observing the feature 'a'. In equation (10) (Lerman et al. 1984) P_i .refers to the probability of the class 'i'.The following types of features are extracted: (i) unigrams, (ii) bi-grams, (iii) bi-tagged and (iv) dependency features as shown in Figure 5. Clustering of features is done using the feature's semantic orientation for which Pointwise Mutual Information (Bouma et al. 2009) is adopted as a similarity measure. The feature scores are calculated using information gain and MID measures. Those features with a score greater than the threshold are extracted as prominent aspects.

Manek et.al. (2017) adopted a decision tree- based Gini index (Lerman et al. 1984) measure as the feature selection method for aspect extraction. The movie reviews are pre-processed, and features are extracted from the reviews. Each feature is weighted using Gini index measure as given in equation (11) (Lerman et al. 1984).

$$Gini\ index = 1 - \sum_i 1 - p_i^2 \ldots\ldots\ldots \tag{11}$$

Gini index measures the level of impurity i.e., a randomly chosen element is wrongly classified under a particular class. p_i indicates the probability that a variable is classified under the class 'i'. The top-k features for opinion classification are extracted based on these Gini index weights.

Deep Learning Based Methods

Figure 6. Aspect extraction using deep neural network

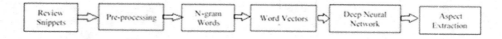

Wang et al. (2015) adopted a deep learning framework for extracting aspects as shown in Figure 6. Bag-of-words based sentence representation is given to a neural network which outputs a probability distribution over aspects. Then these word vectors are scaled based on aspects. CNN (Kim Y. et al. 2014) is then used to perform a convolution (Weighted Sum) operation on a window of 'h' sequential words. After iterating over all the words in a sentence, a feature vector is generated, then Max Pooling operation is performed to select the maximum value as a sentiment orientation associated with each aspect.

Ma et.al. (2018) adopted a Hierarchal LSTM (Hochreiter et al. 1997) for extracting the aspects. Each word in a sentence is converted to its word embeddings (Mikolov et al. 2013). These word vectors are fed into a LSTM network (Hochreiter et al. 1997) which converts the embeddings into a sequence of hidden outputs. A target level attention (Bahdanau et al. 2014) is proposed to obtain a target vector to identify corresponding target expressions (opinion expressions). The aspect embeddings and target vectors are concatenated to represent a sentence vector for each aspect-target pair. Subsequently, this representation is given to a SoftMax layer for sentiment classification. The authors incorporated common sense knowledge from SenticNet (Cambria et al. 2016) to enhance the accuracy of sentiment classification.

Table 2. Summary of supervised methods

Author Name	Year	Method Used	Dataset	Language	Precision (%)	Recall (%)	Limitation of Methodology
Kobayashi, N.	2007	Dependency Tree	Product Reviews (Amazon, 1996a .)	Japanese	72	62	Sentence needs to follow predefined dependency grammar
Jin, W.	2009	Lexicalized HMM	Camera Reviews (Amazon, 1996b.)	English	75	70	Does not deal with out of vocabulary words
Li, F.	2010	Skip tree-CRF	Movie Reviews (Amazon, 1996a.)	English	86	69	Expensive to train
Li, S.	2012	Shallow Semantic Parsing	Web Services (Mitre,1958.)	English	89	52	It takes more processing time to build the semantic graph
Brychcín, T.	2014	CRF+MaxEntropy Classifier	Product Reviews (Cornell,2002.)	English	77	82	Expensive to train
Wang, B.	2015	MLP+CNN	Product Reviews (Cornell,2002.)	English	52	50	Performance degrades when reviews are not available while testing
Agarwal, B.	2016	Information Gain+mrMR	Movie Reviews (Cornell,2002.)	English	78	65	It overfits the model when there are several unique values for an attribute
Manek, A. S	2017	Gini Index+NB+SVM	Movie Reviews (Cornell,2002.)	English	80	81	Time Complexity in building ensemble architecture is quite high.
Ma, Y.	2018	Hierarchal LSTM	Product Reviews (Cornell,2002.)	English	82	81	Requires an extensive training set.

Table 2 shows that we can observe that the shallow semantic parsing-based method achieves a high precision but suffers from a low recall. An ensemble of classifiers achieves a high precision and recall. Deep learning models like Hierarchal LSTM achieves a high precision and recall for the sentiment classification task, as Hierarchal LSTMs are good at sequence modeling which can remember long range dependencies between aspects and opinion words

Semi-Supervised Methods

The semi-supervised approaches for aspect extraction are normally classified as follows:

- Bootstrapping based methods
- Word alignment-based methods

- Graph based methods.

Bootstrapping Based Methods

Wang et.al. (2008) proposed a modified mutual information (Church et al. 1990) measure to find strength of correlation between aspects and opinion words. A seed opinion lexicon is used to identify correlated noun phrases(aspects). Subsequently these aspects are used to generate correlated opinion words. Subsequently aspects with low frequency are pruned by applying some linguistic rules. Implicit aspects are mapped to explicit aspects with the help of opinion words.

Wu et al. (2009) proposed to represent each sentence in the form of a dependency tree using a dependency parser (Stanford, 2008). Adjectives are taken to be the opinion words located near frequent nouns(aspects). After constructing a dependency parse tree, a separate kernel function (Culotta et al. 2004) is adopted to find the lowest common ancestor of aspects and opinion words to identify the relation between them. A kernel function was incorporated into SVM (Mullen et al. 2004) for finally performing an aspect level sentiment classification.

Qiu et.al. (2009) adopted double propagation for the task of aspects and opinion words extraction. The authors have considered a seed opinion lexicon to recognize noun phrases, which have close association with this opinion words. These noun phrases are termed as aspects. The new opinion words are extracted which are closely associated with these aspects. The same procedure is repeated until no new aspects, opinion words are found. As this process propagates through both opinion words and aspects, it is referred to as "Double Propagation".

Zhang et al. (2010) introduced additional patterns like whole-part pattern, no pattern to improve the performance of double propagation. The whole-part relationship is identified to exist between a product and an aspect. For instance, consider the review snippet, "the location of the hotel", whole-part relationship exists between the entity "hotel" and the aspect "location". The "no pattern" is adopted to identify aspects. For example, in the review snippet "no color"," color" is the aspect followed by "no" keyword". HITS algorithm is used (Kleinberg et al. 1999) to measure importance score of aspects and the aspects are finally ranked based on their important scores.

Yu et.al. (2011) recognized the nouns/noun phrases using a Sandford Parser (Stanford, 2008) Then a synonym-based clustering is performed on the aspects. The frequency of each aspect is estimated in reviews expressing both positive and negative sentiments and the opinion orientation of each aspect over all reviews.

d is known as damping factor, typically has value equal to 0.85, N indicates the total count of vertices in a graph. $M(p_i$ indicates number of edges connected to the vertex p_i. $L(p_j)$ denotes the number of outgoing edges the vertex p_j an have. The features with an importance score above a predefined threshold are considered as aspects. The authors expanded each aspect term using a seed synonym lexicon dictionary and identified potential implicit aspects from the expanded synonym sets.

Ansari et.al. (2020) adopted a graph-based approach for aspect extraction task. Each word in reviews is represented as a feature vector containing features such as frequent terms, orthogonal features, stop words etc. which are used as clues for potential aspect terms. Similarity between feature vectors is estimated and a K-nearest Neighbor graph is constructed. Subsequently, some of the terms are labelled as aspects and Label Propagation algorithm (Zhou et al. 2004) is adopted to infer whether a word is an aspect or not.

Table 3. Summary of semi-supervised methods

Author Name	Year	Method Used	Dataset	Language	Precision (%)	Recall (%)
Wang, B.	2008	Bootstrapping	Product Reviews (it168,2017.)	Chinese	56	49
Wu, Y.	2009	Dependency Parsing	Product Reviews (Bing et al. 2004)	English	57	44
Qiu, G.	2009	Double Propagation	Product Reviews (Bing et al. 2004)	English	70	60
Zhang, L.	2010	Rules +Double Propagation	Product Reviews (Bing et al. 2004)	English	72	54
Yu, J.	2011	Shallow Dependency Parser	Product Reviews (cnet, 1994.)	English	68	81
Hai, Z.	2012	Bootstrapping	Product Reviews (Crunchbase, 2015.)	English	68	81
Liu, K.	2013	Word Alignment Model	Product Reviews (Tripadvisor,2000.)	English	80	85
Xu, L.	2013	Partially Supervised Word Alignment Model	Product Reviews (Amazon,1996a.)	English	78	84
Ma, B.	2013	LDA + Seed Lexicon	Product Reviews (Bing et al. 2004)	English	75	73
Yan, Z.	2015	PageRank Model	Product Reviews (jd, 1998.)	English	80	70
Ansari, G.	2020	Label Propagation	Product Reviews (Bing et al. 2004)	English	70	68

Table 3 shows a summary of the different semi supervised methods for aspect extraction. The word alignment model gives an optimal precision and recall among all others. Although extended page rank method provides a good precision it suffers from a low recall because it filters out the terms with low page rank scores.

Reinforcement Learning Based Methods

Wang, T. et.al. (2019) proposed an aspect level sentiment classification using reinforcement learning. Each sentence was divided into segments and each segment is fed into Bi-LSTM (Hochreiter et al. 2004) to get hidden state vectors for each segment, then a multi-layer perceptron (MLP) was used to reduce the dimensionality of each segment hidden state vector and finally it was passed to SoftMax layer for sentiment prediction. Then aspect segments were extracted using a Policy Network which defines a policy for aspect segment extraction and LSTM (Hochreiter et al. 2004) was adopted for state representation. Then policy gradient (Sutton et al. 1999) was used to update the parameters of policy network and cross entropy (Li et al. (1993)) was used as a loss function.

Wang, J. et.al. (2019 b) proposed a hierarchal reinforcement learning (Sutton et al. 1999) for document level aspect sentiment classification. A two-level policy framework was used in which a high-level policy was used to select aspect specific clauses, the cosine similarity was used to select aspect specific clauses in a review sentence whereas low-level policy selects opinion words in each clause. Two LSTM (Hochreiter et al. 2004) networks were used for each of these policies.

Table 4. Summary of reinforcement learning based methods

Author Name	Year	Method Used	Dataset	Language	Precision (%)	Recall (%)
Wang, T.	2019	State Representation LSTM + Policy Network	Product Reviews (SemEval, 2014)	English	83	80
Wang, J.	2019	Hierarchal Reinforcement Learning + LSTM	Product Reviews (SemEval, 2014)	English	80	85

Table 4 shows that the SR-LSTM + Policy Network performs better than LSTM + Hierarchical Reinforcement Learning because the former extracts each aspect segment at a sentence level and assigns polarity to each aspect segment thus improves overall aspect level sentiment classification.

Soft Computing Based Methods

Gupta et al. (2015) proposed to apply PSO (Kennedy et al. 2001) for aspect extraction and CRF (Lafferty et al. 2001) for sentiment prediction. Each review sentence is labelled with the parts of speech tagging and a feature vector of each word is constructed with its context (preceding and following two words), prefix and suffix of length (up to three characters), orthographical features (a word is capitalized or not) etc. as features. Binary Particle Swarm Optimization (PSO) (Kennedy et al. 2001) technique is adopted to find an optimal set of aspects maximizing F-measure as an objective function. CRF (Lafferty et al. 2001) is applied for performing aspect level sentiment analysis. Their approach is domain independent in nature.

Chifu et al. (2015) proposed to apply ant colony optimization (J. Handl et al. 2006) technique to group similar sentences and extract potential aspects that are associated with opinion words. Extended neural network named Growing Hierarchical Self-Organizing Maps (Kohonen et al. 2012) is adopted to represent a hierarchal relationship between aspects and opinion words. The root node is a Product Name, Child nodes are aspect names, whereas the Leaf nodes are Opinion words (Positive, Negative Labels).

Rana, T. et al. (2015) proposed to label each review sentence with a parts of speech tagger, some sequential pattern rules (J. Pei et al. 2004) are used to find correlations between different words and opinion words. Google similarity distance (Cilibrasi et al. 2007) based method was adopted to find synonyms of the extracted aspects. The sets of aspects with a similarity value above a predefined threshold are given to Particle Swarm Optimization algorithm as input (Kennedy et al. 2001) to find an optimal set of aspect clusters.

Akhtar et.al. (2017) taken a set of aspects from a training set and an optimal set of aspects are obtained using PSO (Kennedy et al. 2001) solver with F-measure as the objective function. The three ensemble classifiers namely ME (Nigam et al. 1999), CRF (Lafferty et al. 2001) and SVM (Mullen et al. 2004) are used. A PSO based ensemble with a majority voting and PSO based ensemble with majority weighting methods are used to find a good subset of ensemble classifiers for an accurate sentiment prediction.

Table 5 shows that combining genetic algorithm with traditional aspect extraction approaches yields better results. Combining Conditional Random Field with Particle Swarm Optimization yields a high precision and nominal recall since the aspect and opinion word dependencies in a sentence are better captured through sequence labelling, thus improving the accuracy of the aspect level sentiment classification.

Table 5. Summary of soft computing based methods

Author Name	Year	Method Used	Dataset	Language
Gupta, D.	2015	CRF + PSO	Product Reviews (SemEval, 2014)	English
Chifu, E.	2015	ACO + GHSOM	Product Reviews (SemEval, 2014)	English
Rana, T.	2015	Rule based method + PSO	Product Reviews (Bing et al., 2004)	English
Akhtar,M.	2017	PSO + ensemble classifiers	Product Reviews (SemEval, 2014)	English

Hybrid Methods

Wu et al. (2018) extracted aspects using some dependency rules (Wu et al., 2009). Each review sentence is annotated with its parts of speech and noun phrases are extracted. The domain correlation of the extracted noun phrases is checked using cosine similarity between these phrases and product terms. The noun phrases are extracted as potential aspects which have a frequency greater than a threshold. These aspects are then converted into word embeddings (Mikolov et al., 2013) and are used in training a bidirectional GRU (Cho et al. 2004) for aspect extraction.

Ray et al. (2020) labelled each review sentence with its parts-of-speech. A skip-gram model (Mikolov et al., 2013) is adopted to convert each word into a 300-dimensional word vector. Then these word embeddings are fed into a 7-layer CNN (Kim et al., 2014) to predict the aspect categories in each sentence. CNN is trained with the Stanford dependency rules (Wu et al., 2009) for extracting aspects. Sentiwordnet (Cambria et al., 2014) is used for sentiment prediction. Sentiment scores of aspects are calculated using some predefined rules (Wu et al., 2009).

Chauhan et al. (2020) integrated linguistic rules and deep learning techniques to improve the accuracy of aspect extraction. The noun phrases are fetched from reviews and extended noun phrases are obtained using some linguistic rules. Then a frequency pruning step filtered out the infrequent nouns. Domain correlation pruning is done to prune domain irrelevant terms by measuring cosine similarity between aspects and product terms. Subsequently, these aspects are used to train a bi-directional LSTM network (Hochreiter et al., 1997) with attention (Bahadanu et al., 2014) mechanism for aspect extraction.

Table 6. Summary of hybrid methods

Author Name	Year	Method Used	Dataset	Language	Precision (%)	Recall (%)
Wu, C.	2018	Dependency Parser + Bi GRU	Product Reviews (SemEval, 2014)	English	63	73
Ray, P.	2020	Rule based method + CNN	Product Reviews (SemEval, 2014)	English	90	86
Chauhan, G. S.	2020	Rule based method + Bi LSTM	Product Reviews (SemEval, 2014)	English	68	75

Table 6 illustrates the hybrid methods. Combining two or more existing aspect extraction approaches can yield better results on aspect extraction compared to individual aspect extraction approaches. From the table we can infer that combining rule-based methods with CNN achieves a high accuracy and recall, since CNN can be suitable for finding minimal optimal set of features for sentiment classification.

FUTURE RESEARCH DIRECTIONS

In this section, we outline some research directions which can be pursued by researchers working in the domain of sentiment analysis.

Implicit Aspect Level Opinion Identification

Extracting implicit aspects from review snippets is a challenging task. This is because the user implicitly mentions the occurrence of aspects through opinion words. For example, the review snippet "The phone requires frequent charging" implicitly mentions the aspect "battery" and an opinion "negative" towards the aspect "battery". Extracting implicit opinions corresponding to implicit aspects is underexplored in the literature.

Dynamicity of Aspect Level Sentiment Inference

The preferences of users on different aspects of a product change over time as users change their opinions through their experience of using the product or by consulting with their friends or relatives. Hence, modeling the way sentiments towards aspects change over time is a challenging task.

Aspect Identification from Objective Sentences

Identification of aspects from objective sentences is a challenging task because we do not have any clue words. For example, consider the following hotel review statement "There are many ants in the room" discuss about the aspect "cleanliness".

Multi Implicit Aspect Identification

A review snippet can have more than one implicit aspect in it. For example, consider the following review snippet "The phone display is good, but it is too tiny to put into my pocket", mentions about two aspects namely "screen" and "size".

CONCLUSION

This chapter provided a brief introduction to and motivation behind Aspect Level Sentiment Analysis and then subsequently explored various aspect extraction techniques. We categorized these techniques according to the nature of the statistical model they adopted and provided a summary of these techniques with a relative comparison with respect to the performance metrics like precision and recall. Finally, the chapter highlights some open research challenges to be addressed by researchers in aspect level sentiment analysis. Since Implicit aspect extraction is a challenging task, incorporating domain knowledge into the aspect extraction task can yield a better performance as typically aspects are domain specific in nature. Due to the generic nature of the existing seed opinion lexicon frameworks like Senticnet and WordNet, these frameworks can't be applied to specific domains. It is safe to remark that sentimental inference with the domain specific opinion words can potentially improve the accuracy of the aspect level sentiment classification tasks.

REFERENCES

Agrawal, R., & Srikant, R. (1994). Fast algorithms for mining association rules. *Proc. 20th int. conf. very large data bases, VLDB*, *1215*, 487-499.

Akhtar, M. S., Gupta, D., Ekbal, A., & Bhattacharyya, P. (2017). Feature selection and ensemble construction: A two-step method for aspect-based sentiment analysis. *Knowledge-Based Systems*, *125*, 116–135. doi:10.1016/j.knosys.2017.03.020

Amazon. (1996a). http://www.amazon.com

Amazon. (1996b). http://www.amazon.in

Ansari, G., Saxena, C., Ahmad, T., & Doja, M. N. (2020). Aspect term extraction using graph-based semi-supervised learning. *Procedia Computer Science*, *167*, 2080–2090. doi:10.1016/j.procs.2020.03.249

Bouma, G. (2009). Normalized (pointwise) mutual information in collocation extraction. *Proceedings of GSCL*, 31-40.

Bagheri, A., Saraee, M., & De Jong, F. (2013). Care more about customers: Unsupervised domain-independent aspect detection for sentiment analysis of customer reviews. *Knowledge-Based Systems*, *52*, 201–213. doi:10.1016/j.knosys.2013.08.011

Bahdanau, D., Cho, K., & Bengio, Y. (2014). *Neural machine translation by jointly learning to align and translate*. arXiv preprint arXiv:1409.0473.

Bing, L. (2004). *Opinion Mining, Sentiment Analysis and Opinion Spam Detection*. http://www.cs.uic.edu~liub/FBS/sentiment-analysis.html

Blei, D. M., Ng, A. Y., & Jordan, M. I. (2003). Latent dirichlet allocation. *The Journal of Machine Learning Research, 3*, 993-1022.

Brown, P. F., Della Pietra, S. A., Della Pietra, V. J., & Mercer, R. L. (1993). The mathematics of statistical machine translation: Parameter estimation. *Computational Linguistics*, *19*(2), 263–311.

Brychcín, T., Konkol, M., & Steinberger, J. (2014). Uwb: Machine learning approach to aspect-based sentiment analysis. *Proceedings of the 8th International Workshop on Semantic Evaluation (SemEval 2014)*, 817-822. 10.3115/v1/S14-2145

Cambria, E., Poria, S., Bajpai, R., & Schuller, B. (2016). SenticNet 4: A semantic resource for sentiment analysis based on conceptual primitives. *Proceedings of COLING 2016, the 26th international conference on computational linguistics: Technical papers*, 2666-2677.

Cambria, E., Olsher, D., & Rajagopal, D. (2014). SenticNet 3: a common and common-sense knowledge base for cognition-driven sentiment analysis. *Proceedings of the AAAI Conference on Artificial Intelligence*, 28-35.

Church, K., & Hanks, P. (1990). Word association norms, mutual information, and lexicography. *Computational Linguistics*, 16, 22–29.

Culotta, A., & Sorensen, J. (2004). Dependency tree kernels for relation extraction. *Proceedings of the 42nd Annual Meeting of the Association for Computational Linguistics (ACL-04)*, 423-429. 10.3115/1218955.1219009

Chauhan, G. S., & Meena, Y. K. (2018). Prominent aspect term extraction in aspect based sentiment analysis. *2018 3rd International Conference and Workshops on Recent Advances and Innovations in Engineering (ICRAIE)*, 1-6. 10.1109/ICRAIE.2018.8710408

Chauhan, G. S., Meena, Y. K., Gopalani, D., & Nahta, R. (2020). A two-step hybrid unsupervised model with attention mechanism for aspect extraction. *Expert Systems with Applications*, 161, 113673. doi:10.1016/j.eswa.2020.113673

Chifu, E. Ş., Leţia, T. Ş., & Chifu, V. R. (2015). Unsupervised aspect level sentiment analysis using Ant Clustering and Self-organizing Maps. *2015 International Conference on Speech Technology and Human-Computer Dialogue (SpeD)*, 1-9. 10.1109/SPED.2015.7343075

Cho, K., Van Merriënboer, B., Gulcehre, C., Bahdanau, D., Bougares, F., Schwenk, H., & Bengio, Y. (2014). Learning phrase representations using RNN encoder-decoder for statistical machine translation. doi:10.3115/v1/D14-1179

Cilibrasi, R. L., & Vitanyi, P. M. (2007). The google similarity distance. *IEEE Transactions on Knowledge and Data Engineering*, 19(3), 370–383. doi:10.1109/TKDE.2007.48

cnet. (1994). http://www.cnet.com

Cornell. (2002). *Movie Review Data*. http://www.cs.cornell.edu/people/pabo/movie-review-data/

Crunchbase. (2015.). *lvping*. https://www.crunchbase.com/organization/lvping

Cutting, D., Kupiec, J., Pedersen, J., & Sibun, P. (1992). A practical part-of-speech tagger. *Third Conference on Applied Natural Language Processing*, 33-140.

Deerwester, S., Dumais, S. T., Furnas, G. W., Landauer, T. K., & Harshman, R. (1990). Indexing by latent semantic analysis. *Journal of the American Society for Information Science*, 41(6), 391–407. doi:10.1002/(SICI)1097-4571(199009)41:6<391::AID-ASI1>3.0.CO;2-9

DianPing. (2010). http://www.DianPing.com

Ding, C., & Peng, H. (2005). Minimum redundancy feature selection from microarray gene expression data. *Journal of Bioinformatics and Computational Biology*, *30*(2), 185–205. doi:10.1142/S0219720005001004 PMID:15852500

Dunning, T. E. (1993). Accurate methods for the statistics of surprise and coincidence. *Computational Linguistics*, *19*(1), 61–74.

Eirinaki, M., Pisal, S., & Singh, J. (2012). Feature-based opinion mining and ranking. *Journal of Computer and System Sciences*, *78*(4), 1175–1184. doi:10.1016/j.jcss.2011.10.007

Epinions. (1999). http://www.Epinions.com

Fellbaum, C. (1998). A semantic network of English verbs. *WordNet: An Electronic Lexical Database, 3*, 153-178.

Frantzi, K., Ananiadou, S., & Mima, H. (2000). Automatic recognition of multi-word terms. the c-value/nc-value method. *International Journal on Digital Libraries*, *3*(2), 115–130. doi:10.1007007999900023

Genism. (2009). *Topic Modelling for Humans*. https://radimrehurek.com/gensim/

Gupta, D. K., Reddy, K. S., & Ekbal, A. (2015). Pso-asent: Feature selection using particle swarm optimization for aspect based sentiment analysis. *International conference on applications of natural language to information systems*, 220-233.

Hai, Z., Chang, K., & Cong, G. (2012). One seed to find them all: mining opinion features via association. *Proceedings of the 21st ACM international conference on Information and knowledge management*, 255-264. 10.1145/2396761.2396797

Hochreiter, S., & Schmidhuber, J. (1997). Long short-term memory. *Neural Computation*, *9*(8), 1735–1780. doi:10.1162/neco.1997.9.8.1735 PMID:9377276

Hu, M., & Liu, B. (2004). Mining and summarizing customer reviews. *Proceedings of the tenth ACM SIGKDD international conference on Knowledge discovery and data mining*, 168-177.

Handl, J., Knowles, J., & Dorigo, M. (2006). Ant-based clustering and topographic mapping. *Artificial Life*, *12*(1), 35–62. doi:10.1162/106454606775186400 PMID:16393450

it168. (2017). http://it168.com

jd. (1998). http://www.jd.com

Jin, W., Ho, H. H., & Srihari, R. K. (2009). A novel lexicalized HMM-based learning framework for web opinion mining. *Proceedings of the 26th annual international conference on machine learning*, *10*, 1553374-1553435. 10.1145/1553374.1553435

Joachims, T. (1999). Transductive inference for text classification using support vector machines. ICML, 99, 200-209.

Kaufman, L., & Rousseeuw, P. J. (2009). Finding groups in data: an introduction to cluster analysis. John Wiley & Sons.

Kennedy, J., & Eberhart, R. C. (2001). *Swarm Intelligence*. Morgan Kaufmann Publishers Inc.

Kim, Y. (2014). Convolutional Neural Networks for Sentence Classification. *Proceedings of the 2014 Conference on Empirical Methods in Natural Language Processing (EMNLP)*, 1746-1751. 10.3115/v1/D14-1181

Kleinberg, J. M. (1999). Authoritative sources in a hyperlinked environment. *Journal of the Association for Computing Machinery, 46*(5), 604–632. doi:10.1145/324133.324140

Kobayashi, N., Inui, K., & Matsumoto, Y. (2007). Extracting aspect-evaluation and aspect-of relations in opinion mining. *Proceedings of the 2007 Joint Conference on Empirical Methods in Natural Language Processing and Computational Natural Language Learning (EMNLP-CoNLL)*, 1065-1074.

Kohonen, T. (2012). Self-organizing maps. Science & Business Media, Springer.

Konkol, M. (2014). Brainy: A machine learning library. *International Conference on Artificial Intelligence and Soft Computing*, 490-499. 10.1007/978-3-319-07176-3_43

Lafferty, J., McCallum, A., & Pereira, F. C. (2001). Conditional random fields: Probabilistic models for segmenting and labeling sequence data. *Proceedings of the 18th International Conference on Machine Learning 2001 (ICML 2001)*, 282-289.

Langville, A. N., & Meyer, C. D. (2008). Google's PageRank and beyond: The science of search engine rankings. *The Mathematical Intelligencer, 30*(1), 68–68. doi:10.1007/BF02985759

Lerman, R. I., & Yitzhaki, S. (1984). A note on the calculation and interpretation of the Gini index. *Economics Letters, 15*(3), 363–368. doi:10.1016/0165-1765(84)90126-5

Li, F., Han, C., Huang, M., Zhu, X., Xia, Y., Zhang, S., & Yu, H. (2010). Structure-aware review mining and summarization. *Proceedings of the 23rd International Conference on Computational Linguistics (Coling 2010)*, 653-661.

Li, S., Wang, R., & Zhou, G. (2012). Opinion target extraction using a shallow semantic parsing framework. *Proceedings of the AAAI Conference on Artificial Intelligence, 26*(1).

Li, Y., Qin, Z., Xu, W., & Guo, J. (2015). A holistic model of mining product aspects and associated sentiments from online reviews. *Multimedia Tools and Applications, 74*(23), 10177–10194. doi:10.100711042-014-2158-0

Li, C., & Lee, C. (1993). Minimum cross entropy thresholding. *Pattern Recognition, 26*(4), 617–625. doi:10.1016/0031-3203(93)90115-D

Liu, B. (2011). Opinion mining and sentiment analysis. In *Web Data Mining* (pp. 459–526). Springer. doi:10.1007/978-3-642-19460-3_11

Liu, K., Xu, L., & Zhao, J. (2013). Syntactic patterns versus word alignment: Extracting opinion targets from online reviews. *Proceedings of the 51st Annual Meeting of the Association for Computational Linguistics, 1*, 1754-1763.

Ma, B., Zhang, D., Yan, Z., & Kim, T. (2013). An LDA and synonym lexicon based approach to product feature extraction from online consumer product reviews. *Journal of Electronic Commerce Research, 14*(4), 304.

Ma, Y., Peng, H., & Cambria, E. (2018). Targeted aspect-based sentiment analysis via embedding commonsense knowledge into an attentive LSTM. *Proceedings of the AAAI Conference on Artificial Intelligence, 32*(1).

Manek, A. S., Shenoy, P. D., Mohan, M. C., & Venugopal, K. R. (2017). Aspect term extraction for sentiment analysis in large movie reviews using Gini Index feature selection method and SVM classifier. *World Wide Web (Bussum), 20*(2), 135–154. doi:10.100711280-015-0381-x

Marrese-Taylor, E., Velásquez, J. D., & Bravo-Marquez, F. (2014). A novel deterministic approach for aspect-based media (SocialNLP). *Expert Systems with Applications, 41*(17), 7764–7775. doi:10.1016/j.eswa.2014.05.045

Mikolov, T., Sutskever, I., Chen, K., Corrado, G., & Dean, J. (2013). *Distributed representations of words and phrases and their compositionality.* arXiv preprint arXiv:1310.4546.

Mitre. (1958). https://www.mitre.org/publications/

Moghaddam, S., & Ester, M. (2010). Opinion digger: an unsupervised opinion miner from unstructured product reviews. *Proceedings of the 19th ACM international conference on Information and knowledge management*, 1825-1828. 10.1145/1871437.1871739

Moon, T. K. (1996). The expectation-maximization algorithm. *IEEE Signal Processing Magazine, 13*(6), 47–60. doi:10.1109/79.543975

Mullen, T., & Collier, N. (2004). Sentiment analysis using support vector machines with diverse information sources. *Proceedings of the 2004 conference on empirical methods in natural language processing*, 412-418.

Nakagawa, H., & Mori, T. (2003). Automatic term recognition based on statistics of compound nouns and their components. *Terminology. International Journal of Theoretical and Applied Issues in Specialized Communication, 9*(2), 201–219.

Nigam, K., Lafferty, J., & McCallum, A. (1999). Using maximum entropy for text classification. IJCAI-99 workshop on machine learning for information filtering, 1(1), 61-67.

Nltk. (2002). *Natural Language Toolkit.* https://www.nltk.org/

Pei, J., Han, J., Mortazavi-Asl, B., Wang, J., Pinto, H., Chen, Q., ... Hsu, M. C. (2004). Mining sequential patterns by pattern-growth: The prefixspan approach. *IEEE Transactions on Knowledge and Data Engineering, 16*(11), 1424–1440. doi:10.1109/TKDE.2004.77

Poria, S., Cambria, E., Ku, L. W., Gui, C., & Gelbukh, A. (2014). A rule-based approach to aspect extraction from product reviews. *Proceedings of the second workshop on natural language processing for social media (SocialNLP)*, 28-37. 10.3115/v1/W14-5905

Qiu, G., Liu, B., Bu, J., & Chen, C. (2009). Expanding domain sentiment lexicon through double propagation. *IJCAI (United States), 9*, 1199–1204.

Quan, & Ren, F. (2014). Unsupervised product feature extraction for feature-oriented opinion determination. *Information Sciences, 272*, 16-28.

Raju, S., Pingali, P., & Varma, V. (2009). An unsupervised approach to product attribute extraction. *European Conference on Information Retrieval*, 796-800. 10.1007/978-3-642-00958-7_88

Rana, T. A., & Cheah, Y. N. (2015). Hybrid rule-based approach for aspect extraction and categorization from customer reviews. *2015 9th International Conference on IT in Asia (CITA)*, 1-5. 10.1109/CITA.2015.7349820

Rana, T. A., & Cheah, Y. N. (2017). A two-fold rule-based model for aspect extraction. *Expert Systems with Applications, 89*, 273–285. doi:10.1016/j.eswa.2017.07.047

Ray, P., & Chakrabarti, A. (2020). A mixed approach of deep learning method and rule-based method to improve aspect level sentiment analysis. *Applied Computing and Informatics*, 1-9.

Salton, G., & Buckley, C. (1988). Term-weighting approaches in automatic text retrieval. *Information Processing & Management, 24*(5), 513–523. doi:10.1016/0306-4573(88)90021-0

SemEval. (2014). https://alt.qcri.org/semeval2014/task-4/

Spacy. (2015.). Industrial-Strength Natural Language Processing. https://spacy.io/

Sutton, C., & McCallum, A. (2006). An introduction to conditional random fields for relational learning. *Introduction to Statistical Relational Learning, 2*, 93-128.

Sutton, R. S., McAllester, D. A., Singh, S. P., & Mansour, Y. (1999, November). Policy gradient methods for reinforcement learning with function approximation. NIPs, 99, 1057-1063.

Stanford. (2008). http://nlp.stanford.edu:8080/parser/

Tomokiyo, T., & Hurst, M. (2003). A language model approach to keyphrase extraction. *Proceedings of the ACL 2003 workshop on Multiword expressions: analysis, acquisition and treatment*, 33-40. 10.3115/1119282.1119287

Tripadvisor. (2000). http://www.tripadvisor,in

Tweepy. (2009). https://www.tweepy.org/

Wang, B., & Wang, H. (2008). Bootstrapping both product features and opinion words from chinese customer reviews with cross-inducing. *Proceedings of the Third International Joint Conference on Natural Language Processing*.

Wang, B., & Liu, M. (2015). Deep learning for aspect-based sentiment analysis. Stanford University report

Wang, J., Sun, C., Li, S., Wang, J., Si, L., Zhang, M., . . . Zhou, G. (2019). Human-like decision making: Document-level aspect sentiment classification via hierarchical reinforcement learning. arXiv preprint arXiv:1910.09260. doi:10.18653/v1/D19-1560

Wang, T., Zhou, J., Hu, Q. V., & He, L. (2019). Aspect-level sentiment classification with reinforcement learning. In *2019 International Joint Conference on Neural Networks (IJCNN)*, 1-8.

Webb, G. I. (2010). Naïve Bayes. Encyclopedia of Machine Learning, 15, 713-714.

Wiebe, J., Bruce, R., & O'Hara, T. P. (1999). Development and use of a gold-standard data set for subjectivity classifications. *Proceedings of the 37th annual meeting of the Association for Computational Linguistics*, 246-253. 10.3115/1034678.1034721

Willett, P. (2006). *The Porter stemming algorithm: then and now*. Academic Press.

Wright, R. E. (1995). *Logistic regression*. Springer.

Wold, S., Esbensen, K., & Geladi, P. (1987). Principal component analysis. *Chemometrics and Intelligent Laboratory Systems*, 2(1), 37–52. doi:10.1016/0169-7439(87)80084-9

Wu, C., Wu, F., Wu, S., Yuan, Z., & Huang, Y. (2018). A hybrid unsupervised method for aspect term and opinion target extraction. *Knowledge-Based Systems*, 148, 66–73. doi:10.1016/j.knosys.2018.01.019

Wu, Y., Zhang, Q., Huang, X. J., & Wu, L. (2009). Phrase dependency parsing for opinion mining. *Proceedings of the 2009 conference on empirical methods in natural language processing*, 1533-1541.

Wu, W., Li, H., Wang, H., & Zhu, K. Q. (2012). Probase: A probabilistic taxonomy for text understanding. *Proceedings of the 2012 ACM SIGMOD International Conference on Management of Data*, 81-492. 10.1145/2213836.2213891

Xu, L., Liu, K., Lai, S., Chen, Y., & Zhao, J. (2013). Walk and learn: a two-stage approach for opinion words and opinion targets co-extraction. *Proceedings of the 22nd International Conference on World Wide Web*, 95-96. 10.1145/2487788.2487831

Yan, Z., Xing, M., Zhang, D., & Ma, B. (2015). EXPRS: An extended pagerank method for product feature extraction from online consumer reviews. *Information & Management*, 52(7), 850–858. doi:10.1016/j.im.2015.02.002

Yu, J., Zha, Z. J., Wang, M., & Chua, T. S. (2011). Aspect ranking: identifying important product aspects from online consumer reviews. *Proceedings of the 49th annual meeting of the association for computational linguistics: human language technologies*, 496-1505.

Zar, J. H. (2005). Spearman rank correlation. Encyclopedia of Biostatistics, 7.

Zhang, L., Liu, B., Lim, S. H., & O'Brien-Strain, E. (2010). Extracting and ranking product features in opinion documents. In *Coling 2010* (pp. 1462–1470). Posters.

Zhou, D., Bousquet, O., Lal, T. N., Weston, J., & Schölkopf, B. (2004). Learning with local and global consistency. *Advances in Neural Information Processing Systems*, 16(16), 321–328.

Zhu, J., Wang, H., Zhu, M., Tsou, B. K., & Ma, M. (2011). Aspect-based opinion polling from customer reviews. *IEEE Transactions on Affective Computing*, 2(1), 37–49. doi:10.1109/T-AFFC.2011.2

zol. (2010). https://www.zol.com/

This research was previously published in Data Preprocessing, Active Learning, and Cost Perceptive Approaches for Resolving Data Imbalance; pages 42-65, copyright year 2021 by Engineering Science Reference (an imprint of IGI Global).

Chapter 69
Social Big Data Mining:
A Survey Focused on Sentiment Analysis

Anisha P. Rodrigues

https://orcid.org/0000-0002-3050-4555

NMAM Institute of Technology, Nitte, India

Niranjan N. Chiplunkar

NMAM Institute of Technology, Nitte, India

Roshan Fernandes

NMAM Institute of Technology, Nitte, India

ABSTRACT

Social media is used to share the data or information among the large group of people. Numerous forums, blogs, social networks, news reports, e-commerce websites, and many more online media play a role in sharing individual opinions. The data generated from these sources is huge and in unstructured format. Big data is a term used for data sets that are large or complex and that cannot be processed by traditional processing system. Sentimental analysis is one of the major data analytics applied on big data. It is a task of natural language processing to determine whether a text contains subjective information and what information it expresses. It helps in achieving various goals like the measurement of customer satisfaction, observing public mood on political movement, movie sales prediction, market intelligence, and many more. In this chapter, the authors present various techniques used for sentimental analysis and related work using these techniques. The chapter also presents open issues and challenges in sentimental analysis landscape.

INTRODUCTION

These days use of smart devices and the high speed Internet has led to lots of people to engage in social media sites like Twitter, Facebook, and Instagram. Due to the high social interaction, the data produced by these sites increases drastically. The number of active social media users keeps growing. According

DOI: 10.4018/978-1-6684-6303-1.ch069

to the Global WebIndex statistics the number of people using mobile phones has reached 3.7 billion (Chaffey, D., 2016). According to Facebook, the number of active users has reached 1.59 billion (Tan, W., Blake, M. B., Saleh, I., & Dustdar, S., 2013). A large amount of data is produced by many Internet users while using online social networking media. The term big data is defined as a data with huge volume, complex in nature and inundates business on a day-to-day basis. Big Data is a term that describes data with "3V"s. They are Volume, Variety and Velocity. Volume signifies huge amount of data. Variety signifies various forms of data that is structured, semi-structured and unstructured generated from various sources. Velocity represents the speed at which the data generated. These characteristics were first identified by Doug Laney (Laney, D., 2001). More recently, two additional V's are added to the description of bigdata, namely, Veracity and Value. Hence big data is a data with "5V"s. Figure 1 shows 5vs of big data. Due to these characteristics of data, traditional processing system is unable to process it.

Figure 1. 5vs of big data (Pouyanfar, S., Yang, Y., Chen, S. C., Shyu, M. L., &Iyengar, S. S.,2018)

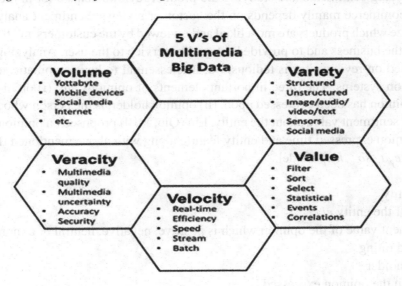

Big Data mining or analytics is the task of analyzing data of 5V's to extract the hidden interesting patterns, market trends, and unknown relations-associations, analyze customer behavior, their preferences and other useful business intelligence information. People share their views on various topics using social media platform. Earlier, before the invention of the Internet or Web, the companies used the techniques like surveys, polls to collect opinions of the people. Now, due to increase in the use of the Web, people openly discuss their ideas on social media and the companies can easily collect people's opinion using the Web. In today's world, there exists a huge competition among the organizations. Within a competitive market, sentiment analysis helps to understand the customer needs. Bigger organizations makes use of social media for promoting their business and marketing purpose. Mining the data generated by social media is called Social Big data mining. Due to the abundance of social media sentiments and emotions, analyzing these sentiments has become challenging. Sentiment analysis attempts to derive the sentiment expressed by an author against an entity. This chapter highlights various techniques used to mine these sentiments.

Outline of the Chapter

In this chapter, we described basic introductory concepts of a sentiment analysis. We focused on different levels of sentiment analysis in Section 3.1 and also explained each techniques used for sentiment analysis, with their applications in section4. Applications of sentiment analysis are outlined in Section 7.Open challenges related to sentiment analysis are discussed in Section 8, which guides interested researchers in their future work. This chapter guides the researchers about the best classifier model in terms of performance for sentiment analysis.

LEVELS OF SENTIMENT ANALYSIS

Sentiment analysis or opinion mining is the learning of people's opinions, attitudes and feelings expressed in the text. Analyzing sentiments and studying the product reviews helps a lot in the growth of the e-commerce as e-commerce mainly depends on the customer reviews. Sentiment analysis helps various retailers to analyze which products are most liked and reviewed by the customers and those details can be used to improve the business and to provide best quality service to the user. Analyzing all the customer opinions expressed on review sites is tedious. So, it is essential to have automatic sentiment analysis and summarization systems. The three important elements of opinions are: (i) opinion target, a target object that the opinion has been expressed upon, (ii) opinion holder, is the person who has expressed the opinion, and (iii) sentiment value about the entity. Liu (Qiu,2010) proposed an opinion quintuple model that includes opinion expressed time and entity feature along with above mentioned three elements.

In *quintuple* $(e_j, a_{jk}, so_{ijkl}, h_i, t_l)$ model,

e_j is the target entity
a_{jk} is the aspect of the entity *ej*
so_{ijkl} is the sentiment value of the opinion which is positive, negative, neutral or a more coarse-grained/ fine-grained rating.
h_i is the opinion holder
t_l is the time when the opinion expressed.

Given an opinionated text, the main objective of sentiment analysis is to find all *quintuple*$(e_j, a_{jk}, so_{ijkl}, h_i, t_l)$ or solve the simpler forms of the problem that is sentiment classification by Document level, Sentence level or Aspect level. Figure 2 shows Levels of sentiment classification.

Figure 2. Levels of sentiment classification

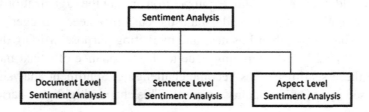

Document Level Sentiment Analysis

In the document level text classification, entire document will be analyzed to detect the emotions expressed (polarity)in the document and whole document is taken as one unit of information. It is assumed that whole document is having opinionated text on one target entity that is on film, book, hotel, and so on. Positive documents will have majority of positive words/sentences (ex. good), which expresses positive sentiments towards the entity. Negative documents will have negative words/sentences (ex. bad), which expresses negative sentiments towards the entity. The entire document will be scanned and polarity of the entire document will be determined and it will be classified as positive or negative.

For example, we consider a customer review on iPhone, "I brought an iPhone a few days back. Although the size is large, it is a nice phone. The voice quality is very clear. The touch screen is cool. I simply love it!". In document level sentiment analysis, this entire review is taken as one document and classified it into positive.

In the document level sentiment analysis, analysis is done by considering entire document contains opinion about on one target entity. Hence, this level of analysis is not suitable, if the document contains opinions on different target entities.

Sentence Level Sentiment Analysis

Sentence level analysis is similar to document level but the opinion summarization is carried out at the sentence level because it assumes that every single sentence in the review document contain the details of one entity. Sentence level analysis emphases on determining the sentiment value of each sentence. There view document will be broken in to a set of sentences and each sentence will be analyzed to determine polarity towards target entity. The sentence polarity is determined by the polarity of word present in the sentence. The word is classified based on whether it is expressing a positive or negative opinion. Some of the opinion words are - amazing, great, excellent, worst, bad, and horrible.

For example, in the sentence "The touch screen is good" the sentence is classified as positive because of positive opinion word "good" present in the sentence.

Aspect Level Sentiment Analysis

Sometimes the users express their opinions on particular feature of the product. Such reviews can also be studied to understand the best and worst features of the product. This kind of analysis names as Aspect/ Feature level sentiment analysis. Aspect level sentiment analysis assumes that the review text comprises opinion on different entities and their respective features. So, the sentence will be analyzed to determine the opinion of the user towards the particular feature of the product. For example, in the review sentence, "The iPhone's battery life is short but voice quality is good", the customer review on iPhone is particularly talking on voice quality and battery of iPhone. In aspect level sentiment analysis, battery life and voice quality are extracted as aspects. After the analysis, the former phrase is classified as positive and latter phrase is classified as negative sentence. Aspect level analysis gives fine grained information of various aspects of a service or product. Some features of product or services are explicitly mentioned in the text like "The battery of this phone is good". In this text, the product aspect – battery, is explicitly mentioned and sentiment on battery is expressed. However, this is not always the case. In the sentence: "The phone lasts all day", we can infer that review is about the product feature-battery even though the word "battery" is not mentioned in the text. These types of aspects are named as implicit aspects and detecting implicit aspects are not easy and open challenges for researchers.

As a summary in the review document: "I feel the latest laptop from Mac is really good overall. It has amazing resolution. The computer is really very sleek and can slide into bags easily. However, I feel the weight is a letdown. The price is a bit expensive given the configurations. I expect an SSD storage. However, the processor seems really good."

At document level text classification, entire review is taken as one entity and it is having many positive sentences compared with negative so classified as positive.

At a sentence level text classification, analysis is done sentence level where document is broke into six sentences. Each sentence is analyzed for subjectivity and classified into positive, negative or class.

At aspect level, sentiment classification is done towards the aspects price, storage, and weight so on.

SENTIMENT ANALYSIS TECHNIQUES

Sentiment analysis techniques can be classified into two major groups namely, the machine learning approach and the lexicon based approach. The machine learning technique makes use of different learning methods for sentiment analysis. The machine learning technique are of two types: supervised learning, which learns from labelled training dataset and predicts the future class and unsupervised learning, identifies hidden pattern from the input data. Different Supervised learning approaches for sentiment classification are shown in Figure 5.Follwing sections briefs sentiment analysis techniques.

Lexicon Based Approach

A Lexicon is means a dictionary which consists of list of words which has a pre-defined polarity. The effectiveness of the Lexical approach strongly depends on Lexical resource that is lexicon dictionary or sentiment corpus. In Lexicon based approach, the dictionaries can be created manually (Tong, 2001) or automatically by means of seed word formation (Turney,2002). Adjectives are taken as indicator for semantic orientation of text in much of lexicon based Research (Hatzivassiloglou, V, McKeown& K. R,1997), (Hu, M., & Liu, B.,2004), (Taboada, M., Brooke, J., Tofiloski, M., Voll, K., & Stede, M., 2011). At the first step, a dictionary formed from an adjective words and their respective sentiment values (polarity). Then, all adjectives are extracted from the given input text and semantic orientation value is obtained from dictionary. These semantic orientation values are aggregated to produce single score for the text. The open lexicon resources such as Sentiwordnet (Baccianella, 2010), (Esuli & Sebastiani, 2006), WordNet-Affect (Valitutti,2004), Q-wordnet (Garcia, 2010) are developed for supporting sentiment analysis. Figure 3 shows the Lexicon based approach. Lexicon based methods does not rely on labelled dataset. So, the sentiment analysis is done without the training dataset. Limitation of lexicon based approach is that, it lags in identifying context specific and domain oriented opinions since it uses sentiment lexicons. This approach requires more manual work on document.

Figure 3. Lexicon based approach

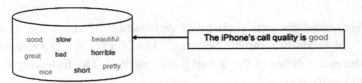

Machine Learning (ML) Approach

In addition to Lexicon based approaches, most research studies on sentiment analysis use supervised machine learning techniques. Dependency on labelled data is major disadvantage of machine learning models. Let the training records be $D = \{X_1, X_2, ..., X_n\}$. Here $X_1, X_2...X_n$ are different features of training record and class label associated with each training record. The classifier is learned from these training records. This classifier is used for the prediction of target value of new observations. There are different algorithms are used to build the classifier. Figure 4 shows the flow of training and prediction phases of supervised machine learning approach.

Figure 4. Machine learning approach

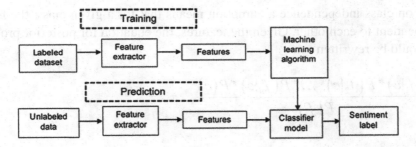

Figure 5 shows different machine learning approaches used to build the classifier for sentiment classification. The following sections briefs about most frequently used supervised classifiers for sentiment analysis.

Figure 5. Machine learning techniques to build the classifier

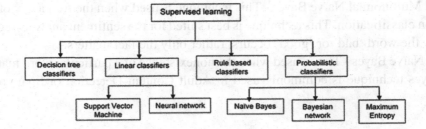

Probabilistic Classifiers

Probabilistic classifier model predicts probability distribution of classes of sample input instead of predicting the most likely class that sample belong to. Let $D = \{f_1, f_2,...,f_n\}$ refers to training document and f_i refers to i^{th} features/attributes of the training document D. The following section discusses three famous probabilistic classifiers.

Naive Bayesian Classifier(NBC)

Using Bayes Theorem, Naïve Bayesian classifier predicts the target class of a random feature set. Equation 1 gives the probability of class c given the features f.

$$P(c \mid f) = \frac{P(f \mid c) * P(c)}{P(f)} \tag{1}$$

$P(c)$ is the prior probability of a class label from the training dataset.
$P(f)$ is the prior probability of a feature set.
$P(f \mid c)$ is the likelihood of feature belong to class.

NBC works on class independence assumption means that for a given class, the features are conditionally independent to each other. Given the features, the equation for posterior probability of class label, $P(c \mid f)$ could be rewritten as:

$$P(c \mid f) = \frac{P(f_1 \mid c) * P(f_2 \mid c) * ... * P(f_n \mid c) * P(c)}{P(f)} \tag{2}$$

The probability of new *feature f* with a *class c* is calculated using equation 2. As per the Bayes rule, the *class c* that achieves highest posterior probability is the outcome. When comparing with other approaches, NBC does sentiment classification with less computing power. So they are frequently used in sentiment classification but feature independent assumptions during the calculation of likelihood will provide inaccurate results. Variants of NBC are include:

1) Multinomial Naïve Bayes –This is used when multiple occurrence of feature matters a lot in sentiment classification. This technique better suits for the topic classification.
2) Binarized Multinomial Naïve Bayes –This technique is used when the frequency of features is not essential in classification. This technique is best suited for the sentiment analysis regardless of how frequently the word 'bad' or 'good' occurs; rather only the fact matters.
3) Bernoulli Naïve Bayes - This is used when the nonexistence of a particular word matters. Bernoulli Naïve Bayes technique is commonly used in Adult Content Detection or Spam and gives good results.

According to (Ye, Q., Zhang, Z., & Law, R., 2009), NBC gives better result for the problems that can be linearly separated but may not work so well for the non-linearly separable problems. The accuracy he achieved by the NBC is 79%.(Pak, A., & Paroubek, P.,2010), builds n-gram sentiment classifier using multinomial Naive Bayes classifier and constructs feature vector using Parts of Speech tagged dataset. N-gram is a combination of adjacent n-words present in the sample text. N-gram of size 1 is denoted as uni-gram, size 2 is denoted as bi-gram, and size 3 as tri-gram. They have tested the classifier on a set of real Twitter posts. They have experimented the effect of orderings of n-grams on the classifier's performance and concluded that bigrams provides good stability between an analysis (unigrams) and has a capacity to capture correct sentiment patterns (trigrams).(Dave, K., Lawrence, S., &Pennock, D. M.,2003), have performed sentiment analysis using NBC method on n-gram patterns and reported that bi-gram and tri-gramgive better result for product reviews.

Bayesian Network

Bayesian Network is the model of variables and their relationships and constructed with the assumption that variables are fully dependent on each other. In sentiment analysis the variables represent feature sets and edges represent dependency between feature sets. Bayesian Network classifier learns structure from training datasets with Conditional Probability Tables (CPT). CPT provides the Condition probability values between the variables of Bayesian Network. Bayesian Network is constructed according to two-step process called search-score model. The first step is carried out to search an element on a search space associated with Bayesian networks and second one to find score function that assesses degree of fitness between each element in a typical search space. Much of the research on Bayesian Network focus on development of scoring function for Bayesian Network classifier (Campos, L. M. D., 2006).In order to extract sentiments from movie reviews, (Airoldi, E., Bai, X., & Padman, R., 2004) and (Bai, X., 2011) proposed Bayesian Network classifier in association with Two-stage Markov Blanket Classifier. It studies Conditional dependencies among an elements in a network and discovers the network part that falls within the range of Markov Blanket. For high cross validated accuracy, (Glover, F., & Laguna, M., 1998) used Tabu Search algorithm to prune the resulting Markov Blanket network. To solve in Bayesian network classifiers (Friedman, N., Geiger, D., & Goldszmidt, M., 1997), Markov Blanket is proved as effective method. But in Markov Blanket Classifier, sentiment dependencies are learned from the existence of words in their original sentiment class only.

Maximum Entropy Classifier

The Maximum Entropy Classifier belongs to a class of exponential model. Unlike the Naive Bayesian, it does not assumes features conditionally independent to each other. Probability distribution function *P(features|class)* is eliminated, instead feature function *f(features|class)* is taken as constraint for classification.λ_i is the weight parameter of the feature function.

$$P(class\,|\,features\lambda) = \frac{\exp\left(\sum_i \lambda_i f_i(features\,|\,class)\right)}{\sum_c \exp\left(\sum_i \lambda_i f_i(features\,|\,class)\right)}$$

To classify tweets, (Parikh, R., &Movassate, M., 2009), used a Maximum Entropy model, Naive Bayes unigram models for unigram and bigram feature sets. Bernoulli and multinomial naïve Bayes are used for the study. To select correct feature sets and to maximize the log-likelihood of tweet test data, they have used preprocessing that smoothens maximum entropy classifier. According to studies, author concluded that multinomial Naive Bayes classifier gave better accuracy compared to Maximum Entropy classifier. (Wang, Y. Y., &Acero, A., 2007), propose that the Maximum Entropy model can obtain global optimization due to the properties of the convex objective function.

Linear Classifier

With the normalized text word frequency $X= \{x_1, x_2,...,x_n\}$, vector of coefficients $A=\{a_1, a_2,..., a_n\}$, and scalar variable b, the linear predictor that is a separator for different classes is defined as $p=AX+b$. This. Among the various linear classifiers, Support Vector Machines is a classifier that gives a better separation between the classes.

Support Vector Machine(SVM) Classifier

The SVM classifiers acts as a best linear separator for the various classes of a given data space. The data points used for classification are termed as support vector. Hyper plane separates different classes of target variable and margin is the width between the hyper plane and support vector. The hyper plane which has maximum margin is selected for classification. Figure 6 shows the set of data points labeled with two classes Yes or No. Where target equals to Yes taken as positive class and target equal to No is taken as negative class.

Figure 6. SVM in a classification

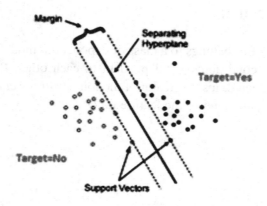

In SVM, hyper plane are found by minute subset of the trained datasets named as support vectors. Due to the correlation nature of the text features, SVM is well suited for text classification. (Pang, B., & Lee, L., 2008), used ML techniques like NBC and SVM. The author has analyzed the movie reviews. For the experiment the author collected the data from the IMDb.com. The author used the unigram feature selection method along with the classifiers. The author successfully got the accuracy of 82.9%. (Dang, Y., Zhang, Y., & Chen, H., 2009),proposed the SVM classifier for sentiment analysis. Along with SVM other famous feature selection methods were also used. The author considered the 305 positive reviews and 307 negative reviews of the camera. Author (Blitzer, J., Dredze, M., & Pereira, F., 2007), performed the experiment using the kitchen appliance reviews. The author used the SVM. The SVM was trained using the domain dependent, domain free, and sentiment features. The author obtained the accuracy of around 84.15%. (Chen, C. C., & Tseng, Y. D., 2011), have used multiclass classifications. People's sentiment towards the digital cameras and MP3 player reviews were studied by them. They have used the Information Quality framework. According to author the SVM works best for analyzing the reviews. It outperforms all other methods. SVMs was also used by (Li, Y. M., &Li, T. Y., 2013) and they focused on more than binary classification problem. Author says that opinions subjectivity also plays an important role in analyzing the reviews. Author used Twitter data for the analysis. The accuracy achieved by the SVM is 88.353%.

Back Propagation Neural Network

Neural Networks (NN) are used in text classification to perform the task such as, sentence modeling, word representation estimation, text generation, vector representation, feature presentation and sentence classification. The neurons are the basic building block of NN which imitates the structure and function of human brain. The neural network is defined by the function:

$$p_i = W^* X_i \tag{3}$$

Where W represents weights of neurons and X_i represents the word frequency. In the multilayer neural network, the output of the earlier layer neurons is fed as input to the next layer neurons. The errors in this model are back propagated in the training process and hence the computation cost becomes heavy. Figure 7shows the structure of neural network.

Neural network has three layers:

1. Input layer: This layer consists of units called as neurons which passes input data X to first hidden layer. This data is then multiplied with hidden layer's weights.
2. Hidden layer: Neurons of this layer will get data from the preceding input layer. This layer is hidden between input and output layer and perform computation on weighted input and produces net output through activation function and passes to the next hidden layer. The more number of hidden layers will increase the complexity.
3. Output layer: Neurons of this layer will get the data from the preceding hidden layer and produces the required output and this is the last layer of neural network.

Figure 7. Structure of neural network

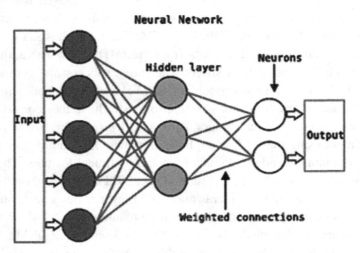

Much of the research [1990] on sentiment analysis using Backpropagation Neural Network used with one or two layers and reported that, as the hidden layer increases, the NN structure becomes more complicated and computationally expensive. Recently from the past 10 years due to the accessibility of computing power and huge set of training data, training "deep" (neural networks with more layers) Neural Networks popularly used for sentiment analysis. Deep learning has networks such as Convolutional Neural Network (CNN), Recurrent Neural Network (RNN), Recursive Neural Network and Deep Belief Networks (DBN).Using Amazon and TripAdviser datasets, (Bespalov, D., Bai, B., Qi, Y., & Shoko-ufandeh, A., 2011) Built neural network classifier with error rate 7.12 and 7.37.Using this classifier, he experimented effect higher order n-gram features in sentiment analysis. Deep learning researchers (Goller, C., & Kuchler, A., 1996) have proposed folding architecture to train recurrent neural networks and got better results compared to simple Recurrent Neural network. Furthermore, to produce more promising result on sentiment analysis task, (Socher, R., Perelygin, A., Wu, J., Chuang, J., Manning, C. D., Ng, A., & Potts, C., 2013) has proposed complex models such as Recursive Neural Tensor Networks and Matrix-Vector RNN.

Rule-Based Classifier

In this technique, set of rules are defined to train the data space. The typical rule is given in the form A→B, where A and B are sentiment patterns. The right hand side of the rule represents the target class label. The left hand side of the rule specifies the condition on the data set which may be given in the disjunctive normal form. The important criteria used in defining these rules are support and confidence. Support is a percentage of transactions containing both A and B. Confidence is the percentage of trans-action D containing A that also contain B. Based on these two parameters the rules are constructed in the training phase. These two parameters judge how closely the data sets are related to each other. These classifiers then tries to predict class label of sample data.(Yang, C. S., & Shih, H. P., 2012),proposed Rule based sentiment analysis and reported that Rule based technique achieves comparable performance with supervised approach in which preparation of training dataset is critical.(Qiu, G., He, X., Zhang,

F., Shi, Y., Bu, J., & Chen, C., 2010),proposed pre-set rule sentiment classification method for targeted advertising to handle consumers' attitude identification and topic word extraction. Experiments show that, for advertising keyword extraction, proposed method beats the term-frequency inverse document frequency method.

Decision Tree Classifier

Decision tree is a hierarchical tree structure for representing training records in which each non-leaf node is split based on attribute condition value. In Decision Tree classifier, each interior node represented by an attribute or features, branches that are leaving the interior node represents test on feature of the dataset and children nodes are the outcome of the test. The leaves of Decision tree are class labels. The training data space is divided recursively till the leaf node ends with the minimum records. The variants of decision tree for text classification are mainly subjected to feature measures used for splitting node such as ID3 and C4. (Li, Y. H., & Jain, A. K., 1998), have used the C5 algorithm for sentiment analysis which is a SuccessorofC4.5 algorithm. The main advantages of decision tree classifier are, it is easier to understand and does not require statistical knowledge to interpret them. Decision tree classifier form complicated trees if poor feature measure methods incorporated in constructing tree and such trees cannot generalized easily.

Some of the popular research articles and sentiment analysis techniques on sentiment analysis are listed in Table1.

Table 1. Popular research articles and sentiment analysis techniques on sentiment analysis

Sentiment analysis Techniques		Data scope	Author
Machine Learning Approach	Naive Bayesian Classifier	Twitter data	(Ye, Zhang, & Law, 2009)
		Product reviews	(Dave, Lawrence, &Pennock, 2003)
	Naive Bayes classifier and Maximum Entropy classifier.	Twitter data	(Parikh & Movassate, 2009)
	Maximum Entropy classifier	Air Travel Information System dataset and Product review	(Wang & Acero, 2007)
	Support vector machine	Twitter posts (blogs)	(Li & Li, 2013)
		Product reviews	(Dang, Zhang, & Chen, 2009), (Blitzer, Dredze, & Pereira, 2007), (Chen & Tseng, 2011)
	Support Vector Machine, Naive Bayesian classifier	Restaurant reviews	(Kang, Yoo, & Han, 2012)
		Movie reviews	(Pang & Lee, 2008)
	Bayesian Networks	Twitter data	(Airoldi, Bai, & Padman, 2004), (Bai, 2011)
	Rule based	Web forums	(Yang & Shih, 2012), (Qiu, He, Zhang, Shi, Bu, & Chen, 2010)
	Neural networks	Amazon and TripAdvisor datasets	(Goller & Kuchler, 1996)
		Movie reviews	Socher, Perelygin, Wu, Chuang, Manning, Ng, & Potts, 2013), (Kim, 2014)
Lexicon-based Approach	Annotated Dictionary and sentiment corpus	Product reviews	(Tong, 2001), (Turney, 2002), (Hatzivassiloglou & McKeown, 1997), (Hu & Liu, 2004), (Taboada, Brooke, Tofiloski, Voll, & Stede, 2011)

Twitter attracts more and more users and analysis of tweets gives useful information for data analytics to make important decisions. Twitter is considered as popular and very rich opinion source and provides user views on various topics. Twitter data can be collected using Twitter API from Twitter source using hashtags as keywords. Twitter analysis offers an entirely different challenge, which is use of nonstandard and short notations used by Twitter users. Preprocessing of dataset has significant impact on the accuracy of an analysis. Many researchers analyzed Twitter data using machine learning techniques because tweet text contain 140 characters and due to the availability of corpus for analysis. Out of different machine learning techniques, Artificial NN, NBC and SVM are popularly used. Artificial NN outperformed in terms of accuracy compared to other sentiment classification techniques but it takes more time for learning phase. So, by considering both execution time and accuracy, SVM and NBC are popularly used for sentiment analysis. In n-gram feature analysis, bigram feature set gives better results. Sarcasm tweets detection and multilingual tweets analysis are highlighted as challenges.

Even the retailer sites provide the user views on different services and products. These reviews are in the document form which can be analyzed using document level, sentence level and aspect level. Product review analysis has its challenges like rating inconsistency, sparse data, skewed data distribution, ambivalence and comparative sentences make sentiment analysis difficult.

PRELIMINARY STEPS OF SENTIMENT ANALYSIS

Information provided by the user may not be in structured format. Sentiment analysis faces various challenges due to this. Data can be of any format, namely, audio, video, or text. To ease the processing of large amount of data many techniques are developed which automates the process of sentiment analysis. Some part of the input dataset may have a structure where as some part may not have any structure. The unstructured data cannot be used as it is as it contains a large amount of unwanted (or unnecessary) information which will slow down the processing. Data acquisition and data pre-processing are the two important steps which helps to reduce the noise in the data.

Data Acquisition

The process of extracting the data from various sources is called Data collection. With an increase in the use of the Internet and other online activities, enormous information is available on the web. The data will be collected from various sources which will then be subjected to various mining techniques. Various microblogs provides the API's to collect public data from their sites. Various APIs are available for collecting and searching the tweets. To search and extract tweets, Twitter provides the search/tweets API. For the search API, keywords are passed as the queries. More than one query can be clubbed together and used together as a comma separated list. Information like user profile information and the user tweets can be extracted from the Twitter source by using Twitter REST API.(Kumar, S., Morstatter, F., & Liu, H.,2014),work discusses about collecting and analyzing the Twitter data and past tweets can be searched using this API. Twitter4J is popularly used for tweet extraction. (Khan, F. H., Bashir, S., & Qamar, U., 2014), worked on Twitter datasets and used the Twitter4J library for data acquisition process.

Pre-Processing Steps

During pre-processing phase, the data will be subjected to cleaning, noise removal and the data will be prepared for the classification process. The data accessed from online is unformatted and contains noise and unwanted information such as tags, advertisements which must be removed for better result. In some cases the words used in a given sentence may not convey any meaning. Many pre-processing techniques are available for removing the stop words and the nouns, adjectives etc. which are present in the sentence. Tokenization is the method which divides the task into words and sentences by removing the punctuation marks. Some example of stop word are the, at, which etc. These parts of speech words present in the text can be removed by using the POS tagging. Some examples of parts of speech are nouns, pronouns, adjectives, adverbs etc. In a sentence large amount of sentiment is described by the adjectives and adverbs.

COMPARATIVE ANALYSIS OF SEVERALTECHNIQUES USED FORSENTIMENT ANALYSIS

(Hailong, Z., Wenyan, G., & Bo, J., 2014), has done survey and comparative study on Lexicon based approaches, Machine learning, cross lingual and cross domain sentiment classification. Author has concluded in his research article, that Machine learning approaches like SVM and NBC gives higher precision results compared to Lexicon based approaches. Even the lexicon based approaches are equally competitive but they require more human efforts and less sensitive to training dataset. Accuracy, Precision, Recall and F-measure are the four performance measurement metrics used of sentiment classification. Accuracy is the number of correct prediction out of the total observation. Precision says out of those predicted positive, how many of them are actual positive. Recall gives the true positive rate that is, what portion of actual positive was identified correctly. F-measure will give the harmonic mean of precision and recall. The calculation are obtained confusion matrix which has True Positive (TP), True Negative (TN), False Positive (FP) and False Negative (FN) instances. Table 2displays the confusion matrix and Equation (4), (5), (6) and (7) shows the formula to calculate performance matrices.

$$Accuracy = \frac{TP + TN}{TP + TN + FP + FN} \tag{4}$$

$$Precision = \frac{TP}{TP + FP} \tag{5}$$

$$Recall = \frac{TP}{TP + FN} \tag{6}$$

$$F1 = \frac{2 * Precision * Recall}{Precision + Recall} \tag{7}$$

Table 2. Confusion matrix

	Predicted Positive	Predicted Negative
Actual Positive	TP	FN
Actual Negative	FP	TN

According to these matrices, many researchers have provided comparative study on sentiment analysis using machine and lexicon approaches. Lexicon sentiment classification techniques rely on tagged Lexicons and sentiment dictionary. But the sentiment resources availability for different languages are uneven. For an instance, English sentiment corpus is freely available in Web but lack of Chinese sentiment corpus availability restricts the progress on sentiment analysis of Chinese text. Domain specific sentiment analysis adds more challenges in sentiment analysis task. Contextual information or topic specific information should be considered while analyzing the sentiments. For cross domain sentiment analysis, dataset will come from different domains and violates the basic assumption of traditional sentiment analysis. This will directly affect the accuracy of sentiment analysis. So, Author has considered research articles on cross-lingual and cross domain sentiment analysis. Table 3 shows the Performance comparison of sentiment classification technique including cross-lingual and cross-domain.

Table 3. Comparison of different sentiment classification techniques

	Data set	Method	Accuracy	Author
Machine Learning Approach	Movie reviews	SVM	86.40%	(Pang & Lee, 2008)
	Twitter	Co-Training SVM	82.52%	(Qiu, He, Zhang, Shi, Bu, & Chen, 2010)
	Standard sentiment Treebank	Deep learning	80.70%	(Socher, Perelygin, Wu, Chuang, Manning, Ng, & Potts,)
Lexicon Approach	Product Reviews	Corpus	74.00%	(Turney, 2002)
	Amazon	Dictionary	---	(Taboada, Brooke, Tofiloski, Voll, & Stede, 2011)
Cross-lingual	Amazon	Ensemble	81.00%	(Wan, 2012)
	Amazon, IT168	Co-Train	81.30%	(Wan, 2009)
	IMDb movie review	EWGA (entropy weighted genetic algorithm)	>90%	(Abbasi, Chen, & Salem, 2008)
	MPQA, NTCIR, ISI	CLMM (Cross lingual Mixture Model)	83.02%	(Meng, Wei, Liu, Zhou, Xu, & Wang, 2012)
Cross-domain	Book, DVD, Electronics, Kitchen	Active learning	80% (average)	(Li & Chen, 2009)
		Thesaurus		(Bollegala, Weir, & Carroll, 2012)
		SFA (spectral feature alignment)		(Pan, Ni, Sun, Yang, & Chen, 2010)

Further author has performed simple lexicon based sentiment analysis using Senti-WordNet lexical resource and evaluated with SVM and NBC. The dataset is taken for sentiment analysis is SFU review Corpus which is shown in Table4.This shows that one of the popular machine learning approach- SVM gives higher degree of accuracy compared to NBC and Senti-WordNet approach.

Table 4. Accuracy comparison of machine learning methods with senti-wordnet

	TP	FP	FN	TN	Accuracy
Senti-WordNet	148	91	52	109	64.25%
NB	156	81	44	119	68.75%
SVM	135	51	65	149	71.00%

APPLICATION OF SENTIMENT ANALYSIS

Stock Market Prediction

Stock market prediction is the act of defining the future value of a company's stock. The successful stock market forecasting helps to gain more profit in the business. The sentiment of the people can be studied to make the stock market prediction. (Liu, B., Hu, M., & Cheng, J., 2005), have proposed a technique called SmeDA-SA, which can be used to analyze and understand the customer opinion. (Hagenau, M., Liebmann, M., & Neumann, D., 2013), has experimented on text data to identify whether the customer opinion affects the stock market.

Prediction Market Box Office Prediction

With the help of the Internet and the Web, people can easily know what is trending in the market. When people express their opinion in the social media it helps other users to know the best quality as well as worst quality of the product. Many people get influenced by the opinion expressed by other people. (Rui, H., Liu, Y., & Whinston, A., 2013), explained how chatter matters in marketing and the influence of tweets on movie sales. The chatting done in the Twitter does matters as it helps the customer to know whether to watch the movie or not. The chatting also provides the kind of advertisement for the movies. (Du, J., Xu, H., & Huang, X., 2014), used a micro blog to predict the box office collection.

Prediction Recommendation System

Recommendation system provides recommendation for the user (Massa, P., &Bhattacharjee, B., 2004). These days, recommendation system shave gained a lot of popularity. With a large amount of information available online the customers have to face the problem of analyzing and selecting only required information. When a customer wants to buy a product with reasonable cost, he has to spend more time in searching various brand products on information search engine to come to a decision. Many approaches were introduced to overcome this problem recommender system is one such case. Usually recommendation system can be classified into two types such as content based system and collaborative system (Massa,

P., &Bhattacharjee, B., 2004), (Albadvi, A., & Shahbazi, M., 2009), (Sharma, R., Nigam, S., & Jain, R., 2014), (Li, Y. M., & Chen, C. W., 2009). In content-based system the user is given recommendation depending upon what he has liked in the past (Yang, W. S., & Dia, J. B., 2008). In collaborative system user with same tastes are identified and recommendation is provided based on their taste. The content based recommendation approach has one drawback that is since the items are displayed based on the past likes of the user, the experiments with SVM e-recommendation will be just based on the past likes which restricts the user from seeing other items. The disadvantage of the collaborative system approach is that, when a user whose tastes are not similar to any other user, it leads to poorer recommendations and also when a new item appears without enough information related to rating or user likes, it cannot be recommended to another user. (Balabanović, M., & Shoham, Y., 1997) proposed a hybrid approach which combines both the approaches for more accurate result. They have discussed the various features of the Fab system.

Online Advertising

The online advertising is also similar to recommender system, it can be seen as application of recommender systems. Recommendation is a very powerful way using which the companies can attract the users. Recommender system assists in understanding the taste of the user and provide the offers only based on the user taste. When a customer decides to buy the item his decision is likely to get affected by the experience shared by other users (Pang, B., & Lee, L., 2008). The purchasing decisions usually gets affected by the other people opinion. Before buying any item customers will go through the reviews or the ratings to do a purchase decision. E-commerce companies allows the user to review the products they purchase. Customer can even chat with other people. Customers can also rate the products. The reviewing and rating helps the other user to decide whether or not to purchase the product.

CHALLENGES AND OPEN ISSUES

Fast growth of Internet and related applications made sentiment analysis as exciting and popular research area among Natural Language Processing. Many researchers have implemented various techniques for automated sentiment analysis but still there is a need of automated sentiment analysis that correctly interpreters the context of text. Some of the challenges in sentiment analysis are: Opinions are written by the user who belong to different culture or zone. So, there is a possibility that opinions have abbreviations, poor spelling and grammar, written in a mixed language. Opinion sentences will have emoticons and short informal text words.

The challenges in the analysis of product reviews are (i) Analysis model constructed on one product or product aspect may not suitable for another product. (ii) Opinion words have positive orientation in one situation might show negative orientation in another situation (Qiu, G., He, X., Zhang, F., Shi, Y., Bu, J., & Chen, C., 2010).For example, the sentence "laptop's battery life was long" is a positive sentence but if the sentence "laptop's start up time was long" then it is a negative sentence. (iii) Sentences expresses sentiments on more than one feature e.g., "The battery life of this phone is short but the voice quality is good" (iv) Comparative opinions will relate similarities and differences between two or more entities. In such cases, finding proper sentiment polarity of one entity is really difficult.

The challenges for analysis of tweets are (i) The volume of data generated by Twitter source very large and needs high processing device for storage and analysis (ii) Retrieving datasets: usage of hashtags or keywords may not retrieve all topic oriented data (iii) Twitter users will post tweets on a particular topic. So, we retrieve text on variety of disciplines(iv)Relevancy of collected data (v) A word, which is subjective in one topic, will be objective in another topic (vi) Occurrence of sarcasm sentences (vii) Analysis of non-English sentences (viii) Fake or spam opinions.

According to many articles sentiment classification are done on direct sentiments. Authors have ignored the opinion sentence expressed in sarcastic way due to its complexity. Sarcastic sentiment detection is very challenging. Sarcasms are very common in movie reviews and political discussions. Some examples of sarcastic opinion are -"I love being ignored". The study of sarcastic sentence still need to be enhanced. They appear with and without sentiment word and express conflicting semantic meaning of what is exactly written.

CONCLUSION

With the increase in the use of Internet the information available on the internet will be more valuable and useful for various business organizations. Sentiment analysis used in many practical applications, more importantly, market prognostication and political polarization. In this chapter, we discussed on social big data mining and about the sentiment analysis and how it evolved. For analyzing the user sentiments several machine learning and lexical approaches are used. But, an abundance of work still remains to be done in the area of sentiment classification and it is a fertile area. This is a survey chapter where we have referred to several research articles to analyze and understand the state-of-art in the area of the sentiment analysis over the past years. This chapter discusses how the sentiment can be analyzed and performance can be made better if it is done at the different levels such as word level, document level, and sentence level. Along with this, various techniques used for sentiment analysis are also studied. Presently there are several techniques available in the field of the sentiment analysis, such as SVM, Lexicon based methods Machine learning, Subjectivity classification, Polarity classification etc. All these techniques try to ease the work of the human by analyzing the sizably voluminous data set. User opinions for sentiment analysis are usually obtained from the micro blogs such as Twitter or e-commerce sites. The information accumulated from the web will be too large and too noisy. Some automatic system must be built to remove the unwanted data from the dataset. Noisy data is one important problem of the Sentiment analysis. Care must take to make sure that data used will be noise free as much as possible to get the best result. While analyzing the popularity of the item the product feature must also be considered for better analysis. Sentiment analysis model for analyzing customer opinion in language other than English (cross-lingual) must also need to be developed.

REFERENCES

Abbasi, A., Chen, H., & Salem, A. (2008). Sentiment analysis in multiple languages: Feature selection for opinion classification in web forums. *ACM Transactions on Information Systems*, 26(3), 12. doi:10.1145/1361684.1361685

Airoldi, E., Bai, X., & Padman, R. (2004, August). Markov blankets and meta-heuristics search: Sentiment extraction from unstructured texts. In *International Workshop on Knowledge Discovery on the Web* (pp. 167-187). Springer.

Albadvi, A., & Shahbazi, M. (2009). A hybrid recommendation technique based on product category attributes. *Expert Systems with Applications, 36*(9), 11480–11488. doi:10.1016/j.eswa.2009.03.046

Bai, X. (2011). Predicting consumer sentiments from online text. *Decision Support Systems, 50*(4), 732–742. doi:10.1016/j.dss.2010.08.024

Balabanović, M., & Shoham, Y. (1997). Fab: Content-based, collaborative recommendation. *Communications of the ACM, 40*(3), 66–72. doi:10.1145/245108.245124

Bespalov, D., Bai, B., Qi, Y., & Shokoufandeh, A. (2011, October). Sentiment classification based on supervised latent n-gram analysis. In *Proceedings of the 20th ACM international conference on Information and knowledge management* (pp. 375-382). ACM. 10.1145/2063576.2063635

Blitzer, J., Dredze, M., & Pereira, F. (2007, June). Biographies, bollywood, boom-boxes and blenders: Domain adaptation for sentiment classification. In *Proceedings of the 45th annual meeting of the association of computational linguistics* (pp. 440-447). Academic Press.

Bollegala, D., Weir, D., & Carroll, J. (2012). Cross-domain sentiment classification using a sentiment sensitive thesaurus. *IEEE Transactions on Knowledge and Data Engineering, 25*(8), 1719–1731. doi:10.1109/TKDE.2012.103

Campos, L. M. D. (2006). A scoring function for learning Bayesian networks based on mutual information and conditional independence tests. *Journal of Machine Learning Research, 7*(Oct), 2149–2187.

Chaffey, D. (2016). *Global social media research summary 2016*. Smart Insights: Social Media Marketing.

Chen, C. C., & Tseng, Y. D. (2011). Quality evaluation of product reviews using an information quality framework. *Decision Support Systems, 50*(4), 755–768. doi:10.1016/j.dss.2010.08.023

Dang, Y., Zhang, Y., & Chen, H. (2009). A lexicon-enhanced method for sentiment classification: An experiment on online product reviews. *IEEE Intelligent Systems, 25*(4), 46–53. doi:10.1109/MIS.2009.105

Dave, K., Lawrence, S., & Pennock, D. M. (2003, May). Mining the peanut gallery: Opinion extraction and semantic classification of product reviews. In *Proceedings of the 12th international conference on World Wide Web* (pp. 519-528). ACM. 10.1145/775152.775226

Du, J., Xu, H., & Huang, X. (2014). Box office prediction based on microblog. *Expert Systems with Applications, 41*(4), 1680–1689. doi:10.1016/j.eswa.2013.08.065

Friedman, N., Geiger, D., & Goldszmidt, M. (1997). Bayesian network classifiers. *Machine Learning, 29*(2-3), 131–163. doi:10.1023/A:1007465528199

Glover, F., & Laguna, M. (1998). Tabu search. In *Handbook of combinatorial optimization* (pp. 2093–2229). Boston, MA: Springer. doi:10.1007/978-1-4613-0303-9_33

Goller, C., & Kuchler, A. (1996, June). Learning task-dependent distributed representations by backpropagation through structure. In *Proceedings of International Conference on Neural Networks (ICNN'96)* (Vol. 1, pp. 347-352). IEEE. 10.1109/ICNN.1996.548916

Hagenau, M., Liebmann, M., & Neumann, D. (2013). Automated news reading: Stock price prediction based on financial news using context-capturing features. *Decision Support Systems, 55*(3), 685–697. doi:10.1016/j.dss.2013.02.006

Hailong, Z., Wenyan, G., & Bo, J. (2014, September). Machine learning and lexicon based methods for sentiment classification: A survey. In *2014 11th Web Information System and Application Conference* (pp. 262-265). IEEE. 10.1109/WISA.2014.55

Hatzivassiloglou, V., & McKeown, K. R. (1997, July). Predicting the semantic orientation of adjectives. In *Proceedings of the 35th annual meeting of the association for computational linguistics and eighth conference of the european chapter of the association for computational linguistics* (pp. 174-181). Association for Computational Linguistics.

Hu, M., & Liu, B. (2004, August). Mining and summarizing customer reviews. In *Proceedings of the tenth ACM SIGKDD international conference on Knowledge discovery and data mining* (pp. 168-177). ACM.

Kang, H., Yoo, S. J., & Han, D. (2012). Senti-lexicon and improved Naïve Bayes algorithms for sentiment analysis of restaurant reviews. *Expert Systems with Applications, 39*(5), 6000–6010. doi:10.1016/j.eswa.2011.11.107

Khan, F. H., Bashir, S., & Qamar, U. (2014). TOM: Twitter opinion mining framework using hybrid classification scheme. *Decision Support Systems, 57*, 245–257. doi:10.1016/j.dss.2013.09.004

Kim, Y. (2014). *Convolutional neural networks for sentence classification*. arXiv preprint arXiv:1408.5882

Kumar, S., Morstatter, F., & Liu, H. (2014). *Twitter data analytics*. New York: Springer. doi:10.1007/978-1-4614-9372-3

Laney, D. (2001). 3D data management: Controlling data volume, velocity and variety. *META Group Research Note, 6*(70), 1.

Li, Y. H., & Jain, A. K. (1998). Classification of text documents. *The Computer Journal, 41*(8), 537–546. doi:10.1093/comjnl/41.8.537

Li, Y. M., & Chen, C. W. (2009). A synthetical approach for blog recommendation: Combining trust, social relation, and semantic analysis. *Expert Systems with Applications, 36*(3), 6536–6547. doi:10.1016/j.eswa.2008.07.077

Li, Y. M., & Li, T. Y. (2013). Deriving market intelligence from microblogs. *Decision Support Systems, 55*(1), 206–217. doi:10.1016/j.dss.2013.01.023

Liu, B., Hu, M., & Cheng, J. (2005, May). Opinion observer: analyzing and comparing opinions on the web. In *Proceedings of the 14th international conference on World Wide Web* (pp. 342-351). ACM. 10.1145/1060745.1060797

Massa, P., & Bhattacharjee, B. (2004, March). Using trust in recommender systems: an experimental analysis. In *International conference on trust management* (pp. 221-235). Springer. 10.1007/978-3-540-24747-0_17

Meng, X., Wei, F., Liu, X., Zhou, M., Xu, G., & Wang, H. (2012, July). Cross-lingual mixture model for sentiment classification. In *Proceedings of the 50th Annual Meeting of the Association for Computational Linguistics: Long Papers-Volume 1* (pp. 572-581). Association for Computational Linguistics.

Pak, A., & Paroubek, P. (2010, May). Twitter as a corpus for sentiment analysis and opinion mining. In LREc (Vol. 10, No. 2010, pp. 1320-1326). Academic Press.

Pan, S. J., Ni, X., Sun, J. T., Yang, Q., & Chen, Z. (2010, April). Cross-domain sentiment classification via spectral feature alignment. In *Proceedings of the 19th international conference on World wide web* (pp. 751-760). ACM. 10.1145/1772690.1772767

Pang, B., & Lee, L. (2008). Opinion mining and sentiment analysis. *Foundations and Trends® in Information Retrieval, 2*(1–2), 1-135.

Parikh, R., & Movassate, M. (2009). *Sentiment analysis of user-generated twitter updates using various classification techniques.* CS224N Final Report, 118.

Pouyanfar, S., Yang, Y., Chen, S. C., Shyu, M. L., & Iyengar, S. S. (2018). Multimedia big data analytics: A survey. *ACM Computing Surveys, 51*(1), 10. doi:10.1145/3150226

Qiu, G., He, X., Zhang, F., Shi, Y., Bu, J., & Chen, C. (2010). DASA: Dissatisfaction-oriented advertising based on sentiment analysis. *Expert Systems with Applications, 37*(9), 6182–6191. doi:10.1016/j.eswa.2010.02.109

Rui, H., Liu, Y., & Whinston, A. (2013). Whose and what chatter matters? The effect of tweets on movie sales. *Decision Support Systems, 55*(4), 863–870. doi:10.1016/j.dss.2012.12.022

Sharma, R., Nigam, S., & Jain, R. (2014). *Opinion mining of movie reviews at document level.* arXiv preprint arXiv:1408.3829

Socher, R., Perelygin, A., Wu, J., Chuang, J., Manning, C. D., Ng, A., & Potts, C. (2013, October). Recursive deep models for semantic compositionality over a sentiment treebank. In *Proceedings of the 2013 conference on empirical methods in natural language processing* (pp. 1631-1642). Academic Press.

Solanki, A., & Pandey, S. (2019). Music instrument recognition using deep convolutional neural networks. *International Journal of Information Technology*, 1-10.

Taboada, M., Brooke, J., Tofiloski, M., Voll, K., & Stede, M. (2011). Lexicon-based methods for sentiment analysis. *Computational Linguistics, 37*(2), 267–307. doi:10.1162/COLI_a_00049

Tan, W., Blake, M. B., Saleh, I., & Dustdar, S. (2013). Social-network-sourced big data analytics. *IEEE Internet Computing, 17*(5), 62–69. doi:10.1109/MIC.2013.100

Tong, R. M. (2001, September). An operational system for detecting and tracking opinions in on-line discussion. In *Working Notes of the ACM SIGIR 2001 Workshop on Operational Text Classification* (*Vol. 1*, No. 6). Academic Press.

Turney, P. D. (2002, July). Thumbs up or thumbs down?: semantic orientation applied to unsupervised classification of reviews. In *Proceedings of the 40th annual meeting on association for computational linguistics* (pp. 417-424). Association for Computational Linguistics.

Wan, X. (2009, August). Co-training for cross-lingual sentiment classification. In *Proceedings of the Joint Conference of the 47th Annual Meeting of the ACL and the 4th International Joint Conference on Natural Language Processing of the AFNLP* (pp. 235-243). Association for Computational Linguistics.

Wan, X. (2012, December). A comparative study of cross-lingual sentiment classification. In *Proceedings of the 2012 IEEE/WIC/ACM International Joint Conferences on Web Intelligence and Intelligent Agent Technology-Volume 01* (pp. 24-31). IEEE Computer Society. 10.1109/WI-IAT.2012.54

Wang, Y. Y., & Acero, A. (2007, December). Maximum entropy model parameterization with TF* IDF weighted vector space model. In *2007 IEEE Workshop on Automatic Speech Recognition & Understanding (ASRU)* (pp. 213-218). IEEE. 10.1109/ASRU.2007.4430111

Yang, C. S., & Shih, H. P. (2012). A Rule-Based Approach For Effective Sentiment Analysis. In PACIS (p. 181). Academic Press.

Yang, W. S., & Dia, J. B. (2008). Discovering cohesive subgroups from social networks for targeted advertising. *Expert Systems with Applications*, *34*(3), 2029–2038. doi:10.1016/j.eswa.2007.02.028

Ye, Q., Zhang, Z., & Law, R. (2009). Sentiment classification of online reviews to travel destinations by supervised machine learning approaches. *Expert Systems with Applications*, *36*(3), 6527–6535. doi:10.1016/j.eswa.2008.07.035

This research was previously published in the Handbook of Research on Emerging Trends and Applications of Machine Learning; pages 528-549, copyright year 2020 by Engineering Science Reference (an imprint of IGI Global).

Chapter 70
Using Sentiment Analysis for Evaluating e–WOM:
A Data Mining Approach for Marketing Decision Making

Zehra Nur Canbolat

https://orcid.org/0000-0001-8359-5713

Istanbul Medipol University, Turkey

Fatih Pinarbasi

https://orcid.org/0000-0001-9005-0324

Istanbul Medipol University, Turkey

ABSTRACT

Electronic word of mouth is one of the keys elements for marketing decision making. e-WOM has been focus of marketing research as technology and social media become larger part of consumers' lives. This study set out to examine e-wom concept with sentiment analysis methodology in service industry context. The structure of study is twofold including theoretical backgound of related concepts and application section. Theoretical backgound section contains electronic word of mouth, new consumer and sentiment analysis concepts, and included selected studies for sentiment analysis. The application section which this study has focus on includes a three-stage plan for sentiment analysis practices. Each stage has three different scenarios. One algorithm and one real-life application for each stage are included. Nine scenarios for different service organizations imply that sentiment analysis supported with other methodologies can contribute to understanding of electronic word of mouth.

DOI: 10.4018/978-1-6684-6303-1.ch070

INTRODUCTION

Communication is the key element of the social being for humankind from the beginning. Exchanging ideas, goods or services, helping to others are always parts of people's lives for ages. As roots of marketing and sales are based on the social exchange theory, communication is still affecting people even the forms of communication changes with increasing technology and communication mediums. A pre-historic age man could exchange goods for the needs before the invention of money. This man and his society lived in a village and they talked to each other about goods/services like the other things they live. Appearing of some "good" sellers in that village is ineviatable. Therefore, this could be a basic form of word of mouth in a historical view. People lives in societies, interacts with each other, no matter communication mediums or exchanging ways change.

Digitalization is a crucial part of people in last of the 20th and 21st century, as habits and behaviors are transferred to digital norms and time passed on online increases. According to We Are Social (2018) 7.593 billion of world population has 53% internet user rate (4.021 billion) and 42% active social media user rate (3.196 billion). That pre-historic man is telling experiences to his neighbor with the messenger on a mobile phone, writes reviews about the treadmill he buys online from another seller which is from another part of the country, chooses the restaurant he wants to go out with his girlfriend by examining the rating scores of local restaurants online. In sum digitalization and communication have strong relationships for people.

Next part of change is taking place for the business side. Thousands of "pre-historic man with digital technology" live online and affect each other for purchasing decisions, in terms of "action and reaction" approach, there must be some reaction on the business side. Marketing and communication plans include not the only company to the customer (one way) communication, but also the customer to the company and customer-to-customer communications, as the nature of communication has changed with web 2.0 technologies. According to Mangold and Faulds (2009), social media has two promotional roles in the marketplace. First one relates to the company to customer communication, while the second role includes communication of consumers to each other. Companies have to take actions regarding changes for the business side.

Word of mouth, a sub-concept of communication is also affected by changes from technology. E-wom concept has a growing interest in marketing and communication contexts, regarding social media and web 2.0 mediums. Review sites, pages of places online are popular for decision making of people. Negative or positive comments written by previous buyers can affect people's decision. According to Nielsen (2015) survey, 83% of participants completely or somewhat trust recommendations of friends or family. It is obvious that successful brands are conscious of digitalization and creates their plans regarding new customers. For e-wom concept, there are three elements to take into for understanding communication. The first element is related to "What" question which refers to the content of the communication. What customers write about your service? What they emphasize, what they do not mind? are the starting questions. The second element is related to "How" question which refers to style or form of communication. How do customers respond to your new service launch? How they do like or do not like your service? How is the mood of customers; happy, angry, excited or hateful? are the questions. The third element is related to "When?" question which refers to the time period of e-wom communication. How long do your customers' reviews take for your new service? Is there any seasonality for your brand? are the starting questions. Beyond these elements there are also customers and communication mediums to consider which are part of the main marketing plan. This study focuses on communication elements of e-wom concept for the brand side.

Previous studies for sentiment analysis concept cover several contexts including emphasizing methodology (Wilson et al., 2005; Pak &Paroubek, 2010; Liu, 2010, Taboada et al., 2011; Dragoni et al., 2018) or contexts (Kucuktunc et al., 2012; Ghiassi et al., 2013; Wen et al., 2014).

Approaches from previous studies mostly refer to technical only studies or limited context marketing studies. The lack of integrated studies in literature will be addressed by this study, as integrated research including both theory and cases is implemented. On the other hand, context-based studies like case researches are helpful for understanding phenomenons. Easton (2010) defines case research as a research method which includes i) investigating one or a small number of social entities/situations, ii) collecting data with using multiple sources of data, iii) developing holistic description by the iterative research process. Thus, example cases and applications will be used for this study.

This study has two-fold aims for evaluating the e-wom concept. The first aim includes theoretical background of e-wom concept and service context, while the second aim has real business cases regarding service industry for managerial side. These aims are integrated into this study as they contribute to a comprehensive approach.

Consistent with aims of the study, this study consists of three parts mainly. First part includes electronic word of mouth, new consumer and sentiment analysis concepts regarding theoretical background. The second part consists of two main sections. The first section includes a three-step pyramid for using sentiment analysis in marketing decision making, these steps are anomaly detection, sentiment analysis and text mining. The second section includes technical steps for sentiment analysis and real-life application. Algorithms for three step-plan are presented and an example case with a dataset is included.

LITERATURE REVIEW

Electronic Word of Mouth

Word of mouth refers to the act of consumers providing information related to goods, services, brands, companies to other consumers (Babić Rosario et al., 2016). e-Wom refers to any positive or negative statement which is available to multiple consumers/companies with the internet. These statements can be made by actual, former or potential consumers (Hennig-Thruau et al., 2004). Comparing word of mouth concept with electronic word of mouth is important since the medium for communication affects significantly. Berger and Iyenyar (2013) conclude that written and oral communication have significant differences as they affect product and brands which consumers discuss. Written communication leads people to write about more interesting products and brands.

One main topic in word of mouth context is related to the motivation side. Sundaral et al (1998) imply that motivations related to engagement about positive wom are product involvement, altruistic and self-enhancement, while motivations for engaging negative wom to include anxiety reduction, altruistic, advice seeking and vengeance. The emotions which play role in word of mouth need to be examined carefully for marketing defcision making. On the other side Hennig-Thurau et al. (2004) study motivations for an electronic word of mouth context and concluded the motivations for e-wom. These motivations include consumers' desire for social interaction, desire for economic incentives, potential to enhance their own self-worth and their concern for others. Yang (2017) examine word of mouth concept in terms of e-wom and finds that an individual's altruistic needs affect positive e-wom and perceived usefulness of website is related to e-wom intentions.

Following motivation side of e-wom, the effect of e-wom also matters. De Langhe et al. (2015) find that customers heavily weight average ratings, rather than a quality like price and number of ratings, even average user ratings have problems with objectivity issues including; inconsistency with Consumer Reports scores, insufficient sample sizes etc. This subjective phenomenon related to online consumer behavior causes new research questions including; How can e-wom be measured? Which contexts e-wom has more effective at? Which content elements have advantages or disadvantages? How e-wom content spread at different platforms?

Recent studies on electronic word of mouth covers different contexts and themes including; hospitality/ tourism (Fine et al., 2017; Liang et al., 2018; Yan et al., 2018; Zhang et al., 2019), ephemeral social media (Wakefield & Bennett, 2018), social networking sites (Aghakhani et al., 2018; Fang et al., 2018) and brand image (Krishnamurty and Kumar, 2018).

This study will follow a technical approach as sentiment analysis and text mining for better measurement of contents related to e-wom. Next section continues with "new" consumer concept and recent communication mediums as they are in relation with the e-wom concept.

"New" Consumer and Communication Mediums

Several changes and advancements effect of today's consumer worldwide for many years. Consumers have different options of communication channels, different ways of purchase actions and most importantly have changing behaviour patterns. Belk (2013) updates the extended-self concept regarding digital world and concludes that the digital world opens new means for self-extension. He summarizes modifications of extended self regarding digital world with five topics including; dematerialization, reembodiment, sharing, co-construction of self and distributed memory. As all changes offer different types of advancements, sharing is related to word of mouth concept. New consumers have several mediums to share their ideas, feelings etc.

In addition to the "new consumer" concept, technological advancements are worth to consider. Changing of web from "read-only" to "read-write" created enthusiastic users who interact/share through web mediums, followingly collective knowledge spread through web (Cambria et al. 2013). Consistent to this, Web 2.0 technologies including user reviews, comments and reports about travel experiences have crucial role as an information source, as they do not include marketing considerations by companies and reflect real experiences (Kasper & Vela, 2011). This "reality" concept contains the potential for marketing researches includes questions about actuality, volume, sentiment. On the other handservice industry is influenced by new communication mediums. Levy et al. (2012) study hospitality context and concluded that social media makes using reviews necessary for hotels. Kim et al. (2015) find that managing process related to reviews on social media is a crucial part of hotel marketing, they also conclude that overall rating and response to negative comments are related to hotel performance. In another study Xie et al. (2014) conclude that hotel performance has a correlation relationship with several factors including overall rating, attribute ratings of purchase value, variation and volume of consumer reviews, location and cleanliness and number of management responses. Therefore, in addition to "new" consumer concept, new mediums for communication are important parts of e-wom concept.

Increasing data posted online and new communication methods makes new researches possible by providing mass information related to consumers and brands. Unlike traditional methods, new research methodologies emerge due to new research possibilities. Latent Dirichlet Allocation for detecting topics (Brody &Elhadad, 2010), text mining for social media competitive analysis (He et al., 2013), eye tracking methodology (Maughan et al., 2007) are some of new methodologies for marketing research.

Sentiment analysis is one of the new methodologies contributing to sensemaking of consumer on web. As more data consumers produce, the need for speed is increasing, thus it makes technical methodologies necessary for better marketing decision making. Next section contains information related to sentiment analysis and sample cases related to sentiment analysis are included followingly.

Sentiment Analysis

Content generated by consumers is increasing day by day with the help of technology and social media. From this fact, it is important for decision makers to discover meanings from the content. Sentiment analysis (opinion mining) is a computational study which examines opinions, attitudes, emotions and appraisals related to individuals, events, issues, topics and their attributes (Liu & Zhang, 2012). On the other hand, Vinodhini and Chandrasekaran (2012) define sentiment analysis as a type of natural language processing which is used to track mood of public related to specific product or topic. It can be a powerful marketing decision making tool for the people-oriented service industry since insights about consumers matter. Pang and Lee (2008) emphasize on the 2001 year regarding history of sentiment analysis and concluded factors related to showing up of sentiment analysis studies. These factors include; the availability of datasets and development of review-aggregation websites, rising of machine learning methods for natural language processing and information retrieval, recognition of intellectual challenges, commercial and intelligence applications. This study uses a public dataset for sample cases in next section.

Sentiment analysis has two approaches for detecting sentiments; first one refers to lexicon-based approach, second one refers to the classification approach (Taboada et al., 2011). Lexicon based approach can be used for document, sentence or entity level, while it can be inefficient since it depends on presence of certain words and can miss sentiments which are not clearly expressed (Zhang et al., 2011). The second approach starts with previously labeled data (positive, negative or neutral), extracts features which model differences between classes and finally infer a function to predict/classify new examples (Kolchyna et al., 2015). It is also useful to integrate approaches for improving accuracy rates. Melville et al. (2009) use lexical knowledge with classification for blogs, Ortigosa et al. (2014) use both lexicon-based, machine learning and hybrid approach for Facebook content, Zhang et al. (2011) combine lexicon based and learning based approach for Twitter. It is important to decide appropriate methodology for contexts.

Contextual differences are crucial for sentiment analysis as it is mainly affected by content. Different languages and different contexts are studied in sentiment analysis context. Tan and Zhang (2008) studied Chinese documents with sentiment analysis and concluded that sentiment classifiers are heavily related to topics or domains. In another study, Duwairi and El-Orfali (2014) examine the Arabic language in sentiment analysis methodology, they investigate different methods and conclude that preprocessing strategies contribute to performance of classifiers. Thus, it is important to investigate further contexts beyond English language and most preferred social media channels. This study includes different scenarios related to different contexts to meet the requirements of different industries.

The combination of sentiment analysis technique with other technique is another research section. Sentiment analysis is studied with different methodologies like bass model for predicting product sales (Fan et al., 2017), with VIKOR approach for measuring customer satisfaction (Kang and Park, 2014). Sentimental analysis can be useful when it is employed alone, but it can be also used as complementary technique. This study included text mining approach as complementary technique to sentiment analysis in next section.

As the history of sentiment analysis includes many significant studies, there are six studies included in Table 1. regarding sentiment analysis context.

Table 1. Selected studies for sentiment analysis context

Author	Subject	Scope	Conclusion
Prabowo and Thelwall (2009)	Combined Method	Movie Reviews, Product Reviews, Myspace Comments	This study combined rule-based classification, machine learning and supervised learning in order to improve classification.
Shi and Li (2011)	Supervised Learning	Hotel Reviews	Online hotel reviews examined with unigram feature with two types of information; frequency and TF-IDF. It is concluded that TF-IDF has better results than frequency information in a supervised learning approach.
Greaves et al. (2013)	Patient Experience	Free-Text Comments	Machine learning is employed to evaluate patient experiences through comments. It is concluded that there is a correlation with results of patient survey and machine learning predictions.
Wen et al. (2014)	Opinions Related to Online Courses	Discussion Forum Posts	Sentiment analysis is employed to evaluate student's opinions regarding online courses. Correlation between sentiment ratio of daily forum posts and a number of drop out students is concluded.
Liu et al. (2017)	Product Ranking	Online Review	The sentiment analysis technique is used with a fuzzy set theory for product ranking system, while identified sentiments are converted to fuzzy numbers. Intuitionistic fuzzy set theory based ranking approach is included.
Mäntylä et al. (2018)	Sentiment Analysis Concept	Literature Review	6996 papers from Scopus related to sentiment analysis are examined. Details about sentiment analysis like historical roots, publication venues and research topics are included.

Overall, these studies show that sentiment analysis has variety in terms of context and subjects. As there are lots of web platforms and content, different algorithms and methodologies have different true detection rates for contexts. For example, recent studies related to sentiment analysis includes differen contexts like; tourism (Alaei et al., 2019), finance (Sohangir et al., 2018; Chiong et al., 2018; Batra &Daudpota, 2018) and sales forecasting (Lau et al., 2018). The second part of this study will continue with real life applications of sentiment analysis.

SAMPLE CASES AND REAL-LIFE APPLICATIONSABOUT EVALUATING WORD OF MOUTH

Sentiment analysis has a wide range of applications for different contexts like website comments, social media pages and blog posts. This makes including sample cases necessary for this study. Three stage-plan for evaluating e-wom is included in this section regarding different phases of examination. The deductive approach is employed in this plan for sensemaking e-wom related interactions.

Figure 1. Three step plan for sentiment analysis

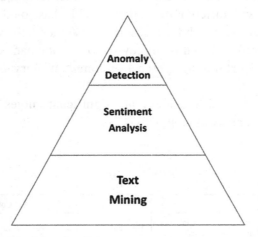

The application section of this study has three cases. Consistent to deductive approach, the first case starts with a general/top-view for evaluating peaks about e-wom content. This process would be a starting point as it includes breakouts about consumer interactions in marketing decision making. The second case starts with either finding of the first case or general e-wom content. The second case includes detecting polarity first and several sentiment types. The third case refers to complementary side of sentiment analysis and it supports with text mining approach. This deductive approach makes each step complete each other to improve sentiment analysis.

Three scenarios will be included in each case. Each scenario has a specific industry, company size, marketing decision making organization, marketing strategies and marketing goals. The selected industries are consistent with Global Industry Forecasts report (Statista, 2016) and top 10 global industries by revenue in 2015. According to this report, financial and insurance activities have 3.609 billion USD revenue, professional, scientific and technical activities have 3.214 billion USD revenue, transportation and storage have 2.486 billion USD revenue, human health and social work activities have 2.002 billion USD revenue, information and communication have 1.771 billion USD revenue. These scenarios contribute to the understanding of sentiment analysis by supporting different examples. In addition to three different marketing scenarios, one algorithm for each stage will be included. This integrative approach would contribute to sentiment analysis concept with real life applications. At the end of this section, nine e-wom scenarios, three algorithms and three examples will integrate for three steps of plan.

Case 1: Detection of Sentiment Anomalies in Social Media for Brands

Markets and web platforms are similiar in terms of action flow, interactions take place moment to moment. Actors of continous events can be also objects of these events and it is important to understand marginal changes for sensemaking process. Due to increase in amount of data in social media and website platforms, sensemaking of data becomes important.

This case refers to a macro view of e-wom content and interactions. Detecting any possible increases or decreases contributes to marketing decision making and findings in this stage are related to Opportunities and Threats topics in SWOT analysis. Detecting periodic changes and correlations in market is crucial for marketing decision making, as there are interesting correlations in market. For example, Bollen et al. (2011) concluded that public mood states are correlated with daily changes in stock market.

The technical aspect of the first case starts with identifying communication mediums and metrics which are related to marketing decision making. These metrics can include interactions on social media, review volume on websites, e-mail communication to company mail and it can be controlled hourly, daily or weekly. Following identification of metrics, possible breakouts must be determined and matched to metrics. For example, communication crisis can be related to increasing negative interactions, new service launch of a competitor can be related to total reviews on website. The third step in first case includes decision of action related to breakout detected in second step. Service companies either have active communication/marketing strategy or passive strategy. The question in this step is related to whether the breakout will be used for further actions or not.

In Table 2, three different scenarios from different company sizes included for first case. Each company has different strategies and goals for first case, therefore demands from first case differ.

Table 2. Scenarios for case 1

	A Dentistry	**B Training**	**C Hotels**
Industry	Health	Business Education	Tourism
Company Size	Small	SME	Large
Marketing Decision Making Organization	Boss plans marketing	Small marketing department.	Outsourcing marketing to agency
Marketing Strategy	Finding opportunities about challenges competitors face.	Detecting potential consumer needs and potential market gaps.	Maintaining top position in market.
Marketing Goals for Case	Evaluating local demand increases on the web. Detecting seasonality about sector.	Evaluating any increase in problems competitors face. Discovering salient seasons related to the education sector.	Examining consumers' problems in macro perspective. Listing industry based seasonalities for marketing campaigns. Controlling possible public relation crisis.

These scenarios have their own parameters and goals for steps in the first case. In first step of first case which mediums and metrics are set, "A Dendistry" can set local review websites and health-theme community forums as mediums and review volume weekly as metrics. "B Training" can set social media groups on Linkedin and business theme news websites as mediums, while group interactions and news and comments volume are set as metrics. Lastly "C Hotels" can set Instagram location pages and Twitter hashtags as mediums, total instagram photos and tweets as metrics.

The second step includes anomalies and breakouts for each company. "A Dentistry" can set weekly 40 reviews on review websites and 100 forum posts as standart metrics. "B Training" can set 10 posts on Linkedin groups and 4 news and 40 comments for a news website as standart metrics. "C Hotels" can set 140 new photos for Instagram location page and 100 tweets for related hashtag as standart metrics.

The third step contains action plan for second step findings, "A Dendistry" can reach users personally, while "B Training" post statuses about related business trends, "C Hotels" can demand advertisement briefs from agency related to uprising consumer concerns.

Case 2: Determination of Sentiments Related to Consumer Reactions Social Media

Understanding e-wom content requires more than quantity, details are also important for marketing decision making. Positive-negative polarities are the first step for sentiment analysis since it reflects main attitude of consumer related to service or product. Specific sentiments including anger, hate, anticipate, joy also crucial for decision making as they are related to specific marketing mix elements. For example, positive e-wom reaction could be an indicator for new consumers but joy and trust have different consequences for consumers.

The technical side of case two starts with deciding sentiment analysis approach since each approach has different features. Lexicon based approach could be useful for general topics, classification-based approach for novelty research and finally hybrid approach can be developed for specific cases. The second step of sentiment analysis includes programming language for analysis. Many programming languages offer sentiment analysis related tools. The third step contains an implementation of sentiment analysis either with polarities or specific sentiments.

Table 3. Scenarios for case 2

	DRestaurant	**EAirlines**	**F Telecom**
Industry	Restaurant	Travel	Telecommunication
Company Size	Middle Size	Large	Large
Marketing Decision Making Organization	In-house marketing team	Marketing Agency manages	Marketing Team
Marketing Strategy	Detecting consumer reactions to existing and potential venues	Evaluating consumer sentiements related to seasonal campaign periodically.	Integrating consumer complaint service with sentiment analysis approach.
Marketing Goals for Case	Discovering existing consumer reactions. Creating a reaction database for potential venues.	Examining different consumer sentiments related to campaigns and take actions.	Assigning negative consumer reactions to complaint service quicker.

These three scenarios from different industries included as sentiment analysis offers different types of sentiments to brands. Since each service industry has its own characteristics, it is useful to use detail sentiments beyond main polarities (positive/negative) for marketing decision making.

The first stage in second case refers to detecting polarities for e-wom content. Positivity and negativty are important starting points for evaluating consumer feedbacks and e-wom. This step could be implemented with the help of main sentiment analysis tools, since it is easier to detect main polarities than detail sentiments. "D Restaurant" can use sentiment polarities for evaluating existing consumer reactions as it is important to monitor different venues periodically. Discovering new venues can be implemented by using location pages on Instagram. In addition to the amount of content shared for location pages, it is also important to consider sentiments in content. Polarities toward positivity at these locations can guide service brands. "E airlines" can use polarities for marketing campaign performance, since it reflects the main reactions of consumer to service company. Launching of a new flight venue can be an example of sentiment analysis which examines consumers' reactions as positive and negative polarities. "F Telecom" can use sentiment analysis for fast feedback consumer complaint service. A helpdesk account on social media can be used for consumer complaint management and reactions toward this account can be examined.

Second stage in second case includes process of detecting different sentiments. This is the next step for sentiment analysis beyond polarities since it contains more consumer insights. "D Restaurant" can measure specific positive sentiments including; joy and suprise. "E Airlines" can use this step for measuring exciteness for specific campaigns. Finally, "F Telecom" can use it for detailing consumer complaints. For example, the ratio of angerness in complaints, the ratio of hate sentiment in complaints have different insights for service marketing, thus managing feedback process requires different approaches. Sentiment analysis with specific sentiments makes these approaches possible.

Case 3: Identifying Word Patterns / N-Gram Detecting for Sentiment Analysis

Although sentiment analysis contributes to marketing decision making by detecting polarity or emotions generally, there are some areas need to be improved. As the content of e-wom includes linguistic elements, it is important to consider the meaning and use of these elements. For example, Agarwal et al. (2008) uses conjunctions for linguistic approach, Subrahmanian et al. (2008) use an integrated approach which combines adjective-verb-adverb combinations for sentiment analysis. These studies confirm the potential of using linguistic approach for sentiment analysis for better results. Therefore, case three focuses on linguistic approach with text mining methodology. As the technical advancements and approaches mostly refers to technical side of sentiment analysis, this study uses more generic methodology consistent with its "marketing" focus. N-gram methodology can contribute to the consumer side of sentiment analysis.

Technical aspect of this case starts with pre-processing raw data from stage 2, as they contain a different type of linguistic elements. Punctations, two spaces, numbers and emojis are removed in the pre-processing stage, thus second stepe there is plain text content to process. Second step starts with finding frequencies for each word for most used words represenatation. Pre-processing step can be implemented backward due to any meaningless words for marketing appears. These words could be "the", "and", "or" etc. Third step refers to the n-gram analysis process. Different from most used words representation it refers to using words together with "n" couple words. 2-grams refer to two words used together in expressions, 3-grams refer to three words used together in expressions.

In Table 4, there are three scenarios included targeting to get insight from text mining approach. Since this process is an advanced process, all three brands have advanced marketing decision making already.

Implementation side of case three starts with setting the content for text mining. This content could be the same as case two or extracted from other marketing sources. "G Agency" can use reviews of hotel websites for their customers, "H Bank" can use the Twitter hashtag for their bank #ilovebanknamedh and lastly "K Website" can use reviews and comments from competitors' websites.

Second step inclures pre-processing of text data for mining. "Noises" in texts including punctations, numbers, emojis and stopwords can mislead methodology, thus this step applies to all three scenarios.

Third step includes calculating frequencies for processed text content. Each word has a frequency number indicating how many times the word used in content. It needs to be checked words before proceeding, as some of the words can still mislead methodology. Finally, most used words in e-wom content are reported. Last step includes examining n-grams from text content. Similiar to third step, words are calculated but with an exception, this time word pairs are considered. Two-word pairs for 2-grams, three words for 3-grams are evaluated. At the end of step, n-grams are reported.

Table 4. Scenarios for case 3

	G Agency	**HBank**	**K Website**
Industry	Marketing Consultancy	Finance	Movie Stream
Company Size	Middle Size	Large	Large
Marketing Decision Making Organization	In-house marketing team	Large marketing department	Large marketing department
Marketing Strategy	Detecting gaps which consumer adressunconciously.	Long-term consumer satisfaction	Service segmentation with the help of text mining and sentiment analysis.
Marketing Goals for Case	Evaulating consumers of parttners expectations with text mining.	Setting an alert system connected to specific n-grams from VIP consumers.	Segment consumers and services with help of descriptive expressions from web.

APPLICATIONS OF SENTIMENT ANALYSIS

Anomaly Detection Application

Anomaly detection application consists of two parts including algorithm and coding implementation. As there are many coding languages available for marketing decision makers, it is useful to include an algorithm for anomaly detection stage. Therefore, any coding language could be implemented through an algorithm, regardless of language choice. Algorithm for application one is indicated in Figure 2.

Figure 2. Algorithm for case 1

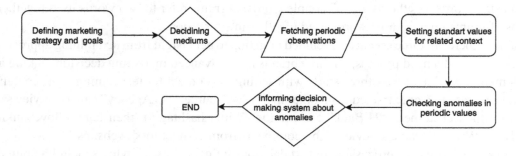

Implementation of first case can be done easily by web technologies. We choose the R programming language for this study and related R packages could be useful for implementation. R code package named "Anomalize" (Dancho & Vaughan, 2018) is used for methodology to detect anomalize and graph them.

The methodology also uses two additional R packages for technical background, including tidyverse (Wickham, 2017) and tibbletime (Vaughan & Dancho, 2019).

Data collection: Google Trends (2019) statistics of search query is used for this application. Since Google Trend statistics signal popularity of specific keywords, it would be a good opportunity for service companies to examine online insights for their marketing decision making. "barcelona hotels" search query is examined with following parameters; area is worldwide, while web search filter is active and last 12 months are examined. Data starts from April 2018 to April 2019.

Analyis: Anomalize package has three main functions for analyzing time series data regarding to anomaly detection. These functions are; time_decompose (), anomalize () and time_recompose().

First function decompose time series for preparing anomaly detection, it has two methods for decomposing, first one is STL and the other one is the Twitter method. According to Dancho and Vaughan (2018), Stl method from "stats" package (R Core Team, 2018) seperates season and trends components from observed component, thus it finds remainder component for anomaly. On the other hand twitter method from Anomaly Detection package (Owen et al., 2014) uses seperating seasonal component, then removes median data. Second function, anomalize(), implements the anomalization process by using two methods, iqr and gesd. According to Dancho and Vaughan (2018) IQR method from foreceast package (Hyndman & Khandakar, 2008; Hyndman et al., 2019) uses innerquartile range of 25 the median, while GESD method from Anomaly Detection package (Owen et al., 2014) eliminates outliers using Student's T-Test which compares teset statistic to a critical value. Last function, time_recompose() uses remainder fields produced at anomalize () function and season, trend/median spans values produced at time_decompose() function for reconstructing band around normal values (Dancho and Vaughan, 2018)

Figure 3 includes anomaly detection results with, stl decomposing method and gesd anomalize method. Red point implies the anomaly section of search query, there is anormal decrease for that point.

Figure 3. Anomaly detection results

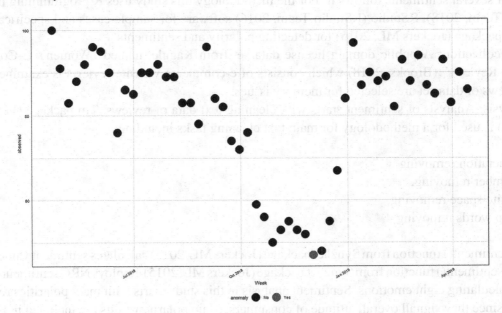

Marketing decision making can use findings of case one as signals for marketing campaigns. Markets have dynamic nature which contains consumer trends and behavior changes. It is crucial for service marketing decision makers to understand changes in consumer attitudes and opinions. Second application will continue with sentiment analysis processes.

Sentiment Analysis Application

Sentiment analysis application consists of two parts, similiar to previous application, one part is algorithm and other part is coding implementation. Algorithm for application two is indicated in Figure 4.

Figure 4. Algorithm for case 2

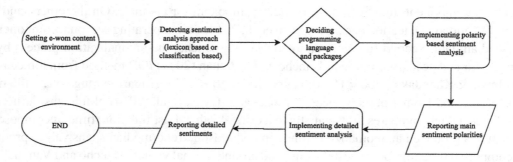

One of the common tasks of sentiment analysis is polarity classification which refers to classification of content between two opposite sentiments (Cambria et al. 2013). Consistent to deductive approach, detection of polarities follows anomaly detection. Case two examines polarities of content firstly, detection of several sentiments follows it. For the methodology this study uses R programming language (R Core Team, 2018), RStudio (RStudio Team, 2016) software for sample cases and specifically uses Syuzhet package (Jockers ML, 2015) for detecting polarity and sentiments.

Data collection: A public domain license data set from Kaggle, named "Women's E-Commerce Clothing Reviews" (Brooks, 2018) which consists of e-commerce website reviews is examined. First, 500 reviews of data set are selected for memory issues.

Analysis: Analysis of sentiment starts with cleaning text data of reviews. Tm package (Feinerer et al., 2008) is used for a methodology for main text cleaning tasks including;

- Punctation removing
- Number removing,
- White space removing,
- Stop words removing

get_sentiment() function from Syuzhet package (Jockers ML, 2015) calculates sentiment values, while get_nrc_sentiment() function from Syuzhet package (Jockers ML, 2015) employs NRC sentiment dictionary for calculating eight emotions. Sentiment analysis in this study starts with main polarities regarding reviews, since they signall overall attitude of consumers. Main polarity results are included in Figure 5.

Figure 5 generated by Syuzhet package implies that most of the reviews refer to positive polarity. This could be an indicator for overall positivity and consumer satisfaction performance. As the information is general, it is important to go further to examine which sentiments regarding to polarities exist. Figure 6 implies different sentiments regarding to reviews.

Figure 6 generated by Syuzhet package implies that the majority of sentiment from review process refers to trust, joy and anticipation categories. The least sentiments from review process refer to disgust, fear and anger sentiments. These findings can be used as signal for consumer sentiment details.

Figure 5. Polarity results of sentiment analysis

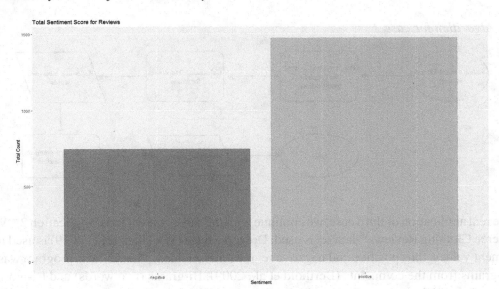

Figure 6. Different sentiment results for case 2

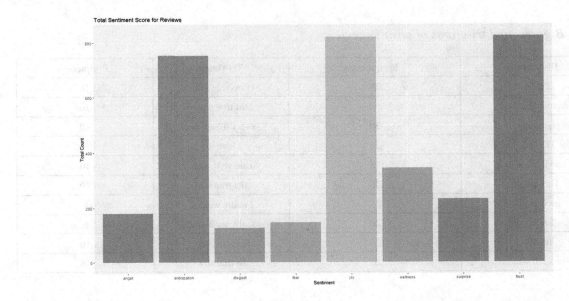

Marketing decision making can use sentiment analysis for managing customer relationships online. It helps decision makers by providing/helping accurate decisions and fast interactions. It can be also implemented to integrate with other steps in marketing decision makings like customer complaint management or advertising campaigns.

Text Mining Application

Text mining application has two parts including algorithm and coding implementation. Algorithm for application is indicated in Figure 7.

Figure 7. Algorithm for case 3

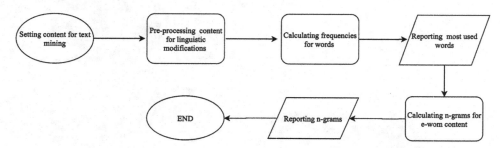

For the real application of third case, we continue with the same content from application 2, "Women's E-Commerce Clothing Reviews" data set is used. Dplyr package (Wickham et al., 2019) is used for filtering sentiment values, thus positive and negative reviews are selected. The KNIME program was used to extract n-grams from the comments (Berthold et al., 2009). Bi-grams (two words) and tri-grams (three words) signal expression of consumers which can be helpful for marketing decision making. Bi-grams related to positive and negative reviews are included in Table 5.

Table 5. Bigrams and tri-grams of positive reviews

Bi-Gram	Frequency	Tri-Gram	Frequency
I love	78	runs true size	16
true size	62	fit true size	16
size small	30	every time wear	10
This top	28	I love top	10
well made	28	cant wait wear	10
This dress	26	fits true size	10
im usually	26	I really wanted	8
I really	26	usually wear small	8
im lbs	26	runs true size	16
ordered size	26	fit true size	16

Bi-grams related to negative reviews are included in Table 6. Tri-grams for negative reviews is not included, as they have all equal values. Table 6 shows that zipper part of product is important for consumers.

Table 6. Bi-Grams for negative reviews

Bi-Gram	Frequency
side zipper	6
needless say	4
Dress runs	2
runs small	2
small esp	2
esp zipper	2
zipper area	2
area runs	2
runs ordered	2
ordered sp	2

Marketing decision making can use stage three for advanced consumer insights. Conclusions are related to expression styles of consumers, therefore many consumer insights can be extracted for different targets. Advertisement taglines, product descriptions, even product slogans can start from consumers' expression. It is a complementary methodology for sentiment analysis and it supports other marketing efforts by providing linguistic conclusions.

SOLUTIONS AND RECOMMENDATIONS

Solutions regarding sentiment analysis for e-wom contains an integrative 3-step plan for marketing decision making. The first step implies observing amount of interactions regardless of polarity or sentiments. This step refers to top-view, most general tracking system for marketing. The determination of possible important events can guide marketing management for reactions. These events can be either brand-related or market-related. For example, competitor of brand can have negative peak moments, this could be a competitive opportunity. Second step which relates to sentimental details of market moments/consumers' interactions includes sentiment analysis processes about polarity and emotions. Sentiment analysis in this step mostly includes positive/negative and neutral polarity, but with help of technology and linguistic approach specific emotions can be examined. This step clarifies previous step by supporting details and helps marketing team sensemaking of market. The final step of the 3-step plan employs text mining methodology for evaluating e-wom content with linguistic approach. This step includes improvements for second step, as sentiment analysis has some accuracy problems regarding context and language specific expressions. In summary 3-step plan from top-view to specific details can help marketing decision making for sensemaking and evaluating e-wom for service industry.

Applications about industries can benefit from this 3-step plan and sentiment analysis. The first step of plan can be implemented of social media tracking tools. These tools can notify when different peaks take place about brand or market. The second and third step requires brand specific efforts regarding differences about markets. Employing human resource for data mining, digital marketing and related departments could be cost-effective in long term. Sentiment analysis and sensemaking of e-wom has long-term nature, therefore decisions related to sentiment analysis mostly refers to strategic decision making. Marketing decision makers must employ strategic planning and long-term goals to maintain and integrate sentiment analysis into their holistic marketing strategy.

FUTURE RESEARCH DIRECTIONS

Future research directions about this study consist of three points which reflects characteristics of sentiment analysis process. These are dynamic nature of electronic word-of-mouth, scope of sentiments in word of mouth and lastly technical advancements of sentiment analysis.

The first research point in sentiment analysis is related to dynamic of electronic word-of-mouth. It would be useful to research increase/decrease periods of consumers's communication. The crisis moments for brands or the positive peaks related to consumers' perceptions contain insights for marketing decision making. Therefore, new research questions can arise from specific events like launching product/store or general events like the Super Bowl.

The second point in sentiment analysis is related to scope of emotions which has different aspects beyond positive/negative/neutral polarities. Specific sentiments like joy, anger, excitement can guide marketing decision makers through e-wom campaign processes. Therefore, characteristics of particular feelings would be next topics.

Third point in sentiment analysis includes technical aspects of research. As sentiment analysis methods include lexicon/dictionary-based techniques, advanced techniques like machine learning could be next point. Regarding usefulness of dictionary-based sentiment analysis, context-based differences could matter. Same word can mean different concepts in different contexts as the tone and theme of communication differs for each context. Therefore developing different dictionaries regarding to different contexts would be next research topics.

CONCLUSION

The study includes e-wom concept in service context in first part and gives information regarding to conceptual structure of related topics. It is concluded that technological advancements and social media change word of mouth concept in terms of electronic word of mouth. New findings related to digital habits and behaviors create new research topics for consumer context. The volume of content related to e-wom, spreading speed, platforms for e-wom, the effects of e-wom are some of the research areas related to e-wom concept.

Second part of study is mostly related to industrial applications regarding to e-wom concept. Three case studies, one algorithm for each and three scenarios for each are included. This three step-plan contributes to an integrated approach which examines and evaluate e-wom comprehensively. Brands from both service and good industies can use e-wom related actions regarding different stages of e-wom process.

Three step-plan for e-wom makes strategic planning necessary for integrating e-wom actions into marketing strategy and plan. The channels/mediums used for e-wom must be selected carefully, examining period, reaction plan and strategy are also important for long-term marketing decision making. The first case is the starting stage of e-wom evaluation which contains anomaly detection. Since each brand and industry has its own standarts for interaction amounts, it is important to detect standarts. Second case is related to main sentiment analysis which includes detecting polarity of content and type of sentiments. This sentiment analysis is mostly descriptive. Last case is supportive of second case in terms of details regarding content of sentiments. Text expressions and related statistics regarding content contributes to better understanding of e-wom. Since the service industry mostly relies on people, it is important to know how people feel with how they express it. The expressions findings can guide to consumer insights and can be used for marketing campaigns like advertisement slogans.

Another part of conclusion refers to technological side of sentiment analysis as it contains different types of methodologies and approaches. Right methodology for sentiment analysis can differ between industries or brands. For global brands methodological differences can take place for local languages. Adapting actions for local languages for sentiment analysis will contribute to accuracy of sentiment analysis.

Another technological issue refers to machine learning and artificial intelligence concepts. Sentiment analysis is mainly based on created dictionaries, but researchers can teach context-based sentiments to machines with machine learning techniques. Health related industry and patient reviews have different vocabulary structure and meanings comparing to hotel industry and tourist reviews. Big data power of social media can guide machine learning for better accuracy. For example, when a specific context like anger expression on social media is choosen for research, hashtags related to consumers' anger expression can be starting points. Collection of thousands of tweets containing anger expressions contributes to detecting and predicting of anger sentiment for further e-wom contents.

REFERENCES

Agarwal, R., Prabhakar, T. V., & Chakrabarty, S. (2008). "I Know What You Feel": Analyzing the Role of Conjunctions in Automatic Sentiment Analysis. In *Advances in Natural Language Processing* (pp. 28–39). Berlin: Springer. doi:10.1007/978-3-540-85287-2_4

Aghakhani, N., Karimi, J., & Salehan, M. (2018). A unified model for the adoption of electronic word of mouth on social network sites: Facebook as the exemplar. *International Journal of Electronic Commerce*, 22(2), 202–231. doi:10.1080/10864415.2018.1441700

Alaei, A. R., Becken, S., & Stantic, B. (2019). Sentiment analysis in tourism: Capitalizing on big data. *Journal of Travel Research*, 58(2), 175–191. doi:10.1177/0047287517747753

Babić Rosario, A., Sotgiu, F., De Valck, K., & Bijmolt, T. H. (2016). The effect of electronic word of mouth on sales: A meta-analytic review of platform, product, and metric factors. *JMR, Journal of Marketing Research*, 53(3), 297–318. doi:10.1509/jmr.14.0380

Batra, R., & Daudpota, S. M. (2018, March). Integrating StockTwits with sentiment analysis for better prediction of stock price movement. In *2018 International Conference on Computing, Mathematics and Engineering Technologies (iCoMET)* (pp. 1-5). IEEE.

Belk, R. W. (2013). Extended self in a digital world. *The Journal of Consumer Research*, *40*(3), 477–500.

Berger, J., & Iyengar, R. (2013). Communication channels and word of mouth: How the medium shapes the message. *The Journal of Consumer Research*, *40*(3), 567–579. doi:10.1086/671345

Berthold, M. R., Cebron, N., Dill, F., Gabriel, T. R., Kötter, T., Meinl, T., ... Wiswedel, B. (2009). KNIME-the Konstanz information miner: Version 2.0 and beyond. *Newsletter*, *11*(1), 26–31.

Bollen, J., Mao, H., & Zeng, X. (2011). Twitter mood predicts the stock market. *Journal of Computational Science*, *2*(1), 1–8. doi:10.1016/j.jocs.2010.12.007

Brody, S., & Elhadad, N. (2010). Detecting salient aspects in online reviews of health providers. *AMIA ... Annual Symposium Proceedings - AMIA Symposium. AMIA Symposium*, *2010*, 202.

Brooks, N. (2018). *Women's E-Commerce Clothing Reviews*. Retrieved from https://www.kaggle.com/nicapotato/womens-ecommerce-clothing-reviews

Cambria, E., Schuller, B., Xia, Y., & Havasi, C. (2013). New avenues in opinion mining and sentiment analysis. *IEEE Intelligent Systems*, *28*(2), 15–21. doi:10.1109/MIS.2013.30

Chiong, R., Fan, Z., Hu, Z., Adam, M. T., Lutz, B., & Neumann, D. (2018, July). A sentiment analysis-based machine learning approach for financial market prediction via news disclosures. In *Proceedings of the Genetic and Evolutionary Computation Conference Companion* (pp. 278-279). ACM. 10.1145/3205651.3205682

Dancho & Vaughan. (2018). *anomalize: Tidy Anomaly Detection*. R package version 0.1.1. Retrieved from https://CRAN.R-project.org/package=anomalize

De Langhe, B., Fernbach, P. M., & Lichtenstein, D. R. (2015). Navigating by the stars: Investigating the actual and perceived validity of online user ratings. *The Journal of Consumer Research*, *42*(6), 817–833. doi:10.1093/jcr/ucv047

Dragoni, M., Poria, S., & Cambria, E. (2018). OntoSenticNet: A commonsense ontology for sentiment analysis. *IEEE Intelligent Systems*, *33*(3), 77–85. doi:10.1109/MIS.2018.033001419

Duwairi, R., & El-Orfali, M. (2014). A study of the effects of preprocessing strategies on sentiment analysis for Arabic text. *Journal of Information Science*, *40*(4), 501–513. doi:10.1177/0165551514534143

Easton, G. (2010). Critical realism in case study research. *Industrial Marketing Management*, *39*(1), 118–128. doi:10.1016/j.indmarman.2008.06.004

Fan, Z. P., Che, Y. J., & Chen, Z. Y. (2017). Product sales forecasting using online reviews and historical sales data: A method combining the Bass model and sentiment analysis. *Journal of Business Research*, *74*, 90–100. doi:10.1016/j.jbusres.2017.01.010

Fang, Y. H., Tang, K., Li, C. Y., & Wu, C. C. (2018). On electronic word-of-mouth diffusion in social networks: Curiosity and influence. *International Journal of Advertising*, *37*(3), 360–384. doi:10.1080/02650487.2016.1256014

Feinerer, I., Hornik, K., & Meyer, D. (2008). Text Mining Infrastructure in R. *Journal of Statistical Software*, *25*(5), 1–54. doi:10.18637/jss.v025.i05

Fine, M. B., Gironda, J., & Petrescu, M. (2017). Prosumer motivations for electronic word-of-mouth communication behaviors. *Journal of Hospitality and Tourism Technology, 8*(2), 280–295. doi:10.1108/JHTT-09-2016-0048

Ghiassi, M., Skinner, J., & Zimbra, D. (2013). Twitter brand sentiment analysis: A hybrid system using n-gram analysis and dynamic artificial neural network. *Expert Systems with Applications, 40*(16), 6266–6282. doi:10.1016/j.eswa.2013.05.057

Greaves, F., Ramirez-Cano, D., Millett, C., Darzi, A., & Donaldson, L. (2013). Use of sentiment analysis for capturing patient experience from free-text comments posted online. *Journal of Medical Internet Research, 15*(11), e239. doi:10.2196/jmir.2721

He, W., Zha, S., & Li, L. (2013). Social media competitive analysis and text mining: A case study in the pizza industry. *International Journal of Information Management, 33*(3), 464–472. doi:10.1016/j.ijinfomgt.2013.01.001

Hennig-Thurau, T., Gwinner, K. P., Walsh, G., & Gremler, D. D. (2004). Electronic word-of-mouth via consumer-opinion platforms: What motivates consumers to articulate themselves on the internet? *Journal of Interactive Marketing, 18*(1), 38–52. doi:10.1002/dir.10073

Hyndman, R., Athanasopoulos, G., Bergmeir, C., Caceres, G., Chhay, L., O'Hara-Wild, M., . . . Yasmeen, F. (2019). *Forecast: Forecasting functions for time series and linear models.* R package version 8.5. Retrieved from http://pkg.robjhyndman.com/forecast>

Hyndman, R. J., & Khandakar, Y. (2008). Automatic time series forecasting: the forecast package for R. *Journal of Statistical Software, 26*(3), 1-22. Retrieved from http://www.jstatsoft.org/article/view/v027i03

Jockers, M. L. (2015). *Syuzhet: Extract Sentiment and Plot Arcs from Text.* Retrieved from https://github.com/mjockers/syuzhet>

Kang, D., & Park, Y. (2014). Review-based measurement of customer satisfaction in mobile service: Sentiment analysis and VIKOR approach. *Expert Systems with Applications, 41*(4), 1041–1050. doi:10.1016/j.eswa.2013.07.101

Kasper, W., & Vela, M. (2011, October). Sentiment analysis for hotel reviews. In Computational linguistics-applications conference (Vol. 231527, pp. 45-52). Academic Press.

Kim, W. G., Lim, H., & Brymer, R. A. (2015). The effectiveness of managing social media on hotel performance. *International Journal of Hospitality Management, 44*, 165–171. doi:10.1016/j.ijhm.2014.10.014

Kolchyna, O., Souza, T. T., Treleaven, P., & Aste, T. (2015). *Twitter sentiment analysis: Lexicon method, machine learning method, and their combination.* arXiv preprint arXiv:1507.00955.

Krishnamurthy, A., & Kumar, S. R. (2018). Electronic word-of-mouth and the brand image: Exploring the moderating role of involvement through a consumer expectations lens. *Journal of Retailing and Consumer Services, 43*, 149–156. doi:10.1016/j.jretconser.2018.03.010

Kucuktunc, O., Cambazoglu, B. B., Weber, I., & Ferhatosmanoglu, H. (2012, February). Large-Scale sentiment analysis for Yahoo! answers. In *Proceedings of the fifth ACM international conference on Web search and data mining* (pp. 633-642). ACM. 10.1145/2124295.2124371

Lau, R. Y. K., Zhang, W., & Xu, W. (2018). Parallel aspect-oriented sentiment analysis for sales forecasting with big data. *Production and Operations Management*, 27(10), 1775–1794. doi:10.1111/poms.12737

Levy, S. E., Duan, W., & Boo, S. (2013). An analysis of one-star online reviews and responses in the Washington, DC, lodging market. *Cornell Hospitality Quarterly*, 54(1), 49–63. doi:10.1177/1938965512464513

Liang, L. J., Choi, H. C., & Joppe, M. (2018). Understanding repurchase intention of Airbnb consumers: Perceived authenticity, electronic word-of-mouth, and price sensitivity. *Journal of Travel & Tourism Marketing*, 35(1), 73–89. doi:10.1080/10548408.2016.1224750

Liu, B. (2010). Sentiment Analysis and Subjectivity. Handbook of natural language processing, 2(2010), 627-666.

Liu, Y., Bi, J. W., & Fan, Z. P. (2017). Ranking products through online reviews: A method based on sentiment analysis technique and intuitionistic fuzzy set theory. *Information Fusion*, 36, 149–161. doi:10.1016/j.inffus.2016.11.012

Mangold, W. G., & Faulds, D. J. (2009). Social media: The new hybrid element of the promotion mix. *Business Horizons*, 52(4), 357–365. doi:10.1016/j.bushor.2009.03.002

Mäntylä, M. V., Graziotin, D., & Kuutila, M. (2018). The evolution of sentiment analysis—A review of research topics, venues, and top cited papers. *Computer Science Review*, 27, 16–32. doi:10.1016/j.cosrev.2017.10.002

Maughan, L., Gutnikov, S., & Stevens, R. (2007). Like more, look more. Look more, like more: The evidence from eye-tracking. *Journal of Brand Management*, 14(4), 335–342. doi:10.1057/palgrave.bm.2550074

Melville, P., Gryc, W., & Lawrence, R. D. (2009, June). Sentiment analysis of blogs by combining lexical knowledge with text classification. In *Proceedings of the 15th ACM SIGKDD international conference on Knowledge discovery and data mining* (pp. 1275-1284). ACM. 10.1145/1557019.1557156

Nielsen. (2015). *Nielsen Global Trust in Advertising Survey*. Retrieved from https://www.nielsen.com/content/dam/nielsenglobal/apac/docs/reports/2015/nielsen-global-trust-in-advertising-report-september-2015.pdf

Ortigosa, A., Martín, J. M., & Carro, R. M. (2014). Sentiment analysis in Facebook and its application to e-learning. *Computers in Human Behavior*, 31, 527–541. doi:10.1016/j.chb.2013.05.024

Pak, A., & Paroubek, P. (2010, May). Twitter as a corpus for sentiment analysis and opinion mining. In LREc (Vol. 10, No. 2010, pp. 1320-1326). Academic Press.

Pang, B., & Lee, L. (2008). Opinion mining and sentiment analysis. *Foundations and Trends® in Information Retrieval*, 2(1–2), 1-135.

Prabowo, R., & Thelwall, M. (2009). Sentiment analysis: A combined approach. *Journal of Informetrics*, 3(2), 143–157. doi:10.1016/j.joi.2009.01.003

R Core Team. (2018). *R: A language and environment for statistical computing*. Author.

R Foundation for RStudio Team. (2016). *RStudio: Integrated Development for R*. RStudio, Inc. Retrieved from www.rstudio.com/

Shi, H. X., & Li, X. J. (2011, July). A sentiment analysis model for hotel reviews based on supervised learning. In *Machine Learning and Cybernetics (ICMLC), 2011 International Conference on* (Vol. 3, pp. 950-954). IEEE. 10.1109/ICMLC.2011.6016866

Sohangir, S., Wang, D., Pomeranets, A., & Khoshgoftaar, T. M. (2018). Big Data: Deep Learning for financial sentiment analysis. *Journal of Big Data*, *5*(1), 3. doi:10.118640537-017-0111-6

Statista. (2016). *Global Industry Forecasts Report*. Retrieved from https://cdn.statcdn.com/static/promo/Statista_Global_Industry_Forecast_Summary_2016.pdf

Statistical Computing, Vienna, Austria. (n.d.). Retrieved from https://www.R-project.org/

Subrahmanian, V. S., & Reforgiato, D. (2008). AVA: Adjective-verb-adverb combinations for sentiment analysis. *IEEE Intelligent Systems*, *23*(4), 43–50. doi:10.1109/MIS.2008.57

Sundaram, D. S., Mitra, K., & Webster, C. (1998). *Word-of-mouth communications: A motivational analysis*. ACR North American Advances.

Taboada, M., Brooke, J., Tofiloski, M., Voll, K., & Stede, M. (2011). Lexicon-based methods for sentiment analysis. *Computational Linguistics*, *37*(2), 267–307. doi:10.1162/COLI_a_00049

Tan, S., & Zhang, J. (2008). An empirical study of sentiment analysis for chinese documents. *Expert Systems with Applications*, *34*(4), 2622–2629. doi:10.1016/j.eswa.2007.05.028

TrendsG. (2019). Retrieved from https://trends.google.com/trends/explore?q=barcelona%20hotels

Vaughan & Dancho. (2019). *tibbletime: Time-Aware of Tibbles*. R package version 0.1.2. Retrieved from https://CRAN.R-project.org/package=tibbletime

Vinodhini, G., & Chandrasekaran, R. M. (2012). Sentiment analysis and opinion mining: A survey. *International Journal (Toronto, Ont.)*, *2*(6), 282–292.

Wakefield, L. T., & Bennett, G. (2018). Sports fan experience: Electronic word-of-mouth in ephemeral social media. *Sport Management Review*, *21*(2), 147–159. doi:10.1016/j.smr.2017.06.003

We Are Social. (2018). *Global Digital Report 2018*. Retrieved from https://digitalreport.wearesocial.com/

Wen, M., Yang, D., & Rose, C. (2014, July). Sentiment Analysis in MOOC Discussion Forums: What does it tell us? Educational data mining 2014.

Wickham, H. (2017). *tidyverse: Easily Install and Load the 'Tidyverse'*. R package version 1.2.1. Retrieved from https://CRAN.R-project.org/package=tidyverse

Wickham, H., François, R., Henry, L., & Müller, K. (2019). *dplyr: A Grammar of Data Manipulation*. R package version 0.8.0.1. Retrieved from https://CRAN.R-project.org/package=dplyr

Wilson, T., Wiebe, J., & Hoffmann, P. (2005). Recognizing contextual polarity in phrase-level sentiment analysis. *Proceedings of Human Language Technology Conference and Conference on Empirical Methods in Natural Language Processing*. 10.3115/1220575.1220619

Xie, K. L., Zhang, Z., & Zhang, Z. (2014). The business value of online consumer reviews and management response to hotel performance. *International Journal of Hospitality Management, 43*, 1–12. doi:10.1016/j.ijhm.2014.07.007

Yan, Q., Zhou, S., & Wu, S. (2018). The influences of tourists' emotions on the selection of electronic word of mouth platforms. *Tourism Management, 66*, 348–363. doi:10.1016/j.tourman.2017.12.015

Yang, F. X. (2017). Effects of restaurant satisfaction and knowledge sharing motivation on eWOM intentions: The moderating role of technology acceptance factors. *Journal of Hospitality & Tourism Research (Washington, D.C.), 41*(1), 93–127. doi:10.1177/1096348013515918

Zhang, L., Ghosh, R., Dekhil, M., Hsu, M., & Liu, B. (2011). *Combining lexiconbased and learning-based methods for twitter sentiment analysis.* HP Laboratories, Technical Report HPL-2011, 89.

Zhang, S. N., Li, Y. Q., Liu, C. H., & Ruan, W. Q. (2019). Critical factors in the identification of word-of-mouth enhanced with travel apps: The moderating roles of Confucian culture and the switching cost view. *Asia Pacific Journal of Tourism Research, 24*(5), 422–442. doi:10.1080/10941665.2019.1572630

ADDITIONAL READING

Analytics, P. (2018). *Twitter Sentiment Analysis Using R.* Retrieved from http://dataaspirant.com/2018/03/22/twitter-sentiment-analysis-using-r/

Baccianella, S., Esuli, A., & Sebastiani, F. (2010, May). Sentiwordnet 3.0: an enhanced lexical resource for sentiment analysis and opinion mining. In Lrec (Vol. 10, No. 2010, pp. 2200-2204). Academic Press.

Gupta, S. (2018). *Sentiment Analysis: Concept, Analysis and Applications.* Retrieved from https://towardsdatascience.com/sentiment-analysis-concept-analysis-and-applications-6c94d6f58c17

Hutto, C. J., & Gilbert, E. (2014, May). Vader: A parsimonious rule-based model for sentiment analysis of social media text. *Eighth international AAAI conference on weblogs and social media.*

JockersM. (2017). *Package 'syuzhet'.* Retrieved from https://cran. r-project. org/web/packages/syuzhet

Loria, S., Keen, P., Honnibal, M., Yankovsky, R., Karesh, D., & Dempsey, E. (2014). Textblob: simplified text processing. *Secondary TextBlob: Simplified Text Processing.*

Pak, A., & Paroubek, P. (2010, May). Twitter as a corpus for sentiment analysis and opinion mining. In LREc (Vol. 10, No. 2010, pp. 1320-1326). Academic Press.

Pang, B., & Lee, L. (2008). Opinion mining and sentiment analysis. *Foundations and Trends® in Information Retrieval, 2*(1–2), 1-135.

Silge, J. (2015). *Joy to the world, and also anticipation, disgust, surprise...* Retrieved from https://juliasilge.com/blog/joy-to-the-world/

KEY TERMS AND DEFINITIONS

Electronic Word-of-Mouth: The communication action of consumers which uses technological channels as mediums.

Sentiment Analysis: Methodology for detecting emotions in content.

Social Media: The communication platform which makes people connected on web.

Word-of-Mouth: The activity of communication regarding goods and services.

Chapter 71
Using E–Reputation for Sentiment Analysis:
Twitter as a Case Study

Dhai Eddine Salhi

https://orcid.org/0000-0002-4025-2806

LIMOSE Laboratory, University of Mhamed Bougara, Boumerdes, Algeria

Abelkamel Tari

LIMED Laboratory, University Abderrahmane Mira, Bejaia, Algeria

Mohand Tahar Kechadi

Insight Centre for Data Analytics, University College Dublin, Dublin, Ireland

ABSTRACT

In a competitive world, companies are looking to gain a positive reputation through these clients. Electronic reputation is part of this reputation mainly in social networks, where everyone is free to express their opinion. Sentiment analysis of the data collected in these networks is very necessary to identify and know the reputation of a companies. This paper focused on one type of data, Twits on Twitter, where the authors analyzed them for the company Djezzy (mobile operator in Algeria), to know their satisfaction. The study is divided into two parts: The first part was the pre-processing phase, where this research filtered the Twits (eliminate useless words, use the tokenization) to keep the necessary information for a better accuracy. The second part was the application of machine learning algorithms (SVM and logistic regression) for a supervised classification since the results are binary. The strong point of this study was the possibility to run the chosen algorithms on a cloud in order to save execution time; the solution also supports the three languages: Arabic, English, and French.

DOI: 10.4018/978-1-6684-6303-1.ch071

1. INTRODUCTION

Nowadays, given the strong competition and the diversity of the products offered, each company focuses on its image and its impact in the market. In order to attract the most customers and increase its turnover, the company's reputation on the web in general, and social networks more precisely, is a factor. And its success depends heavily on it. To maintain a good E-Reputation, the economic structures study and analyze the number of positive and negative opinions on their companies, products and services.

E-Reputation is a concept that has emerged as a result of the evolution of web 2.0 and interactions. Of Internet users. According to Digimind: The Leading Social Media Listening and Analytics Solution, a specialist in business intelligence software (Tran, 2019), E-reputation is "the perception that Internet users have of your company, your brand or people who collaborate (managers, employees) and which is potentially visible on many supports of the net" (Uikey & Bhilare, 2017). 66% of consumers seek advice before buying a product and 96% seek advice before buying a product are influenced by the E-reputation of a brand during a purchase. From the moment companies became aware of the importance of mastering their E-Reputation, the construction of a strategy to manage their E-Reputation became a key element for their communication. However, companies must face the lack of control over Internet users' conversations on the web and as a result, the fear of a crisis on the net is growing because, faced with real-time information relays and the resulting chain reactions (Louisot & Girardet, 2012), An on-line crisis can have a catastrophic and devastating effect on a company's e-reputation, but also on its turnover. Companies must then analyze any data that may impact their E-reputation (Pan, 2011). It is in this context of E-reputation that our work is part of it.

In our project, we propose a case study at the level of a telecom leader in Algeria, namely: Djezzy the aim is to analyze the different opinions that are in the form of comments found on social network: Twitter, use Automatic Learning (Tran, 2019) and Data Mining techniques (Tran, 2019) To detect strengths and anomalies of the company, and create a dashboard offering an overview of its E-reputation (positive or negative) and its distribution by geographical area. The proposed solution can be implemented on a Cloud server for various advantages, such as execution time, storage capacity and above all ease of access, for which a solution based on cloud computing is highly recommended.

2. BACKGROUND

In this section, we present the principle of E-reputation and sentiment analysis

2.1. E-Reputation

Boistel (2008) reminds us that two theoretical trends contribute to the definition of reputation. A first approach consists in considering that reputation results from the different images of the company (Fombrun, (1996)), from the perceptions that all stakeholders develop (Davies et al., 2002; Chan et al., 2006). The second posits that reputation is "a reflection of the history of accumulated perceptions of observed identity and experiences". Whatever the approach chosen, it emerges that the reputation of an object (company, brand, and product) is built through the different signals emitted by the object, the experiences that each member of the stakeholders has lived in relation to this object. This last point is fundamental (Boistel (2008)).

2.1.1. E-Reputation Through Social Networks

Reputation being the opinion we have of a company or a brand. Just as companies insure their staff and property, it is important to essential to ensure their image on the Internet because the risks to which the company or the brand is exposed through social media (social networks (Jeanjean et al., n.d.), blogs, web forums (Linton, 2016), websites videos, etc.) are countless, especially for companies that are unaware of the news technologies or who do not take seriously the influence of the web and social networks on their representation (Woldemariam, 2016).

Since the popularization of the Internet, the arrival of smartphones and tablets and access to 3G, information has spread exponentially and at a high speed (Lemoine, 2014). Since then, we have been talking about the digital reputation that the most "connected" companies consider as the most important for their image. Thus, in an economic sector open to competition, the reputation of companies is weakened by the criticisms of Internet users who are able to damage their image. It is to face competition and maintain its image that more and more companies are investing in e-reputation through social networks and in particular Facebook (Woldemariam, 2016).

2.1.2. Sentiment Analysis

Sentiment analysis is a type of Automatic Natural Language Processing to track the mood of the audience about a particular product or topic. Sentiment Analysis (Ouchiha, 2018), which is also called "Opinion Mining", involves building a system to collect and examine opinions about the product put in blog articles (Lemoine, 2014), comments, reviews or tweets.

The analysis of feelings presents several challenges. The first is a word of opinion that is considered positive in one situation, and can be considered negative in another. A second challenge is that people do not always express their opinions in the same way. Most traditional word processors are based on the fact that small differences between two pieces of text do not significantly change the meaning. In the analysis of feelings, however, "the picture was excellent" is very different from "the picture was not good". People can be contradictory in their statements. Most of them opinions will have both positive and negative comments, which is relatively manageable by analyzing the sentences one at a time. However, in a more informal medium such as Twitter or blogs, it is more likely that people associate different opinions in the same sentence, which is easy for a human to understand, but more difficult to analyze for a computer. Sometimes even other people have trouble understanding what someone is saying was based on a short text because it lacks context. For example, "This film was as good as that his last film" depends entirely on what the person expressing the opinion thought of the previous model (Woldemariam, 2016).

The classification of feelings consists in organizing entire documents according to opinions on certain objects. On the other hand, the classification of feelings based on characteristics takes into account opinions on the characteristics of certain objects. The task of opinion synthesis differs from traditional text synthesis because only the product features on which customers have expressed their opinions are used. The synthesis of opinions does not summarize the criticisms by selecting a subset or rewriting some of the original sentences of the criticisms to capture the main points as in the classic text synthesis. As for the languages studied in the work on the analysis of feelings, we find mainly English and Chinese (Jeanjean et al., n.d.). Currently, very little research has been conducted on the classification of feelings for other languages such as Arabic.

3. RELATED WORK

Referring to the existing works in literature, which are related to our study, we have divided the papers into three categories, the first one is E-reputation, and the second one is sentiment analysis and the last one present about cloud-based solutions.

3.1. E-Reputation

In this section we find several studies, the first (De Oliveira & Alturas, 2016) is written by L. de Oliveira et Al is based on a quiz study on social networks about a company X, then find the level of reputation, and compare it with the competitors of company X. The second article (Fourati-Jamoussi, 2015), F. FOURATI-JAMOUSSI deals with the reputation of the four cosmetic companies competing, the work compares their E-reputation by manually processing comments, then calculating the percentage of negative or positive reputation of each company. Also propose recommendations for each according to the weaknesses detected. There is another vision in article (Kikuchi & Bhalla, 2014) established by S.Kikuchi et Al, is to analyze the emissions through smart TV and IPTV, in order to recommend the type of emissions most solicited, by storing the histories in a database, after analyzing them by statistical techniques, to find the most viewed emissions. Another use of electronic reputation in P2P (peer to peer) sharing systems. Li and Al (Li & Su, 2018) have created a new mechanism to analyze reputation based on the interests of nodes in a P2P network, which is based on sending and receiving history. Compared with other mechanisms such as Eigen Trust Model and SupRep Model, the new model gives the best accuracy and satisfaction. In the same context, another study by Wang.S and Al (2017) talk about electronic credit, where they found a method of risk analysis based on known platforms, in order to decide whether or not to make credit. Looking at the works cited on E-reputation, we see that all the results found are from manual analysis, we do not find Machine learning or Deep Learning.

3.2. Sentiment Analysis

In the second part of related work, we deal with sentiment analysis on social networks, specially on Twitter, where we found some interesting work, The first paper cited (Ramanathan & Meyyappan, 2019), V. Ramanathan et Al worked on anthologies in the field of tourism, they created an ontology that composes the positive words on tourism, and compare it with comments on social networks. And there are also works based on artificial intelligence, paper (Park & Seo, 2018) and its authors C. Won Park et Al the tweets on Twitter are collected, analyzed by a Value Aware Dictionary algorithm, to detect negative, positive and neutral tweets. Arabic is one of the most complicated languages to treat automatically. For this purpose, authors Khaled S. Sabra et Al in their paper (Sabra et al., 2017) found a new method of processing, based on semi- supervised learning, using WordNet software. The use of new technologies is necessary. For this purpose, the authors M. Trupthi et Al in their paper (Trupthi et al., 2017), used Hadoop for the recovery, storage and filtering of tweets. Then, they used Data Mining techniques to analyze reputation. Cross media is a very efficient and well-known framework. For this purpose, the author Yonas Woldemariam (2016) had the idea of integrating a pipeline into the global Cross media process, ensuring E-reputation. It has produced very good results. According to a study that did Al smadi and Al (2018), where they analyzed users' feelings on Arab hotel platforms. The authors compared the results obtained by several algorithms such as: CNN, SVM, etc., and found that the results were similar.

At the end of the study they found that SVM gives better results in this field than neural networks. We have two general remarks concerning the work mentioned. The first is that all papers are based on the processing of a unique language. The second, we did not find a paper that gives importance to the pre-treatment phase to eliminate noise, in order to find better results, and this is the strength of our study presented in the next section.

3.3. Cloud Based Solutions

In this section, we present the most cited works based on Cloud Computing technology, processing data for semantic analysis. Arulmurugan (2017) made a comparison study on 3 Machine Learning algorithms ANN, SVM and naive Bayes. Most in this study, he introduced the notion of cloud computing to do pre- processing and processing. Where he used an execution space at a remote Cloud server. Or he saved 80% execution time. SVM also gives more accuracy compared to the other two algorithms. Benedetto (2016) treated a new learning technique, is the comparison between sentiment analysis (Reputation) and its influence on user reactions on social networks by techniques and an existing algorithm on Cloud computing (SVM). The author found that reputation studies influence up to 80% on users' opinions and reactions. Krishna (2013) in his paper proposes a recommendation model based on reputation on social networks. The idea is to collect as much data as possible from several sites on a specific topic and then analyze the content in order to decide whether or not to offer it to applicants. The solution is implemented on a public cloud server to save time. Xiao Liu (2016) proposes a prediction study, starting to collect data from social networking sites, he implemented a machine learning algorithm (he did not mention the name of the algorithm) on a public cloud server, and then he created a prediction model on different topics, with feedback from people using the proposed system. Satisfaction reached 77%. Qaisi (2016) made an analysis of data (comments) retrieved from Twitter and applied Machine Learning algorithms on two different Cloud Computing platforms Microsoft Azure and AWS. At the end of the study the author found that there is a higher satisfaction in Azure than in AWS on different datasets.

4. APPROACH PROPOSAL

Based on existing works in the literature, we proposed a study on the analysis of Twitter users' feelings, in order to analyze their opinions on the Djezzy society mentioned before. The proposed study is based on a set of important phases, starting with the first phase, where we collect twits from Djezzy's page on Twitter. The second phase is the manual exploration, where we decide each comment is what it is positive or negative in a manual way. The third phase is the pre-processing where we select the most relevant attributes, removing parts of unnecessary comments and special characters, tokenization and vectorization. The fourth phase is the implementation, where we test the Machine Learning algorithms and their created models, in order to find the most accurate solution. We end this approach by interpreting the results through graphical interfaces. The is explained in detail in Figure 1.

4.1. Comments Collection

There are several techniques that allow data collection through social networks.

Figure 1. The approach proposal

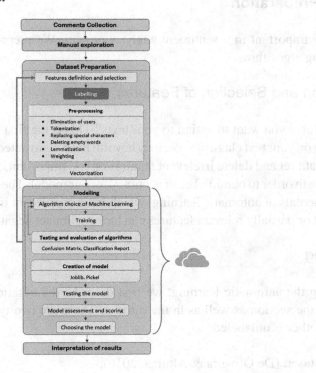

4.1.1. Web Scrapping

Web scraping is a technique of extracting content from websites, via a script or program, in order to transform it to allow its use in another context. Data collection is the systematic approach to collecting and measuring information from a variety of sources. In many cases, data science uses existing data collected during other projects. Our work consists in collecting the tweets and comments from different social networks (Ramanathan & Meyyappan, 2019).

4.1.2. Tweepy API

Tweepy is a Python library that provides access to the Twitter API. It's perfect for simple automation and creating Twitter robots. Tweepy has many features:

- Receive tweets.
- Creating and deleting tweets.
- Track and no longer track users.

4.2. Manual Scanning

Manual exploration is a very important step in the analysis of our comments, because it allows us to know the nature and language in which they are written, and it is a crucial step in the choice of features (Trupthi et al., 2017).

4.3. Dataset Preparation

This step is very important in a sentiment analysis project. We prepare the dataset to then apply the Machine Learning algorithms.

4.3.1. Selection and Selection of Features

What are the features you want to assign to your texts? This is the first question you must answer when you start working on your text classifier. We may have all been confronted with this identification problem features from a data set and delete irrelevant features or less important, which do not contribute much to our target variable in order to obtain a better accuracy for our model. The selection of features is one of the concepts fundamentals of automatic learning, which has a significant impact on the performance of our model. Irrelevant or partially relevant features can have an impact negative on the model's performance.

4.3.2. Labelling

Before deepening the automatic learning, we first describe the notation of the dataset, which will be used throughout the section as well as in the tutorial. There are two types of general data sets. One is labelled and the other is unlabeled:

- Labeled Dataset: (De Oliveira & Alturas, 2016):

$$D : X = \left\{ x^{(n)} \in R^d \right\}_{n=1}^{N}, Y = \left\{ y^{(n)} \in R \right\}_{n=1}^{N}$$

- Unlabeled Dataset: (De Oliveira & Alturas, 2016):

$$D : X = \left\{ x^{(n)} \in R^d \right\}_{n=1}^{N}$$

4.3.3. Data Preprocessing

This step consists of four tasks:

- Tokenization (converts sentences into words;
- Removal of punctuation marks and unnecessary aliases (users, links);
- Deletion of empty words - frequent words such as "the", "is", etc. that do not have specific semantics;
- Lemmatization - Another approach to removing inflection is to determine the part of the speech and use a detailed language database.

4.3.4. Vectorization

In word processing, words in the text represent discrete and categorical characteristics. How to encode such data in a way that is ready for use by algorithms? In another way we prepare the words to be applied by Machine Learning algorithms.

Mapping text data to real value vectors is called feature extraction. One of the simplest techniques for digitally representing a text is the Bag of Words, there are many approaches to do this and the most popular is to use the TF-IDF (Term Frequency-Inverse Document Frequency) technique.

Figure 2. Example of Word2Vec

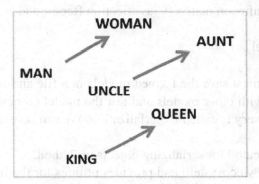

Word2Vec (Figure 2) is well known for capturing meaning and demonstrating it on tasks such as analogy calculation, questions of the form is for b as it is for"?". For example, the man belongs to the woman as uncle is for"?" (Aunt) using a simple vector shift method based on cosine distance. (Pan, 2011).

4.4. Modelling

In this section, the execution of the algorithms and the creation of the models can be on a Cloud server like a local station. The advantage of using a remote Cloud server is to save storage space or we can use large datasets (Big Data), saving execution time.

4.4.1. Choice of Machine Learning Algorithms

There are different algorithms for creating ML models for different text-based applications, depending on the nature of the problem and the data available. Among the algorithms most commonly used in a sentiment analysis project: Naive Bayes, Support Vector Machines (SVM), Logistic Regression, Neural Network. The choice of algorithms is based on several criteria: The first is the state of the art or 90% (Fombrun & Rindova, 1996) of the articles have used the algorithms proposed above. The second criterion, we are working on a supervised classification, because as a result we get two answers: either the comment is positive or negative (Yes/No) the third criterion is the possibility to run the algorithms on the Cloud Computing. The last criterion is to support the three languages Arabic, English and French.

4.4.2. Training

The process of forming a machine learning model (ML) involves providing a machine learning algorithm (i.e., the learning algorithm) with training data that often represents 80% of the dataset data and will be used for learning. The term machine learning model refers to the model artifact that is created by the training process.

4.4.3. Testing and Evaluation of Algorithm

Testing: When the training phase is finished, the model is tested with the rest of the data from the dataset (20%). Evaluation of Algorithm: This is the last step to go through when creating the model. Using several techniques such as confusion matrix, Classification Report and precision calculation.

4.4.4. Creating the Model

Once the model is ready we must save the formed models in a file and restore them in order to reuse them to compare the model with other models and test the model on new data. Data backup is called Serialization, while data recovery is called Deserialization. We can save a template in two ways:

- Pickle is the standard method for serializing objects in Python.
- Joblib is part of the SciPy ecosystem and provides utilities for the pipeline processing of Python jobs.

4.4.5. Test the Model

Apply the model to new data, allowing the model to be evaluated. The difference between algorithm test and model test: algorithm test is to check if the algorithm works well on the training dataset. Testing the model is checking the accuracy of the results on the test dataset.

4.4.6. Choice of Model

After comparing the models created, we choose the one that best meets our needs.

4.5. Interpretation of the Results

This is the last step of the project where we present the results obtained in graphical mode via histograms and graphs.

5. RESULTS AND DISCUSSION

In this step we follow the same steps mentioned in the approach. We apply different techniques to achieve the final results, the phases are explained as follows.

5.1. Comments Collection

We used web scrapping to extract comments on Twitter, the following python code in Figure 3 illustrates how we did the extraction.

Figure 3. Scrapping code

Figure 4 shows the tweets retrieved from the Internet in Json form.

Figure 4. Tweets retrieve on Json

[{"usernameTweet": "Jasminkoratela1", "ID": "1000004957473529861", "text": "Amine", "url": "/Jasminkoratela1/status/1000004957473529861", "nbr_retweet": 0, "nbr_favorite": 0, "nbr_reply": 0, "datetime": "2018-05-25 15:25:35", "is_reply": true, "is_retweet": false, "user_id": "945413186890665985"}, {"usernameTweet": "Mak6613", "ID": "1000008468949078016", "text": "Djezzy a proposer mieux", "url": "/Mak6613/status/1000008468949078016", "nbr_retweet": 0, "nbr_favorite": 0, "nbr_reply": 0, "datetime": "2018-05-25 15:39:32", "is_reply": true, "is_retweet": false, "user_id": "945026532166328320"}, {"usernameTweet": "emploiest_dz", "ID": "1000020165856145408", "text": "\u0627\u0639\u0644\u0627\u0646 \u062a\u0648\u0638\u064a\u0641 \u0628\u0627\u0624\u0633\u0633\u0629 \u062c\u064a\u0632\u064a- \u0645\u0627\u064a djezzy recrutement 2018 http:// dlvr.it/QV4jvB \u00a0", "url": "/emploiest_dz/status/1000020165856145408", "nbr_retweet": 0, "nbr_favorite": 0, "nbr_reply": 0, "datetime": "2018-05-25 16:26:01", "is_reply": false, "is_retweet": false, "user_id": "4099590713"}, {"usernameTweet": "MNPRONET", "ID": "1000048391592861696", "text": "\u062e\u0628\u0631 \u0635\u0627\u062f\u0645 \u0644\u062c\u0627\u0632\u064a \u0644\u064a\u0646 \u0631\u0644\u0639\u0631 \u062a\u0639\u0628\u0626\u0629 \u0631\u0635\u064a\u062f \u0644\u0647\u0648\u0627\u0641 \u0627\u0644\u0646\u0642\u0627\u0644\u0629 Djezzy Ooredoo Mobilis:", "url": "/MNPRONET/status/1000048391592861696", "nbr_retweet": 0, "nbr_favorite": 1, "nbr_reply": 0, "datetime": "2018-05-25 18:18:11", "is_reply": false, "is_retweet": false, "user_id": "821406823681036291"}, {"usernameTweet":

5.2. Dataset Preparation

The preparation of our dataset goes through several steps.

5.2.1. Definition and Selection of Features

We developed a python script that allows the extraction of dataset features from the file recovered in Json and convert it to CSV format. After executing the script we will get the dataset in Figure 5.

Figure 5. Tweets converted on CSV

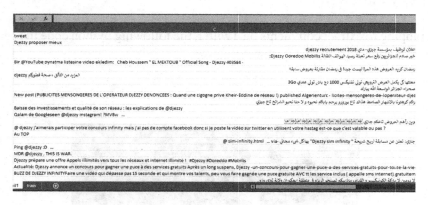

5.2.2. Labelling

In this step, we decide for each comment manually if it is positive or negative for the preparation of the dataset for the training phase. We gave the number 1 for positive tweets and 0 for negative tweets. Figure 6 shows how to label tweets.

Figure 6. Adding label column

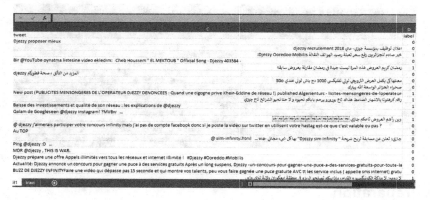

5.2.3. Pre-Processing

This step is based on three essential phases:

- **Elimination of users:** We keep only the necessary information in a tweet (tweet Id, tweet text);
- **Elimination of special characters and empty words:** This phase is a continuation of the previous phase, we eliminate empty words, articulators and special characters;
- **Tokenization:** This phase consists in taking the tweets resulting from the previous phase, converting them into separate words, to find the importance and weight of each word. Also to find the length of each tweet.

Figure 7 illustrates the result of this step after the application of the three points mentioned.

Figure 7. Processed dataset

id	lenght	tweet	tidy_tweet
0	3.0	Djezzy proposer mieux	Djezzy proposer mieux
1	8.0	اعلن توظيف بمؤسسة جيزي- ماي djezzy recrutemen...	اعلن توظيف جيزي djezzy recrutement
2	12.0	...خبر صادم للجزائريين رفع سعر تعبئة رصيد الهواتف	Djezzy Oo... مادم للجزا ريين رصيد الهواتف النقاله
4	12.0	...رمضان كريم العروض هذه المرة ليست جيدة في رمضان	...رمضان كريم العروض المرة ليست جيدة رمضان مقارنة

5.2.4. Vecorization

In this step. To apply vectorization, we use the Bag of words algorithm mentioned earlier. Bag of Words is based on two techniques Count Vectorizer and TF-IDF Verctorizer.

The next step is the application of a Machine Learning algorithm to test our approach.

5.3. Modelling

In this step, we decided to use 2 Machine Learning algorithms among those already mentioned in the previous section, the first one is Logistic regression and the second one is SVM (Support Vector Machine).

The purpose of our article is to test the reputation of the Djezzy company (negative or positive) in the tweets treated at the previous stage, where we make a comparison between the two algorithms mentioned earlier to find the best between them, going through the test methods (precision, scoring and confusion matrix).

Before presenting the results, here is a Figure 8 comparing the two algorithms. Where the first line presents the accuracy of each algorithm and the second line displays the scoring. Another very important criterion is the confusion matrix, it represents the result found by the machine learning algorithms compared to the original tweets. We used a dataset of 1510 tweets in this study. According to the manual exploration we had 840 positive tweets and 670 negative tweets, so the confusion matrix presented in Table 1 is the percentage of tweets found by Machine Learning algorithms (Logistic Regression and SVM) compared to the manual exploration.

From the results displayed, Logistic Regression and SVM give very close values, with a small superiority for SVM. For this reason we have chosen the SVM to continue in our work. The result found after applying SVM is shown in the following Figure 9, where 62.91% of the tweets are positive in red, while 37.09% of the tweets were detected as negative in green. The creation of the final model of the program is a very important step to better visualize the results, for this we use Pickel (cited in the previous section), and here is the final code written in Python language, presented in the Figure 10.

Figure 8. Comparison between Logistic regression and SVM

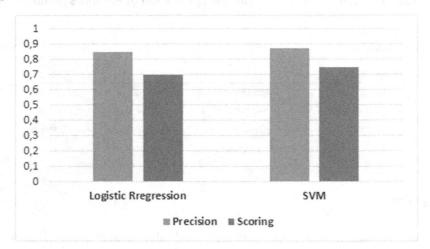

Table 1. Confusion Matrix

		LR Algorithm		SVM Algorithm	
		Positive	**Negative**	**Positive**	**Negative**
Manual exploration	*positive*	840	0	830	10
	negative	150	520	120	550

5.3.1. Results Visualization

After analyzing the tweets and applying the SVM algorithm, we were able to find Djezzy's e- reputation compared to the two competitors in the Algerian market (Ooredoo and Mobilis). The overall view of our system is shown in Figure 11.

The dashboard is composed of several graphs. The first graph presented in Figure 12 is to check the reputation by city in the Algerian territory. Each city has a set of positive, negative and neutral tweets.

The second one is the comparison of offers: it allows the estimation and propagation of offers of the same value from Djezzy in relation to the competition, it's illustrated in the following Figure 13.

The last graph presented in Figure 14 gives the e-reputation of the three Mobile operators (Djezzy, Ooredoo and mobilis).

6. CONCLUSION

In a world where the Internet has become the primary means of communication between people, companies are interested in knowing their opinions through social networks. This paper is based on a detection study of the e-reputation of the leading mobile operator in Algeria "Djezzy", by analyzing the tweets that speak about the company on the social network Twitter.

Figure 9. SVM Results

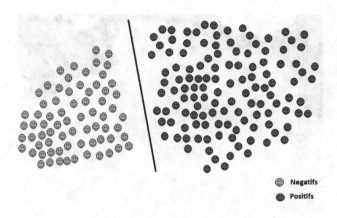

Figure 10. Creation of the model

```
# Save Model Using Pickle
import pandas as pd
from sklearn import model_selection
from sklearn import svm
import pickle

dataframe =  pd.read_csv('testDataSet.csv')
array = dataframe.values
X = array[:,0:8]
Y = array[:,8]
test_size = 0.33
seed = 7
X_train, X_test, Y_train, Y_test = model_selection.train_test_split(X, Y, test_size=test_size, random_state=seed)

# Fit the model on 33%
svc = svm.SVC(kernel='linear', C=1, probability=True).fit(X_train, Y_train)
```

Figure 11. Global dashboard

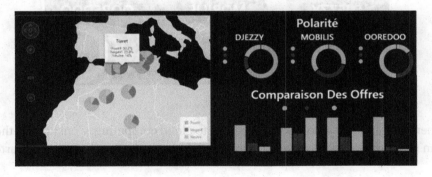

The first phase of the study was the pre-treatment, where we cleaned the tweets and kept only the necessary information. The second phase was the application of a Machine Learning algorithm which is SVM, the result of the algorithm was the obtaining of three categories of positive, negative or neutral tweets. For the future we aim to prevent the level of acceptance of subscribers to Djezzy's offers before launching them.

Figure 12. Djezzy's E-reputation by city

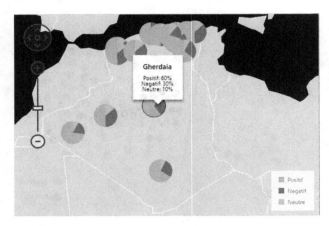

Figure 13. Offers comparison

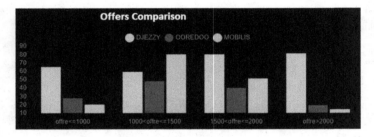

Figure 14. Mobile operator's comparison

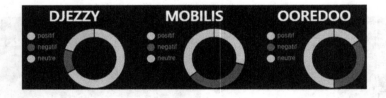

Our implemented solution is a solution applicable to cloud computing. Considering the implementation part we can run it on a remote server. This will be the next phase of the studies started.

REFERENCES

Al-Smadi, M., Qawasmeh, O., Al-Ayyoub, M., Jararweh, Y., & Gupta, B. (2018). Deep Recurrent neural network vs. support vector machine for aspect-based sentiment analysis of Arabic hotel reviews. *Journal of Computational Science*, *27*, 386–393. doi:10.1016/j.jocs.2017.11.006

Arulmurugan, R., Sabarmathi, K. R., & Anandakumar, H. (2017). Classification of sentence level sentiment analysis using cloud machine learning techniques. *Cluster Computing*, 1–11.

Benedetto, F., & Tedeschi, A. (2016). Big data sentiment analysis for brand monitoring in social media streams by cloud computing. In *Sentiment Analysis and Ontology Engineering* (pp. 341–377). Springer. doi:10.1007/978-3-319-30319-2_14

Boistel, P. (2008). La réputation d'entreprise: Un impact majeur sur les ressources de l'entreprise. *Management Avenir*, (3), 9-25.

De Oliveira, L. S., & Alturas, B. (2016, June). Using social networks: Impact on enterprise reputation. In *2016 11th Iberian Conference on Information Systems and Technologies (CISTI)* (pp. 1-6). IEEE.

Fombrun, C. J., & Rindova, V. (1996). *Who's tops and who decides? The social construction of corporate reputations*. New York University, Stern School of Business, Working Paper, 5-13.

Fourati-Jamoussi, F. (2015, February). E-reputation: a case study of organic cosmetics in social media. In *2015 6th International Conference on Information Systems and Economic Intelligence (SIIE)* (pp. 125-132). IEEE.

Jeanjean, T., Martinez, I., & Davrinche, G. (n.d.). *Policy Paper Utilisation du résultat pro forma pour la prädiction des flux de trãsorerie futurs: Importance de la présentation du compte de résultat*. Academic Press.

Kikuchi, S., & Bhalla, S. (2014, October). Data model for reputational analysis for combined Medias, social networks and IPTV. In *2014 IEEE 3rd Global Conference on Consumer Electronics (GCCE)* (pp. 51-52). IEEE. 10.1109/GCCE.2014.7031116

Krishna, P. V., Misra, S., Joshi, D., & Obaidat, M. S. (2013, May). Learning automata based sentiment analysis for recommender system on cloud. In *2013 International Conference on Computer, Information and Telecommunication Systems (CITS)* (pp. 1-5). IEEE. 10.1109/CITS.2013.6705715

Lemoine, P. (2014). *La nouvelle grammaire du succès. La transformation numérique de l'économie française*. Rapport au gouvernement.

Li, S., & Su, W. (2018). The research of reputation incentive mechanism of P2P network file sharing system. *International Journal of Information and Computer Security, 10*(2-3), 149-169.

Linton, I. (2016). *Taking technology to the market: a guide to the critical success factors in marketing technology*. Routledge.

Liu, X., Singh, P. V., & Srinivasan, K. (2016). A structured analysis of unstructured big data by leveraging cloud computing. *Marketing Science, 35*(3), 363–388. doi:10.1287/mksc.2015.0972

Louisot, J. P., & Girardet, C. (2012). Managing risk to reputation a model to monitor the key drivers. A key to long term solvency for insurance and reinsurance companies. International Journal of Banking. *Accounting and Finance, 4*(1), 4–47.

Ouchiha, T. (2018). *Les réseaux sociaux et la participation politique en Algérie. Analyse de la campagne de boycottage des législatives de mai 2017 Ã Travers Facebook*. Communication. Information médias théories pratiques.

Pan, Y. (2011). Eliminating the cyber 'lemons' problem with the e-reputation in e- commerce market: Theoretical model and practice. *International Journal of Networking and Virtual Organisations*, 8(3/4), 182–191. doi:10.1504/IJNVO.2011.039993

Park, C. W., & Seo, D. R. (2018, April). Sentiment analysis of Twitter corpus related to artificial intelligence assistants. In *2018 5th International Conference on Industrial Engineering and Applications (ICIEA)* (pp. 495-498). IEEE. 10.1109/IEA.2018.8387151

Qaisi, L. M., & Aljarah, I. (2016, July). A twitter sentiment analysis for cloud providers: A case study of Azure vs. AWS. In *2016 7th International Conference on Computer Science and Information Technology (CSIT)* (pp. 1-6). IEEE. 10.1109/CSIT.2016.7549473

Ramanathan, V., & Meyyappan, T. (2019, January). Twitter Text Mining for Sentiment Analysis on People's Feedback about Oman Tourism. In *2019 4th MEC International Conference on Big Data and Smart City (ICBDSC)* (pp. 1-5). IEEE.

Sabra, K. S., Zantout, R. N., El Abed, M. A., & Hamandi, L. (2017, September). Sentiment analysis: Arabic sentiment lexicons. In *2017 Sensors Networks Smart and Emerging Technologies (SENSET)* (pp. 1-4). IEEE.

Tran, H. (2019). *A survey of machine learning and data mining techniques used in multimedia system*. Academic Press.

Trupthi, M., Pabboju, S., & Narasimha, G. (2017, January). Sentiment analysis on twitter using streaming API. In *2017 IEEE 7th International Advance Computing Conference (IACC)* (pp. 915-919). IEEE. 10.1109/IACC.2017.0186

Uikey, C., & Bhilare, D. S. (2017, August). Security and trust life cycle of multi-domain cloud environment. In *2017 International Conference on Energy, Communication, Data Analytics and Soft Computing (ICECDS)* (pp. 2670-2678). IEEE. 10.1109/ICECDS.2017.8389938

Wang, S., Fu, B., Liu, H., Jiang, Z., Wu, Z., & Hsu, D. F. (2017). Feature engineering for credit risk evaluation in online P2P lending. *International Journal of Software Science and Computational Intelligence*, 9(2), 1–13. doi:10.4018/IJSSCI.2017040101

Woldemariam, Y. (2016, March). Sentiment analysis in a cross-media analysis framework. In *2016 IEEE International Conference on Big Data Analysis (ICBDA)* (pp. 1-5). IEEE. 10.1109/ICBDA.2016.7509790

This research was previously published in the International Journal of Cloud Applications and Computing (IJCAC), 11(2); pages 32-47, copyright year 2021 by IGI Publishing (an imprint of IGI Global).

Chapter 72
Ontology–Based Opinion Mining for Online Product Reviews

Farheen Siddiqui
Jamia Hamdard, India

Parul Agarwal
Jamia Hamdard, India

ABSTRACT

In this chapter, the authors work at the feature level opinion mining and make a user-centric selection of each feature. Then they preprocess the data using techniques like sentence splitting, stemming, and many more. Ontology plays an important role in annotating documents with metadata, improving the performance of information extraction and reasoning, and making data interoperable between different applications. In order to build ontology in the method, the authors use (product) domain ontology, ConceptNet, and word net databases. They discuss the current approaches being used for the same by an extensive literature survey. In addition, an approach used for ontology-based mining is proposed and exploited using a product as a case study. This is supported by implementation. The chapter concludes with results and discussion.

INTRODUCTION

Opinion mining is also referred as Sentiment Analysis, is a study that comprises of people's emotions, sentiments, behavioral patterns, opinions towards objects like situations, events, products, persons, organizations and similar objects in nature around us. Closely related terms with opinion mining or sentiment analysis but meant for different tasks and purpose are sentiment mining, affect analysis, review mining, opinion extraction, etc. Since, the growth of e-commerce sentiment analysis has become a strong area of research so in this chapter we shall define and discuss the problems associated, along with their solutions by describing the techniques for solving them. Sentiment analysis and opinion mining mainly focuses on opinions which express or imply positive or negative sentiments. The research gained its demand and has become an area of research for the fact that e-commerce gained its popularity. It has kind of binded

DOI: 10.4018/978-1-6684-6303-1.ch072

and shrunk the world. All of us have drifted from the conventional means of buying and shifted to usage of e-commerce. This resulted in proliferation of commercial applications. Secondly, this factor led to a series of challenging research problems one of them being opinion mining. These have led to enormous opinionate data being generated in the Web, more so because of social media influence.

Opinions, which are important influencers of our behaviors, form a focus in all human activities that we perform. Any decision making that we do, we seek the opinions of others. Though, the process of collecting opinions has changed with time. In the past, opinions were collected from friends, family members, surveys, polls and questionnaires. These were useful for businesses like marketing, public relations and even for political campaigns. But today, in e-commerce context and due to the explosive advent of social media, whenever a buying decision has to be made for a product, we are not limited to consulting the above means for opinions; rather the user reviews and discussions on the public forums available on the Web are useful. People make their buying decisions on reviews. The reason is quite obvious, consumer products and services that include movies, clothing, electronic items and hotels are frequently being discussed by the websites in the form of shared opinions (Deshpande & Sarkar, 2010). Famous examples of websites having reviews include www.amazon.com, www.flipkart.com, www.ebay. com and many others. These websites allow the users to express their opinions about the product bought. Thus, when a buying decision has to be made by a new user, he/she reads the reviews and benefits from these reviews. Customer's comment usually covers various issues that are related to different types of products. Some comments are termed as general comments but some focus on certain types of specific technical issues related to any particular product.

Ontology, generally refers to the domain being studied (Gruber, 1993).Its main aim is to provide an insight into the concepts and knowledge which both the developers and the computers can understand. Thus it enumerates the concepts related to domain and explains the relationships that exist between the concepts (Guarino, 1995). Ontology can lead to remarkable improvement in information or feature extraction and reasoning (Pang & Lee, 2008) and also make data interoperable in several applications (Baziz, Boughanem, Aussenac-Gilles, & Chrisment, 2005; Duo, Juan-Zi, & Bin, 2005; Fensel, 2002; Zhou&Chaovalit, 2007). Meersman (2005) suggested that ontologies in context of information also known as data models can be helpful in the construction of a narrow application domain. This paper also highlights that ontologies which include lexicons and thesauri is a useful step for formalization of semantics of information representation. If Lexicon on one hand is language specific ontology, then thesaurus on the other hand is either domain specific or application specific ontology. Ontology theory, manufacturing are domain specific and airlines reservations, Inventory control are a few examples of application specific Ontology.

This chapter shall perform ontology based opining mining for online product reviews. First and foremost, we shall perform preprocessing, which is necessary as presence of irrelevant and incorrect data cannot be ruled out. Several methods like stemming, sentence splitting, and tokenization shall be explored. The next step would be to construct ontology to extract product features in the reviews and thus generate a feature based summary. In order to construct this, we may use ConceptNet (Speer, 2016).

BACKGROUND

The term sentiment analysis was suggested in Nasukawa and Yi, (2003), and opinion mining in Kushal, Lawrence and Pennock, (2003). But related research or concept can be found in Das and Chen (2001);

Morinaga et al., (2002); Pang, Lee and Vaithyanathan, (2002); Tong, (2001); Turney, (2002); and Wiebe, (2000). As explained above, some comments may be positive, negative or neutral and have been reported in Yaakub et al., (2011).Since the birth of sentiment analysis can be attributed to social media research so research in opinion mining finds its applications in political sciences, social sciences, economics, management sciences and Natural language processing to name a few. The initial works related to these can be found in Hatzivassiloglou and McKeown, (1997); Hearst, (1992); Wiebe, (1990); Wiebe, (1994); and Wiebe, Bruce and O'Hara, (1999). This chapter shall comprehensively study the related work in this area. In organizations, enormous amount of information is generated by different processes (Sukumaran & Sureka,2006). This enormous information comprises of both structured and unstructured data. Structured data is the numeric data collected typically from transactional data and is useful for capturing quantitative and transactional information (Lahl, 2011). Unstructured data on the other hand, comprises of heterogenous data in form of text found in e-mails, SMS, Customer service surveys, PDF files, comments recorded by call centers and may also include images, vieos and audios represent d in varied formats (Lahl, 2011;Yaakub et al., 2011;Sukumaran & Sureka,2006).But Decision making has to be done on the basis of both structured and unstructured data by using some mining technique (Negash & Grey, 2008). Unstructured data is of heterogenous type and manging such data is a difficult task and can only be manage by using file systems and through document management(Castellanos et al., 2010). In contrast, Structure data has a predefined schema and stored in Data Warehouses or in RDBMS(Relational Database management systems). The main task associated is difficulty in search, retrieval and analysis of unstructured data and its integration with the structured data(Sukumaran & Sureka, 2006).

Further, monitoring and identifying opinion sites and distilling the information is a daunting task as each site contains enormous data in the form of opinion text that is difficult to decipher in long blogs and postings. It is difficult for an average human to identify relevant sites and then extract opinions and further use it for decision making. Many big companies like Microsoft, Google, SAS, SAP, HP and many others have their own in house capabilities. Since Sentiment Analysis has varied applications, so these find its place in various research papers. For ranking products reviews have been used in McGlohon, Glance and Reiter (2010). Twitter sentiments were linked with opinion polls and have been explained in O'Connor et al. (2010). For predicting the election results twitter sentiments have been described in Tumasjan et al. (2010). Twitter data and movie reviews can be used to predict box office revenues in case of movies. This has been explained in Asur and Huberman, (2010); Joshi et al., (2010); Sadikov, Parameswaran and Venetis, (2009). Interesting applications like identifying the gender difference in context of emotional axes on the basis of sentiments in mails are described in Mohammad and Yang (2011). The stock market predictions on the basis of twitter moods have been explained in Bollen, Mao and Zeng, (2011). In Groh and Hauffa, (2011), social relations have been characterized using opinion mining. Social influences for online book reviews have been studied in Sakunkoo and Sakunkoo, (2009). An extensive opinion mining or sentiment analysis system and several case studies have been described in Castellanos et al., (2011). The following subsection describes basic steps for ontology based opinion mining .

Preprocessing Data for Opinion Mining

Preprocessing stage is the important stage at feature level opinion mining classification, It includes sentence splitting, tokenizing strings of words, part of speech (POS) tagging technique and finally applying the suitable term of stemming. The following preprocessing process was used in the present work (Lazhar & Yamina, 2012).

1. Remove irrelevant data: This can be done by removing reviews which do not have any feature.
2. Sentence Splitting: The sentence can be split on the use of delimiters such as ".", ",".
3. Tokenization: The reviews can be broken down into smallest units which we identify as tokens. Thus, each word can be associated as a token.
4. Stemming: This step is an important preprocessing step for input document reviews. Root stemming means to reduce words to their roots.

Construct the Ontology

In ontology based methodology, there is a need to build ontology so as toenable feature selection. Lazhar and Yamina, (2012) focused on domain ontology performing structuring of features, representation of semantic information, extraction the features, and then producing a summary of features. Once, the features have been associated with opinions, these are then classified as positive, negative by using supervised classification techniques. In Yaakub et al., (2011), the authors propose an architecture that uses a multi dimensional model so as to integrate customers' characteristics along with their comments about the products. They first identify the entities, study the reviews for identifying the sentiments and then construct an attribute table by assigning a polarity ranging from -3 to 3. Each polarity denotes negative to positive opinion. For example, if -3 represents poor, then 0 represents neutral opinion and 1 would then represent accept.

Thus, on the basis of customer's comments and reviews for an entity on the basis of its features, a model is the produced based on the dimensions. For example product, customer, time and opinion. The extracted opinions from the reviews in the form of their strength of polarities are included in the opinion table. The opinion polarity was then calculated using their suggested formula. Their study includes short customer comments for extracting sentiments manually. The ontology proposed by the author covers features and its characteristics of mobile phone in general and in other technical terms . We generally write comments in the form of sentences like:

The camera is good, picture clarity excellent, battery life poor, accessories good and so on. These reviews can be collected from websites like www.amazon.com, www.flipkart.com, www.ebay.com.

In Yaakub, Li, Algarni, and Peng (2012) ontology has been constructed for opinion mining of customer reviews for the smart phones.Yaakub developed an ontology to do feature based opinion mining of customer's review on smart phones. The main objective of their work is to transfer reviews to structure table that includes several dimensions, such as, customers, products, time and locations. Polarity of portugese user product reviews based on the the features described in the domain ontology has been reported in Freitas and Vieira (2013).

In Mukherjee and Joshi (2013) ConceptNet database has been exploited for the construction of domain specific ontology for product reviews using lexicons to determine the polarity of opinion words in reviews. Then using the ontological information, the features and its polarity are integrated using the bottom up approach.In Agarwal, Mittal, Bansal, and Garg (2015) they use ConceptNet and WordNet databases for constructing the ontology. They used ontology to determine the domain specific features which in turn produced the domain specific important features. Then, the polarity of the extracted features are determined using more than one lexicons In Cadilhac, Benamara, and Aussenac-Gilles (2010), a hierarchy of features is used which the performance of features based identification systems.But the research papers that are domain ontology based use the ontology as a taxonomy using only "is a" relations between concepts. The opinion words are extracted using rule based approach. In Zhao and Li (2009) the ontology describes the semantics of domain and the concepts with their relation. The features are classified as frequent and infrequent. A random 60-0 positive and negative review was selected for their study and obtained accuracy of 88.30% in positive reviews and 81.7% in negative reviews. In Lau, Lai, Ma, and Li (2009) an automated analysis of the sentiments which can be found in customer's feedbacks was described. They also proposed a model of their Ontology Based Product Review Miner (OBPRM).

Use an Approach for Opinion Mining Classification

Lexicon Based Approach

The lexicon-based approach has concentrated on using adjectives as indicators the polarity of text. First, a list of adjectives and corresponding score values are compiled into a dictionary. Then, for any given text, all adjective words are extracted and annotated with their polarity, using the dictionary scores. The polarity scores are aggregated into a final score for the review.

Wordnet contains words with three scores as given below, that is: 1. Positive score. 2. Negative score. 3. Objective score. For every word, positive, negative and neutral scores are having values between 0.0 and 1.0 and the addition of all the scores, that is, positive score, negative score, and objective score for a word, is 1. The objective score of 1.0 denotes that it is a neutral word and does not express any opinion.

Machine Learning (ML) Approach

Like a human learns from the past experiences, a computer doesn't have experiences, but it learns from data, which represent some past experiences of the application domain. Machine learning defined as "field of study that gives computers the ability to learn without being explicitly programmed." The machine learning approach for opinion mining often relies on supervised classification methods. In this approach, labeled data is used to train classifier. In supervised machine learning, two datasets are used: train and test data. The training data contains a set of training sets. A test data is the unseen data to evaluate classifier accuracy. In classification, the most commonly features used in most methods are the following: Boolean model: Which indicates the presence or absence of a word with Booleans one or zero respectively. Term Frequency: Is the number that the term T occurs in the document D. Term Frequency Inverse Document Frequency (TF-IDF): Is a common weight scheme that is more meaningful, where large weights are assigned to terms that are occurred frequently in relevant documents.

Decision Tree (DT)

The decision tree is supervised machine learning, where it is an active method for make classifiers from data. It is also a flow-chart-like tree structure, where each node denotes a test on an attribute value, each branch represents an outcome of the test and tree leaves represent label classes. In addition, it is used in determining the best course of action, in situations having several possible alternatives with uncertain outcomes. A decision tree classifier is modeled in two stages: tree building and tree pruning. In tree building stage, the decision tree model is built by recursively splitting the training data set and assigning a class label to leaf by the most frequent class. Pruning a sub tree with branches if error is obtained.

Naïve Bayes (NB)

The NB is important for several reasons. It is very easy to construct, and not needing any difficult iterative parameter estimation schemes. This means it may be readily applied to large data sets. It is easy to interpret, understand, it often does surprisingly well and can usually be relied on to be robust and to do quite well. The NB classifier, works as follows

- Let D be training set of tuples and their associated class labels. As usual, each tuple is represented by a n-dimensional attribute vector, $X = (X1, X2,...., Xn)$, n measurements made on the tuple from n attribute, respectively, A1, A2...An.
- Assume that there are m classes, C1, C2...Cm. Given a tuple, X, the classifier will predict that X belongs to the class having the highest probability, conditioned on X. That is, the NB classifier predicts that tuple X belongs to the class Ci if and only if

$(Ci|X) > (Cj|X)$ $1 \leq j \leq m, \neq I$

Thus we maximize P(Ci|X). The class Ci for which P(Ci|X) is the maximized, is called the maximum posteriori hypothesis. By Bayes' theorem

$(Ci|X) = P(X|Ci)P(Ci) P(X)$

K-Nearest Neighbor (K-NN)

K-nearest neighbor finds a group of k objects in the training set that are closest to the test object, and bases the assignment of a label on the predominance of a particular class in this neighborhood. To classify an unlabeled object, the distance of this object to the labeled objects is computed, its k-nearest neighbors are identified, and the class labels of these nearest neighbors are then used to determine the class label of the object. Once the k-nearest neighbor list is obtained, the test object is classified based on the majority class of its nearest neighbors.

Combined Approach

In combined approach use both lexicon base and machine learning approach. The lexicon based approach uses opinion words and phrases to determine the semantic orientation of the whole document or sentence. Then, using these words to classify the entire sentence in document and then classify the entire document. The next step is to use machine learning approach. The documents that have been classified from the previous step are then used as a training set for the classifier.

USER CENTRIC ONTOLOGY BASED OPINION MINING

Ontology, commonly referred to the concept of a domain aims to provide knowledge and concepts about specific domains that are understandable by both developers and computers. In particular, ontology enumerates domain concepts and relationships among the concepts and provides a sound semantic ground of machine-understandable description of digital content. Ontology is popular in annotating documents with metadata, improving the performance of information extraction and reasoning, and making data interoperable between different applications. Using ontology in opinion mining offers several advantages which are: structuring of the features and extraction of features. In order to build ontologies in our method, we will use domain ontology, ConceptNet and WordNet databases. The main objective of our work is to provide technique that improves the performance of opinion mining classification technique by first using ontology to select features in a user centric way for the review having different features with diverse opinion strengths and then exploit these selected features to determine the proper polarity of the review. The methodology for user centric ontology based opinion mining is:

1. Retrieve customer's reviews for particular product from online social forums.
2. Decide an optimal data preprocessing method for opinion mining.
3. Select a domain ontology tree for the product domain.
4. Determine the user centric features from the review using the ontology selected.
5. Add user specific product features in the product domain ontology.
6. Determine the opinions of the user centric features using public lexicon.
7. Exploit extracted features and opinions to determine the overall polarity of review.
8. Summarization is done to generate feature-based summaries of document reviews.
9. Evaluate the performance using different performance metrics such as accuracy, precision, recall and f-measure.

The significance of this research is in improving the performance of opinion mining at feature level classification and generate complete feature-based summary can be utilized for e-commerce and many businesses' benefit. It can be taken into account in product quality improvement by understand what the customer like and dislike in the product. Also, for the customer who wants to buy a product would like to know the opinions about features in specific product from the existing users. Feature summary can save efforts and time by helping the manufactures to find which features will be improved in the product that customer dislike it.

Challenges

Though opinion mining is deeply researched field, still issues arise for review having dissimilar features with unlike opinion priorities. All opinion mining methodologies consider features recognized from the customer's review to be of equal priority and thus are unable to calculate the correct polarity of the customer's review. Also the opinion summary generation for each feature doesn't consider the user centric features that are present it in the ontology or any additional user specific feature and thus making the feature-based summary is unfinished. In this research, we use ontology structure to determine the important feature in the review and to generate an opinion summary for each feature. Also any feature that is not present in product ontology can be added through the user interactively in the final ontology tree constructed.

In this work, we focus on some of the issues for product opinion mining technique:

1. For analyzing customer's review on a product having different features with diverse opinion strengths most of the techniques considers all features extracted from the reviews to be equally important in

failing to determine the proper polarity of the review and makes the review's sentiment classification less accurate.

2. Opinion summary for each feature doesn't consider user centric features that are present it in the ontology.

3. Additional user specific feature can be added dynamically to the ontology for generating polarity of a customer product review.

This research presents a technique using ontology that selects user centric feature from product ontology, assign priority to them and also possibly adds new features to the product ontology to determine polarity of user generated product reviews.

SOLUTIONS AND RECOMMENDATIONS

In this section, we explain our methodology to classify product opinion reviews which we followed in this research. The section organized into six sections. Section discusses about overview of our methodology and short description about each steps document reviews, preprocessing steps that we followed, description of building ontology tree, about determine important additional features, opinion of extracted features, the polarity of opinion word and the overall polarity of review. Also we will discuss performance by comparing proposed method with other supervised and unsupervised techniques.

Methodology Overview

We proposed to use a methodology which is divided into five stages: stage one preparation which contain document reviews and preprocessing steps, stages two ontology construction which contain feature extraction and determine important features, stage three opinion mining which contain determine the opinion of word and overall review, stage four summarization, stage five evaluation

Stage 1: Preparation and Document Reviews

For demonstration of our proposed methodology, we must choose a product domain with features that is available online with English language reviews. Therefore a dataset was selected from domains namely, hotel from review dataset from trip advisor (2016) which contains reviews about hotels and its features such as room,"room service "food"etc. and also pizza dataset from online sources. We collect corpus consists of 2000 reviews. Polarity of the review documents is classified as equal size positive and negative. Table 1 describes the hotel data.

Table 1. Number of positive and negative class with their source

Domain	Positive	Negative
Hotel	1000	1000
Pizza	1000	1000

Preprocessing

Preprocessing is a indispensable component for our approach. There always exist few irrelevant missing and incorrect data thus we employ preprocessing methods to reach our goal, the steps employed are:

- Ignore beside the relevant point data: numeric terms and non-english terms are useless for our method. we exclude product reviews not having a few feature.
- Divide sentence on the basis of use of delimiters such as ".", ",".
- Divide the product reviews into tokens. The simplest meaningful token is a term or word that is being used in proposed approach.
- English pos tagger: we used available online tools to produce the part-of-speech tag for each term that can be noun, verb or an adjective
- Stemming: Stemming at root level implies reducing terms to their roots. In proposed approach root stemming methods are employed to produce effective correspondence of features in the product ontology. Also language sentiment lexicon comprise of words at root level.

Stage 2: Ontology

Constructing Automatic Domain Specific Ontology Tree

In our opinion mining technique, ontology in built in a user centric way by extracting user specific product features in the reviews from the product domain ontology. Also all features are assigned a positive priority value, to denote which selected feature is how much important and to finally create feature guided summary. For the purpose of constructing ontology, ConceptNet (Speer, 2016) as a knowledge resource and domain ontology is used to automatically construct in domain-specific ontology tree for a product. ConceptNet relations consist of inbuilt structures that assist in the construction of an ontology tree from the resource. The sample ontology for "hotel" domain using ConceptNet database demonstrated in Figure 1. In the next step, we expand our ontology by merging with each node in the ontology with synonyms words of English Language using WordNet (Princeton University, 2010) database, the useful of using WordNet to better coverage of domain specific features in english language. Pseudocode was proposed in algorithm described in following section that construct automatic ontology tree. This algorithm is a recursive function used to build automatic ontology tree. It takes the domain name (root) and number of levels of the ontology tree as input parameters. The get_features function using the SQL query to return a list of features from ConceptNet database that subclass of the root name parameter as seen in Table 2. The get_synonyms function also uses a SQL query to return Arabic synonyms words from WordNet database for the feature parameter. Finally, the output of function return ontology tree for specific domain.

Table 2. Concepts with relations in the ConceptNet database for hotel domain

Start Concept	Relation	End Concept	Weight
Hotel	Used For	Sleep	1
Hotel room	HasA	room service	1
hotel room	part of	Hotel	1

Figure 1.Hotel ontology tree

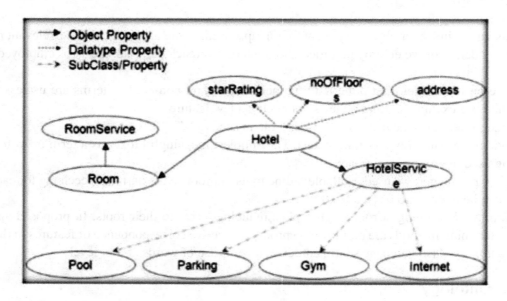

Algorithm (4.1): Algorithm for Creation of Ontology Tree

Algorithm: Function Build Ontology Tree Function createOntologyTree (p_rootName, p_levelNo)

```
Input: p_rootName parameter. // name root of ontology.
p_levelNo parameter. // number of ontology tree level.
Output: Ontology tree represents the concepts and their synonyms.
Root p_rootName //A root node of tree that created recursively. No_of_level p_
levelNo //The number of levels to deep into ontology searching for appropriate
meaning for the root concept.
If No_of_level = 0
then
Return root;
List_features=get_features(Root). //return the features that subclass from root
For each feature ∈ List_features do
Root.Add (feature); // append a node to the root
List_synonyms = Get_synonyms(feature);//return the synonyms for these feature
For each synonym ∈ List_ synonyms do
Root. addSibling (synonym); // add Sibling a node to the root
Return createOntologyTree (feature, No_of_level-1);
*************************************************************
Function get_features (root_parameter, ConceptNetDatabase)
return list
{
Input: root_parameter. // root name or node in the ontology tree. ConceptNet-
```

```
Database parameter. // database have two concepts with their relation.
Output: return features that sub-class from root feature.
V_list list; // variable list of nodes type;
Select start into V_list from ConceptNetDatabase
where end = root and rel = 'PartOf' and weight = 1
Union
Select end into V_list from ConceptNetDatabase
where start = root and rel = 'hasA';
Union
Select start into V_list from ConceptNetDatabase
where end = root and rel = 'AtLocation' etc.
return V_list;
}
Function get_synonyms (feature, WordNetDatabase)
return list
{
Input: feature parameter. // feature name or node in the ontology tree.
WordNetDatabase parameter. // database have synonym words for any word.
Output: return synonyms that related to feature parameter. V_list list; //
variable list of nodes type.
Select Ar_Synonyms into V_list from WordNetDatabase where word = feature;
return V_list;
}
```

Extract Product Features

In our methodology, constructed ontology from previous step is used to extract product features in a user centric manner interactively. Feature is actually a concept upon which an opinion is submitted by the reviewer of a product. To identify the feature term, all the noun terms are extracted from review. We used the online parser tool to parse each review and to produce the pos tag for each word (whether the word is a noun, verb, adjective, etc.).

Select User Centric Product Features

The main contribution of this research is to determine important features about which any opinion is expressed and identify which features is important than other features on the basis of interactively build user centric ontology. The feature importance is captured by the height or level of a feature node in the ontology tree. For example, in the review:

The hotel is good for staying but I have a remark about its TV. It's kind of an old version and doesn't match with the hotel

Using baseline dictionary, the overall polarity of the review is neutral "but upon checking in the review will see the feature, "staying" is not the same important compared with feature, "television" which means the overall polarity of the review is positive. For this reason, using ontology tree help us to determine the polarity of the review by determine the important features. Two important interactive step takes at this stage. First user select features from ontology and also possibly adds additional features to the ontology. As shown in Figure 2, the level in the hotel ontology presents the important features for example, the feature, "staying" was placed in level 2, but feature "TV" was placed in level 1.

Figure 2. Hotel Ontology depicted with 2 levels from ConceptNet

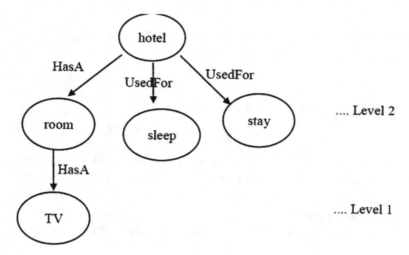

Stage 3: Opinion Mining

Calculate Opinion for Selected Feature

After identifying the features in the review and determine the important features. The next step is to get opinion word related to specific feature. Determine polarity of the feature can get by identify the opinion word related to it's feature. Opinion words may be adjectives, verb and noun, for example "excellent", "love", "prefer", "excellent", "not good" are considered opinion words.

Determine Polarity of Opinion Words

After opinion words extracted from previous steps, the polarity (positive or negative) of these words must be identified and these opinion words can be used to calculate the overall polarity of the review.

Determine the Overall Polarity (OP) of the Review

After features are extracted from the review document, it is matched in the ontology. The level of ontology where it is located determines the importance of the feature. The features located at higher level near to the root of the ontology are considered to be more important as compared to the lower level features. Finally, the overall polarity of the review is determined by summing up the opinion polarity multiplied by the height of ontology for each feature with respect to c factor that mentioned in previous section. In general, the following formula was proposed to determine the overall polarity of the review:

$$OP = \sum ((P * h) + c) \; ; 1$$

where summation is from k=1 to fn(number of feature), P is polarity of opinion, h is height of feature in ontology and c if exist, is intensifier factor that effect to opinion polarity.

"The hotel is good for staying but I have a remark about its TV. It's kind of an old version and doesn't match with the hotel"

OP=4*(1) +3*(-1) =1; //Positive with determine important the features.

Stage 4: Feature-Based Opinion Summary

Finally, after the feature and opinion extraction process is done, we are ready to generate the final feature-based summary. Our summary depends on the ontology to identify the opinion summary of each feature in the whole corpus by identifying the opinion of its sub-class terms in the ontology

Stage 5: Evaluate the Performance

In this section we discuss the evaluation of our method. The measures evaluating of the performance of classification are a confusion matrix, which is also called a performance vector that contains information about realistic and predicted classifications (Holte, 1993).

- The number of correct predictions that an instance is positive (TP).
- The number of correct predictions that an instance is negative (TN).
- The number of incorrect predictions that an instance is positive (FP).
- The number of incorrect predictions that an instance is negative (FN).

From the entries in the confusion matrix several concepts have been computed. These include Recall, Precision, F-Measure, and accuracy. Accuracy: Is the proportion of the total number of predictions that were correct. It is determined using this equation (Holte, 1993).

$$Accuracy = TP+FN+FP+TN/(TP+TN) \; 2$$

Recall: True *positive* rate, Recall, or Sensitivity which is the proportion of Real Positive cases that are correctly predicted positive. This measures the Coverage of the Real Positive cases by the (Predicted Positive) rule. Recall is defined, with its various common appellations, by equation (Holte, 1993).

$$Recall=TP/(TP+FN) \; 3$$

Precision: True *False Acc*uracy, Precision or Confidence (as it is called in Data Mining) denotes the proportion of Predicted Positive cases that are correctly Real Positives. This is what Machine Learning,

Data Mining, and Information Retrieval focus on; Precision is defined, with its various common appellations, by equation (Holte, 1993).

$$\text{Precision} = TP/(TP+FP) \quad 4$$

F-Measure: F-Measure *or F-Fac*tor is the ratio between recall and precision measurements F-Measure is defined, with its various common appellations, by equation (Holte, 1993)

$$F - \text{Measure} = 2*((\text{Precision} * \text{Recall})/(\text{Precision} + \text{Recall})) \quad 5$$

EXPERIMENTATION

In this section, we describe the conducted experiments to evaluate our approach. We made experiments with ontology considering important feature in the review. In order to compare our result, we used three classifiers which are Decision Tree (DT), Naïve Bayes (NB), and K-Nearest Neighbor (K-NN). We explain the machine environment, and the tools used in our experiment.

Datasets

Our method is performed in two domains corresponding t o hotels and pizza. The two corpora each consists of 2000 reviews of equal number of positive and negative datasets as shown in table 4.1. All the features/words extracted from the review documents are reduced to their root form for better matching of features in the ontology.

Experiments Setup

In this section, a description about the experimental environment, tools used in experiments, measures of performance evaluation of classification methods.

Experimental Environment and Tools

We applied experiments on a machine with properties that is Intel (R) Core (TM) i3- 3110M CPU @ 2.40 GHz, 4.00 GB RAM, 320 GB hard disk drive and Windows 7 operating system installed. To carry out our work (including the experimentation), special tools and programs were used which are:

- Eclipse IDE 3.8: to build and evaluate our method
- Ontology editor protégé 4.3.
- RapidMiner application program (RapidMiner Studio, 2016): used to do supervised classification methods, and extracting the required results that compared with our method.
- MySQL 6.3 (Workbench, 2016): to handle with ConceptNet database and sentiment lexicon database

Ontology Construction

The ontology construction is done using ConceptNet. We extract the concepts/features from the ConceptNet up to level 4 and domain ontology.The domain ontology for pizza is depicted in Figure 3 We notice from our experiment that some features/concepts don't exist in ConceptNet database, therefore we manually add it in domain ontology as shown in Figure 4. Also in Figure 5 the main novel contribution of interactive user centric ontology construction with feature selection and addition is shown.

Figure 3. Example of ontology tree in the pizza domain

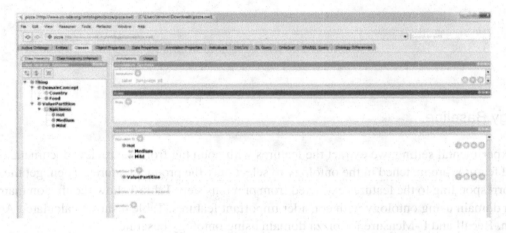

Figure 4. Example of user centric feature selection for pizza domain

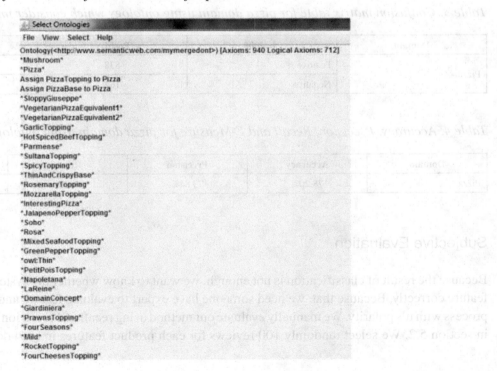

Figure 5. Interactive feature addition in ontology

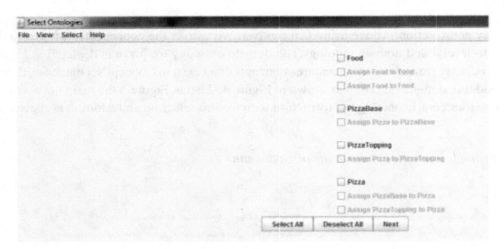

Ontology Baseline

In this experimental setting, we extract the features with noun tag from the review documents; further, extracted features are matched in the ontology to select only the product features. Then, get the opinion words corresponding to the features extracted from previous step. Table 3 shows confusion matrix table for pizza domain using ontology with consider important features. Table 4 shows calculated Accuracy, Precision, Recall and F-Measure for pizza domain using ontology baseline.

Table 3. Confusion matrix table for pizza domain using ontology which consider important features

Domain	N=2000	Positive	Negative
Pizza	Positive	838	288
	Negative	162	712

Table 4. Accuracy, Precision, Recall and F-Measure for pizza domain using ontology baseline

Domain	Accuracy	Precision	Recall	F-measure
Pizza	78.20%	73.84%	81.00%	77.25%

Subjective Evaluation

Because the result of classification is not enough, we want to know whether the system has extracted the feature correctly. Because that, we need someone have expert to evaluate feature and opinion extraction process with it's polarity. We manually evaluate our method using recall and precision formula that shown in section 5.2. We select randomly 100 reviews for each product features in both domains and manual extract tuple (feature, opinion, polarity) for the reviews with the help of someone who has experience. We choose two product features in hotel domain, such as: "room" and "restaurant" and two product feature in pizza domain "toppings"and "base". Table 5 shows the result for pizza ontology.

Table 5. Recall, precision and F-measure for feature, opinion and polarity generation for two features in hotel domain.

Features	No. of tuple extracted by Human	No. of system tuple Extracted	Correct system	Recall	Precision	F-Measure
Base	78	70	64	82.05%	91.43%	86.49%
Toppings	76	69	60	78.95	86.96	82.76

FUTURE RESEARCH DIRECTIONS

In future, this work can be extended to discover methods to enrich the ontology. Extracting ontology from reviews is also a big task to deal with in future. Also, we want to take more benefit from the ontology by expanding our ontology from more than one ontology to improve the performance. Also, we want to incorporate our method with supervised classification approaches. We need to apply our method in different domains such as mobile, computer and cars etc. We will try to apply the light stemming technique for our datasets and evaluate the performance of our method used large data set. Evaluating the effectiveness of feature and opinion extraction process used more than two features can also be considered.

CONCLUSION

Table 5 shows the recall and precision result for pizza domain in two distinct product features. Column 1, lists of each product features. Column 2, number of tuple generated manually. Column 3, number of tuple generated by our system. Columns 4, number of correct tuple generated by our system. Columns 5 and 6 give the recall and precision of our method generation for each product feature. We notice from the results that our system has good recall and precision in predicting of features with their opinion. The average f-measure of product features in pizza domain is 84.62% . Results show us the effectiveness of our method. Research in opinion mining has been very limited for the user centric feature level classification. In this work, we proposed approach work at feature level opinion mining classification to detect polarity of on-line product opinion reviews. Furthermore, we combined our approach with ontology information to give better opinion mining classification performance. Using ontology in our method has several advantages, such as extract explicit product features from the review, also to determine the important features from the review. Our approach is very applicable for any product domain that requires a domain name and number of level of the ontology parameter and using ConceptNet and WordNet databases to automatically construct domain specific ontology tree. All the experiments are performed on two review datasets, namely, hotels and pizzas. The data were collected from the websites, obtaining a total of 2000 reviews in both hotel and pizza domain with equal number of positive and negative reviews. We notice from our experiments that our method improves the performance over supervised and unsupervised approaches.

REFERENCES

Agarwal, B., Mittal, P., & Garg, S. (2015). Sentiment Analysis Using Common-Sense and Context Information. *Computational Intelligence and Neuroscience*, *2015*, 1–9. doi:10.1155/2015/715730 PMID:25866505

Asur, S., & Bernardo, A. H. (2010). *Predicting the future with social media.* Arxiv preprint arXiv:1003.5699, 2010.

Baziz, M., Boughanem, M., Aussenac-Gilles, N., & Chrisment, C. (2005). Semantic cores for representing documents in IR. *Proceedings of the 2005 ACM symposium on Applied computing.* 10.1145/1066677.1066911

Bollen, J., Mao, H., & Zeng, X.-J. (2011). Twitter mood predicts the stock market. *Journal of Computational Science*, *2*(1), 1–8. doi:10.1016/j.jocs.2010.12.007

Castellanos, M., Dayal, U., Wang, S., & Chetan, G. (2010). Information Extraction, Real-Time, Processing and DW2.0 in Operational Business Intelligence, Databases in Networked *Information Systems. Lecture Notes in Computer Science*, *5999*, 33–45. doi:10.1007/978-3-642-12038-1_4

Das, S., & Chen, M. (2001). Yahoo! for Amazon: Extracting market sentiment from stock message boards. *Proceedings of APFA-2001.*

Dave, K., Lawrence, S., & Pennock, D. M. (2003). Mining the peanut gallery: Opinion extraction and semantic classification of product reviews. *Proceedings of International Conference on World Wide Web (WWW-2003).* 10.1145/775152.775226

Duo, Z., Juan-Zi, L., & Bin, X. (2005). *Web service annotation using ontology mapping.* Paper presented at the Service-Oriented System Engineering, SOSE 2005, IEEE International Workshop.

Fensel, D. (2002). Ontology-based knowledge management. *Computer*, *35*(11), 56–59. doi:10.1109/MC.2002.1046975

Freitas, L. A., & Vieira, R. (2013). Ontology based feature level opinion mining for portuguese reviews. *Proceedings of the 22nd international conference on World Wide Web companion.* 10.1145/2487788.2487944

Groh, G., & Hauffa, J. (2011). Characterizing Social Relations Via NLP-based Sentiment Analysis. *Proceedings of the Fifth International AAAI Conference on Weblogs and Social Media (ICWSM-2011).*

Gruber, T. R. (1993). A Translation Approach to Portable Ontology Specifications Acquisition. *Current Issues in Knowledge Modeling, 5*(2), 199-220.

Guarino, N. (1995). Formal ontology, conceptual analysis and knowledge representation. *International Journal of Human-Computer Studies*, *43*(5), 1–15.

Lahl, D. (2011). Better Decisions by Analyzing Structured and Unstructured Data Together. *Business Intelligence Journal*, *16*(1), 9–1.

Hatzivassiloglou, V., & McKeown, K. R. (1997). Predicting the semantic orientation of adjectives. *Proceedings of Annual Meeting of the Association for Computational Linguistics (ACL-1997)*.

Hearst, M. (1992). Direction-based text interpretation as an information access refinement. In P. Jacobs (Ed.), *Text-Based Intelligent Systems* (pp. 257–274). Lawrence Erlbaum Associates.

Holte, R. C. (1993). Very simple classification rules perform well on most commonly used datasets. *Machine Learning*, *11*(1), 1–27. doi:10.1023/A:1022631118932

Joshi, M., Das, D., Gimpel, K., & Smith, N. A. (2010). *Movie reviews and revenues: An experiment in text regression. Proceedings of the North American Chapter of the Association for Computational Linguistics Human Language Technologies Conference (NAACL 2010)*.

Lahl, D. (2011). Better Decisions by Analyzing Structured and Unstructured Data Together. *Business Intelligence Journal*, *16*(1), 9–1.

Lau, R. Y., Lai, C. C., Ma, J., & Li, Y. (2009). Automatic domain ontology extraction for context-sensitive opinion mining. *ICIS 2009 Proceedings*, 1-18.

Lazhar, F., & Yamina, T. G. (2012). Identification of Opinions in Arabic Texts using Ontologies. *J Inform Tech Soft Engg*, *2*(2), 1–4. doi:10.4172/2165-7866.1000108

Malviya, N., Mishra, N., & Sahu, S. (2011). Developing University Ontology using protégé OWL Tool: Process and Reasoning. *International Journal of Scientific & Engineering Research*, *2*(9), 1–8.

McGlohon, M., Natalie, G., & Zach, R. (2010). Star quality: Aggregating reviews to rank products and merchants. *Proceedings of the International Conference on Weblogs and Social Media (ICWSM-2010)*.

Meersman, M. (2005). The use of lexicons and other computer-linguistic tools in semantics, design and cooperation of database systems. *Star Lab Technical Report*. Available at: http://www.starlab.vub.ac.be/website/files/STAR-1999-02_0.pdf

Mohammad, S., & Tony, Y. (2011). Tracking Sentiment in Mail: How Genders Differ on Emotional Axes. *Proceedings of the ACL Workshop on ACL 2011:Workshop on Computational Approaches to Subjectivity and Sentiment Analysis*.

Mukherjee, S., & Joshi, S. (2013). *Sentiment aggregation using conceptnet ontology*. Paper presented at the 6th International Joint Conference on Natural Language Processing.

Nasukawa, T., & Yi, J. (2003). *Sentiment analysis: Capturing favorability using natural language processing. Proceedings of the K-CAP-03, 2nd Intl. Conf. on Knowledge Capture*. 10.1145/945645.945658

Negash, S., & Gray, P. (2008). Business intelligence. In F. Burstein & C. Holsapple (Eds.), Handbook of decision support systems. Springer Link.

O'Connor, B., Balasubramanyan, R., Routledge, B. R., & Smith, N. A. (2010). From Tweets to Polls: Linking Text Sentiment to Public Opinion Time Series. *Proceedings of the International AAAI Conference on Weblogs and Social Media (ICWSM 2010)*.

Pang, B., & Lee, L. (2008). Opinion mining and sentiment analysis. *Foundations and Trends in Information Retrieval, 2*(1-2), 1–135. doi:10.1561/1500000011

Pang, B., Lee, L., & Vaithyanathan, S. (2002). Thumbs up? Sentiment Classification Using Machine Learning Techniques. *Proceedings of the conference on Empirical Methods in Natural Language Processing (EMNLP),* 79-86. 10.3115/1118693.1118704

Princeton University. (2010). *WordNet Software.* Retrieved February 1, 2016 from: http://wordnet.princeton.edu/wordnet/license/

Rob Speer, L. F. (2016). *ConceptNet Database.* Retrieved February 1, 2016 from: http://conceptnet5.media.mit.edu/

Sadikov, E., Parameswaran, A., & Venetis, P. (2009). Blogs as predictors of movie success. *Proceedings of the Third International Conference on Weblogs and Social Media (ICWSM-2009).*

Sakunkoo, P., & Sakunkoo, N. (2009). Analysis of Social Influence in Online Book Reviews. *Proceedings of third International AAAI Conference on Weblogs and Social Media (ICWSM-2009).*

Sukumaran, S., & Sureka, A. (2006). Integrating Structured and Unstructured Data Using Text Tagging and Annotation. *Business Intelligence Journal, 11*(2), 8–16.

Tong, R. (2001). An Operational System for Detecting and Tracking Opinions in on-line discussion. *Proceedings of SIGR Workshop on operational Text Classification.*

Tripadvisor. (2016). *Hotel reviews.* Retrieved January 1, 2016 from: https://www.tripadvisor.com/

Tumasjan, A., Sprenger, T. O., Sandner, P. G., & Welpe, I. (2010). Predicting elections with twitter: What 140 characters reveal about political sentiment. *Proceedings of the International Conference on Weblogs and Social Media (ICWSM-2010).*

Turney, P. (2002). Thumbs Up or Thumbs Down? Semantic Orientation Applied to Unsupervised Classification of Reviews. *Proceedings of the 40th Annual Meeting of the Association for Computational Linguistics (ACL),* 417-424.

Wiebe, J. (1990). Identifying subjective characters in narrative. *Proceedings of the International Conference on Computational Linguistics (COLING-1990).*

Wiebe, J. (1994). Tracking point of view in narrative. *Computational Linguistics, 20,* 233–287.

Wiebe, J., Rebecca, F. B., & Thomas, P. O. (1999). Development and use of a gold-standard data set for subjectivity classifications. *Proceedings of the Association for Computational Linguistics (ACL-1999).* 10.3115/1034678.1034721

Wiebe, J. (2000). Learning subjective adjectives from corpora. In *Proceedings of National Conf. on Artificial Intelligence* (pp. 735-740). AAAI Press.

Yaakub, Li, & Feng. (2011). Integration of Opinion into Customer Analysis Model. *Proceedings of Eighth IEEE International Conference on e-Business Engineering,* 90-95.

Zhou, L., & Chaovali, P. (2008). Ontology-Supported Polarity Mining. *Journal of the American Society for Information Science and Technology*, *59*(1), 98–110. doi:10.1002/asi.20735

Zhao, W. X., Jing, J., Hongfei, Y., & Xiaoming, L. (2010). Jointly modeling aspects and opinions with a MaxEnt-LDA hybrid. *Proceedings of Conference on Empirical Methods in Natural Language Processing*, 56-65.

Chapter 73

Assessing Public Opinions of Products Through Sentiment Analysis: Product Satisfaction Assessment by Sentiment Analysis

C. Y. Ng

Lee Shau Kee School of Business and Administration, The Open University of Hong Kong, Hong Kong

Kris M. Y. Law

iD https://orcid.org/0000-0003-3659-0033

School of Engineering, Deakin University, Australia

Andrew W. H. Ip

iD https://orcid.org/0000-0001-6609-0713

Department of Mechanical Engineering, University of Saskatchewan, Canada

ABSTRACT

In the world of social networking, consumers tend to refer to expert comments or product reviews before making buying decisions. There is much useful information available on many social networking sites for consumers to make product comparisons. Sentiment analysis is considered appropriate for summarising the opinions. However, the sentences posted online are generally short, which sometimes contains both positive and negative word in the same post. Thus, it may not be sufficient to determine the sentiment polarity of a post by merely counting the number of sentiment words, summing up or averaging the associated scores of sentiment words. In this paper, an unsupervised learning technique, k-means, in conjunction with sentiment analysis, is proposed for assessing public opinions. The proposed approach offers the product designers a tool to promptly determine the critical design criteria for new product planning in the process of new product development by evaluating the user-generated content. The case implementation proves the applicability of the proposed approach.

DOI: 10.4018/978-1-6684-6303-1.ch073

1. INTRODUCTION

Social networking sites are internet-based applications supporting communications for social and business purposes. These sites enable an individual user to interact with others to efficiently share personal interest, ideas, thoughts, or activities. One unique commonality to the existing social networking sites is that the user-generated content, in different forms such as photos, videos, blogs, emoticons, or text posts, is openly shared. Text posts like comments or reviews of a target product are embedded with sentiment words that can be extracted for further analyse for making purchase decisions (Goldsmith & Horowitz, 2006). The analysis on opinion strengths would be very useful to product review references because these comments are directly from the consumers (Hu and Liu, 2004; Kim and Moon, 2011; Yoo et al., 2018) and can be utilised to support product design evaluations. The number of user-generated contents in the social networking sites is increasing drastically, the sentiment analysis is emerging as a topic among researchers, regarding the capturing or summarising the text posts (Cambria et al., 2013).

Sentiment analysis, which focuses on the processing of the text for the identification of opinionated information, can handle large volumes of text posts (Mali et al., 2016). It can be used for the determination of the contextual polarity as well as the measurement of opinion strengths by searching the sentiment words in a set of text posts. Many applications using sentiment word analyses to summarise customer text posts have been successfully carried out for different product categories including digital cameras, laptops, cell phones, books, and health care products (Hu and Liu, 2004; Bucur, 2015; Kim et al., 2018).

The SentiWordNet (Guerini et al., 2013) is one of the commonly used for the determination of polarity and opinion strength. It is done by counting the number of sentiment words or summing up the sentiment scores. However, it may not be sufficient to classify a comment to be positive or negative by merely counting the number of sentiment words or determining the sentiment scores. Thus, an algorithm for categorising the comments into different polarities to support decision making is needed.

K-means (MacQueen, 1967) is a simplified approach to perform cluster analyses for multiple dimensional data. It aims to classify several data into *k* clusters. With its advantages for grouping the unlabeled data efficiently, the use of *k*-means for clustering the text posts is proposed. The text posts can be classified into three different groups, i.e. positivity, negativity, and objectivity, using sentiment analysis with the *k*-means algorithm. K-means can also be employed to facilitate the classification of various comments into corresponding design criteria.

The approach proposed has two distinct features. First, it offers an immediately applicable instrument for the evaluation of sentiment scores to present the results of sentiment analysis. Second, it helps to identify the critical design criteria and opinion strengths based on the user-generated content without reading all the text posts. Also, it offers a practical and prompt means for collecting feedback from the customers' perspective. The results are valuable for decision-makers to perform product analysis, especially for generating new design alternatives or revised models at the initial product development stage. The subsequent sections of the paper are organised as follows: Section 2 describes the related work of sentiment analysis and *k*-means for product evaluations. Section 3 outlines the procedure of the approach. Section 4 demonstrates the applicability of the method approach using a case application. Section 5 presents the results and conclusion.

2. BACKGROUND

2.1. Consumer Reviews and Product Development

In the new product development processes of consumer products, the product design stage is the most challenging, to gather customer concerns to support the decision-making on product design (He et al., 2015; Chang et al., 2018; Ng and Law, 2019), by collecting feedback from consumers (Liu et al., 2019).

The traditional product evaluation based on customer survey incurs time lag and significant resources for data processing (Pournarakis et al., 2017). It requires the pro-active participation of the users in the survey; thereby, those studies are conducted on a relatively smaller scale (Wang et al., 2018). Besides, the questions are set from the experts' point of view before conducting the survey rather than from the customers' perspectives (Hsiao et al., 2017). Thus, the interviewees are only able to provide their opinions in a specific context. In contrast, social networking sites enable customers to provide feedback and concerns about the products with relatively fewer restrictions. The product can gather constructive feedback through maintaining product pages for consumers to post product reviews. The consumers post their comments on a product concerning a specific product feature based on their qualitative judgement. These reviews, written by consumers or products end-users, reveal their expectations of the products (Li et al., 2014). Manufacturers can, therefore, obtain some reflection for the redesign of the product according to consumer's feedbacks (Gallaugher & Ransbotham, 2010; Helander and Khalid, 2006). Hence, gathering opinions from consumers contributes significantly to the core processes of product design and development, which are critical in the value chain of the consumer product. The analysis on the consumer opinions is useful for identifying product life cycle criteria, to support product innovation (Muninger et al., 2019; Suseno et al., 2018) and new product development (Bashir et al., 2017; Poecze et al., 2018). The consumer opinions can be done by analysing the online reviews and ranking the options available (Liu et al., 2017). The analysis of the online review is to identify product features by assessing the sentiment strengths of user-generated content. The ranking of options helps interpret the results after carrying out the analysis of the online reviews. The text mining approach can then be applied for analysing the user-generated content using natural language processing and machine learning (Wang et al. 2017). The sentiment analysis involves the search, extraction, and evaluation of the unstructured text written by the writers to understand the writers' attitudes (Yadollahi et al., 2017).

2.2. Sentiment Analysis

Sentiment analysis is well known for summarising the public opinion. Opinionated information can be captured using corpus-based methods, machine learning-based methods, and hybrid (Tang et al., 2009; Liu, 2010; Yan et al., 2017; Basili et al., 2017; Tang et al., 2018; Yoo et al., 2018). The machine learning approaches often require a significant amount of training documents for text classification (Medhat et al., 2014). In contrast, the corpus-based approach can simply begin with a set of opinion words collected and then expanded the set of words by searching the synonyms and antonyms, according to the thesaurus. It starts with a list of sentiment words and then searches for the additional sentiment words with similar meaning to build a large corpus.

While previous studies have attempted to address this problem, they mainly rely on traditional sentiment classification methods, including lexicon-based methods [6], which are economical, expandable, and straightforward. The limitations in traditional sentiment classification stem from its dependence on human effort in labelling documents, time-intensive activities, low coverage, and limited effectiveness resulting from the ordinary and unstructured text in tweets [7], [8], [9]. Many researchers claim that employing a mix of lexicon-based and machine learning methods can produce improved results [10].

For the public opinion on a target topic, several automatic text classification techniques are introduced to classify the subjective words into different sentiment polarities (Dave, Lawrence, & Pennock, 2003; Pang & Lee, 2008; Yang and Lin, 2018) and to summarise the public opinions for the user reviews from social networking sites regarding their experiences on movies, electronic products, restaurants, or hotels (Hu and Liu, 2004; Thet et al., 2008; Yan et al., 2015; Ali et al., 2016; Tjahyanto and Sisephaputra, 2017). Numerous studies have attempted to apply the lexicon-based approach for conducting the sentiment analysis because of the simple and expendable (Naseem et al., 2020). However, the lexicon-based approach requires extensive use of resources in tagging the words for the unstructured content posted (Saeed et al., 2018). This limitation can be remedy by the adoption of the integration of the lexicon-based approach with learning algorithm (da Silva et al., 2014; Naseem et al., 2020).

2.2.1. Classifying and Polaritizing

The mechanism of classifying subjective words into different polarities is important in the sentiment analysis. The polarities of the subjective or emotional words are determined, while the sentiment strengths of the text are assigned with linguistic terms of preferences (Wilson et al., 2004). The lexical databases such as SentiWordNet (Guerini et al., 2013), SenticNet (Cambria et al., 2010) and Opinion Lexicon (Hu and Liu, 2004) are developed to support sentiment words searching. Liu and Hu Opinion Lexicon has over 6800 positive and negative opinion words (Hu and Liu, 2004) to facilitate the sentiment analysis. The opinion words are categorised into either positive or negative polarity to support the analysis of customer reviews. Another tool for sentiment analysis called SentiWords (Guerini et al., 2013) has been developed recently. This lexical tool contains about 155,000 words. Each opinion word is classified as positivity, negativity, or objectivity. The opinion strength is associated with a sentiment score ranging from -1 to 1. For example, the word "bad" is associated with a sentiment score -0.625 in negative polarity with 0.375 in objective polarity (1-|-0.625|=0.375). The sentiment scores enable a practical approach to support sentiment word searches for summarising customer reviews. Many case applications using SentiWords have been reported including opinion mining in tourism products (Bucur, 2015), development of intercity safe travelling plans (Ali et al., 2017), and extraction of public opinion in financial services (Ravi et al., 2017).

SentiWordNet (Guerini et al., 2013) is capable of supporting the analysis of sentiment strengths. SentiWordNet assigns each word with three values, called triplets, ranging from -1 to 1 for indicating a sentiment strength of a subjective word and the sum of the absolute values of the triplets should be 1.0. SentiWordNet has been employed for many case applications (Zhao and Li, 2009; Jahiruddin et al., 2009; Dalal and Zaveri, 2013; Bucur, 2015; Ali et al., 2016). Extending the existing SentiWordNet lexical database with the triplets is a valuable approach for performing sentence-based analyses.

However, one of the disadvantages is that scores obtained from objective sentiment are often ignored when determining the sentiment polarity (Gonçalves et al., 2013). It is because merely summing up or taking averages on the sentiment scores for concluding the sentiment polarity of a review, the score of objectivity is always very high that affects the polarity determination, even the polarity of the text post can be classified to positivity or negativity. The use of an unsupervised learning approach for determining the polarity of the text posts based on sentiment scores thus remains open for discussions.

2.2.2. K-Means For Vector Quantisation

K-means is a type of unsupervised learning technique for vector quantisation to partition unlabeled data for data mining. The term k-means was first applied for analysing multivariate observations (MacQueen, 1967), and the standard algorithm was proposed to support the analysis of pulse-code modulation (Lloyd, 1982). It is used to group many observations n into groups or clusters k that each observation is partitioned to a cluster with the nearest mean. The centroids of the k non-intersection clusters, as well as the groupings of observations, can be determined by iterating the algorithm to search for the minimum value of the squared Euclidean differences (between the centroids of clusters and the corresponding clustered observations). The number of "k" clusters can be pre-determined or obtained by searching the "elbow point" (Ketchen & Shook, 1996). Once the value of k is determined, the initial centroids of clusters can be either generated or selected randomly from the observations.

The results of the k-means++ algorithm are found more reliable than the standard k-means algorithm (Bahmani et al., 2012; Öztürk et al., 2015). The k-means++ approach can overcome the deficiencies associated with determining the initial centroids for k-means. A study on different dataset has been conducted to demonstrate that k-means++ is capable of providing more reliable results, even the number of clusters is increased (Shindler, 2008).

2.2.3. Integration of K-means and Sentiment Analysis

Though k-means is straightforward with some lexical resources for performing sentiment analysis available, the combined k-means with sentiment analysis for summarising public opinions of product reviews has not been well explored until recent years. The combined approach has been employed for the evaluations of emotional signals based on emoticon or text posts obtained from Twitter (Hu et al., 2013), and this is probably more suitable for summarising the crowd responses on an incidence. It has been used for analysis on the impact of the economic costs of violence (Pejić Bach et al., 2018). Besides, it has also been applied for opinion mining (AL-Sharueea et al. 2018), where the online reviews are crawled from an Australia consumer opinion website, for processing a vast amount of data with no training or manual work is involved.

This combined approach can categorise the reviews into different rating for supporting purchase decisions (Riaz et al., 2017). However, specifically for evaluating online review for a target product or service, the assessment criteria often are not with equal importance, as well as the weights of the criteria. Result simply based on the majority of voting of polarities or the summation of sentiment scores is not sufficient to conclude a design evaluation of a target product or service. Hence, a new approach is proposed, and the details are discussed in the subsequent sections.

3. THE PROPOSED APPROACH

Customers may have different perceptions of the product models. Some of them would post their comments or reviews about the product models on the corresponding fans' pages. These comments or reviews posted on social networking sites help the decision-makers to evaluate different product models and identify the importance among different attributes by extracting the ideas from the crowd. The development of text mining approach supports automatically evaluate and summarise a vast amount of comments.

The proposed opinion mining approach starts with the determination of the assessment criteria of the target products (Figure 1). It includes the extraction of text posts from social networking sites, identifying keywords to form a corpus for the product category, the adoption of K-means for classifying the posts according to different design attributes, and evaluating the posts using sentiment analysis.

Figure 1.

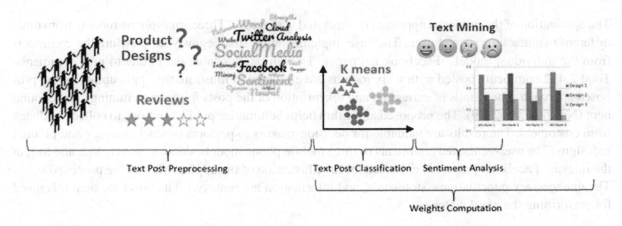

The decision-makers firstly determine the assessment criteria and the number of criteria (i.e. clusters) for the implementation of the approach. The text posts are crawled from the corresponding social networking sites for further processing. The unnecessary information of the text posts such as the post identification numbers, writers' nicknames, date information, and query times are removed. The stop words are deleted to reduce the searching time. The words of the posts are stored in an array through tokenisation to support the search of sentiment words. In the second stage, the key phrases related to the assessment criteria are tagged manually and extracted into the corresponding arrays to facilitate criteria classification processes.

A search process is then carried out for counting the number of occurrences of key phrases. For example, three assessment criteria related to mobile devices, namely "Display", "Specifications", and "Camera" are identified. The associated key phrases are pre-determined, with a text post *"Nice screen but the fingerprint sensor is useless and plz solve the overheating problem"* extracted. The extracted post contains three key phrases that can be associated with the assessment criteria. They are "display", "fingerprint", and "overheat". Further details of employing *k*-means to categorise the text posts into assessment criteria will be presented in the subsequent section.

In the third stage, sentiment analysis would be conducted using SentiWordsNet (Guerini et al., 2013). Suppose a sentiment word "superb" is found in a text post, the corresponding sentiment scores are (P: 0.875, N: 0, O: 0.125) and a three-dimensional vector can represent the scores. The *k*-means iteration then can be carried out to categorise the text posts into the three polarities of sentiment analysis (i.e. positivity, negativity, and objectivity). The fourth stage is to finalise the weights for ranking the product models of the target product. The priority weights of polarities can be determined through normalisation. The overall priority weights can be obtained by multiplying the corresponding criteria weights with the sum of sentiment scores. A higher total priority weight of a product model scored indicates that it is preferred than the other assessed models.

4. CASE IMPLEMENTATION

4.1. The Case

The application of the proposed approach is illustrated with a case. Three smartphone models from three different manufacturers are chosen. The case implementation first begins with crawling the comments from the individual models' Facebook fan pages. The fan pages enable the public to post comments. Total 2,412 comments posted within six months are extracted to illustrate the applicability of the proposed approach. The details of extraction and tokenisation of the posts for opinion mining can be found here (Ng and Law, 2019). The proposed algorithm helps summarise public opinions to collect feedback from customers. The results are valuable for decision-makers to perform product analyses and product redesigns. The user-generated comments of three mobile phone models, denoted as M1, M2, and M3, in the relevant FaceBook pages are extracted for the illustration of the applicability of the proposed work. The unnecessary punctuations, stopwords, and information are removed. The posts are then tokenised for performing the word matches.

4.2. The Process

4.2.1 Select The Assessment Criteria and Determine The Number of Criteria (The Value of K)

Six assessment criteria of the mobile phone devices namely Specifications (A1), Display (A2), Camera and Storage (A3), Battery (A4), Design (A5), and Software (A6) are identified. These criteria often employed for the evaluations of mobile phones performances in related websites or magazines for consumers. Thus, the value, $k=6$, is assumed. As the objective of this paper is to showcase the use of k-means for summarising user-generated content from the social networking sites, the details of selecting the assessment criteria are not given here. The three mobile phone models will be assessed based on these six criteria.

4.2.2 Identify The Key Phrases of The Selected Assessment Criteria

A set of key phrases concerning each assessment criterion are identified by tagging the phrases based on the posts extracted from the fan pages by manual. The key phrases are identified by counting the number of occurrences, and then tag the phrases, which are with a higher number of occurrences, for grouping them into the corresponding assessment criteria. For example, a text post is read as "Its' "camera" "has" "a" "wider" "aperture". The key phrases "camera" and "aperture" are included in the array of key phrases under A3. Over 500 phrases are categorised into the six criteria using the method of word count. Table 1 shows some of the key phrases used in this case application. The next step is to search the text posts using the key phrases in the arrays. The results are represented by a vector defined as:

$$p_i = \{A_j\} \ i=1,2,\ldots, n \text{ and } j=1,2,\ldots, k=6 \tag{3}$$

where p and A are denoted as the text posts and assessment criteria respectively, n is the number of text posts for evaluation, and k is the number of clusters. Using the case example, while the words "camera" and "aperture" are the key phrases of A3, the text post, p_{ex}, can then be represented by a vector, $p_{ex}=\{$ 0, 0, 2, 0, 0, 0$\}$.

Table 1. Assessment criteria and their corresponding key phrases

Assessment Criteria	Related areas of assessment	Key phrases
Specifications, A1	Processing power, CPU and GPU performance, rom, ram, sim card slots, wireless connectivity, sound and speaker quality	quad, octa, processor, qualcomm, snapdragon, LTE, Bluetooth, DAC, sim, B&O, speaker, fingerprint, jack, heat, overheat, feature, spec, hardware, core, ram, rom, 2GB, 4GB, 6GB, IP68, etc.
Display, A2	Resolution, screen size, durability, glass type, surface, hardness,	720p, 1080p, 4k, 18.5:9, ppi, 5", 6" 720p, amoled, oled, IPS, breakable, broke, display, screen, curve, edge, brightness, brittle, crack, fragile, scratch, glass, gorilla, hard, protector etc.
Camera and Storage, A3	Aperture value, photo quality, flash, optical zoom, expandable memory, sd card size,	32gb, 64gb, 128gb, 256gb, SD, sdcard, microsd, aperture, megapixel, 16mp, 5mp, fps, hdr, camera, cam, capture, blue, exposure, flash, motion, optic, optical, pics, photo, pictures, portrait, zoom, shoot, redeye, slow-motion, stabilisation, shot, selfies, movie, etc.
Battery, A4	Battery endurance, charging time,	battery, charger, charging, detachable, mah, explode, bomb, etc.
Design, A5	Design, materials, size, weight, shape, colour	Bezel, borderless, colour, plastic, metal, metallic, stylus, aesthetic, design, shape, materials, size, weight, square, pretty, comfortable, heavy, light, etc.
Software, A6	Firmware update, software, user interface, Apps of the hardware modules	App, software, firmware, android, app, bug, bootloader, oreo, os, setting, version, root, interface, etc.

4.2.3 Use The K-Means++ Algorithm To Determine The Centroids and Obtain Criteria Weights

The k-means algorithm supplemented by k-means++ is employed to categorise the extracted posts into various clusters for each product model. As mentioned in section 2.2.2, the results generated by the standard k-means algorithm are sensitive to the initial values of centroids assigned, and the proposed approach uses k-means++ for determining the initial seeds to improve the reliability of the results. The centroids for clusters A1, A2, ..., A6 can be determined using k-means++. The detailed steps of calculations can be found in the Appendix section.

The adoption of k-means algorithms can be used to categorise the data points into corresponding clusters by minimising the sum of squared differences within the clusters. It can be done by calculating the Euclidean distance between a data point and the six centroids. The optimum clustering solution can be determined by selecting the data point with the minimum value of the sum of the Euclidean distances. The optimum values of centroids can be calculated using the equation (2) if a new minimum distance can be found in that particular iteration. The iterations will be terminated if no further minimum value is found. After looping the equations (1) and (2) for the data points, the posts are then categorised into the six assessment criteria, as shown in Table 2.

Table 2. Summarised results after the k-means iterations of assessment criteria categorisation for the three models

Assessment Criteria	M1		M2		M3	
	No. of Post	Normalised	No. of Post	Normalised	No. of Post	Normalised
A1	205	0.1902	134	0.2306	192	0.2465
A2	85	0.0788	119	0.2048	62	0.0796
A3	158	0.1466	61	0.1050	122	0.1566
A4	91	0.0844	97	0.1670	34	0.0436
A5	478	0.4434	123	0.2117	325	0.4172
A6	61	0.0566	47	0.0809	44	0.0565

4.2.4 Use The k-Means/ k-Means++ Algorithms To Categorize Sentiment Polarities

The sentiment analysis on the extracted text posts is conducted by searching the sentiment words using the lexical resource databases. In our case, we use SentiWordNet (Guerini et al., 2013) for illustrating the applicability of the proposed approach. Some other lexical-based tools for determining the sentiment scores such as Sentic Net (Cambria et al., 2017), TextBlob (Subirats et al., 2018), and Valence Aware Dictionary and sEntiment Reasoner (2014) can also be applied in the proposed k-means approach. By the adoption of these tools, the sentiment strengths of the words are represented by sentiment polarities and scores. In our proposed approach, a vector can be defined, given in equation (4), for representing the sentiment strengths of each post,

$$s_i = \{P_i, N_i, O_i\} \; i=1,2,3\ldots, n \tag{4}$$

where s_i is a 3-dimensional vector for representing sentiment strengths, P, N, O are denoted as the sum of positivity, negativity, and objectivity sentiment strengths respectively; n is the number of text posts extracted of a target product model.

The posts of each product model are categorised into three polarities by iterating the k-means and k-means++ algorithms. The normalised weights are shown in Table 3 and Table 4. The ranking of the product models can be prioritised by multiplying the criteria weights with the weights of sentiment polarities. The ranking of the models remains unchanged when the value of f_p is increased by 0.01 within [0, 1] (Figure 2).

Table 3. Summarised results of sentiment analysis for the three models

Assessment Criteria		M1			M2			M3		
		Positivity	Negativity	Objectivity	Positivity	Negativity	Objectivity	Positivity	Negativity	Objectivity
A1	No. of posts	68	112	25	64	43	29	104	63	25
	Normalised	0.3317	0.5463	0.122	0.4706	0.3162	0.2132	0.5417	0.3281	0.1302
A2	No. of posts	35	36	14	50	33	36	19	18	25
	Normalised	0.4118	0.4235	0.1647	0.4202	0.2773	0.3025	0.3065	0.2903	0.4032
A3	No. of posts	92	45	21	15	32	13	49	49	24
	Normalised	0.5823	0.2848	0.1329	0.25	0.5333	0.2167	0.4016	0.4016	0.1967
A4	No. of posts	26	43	22	62	25	10	12	17	5
	Normalised	0.2857	0.4725	0.2418	0.6392	0.2577	0.1031	0.3529	0.50	0.1471
A5	No. of posts	247	74	157	36	68	18	91	195	39
	Normalised	0.5167	0.1548	0.3285	0.2951	0.5574	0.1475	0.2800	0.60	0.120
A6	No. of posts	30	19	12	13	22	12	23	14	7
	Normalized	0.4918	0.3115	0.1967	0.2766	0.4681	0.2553	0.5227	0.3182	0.1591

Table 4. A summary of weights for the product models ($f_p = 0.5$)

Model Criteria	M1	M2	M3
A1	-0.0088	0.0424	0.0424
A2	0.0061	0.0456	0.0167
A3	0.0315	-0.0035	0.0154
A4	0.0023	0.0404	6.06E-6
A5	0.1531	-0.0121	-0.0417
A6	0.0107	0.00258	0.01026
Overall weights	0.1948	0.1154	0.0430

Figure 2.

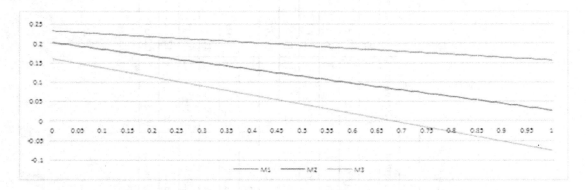

5. DISCUSSIONS OF THE PROPOSED K-MEANS AND SENTIMENT ANALYSIS APPROACH

5.1 Rapid Production Evalution

The adoption of the *k-means* algorithm in summarising the user-generated contents extracted from social media sites to support a fast-track product evaluation is illustrated in the case example in Section 4.

Results, as shown in Table 4, show that the majority of the posts are related to the Design (A5) and Specifications (A1). The next critical criterion is Display (A2) because many positive comments are posted concerning its high-density display of the model M2. In contrast, the model M1 is ranked as the best among the candidates.

The factor, f_p, is determined intuitively by decision-makers for combining the weights of assessment criteria with the weights of sentiment polarities. A sensitivity analysis is conducted to verify that the final ranking would not be affected by changing the values of vector *f,* as shown in Figure 3.

Our results show that Design (A5) and Specifications (A1) are the most critical assessment criteria, implying that users are concerned more about these two criteria. Consumers pay more attention to the aesthetics of the products such as colour and finishing. Manufacturers may need to put more efforts into developing new phones with better specifications such as the processing power of microprocessors capacity of RAM/ ROM, and sound quality. Some product models emphasised on the image quality, however, the amount of comments obtained is relatively less than the other criteria, and this may imply the 'image quality' is not the foremost concern of consumers. Putting more efforts in enhancing the performances in these criteria may not be leading to inc increase the overall attractiveness of these product models.

5.2 Linking The Sentiment Analysis and product Development

The adoption of sentiment analysis on the user-generated comment to support the evaluation of product design, from a customer perspective, can help to collect the feedback and public views efficiently. This proposed approach is a new initiative on the topic of sentiment analysis and product design evaluation.

In the proposed approach, the sentiment polarities of the text posts, which are categorised by k-means, eliminate the drawbacks related to majority votes or summation of the sentiment scores. Each text post is represented as a data point and categorised into a cluster, the problem related to unreasonably high sentiment score of a particular polarity, which is boosted by posts that contains a large number of sentiment words, can be eliminated. Thus, the confidence in the results of sentiment analysis is enhanced.

Launching a new product to the market is a crucial driver to support a company's long term growth and success (Battistoni et al., 2013). The new product development process consists of a series of the identification on the necessary changes or improvement on existing products, products' idea generation, design of the products, and making the products real and beneficial. The new product development is, therefore,e crucial to product success (Suharyanti et al., 2017).

The proposed approach supports the product designers to promptly determine the critical design criteria for new product planning in the process of new product development by evaluating the user-generated content. Improvement areas of the existing product model can be identified from the end-users opinions without traditional product surveys, and this is a significant contribution to the rapid product development.

6. CONCLUSION

The proposed approach provides a practical way to perform product evaluations by considering the sentiment words of the text posts uploaded to the social networking sites. It offers the product designers a tool to promptly determine the important design criteria for new product planning in the process of new product development by evaluating the user-generated content. The more the comments on a specific product model posted online, the more attention it attracts from the public. However, counting the number of sentiment words and summing up the corresponding sentiment scores are not sufficient to support product evaluation as the design criteria are very often not with equal importance. The use of k-means to identify the significance among different design criteria is a novelty of the proposed approach. Improvement areas of the existing product model can be identified from the end-users' opinions without traditional product surveys, and this is a significant contribution to the rapid product development.

6.1 Contributions

The approach combining the k-means algorithm with the lexical resource database offers a logical and practical solution to summarise the customer-generated comments without reviewing thousands or more text posts, which is certainly a time and resource-consuming process. Another contribution is the integration of text mining using sentiment analysis and new product development. The use of k-means for clustering the product design criteria along with the SentiWordNet for summarising the user-generated content is a new attempt in the field of opinion mining.

6.2 Limitation and Future Works

The proposed approach has some limitations. It requires users to select the product models or alternatives for comparison purposes, and the selection of suitable referencing product models may affect the overall results. In the case implementation, three android mobiles phones with more or less the same price and specifications are selected. In contrast, phones driven by iOS are not chosen because of different user-interface. Therefore, expert judgement is needed when selecting appropriate product models for product comparison. Furthermore, the sentiment scores are given by the lexical resource sometimes may not be sufficient or precise enough because the sentiment words chosen to represent opinions vary among different persons. Therefore, the use of uncertainty analysis in conjunction with sentiment analysis and clustering algorithms are the possible direction for the future works.

REFERENCES

Al-Sharuee, M. T., Liu, F., & Pratama, M. (2018). Sentiment analysis: An automatic contextual analysis and ensemble clustering approach and comparison. *Data & Knowledge Engineering*, *115*, 194–213. doi:10.1016/j.datak.2018.04.001

Ali, F., Daehan, K., Pervez, K., Riazul, S. M., Kim, K. H., & Kwak, K. S. (2017). Fuzzy Ontology-based Sentiment Analysis of Transportation and City Feature Reviews for Safe Traveling. *Transportation Research Part C, Emerging Technologies*, *77*, 33–48. doi:10.1016/j.trc.2017.01.014

Arthur, D., & Vassilvitskii, S. (2007). k-means++: the advantages of careful seeding. *Proceedings of the eighteenth annual ACM-SIAM symposium on Discrete algorithms*, 1027–1035.

Bahmani, B., Moseley, B., Vattani, A., Kumar, R., & Vassilvitskii, S. (2012). Scalable k-means++. *Proceedings of the VLDB Endowment International Conference on Very Large Data Bases*, *5*(7), 622–633. doi:10.14778/2180912.2180915

Basili, R., Croce, D., & Castellucci, G. (2017). Dynamic polarity lexicon acquisition for advanced Social Media analytics. *International Journal of Engineering Business Management*, *9*, 1847979017744916. doi:10.1177/1847979017744916

Battistoni, E., Fronzetti Colladon, A., Scarabotti, L., & Schiraldi, M. M. (2013). Analytic hierarchy process for new product development. *International Journal of Engineering Business Management*, *5*, 5-42.

Bucur, C. (2015). Using Opinion Mining Techniques in Tourism. *Procedia Economics and Finance*, *23*, 1666–1673. doi:10.1016/S2212-5671(15)00471-2

Cambria, E., Poria, S., Gelbukh, A., & Thelwall, M. (2017). Sentiment analysis is a big suitcase. *IEEE Intelligent Systems*, *32*(6), 74–80. doi:10.1109/MIS.2017.4531228

Cambria, E., Schuller, B., Xia, Y., Havasi, C. (2013, Mar.). New Avenues in Opinion Mining and Sentiment Analysis. *IEEE Computer Society*, 15-21.

Cambria, E., Speer, R., Havasi, C., & Hussain, A. (2010) SenticNet: A publicly available semantic resource for opinion mining In *Commonsense Knowledge: Papers from the AAAI Fall Symposium*. AAAI Press.

da Silva, N. F., Hruschka, E. R., & Hruschka, E. R. Jr. (2014). Tweet sentiment analysis with classifier ensembles. *Decision Support Systems, 66*(C), 170–179. doi:10.1016/j.dss.2014.07.003

Goldsmith, R. E., & Horowitz, D. (2006). Measuring motivations for online opinion seeking. *Journal of Interactive Advertising, 6*(2), 2–14. doi:10.1080/15252019.2006.10722114

Gonçalves, P., Araújo, M., Benevenuto, F., & Cha, M. (2013). Comparing and combining sentiment analysis methods. *COSN '13 Proceedings of the first ACM conference on Online social networks*, 27-38.

Hsiao, Y. H., Chen, M. C., & Liao, W. C. (2017). Logistics service design for cross-border e-commerce using Kansei engineering with text-mining-based online content analysis. *Telematics and Informatics, 34*(4), 284–302. doi:10.1016/j.tele.2016.08.002

Hu, M., & Liu, B. (2004). Mining and summarising customer reviews. *Proceedings of the tenth ACM SIGKDD international conference on Knowledge discovery and data mining*, 168-177.

Hu, X., Tang, J., Gao, H., & Liu, H. (2013). Unsupervised sentiment analysis with emotional signals. *Proceedings of the 22nd international conference on World Wide Web*, 607-618. 10.1145/2488388.2488442

Hutto, C. J., & Gilbert, E. (2014). VADER: A parsimonious rule-based model for sentiment analysis of social media text. *Eighth International AAAI Conference on Weblogs and Social Media.*

Ketchen, D. J. Jr, & Shook, C. L. (1996). The application of cluster analysis in Strategic Management Research: An analysis and critique. *Strategic Management Journal, 17*(6), 441–458. doi:10.1002/(SICI)1097-0266(199606)17:6<441::AID-SMJ819>3.0.CO;2-G

Kim, A. R., Lee, S., & Song, M. (2018). Incorporating product description to sentiment topic models for improved aspect-based sentiment analysis. *Information Sciences, 454-455*, 200–215. doi:10.1016/j.ins.2018.04.079

Kim, Y., & Moon, I. (2011). A study on algorithm for selection priority of contents in social network service. *Proceedings of the Korean Institute of Information and Communication Sciences Conference.*

Kreutzer, J., & Witte, N. (2013). *Opinion Mining Using SentiWordNet*. Uppsala University. http://stp.lingfil.uu.se/~santinim/sais/Ass1_Essays/Neele_Julia_SentiWordNet_V01

Liu, Y., Bi, J. W., & Fan, Z. P. (2017). Ranking products through online reviews: A method based on sentiment analysis technique and intuitionistic fuzzy set theory. *Information Fusion, 36*, 149–161. doi:10.1016/j.inffus.2016.11.012

Lloyd, S. P. (1982). Least squares quantisation in PCM. *IEEE Transactions on Information Theory, 28*(2), 129–137. doi:10.1109/TIT.1982.1056489

MacQueen, J. B. (1967). Some Methods for classification and Analysis of Multivariate Observations. *Proceedings of 5th Berkeley Symposium on Mathematical Statistics and Probability*, 281–297.

Mali, D., Abhyankar, M., Bhavarthi, P., Gaidhar, K., & Bangare, M. (2016). Sentiment Analysis of Product Reviews for E-commerce Recommendation. *International Journal of Management and Applied Science, 2*(1).

Medagoda, N., Shanmuganathan, S., & Whalley, J. (2015). Sentiment Lexicon Construction Using SentiWordNet 3.0. *11th International Conference on Natural Computing*. 10.1109/ICNC.2015.7378094

Medhat, W., Hassan, A., & Korashy, H. (2014). *Sentiment analysis algorithms and applications: a survey*. Ain Shams Eng. Journal.

Naseem, U., Razzak, K., Musial, K., & Imran, N. (2020). Transformer based Deep Intelligent Contextual Embedding for Twitter sentiment analysis. *Future Generation Computer Systems*.

Ng, C. Y., & Law, K. M. (2019). Investigating Consumer Preferences on Product Designs by Analysing Opinions from Social Networks using Evidential Reasoning. *Computers & Industrial Engineering*, 106180.

Öztürk, M. M., Cavusoglu, U., & Zengin, A. (2015). A novel defect prediction method for web pages using k-means++. *Expert Systems with Applications*, *42*(19), 6496–6506. doi:10.1016/j.eswa.2015.03.013

Pejić Bach, M., Dumičić, K., Jaković, B., Nikolić, H., & Žmuk, B. (2018). Exploring impact of economic cost of violence on internationalisation: Cluster analysis approach. *International Journal of Engineering Business Management*, *10*, 1847979018771244. doi:10.1177/1847979018771244

Ravi, K., Ravi, V., & Krishna, P. (2017). Fuzzy formal concept analysis based opinion mining for CRM in financial services, Research article. *Applied Soft Computing*, *60*, 786–807. doi:10.1016/j.asoc.2017.05.028

Riaz, S., Fatima, M., & Kamran, M. (2017). *Cluster Computing*. Advance online publication. doi:10.100710586-017-1077-z

Saeed, Z., Abbasi, R. A., Sadaf, A., Razzak, M. I., & Xu, G. (2018). Text stream to temporal network-a dynamic heartbeat graph to detect emerging events on Twitter. In *Pacific-Asia Conference on Knowledge Discovery and Data Mining*. Springer.

Shindler, M. (2008). *Approximation algorithms for the metric k-median problem. Written Qualifying Exam Paper*. University of California.

Silva, N. F. F. D., Coletta, L. F., & Hruschka, E. R. (2016). Survey and Comparative Study of Tweet Sentiment Analysis via Semi-Supervised Learning. *ACM Computing Surveys*, *49*(1), 49–15. doi:10.1145/2932708

Subirats, L., Reguera, N., Bañón, A., Gómez-Zúñiga, B., Minguillón, J., & Armayones, M. (2018). Mining facebook data of people with rare diseases: A content-based and temporal analysis. *International Journal of Environmental Research and Public Health*, *15*(9), 1877. doi:10.3390/ijerph15091877 PMID:30200209

Suharyanti, Y., Subagyo, Masruroh, N. A., & Bastian, I. (2017). A multiple triangulation analysis on the role of product development activities on product success. *International Journal of Engineering Business Management*, *9*, 1847979017723544. doi:10.1177/1847979017723544

Thet, T., Na, J., & Khoo, C. (2008). Sentiment classification of movie reviews using multiple perspectives. *Proceedings of the international conference on Asian digital libraries (ICADL)*, 184–193. 10.1007/978-3-540-89533-6_19

Wang, W. M., Li, Z., Tian, Z. G., Wang, J. W., & Cheng, M. N. (2018). Extracting and summarizing affective features and responses from online product descriptions and reviews: A Kansei text mining approach. *Engineering Applications of Artificial Intelligence*, *73*, 149–162. doi:10.1016/j.engappai.2018.05.005

Yadollahi, A., Shahraki, A. G., & Zaiane, O. R. (2017). Current state of text sentiment analysis from opinion to emotion mining. *ACM Computing Surveys*, *50*(2), 1–33. doi:10.1145/3057270

Yoo, S. Y., Song, J. I., & Jeong, O. R. (2018, September). Social media contents based sentiment analysis and prediction system. *Expert Systems with Applications*, *105*(1), 102–111. doi:10.1016/j.eswa.2018.03.055

This research was previously published in the Journal of Organizational and End User Computing (JOEUC), 33(4); pages 125-141, copyright year 2021 by IGI Publishing (an imprint of IGI Global).

APPENDIX A

Use The k-Means++ Algorithm To Determine The Centroids

The k-means algorithm supplemented by k-means++ is employed to categorise the extracted posts into various clusters for each product model. As mentioned in section 2.2.2, the results generated by the standard k-means algorithm are sensitive to the initial values of centroids assigned, and the proposed approach uses k-means++ for determining the initial seeds to improve the reliability of the results.

Suppose we have 10 data points $(d_1, d_2, d_3, \ldots, d_{10})$ for the model M1 and each data point can be represented by a vector with 6 dimensions as shown in Table 5. Firstly, $d_3 = \{0, 0, 2, 0, 0, 0\}$ is randomly picked as the first centroid among the 10 data points. Second, for each data point, calculate the squared distances between the data and centroid. The results are listed in the column "Dist$(d_3)^2$". Third, a new centroid is selected randomly according to the cumulative probability distribution of "Dist$(d_3)^2$". Here, d_8 is selected based on a random number, 95, which is within an interval 0 to 129. The squared distances and the cumulative probability distribution are then calculated and listed in the column "Dist$(d_8)^2$". To exclude those data points which have already been selected as centroids in the previous rounds, the minimum values between "Dist$(d_3)^2$" and "Dist$(d_8)^2$" is chosen for calculating the column "Cum. Dist$(d_8)^2$". The next step is to generate new random numbers for determining the next centroids and calculate the squared distances as well as compute the cumulative probability distributions until the initial values for all the k centroids are determined. The centroids for clusters A1, A2, …, A6 determined by k-means++ are d_{10}, d_6, d_3, d_2, d_7, and d_8 respectively.

Table 5. Dataset for the illustration of the procedure of k-means++

Data_no. (M1)	A1	A2	A3	A4	A5	A6	Dist$(d_3)^2$	Cum. Dist$(d_3)^2$	Dist$(d_8)^2$	Cum. Dist$(d_8)^2$
d_1	1	4	0	0	0	0	21	21	21	21
d_2	1	0	0	3	0	0	14	35	14	35
d_3	0	0	2	0	0	0	0	35	8	35
d_4	0	0	0	0	3	0	13	48	13	48
d_5	1	0	0	0	0	2	9	57	1	49
d_6	1	3	0	0	0	0	14	71	14	63
d_7	1	0	0	0	4	0	21	92	21	84
d_8	0	0	0	0	0	2	8	100	0	84
d_9	2	0	0	0	0	0	8	108	8	92
d_{10}	4	0	0	0	1	0	21	129	21	113

APPENDIX B

Apply The K-Means Algorithm For Obtaining The Criteria Weights

The adoption of k-means algorithms can be used to categorise the data points into corresponding clusters by minimising the sum of squared differences within the clusters. Using d_1 as an example, the Euclidean distance between d_1 and the six centroids are first calculated, and the corresponding distances are 5.099, 1.0, 4.583, 5.0, 5.657, and 4.583. The minimum value is 1.0, and therefore, d_1 is initially categorised into cluster A2. The remaining data points can be partitioned into the clusters by repeating this procedure. The initial solution can be obtained with all the data points clustered into the criteria. The next step is, to sum up, the minimum distances of all data points and look up the optimum clustering solution based on the objective of minimising the sum of distances. The values of centroids would then be updated immediately using the equation (2) if a new minimum distance can be found in that particular iteration. The iterations would be terminated until no further minimum value can be obtained. After looping the equations (1) and (2) for the 10 data points, the solution can be obtained {A1: d_9 and d_{10}; A2: d_1 and d_6; A3: d_3; A4: d_2; A5: d_4 and d_7; A6: d_5 and d_8}. Once the iterations of the k-means algorithms for each product model (M1, M2, and M3) are completed, the posts are then categorised into the six assessment criteria. The results can be found in Table 2 under section 4.2.3.

Calculate The Sentiment Scores of Text posts and use The k-Means/k-Means++ Algorithms To Categorise Sentiment Polarities

The sentiment analysis on the extracted text posts is conducted by searching the sentiment words using the lexical resource databases. The SentiWordNet (Guerini et al., 2013) is used here. A post extracted as "I" "love" "the" "performance" "specially" "its" "photo" "quality", the positive sentiment words are "love", "performance", and "quality" and the positive, negative, and objective sentiment strengths are 0.375, 0, and 2.625 respectively. A vector can be defined, given in equation (4), for representing the sentiment strengths of each post,

$$s_i = \{P_i, N_i, O_i\} \quad i=1,2,3\ldots, n \tag{4}$$

where s_i is a 3-dimensional vector for representing sentiment strengths, P, N, O are denoted as the sum of positivity, negativity, and objectivity sentiment strengths respectively; n is the number of text posts extracted of a target product model.

After the determination of the centroids, the posts of each product model are categorised into three polarities by iterating the k-means and k-means++ algorithms. Thus, the posts can then be categorised. The normalised weights have been presented in Table 3.

Calculate The Overall Weights and Prioritise Products

The final step is to rank the product models by combining the weights obtained. It can be done simply by multiplying the criteria weights with the weights of sentiment polarities. For multiplying the values, a 3-dimensional vector, f, is introduced: $\underline{f} = \{fp, fn, fo\}$, where $fp = fn \, (-1)$, and $fp = 1-fo$, where fp is a within [0, 1] determined by the decision-maker subjectively. Taking M_1 as an example, the normalized weights obtained are, $A_1=0.1902$ and $s_{A1} = \{0.3317, 0.5463, 0.122\}$. Assuming $fp = 0.5$, the factor, f, would then be equal to $\{0.5, -0.5, 0.5\}$, and we can obtain -0.0088 for the criterion A_1. By repeating the multiplication processes, the overall weights of all assessment criteria are 0.1948, 0.1154, and 0.043 for the three models, respectively. That means, based on the result summarised from user-generated comments, M_1 is considered as the best model, then followed by M_2 and M_3. Table 4 summarises the weights for the target product models. Besides, a sensitivity analysis is conducted to verify whether the final ranking is sensitive to the value of fp.

Index

M

N

O

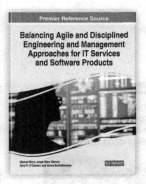

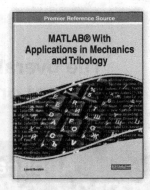

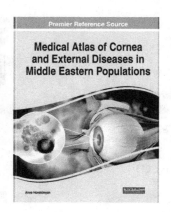

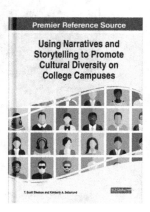

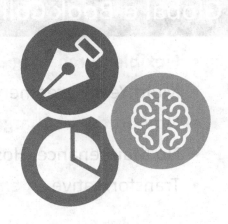

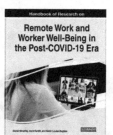